Microsoft® Visual Basic® 5.0

Developer's Workshop

Fourth Edition

John Clark Craig
and Jeff Webb

Microsoft Press

PUBLISHED BY
Microsoft Press
A Division of Microsoft Corporation
One Microsoft Way
Redmond, Washington 98052-6399

Library of Congress Cataloging-in-Publication Data
Craig, John Clark.
   Microsoft Visual Basic 5.0 Developer's Workshop / John Clark
Craig, Jeff Webb. -- 4th ed.
     p. cm.
   Rev. ed. of: Microsoft Visual Basic 4.0 Developer's Workshop. 3rd
ed. c1996.
   Includes index.
   ISBN 1-57231-436-2
   1. BASIC (Computer program language) 2. Microsoft Visual BASIC.
I. Webb, Jeff, 1961–   . II. Craig, John Clark.   Microsoft Visual
Basic 4.0 Developer's Workshop.
QA76.73.B3C713   1997
005.26'8--dc21   97-837
                                           CIP

Printed and bound in the United States of America.

1 2 3 4 5 6 7 8 9 WCWC 2 1 0 9 8 7

Distributed to the book trade in Canada by Macmillan of Canada, a division of Canada Publishing Corporation.

A CIP catalogue record for this book is available from the British Library.

Microsoft Press books are available through booksellers and distributors worldwide. For further information about international editions, contact your local Microsoft Corporation office. Or contact Microsoft Press International directly at fax (206) 936-7329.

Macintosh and TrueType fonts are registered trademarks of Apple Computer, Inc. Microsoft, MS-DOS, Visual Basic, Visual C++, Win32, Windows, and Windows NT are registered trademarks and ActiveX, MSN, Visual FoxPro, and Visual SourceSafe are trademarks of Microsoft Corporation. Java is a trademark of Sun Microsystems, Inc. Other product and company names mentioned herein may be the trademarks of their respective owners.

Acquisitions Editor: Eric Stroo
Project Editor: Patricia Draher
Manuscript Editor: Jennifer Harris
Technical Editor: Robert Lyon

CONTENTS

PART I: GETTING STARTED WITH VISUAL BASIC 5

CHAPTER ONE

What's New in Visual Basic 5? **3**

CHAPTER TWO

Programming Style Guidelines **17**

PART II: DEAR JOHN, HOW DO I...?

CHAPTER THREE

Variables **29**

CHAPTER FOUR

Parameters **55**

CHAPTER FIVE

Object-Oriented Programming **63**

CHAPTER THIRTEEN

File I/O **263**

CHAPTER FOURTEEN

The Registry **281**

CHAPTER FIFTEEN

Help Files **293**

CHAPTER TWENTY

Multiple Document Interface   **353**

CHAPTER TWENTY-ONE

Database Access   **359**

CHAPTER TWENTY-TWO

ActiveX Objects in Other Applications   **373**

CHAPTER TWENTY-SIX

Miscellaneous Techniques **451**

PART III: SAMPLE APPLICATIONS

CHAPTER TWENTY-SEVEN

Graphics **465**

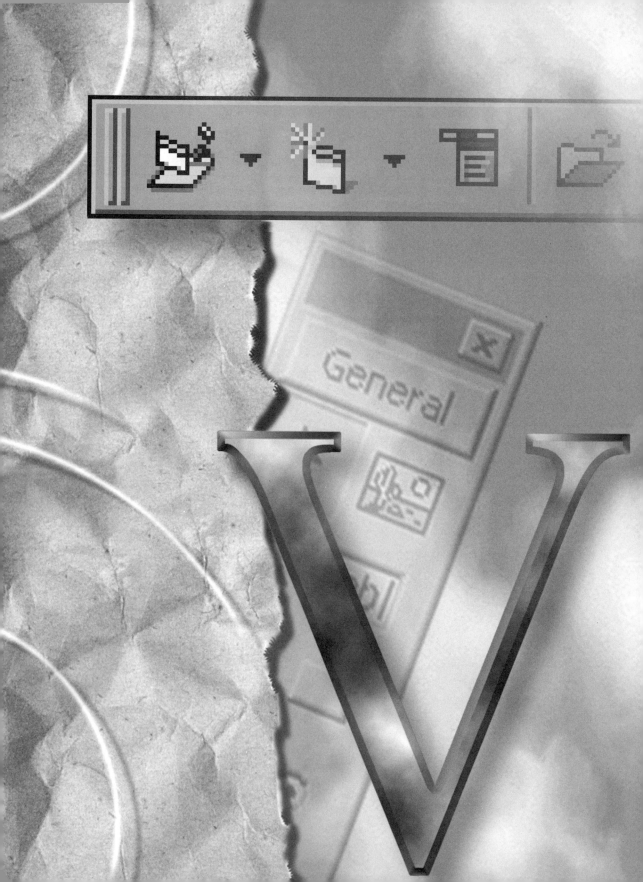

ACKNOWLEDGMENTS

Well, they did it! Microsoft Visual Basic 5.0 now gives us Microsoft Windows programmers what we want, as well as providing us with what Microsoft wants us to want. Let me explain. A few years ago, the Visual Basic product was turned over to the Microsoft Office development people during the initial design phase of Visual Basic 4.0. At first, during the beta program for version 4.0, it was obvious (and frustrating) to many of us that Visual Basic was being turned into a kind of super macro language in support of the Office products at the expense of those capabilities valued for creating stand-alone applications. Fortunately, voices of concern from both inside and outside Microsoft were heard and Visual Basic 4.0 design and development were redirected.

Visual Basic 5.0, I'm extremely pleased to report, satisfies the needs, requirements, and goals of both camps. It's a great tool for creating ActiveX components in support of the various Office products (and, indeed, many other Windows applications as well), and it's also a great tool for development of stand-alone 32-bit Windows applications. As just one example, the ability to create native code compiled ActiveX DLLs is one of the many new features that everyone's excited about. Visual Basic 5.0 does it all!

I want to thank all the great people behind the scenes at Microsoft Press for helping create this book. Several people played major roles and deserve special thanks. Patricia Draher's guidance and editing, Robert Lyon's technical expertise, and Jennifer Harris's editing skills all were appreciated more than they'll ever know. Eric Stroo's direction and patience helped immensely during the struggle to keep the project on track.

This is the first edition of this book with Jeff Webb as coauthor, and I'm not sure how to begin to thank him for his help and expertise. It's been a true pleasure working with Jeff, and I know this book contains much improved content and coverage because of his talent, skills, and knowledge. Jeff, thank you!

The classic picture of dairy cows in Chapter 31 is courtesy of Greg Nelson, who snapped this fascinating photo a few years ago in New South Wales. I also want to thank my grandson Dakotah for letting me use his bright and shining photogenic face.

Finally, I want to thank all the kind, gentle readers. I hope you enjoy Visual Basic programming as much as I did while working on this book.

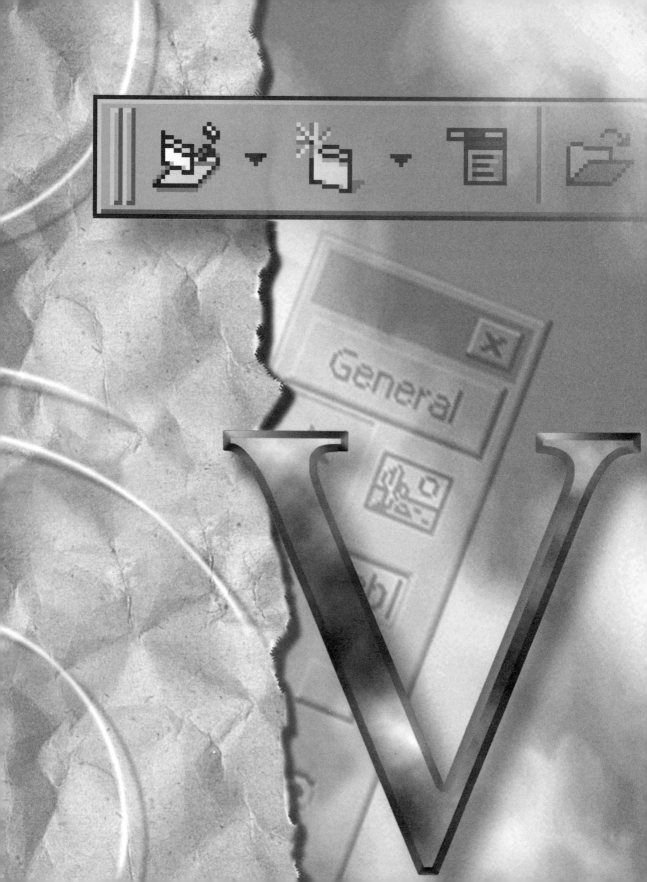

INTRODUCTION

This book evolved from the previous editions of *Microsoft Visual Basic Developer's Workshop*. Perhaps the biggest change this time around is that there are now two of us working on the book—myself and Jeff Webb. Jeff is the author of several other fine books on topics related to Visual Basic, and it's been a pleasure to have his expertise on board. With two of us working on the book, we've been able to improve the accuracy, content, and scope of our discussion of Visual Basic 5. Visual Basic has become such a diverse and wide-ranging product that a team effort is much more effective to provide proper coverage and perspective. We've learned a lot in our research, and we hope you'll find many useful tidbits of Visual Basic programming information in these pages as a result!

Right up front, you'll find a concise description of the new features in Visual Basic 5. This will help you sift through all the hype to see just how Visual Basic can help you become more efficient in the development of your projects. There have been many major changes to Visual Basic in this version, so be sure to at least skim Chapter 1, "What's New in Visual Basic 5?" to become familiar with the new capabilities.

Programming Style

We've also included information about standard programming style, as gleaned from experts at Microsoft and elsewhere. These suggestions are not intended to be too rigorous—indeed, software development teams that are too strict tend to be uncreative, boring, and unproductive—but rather are meant to provide guidelines to help groups of developers more easily understand and share code. All of the source code presented in this book pretty much follows these guidelines.

What's Been Left Out

Introductory material on the history of Basic has been left out of this book, along with some beginner-level instructions for using Visual Basic. This leaves more room for the good stuff! There's plenty of introductory material for beginners in several popular introductory books on the Basic programming language. We've found that most of our readers are already somewhat familiar with Visual Basic and are looking for new information to improve their skills and to add to their personal toolboxes of techniques.

How-To

In our presentations on Visual Basic, we've noticed that the majority of questions asked by the audience are of a "How do I…?" nature. Visual Basic programmers have discovered a wealth of powerful, but sometimes not too well documented, tricks and techniques for getting things done. We've added new, up-to-date material to the "Dear John, How Do I…?" section of this book. Often Visual Basic 5 provides better solutions to these questions than earlier versions of the language did, so the information in Part II is more current than in many other books.

By the way, after much debate it was decided for the sake of simplicity to leave these questions in their "Dear John…" format, but do note that in many cases "Dear Jeff…" would have been more accurate. "Dear J & J…," "Dear Jeff and John…," and "Hey, you guys!…" were all ruled out, so "Dear John…" it remains. For the same reason, we use *I* instead of *we* in the text, even though there are two authors speaking.

Sample Programs

The CD-ROM that accompanies this book is improved from the previous edition. You'll now find the code from all parts of this book, including the code snippets in the "Dear John, How Do I…?" section as well as the full-blown sample applications found in Part III. Visual Basic is a rich, diversified development environment, and we've tried to provide useful, enlightening examples that cover all the major subject areas. This does impose limits on the depth of coverage possible in a single book, however. For example, we've provided a real, working example of a complete but relatively simple database program, but there's no way one book can cover all aspects of the rich set of database programming features now built into Visual Basic. This book can provide a quick start in the fundamentals of database programming with Visual Basic, but you might want to supplement it with a book devoted entirely to the subject if that is your main area of interest.

Windows 95 and 32-Bit Programming

Visual Basic 4 was provided in both 16-bit and 32-bit flavors, designed to run on the Microsoft Windows version 3.1 operating system and on Microsoft Windows 95 and Microsoft Windows NT. Visual Basic 5, however, completes the migration of the product to the 32-bit world and does not provide a version for 16-bit programming. This book focuses primarily on Visual Basic 5 programming for Windows 95, as this is the most popular operating system around right now.

If you are developing code for Windows NT, this book will still suit your needs well. Some application programming interface (API) system-level calls will need slight adjustments, but most of the programs and examples here will work just fine under Windows NT.

Using the Companion CD-ROM

Bound into the back of this book is a companion CD-ROM that contains all the code snippets described in the text. The code snippets have been incorporated into Hypertext Markup Language (HTML) pages so that each snippet can be easily located and then copied and pasted into your Visual Basic project. To view the HTML files, you will need a Web browser. If you don't have a Web browser installed, Microsoft Internet Explorer version 3.01 is available on the CD-ROM.

Also on the CD-ROM are all the source code, projects, forms, and associated files described in Part III of this book. This code is ready to be compiled into executable files, integrated into your own applications, or torn apart to see how it works. You can copy and paste the code or load the project files directly into your Visual Basic environment from the CD-ROM. If you would like to copy the project files from the CD-ROM to your hard drive, we've arranged them in a chapter-based directory structure to help you locate them. For additional information about using the companion CD-ROM, see the README.TXT file on the CD-ROM.

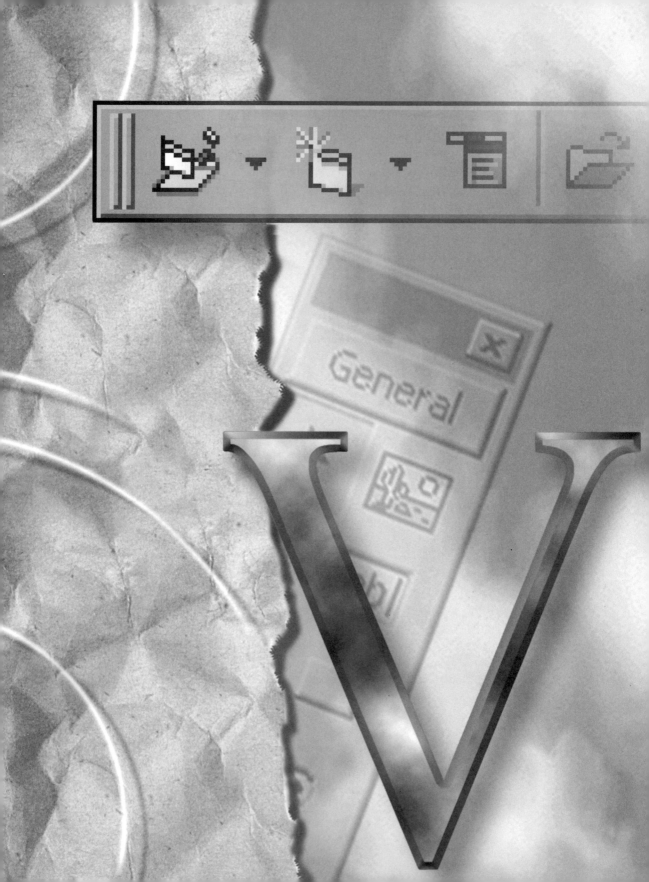

PART I

GETTING STARTED WITH VISUAL BASIC 5

The Basic programming language, created in 1963, was the first language that let the programmer concentrate on the methods and algorithms for solving programming tasks rather than on the methods and algorithms that the computer hardware needed to build and debug programs. Visual Basic has evolved far beyond the original design, but the underlying philosophy has remained consistent. Programming Microsoft Windows using C or C++ is notoriously complicated, yet Visual Basic allows programmers to accomplish the same results with a much shorter learning curve. Visual Basic is the ultimate high-productivity Windows development system for cost-effective and timely results.

C H A P T E R   O N E

What's New in Visual Basic 5?

When you launch Visual Basic 5, you are greeted by the New Project dialog box, shown in Figure 1-1. This is the first indication that Microsoft has made some major technical revisions to the Visual Basic language this time around.

Figure 1-1.
The Visual Basic 5 New Project dialog box.

In this chapter, I list many of the major new features and improvements found in Visual Basic 5, as well as some of the little enhancements that make Visual Basic a powerful and easy-to-use tool. Many of these new features are demonstrated throughout this book. Although I cover a lot of territory in this chapter and in the rest of this book, there may be a particular topic for which you require more detailed information. In this case, I recommend that you consult the Visual Basic documentation, Visual Basic's Books Online, and Microsoft's Web site.

Edition Enhancements

Visual Basic now comes in three 32-bit flavors, or editions; each edition is an enhancement of its equivalent predecessor. All editions include Visual Basic Books Online, which is the complete documentation for Visual Basic in an easy-to-navigate, CD-ROM multimedia format.

The Visual Basic Learning Edition allows programmers to easily create powerful 32-bit applications for Microsoft Windows 95 and Microsoft Windows NT. It includes all the intrinsic controls, plus grid, tab, and data-bound controls.

The Professional Edition has all the features of the Learning Edition, plus additional ActiveX controls, including Internet controls and the Crystal Report Writer. Additional documentation includes *Component Tools Guide* and *Crystal Reports for Visual Basic User's Manual.*

The Enterprise Edition includes everything in the Professional Edition, plus the Automation Manager, the Component Manager, database management tools, the Microsoft Visual SourceSafe project-oriented version control system, and more.

Integrated Development Environment

Visual Basic's Integrated Development Environment (IDE) has been overhauled in several ways. The two most noticeable changes are an option that lets you run the environment in Single Document Interface (SDI) mode or in Multiple Document Interface (MDI) mode, and the capability to simultaneously load multiple projects into the environment as a single project group. SDI mode is what you're familiar with if you've used earlier versions of Visual Basic; in SDI mode, shown in Figure 1-2, the various windows open independently on your display, with the desktop or previously opened applications visible behind and between the Visual Basic windows. The new MDI mode (now the default mode), shown in Figure 1-3, behaves more like Microsoft Word, Microsoft Excel, or Microsoft Access, with one large window for the overall application and multiple child windows displayed in and limited to the area of the main window. At first this new MDI mode feels strange, but do give it a try—you'll probably like it much better than the old SDI mode once you get used to it.

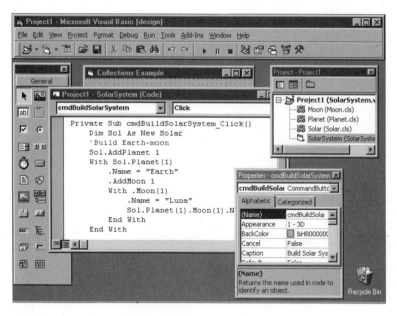

Figure 1-2.

The Integrated Development Environment in SDI mode.

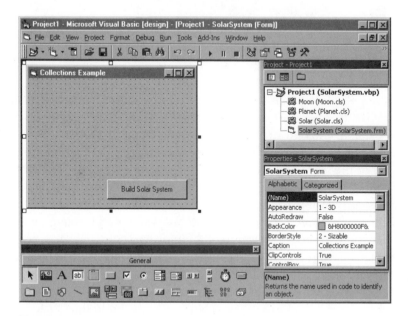

Figure 1-3.

The Integrated Development Environment in MDI mode.

The Object Browser has been enhanced in Visual Basic 5. From the Object Browser, shown in Figure 1-4, you can now quickly jump to modules and procedures in your project and to the References dialog box. With built-in search capabilities, a description pane, and other new features, the Object Browser makes it much easier to locate and understand all the component elements that are in your project or available to your project.

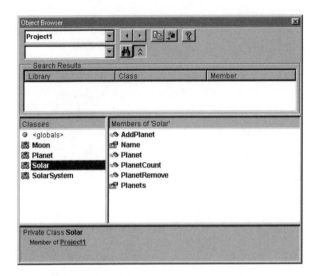

Figure 1-4.
The enhanced Object Browser.

The Code Editor has some interesting new features that are really slick! As you type, drop-down lists appear that help you complete the spelling of keywords, help you determine the properties or methods available for a control or an object, and provide other appropriate options. Figure 1-5 shows an example of the Auto List Members feature. Another helpful feature is Auto Quick Info. The Auto Quick Info feature displays the syntax for statements and functions, as shown in Figure 1-6.

Numerous other enhancements include improved Debugging windows, improved toolbars, dockable windows, an improved color palette, a new Project dialog box, margin indicators that assist in code editing (such as creating breakpoints), a quick menu link to Microsoft's help information on the Internet, and the capability to add comment characters to and remove comment characters from all lines in a selected block of code. I find the block commenting capability especially useful during the development process. (Look on the Edit toolbar for the Comment Block and Uncomment Block buttons.)

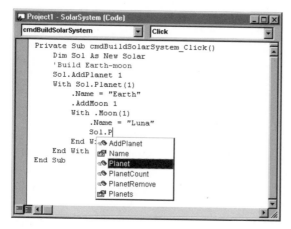

Figure 1-5.
Example of the Auto List Members feature.

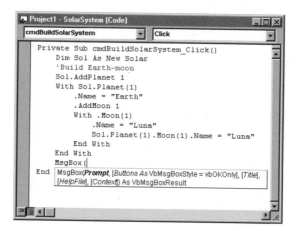

Figure 1-6.
Example of the Auto Quick Info feature.

Utilities that assist you during the development process have been included. For example, the Application Performance Explorer (APE), a new software utility written in Visual Basic, is included in the Enterprise Edition of Visual Basic. The APE aids you in the design, deployment planning, and performance tuning of distributed client/server applications. The APE lets you easily run automated "what-if" tests to profile the performance of a multitier application in different network topologies, taking into consideration such factors as network bandwidth, request frequency, data transfer requirements, server capacity, and so on. All of the source code for this application is provided with your Visual Basic installation for your study and/or modification.

Native Code Compiler

The native code compiler is one of the most important new features of Visual Basic 5, partly because it helps Visual Basic gain respectability in the eyes of the many developers who've resisted trying Visual Basic simply because of its "toy language" image, but mostly because it lets Visual Basic do new things that simply weren't appropriate in the past. For example, until now Basic was a poor choice for tasks such as high-speed animated games, three-dimensional graphics transformations, ray-tracing algorithms, and so on. Figure 1-7 shows the compiler options on the Compile tab of the Project Properties dialog box, which is displayed when you choose Project Properties from the Project menu.

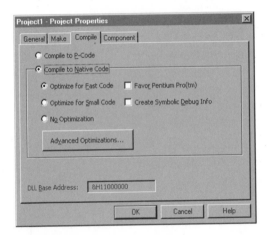

Figure 1-7.
The Compile tab of the Project Properties dialog box.

High-speed number crunching, three-dimensional graphics creation, and similar computations will benefit the most from the compiler, but all Visual Basic applications will now run faster when compiled. Visual Basic uses the same compiler technology as found in Visual C++, and you can even debug your compiled code using the Visual C++ environment if you want.

ActiveX

ActiveX is a new buzzword that refers to technologies that previously may have been associated with the term *OLE*. ActiveX is Microsoft's name for technologies that are based on the Component Object Model (COM). Visual Basic now lets you create ActiveX controls, ActiveX documents, ActiveX dynamic link libraries (DLLs), applications that expose ActiveX objects for other applications to use, and on and on. Even Visual Basic itself, and its IDE, are composed of ActiveX components. You'll hear a lot about ActiveX technology in this book, and in just about everything else you read about Visual Basic. Think of ActiveX as the technology behind all the components you use and all the components you can create in Visual Basic.

New Internet Features

It's obvious that the Internet and intranet technologies are now an extremely important part of Microsoft's vision and long-term goals. To jump-start this very important and significant use of Visual Basic for Internet and intranet applications, a special Control Creation Edition of Visual Basic became available as a free download from Microsoft's World Wide Web site before Microsoft released the full-blown version of Visual Basic 5. This limited edition of Visual Basic provides the capability to create ActiveX controls designed to work hand in hand with Microsoft's Internet Explorer. Visual Basic 5 includes all the features of the special Control Creation Edition and more. Visual Basic's Internet capabilities let you create powerful applications hosted by standard browsers, going far beyond the limitations of standard, relatively flat-looking Hypertext Markup Language (HTML) documents.

Visual Basic 5 lets you build your own ActiveX documents. ActiveX documents are created in much the same way as any other Visual Basic form, but they are designed to be hosted by ActiveX document containers such as Microsoft Internet Explorer version 3.0 and later. These documents support hyperlink navigation, menu negotiation with the hosting browser, help menu merging, and other powerful features. Perhaps the most significant feature is simply the capability to create complete, fully developed applications that run over the Internet or your intranet.

New and Enhanced Controls

Controls are an integral part of the Visual Basic 5 experience. As with the earlier versions of Visual Basic, new and enhanced controls are an important incremental improvement to the language.

Generally speaking, the ActiveX controls in Visual Basic 5 are the hottest new concept. You can combine one or more existing controls or develop your own controls from scratch to create ActiveX controls deployable locally or over the Internet. You'll hear a lot about ActiveX controls and their use on the Internet over the next few years. There are several new ActiveX controls in the Visual Basic package, as follows:

■ The new Animation control lets you display silent Audio Video Interleaved (AVI) clips, creating a type of movie. This control is designed to display animation clips such as the ones you see when you copy files (those little documents flying from one folder to another) or when you empty the Recycle Bin when it contains many files (those documents that fly out of the bin and go "poof").

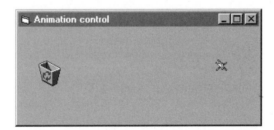

■ The FlexGrid control is similar to the original Grid control, but due to popular request, this grid now supports individual cell formatting, sorting, and many other new features that the original Grid control lacked.

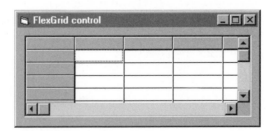

■ You can now add Hypertext Transfer Protocol (HTTP) and File
Transfer Protocol (FTP) capabilities to your Internet-enabled and
intranet-enabled applications, thanks to the new Internet Transfer
control.

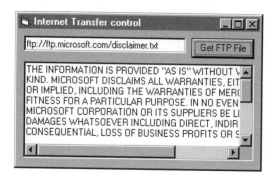

■ Another Internet-enabled control is the WebBrowser control. This
control enables you to browse the World Wide Web from within a
Visual Basic application. You might find this control especially useful
for a custom-designed corporate intranet solution. The Internet
Explorer object allows you to create an instance of the full-blown
Microsoft Internet Explorer version 3.0 or later in your applications.

■ For lower-level communications tasks, the WinSock control lets
your applications connect to remote machines and exchange data
using either the User Datagram Protocol (UDP) or the Transport
Control Protocol (TCP).

In addition to new controls, many of the existing controls in Visual Basic have been enhanced with new properties, methods, and events. A quick

scan of the Visual Basic Books Online documentation shows a long list of such improvements. For complete, detailed information, I suggest spending some time reading through this list.

Figure 1-8 shows one example of the kinds of changes made by Microsoft in this version of Visual Basic: you'll now find that almost all visual controls have a ToolTips property. Also, more and more controls are now enhanced for common features such as data-access binding, all kinds of Internet capabilities, and OLE drag-and-drop.

Figure 1-8.
The ToolTips property is now standard on most controls.

One of my favorite new features is the capability of the PictureBox control to load and display JPEG and GIF graphics images such as are found all over the Internet, as shown in Figure 1-9.

Figure 1-9.
JPEG and GIF images are now supported.

Be sure to carefully check through the lists of properties, methods, and events for the controls as you get ready to implement them—you'll probably discover many other exciting and powerful new features!

Object-Oriented Features

Class modules in Visual Basic 4 gave you the ability to create and use objects for the first time. Visual Basic 5 enhances the features of class modules and adds many new object-oriented programming (OOP) capabilities to the language. For example, Visual Basic now supports a form of *polymorphism*. In addition to their default interface (an object's set of properties and methods), Visual Basic objects can implement extra interfaces to provide polymorphism. Polymorphism lets you manipulate different kinds of objects in the same way without worrying about what kind each object is. These multiple interfaces are a feature of the Component Object Model; they allow you to develop your programs over time, adding new functionality without breaking old code.

A whole new set of terminology comes with object-oriented programming. If the terms *polymorphism, friend functions, encapsulation, interfaces, collections,* and so on are not all that clear to you, don't panic! I explain these concepts in more detail later and provide working examples to help you get a firm grasp on this important new part of the language.

One really cool new feature that I'll mention right away is the ability to create global objects. Global objects let you create a set of methods and properties that don't require an explicit instancing of the defined object. These global objects let you effectively extend Visual Basic by adding new commands and features that appear to be part of the language.

Language Enhancements

Many new features are designed to aid in the manufacture of add-ins for the Visual Basic development environment. Most restrictions and limitations in the extensibility object model exposed by Visual Basic 4 have been lifted.

Optional arguments can now be an explicit data type. (Before, arguments had to be entered as Variants.) This change is significant for arguments used in the Property Let and Property Get procedures defining properties in a class module.

As mentioned, object-oriented programming features have been expanded to include a form of polymorphism. Most OOP languages implement an inheritance mechanism to support polymorphism, whereas Visual Basic provides a mechanism based on ActiveX interfaces. For now, be aware that the Implements keyword is used to provide and share common interface elements between your objects.

The new Enum keyword provides a way to expose constants publicly in type libraries. This means that your objects can now come complete with a list of related constants for their properties that show up in the Object Browser.

The Event and RaiseEvent keywords provide a way to add events to your objects. These events can be raised programmatically as desired.

The new AddressOf operator permits the address of a procedure to be passed to an API function in a DLL. The API function can then use the address to call the Visual Basic procedure, a process known as a *callback*. The AddressOf operator provides the first direct way for Visual Basic to use a form of pointers, although there are some limitations. For API functions that expect a callback address, AddressOf works miracles!

The new Decimal data type provides a huge range of precision. This 12-byte Variant-based data type holds decimal numbers with up to 28 digits of accuracy and with a decimal point located anywhere in the range of those 28 digits. The behavior of this data type is rather bizarre in that it can be used only within a Variant, but it is useful in situations in which high precision is required.

OLE drag-and-drop is now supported in Visual Basic. For example, you can now provide your applications with the capability to handle a Word document dragged and dropped into a text box.

Data Access

The data access components have been enhanced in Visual Basic 5. The Jet engine, for example, can be more finely controlled through the use of several new methods and properties: The SetOption method lets your applications temporarily override the Jet Registry settings. The MaxRecords property halts the query processor when a given number of matching records is returned, even if more records would qualify. The MaxRecords property can be useful on systems with limited resources. See the Visual Basic documentation for more information about data access.

For Remote Data Object (RDO) data access, you'll find many new and enhanced features. There's a new Rushmore technology–based library to implement high-speed local cursors and to enhance batch updates. (Rushmore is a technology that improves data access.) RDO now exposes many new events that can be used to control all aspects of connection, query, and row access processes. The list goes on and on, so be sure to browse the Visual Basic documentation for all the new RDO language elements if data access is important to your development goals.

Wizards

Everywhere you look in Visual Basic 5, you'll find useful wizards! As you get into new areas of development with Visual Basic, I strongly suggest that you first give the wizards a shot at what you're trying to do. You'll learn a lot about the flow of the development process by watching closely as the wizards take you step by step through the various stages. Later you can "think like a wizard," following the same basic steps and adding a human element as you make adjustments and further customize your applications.

As mentioned, when you start Visual Basic one of the first things you'll see is the New Project dialog box. One of the options presented in this dialog box is the Application Wizard. Choose this option to start the Application Wizard, shown in Figure 1-10.

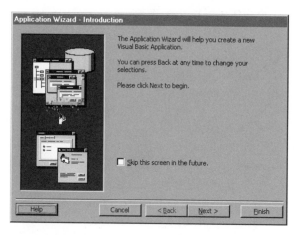

Figure 1-10.
The Application Wizard is just one of many useful wizards.

You should spend some time experimenting with this wizard; it provides a shortcut to setting up the forms and code for many of the common programming tasks you'll encounter time after time. Want to add a standard dialog box to your application? Let the Application Wizard do it for you! Or how about creating an MDI application with all the standard menus and other bells and whistles? No problem—let the Application Wizard set it up for you!

There are wizards available throughout Visual Basic to help with all kinds of development tasks, such as setting up a data access form, or creating a setup program. On the following page is a list of some features related to Visual Basic wizards.

- ActiveX Control Interface Wizard: Assists in creating ActiveX control properties, methods, and events.

- ActiveX Document Migration Wizard: Assists in converting your existing forms to ActiveX documents.

- Application Wizard: Assists in generating an application.

- Data Form Wizard: Assists in creating forms for a database.

- Property Page Wizard: Assists in creating property pages for an existing control.

- Setup Wizard: Assists in creating a setup program to distribute your program. Also assists in packaging files for distribution over the Internet.

- Wizard Manager: Assists in creating your own wizards. (Aficionados of self-referencing logic will love this one!)

Many of these wizards are not available until you enable them. To do so, choose Add-In Manager from the Add-Ins menu, and select the wizards you want to have available on the Add-Ins menu.

Extensibility

Visual Basic's development environment can be extended by creating *add-ins* written in Visual Basic. Add-ins were enabled in Visual Basic 4, but in version 5 the language elements and tools are much more extensive. There are literally hundreds of new objects, collections, properties, methods, and events providing information about and hooks into all aspects of Visual Basic's environment. I'm sure that we'll soon see an increasingly creative offering of third-party tools to enhance Visual Basic, all written and created using Visual Basic itself!

There are a multitude of other new capabilities, objects, and enhancements in Visual Basic 5, and the best way to learn about them is to browse through the Visual Basic documentation. Throughout this book, I will provide working examples of many of these new features.

CHAPTER TWO

Programming Style Guidelines

Visual Basic's ease of use can mask the need for a consistent programming style, but that need grows with the size of the programs you create. It's easy to debug a 100-line program, harder at 1000 lines, and almost impossible at 10,000 lines unless you've used some system of organization. The need for rules grows further when more than one person is writing the code or when the project needs to be maintained over long periods of time.

The goal of programming style is consistency and clarity. Good programming style will reduce the possibility of bugs and shorten the time it takes to read and understand code. Programming style guidelines must address naming, type checking, scope, and comments. Remember the following guidelines:

- Name items descriptively.
- Always use the Option Explicit statement.
- Use the most appropriate data type for each variable and parameter.
- Limit scope by using property procedures instead of global data.
- Write comments while you create code.

These rules bear repeating until they become so automatic that you don't have to think about them. This chapter expands on these guidelines and provides specific details.

Descriptive Naming

Is the Basic programming language easy to read or hard to read? It depends on who you talk to, what your background is, and how clean your programming habits are. In the old days, line numbers and GOTO statements made it easy to create obscure spaghetti code. Fortunately, today's versions of Basic are much more structured and object oriented, although you can still mangle the readability of your code if you really want to!

A lot of suggestions for standard coding style have been floated over the past few years, some good and some not so useful. In my opinion, it's not worth getting uptight about. If you simply get into the habit of using a few relatively simple and standard techniques, you can gain a reputation for creating easy-to-read code. If you're part of a team programming effort, which often seems to be the case for Visual Basic programmers today, efforts at making code easier to read can greatly enhance productivity.

Control Prefixes

One of the easiest techniques to master is naming each control with a standard three-letter prefix that identifies references to the control in the source code. This really does improve the readability of your code. Consider, for example, an event-driven procedure named Buffalo_Click. Does this refer to a command button? A picture? An option button? Until you figure out just what object on the form the name refers to, you are pretty well buffaloed. However, *cmdBuffalo_Click* is easily recognized as belonging to a command button, *picBuffalo_Click* belongs to a Picture Box control, and so on. A widely accepted list of standard prefixes has already been published in several places, and I'll repeat the list here with some additions to help propagate the standard.

Control-Naming Prefix Conventions for Visual Basic

Prefix	Control
ani	Animation button
cbo	Combo box
ch3	3D check box
chk	Check box
clp	Picture clip
cm3	3D command button
cmd	Command button
com	Communications
ctr	Control (specific type unknown)
dat	Data
db	ODBC database
dbc	Data-bound combo box
dbg	Data-bound grid
dbl	Data-bound list box
dir	Directory list box

(continued)

Control-Naming Prefix Conventions for Visual Basic *continued*

Prefix	Control
dlg	Common dialog box
drv	Drive list box
ds	ODBC dynaset
fil	File list box
fr3	3D frame
fra	Frame
frm	Form
gau	Gauge
gpb	Group push button
gra	Graph
grd	Grid
hsb	Horizontal scrollbar
img	Image
iml	Image list
key	Key status
lbl	Label
lin	Line
lst	List box
lsv	ListView
mci	Multimedia MCI
med	Masked edit
mnu	Menu
mpm	MAPI message
mps	MAPI session
ole	OLE client
op3	3D option button
opt	Option button
out	Outline
pic	Picture box
pnl	3D panel
prb	ProgressBar
rtf	RichTextBox
shp	Shape
sli	Slide

(continued)

Control-Naming Prefix Conventions for Visual Basic *continued*

Prefix	Control
spn	Spin button
sst	SSTab
stb	StatusBar
tbs	TabStrip
tlb	Toolbar
tmr	Timer
trv	TreeView
txt	Text box
vsb	Vertical scrollbar

Variable Names

Some people, particularly those coming from the world of C programming, suggest naming all variables using Hungarian Notation prefixes, which are similar to the control prefixes listed above. I have mixed feelings about this technique. On the one hand, it's nice to know what type of variable you're dealing with as you read it in the code, but on the other hand, this can sometimes make for cluttered, less readable syntax.

Since day one, Microsoft Basic programmers have had the option of naming variables using a suffix to identify the data type. For example, $X\%$ is an integer, $X!$ is a single-precision floating-point number, and $X\$$ is a string. It's a matter of opinion whether these are better names than those using Hungarian Notation prefixes. I've even seen schemes for keeping track of the scope of variables using part of the prefix, which is an advantage of Hungarian Notation, but this much detail in the name of a variable might be overkill.

The following table lists the suffixes for various data types. It also lists the newer data types, which have no suffix, supporting my contention that Microsoft is heading away from the use of these suffixes.

Standard Suffixes for Data Types

Suffix	Data Type
%	2-byte signed integer
&	4-byte signed integer
@	8-byte currency

(continued)

Standard Suffixes for Data Types *continued*

Suffix	Data Type
!	4-byte single-precision floating-point
#	8-byte double-precision floating-point
$	String
None	Boolean
None	Byte
None	Collection
None	Date
None	Decimal (a 28-digit variant)
None	Object
None	Variant

You might think that Hungarian Notation prefixes for all variable names are an absolute must, so I'll list the suggested prefixes here. Notice that some data types are indicated by more than one prefix—this lets you keep track of the intended use of the variable. For example, the standard 16-bit signed integer data type can be called Boolean, Handle, Index, Integer, or Word, depending on how you want to look at a given variable.

Hungarian Notation Prefixes for Data Types

Prefix	Data Type
a	Array
b	Boolean
by	Byte
c	Currency
col	Collection (generic)
d	Double
dc	Decimal
dt	Date
f	Float/Single
h	Handle
i	Index
l	Long

(continued)

Hungarian Notation Prefixes for Data Types *continued*

Prefix	Data Type
n	Integer
obj	Object (generic)
s	String
u	Unsigned quantity
ul	Unsigned Long
vnt	Variant
w	Word

The Collection and Object data types refer only to generic collections and objects, not to specific objects that you know the name of—for example, a procedure might receive an object as a parameter but might not know what type of object it is. When you do know an object's type, use a prefix based on the object's class name. (See the section "Class Names" on the following page for more information.)

Variable Declarations

As mentioned at the beginning of this chapter, one very important technique for keeping track of variable names is the use of the Option Explicit statement. You can choose to automatically add the Option Explicit statement whenever a new module is created, and I'd strongly recommend using this option. From the Tools menu, choose Options, select the Editor tab, and check the Require Variable Declaration check box.

The Option Explicit statement forces you to declare all variables before they are referenced. The Dim statement for each variable is an excellent place to explicitly declare the data type of the variable. This way, a variable name can be easy to read and easy to differentiate from the names of controls and other objects that do have prefixes, and its type can be easily determined by a quick glance at the block of Dim statements at the head of each module or procedure. This is the technique I've chosen for the source code examples in this book, but feel free to use the standard Hungarian Notation prefixes if they suit your style better.

WARNING: A very common and dangerous mistake, especially for those familiar with the C programming language, is to incorrectly combine the declarations of several variables of one data type into one statement. This won't cut the mustard! You must explicitly define the data type for each variable in a Dim statement. Read on!

The following explicit variable declarations are all OK, and you'll get what you expect:

```
Dim a As Integer, b As Single, c As Double
Dim a%, b!, c#
```

However, the following declaration will create two Variant variables (i and j) and one Integer variable (k) instead of the expected Integers:

```
Dim i, j, k As Integer
```

Your program might or might not work as expected, and the reason for any unexpected behavior can be very hard to track down.

Menus

There are several schemes for naming menu items too. I've chosen to name all menu items with the now-standard *mnu* prefix. You might want to add letters to identify which drop-down menu a given menu item is associated with. For example, a menu item named *mnuHelpAbout* refers to the About item selected from the Help menu. I've chosen to keep things slightly simpler—I usually shorten the name to something like *mnuAbout*. When you see *mnu* as a prefix in the source code in this book, you'll know immediately that it's a menu item. It's usually quite simple to figure out where in the menu structure the item is positioned, so I don't confuse the issue with extra designators.

Class Names

When creating new classes, name the class descriptively and then name the objects you create from that class using a descriptive prefix. Typically, a unique three-character prefix is used, but if necessary, use a longer prefix to be more descriptive. In other words, create your own object-naming scheme. Microsoft suggests using whole words and standard capitalization when naming classes, as shown in the table on the following page.

Examples of Class-Naming and Object-Naming Conventions

Class Name	Object Name Prefix	Sample Object
Loan	*lon*	*lonBoat*
Planet	*plnt*	*plntEarth*
EmployeeRecord	*erc*	*ercSales*
DailySpecial	*dspec*	*dspecTuesday*

Checking Data Types

You should strive to use the data type that is most appropriate for each variable. This is a little different from using the "smallest possible" data type. For example, the Boolean data type should consume only 1 bit—*True* or *False*, right? But a Boolean variable is actually the same size as an Integer variable, 2 bytes.

So why carry around extra baggage? Because these days it is better to be safe than small. Even if you might be developing code that will be used on the Internet, it is better to use appropriate data types to make your code safer and more understandable. A Boolean variable will always contain one of two values: *True* or *False.* The smallest type, Byte, might always evaluate to *True* or *False,* but there's no guarantee that that's what the value represents. Using Boolean is a clearer and therefore safer way to program.

Using the most appropriate data type is especially important when you declare object variables. Declaring an object variable as a specific class name rather than using the generic Object or Collection data type allows the compiler to optimize the use of that object. (The specifics of this are a little too complicated to discuss here; for more information, see Chapter 22, "ActiveX Objects in Other Applications.")

Always specify data types for each parameter in a procedure. This helps detect the inappropriate use of a procedure. Remember, Optional parameters can now have data types other than Variant. This feature was missing in Visual Basic 4, so it's a good idea to go back over procedures you created with that version to see whether you can tighten things up a bit.

Scoping Things Out

Scope refers to the visibility of a variable, a procedure, or an object to other procedures in a program. In the old days, all data was global—that is, you could get or change the value of any variable anywhere in a program. Later, when subroutines and function procedures were added to Basic, data could be global or local to a procedure. Today there are four levels of scope, listed here:

- Universal: Visible to other running applications through Microsoft ActiveX

- Global: Visible to all procedures in all modules of a project

- Module: Visible to all procedures in the same module

- Local: Visible only to the procedure that contains the variable

Limiting the scope of an item provides control over how the item can be changed. The wider the scope, the more careful you have to be. It makes sense to limit the scope of items as much as possible. In fact, global variables can be eliminated entirely using property procedures. These procedures provide an additional level of control over global data by checking whether a value is valid and whether the calling procedure has permission to change the data.

Commenting While You Code

Good comments are a pleasant surprise for anyone who's ever tried to revise someone else's program. Not too long ago, I landed a contract writing a guide for a new, company-internal programming language. Was there a spec? No. Were there sample programs? Not really. Comments in the source code? No— strike three. The lead developer and I spent a lot more time with each other than with our families for a number of weeks—good thing we got along. But why take that chance? Better to write your comments as you go. Here are some ways to structure comments within a procedure:

- In procedure headers, define what the procedure does and list the other procedures or global data the procedure uses.

- Before Case statements and other decision structures, briefly summarize the choices and the possible actions taken.

- Before loops, describe the processing that is performed and the exit conditions.

- Warn about assumptions by using the word *ASSUMPTION:* followed by a description of what is assumed. Use *UNDONE* to mark anything you need to get back to, and then use the Find command to return to these lines and resolve problems before releasing your code.

For More Information

You can find more information about standard naming schemes and programming style on the Microsoft Developer Network CD-ROM. If you're part of a large programming team and this is an important subject for you, I'd suggest this CD-ROM as a good reference for a standard set of techniques. Many corporations and programmers use this same set of standards, so there's no sense in setting out alone on a dead-end road with your own "standards."

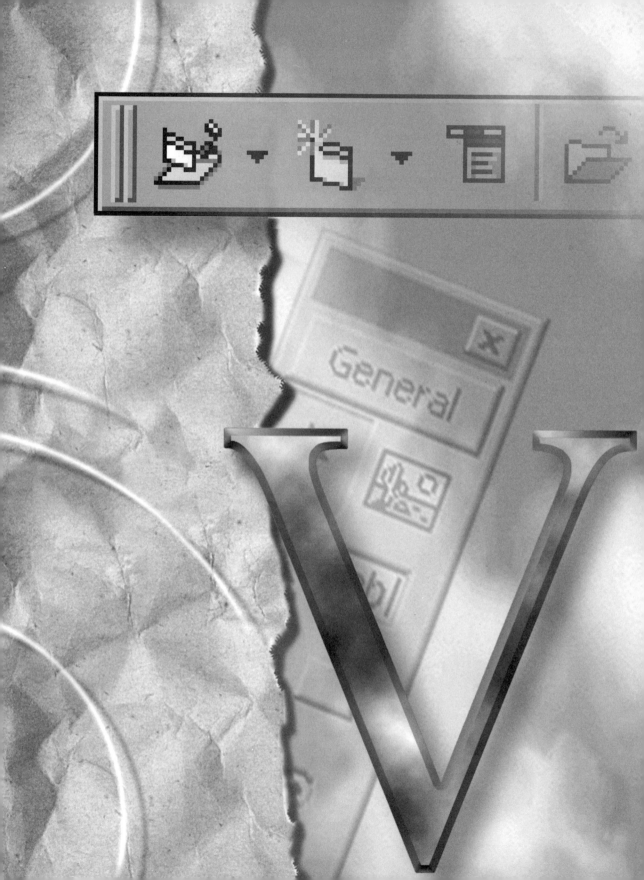

PART II

DEAR JOHN,
HOW DO I...?

One of the great strengths of Visual Basic is its flexibility. If there's some programming goal you want to accomplish and Visual Basic doesn't provide a direct, built-in solution, you can invariably come up with a "trick" that uses application programming interface (API) function calls or that uses controls in creative ways that take them beyond what they were originally designed to do.

In this part of the book, I've collected some of my favorite "Dear John, how do I…?" questions and answers, and I've been careful to use the most up-to-date techniques. For example, although it is possible in Visual Basic 4 to use API calls requiring pointers by including the Message Blaster custom control, Visual Basic 5 includes a built-in AddressOf operator. Don't use the old technique—use Visual Basic 5's better way!

CHAPTER THREE

Variables

Visual Basic's new Decimal data type provides a great excuse to use the word *octillion* in a sentence. The Decimal data type is a 28-digit variant. Numbers this large are used in database applications; you might also sometimes use them when you're on vacation in Italy, as in "Bob's hotel bill was only 79 octillion lire because he steered clear of the minibar."

Visual Basic 5 also adds *enumerations (Enums),* which let you define a block of constants using sequential values. Enums are also used to create predefined constants for reusable components that can be viewed in the Object Browser. This is important because constants defined with Const are not visible across components.

This chapter covers the uses of these new features and discusses some tricks for working with variables that are not new to this version of Visual Basic, such as using Variants and using classes to create new data types. Also covered in this chapter are working with predefined constants and creating Type structures.

Dear John, How Do I...

Simulate Unsigned Integers?

Unfortunately, Visual Basic does not support unsigned 16-bit integers, a data type often encountered in API calls. But don't despair—there are ways to compensate for this lack.

Visual Basic's integer data types come in three distinct flavors: Long, Integer, and Byte. Long variables are 32-bit signed values in the range −2,147,483,648 through +2,147,483,647. The most frequently used of the three data types is Integer, which stores 16-bit signed integer values in the range −32,768 through +32,767. Byte variables hold unsigned 8-bit numeric values in the range 0 through 255. Notice that the only unsigned integer data type is Byte.

Unsigned 16-bit integers are useful in many API function calls. You can go ahead and pass signed integer variables to and from these functions instead, but you must develop a mechanism to deal with negative values when they show up. There are several approaches to simulating unsigned 16-bit integers, and I'll cover two of the best.

NOTE: If you are compiling your program using the native code compiler, be aware that you can turn off integer overflow detection. This allows incorrect integer computation in some cases, so you should carefully consider your application before turning off this option. On the positive side, turning off integer overflow detection allows faster integer math calculations and, for certain types of calculations, effectively allows unsigned integer results.

Transferring to and from Long Variables

In some cases, you can manipulate unsigned integers in the range 0 through 65,535 by storing them in Long integers. When it comes time to assign the 16-bit values into a signed Integer variable that will simulate an unsigned 16-bit variable, use the following calculation:

```
iShort = (iLong And &H7FFF&) - (iLong And &H8000&)
```

Here *iShort* is a signed Integer variable to be passed to the API, and *iLong* is the Long variable containing the stored value to be passed. The calculation uses the logical And operator and hexadecimal-based bit masks to execute bitwise operations to convert the 32-bit value to a 16-bit unsigned value.

To store the value of a signed integer that has been used to simulate an unsigned 16-bit integer as a Long integer (the inverse of the calculation just shown), use this calculation:

```
iLong = iShort And &HFFFF&
```

Be aware that the 16-bit unsigned value (*iShort*), although stored in a 16-bit signed Integer variable, might be interpreted as a negative value if you print or calculate with it. Use these two calculations to convert the values just before and just after calling API functions that expect a 16-bit unsigned integer. Work with the Long integer version (*iLong*) of the unsigned integers in your code, and pass the Integer version (*iShort*) of the value to API functions.

Packing Unsigned Byte Values Using Data Structures

Visual Basic doesn't have a Union construct as C does, but you can simulate the construct's functionality by copying bytes between user-defined data Type structures using the LSet statement. This makes it easy to pack and unpack unsigned Byte values into and out of a signed integer. The following code fragments demonstrate this technique:

```
Option Explicit

Private Type UnsignedIntType
    lo As Byte
    hi As Byte
End Type

Private Type SignedIntType
    n As Integer
End Type
```

These two Type structures define storage for 2 bytes each. Although the memory allocation is not overlapping, as would be true in a C union, the binary contents can be shuffled between variables of these types, as the next block of code demonstrates:

```
Private Sub Form_Click()
    'Create variables of user-defined types
    Dim u As UnsignedIntType
    Dim s As SignedIntType
    'Assign high and low bytes to create integer
    u.hi = 231
    u.lo = 123
    'Copy binary data into the other structure
    LSet s = u
    Print s.n, u.hi; u.lo
    'Assign integer and extract high and low bytes
    s.n = s.n - 1   'Decrement integer for new value
    'Copy back into the other data structure
    LSet u = s
    Print s.n, u.hi; u.lo
End Sub
```

If you put these two code fragments in a form and click on it, the signed integer value (−6277) and the two byte values (231 and 123) on which it is based are printed on the form. After conducting an operation on the integer—in this case, subtracting 1—the result of the reverse operation is also printed: the new signed integer value (−6278) and the high and low bytes (231 and 122) of the integer. This is accomplished by first declaring two variables, *u* and *s*, using the declared Type structure definitions. The *u.hi* and *u.lo* bytes are used to assign values to the high and low bytes of the *u* variable. The binary contents of *u* are then copied into *s* using LSet, and the resulting signed integer is printed out. Finally, the integer value in *s* is decremented to provide a value different from the original, and *s* is copied back into *u* to show how a signed integer can be split into two unsigned byte values.

By adding text boxes and labels to your form, it's easy to transform the code fragments into a working integer-byte calculator, as shown in Figure 3-1.

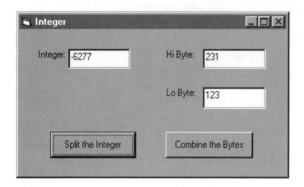

Figure 3-1.
A signed integer comprising two unsigned bytes.

Note that LSet can be used to copy any binary contents of one user-defined Type structure to another. This provides an efficient way to treat the binary contents of memory as different types of data.

WARNING: In Microsoft Windows 95 and Microsoft Windows NT, the elements in your Type structures might not line up in memory exactly as you expect. This is because each element is aligned on a 4-byte boundary, with extra padding bytes inserted to accomplish the alignment. When using LSet to move data from one Type structure to another, experiment to verify that the bytes end up where you want them to go. Be careful!

See Also...

- "Dear John, How Do I...Use C to Create a DLL?" in Chapter 25, "Advanced Programming Techniques," for information about creating a DLL using Visual C++. The C language is ideally suited to the packing and unpacking of bytes within integers.

Dear John, How Do I...

Work with *True/False* Data?

The Boolean data type stores either the value *True* or the value *False* and nothing else. Typically, Boolean variables are used to store the results of comparisons or other logical tests. For example, the following procedure assigns the result of a logical comparison of two values to a Boolean variable named *TestResult* and then prints this variable to the display:

```
Private Sub Form_Click()
    Dim TestResult As Boolean
    TestResult = 123 < 246
    Print TestResult
End Sub
```

Notice that the displayed result appears as *True* in this case. When you print or display a Boolean variable, you print or display either *True* or *False*.

> **WARNING:** Watch out for strange variable type coercions! Read on...

Visual Basic supports many types of automatic variable type coercions, which means you can assign just about anything to just about anything. For example, even though Boolean variables hold only the values *True* and *False*, you can assign a number or even a string to a Boolean variable. The results might not be what you'd expect, though, so be careful!

Here's one short example of this rather strange behavior. The following code will display *True, True,* and *False,* which implies that *a* equals *True* and *b* equals *True* but that *a* does not equal *b*! The reason for the final result of *False* might not be obvious; it results from the internal conversions of the unlike variables *a* and *b* to like data types during the test to see whether they equal each other.

```
Private Sub Form_Click()
    Dim a As Byte
    Dim b As Integer
    a = True
    b = True
    Print a = True
    Print b = True
    Print a = b
End Sub
```

Use the operators And, Or, and Not to perform logical operations with Booleans. Logical operations combine several conditions in a single statement, creating a result that is either *True* or *False*. For example:

```
If bExit And Not bChanged Then End
```

This line of code ends a program if *bExit* is *True* and *bChanged* is *False*. You can use mathematical operators for the same task, but the logical operators make the code shorter and more readable. By using Boolean variables exclusively in these tests, you also avoid unexpected type coercion.

Dear John, How Do I...

Use Byte Arrays?

One of the main reasons Byte arrays were created was to allow the passing of binary buffers to and from the 32-bit API functions. One of the differences to be aware of between 16-bit and 32-bit Visual Basic applications is that 32-bit version strings are assumed to contain Unicode characters, which require 2 bytes for each character. The system automatically converts Unicode 2-byte sequences to 1-byte ANSI characters, but if the string contains binary data the contents can become unintelligible. To prevent problems, you should get into the habit of passing only printable string data in strings and passing binary data in Byte arrays.

Passing Byte Arrays Instead of Strings

Byte arrays contain only unsigned Byte values in the range 0 through 255. Unlike the contents of strings, Byte array contents are guaranteed not to be preprocessed by the system. You can pass Byte arrays in place of strings in many API functions.

For example, the following code, which uses the GetWindowsDirectory Windows API function to find the path to the Windows directory, demonstrates the changes you'll need to make to the function declarations and function parameters. The code is shown in two versions: the first passes a string for the API function to return the Windows directory in, and the second passes a Byte array instead. When you place either of these code examples in a form, run it, and click on the form, you'll see the path to your Windows directory, as shown in Figure 3-2.

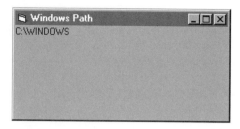

Figure 3-2.
The API function that returns the path to your Windows directory.

By carefully noting the differences in these two examples, you'll gain insight into the differences between string and Byte array parameters. The string example is shown here:

```
Option Explicit

Private Declare Function GetWindowsDirectory _
Lib "kernel32" _
Alias "GetWindowsDirectoryA" ( _
    ByVal lpBuffer As String, _
    ByVal nSize As Long _
) As Long

Private Sub Form_Click()
    Dim n As Integer
    Dim strA As String
    'Size the string variable
    strA = Space$(256)
    n = GetWindowsDirectory(strA, 256)
    'Strip off extra characters
    strA = Left$(strA, n)
    Print strA
End Sub
```

In this first code example, the string parameter *lpBuffer* returns the path to the Windows directory. I presized the variable *strA* to 256 characters before calling the function, and I stripped off the extra characters upon returning from the function.

WARNING: Before making the function call, always presize a string or a Byte array that an API function fills with data. Your program will probably crash if you forget to do this!

Here's the Byte array example:

```
Option Explicit

Private Declare Function GetWindowsDirectory _
Lib "kernel32" _
Alias "GetWindowsDirectoryA" ( _
    ByRef lpBuffer As Byte, _
    ByVal nSize As Long _
) As Long

Private Sub Form_Click()
    Dim n As Integer
    Dim Buffer() As Byte
    Dim strA As String
    'Size the Byte array
    Buffer = Space$(256)
    n = GetWindowsDirectory(Buffer(0), 256)
    strA = StrConv(Buffer, vbUnicode)
    'Strip off extra characters
    strA = Left$(strA, n)
    Print strA
End Sub
```

Take a close look at the function declaration for the GetWindows-Directory API function in this second example. I changed the declaration for the first parameter from a ByVal string to a ByRef Byte array. The original parameter declaration was:

```
ByVal lpBuffer As String
```

I changed the ByVal keyword to ByRef and changed String to Byte in the new form of this declaration:

```
ByRef lpBuffer As Byte
```

A ByVal modifier is required for passing string buffers to API functions because the string variable actually identifies the place in memory where the address of the string contents is stored—in C terminology, a pointer to a pointer. ByVal causes the contents of the memory identified by the string name to be passed, which means that the value passed is a memory address to the actual string contents. Notice that in my function call I pass *Buffer(0)*, which, when passed using ByRef, is passed as the memory address for the contents of the first byte of the array. The result is the same, and the GetWindows-Directory API function will blindly load the addressed buffer memory with the path to the Windows directory in both cases.

Further along in the code is this important line which requires some explanation:

```
strA = StrConv(Buffer, vbUnicode)
```

This command converts the Byte array's binary data to a valid Visual Basic string. Dynamic Byte arrays allow direct assignment to and from strings, which is accomplished like this:

```
Buffer = strA
strB = Buffer
```

When you assign a string to a dynamic Byte array, the number of bytes in the array will be twice the number of characters in the string. This is because Visual Basic strings use Unicode, and each Unicode character is actually 2 bytes in size. When ASCII characters are converted to a Byte array, every other byte in the array will be a 0. (The second byte is used to support other character sets, such as for European or Asian languages, and becomes important when internationalization of your applications is necessary.) In the case of the GetWindowsDirectory API function, however, the returned buffer is not in Unicode format, and we must convert the Byte buffer's binary contents to a Unicode string ourselves, using the StrConv function as shown above. In the first code example, we let Visual Basic perform this housekeeping chore automatically as it filled our string parameter.

The conversion to Unicode converts each character in the buffer to 2 bytes and actually doubles the number of bytes stored in the resulting string. This isn't readily apparent when you consider that the function Len(*strA*) reports the same size as would UBound(*Buffer*) after the Unicode conversion in the above case. However, the function LenB(*strA*) does report a number twice the size of the number reported by the Len(*strA*) function. This is because the Len function returns the number of characters in the string, whereas the LenB function returns the number of bytes in the string. The character length of a Unicode string (remember, this includes all 32-bit Visual Basic strings) is only half the number of actual bytes in the string because each Unicode character is 2 bytes.

To summarize, when converting an API function parameter from a string buffer to the Byte array type, change the ByVal keyword to ByRef, pass the first byte of the array instead of the string's name, and if the binary data is to be converted to a string, remember to use StrConv with the *vbUnicode* constant.

Copying Between Byte Arrays and Strings

To simplify the transfer of data between Byte arrays and strings, the designers of Visual Basic decided to allow a special case assignment between any dynamic Byte array and any string.

> **NOTE:** You can assign a string to a Byte array only if the array is dynamic, not if it is fixed in size.

The easiest way to declare a dynamic Byte array is to use empty parentheses in the Dim statement, like this:

```
Dim Buffer() As Byte
```

The following Dim statement creates a fixed-size Byte array, which is useful for a lot of things but not for string assignment. It will, in fact, generate an error if you try to assign a string to it.

```
Dim Buffer(80) As Byte
```

Dear John, How Do I...

Work with Dates and Times?

Internally, a Date variable is allocated 8 bytes of memory that contain packed bit patterns for not only a date but also an exact time. Magically, when you print a Date variable, you'll see a string designation for the year, month, day, hour, minute, and second that the 8-byte internal data represents. The exact format for the displayed or printed date and time is dependent on your system's regional settings. For all the sample calculations that follow, I've assumed that date and time values are always stored in Date variables.

Loading a Date Variable

To load date and time values directly into a variable, enclose the information between two # characters. As you enter a program line with date values in this format, Visual Basic checks your syntax. If the date or time is illegal or nonexistent, you'll immediately get an error. Here's an example in which a Date variable, *D*, is loaded with a specific date and time:

```
Dim D As Date
D = #11/17/96 6:19:20 PM#
```

We'll use this value of *D* throughout the following examples.

Several functions convert date and time numbers to Date type variables. DateSerial combines year, month, and day numbers in a Date value. In a similar way, TimeSerial combines hour, minute, and second numbers in a Date value:

```
D = DateSerial(1996, 11, 17)
D = TimeSerial(18, 19, 20)
```

To combine both a date and a time in a Date variable, simply add the results of the two functions:

```
D = DateSerial(1996, 11, 17) + TimeSerial(18, 19, 20)
```

To convert a string representation of a date or time to a Date value, use the DateValue and TimeValue functions:

```
D = DateValue("11/17/96")
D = TimeValue("18:19:20")
```

Again, to convert both a date and a time at the same time, simply add the results of the two functions:

```
D = DateValue("Nov-17-1996") + TimeValue("6:19:20 PM")
```

A wide variety of legal formats are recognized as valid date and time strings, but you do need to be aware of the expected format for the regional setting on a given system. In some countries, for example, the month and day numbers might be expected in reverse order.

Displaying a Date or a Time

The Format function provides great flexibility for converting a Date variable to a printable or displayable string. The following block of code shows the predefined named formats for these conversions:

```
Print Format(D, "General Date") '11/17/96 6:19:20 PM
Print Format(D, "Long Date")    'Sunday, November 17, 1996
Print Format(D, "Medium Date")  '17-Nov-96
Print Format(D, "Short Date")   '11/17/96
Print Format(D, "Long Time")    '6:19:20 PM
Print Format(D, "Medium Time")  '06:19 PM
Print Format(D, "Short Time")   '18:19
```

Be aware that the results depend on your system's regional settings. You should run this code to see whether your results differ from mine.

In addition to the named formats, you can create your own user-defined formats for outputting date and time data. For example, the line of code on the following page formats each part of the date and time in a unique way and stores the result in a string variable.

```
A$ = Format(D, "m/d/yyyy hh:mm AM/PM")   '11/17/1996 06:19 PM
```

These user-defined formats are extremely flexible. For example, here's how you can generate the textual name of the month for a date:

```
MonthName$ = Format(D, "mmmm")   'November
```

See the online help for the Format function for a detailed description of the many combinations of user-defined date and time formats you can use.

Extracting the Details

Several functions are available to extract parts of the Date variable. The following lines of code provide a quick reference to this group of related functions:

```
Print Month(D)       '11
Print Day(D)         '17
Print Year(D)        '1996
Print Hour(D)        '18
Print Minute(D)      '19
Print Second(D)      '20
Print WeekDay(D)     '1
```

A set of built-in constants is provided by Visual Basic for the WeekDay result; *vbSunday* is 1, *vbMonday* is 2, and so on through *vbSaturday*, which is 7.

Date and Time Calculations

Date variables can be directly manipulated in a mathematical sense if you keep in mind that the unit value is a day. For example, you can easily create an application to calculate your age in days, as shown in Figure 3-3. To do so, simply subtract your date of birth (stored in a Date variable) from Now, the function that returns today's date.

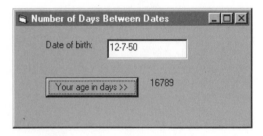

Figure 3-3.
Using Date variables to calculate the number of days between dates.

To calculate date values using hours, minutes, or seconds, you could multiply or divide the date value by 24, 60, and 60, but the DateSerial and TimeSerial functions provide a better way. Let's say, for instance, that you want to calculate the exact date and time 10,000 minutes from the current moment. Here's how to do this without getting tangled up in a lot of math:

```
D = Now + TimeSerial(0, 10000, 0)
```

The TimeSerial function returns a value representing no hours, 10,000 minutes, and no seconds. This value is added to Now to calculate a Date variable containing the desired date and time. If you print the value of *D*, you'll see a date and time that's roughly one hour short of exactly a week from now.

Date and Time Validity Checking

You can use an error trap when assigning a user-entered date or time string to a Date variable. If the date or time is not recognizable as a valid date or time, a "Type mismatch" error is generated by Visual Basic. Another approach to getting a valid date from the user is to use a calendar control. This prevents errors by letting the user interactively select only a valid date from a one-month calendar page.

See Also...

- The VBCal application in Chapter 29, "Date and Time," for a date selection dialog box that you can plug into your own applications

Dear John, How Do I...

Work with Variants?

Variants are extremely flexible (some say too flexible), but they do allow for some clever new ways to structure and organize your data.

If not declared as something else, all variables default to Variant. You can store just about anything in a Variant variable, including arrays, objects, Type structures, and other Variants. Arrays always contain like elements, which means you normally can't mix strings and numbers in the same array, for instance. But an array of Variants gets around this limitation. Consider the code on the following page, which creates a Variant array and loads it with an integer, a string, and another Variant. To hint at the flexibility here, I've even stored a second Variant array in the third element of the primary Variant array. Remember, you can store just about anything in a Variant!

```
Option Explicit

Private Sub Form_Click()
    Dim i        'Note that this defaults to Variant
    Dim varMain(1 To 3) As Variant
    Dim X As Integer
    Dim A As String
    Dim varAry(1 To 20) As Variant
    'Fill primary variables
    A = "This is a test."
    For i = 1 To 20
        varAry(i) = i ^ 2
    Next i
    'Store everything in main Variant array
    varMain(1) = X
    varMain(2) = A
    varMain(3) = varAry()
    'Display sampling of main Variant's contents
    Print varMain(1)          '0
    Print varMain(2)          'This is a test
    Print varMain(3)(17)      '289
End Sub
```

Notice, in the last executable line of the procedure, how the Variant array element within another Variant array is accessed. The *varMain(3)(17)* element looks, and indeed acts, somewhat like an element from a two-dimensional array, but the subscripting syntax is quite different. This technique effectively lets you create multidimensional arrays with differing dimensions and data types for all elements.

For Each Loops

Variants serve an important role in For Each...Next loops. You can loop through each member of a collection, or even through a normal array, using a For Each statement. The only type of variable you can use for referencing each element is an Object or a Variant. When looping through arrays you *must* use a Variant. When looping through a collection you *may* use an Object variable, but you always have the option of using a Variant.

Flexible Parameter Type

The Variant type is useful as a parameter type, especially for object properties for which you want to set any of several types of data in a single property. You can pass just about anything by assigning it to a Variant variable and then passing this data as an argument.

Variant-Related Functions

You should be aware of several useful functions for working with Variants. TypeName returns a string describing the current contents of a Variant. The family of Is functions, such as IsNumeric and IsObject, provides fast logical checks on a Variant's contents. Search the online help for more information about these and other related functions.

Empty and Null

Be careful of the difference between an *Empty* Variant and a *Null* one: a Variant is Empty until it's been assigned a value of any type; Null is a special indication that the Variant contains no valid data. A Null value can be assigned explicitly to a Variant, and a Null value propagates through all calculations. The Null value most often appears in database applications, where it indicates unknown or missing data.

Data Type Coercion

Variants are very flexible, but you need to be careful when dealing with the complexities of automatic data conversions. For example, some of the following program steps may surprise you:

```
Option Explicit

Private Sub Form_Click()
    Dim a, b
    a = "123"
    b = True
    Print a + b             '122
    Print a & b             '123True
    Print a And b = 0       '0
    Print b And a = 0       'False
End Sub
```

The first Print statement treats the contents of the two Variants as numeric values, and the second Print statement treats them as strings. The last two Print statements produce considerably different results based on the operational hierarchy, which isn't at all obvious. The best advice I can provide is this: Be cautious and carefully check out the results of your coding to be sure that the results you get are what you expect.

Dear John, How Do I...

Work with Objects?

Object variables not only store information but also perform actions. This makes them a very special sort of variable, and there are special considerations you should take into account when working with them.

New Objects

Objects are declared slightly differently than other variables. Visual Basic initializes most variables when they are first used. For instance, you declare a new Integer variable with Dim, and then when you first use the variable Visual Basic initializes its value to *0* automatically. Objects aren't initialized this way. If you declare an Object variable and then check its type name, you'll get the answer "Nothing":

```
Dim x As Form1
Debug.Print TypeName(x)     'Displays "Nothing"
```

You can't do anything with an Object variable until you create an instance of it. Use the New keyword to create a new object:

```
Dim x As New Form1
Debug.Print TypeName(x)     'Displays "Form1"
```

Existing Objects

An Object variable only *refers* to an object—this isn't the same thing as *being* the object. You can reassign which object an Object variable refers to by using the Set statement, as shown here:

```
Dim x As New Form1      'Create a new object
Dim y As New Form1      'Create another object
Set x = y               'x and y both refer to the same object
```

You must use Set rather than simple assignment to assign an object reference to a variable. Most objects have a default property. Set tells Visual Basic to perform an object assignment rather than a property assignment.

Object Operations

You compare objects using the Is operator. Is tells you whether two Object variables refer to the same object. The following code shows how this works:

```
Dim x As New Form1      'Create a new object
Dim y As New Form1      'Create another object
```

(continued)

```
Debug.Print x Is y      'Displays "False"
Set x = y               'x and y both refer to the same object
Debug.Print x Is y      'Displays "True"
```

Dead Objects

How long do objects live? Until they become Nothing!

Objects stick around as long as they have a variable that refers to them or, as is the case with Form objects, as long as they are visible. You can usually control the visibility of an object using its Visible property. You can get rid of an object by setting its variable to another object or to Nothing:

```
Dim x As New Form1  'Create a new object
Dim y As Object     'Declare a variable of type Object
Set y = x           'x and y both refer to same object
Set x = Nothing     'y is still valid; object persists
Set y = Nothing     'Object goes away
```

At least, that's what's supposed to happen. Some objects aren't so careful. Early versions of some objects (including some from Microsoft) weren't so good about going away. Most objects are better behaved today, but it's still a good idea to be careful when working with objects you can't see. In general, objects you create in Visual Basic are well behaved, and objects in other products are usually, but not always, well behaved.

See Also...

• Chapter 5, "Object-Oriented Programming," for more information about objects

Dear John, How Do I...

Work with Predefined Constants?

There are actually several types of constants in Visual Basic, including some predefined constants provided by the system.

Compiler Constants

If you need to develop your applications in both 16-bit and 32-bit versions, you must use Visual Basic 4. That version is the only one that provides a development environment for Windows version 3.1 (16-bit), Windows 95 (32-bit), and Windows NT version 3.51 (32-bit). To create applications that will run on both 16-bit and 32-bit operating systems, you'll need to use the Win16 and Win32 compiler constants. These constants indicate the system currently in use during development of your Visual Basic applications and let you select appropriate blocks of code to suit the conditions.

These constants are used with the #If...Then...#Else directives to select or skip over sections of code during compilation. Visual Basic 5 still supports these constants, but Win32 is always *True* and Win16 is always *False* because Visual Basic 5 runs only on 32-bit versions of Windows.

Visual Basic Constants

A huge list of predefined constants is provided automatically by Visual Basic for virtually every need. To see what's available, click the Object Browser button, select VBA or VB from the top drop-down list, and click on the appropriate group of constants in the Classes list. A list of constants, each identifiable by the Constant icon and the *vb* prefix, is shown on the right side in the Members list, as you can see in Figure 3-4.

Figure 3-4.
Built-in constants, as shown in the Object Browser.

Notice that many components provide constants, and this is the place to locate them when you need them.

You'll find that there are predefined constants for almost every control and function parameter imaginable—for example, *vbModal* and *vbModeless* for the form's Show method; *vbRed, vbBlue,* and *vbGreen* for color constants used in most graphics methods; and even *vbCr, vbLf, vbCrLf,* and *vbTab* for common text characters. The following code shows how to insert a carriage return/ linefeed character into a string:

```
a$ = "Line one" & vbCrLf & "Line two"
```

Anytime you find yourself starting to type a numeric value for a property or a method argument, you should stop yourself and check to see whether there is already a constant defined by the system that you could use instead. This can help make your programs self-documenting, easier to read, and easier to maintain.

User-Defined Constants

As in earlier versions of Visual Basic, you can define your own constants in your programs by using the Const keyword. You can also create conditional compiler constants using the #Const directive, which looks similar but is actually quite different. Constants created by #Const are to be used only with the #If...Then...#Else directives described earlier. Conversely, user-defined constants created with the Const keyword are not to be used as conditional compiler constants.

Some of the predefined constants are extremely helpful for building complex string constants. For example, the following code prints one constant to display digits in a column on a form. This same formatting was impossible without extra coding in earlier versions of Visual Basic. Now you can do all this formatting at design time. Note that only one executable statement is executed in the following procedure at runtime:

```
Option Explicit

Private Sub Form_Click()
    Const DIGITS = _
        "1" & vbCrLf & _
        "2" & vbCrLf & _
        "3" & vbCrLf & _
        "4" & vbCrLf & _
        "5" & vbCrLf & _
        "6" & vbCrLf & _
        "7" & vbCrLf & _
        "8" & vbCrLf & _
        "9" & vbCrLf
    Print DIGITS
End Sub
```

Use the Private and Public keywords to define the scope of constants declared at the module level. If declared Private, the constants will be local to the module only, whereas Public constants are available project-wide. These keywords cannot be used for defining constants inside procedures. A constant declared within a procedure is always local to that procedure.

Enumerations

An enumeration (Enum for short) is a way that you can associate integer values with names. This can be helpful with property procedures. For example, a SpellOption property might have these valid settings:

```
'MailDialog class module-level declarations
Public Enum CheckedState
    Unchecked           'Enums start at 0 by default
    Checked             '1
    Grayed              '2, and so on
    'CantDeselect = 255 (You can set specific values too)
End Enum
```

The properties that set or return the state of check boxes in a dialog box would then be defined using the Enum in the property's parameter declaration:

```
Public Property Let SpellOption(Setting As CheckedState)
    'Set the state of the Check Spelling check box
    frmSendMail.chkSpelling.Value = Setting
End Property

Public Property Get SpellOption() As CheckedState
    'Return the state of the Check Spelling check box
    SpellOption = frmSendMail.chkSpelling.Value
End Property
```

You can use Enums in any type of module. They appear in the Object Browser in the Classes list box; their possible settings are shown in the Members list box. Only the public Enums in public class modules are visible across projects, however.

Flags and Bit Masks

The operators And, Or, and Not are most often used for logical comparisons in decision structures. For example, an If statement can test several conditions using the And operator, as shown here:

```
If bExit And Not bChanged Then End
```

Logic is great, but to be a really smooth operator you'd better be bitwise too. *Bitwise* operations are bit-by-bit comparisons of two numbers to create a result. Bitwise operations are used when you want to stuff more than one meaning into a single numeric value. These values are referred to as *flags*. A good example is the Print dialog box's Flags property:

```
dlgPrint.Flags = cdlPDCollate Or cdlPDNoSelection
```

In most cases, using Or to combine flags is equivalent to using the addition operator (+). However, when flags conflict you'll get a different result using addition—for example, $1 + 1 = 2$, but 1 Or 1 = 1. This shouldn't happen if flag values are well thought out, but it's safer to use Or.

To reset flags to *0* or to check the value of a flag, use And. This code checks whether Print To File is selected in the Print dialog box:

```
'Check whether Print To File
If dlgPrint.Flags And cdlPDPrintToFile Then
```

The And operation above checks whether bit 32 is on (&H20 is the value of cdlPDPrintToFile); if it is, the statement is *True.* Checking flags this way is known as using a *bit mask.* A bit mask is the collection of bits you are checking—for example, 01101101 (in binary; &H6D in hex). If the value in question has 1s in all the same bit positions as the mask, the mask "fits."

Masking is how a signed integer was converted to an unsigned number earlier in this chapter. Signed integers have values from &H8000 (−32,768 in decimal) to &H7FFF (+32,767 in decimal). By masking out the proper bits, you can convert a signed integer to an unsigned value:

```
iShort = (iLong And &H7FFF&) - (iLong And &H8000&)
```

Dear John, How Do I...
Create Type Structures?

The Type keyword is used to declare the framework of a Type data structure. Notice that the Type command doesn't actually create a data structure; it only provides a detailed definition of the structure. You use a Dim statement to actually create variables of the new type.

You can declare a Type structure at the module level only. Within a form or a class module, you must declare the Type structure as Private to its module. When combined with Variants, amazingly dynamic and adjustable data structures can result. The following code demonstrates a few of these details:

```
Option Explicit

Private Type typX
    a() As Integer
    b As String
    c As Variant
End Type
```

(continued)

```
Private Sub Form_Click()
    'Create a variable of type typX
    Dim X As typX
    'Resize dynamic array within the structure
    ReDim X.a(22 To 33)
    'Assign values into the structure
    X.a(27) = 29
    X.b = "abc"
    'Insert entire array into the structure
    Dim y(100) As Double
    y(33) = 4 * Atn(1)
    X.c = y()
    'Verify a few elements of the structure
    Print X.a(27)      '29
    Print X.b          'abc
    Print X.c(33)      '3.14159265358979
End Sub
```

Notice the third element of the *typX* data structure, which is declared as a Variant. Recall that we can store just about anything in a Variant, which means that at runtime we can create an array and insert it into the Type data structure by assigning the array to the Variant.

Replacing Type Structures with Classes

You can't pass Type structures between components such as objects or controls created with Visual Basic. You can, however, create classes that contain similar structures and then pass the data as an object. The following class module is equivalent to the *typX* structure:

```
'Class objX module level
Option Explicit

'These declarations are read/write properties of objX
Private mA() As Integer
Public b As String
Public c As Variant

Property Get a(Index As Integer) As Integer
    a = mA(Index)
End Property

Property Let a(Index As Integer, setting As Integer)
    mA(Index) = setting
End Property
```

(continued)

```
Sub RedimA(LB As Integer, UB As Integer)
    ReDim mA(LB To UB)
End Sub
```

Declare a variable with the *objX* type, being sure to use the New keyword. This creates an instance of the object, allocating storage for its data members:

```
Private Sub Form_Click()
    'Create a new instance of the object
    Dim X As New objX
    'Use ReDimA method to change bounds of array
    X.ReDimA 22, 33
    'Rest of code works same as before
    'Assign values into the structure
    X.a(27) = 29
    X.b = "abc"
    'Insert entire array into the structure
    Dim y(100) As Double
    y(33) = 4 * Atn(1)
    X.c = y()
    'Verify a few elements of the structure
    Print X.a(27)    '29
    Print X.b        'abc
    Print X.c(33)    '3.14159265358979
End Sub
```

Note that arrays can't be public members of a class. You need to create a special method to handle resizing the array and a property to return values from the array. Objects also take more time and memory to create than Type structures. Objects only make useful replacements for Type structures when you need to move those structures of data across components.

Memory Alignment

32-bit Visual Basic, in its attempt to mesh well with 32-bit operating system standards, performs alignment of Type structure elements on 4-byte boundaries in memory (known as *DWORD alignment*). This means that the amount of memory your Type structures actually use is probably more than you'd expect. More important, it means that the old trick of using LSet to transfer binary data from one Type structure to another might not work as you expect it to.

Again, your best bet is to experiment carefully and remain aware of this potential trouble spot. It could cause the kind of bugs that are hard to track down unless you're lucidly aware of the potential for trouble.

Dear John, How Do I...

Create New Data Types with Classes?

As shown in the section titled "Replacing Type Structures with Classes" earlier in this chapter, you can use class modules instead of Type structures when you need to pass structures of data between components. But that doesn't even scratch the surface of what you can do.

First, a little terminology. *Classes* or *class modules* are where objects are defined, just as Type structures are where user-defined data types are defined. The actual object is an *instance* of the class. Classes define what kind of data the object can contain in its *properties* and how the object behaves through its *methods*.

Classes can range from very simple to vastly complex. Of course, it's best to start with the simple. This section shows you how to create an unsigned Integer data type using a class module. Chapter 5, "Object-Oriented Programming," covers more complex aspects of object-oriented programming.

Creating a New Data Type

The first section of this chapter showed you how to simulate unsigned integers in Visual Basic code. You can put that code into a UInt class to create a new, "fundamental" data type for working with unsigned integers.

The module level of the UInt class, shown below, defines the Type structures and private variables used to return the high and low bytes from the integer. It's a good idea to specify the uses of a class, as well as include comments within the class module. This makes the class more easily understood and more likely to be reused.

```
'Class UInt module level
'Provides an unsigned integer type
'Methods:
'    None
'Properties:
'    Value (default)
'    HiByte
'    LoByte

'Type structures used for returning high/low bytes
Private Type UnsignedIntType
     lo As Byte
     hi As Byte
```

(continued)

```
End Type

Private Type SignedIntType
    n As Integer
End Type

'Internal variables for returning high/low bytes
Private mnValue As SignedIntType
Private muValue As UnsignedIntType
```

The class uses the private module-level variable *mnValue* to store the actual value of the property, but access to this variable is controlled through the Let Value and Get Value property procedures, as shown below. These procedures perform the conversions needed to simulate an unsigned integer.

```
Property Let Value(lIn As Long)
    mnValue.n = (lIn And &H7FFF&) - (lIn And &H8000&)
    LSet muValue = mnValue
End Property

Property Get Value() As Long
    Value = mnValue.n And &HFFFF&
End Property
```

Each property has a Let procedure in which the value of the property is assigned and a Get procedure in which the property value is returned. The HiByte and LoByte properties, for example, are implemented using Let and Get procedures, as shown here:

```
Property Let HiByte(bIn As Byte)
    muValue.hi = bIn
    LSet mnValue = muValue
End Property

Property Get HiByte() As Byte
    LSet muValue = mnValue
    HiByte = muValue.hi
End Property

Property Let LoByte(bIn As Byte)
    muValue.lo = bIn
    LSet mnValue = muValue
End Property

Property Get LoByte() As Byte
    LSet muValue = mnValue
    LoByte = muValue.lo
End Property
```

Using the New Data Type

To use the UInt class, be sure to declare the object variable as New, as shown below. This creates a new instance of the class.

```
Dim uNewVar As New UInt
```

The Value property of the UInt class is the *default* property. (For information about how to set the default property of a class, see Chapter 5, "Object-Oriented Programming.") You can omit the property name Value when using the property, as shown here:

```
'Set the default property
uNewVar = 64552
```

The HiByte and LoByte properties can be called just like any other Visual Basic property, as shown here:

```
'Set the high byte
uNewVar.HiByte = &HFF

'Return the low byte
Print Hex(uNewVar.LoByte)
```

Parameters

Visual Basic 5 removes data type restrictions on optional parameters and adds default values and enumeration (Enums) to parameter declarations. These improvements let you be a lot more strict about the values your procedures accept, helping you tighten up your code.

> NOTE: In this chapter, an *argument* is a constant, a variable, or an expression that is passed to a procedure. A *parameter* is the variable that receives the argument when it is passed to the procedure.

Dear John, How Do I...

Use Named Arguments?

The most common way to pass arguments in Visual Basic, and indeed in almost every programming language, is by position in a comma-delimited list. So, for instance, if you create a procedure that expects the parameters (*Red, Green, Blue*), you always pass three values to the procedure and it's understood that the first argument will always represent *Red*, the second *Green*, and the last *Blue*.

Now take a look at the following procedure and the code that calls it. Here I've used explicit parameter names to pass the three arguments, but in reverse order!

```
Option Explicit

Private Sub FormColor(Red, Green, Blue)
    BackColor = RGB(Red * 256, Green * 256, Blue * 256)
End Sub

Private Sub Form_Click()
    FormColor Blue:=0, Green:=0.5, Red:=1     'Brown
End Sub
```

The real value of named arguments lies not so much in their ability to be passed in any order as in their ability to clearly pass a subset of parameters to a procedure that expects any of a large number of parameters. To take full advantage of named arguments in your applications, you need to make some or all of your parameters optional, which takes us right into the next question.

Dear John, How Do I...

Use Optional Parameters?

Optional parameters are especially useful when you have a relatively long list of parameters for a procedure. Here's a simple modification of the previous example to show you how this works:

```
Option Explicit

Private Sub FormColor( _
    Optional Red = 0, _
    Optional Green = 0, _
    Optional Blue = 0 _
)
    BackColor = RGB(Red * 256, Green * 256, Blue * 256)
End Sub

Private Sub Form_Click()
    FormColor Green:=0.5    'Medium green
End Sub
```

By adding the keyword Optional to the parameter declarations in the FormColor procedure, you can pass any or all of the parameters as named arguments to clearly indicate which parameters are passed. In this example, I've passed only the *Green* parameter, knowing that the procedure will default to the value *0* for the optional parameters I didn't pass.

Notice that the default values are set in the parameter list. In Visual Basic 4, you had to check each optional parameter by using an IsMissing function and then setting a default value. In Visual Basic 5, optional parameters can now have specific data types other than Variant. However, you still have to be sure that once a parameter is defined with the Optional modifier, all remaining parameters in the list are also declared as optional.

See Also...

- The Metric application in Chapter 28, "Development Tools," for a demonstration of the use of optional parameters

Dear John, How Do I...

Pass Parameter Arrays?

If you declare the last parameter in the parameter list of a procedure as a Variant array with the ParamArray keyword, you can pass a flexible number of arguments. The following code demonstrates this by converting any number of arguments passed into a vertically formatted string list of all items:

```
Option Explicit

Private Function MakeVerticalList(ParamArray N()) As String
    Dim A$, i
    For i = LBound(N) To UBound(N)
        A$ = A$ + vbCrLf + CStr(N(i))
    Next i
    MakeVerticalList = A$
End Function

Private Sub Form_Click()
    Dim A As Integer
    Dim B As Single
    Dim C As String
    A = 123
    B = 3.1416
    C = "This is a test."
    Print MakeVerticalList(A, B, C)
    Print
    Print MakeVerticalList("This", "time", "we'll", "pass five", _
        "string arguments.")
End Sub
```

Notice that I called MakeVerticalList twice, the first time with a variety of types of arguments—three in all—and the second time with five string arguments.

Figure 4-1 on the following page shows the results displayed when you click on the form.

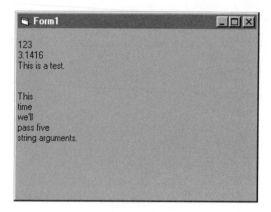

Figure 4-1.
Results of passing first three and then five arguments to the MakeVerticalList function.

Dear John, How Do I...

Pass Any Type of Data in a Parameter?

Remember that Variant variables can contain just about any kind of data imaginable. This opens the door to passing any type of data you want to a parameter as long as the parameter has been declared as Variant. For example, in this code sample I've passed an integer, a string, and an array to a small procedure:

```
Option Explicit

Private Sub varTest(V)
    Print TypeName(V)
End Sub

Private Sub Form_Click()
    Dim A(3, 4, 5, 6, 7) As Double
    varTest 123
    varTest "This is a test string."
    varTest A
End Sub
```

The Variant parameter *V*, defined as the only parameter in the varTest procedure, accepts whatever you want to pass it. The TypeName function is then used to display the type of data that was passed.

Figure 4-2 shows the results of running this sample code.

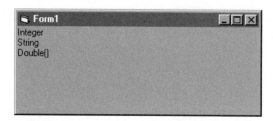

Figure 4-2.
Results of a procedure that uses a Variant parameter.

Dear John, How Do I...

Use Enums in Parameters?

You use enumerations (Enums) to restrict parameters to a predefined set of values. An Enum defines a set of symbolic values, much the same as Const, but the name of the Enum can be included in a procedure's parameter type declaration. When you use the procedure, Visual Basic's Auto List Members feature displays a list of the possible values for the argument. To see how this works, type in the following code:

```
Enum Number
    Zero
    One
    Two
    Three
End Enum

Sub ShowNumber(Value As Number)
    MsgBox Value
End Sub

Sub Form_Load()
    ShowNumber One
End Sub
```

After you type *ShowNumber* in the Form_Load event procedure, Visual Basic displays the list of Enums to choose from. A similar thing happens when you use an Enum in the parameter list of a user control property. The following code shows a simple Value property in a user control:

```
Enum Number
    Zero
    One
    Two
End Enum

Dim mValue As Number

Property Get Value() As Number
    Value = mValue
End Property

Property Let Value(Setting As Number)
    mValue = Setting
End Property

Private Sub UserControl_ReadProperties(PropBag As PropertyBag)
    mValue = PropBag.ReadProperty("Value", One)
End Sub

Private Sub UserControl_WriteProperties(PropBag As PropertyBag)
    PropBag.WriteProperty "Value", mValue, One
End Sub
```

The ReadProperties and WriteProperties event procedures maintain the Value property setting in the Properties window. When you select the Value property in the Properties window, you will see a list of possible values from the Number Enum: *Zero, One,* and *Two,* as shown in Figure 4-3.

Another bit of helpful information to know about Enums is that Enums automatically coerce floating-point values to long integer values. For example, if you pass the value *0.9* to the ShowNumber procedure shown earlier, it will display *1.* Also, Enums don't provide any special type checking—invalid settings are gleefully accepted. You'll have to write code to check whether a passed-in value is valid.

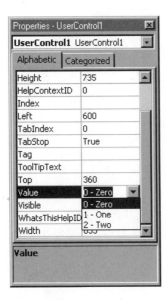

Figure 4-3.
List of possible values for the Value property from the Number Enum in the
Properties window.

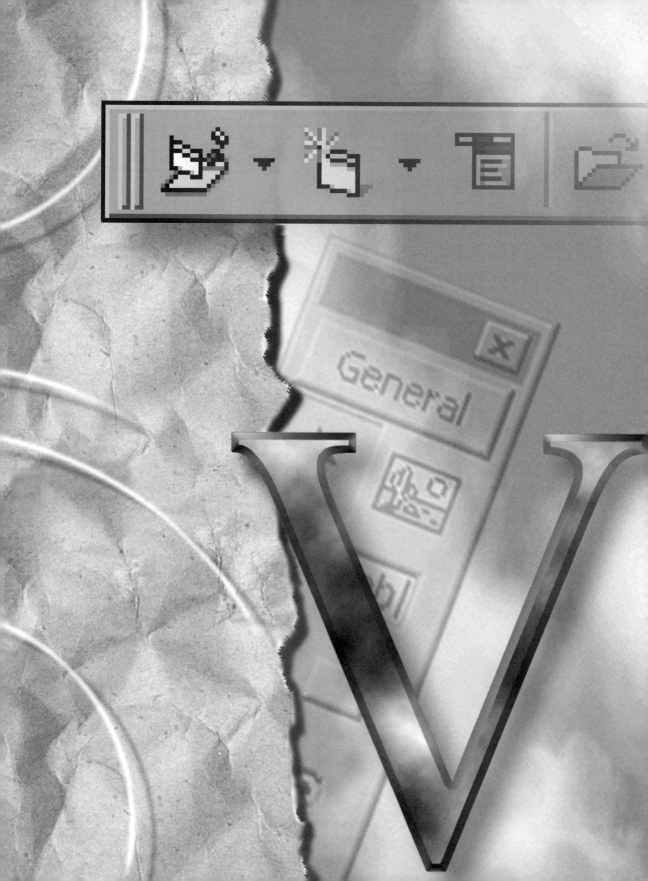

CHAPTER FIVE

Object-Oriented Programming

Perhaps the most important new features in Visual Basic are those that allow you to do true object-oriented programming (OOP). This is a huge topic, and indeed many pages of Microsoft's manuals deal with this important subject in great detail. Instead of repeating all these details, in this chapter I'll highlight the main concepts, provide simple code examples, and give you a foundation from which to further your studies.

Object-oriented programming in Visual Basic is a fascinating subject. Class modules let you structure your applications in ways that you never could before, collections provide a way to flexibly organize and structure the objects you create, and ActiveX technology provides the mechanism to share and use objects across the board. You'll find yourself able to grasp the organization of much bigger projects and keep this structure clearly in mind as you work with objects. Team programming and single programmer projects alike are made easier by this object-oriented approach.

There's a lot of new information to be absorbed when you first get into the object-oriented programming aspects of using Visual Basic. With a little persistence, and by experimenting with the examples provided in this book or elsewhere, you'll soon start to get the hang of it. For me, the moment of enlightenment came when I suddenly realized that creating objects is actually a lot of fun!

In this chapter, we'll create a sample object and a sample ActiveX EXE, and we'll take a look at one way to work with collections of objects. We will also discuss two new features supported in Visual Basic 5, polymorphism and friend methods.

Dear John, How Do I...
Choose Between an ActiveX EXE and a DLL?

ActiveX EXEs and ActiveX dynamic link libraries (DLLs) let you combine your objects into components that can provide these objects to other applications (clients) through Automation. Both types of ActiveX components expose some or all of their objects to external applications.

A client application that creates and uses instances of an ActiveX EXE's exposed objects uses them *out-of-process,* which means that the code in the ActiveX EXE runs in its own thread and in its own workspace, separate from the code space of the client application.

On the other hand, an ActiveX DLL can't run as a stand-alone application but instead provides a dynamic link library of objects for applications to use *in-process.* This means that the code from the ActiveX DLL runs in the same single-threaded code space as the calling application, resulting in faster, more efficient program execution. Both types of ActiveX components are useful, and Visual Basic lets you build both types without resorting to C or other languages.

Dear John, How Do I...
Create All My Objects in External ActiveX Components?

You don't have to! There's a lot of hype and interest and great reasons to create and use objects in ActiveX components, but an excellent way to get started creating your own objects is to simply add class modules to your standard EXE Visual Basic projects.

Objects defined by class modules within your project are automatically private to your application. (If you want to let other applications create instances of your objects, well then, we're back to talking about ActiveX components.) Your application can create one or multiple instances of each class module–defined object, and each copy has its own set of data. One of the advantages of these objects is that the memory used by each instance is recovered immediately when the object is destroyed. Probably the biggest advantage, however, is the increased structure, understandability, and organization that OOP techniques bring to your programming efforts. Getting rid of Basic's line numbers a few years back was a huge step in the right direction, and the addition of objects is another one.

The next two sections provide a relatively simple example of an object created in a standard EXE. This is the simplest way to start working with objects.

Dear John, How Do I...

Create a New Object?

The short answer is: create a class module. Class modules open the door to some powerful new ways of structuring programs. The printed manuals and online help are the best resources to study for all the intricacies of class modules and the objects you can create with them. Here I'll present a simple example, just enough to whet your appetite and provide a framework for learning. Throughout this book, you'll find numerous working examples of class modules—they provide a great way to create structured code, and I like using them.

Loan—A Class Module Example

To demonstrate many of the most important features of objects, I've built a relatively simple class module that lets you create Loan objects. The Loan object is used to calculate the payment schedule over the life of a loan. You could easily add more methods and properties to this class or restructure the way it works, but I kept it fairly simple on purpose, to provide a working model for you to study.

To create a class module, start a new Standard EXE project, choose Add Class Module from the Project menu, and double-click the Class Module icon. Add the following code, change the Name property to *Loan*, and save the module as LOAN.CLS. The code for the Loan class is followed by explanations of the different parts of the code.

```
'LOAN.CLS - This is a class module that provides a
'blueprint for creating Loan objects

Option Explicit

'These variables are public properties of Loan object
Public Principal As Currency
Public AnnualInterestRate As Single

'These variables are known only within this class module
Private Mo As Integer      'Number of months of loan
Private Ba() As Currency   'Amortized balance array

'Lets user assign a value to Months property
Property Let Months(M)
    Mo = M
End Property
```

(continued)

```
'Gets current value of Months property for user
Property Get Months()
    Months = Mo
End Property

'Lets user assign a value to Years property
Property Let Years(Y)
    Mo = Y * 12
End Property

'Gets current value of Years property for user
Property Get Years()
    Years = Mo / 12
End Property

'Gets calculated Payment property for user
Property Get Payment()
    Dim MonthlyInterestRate As Single
    'Verify that all properties are loaded
    If Principal = 0 Or AnnualInterestRate = 0 Or Mo = 0 Then
        Payment = 0
    Else
        MonthlyInterestRate = AnnualInterestRate / 1200
        Payment = (-MonthlyInterestRate * Principal) / _
            ((MonthlyInterestRate + 1) ^ (-Mo) - 1)
    End If
End Property

'Method to fill amortized balance array
Public Sub Amortize()
    Dim i
    Dim Balance As Currency
    Dim Paid As Currency
    ReDim Ba(0)
    Ba(0) = Principal
    Paid = CCur(Payment / 100) * 100      'Rounds to nearest penny
    Do Until Ba(i) <= 0
        i = i + 1
        ReDim Preserve Ba(i)
        Ba(i) = Ba(i - 1) * (1 + AnnualInterestRate / 1200)
        Ba(i) = Ba(i) - Paid
        Ba(i) = CCur(Ba(i) / 100) * 100
    Loop
End Sub

'Gets balance of loan after N months for user
Property Get Balance(N)
```

(continued)

66

```
   If N > UBound(Ba) Or N < 1 Then
       Balance = 0
   Else
       Balance = Ba(N)
   End If
End Property
```

The Loan objects created in the main program will have properties and methods, just like other objects. The simplest way to create a property is to declare public variables. Principal and AnnualInterestRate, declared at the top of the LOAN.CLS listing, are two such properties:

```
Public Principal As Currency
Public AnnualInterestRate As Single
```

Two variables, *Mo* and *Ba()*, are declared as Private, as shown below, so that the outside world will be unaware of their existence. Within the Loan object, you can be assured that the values contained in these variables are always under direct control of the object's internal code.

```
Private Mo As Integer      'Number of months of loan
Private Ba() As Currency   'Amortized balance array
```

Mo stores the number of months of the loan. I could have made this a simple public variable, but I've designed the Loan object with two related public properties, Years and Months, either of which can be set by the user to define the length of the loan. These properties then internally set the value of *Mo*. Read on to see how these two properties are set up to do this.

The Property Let statement provides a way to create a property in your object that can take action when the user assigns a value to it. Simple properties, such as Principal, just sit there and accept whatever value the user assigns. The Months property, on the other hand, is defined in such a way that you can add code that will be executed whenever a value is assigned to the property. In this case, the code is a simple assignment of the number of months to the local *Mo* variable for safekeeping:

```
Property Let Months(M)
    Mo = M
End Property
```

The Property Let and Property Get statements work hand in hand to build one writable and readable property of an object. Here the Property Get Months statement provides a way for the user to access the current contents of the Months property:

```
Property Get Months()
    Months = Mo
End Property
```

Stop and think about what I've just done here. From the outside world, the Months property appears to be a simple variable that can store values assigned to it, and it supplies the same value when the property is accessed. But when you look at the implementation of the Months property from a viewpoint inside the Loan class module, you see a lot more going on. Months is not just a simple variable. Code is activated when values are written to or read from the property, and it's possible for this code to take just about any action imaginable. It's a powerful concept!

If you don't add a corresponding Property Get statement to go along with a Property Let, the defined property will be write-only. Conversely, a Property Get without a corresponding Property Let results in a read-only property. For some properties, this can be a good thing. This is true for the Payment property, which is described later.

The Years property, shown below, provides a second, alternative, property that the user can set to define the length of the loan. Notice that the value set into the Years property is multiplied by 12 internally to convert it to months. This detail is hidden from the user.

```
Property Let Years(Y)
    Mo = Y * 12
End Property

Property Get Years()
    Years = Mo / 12
End Property
```

Compare the Years and Months property procedures to see why I created the local variable *Mo* to store the actual length of the loan separately from the properties used to set this value. Again, the implementation of the Years and Months properties is encapsulated within the Loan object, and the details of how these properties do their thing is hidden from the outside world.

When the user accesses the value of the Loan object's Payment property, shown below, a complicated calculation is triggered, and the payment amount is computed from the current value of the other property settings. This is a clear example that shows why Property Get statements add useful capabilities beyond those provided by properties that are created by simply declaring a public variable in a class module.

```
Property Get Payment()
    Dim MonthlyInterestRate As Single
    If Principal = 0 Or AnnualInterestRate = 0 Or Mo = 0 Then
        Payment = 0
    Else
```

(continued)

```
        MonthlyInterestRate = AnnualInterestRate / 1200
        Payment = (-MonthlyInterestRate * Principal) / _
            ((MonthlyInterestRate + 1) ^ (-Mo) - 1)
    End If
End Property
```

The Amortize procedure, shown below, defines a method of the Loan object. When the user calls this method, the Loan object expands and fills the local dynamic array *Ba()* with monthly balances until the balance goes to 0 or below. This array is filled just once, when this method is called, and then values are returned one at a time by the Balance property, which follows.

```
Public Sub Amortize()
    Dim i
    Dim Balance As Currency
    Dim Paid As Currency
    ReDim Ba(0)
    Ba(0) = Principal
    Paid = CCur(Payment / 100) * 100        'Rounds to nearest penny
    Do Until Ba(i) <= 0
        i = i + 1
        ReDim Preserve Ba(i)
        Ba(i) = Ba(i - 1) * (1 + AnnualInterestRate / 1200)
        Ba(i) = Ba(i) - Paid
        Ba(i) = CCur(Ba(i) / 100) * 100
    Loop
End Sub
```

The Balance property, which is set up as a read-only property because I define it only in a Property Get statement with no corresponding Property Let, is shown here. The Balance property returns a precalculated value from the monthly balances array.

```
Property Get Balance(N)
    If N > UBound(Ba) Or N < 1 Then
        Balance = 0
    Else
        Balance = Ba(N)
    End If
End Property
```

If anything goes wrong here—if the month number is out of range, or if the user hasn't called the Amortize method first, for example—the property will return the value *0.* This is a simplified way to handle potential errors. My intent is not to cover the best ways to handle all potential errors here but simply to show you an example class object in a simplified, straightforward manner.

See Also...

- The next section, "Dear John, How Do I...Use My New Object?" for a demonstration of how to use objects

Dear John, How Do I...

Use My New Object?

The Loan class module doesn't actually create an object; it just provides a blueprint, or a definition, that lets your program stamp out one or more real Loan objects as needed. Let's complete the example by adding the LOAN.CLS module to a simple project and doing something with it.

Start with a new Standard EXE project containing just a single form. I'll keep this form very simple as its only purpose is to create and demonstrate a Loan object. Change the form's Caption property to *Please Click on This Form.* Add the LOAN.CLS class module created in the previous section to your project, and add the following lines of code to your form. Following the code listing are explanations of the different parts of this code.

```
Option Explicit

Private Sub Form_Click()
Dim loanTest As New Loan
Dim Mon As Integer
Dim Bal As Currency

    'Set loan parameters
    Me.Cls
    loanTest.Principal = 1000
    loanTest.Months = 12
    loanTest.AnnualInterestRate = 9.6
    'Display parameters used
    Print "Principal: ", , Format(loanTest.Principal, "Currency")
    Print "No. Months: " , , loanTest.Months
    Print "Interest Rate:", , Format(loanTest.AnnualInterestRate _
        / 100, "Percent")
    Print "Monthly Payment: ", Format(loanTest.Payment, "Currency")
    Print
    loanTest.Amortize
    'Display payment schedule
    Do
```

(continued)

```
        Mon = Mon + 1
        Bal = loanTest.Balance(Mon)
        If Bal <= 0 Then Exit Do
        Print "Month: "; Mon,
        Print "Balance: "; Format(Bal, "Currency")
      Loop
End Sub
```

Figure 5-1 shows the form during development.

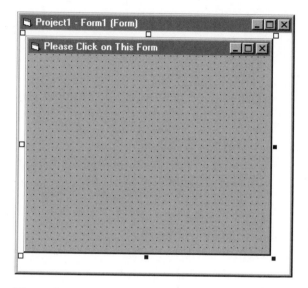

Figure 5-1.
The form used to demonstrate the Loan object.

A new Loan object named loanTest is created when you click on the form, as shown in the code below. The Loan object will be destroyed automatically, just like any other local variable, when it goes out of scope.

```
Dim loanTest As New Loan
```

The following three lines assign values to three of the properties we've created for the Loan object. Review the Loan class module to see how the Months property works differently from the Principal and AnnualInterestRate properties.

```
loanTest.Principal = 1000
loanTest.Months = 12
loanTest.AnnualInterestRate = 9.6
```

As you output results, various properties of the Loan object are accessed as required, as shown in the following code. In most cases, the loanTest object simply hands back each value as it is currently stored in the object. In the case of the loanTest.Payment property, however, a complex calculation is triggered. The calling code is blissfully unaware of when, where, and how the calculations are performed.

```
Print "Principal: ", , Format(loanTest.Principal, "Currency")
Print "No. Months: ", , loanTest.Months
Print "Interest Rate:", , Format(loanTest.AnnualInterestRate _
    / 100, "Percent")
Print "Monthly Payment: ", Format(loanTest.Payment, "Currency")
Print
```

Calling the Amortize method, shown here, tells the loanTest object to go ahead and internally prepare a table of loan balances, in preparation for accessing each month's balance in the next few lines of the program:

```
loanTest.Amortize
```

The last few lines of our sample program display an amortized table of the loan's balance at the end of each month of the loan:

```
Do
    Mon = Mon + 1
    Bal = loanTest.Balance(Mon)
    If Bal <= 0 Then Exit Do
    Print "Month: "; Mon,
    Print "Balance: "; Format(Bal, "Currency")
Loop
```

When the end of the Form_Click event procedure is reached, all variables declared in the procedure are automatically destroyed by the system. This includes the instance of the Loan object, with all its code and data.

Figure 5-2 shows the displayed results of running this program. Notice that you could greatly improve and expand on this simple program without ever having to touch the contents of the Loan class module.

A carefully designed object, in the form of a class module, lets you extend Visual Basic by adding some new programmable objects to your bag of tricks. Once you get an object the way you want it, all you need to document for future reference and use is the object's *interface,* which is its set of public properties and methods. The internal workings and implementation of the object can be mentally "black-boxed" and ignored. Imagine the object encased in a hard shell, with just the defined interface visible from the outside world. This is what is meant by the object-oriented programming term *encapsulation.* The object itself is responsible for the correct implementation of its features and behavior, and the calling application is responsible for understanding and correctly using the object's interface. This encapsulation makes it much easier to create and debug larger applications. That demonstrates the true power and beauty of object-oriented programming!

Please Click on This Form

Principal:	$1,000.00
No. Months:	12
Interest Rate:	9.60%
Monthly Payment:	$87.73

Month: 1   Balance: $920.27
Month: 2   Balance: $839.90
Month: 3   Balance: $758.89
Month: 4   Balance: $677.23
Month: 5   Balance: $594.92
Month: 6   Balance: $511.95
Month: 7   Balance: $428.32
Month: 8   Balance: $344.02
Month: 9   Balance: $259.04
Month: 10 Balance: $173.38
Month: 11 Balance: $87.04
Month: 12 Balance: $0.01

Figure 5-2.
Output generated by using a Loan object.

The Loan class was simply added as another module to the sample application. This is a great way to use class modules, but you can also combine one or more class modules into ActiveX components.

See Also...

- The section "Dear John, How Do I...Create and Use an Active EXE?" later in this chapter, and Chapter 25, "Advanced Programming Techniques," for more information about ActiveX components

- The Lottery application in Chapter 27, "Graphics," for a demonstration of the use of objects

Dear John, How Do I...

Set a Default Property for My Object?

I prefer to always set all properties explicitly rather than by using the shortcut for an object's default property, but some people prefer to do it the other way. For example, the Text property is the default for the TextBox control, which means that you can set the Text property explicitly or by default. Both of these lines have exactly the same effect:

```
Text1.Text = "This string is assigned to the Text property."
Text1 = "This string is assigned to the Text property."
```

It's not well documented, but Visual Basic now lets you assign a default property to your own objects, if you like to use this technique. Let's see how this is done by setting the Loan object's Principal property as its default property. Bring up the code for the Loan class, and from the Tools menu choose Procedure Attributes to display the Procedure Attributes dialog box. From the Name drop-down list, select the Principal property. Click the Advanced button, select the (Default) option from the Procedure ID drop-down list, and click OK. The Principal property is now the default for the Loan object.

To verify the correct operation of this default property, bring up the code for the form you created to test the Loan object. Find the line on which the Principal property is set to *1000*, and edit the line to remove the .Principal part, as shown here:

```
loanTest = 1000
```

Run the test application, and verify that it still calculates the loan values correctly.

Dear John, How Do I...
Create and Use an ActiveX EXE?

ActiveX EXEs and ActiveX DLLs are similar creatures. In Chapter 25, "Advanced Programming Techniques," I'll walk you through the creation of an ActiveX DLL; here I'll walk you through the creation of an ActiveX EXE. An ActiveX EXE can run by itself, yet it also provides objects for use by external applications. As mentioned, these objects run out-of-process, which means that they run in their own code space and on different threads of execution than a client application.

Chance—An ActiveX EXE Example

In this example, we'll build a very simple ActiveX EXE containing the definition for one type of object. Or, to use the correct terminology, we'll create one *class*. The class can then function as a template to produce copies of the object. Once the ActiveX EXE is up and running and automatically registered with the system, we'll build a second, more conventional Visual Basic application that will create a couple of these objects on the fly, and properties and methods of these objects will be manipulated to get the desired results.

We'll create an object named Dice in an ActiveX EXE component named Chance. Even though I've named the object Dice, I've provided properties that let the calling application set the number of sides so that each die can act more like a coin (if it has two sides), like a dodecahedron-shaped die (if the number of sides is set to 12), and so on.

DICE.CLS

Let's jump right in and start building the ActiveX EXE. Start a new project, and double-click the ActiveX EXE icon in the New Project dialog box. Add the following lines of code to the class module, change its Name property to *Dice*, save this class module as DICE.CLS, and save the project as CHANCE.VBP:

```
Option Explicit

'Declare properties that define the range of possible values
Public Smallest As Integer
Public Largest As Integer

'Declare a read-only property and define its value
'as a roll of the die
Public Property Get Value()
    Value = Int(Rnd * (Largest - Smallest + 1)) + Smallest
End Property

'Use a method to shuffle the random sequence
Public Sub Shuffle()
    Randomize
End Sub
```

This class module defines three properties and one method for the Dice object. Smallest and Largest are two properties that I've declared as public variables so that the client application (which is created a little later on) can set the range of returned values—in this case, the number of sides of the die. Properties of objects are often simply declared as public variables in this way.

Value is another property of the Dice object, but in this case we want to perform a little calculation before handing a number back to the client application. The Property Get statement provides the mechanism for performing any extra steps we specify when the property's value is requested. In this case, a random number is generated to simulate a roll of the die, and this number is returned as the value of the property. (For the mathematical purists among us, the number is not truly random, but it's close enough for our needs.) The Value property is read-only by the client application because the Property Get statement was used but there is no corresponding Property Let statement. Adding a Property Let statement would enable the client application to write a new value to the Value property. In this example, we just want to return a random roll of the die, so we have no need to let the client application set a value for this property.

Shuffle is a simple method I've added so that the object will have at least one method to show for itself. When this method is called, the object will randomize the random number generator to effectively shuffle the outcome of rolls of the die.

Let's add a little code that runs when the Chance ActiveX EXE starts up. This will make it easier to follow the action later on. From the Project menu, choose Add Module, and then double-click the Module icon in the Add Module dialog box. Add the following code to this module, and save it as CHANCE.BAS:

```
Option Explicit

Sub Main()
    Dim diceTest As New Dice
    diceTest.Smallest = 1
    diceTest.Largest = 6
    diceTest.Shuffle
    MsgBox "A roll of two dice: " & _
        diceTest.Value & "," & diceTest.Value, _
        0, "Message from the Chance ActiveX EXE"
End Sub
```

From the Project menu, choose Project Properties to open the Project Properties dialog box. From the Startup Object drop-down list, select Sub Main, enter *Chance* in the Project Name field, enter *Chance - ActiveX EXE Example* in the Project Description field, and then click OK. Finally, from the File menu choose Make Chance.exe. In the displayed Make Project dialog box, select a location and click OK. This will compile and automatically register the Chance ActiveX EXE.

Testing the ActiveX EXE Component

Now that the Chance ActiveX EXE is compiled and registered, we can reference it and use its objects from any application that supports ActiveX programming. Let's demonstrate this by creating a second Visual Basic application that uses the ActiveX EXE we just created.

Start a new Standard EXE project, and save it as DICEDEMO.VBP. We'll keep this test program simple, so don't bother to rename the Form1 file. Change the form's Caption property to *Taking a Chance with Our ActiveX EXE,* and add a single command button. I changed the button's Caption to *Roll 'em* and moved it off to the upper right side of the form. Add the following code to the form to complete it, and save your work:

```
Option Explicit

Dim diceTest As New Dice

Private Sub Command1_Click()
    diceTest.Shuffle
    diceTest.Smallest = 1
    diceTest.Largest = 2
    Me.Print "Coin:" & diceTest.Value,
    diceTest.Largest = 6
    Me.Print "Dice:" & diceTest.Value,
    diceTest.Largest = 12
    Me.Print "Dodecahedron:" & diceTest.Value
End Sub
```

Figure 5-3 shows the form during development.

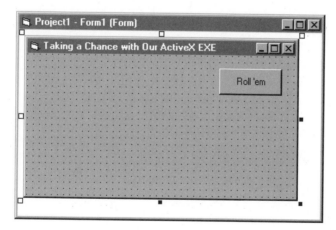

Figure 5-3.
The DiceDemo form.

This form creates an instance of our new Dice object, so we need to add a reference to the Chance ActiveX EXE in order for the current project to know where the Dice object is defined. Choose References from the Project menu, and locate the check box labeled Chance - ActiveX EXE Example in the References dialog box. (Recall that this is the project description we gave the Chance project.) Check this box and click OK to add this reference to the DiceDemo project.

That should do it! Run the program, and notice what happens. First our new test form opens, ready for us to click the Roll 'em button. When you click this button, the Dice object is created, and rolls of 2-sided, 6-sided, and 12-sided dice are tallied and displayed on the form. Each click creates another line of pseudorandom values. Figure 5-4 shows the results of clicking this button several times.

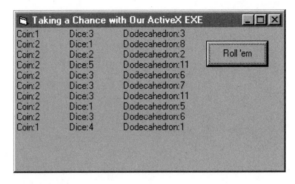

Figure 5-4.
The DiceDemo application after the Roll 'em button has been clicked several times.

One other significant message appears the first time you click the Roll 'em button. As the Chance ActiveX EXE loads into memory, its Sub Main startup code displays a message box, and it also rolls a pair of dice using the Dice object defined within its own interior. The result is shown in Figure 5-5.

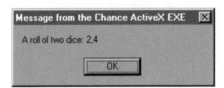

Figure 5-5.
The Chance ActiveX EXE displays this message when it loads.

This message box appears only once, when the Chance component first loads. In case you're wondering, the Chance ActiveX component will unload from memory when the last reference to any of its objects goes away—which happens when we terminate the DiceDemo application.

Dear John, How Do I...

Create an Object That Displays Forms?

The Loan and Dice sample objects shown earlier in this chapter don't display a visible interface, such as a form, to the user. Many objects don't present a visible interface, but there will be cases in which you'll want to create objects that use forms to collect data from the user.

It's very easy to add a form to an ActiveX EXE or ActiveX DLL project, but you need to be aware of one major gotcha—objects that display forms need to carefully manage the creation and destruction of those forms. A client application will never interact directly with a form in an ActiveX component (these forms are private to the component), so it's important that all house-keeping of the form be correctly implemented by the object within the component that is responsible for the form. Otherwise, instances of the object can remain hidden in memory, consuming resources and occasionally causing unexpected results.

The following code shows the class module definition for an object named User. This object is used to gather name and password information and displays a modal form with two text boxes, named *txtName* and *txtPassword,* and an OK button, named *cmdOK.*

```
'USER.CLS
'~~~.Name
Property Get Name()
    Name = frmPass.txtName
End Property

'~~~.Password
Property Get Password()
    Password = frmPass.txtPassword
End Property

'~~~.Show
Sub Show()
    frmPass.Show vbModal
End Sub

Private Sub Class_Terminate()
    'Unload form when object is destroyed
    Unload frmPass
End Sub
```

The form, named *frmPass,* contains only one event procedure, shown on the following page, to hide the form when the user clicks OK. This lets the object's creator validate the user name and password and quickly redisplay the form if the entered data is incorrect. The data on the form isn't cleared, making it easier for the user to make corrections.

```
'FRMPASS.FRM
Private Sub cmdOK_Click()
    Me.Hide
End Sub
```

To use this object, another application simply creates an instance of the object and then calls the Show method. The code below shows an example of how this can be done on a form containing a command button named *cmdSignOn*. Note the syntax for referencing the User class in the project named PasswordSample.

```
Private Sub cmdSignOn_Click()
    'Create an instance of the object
    Dim usrSignOn As New PasswordSample.User
    'Loop until user enters Guest password
    Do While usrSignOn.Password <> "Guest"
        'Display dialog box
        usrSignOn.Show
    Loop
End Sub
```

Figure 5-6 shows an example of the User Object form.

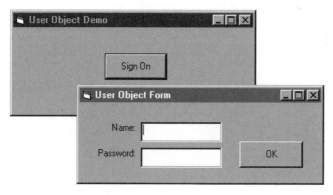

Figure 5-6.
Example of an object that displays a form.

To see the importance of managing form creation and destruction, remove the User object's Class_Terminate event procedure, and then create the object from another application, as shown above. When the cmdSignOn_Click event procedure ends, the *usrSignOn* variable loses scope and is destroyed, but the *frmPass* form remains loaded, running in a hidden instance of the object's application.

If the object's application is an EXE file, you can view this hidden instance in the Windows Task Manager by pressing Ctrl-Alt-Delete. You'll have to end the task from the Task Manager so that you can correct this problem and recompile a corrected version. Don't leave a "bad" version of this object around to cause problems later—hidden instances of object applications can be difficult to detect.

In general, you use the Class_Initialize and Class_Terminate event procedures to manage the creation and deletion of forms. Because this sample was so short, I let the form be created implicitly by whichever property or method was called first. I could just as easily have been explicit by including this Class_Initialize event procedure:

```
'Add to USER.CLS to be explicit
Private Sub Class_Initialize()
    'Create form when object is created
    'by calling Show method
    Me.Show
End Sub
```

It's a good idea to *always* be explicit when you create and destroy forms in objects. This will save time down the road when you are debugging.

Event, WithEvents, and RaiseEvent

There are several new, related Visual Basic statements that let you add your own user-defined events to your objects. I mention this here because one of the best uses for this new technique is to provide a way for private forms owned by objects in ActiveX components to immediately react with client applications. An event raised in a private form can trigger an immediate response in the ActiveX object responsible for that form, and that object can in turn raise an event back in the client application. The Books Online documentation topic Adding a Form to the ThingDemo Project provides a good example of this scenario.

Dear John, How Do I...
Work with Collections of Objects?

Visual Basic's Collection object lets you combine objects—or items of any data type for that matter—into a set that can be referred to as a single unit. You might think of a Collection object as an extremely flexible array that contains just about anything you want to put in it, including objects and other collections.

There are many ways to use collections in the Visual Basic objects you create. Some techniques are more "dangerous" than others, and depending on how much you want to protect yourself or other programmers, you can implement collections of objects in simple ways or in somewhat intricate but safe configurations. I suggest you thoroughly read the Books Online topics covering this subject to get a solid understanding of Microsoft's suggested approach and then give my approach a try. (Search Books Online for *House of Straw, House of Sticks,* and *House of Bricks* to locate these topics.)

I've found a simple method for implementing collections of user-defined objects within other objects. This method is fairly robust, and the technique can be easily duplicated or modified as desired. Within each type of object collection, you'll be responsible for manually renaming the collection properties and methods, but the pattern is straightforward and clear. The following example project demonstrates how it all works. We'll create a solar system structure comprising a top-level Solar object that contains a Planets collection. Each Planet object within this collection contains a Moons collection, and each Moon object is a very simple object consisting of just a Name property.

SolarSystem—A Collections Example

Start up Visual Basic, and open a new Standard EXE project. Set the form's Name property to *SolarSystem,* and save this form as SOLARSYSTEM.FRM. Save the project using the name SOLARSYSTEM.VBP. Change the form's Caption property to *Collections Example,* and add a command button named *cmdBuildSolarSystem.* Edit the button's Caption property to read *Build Solar System.* Add the following code to the form, and then save your work:

```
Option Explicit

Private Sub cmdBuildSolarSystem_Click()
    Dim Sol As New Solar
    'Build Earth and Moon
    Sol.AddPlanet 1
    With Sol.Planet(1)
        .Name = "Earth"
        .AddMoon 1
        With .Moon(1)
            .Name = "Luna"
        End With
    End With
    'Build Jovian system
    Sol.AddPlanet 2
    With Sol.Planet(2)
        .Name = "Jupiter"
```

(continued)

```
            .AddMoon 1
            With .Moon(1)
                .Name = "Callisto"
            End With
            .AddMoon 2
            With .Moon(2)
                .Name = "Io"
            End With
        End With
        'Display some of the info
        Print Sol.Planet(1).Name
        Print , Sol.Planet(1).Moon(1).Name
        Print Sol.Planet(2).Name
        Print , Sol.Planet(2).Moon(1).Name
        Print , Sol.Planet(2).Moon(2).Name
End Sub
```

Figure 5-7 shows the SolarSystem form during development.

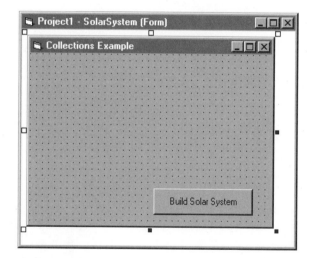

Figure 5-7.
The SolarSystem form, used to demonstrate nested collections of objects.

We'll refer back to this code in a minute, but first let's define the objects and collections of objects that this code creates and manipulates.

The Solar Class

From the Project menu, choose Add Class Module, and double-click the Class Module icon. Set the class module's Name property to *Solar*, add the code on the following page, and then save the module as SOLAR.CLS.

```
Option Explicit

Public Name As String

Private Planets As New Collection

'~~~~~~~~~~~~~~~~~~Planets

Public Function AddPlanet(nIndex As Integer) As Planet
    Dim newPlanet As New Planet
    Planets.Add newPlanet, CStr(nIndex)
    Set AddPlanet = newPlanet
End Function

Public Sub PlanetRemove(nIndex As Integer)
    Dim lLast As Long
    lLast = Planets.Count
    Planets.Remove CStr(nIndex)
    Planets.Add Planets.Item(CStr(lLast)), CStr(nIndex)
    Planets.Remove CStr(lLast)
End Sub

Public Function PlanetCount() As Integer
    PlanetCount = Planets.Count
End Function

Public Function Planet(nIndex As Integer) As Planet
    Set Planet = Planets.Item(CStr(nIndex))
End Function
```

Take a close look at the code in this module—it will be duplicated in a nearly identical layout to create the Planet object and can be copied and edited in the same pattern to make other objects containing collections.

The Solar class has one public property unrelated to the collection it contains. The Name property can be used by a client application to name each instance of the Solar object it might create. Notice that this Name property has nothing to do with the class Name property or with the name of the file used to save the class. The Name property here is readable and writable at runtime by the client application, unlike the other names I just mentioned.

The next line in the listing creates a private Planets collection object, visible only to code within this class. The remaining properties and methods all act on this hidden collection. I've set up the Planets collection in this private way to provide encapsulation, or protection, from the outside world. The Solar object itself is entirely responsible for maintaining the Planets collection it contains, and a client application can't mess with this collection directly.

The remaining methods and properties are used by a client application to tell the Solar object to add and remove Planet objects from its collection, to provide a count of the Planet objects currently in the collection, and to provide a reference to a specific Planet object within the collection. Take a look at the first few lines of code in the SolarSystem form. There you'll see the following line, which tells the Solar object to add the first Planet object to its collection using the AddPlanet method:

```
Sol.AddPlanet 1
```

The index number *1* is converted to a text tag to identify the particular Planet object created here, but you could theoretically use any number you want. To keep things simple and straightforward, I decided to let the client add Planet objects sequentially, starting with an integer index identifier of *1*. (If the client were to create Planet objects from within a loop, say from index numbers 1 through 100, the loop counter could be used as the identifier for each planet.) I suggest always using sequential integer identifiers for the method of nested object collections presented here.

The PlanetRemove method deletes any Planet object from within the Planets collection. In order to maintain a sequential 1-to-*N* identifier tag for all Planet objects within the collection, there are two ways to maintain the collection after a planet is deleted: you can shuffle Planet objects one notch each, effectively filling the *N*th gap created when the *N*th planet is removed, or you can copy the last Planet object in the list to the *N*th spot left open by the deleted planet and then shrink the collection by one member. The latter is the method I've chosen because it's faster, especially when the collections get larger. Notice in the PlanetRemove method that the intrinsic Remove, Count, and Item collection methods are used to grab the last Planet object in the collection to replace the deleted one.

To isolate the client application from the collection's built-in methods, I've provided an explicit PlanetCount property to return the collection's Count value and a Planet property to return a specific planet from the collection using the collection's Item method.

The Planet Class

Add a second class module to the SolarSystem project, set its Name property to *Planet,* and save the module as PLANET.CLS. This class defines the Planet objects that are collected within the Solar object. Add the code on the following page to this class module.

```
Option Explicit

Public Name As String

Private Moons As New Collection

'~~~~~~~~~~~~~~~~~~Moons

Public Function AddMoon(nIndex As Integer) As Moon
    Dim newMoon As New Moon
    Moons.Add newMoon, CStr(nIndex)
    Set AddMoon = newMoon
End Function

Public Sub MoonRemove(nIndex As Integer)
    Dim lLast As Long
    lLast = Moons.Count
    Moons.Remove CStr(nIndex)
    Moons.Add Moons.Item(CStr(lLast)), CStr(nIndex)
    Moons.Remove CStr(lLast)
End Sub

Public Function MoonCount() As Integer
    MoonCount = Moons.Count
End Function

Public Function Moon(nIndex As Integer) As Moon
    Set Moon = Moons.Item(CStr(nIndex))
End Function
```

Notice that this code listing is very much like the listing for the Solar object. Basically, each Planet object has a Name property, and each contains Moon objects in a Moons collection. The methods and properties used to maintain the Moons collection are the same (only the names have been changed to protect the innocent). Actually, I created this code by copying and pasting from the Solar class code and then changing all occurrences of the text *Planet* to *Moon*. You can use this same technique to mass-produce your own collections and objects.

So, just as the Solar objects contain 1 to *N* Planet objects, each Planet object maintains a collection of 1 to *M* Moon objects. There's nothing to stop us from nesting collection objects within other collection objects to even greater levels, but we've probably gone far enough here. We do still need to define a Moon object, but we'll resist the temptation to add a Craters collection to each Moon.

The Moon Class

This class is ultra-simple. Each Moon object will have a Name property, and that's all. Add another class module to the project, set its Name property to *Moon*, save it as MOON.CLS, and add the following code to create the public Name property:

```
Option Explicit

Public Name As String
```

How the Nested Collections Work

Let's take a closer look at the top-level code in the SolarSystem form. When the *cmdBuildSolarSystem* command button is clicked, a new Solar object, named Sol, is created. Since we aren't concerned with creating more than one of these Solar objects, we won't bother to set its Name property. (If we were creating a program to catalog all star systems in a collection of science fiction stories, we might want to create multiple Solar objects, and unique names for each would probably be appropriate.)

To greatly simplify the code, I decided to add just two of our solar system's planets and just a handful of moons. Feel free to build up the whole solar system if you feel so inclined! The following code adds a Planet object named Earth and a single Moon object named Luna:

```
'Build Earth and Moon
Sol.AddPlanet 1
With Sol.Planet(1)
    .Name = "Earth"
    .AddMoon 1
    With .Moon(1)
        .Name = "Luna"
    End With
End With
```

I've used the With statement to simplify the object references because we're going several layers deep here. However, we could access the Moon object's Name property by explicitly using dot notation to get to it. Here's what the line to set the Moon object's Name property would look like using the complete dot notation:

```
Sol.Planet(1).Moon(1).Name = "Luna"
```

Paraphrased, this says to set the string *Luna* as the Name property of the first Moon object in the collection maintained by the first Planet object in the collection maintained by the Solar object named Sol. Whew! You can see why

the With statement is useful. In addition to being easier for humans to com-
prehend, With blocks reduce the number of dereferencing steps required to
access each object and its properties, thus speeding things up.

The next block of code repeats the process, adding a second Planet
object, named Jupiter, and a couple of its Moon objects. Notice that index tags
are used to reference specific Planet and Moon objects in the nested collections.

```
'Build Jovian system
Sol.AddPlanet 2
With Sol.Planet(2)
    .Name = "Jupiter"
    .AddMoon 1
    With .Moon(1)
        .Name = "Callisto"
    End With
    .AddMoon 2
    With .Moon(2)
        .Name = "Io"
    End With
End With
```

Once this simplified model of our solar system is built up as a set of
collections of objects contained within other collections of objects, the next
few lines of code access this structure to display the names of all the nested
objects it contains:

```
'Display some of the info
Print Sol.Planet(1).Name
Print , Sol.Planet(1).Moon(1).Name
Print Sol.Planet(2).Name
Print , Sol.Planet(2).Moon(1).Name
Print , Sol.Planet(2).Moon(2).Name
```

Figure 5-8 shows these object names as displayed on the SolarSystem form
after the command button is clicked.

There are a lot of ways you could modify the technique presented here
to suit your needs. As mentioned, you can change the way objects are deleted
from their collections in order to maintain the original order. My method
relies on the client application's accuracy with the index tags. You might want
to add some code to check for the existence of an indicated object and handle
missing objects in a more robust fashion. This method serves as a strong con-
ceptual foundation on which you can build without getting too lost in all the
possible complexities. For many programming situations, this method can
provide everything you need.

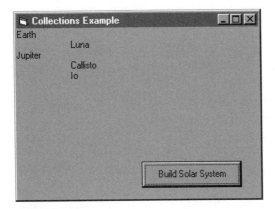

Figure 5-8.
The simplified solar system's Planets and Moons collections.

Dear John, How Do I...

Understand and Use Polymorphism?

This new OOP world is just full of new terminology and concepts! Let's take a look at *polymorphism*—what it means and how it can help you in your development efforts.

Simply put, polymorphism means that multiple objects will provide the same interface elements. For example, you might create a set of objects for your business that all provide a "standard" set of file functions. All of these objects would provide related methods and properties with predictably identical names, such as FileName, Read, and Write. This would simplify, standardize, and coordinate these objects, making them easier to use, and it would make them more predictable and consistent.

Visual Basic handles polymorphism a little differently than C++ does, for instance. Historically, in most OOP languages, methods and properties of one object are inherited by a new object. The new object can then optionally modify the inherited interface elements or expose them "as is" to client applications.

Visual Basic, on the other hand, doesn't use inheritance to provide polymorphism. Instead, Visual Basic lets us create an interface, which as mentioned is a set of related property and method definitions, contained in an *abstract class*. An abstract class is simply a class module containing empty, ghost-like definition shells of methods and properties. This special class is then declared in class modules that agree to implement these interface items using the Implements keyword.

I like to think of the abstract class as a kind of contract. Multiple class modules can each agree to abide by this shared contract by using the Implements keyword. A client application can then declare instances of these objects, including an object variable defined by the special abstract class. By accessing each object's implemented interface elements through the abstract class–defined object, it's guaranteed that each object will handle the agreed-upon method or property in its own way.

The best way to master these concepts is to try them and work with them. The example provided in the Books Online documentation provides a great way to experiment and learn how they work. Search Books Online for *Tyrannosaur*, or if you're in a hurry or don't feel like typing that much, search for *Flea*. The explanation of how a Tyrannosaur object and a Flea object each agree to implement a Bite method through Visual Basic's form of polymorphism is a great way to learn—and to remember—how this all works.

Dear John, How Do I...
Use Friend Methods?

Visual Basic 4 first introduced us to class module–defined objects and their methods and properties. Users soon noted a minor shortcoming in the way a component exposes properties and methods of its set of class modules to client applications. There was no way for a class to expose methods to other objects within the same component without also exposing these methods to the whole world.

Visual Basic 5 solves this problem by providing the Friend keyword, which modifies a method so that it is exposed and visible to all classes within the same component but not to external, client applications.

Components often provide a related set of objects that have a lot in common with each other. The Friend methods let these objects communicate in a structured way among themselves, without requiring their intercommunication methods to be exposed to other applications. These methods are not added to the ActiveX component's type library and hence are not accessible to client applications.

CHAPTER SIX

ActiveX Controls

Many analysts credit the early success of Visual Basic to custom controls. It's easy to see why—custom controls mean that you aren't limited to one vendor for all your programming tools. You can choose the best tools from a free and competitive marketplace.

With Visual Basic 5, you can now create your own custom controls (called *ActiveX controls*) using Visual Basic itself. ActiveX controls written in Visual Basic look and behave just like controls written in C. In fact, you can distribute them to your C-programming friends for use in Microsoft Visual C++.

ActiveX controls can be used just about everywhere: on Web pages viewed by Microsoft Internet Explorer; in Microsoft Excel 97 and Microsoft Word 97 documents; in Microsoft Access and Visual FoxPro database applications; and, of course, in Visual Basic, Visual C++, and Borland Delphi.

This chapter shows you how to create ActiveX controls and discusses the programming issues that are unique to these controls. The sample code presented in this chapter is available on the companion CD-ROM.

Dear John, How Do I...

Create an ActiveX Control?

The ActiveX Control Interface Wizard lets you base new controls on existing controls. The code generated by the wizard can be difficult to understand, however, so this section shows you how to create an ActiveX control manually. Once you understand the parts of an ActiveX control, it's easier to use the ActiveX Control Interface Wizard.

ActiveX Control Design Steps

To create an ActiveX control, follow these steps:

1. Create a new ActiveX control project.

2. In the UserControl window, draw the visual interface of the control using graphics methods and controls from the Toolbox, just as you would for a form.

3. In the code window, add an event procedure to resize the visible aspects of the control when the user resizes the control on a form.

4. Add the properties, methods, and events that your control will expose to applications using it. These elements define the interface of your control.

5. Write code that implements your control's functionality. This code determines the behavior of your control.

6. Add a new Standard EXE project within Visual Basic to provide a way to debug the control.

7. From the File menu, choose Make to compile the control into an OCX file.

The following text discusses the first five steps in greater detail while providing instructions on how to build a sample control named Blinker (BLINKER.VBP). The Blinker control is used to flash controls or windows on screen for emphasis. Debugging and compiling the control are discussed in the two sections that follow, "Dear John, How Do I...Debug a Control?" and "Dear John, How Do I...Compile and Register a Control?"

Creating the ActiveX Control Project

To create an ActiveX Control project, follow these steps:

1. From the File menu, choose New Project to display the New Project dialog box.

2. Double-click the ActiveX Control icon. Visual Basic creates a new project and displays the UserControl window.

3. From the Project menu, choose Project Properties to display the Project Properties dialog box.

4. In the Project Name text box, type *VB5WkSamp*. In the Project Description text box, type *VB5 Workshop Blinker Sample Control*, and then click OK. The project name is used to name the OCX file; the project description is displayed in the Components dialog box.

5. In the UserControl Properties window, set the Name property to *Blinker*. This is the class name for the control. It will be used when naming instances of the control as they are drawn on a form: *Blinker1*, *Blinker2*, and so on.

6. Choose Save Project from the File menu, and save the Blinker control as BLINKER.CTL and the project as BLINKER.VBP.

Drawing the Interface

The Blinker control flashes other controls or windows in your application in order to draw the user's attention. This isn't spectacularly hard to do—which is one reason it makes a good sample. The Blinker control uses an ActiveX UpDown control, an intrinsic TextBox control, and an intrinsic Timer control, as shown in Figure 6-1.

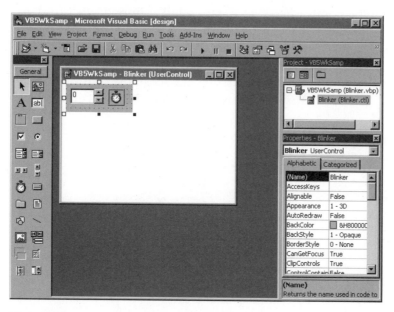

Figure 6-1.
The visual interface of the Blinker control, which contains one ActiveX control and two intrinsic controls.

93

To create the visual interface of the Blinker control, follow these steps:

1. From the Project menu, choose Components to display the Components dialog box.

2. On the Controls tab, check the Microsoft Windows Common Controls-2 (COMCT232.OCX) checkbox and click OK. Visual Basic adds the UpDown control and other common Windows controls to the Toolbox.

3. In the UserControl window, draw a text box. In the Properties window, set its Name property to *txtRate* and its Text property to *0*.

4. Draw an UpDown control next to the text box, and set its Name property to *updnRate*. Set the UpDown control's AutoBuddy property to *True*, its BuddyControl property to *txtRate*, and its Buddy-Property property to *(Default)*.

5. Draw a Timer control, and set its Name property to *tmrBlink*.

Resizing the Control

You can be sloppy when drawing the Blinker interface because the size and position of the visible controls must be handled in code anyway. When users draw the Blinker control on a form, they can click and drag the control to make it the size they want. Resizing triggers the UserControl_Resize event procedure, which positions and sizes the visible interface of the control appropriately.

The following code handles resizing the Blinker control:

```
'Code for control's visual interface
Private Sub UserControl_Resize()
    'Be sure visible controls are
    'positioned correctly within the
    'UserControl window
    updnRate.Top = 0
    txtRate.Top = 0
    txtRate.Left = 0
    'Resize visible controls
    'when user control is resized
    updnRate.Height = Height
    txtRate.Height = Height
    'Adjust UpDown control's width up
    'to a maximum of 240 twips
    If Width > 480 Then
        updnRate.Width = 240
```

(continued)

```
    Else
        updnRate.Width = Width \ 2
    End If
    'Set width of text box
    txtRate.Width = Width - updnRate.Width
    'Move UpDown control to right edge of
    'text box
    updnRate.Left = txtRate.Width
End Sub
```

As you can see, I got a little fancy with the resize code for the UpDown control. Rather than fix it at 240 twips, I let it scale down if the user makes the Blinker control less than 480 twips. Your resize code can be as simple or as complicated as you want.

Adding Properties, Methods, and Events

In addition to the standard size, position, and visibility properties provided with all controls, the Blinker control has a TargetObject property, which specifies the object that will blink, and an Interval property, which specifies how many times per second the object should blink. The Blinker control also includes a Blinked event, which occurs after the object blinks, and a Blink method, which sets the TargetObject and Interval properties.

ActiveX control properties, methods, and events are defined in the same way as they are for any object. The following code shows the TargetObject, Interval, Blinked, and Blink members of the control:

```
Option Explicit

'Windows API to flash a window
Private Declare Function FlashWindow _
Lib "user32" ( _
    ByVal hwnd As Long, _
    ByVal bInvert As Long _
) As Long

'Blinked event definition
Public Event Blinked()

'Internal variables
Private mobjTarget As Object
Private mlForeground As Long
Private mlBackground As Long
Private mbInitialized As Boolean
```

(continued)

```
'Public error constants
Public Enum BlinkerErrors
    blkCantBlink = 4001
    blkObjNotFound = 4002
End Enum

'Code for control's properties and methods
'~~~.TargetObject
Public Property Set TargetObject(Setting As Object)
    If TypeName(Setting) = "Nothing" Then Exit Property
    'Set internal object variable
    Set mobjTarget = Setting
End Property

Public Property Get TargetObject() As Object
    Set TargetObject = mobjTarget
End Property

'~~~.Interval
Public Property Let Interval(Setting As Integer)
    'Set UpDown control--updates TextBox and
    'Timer controls as well
    updnRate.Value = Setting
End Property

Public Property Get Interval() As Integer
    Interval = updnRate.Value
End Property

'~~~.Blink
Sub Blink(TargetObject As Object, Interval As Integer)
    'Delegate to TargetObject and Interval properties
    Set Me.TargetObject = TargetObject
    Me.Interval = Interval
End Sub
```

The TargetObject Property Set procedure sets the target object that should blink by assigning an internal object variable. The Interval property merely sets or returns the value of the UpDown control—this changes the value in the text box and thereby changes the Timer control's Interval property. The Blinked event is defined here but is triggered from the Timer event. Next I'll show you the event procedures for the Timer and TextBox controls—where the real work is done.

Programming the Control's Behavior

So far, the Blinker control looks nice, but it doesn't do anything. The control's behavior—flashing a control or window—is determined by code in the timer's Timer event procedure and the text box's Change event procedure, as shown here:

```
'Code for control's behavior
Private Sub tmrBlink_Timer()
    'Counter to alternate blink
    Static bOdd As Boolean
    bOdd = Not bOdd
    'If the object is a form, use FlashWindow API
    If TypeOf mobjTarget Is Form Then
        FlashWindow mobjTarget.hwnd, CLng(bOdd)
    'If it's a control, swap the colors
    ElseIf TypeOf mobjTarget Is Control Then
        If Not mbInitialized Then
            On Error GoTo errTimer
            mlForeground = mobjTarget.ForeColor
            mlBackground = mobjTarget.BackColor
            mbInitialized = True
        End If
        If bOdd Then
            mobjTarget.ForeColor = mlBackground
            mobjTarget.BackColor = mlForeground
        Else
            mobjTarget.ForeColor = mlForeground
            mobjTarget.BackColor = mlBackground
        End If
    Else
        Set mobjTarget = Nothing
        GoTo errTimer
    End If
    'Trigger the Blinked event
    RaiseEvent Blinked
    Exit Sub
errTimer:
    If TypeName(mobjTarget) = "Nothing" Then
        Err.Raise blkObjNotFound, "Blinker control", _
            "Target object is not valid for use with this control."
    Else
        Err.Raise blkCantBlink, "Blinker control", _
            "Object can't blink."
    End If
End Sub
```

(continued)

```
Private Sub txtRate_Change()
    'Set Timer control's Interval property
    'to match value in text box
    If txtRate = 0 Then
        tmrBlink.Interval = 0
        tmrBlink.Enabled = False
        mbInitialized = False
        'If blinking is turned off, be sure object
        'is returned to its original state
        If TypeOf mobjTarget Is Form Then
            FlashWindow mobjTarget.hwnd, CLng(False)
        ElseIf TypeOf mobjTarget Is Control Then
            mobjTarget.ForeColor = mlForeground
            mobjTarget.BackColor = mlBackground
        End If
    Else
        tmrBlink.Enabled = True
        tmrBlink.Interval = 1000 \ txtRate
    End If
End Sub
```

The timer's Timer event procedure handles the flashing by using the FlashWindow API function for forms or by swapping the ForeColor and BackColor properties for visible controls. Using the FlashWindow API function is more effective than swapping the ForeColor and BackColor properties. The text box's Change event procedure handles the blinking rate.

See Also...

- Chapter 10, "Dialog Boxes, Windows, and Other Forms," for more information about the FlashWindow API function

Dear John, How Do I...

Debug a Control?

Once you've created an ActiveX control, you'll want to debug it. Because a control can't run on its own, you'll have to debug it in-process. To do so, follow these steps:

1. With the control's project already loaded, add a new project to create a project group. From the File menu, choose Add Project to display the Add Project dialog box.

2. Double-click the Standard EXE icon. Visual Basic creates a new project with a single form that you can use to test your ActiveX control.

3. Close the UserControl window if it is open. Once the window is closed, Visual Basic activates the control's Toolbox icon.

4. Click the ActiveX control's Toolbox icon, and draw the control on your test project's form.

5. Write code in the test project to access the control's properties and methods.

6. Run the test project.

The following code tests the Blinker control on a form that also contains a text box named *Text1*:

```
Option Explicit

Private Sub Form_Load()
    'Set the object to blink
    Blinker1.Blink Text1, 1
End Sub

Private Sub Form_Click()
    'Stop the blinker
    Blinker1.Interval = 0
End Sub

Private Sub Blinker1_Blinked()
    Static i As Integer
    i = i + 1
    Caption = "Blinked " & i & " times"
End Sub
```

Figure 6-2 shows an example of the Blinker control being tested.

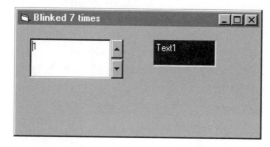

Figure 6-2.
Testing the Blinker control.

While debugging a control in-process, you can trace execution from the test project into the ActiveX control's code. You can test the code in your

ActiveX control by stepping through execution, setting breakpoints, and using watches, as shown in Figure 6-3.

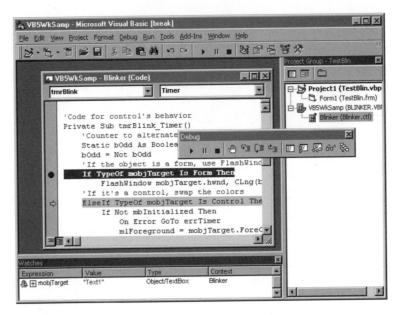

Figure 6-3.
The Blinker control being debugged in-process.

Some of the code in the control runs before you run your test project. To see this, set a breakpoint in the UserControl_Resize event procedure before you draw the control. Visual Basic will jump to the breakpoint when you release the mouse button after drawing the control.

You can modify the code in your ActiveX control at any time, but if you open the UserControl window, the control is disabled on your test form and in the Toolbox. Close the UserControl window to reenable the control.

If you draw a control on your test form and then add design-time properties to the control, Visual Basic disables the control on the form. Terminating code running in the control has the same effect. You can reactivate the control by running the test project.

NOTE: When the ActiveX control is initialized at runtime, properties from other controls on the form might or might not be available to code in the ActiveX control. Referring to a control that was drawn on the form before the ActiveX control was drawn may cause your application to stop responding. This appears to be a bug in Visual Basic.

Dear John, How Do I...

Compile and Register a Control?

Compiling the control is straightforward, but before you compile you should decide whether the control should be compiled to native code or pseudocode (p-code). Native code executes faster, but p-code results in a smaller OCX file.

In the case of the Blinker control, the differences are minimal. Because the control relies on Timer events, execution speed isn't much of an issue and the difference between a native code OCX file and a p-code OCX file is only 5 kilobytes (KB).

Of course, even 5 KB can make a difference when you are downloading a control across the Internet. It's generally a good idea to use p-code for any controls you plan to use in Internet applications.

To set the compiler options and compile your control, follow these steps:

1. Select the control project in the Project Explorer window. From the File menu, choose the Make option for your project—for example, Make Blinker.OCX—to display the Make Project dialog box.

2. Click Options to display the Project Properties dialog box.

3. Click on the Compile tab, and then select the compilation method and any optimization options. Click OK.

4. In the Make Project dialog box, select the location in which to save the control, and then click OK to compile the control.

Once the control is compiled, Visual Basic automatically registers it on your machine. Registering the control adds it to the Components dialog box, as shown in Figure 6-4 on the following page.

If your control is part of an application that you are distributing, the Setup Wizard will handle registering your control when the application is installed on other machines. If you are distributing your control without a setup program, you'll need to install the Visual Basic runtime DLL, COMCT232.OCX, and BLINKER.OCX and then use the REGOCX32.EXE utility to register COMCT232.OCX and BLINKER.OCX. REGOCX32.EXE is found in the \TOOLS\REGUTILS directory on the Visual Basic CD-ROM. The following command line registers the Blinker ActiveX control:

```
REGOCX32.EXE BLINKER.OCX
```

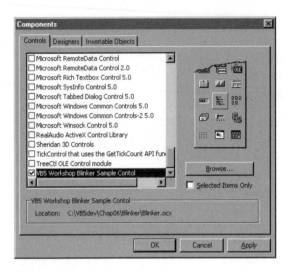

Figure 6-4.
The Components dialog box, which lists all registered controls.

Dear John, How Do I...

Create a Design-Time Property?

The TargetObject and Interval properties of the Blinker control can be set at runtime. To create a property that can be set from the Properties window at design time, you need to use the PropertyBag object in the ReadProperties and WriteProperties events, as shown here:

```
'Make Interval a design-time property
Private Sub UserControl_ReadProperties(PropBag As PropertyBag)
    updnRate.Value = PropBag.ReadProperty("Interval", 0)
End Sub

Private Sub UserControl_WriteProperties(PropBag As PropertyBag)
    PropBag.WriteProperty "Interval", updnRate.Value, 0
End Sub
```

This code adds the Interval property to the Blinker control's list of properties in the Visual Basic Properties window, as shown in Figure 6-5.

You need to add a PropertyChanged statement to the control's Interval Property Let procedure so that Visual Basic will save changes to the property at design time. The following code shows the modified procedure:

```
'~~~.Interval
Public Property Let Interval(Setting As Integer)
    'Set UpDown control--updates TextBox and
    'Timer controls as well
    updnRate.Value = Setting
    'Update design-time setting
    PropertyChanged "Interval"
End Property
```

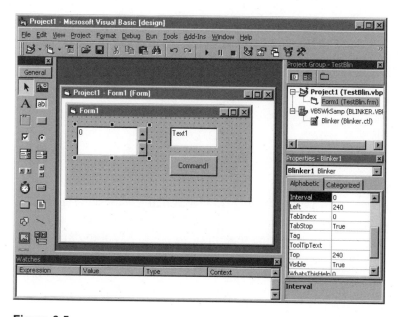

Figure 6-5.

The PropertyBag object being used to add properties to the Properties window.

Finally, you need to ensure that design-time changes to the Interval property don't start the Timer event firing. You can tell whether a control is in design mode or user mode by checking the UserControl object's Ambient.UserMode property. UserMode is *False* during design time and *True* at runtime. The following changes to the TextBox's Change event procedure prevents "Object variable or With block variable not set" errors from occurring at design time when Interval is set to a nonzero value:

```
Private Sub txtRate_Change()
    'Exit if in design mode
    If Not UserControl.Ambient.UserMode Then Exit Sub
```

(continued)

```
'Set Timer control's Interval property
'to match value in text box
If txtRate = 0 Then
    tmrBlink.Interval = 0
    tmrBlink.Enabled = False
    'If blinking is turned off, be sure object
    'is returned to its original state
    If TypeOf mobjTarget Is Form Then
        FlashWindow mobjTarget.hwnd, CLng(False)
    ElseIf TypeOf mobjTarget Is Control Then
        mobjTarget.ForeColor = mlForeground
        mobjTarget.BackColor = mlBackground
    End If
Else
    tmrBlink.Enabled = True
    tmrBlink.Interval = 1000 \ txtRate
End If
End Sub
```

NOTE: The UserMode property is not available within the control's Initialize event.

Making the TargetObject property available at design time is tricky. Since Visual Basic Properties windows can't display objects, you need to create a new property that accepts a string that, in turn, sets the TargetObject property. The TargetString property shown here can appear in the Properties window:

```
'~~~.TargetString
Public Property Let TargetString(Setting As String)
    If UserControl.Parent.Name = Setting Then
        Set TargetObject = UserControl.Parent
    ElseIf Setting <> "" Then
        Set TargetObject = UserControl.Parent.Controls(Setting)
    End If
End Property

Public Property Get TargetString() As String
    If TypeName(mobjTarget) <> "Nothing" Then
        TargetString = mobjTarget.Name
    Else
        TargetString = ""
    End If
End Property
```

You also need to add a PropertyChanged statement to the control's TargetObject property, as shown in the following code:

```
'~~~.TargetObject
Public Property Set TargetObject(Setting As Object)
    If TypeName(Setting) = "Nothing" Then Exit Property
    'Set internal object variable
    Set mobjTarget = Setting
    'Property has changed
    PropertyChanged "TargetObject"
End Property
```

To add the TargetString property to the Properties window, edit the control's ReadProperties and WriteProperties event procedures as follows:

```
'Get design-time settings
Private Sub UserControl_ReadProperties(PropBag As PropertyBag)
    updnRate.Value = PropBag.ReadProperty("Interval", 0)
    TargetString = PropBag.ReadProperty("TargetString", "")
End Sub

'Save design-time settings
Private Sub UserControl_WriteProperties(PropBag As PropertyBag)
    PropBag.WriteProperty "Interval", updnRate.Value, 0
    PropBag.WriteProperty "TargetString", TargetString, ""
End Sub
```

Dear John, How Do I...

Display a Property Pages Dialog Box?

Property pages let you set the design-time properties of an ActiveX control from a tabbed dialog box rather than from the Visual Basic Properties window. You may want to add property pages to controls that have groups of related properties so that you can access them easily, without having to scroll around in the Properties window.

You can also use property pages to display lists of valid settings that are determined at design time. For example, the Blinker control's property page displays a list of the objects on a form for the TargetString property, as shown in Figure 6-6 on the following page.

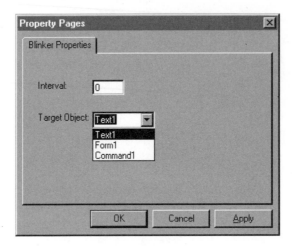

Figure 6-6.
The Blinker control's property page.

To add a property page to a control project, select the control project in the Project Explorer window, choose Add Property Page from the Project menu, and double-click the Property Page icon. You can name the property page and specify the text to appear on the property page tab when it is being used by setting the Name and Caption properties, respectively, in the Properties window. To connect a property page to a control, first open the control's UserControl window and select the control. In the Properties window, double-click on the PropertyPages property to display the Connect Property Pages dialog box, as shown in Figure 6-7. Check the appropriate property page in the Available Property Pages list, and then click OK.

When you connect a property page to an ActiveX control, Visual Basic adds a (Custom) item to the list of design-time properties displayed for that control. Double-clicking on (Custom) displays the control's property page in run mode.

As in the case with the UserControl window, while the property page window is open it is in design mode. You can draw controls on the property page and write code to respond to events just as you would on a form. The property page has a built-in SelectedControls collection that you use to get the instance of the control that the property page refers to. Use the property page's SelectionChanged event procedure to initialize the data you display in the controls on a property page. The following code sets the initial values for the Interval and Target Object properties displayed on the Blinker property page.

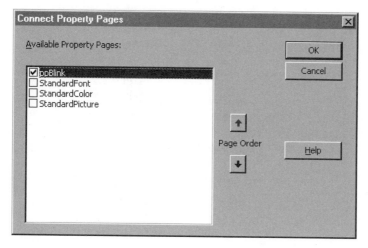

Figure 6-7.
Using the Connect Property Pages dialog box to connect a property page to a control.

The Blinker property page contains a TextBox named *txtInterval* and a ComboBox named *cmbTargetString*.

NOTE: Originally, an UpDown control was also used on the Blinker property page to set the interval, but the UpDown control does not respond to events if it is placed on a property page. This appears to be a bug in Visual Basic.

```
Private Sub PropertyPage_SelectionChanged()
    'Set property page interval to match
    'control's setting
    txtInterval = SelectedControls(0).Interval
    'Build a list of objects for TargetString
    Dim frmParent As Form
    Dim ctrIndex As Control
    Dim sTarget As String
    'Get form the control is on
    Set frmParent = SelectedControls(0).Parent
    sTarget = SelectedControls(0).TargetString
    If sTarget <> "" Then
        'Add current property setting to
        'combo box
        cmbTargetString.List(0) = sTarget
    End If
```

(continued)

```
    If frmParent.Name <> sTarget Then
        'Add form name to combo box
        cmbTargetString.AddItem frmParent.Name
    End If
    'Add each of the controls on the form to
    'combo box
    For Each ctrIndex In frmParent.Controls
        'Exclude Blinker control
        If TypeName(ctrIndex) <> "Blinker" Or _
            ctrIndex.Name = sTarget Then
            cmbTargetString.AddItem ctrIndex.Name
        End If
    Next ctrIndex
    'Display current TargetString setting
    cmbTargetString.ListIndex = 0
End Sub
```

NOTE: The SelectedControls collection is not available within the property page's Initialize event.

Notice that SelectedControls(0) returns the currently selected object—in this case, the Blinker control. I had to add a Parent property to the Blinker control so that this property page can get information about the Blinker control's container. The following code shows the Blinker control's Parent property:

```
'~~~.Parent
Public Property Get Parent() As Object
    Set Parent = UserControl.Parent
End Property
```

You use the property page's ApplyChanges event procedure to write the settings on the property page to the ActiveX control's properties. The following code retrieves the settings from the property page and stores them in the ActiveX control's properties:

```
Private Sub PropertyPage_ApplyChanges()
    'Save settings on the property page
    'in the control's properties
```

(continued)

```
SelectedControls(0).Interval = txtInterval.Text
SelectedControls(0).TargetString = _
    cmbTargetString.List _
    (cmbTargetString.ListIndex)
End Sub
```

You need to notify the property page if the user changes any of the settings on the property page. The built-in Changed property tells Visual Basic to apply the property changes when the user clicks OK or Apply. The following code sets the Changed property if either setting on the Blinker control's property page changes:

```
Private Sub txtInterval_Change()
    Changed = True
End Sub

Private Sub cmbTargetString_Change()
    Changed = True
End Sub
```

Property pages can be displayed by right-clicking on a control and choosing Properties from the context menu, by double-clicking on the (Custom) property in the Properties window, or by clicking the ellipsis button in the property's setting field in the Properties window.

To add an ellipsis button to a property in the Properties window, follow these steps:

1. Select the Code window of the ActiveX control.

2. From the Tools menu, choose Procedure Attributes to display the Procedure Attributes dialog box.

3. Click Advanced to expand the dialog box.

4. Select the name of the property in the Name drop-down list, and select the property page to display in the Use This Page In Property Browser drop-down list, as shown in Figure 6-8 on the following page.

5. Click OK.

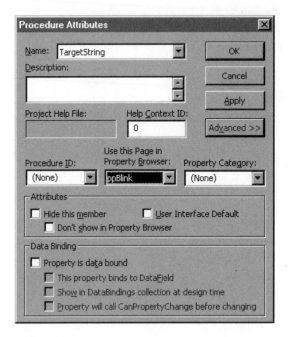

Figure 6-8.

Using the Procedure Attributes dialog box to associate a property page with a specific property.

To display the Blinker control's property page, shown in Figure 6-9, click the ellipsis button in the TargetString property.

When a user displays a Property Pages dialog box by clicking the ellipsis button, the property page should set the focus on the appropriate field. The property page EditProperty event procedure shown here sets the focus on the appropriate control when the user clicks the ellipsis button in the TargetString or Interval property of the Blinker control:

```
Private Sub PropertyPage_EditProperty(PropertyName As String)
    'Set focus on the appropriate control.
    Select Case PropertyName
        Case "TargetString"
            cmbTargetString.SetFocus
        Case "Interval"
            txtInterval.SetFocus
        Case Else
    End Select
End Sub
```

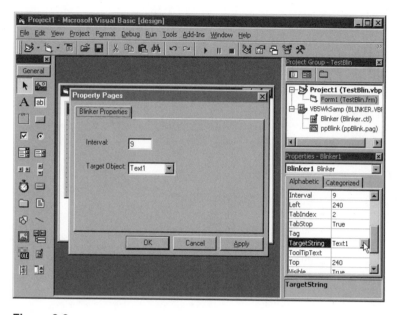

Figure 6-9.
The Blinker control's Property Pages dialog box as displayed by clicking the ellipsis button.

Dear John, How Do I...

Load a Property Asynchronously?

ActiveX controls used on Web pages may need to load property settings asynchronously. This allows the user's Web browser to display the contents of a Web page while transferring graphics or other large pieces of data in the background.

Figure 6-10 shows an Asynchronous Animation control based on the Animation control found in the Microsoft Windows Common Controls-2 (COMCT232.OCX).

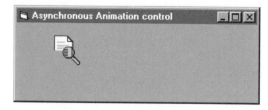

Figure 6-10.
The Asynchronous Animation control playing an AVI file that was downloaded in the background.

The Asynchronous Animation control's AVIFile property takes a string argument that can be a local file specification or a uniform resource locator (URL). The AsyncRead method begins the transfer of the file to the local machine, saving the file in the Windows Temp directory with a name generated by Visual Basic. The following code shows the AVIFile property:

```
Option Explicit

Dim mstrAVISourceFile As String
Dim mstrTempAVIFile As String

'~~~.AVIFile
Property Let AVIFile(Setting As String)
    If UserControl.Ambient.UserMode _
        And Len(Setting) Then
        AsyncRead Setting, vbAsyncTypeFile, "AVIFile"
        mstrAVISourceFile = Setting
    End If
End Property

Property Get AVIFile() As String
    AVIFile = mstrAVISourceFile
End Property
```

The AsyncRead method triggers the AsyncReadComplete event when the transfer is complete. The AsyncReadComplete event procedure is a general handler that runs for all asynchronous events. Use the AsyncProp.Property-Name value in a Select Case statement to execute specific code for each asynchronous property in your control. The AsyncReadComplete event procedure for the sample control opens and plays the AVI file by using an Animation control named *aniControl*, as shown here:

```
'General event handler for all async read complete events
Private Sub UserControl_AsyncReadComplete _
    (AsyncProp As AsyncProperty)
    Select Case AsyncProp.PropertyName
        'For AVIFile property
        Case "AVIFile"
            'Store temporary filename
            mstrTempAVIFile = AsyncProp.Value
            'Open file
            aniControl.Open mstrTempAVIFile
            'Play animation
            aniControl.Play
        Case Else
    End Select
End Sub
```

When the control terminates, be sure to clean up any temporary files you created. Well-behaved Internet applications should not fill up the user's disk with unneeded temporary files. The following code closes the animation and deletes the temporary file containing the data:

```
Private Sub UserControl_Terminate()
    'Delete temporary file
    If Len(mstrTempAVIFile) Then
        aniControl.Close
        Kill mstrTempAVIFile
    End If
End Sub
```

To use the Asynchronous Animation control named *AsyncAni*, simply draw the control on a form and set the AVIFile property from an event procedure. For example, the following code loads the Find File animation from the Visual Basic CD-ROM:

```
Private Sub Form_Load()
    AsyncAni1.AVIFile = "d:\vb\graphics\avis\findfile.avi"
End Sub
```

See Also...

- Chapter 7, "The Internet Connection," for information about embedding the Asynchronous Animation control in a Web page

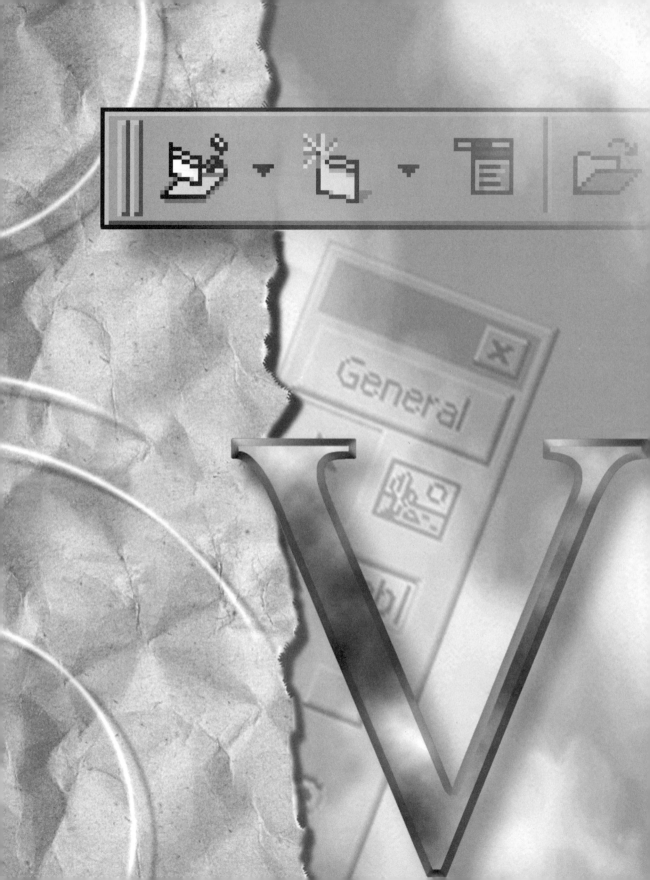

The Internet Connection

It's hard to know what people are referring to when they talk about an Internet application—there are so many different types. Visual Basic provides specific technologies for different aspects of the Internet, so it's important to know what type of application you want to create before you decide on your tool set. The following table categorizes the different uses for the Internet and lists the Visual Basic tools appropriate for each task.

Internet Task	Visual Basic Tool
Direct computer-to-computer communication	WinSock control (MSWINSCK.OCX)
File transfer	Internet Transfer control (MSINET.OCX)
Browsing of the Web	WebBrowser control (SHDOCVW.DLL)
Deployment of applications that run in Microsoft Internet Explorer	ActiveX documents
Distribution of applications using Internet setup	Setup Wizard
Deployment of components for use in Hypertext Markup Language (HTML) pages	ActiveX controls
Database applications	ActiveX documents with data controls or Active Server Pages using the ADODB object
Transactions/data transfer from server to clients	Active Server Pages

The following sections cover each of these topics in turn. In many cases, the Visual Basic documentation provides an excellent example of the particular type of application, so I'll point you there. However, I have learned some tips and tricks of my own that I think you'll find handy.

One other thing: I use the term *Internet* throughout this chapter, but each task applies equally well to intranet applications. In fact, intranet applications probably already outnumber Internet applications and will continue to do so.

Dear John, How Do I...
Use the Internet Controls?

The Visual Basic Professional and Enterprise Editions include three ActiveX controls that provide access to every level of Internet communication:

- The WinSock control (MSWINSCK.OCX) provides low-level access to the Transport Control Protocol (TCP) and User Datagram Protocol (UDP) network protocols used on the Internet. WinSock is used to create chat applications and to perform direct data transfers between two or more networked computers.

- The Internet Transfer control (MSINET.OCX) lets you copy files from WWW and File Transfer Protocol (FTP) servers and lets you browse directories of files and retrieve data synchronously or asynchronously. This control is used to create FTP browsing and file transfer applications.

- The WebBrowser control (SHDOCVW.DLL) packs all the capabilities of Internet Explorer into a single control. Use it to add an Internet browser to an existing application or to control Internet Explorer from another application through Automation.

NOTE: The WebBrowser control is called Microsoft Internet Controls in the Visual Basic Components dialog box. It is installed as part of the Internet Explorer setup. Microsoft Internet Explorer version 3.01 is included on the Visual Basic CD-ROM in the \TOOLS\MSIE directory.

Visual Basic provides samples for each of these controls, but the samples aren't part of the SAMPLES directory. Instead, they are found in Books Online topics or (in the case of WebBrowser) as part of a form template. The following table lists where you'll find samples for each control.

Control	Books Online Topic	Sample Description
WinSock	Using the WinSock Control	Chat application using either TCP/IP or UDP protocols.
Internet Transfer	Using the Internet Transfer Control	Samples for transferring files, executing FTP commands, and logging on to a server.
WebBrowser	(none)	The Browser form template and Application Wizard create a form-based browser for use in your application.

The chat sample application provided for the WinSock control covers that control thoroughly. The samples for the Internet Transfer and WebBrowser controls are less thorough. The following sections attempt to remedy that.

Creating an FTP Browser

The Books Online documentation for the Internet Transfer control demonstrates the pieces you would use to create an FTP browser, but it doesn't assemble those pieces. This is a problem because the Internet Transfer control is asynchronous—how the events and error handling interact is the most difficult aspect of using the control.

Figure 7-1 on the following page shows a simple FTP browser I've created using two text boxes and an Internet Transfer control. You enter the Uniform Resource Locator (URL) of an FTP server in the Address text box and then select a file or directory from the contents text box. If the selection is a directory, the application displays that directory. If the selection is a file, the browser saves the file in the Windows Temp directory.

The Address text box executes requests when the user presses Enter by setting the Internet Transfer control's URL property and calling the Execute method. The OpenURL method performs the same action when requesting a specific file. However, when you use the OpenURL method to return the contents of a directory, typically HTML source code indicating the directory contents is returned. Therefore, in this example, I have steered clear of the OpenURL method. The code on the following page shows the KeyPress event procedure for the *txtAddress* text box.

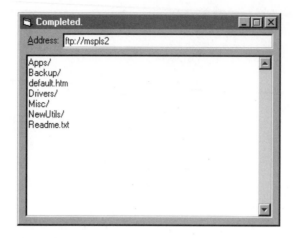

Figure 7-1.
A simple FTP browser created using the Internet Transfer control.

```
Private Sub txtAddress_KeyPress(KeyAscii As Integer)
    If KeyAscii = Asc(vbCr) Then
        'Eat keystroke
        KeyAscii = 0
        'Select text
        txtAddress.SelStart = 0
        txtAddress.SelLength = Len(txtAddress)
        On Error GoTo errOpenURL
        'Set FTP address to view
        inetBrowse.URL = txtAddress.Text
        'Get directory
        inetBrowse.Execute , "Dir"
        'Display address
        Caption = inetBrowse.URL
    End If
    Exit Sub
errOpenURL:
    Select Case Err.Number
        Case icBadUrl
            MsgBox "Bad address. Please reenter."
        Case icConnectFailed, icConnectionAborted, _
                icCannotConnect
            MsgBox "Unable to connect to network."
        Case icInetTimeout
            MsgBox "Connection timed out."
        Case icExecuting
            'Cancel previous request
```

(continued)

```
            inetBrowse.Cancel
            'Check whether cancel worked
            If inetBrowse.StillExecuting Then
                Caption = "Couldn't cancel request."
            'Resubmit current request
            Else
                Resume
            End If
        Case Else
            Debug.Print Err.Number, Err.Description
    End Select
End Sub
```

It's important to trap the errors that can occur when you submit a request. The icExecuting error is particularly important. The Internet Transfer control processes all requests asynchronously; however, it can process only one request at a time. If you cancel a pending request, be sure to check the StillExecuting property before resuming, as shown above. Some requests can't be canceled, and simply using a Resume statement will result in an infinite loop!

The following code shows the DblClick event procedure for the *txtContents* text box, in which directory listings are displayed. This code builds the URL string and executes a Dir command if the selection is a subdirectory or a Get command if the selection is a file.

```
Private Sub txtContents_DblClick()
    'Browse selected directory
    If txtContents.SelLength Then
        'If selection is a directory...
        If Right(txtContents.SelText, 1) = "/" Then
            'Add selected item to address
            txtAddress = txtAddress & "/" & _
                Left(txtContents.SelText, _
                txtContents.SelLength - 1)
            'Trap errors (important!)
            On Error GoTo errBrowse
            'Show directory
            msDir = Right(txtAddress, Len(txtAddress) _
                - Len(inetBrowse.URL))
            inetBrowse.Execute , "Dir " & msDir & "/*"
        'Otherwise, it's a file, so retrieve it
        Else
            'Build the path name of the file
            msDir = Right(txtAddress, Len(txtAddress) _
                - Len(inetBrowse.URL)) & "/" & _
                txtContents.SelText
```

(continued)

119

```
                    msDir = Right(msDir, Len(msDir) - 1)
                    'Retrieve file
                    inetBrowse.Execute , "Get " & msDir & _
                        " " & msTempDir & txtContents.SelText
                End If
            End If
    Exit Sub
    errBrowse:
        If Err = icExecuting Then
            'Cancel previous request
            inetBrowse.Cancel
            'Check whether cancel worked
            If inetBrowse.StillExecuting Then
                Caption = "Couldn't cancel request."
            'Resubmit current request
            Else
                Resume
            End If
        Else
            'Display error
            Debug.Print Err & " " & Err.Description
        End If
    End Sub
```

The Execute and OpenURL methods trigger the StateChanged event. It's important to remember that both methods do this, because OpenURL appears to be a synchronous method; however, StateChanged events still occur and can cause problems with reentrancy.

NOTE: I have steered clear of OpenURL because it seems to have bugs at the time of this writing.

The following code updates the form's caption to keep you abreast of the request's progress and then uses the GetChunk method to retrieve a directory listing if the command executed was Dir:

```
Private Sub inetBrowse_StateChanged(ByVal State As Integer)
    Select Case State
        Case icError
            Debug.Print inetBrowse.ResponseCode & " " & _
                inetBrowse.ResponseInfo
        Case icResolvingHost, icRequesting, icRequestSent
            Caption = "Searching..."
        Case icHostResolved
            Caption = "Found."
        Case icReceivingResponse, icResponseReceived
            Caption = "Receiving data."
```

(continued)

120

```
Case icResponseCompleted
    Dim sBuffer As String
    'Get data
    sBuffer = inetBrowse.GetChunk(1024)
    'If data is a directory, display it
    If sBuffer <> "" Then
        Caption = "Completed."
        txtContents = sBuffer
    Else
        Caption = "File saved in " & _
            msTempDir & "."
    End If
Case icConnecting, icConnected
    Caption = "Connecting."
Case icDisconnecting
Case icDisconnected
Case Else
    Debug.Print State
End Select
End Sub
```

NOTE: The current documentation suggests that GetChunk will work with the Execute method's Get command, but that does not seem to be the case. The Get command's syntax specifies a source file and a destination file, so GetChunk is not needed when you are copying a file from a server.

The complete code for the FTP browser, including the GetTempPath API function declaration and the Form_Load event procedure, can be found on the companion CD-ROM.

Creating a Browser Add-In

An interesting feature of the WebBrowser control is the fact that its source file, SHDOCVW.DLL, is also a type library for Internet Explorer. You can reference this file in code to create and control instances of the Internet Explorer application through Automation (formerly called OLE Automation).

This technique is of practical use when you are debugging Internet applications written in Visual Basic. By default, Internet Explorer caches Web pages; however, you will usually want fresh copies of each Web page when debugging. The Browser add-in sample, shown in Figure 7-2 on the following page, starts an instance of Internet Explorer with caching turned off, making it easier to debug Internet applications in Visual Basic.

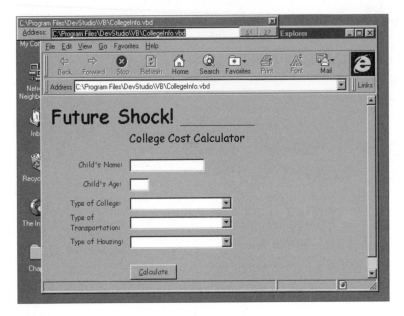

Figure 7-2.
The Browser add-in always loads fresh Web pages, rather than using cached pages.

In addition to the standard connection class (CLS) and registration startup module (BAS) used by all add-ins, the Browser add-in (WEBTOOL.VBP) includes a single form with a text box for entering URLs and Forward and Back command buttons.

The following code creates an instance of Internet Explorer and sets the *txtAddress* text box to the path in which Visual Basic stores temporary VBD files while debugging Internet applications. VBD files are discussed in detail in the next section.

```
Option Explicit

'Specify the path where VB5.EXE is installed
Const VBPath = "file://C:\Program Files\DevStudio\VB\"

'Create an Internet Explorer object variable
Dim WithEvents ieView As InternetExplorer

Private Sub Form_Load()
    'Establish a reference to application object
    Set ieView = GetObject("", "InternetExplorer.Application")
    'Be sure Internet Explorer is visible
```

(continued)

```
        ieView.Visible = True
        'Start with VB.EXE path since that's where VBD
        'files are stored during debugging
        txtAddress = VBPath
End Sub
```

Unfortunately, you can't use the GetObject function with the first argument empty to get a running instance of Internet Explorer. The application doesn't allow it, so you need to start a new instance when you establish your object reference. You also need to be sure to make the instance visible.

The following code does the navigation work. Notice the navNoRead-FromCache flag in the Navigate method. You can control how Internet Explorer navigates to a URL using this and other flags.

```
Private Sub txtAddress_KeyPress(KeyAscii As Integer)
    If KeyAscii = Asc(vbCr) Then
        'Eat keystroke
        KeyAscii = 0
        'Select text
        txtAddress.SelLength = Len(txtAddress)
        'Navigate to address without reading from cache
        ieView.navigate txtAddress, navNoReadFromCache
    End If
End Sub
```

The *ieView* object variable is declared using WithEvents, so this form can intercept events from Internet Explorer. The CommandStateChange event is used here to enable or disable the Forward and Back command buttons:

```
Private Sub ieView_CommandStateChange( _
    ByVal Command As Long, _
    ByVal Enable As Boolean _
)
    'Enable or disable Back and Forward command buttons
    'based on whether there is an address to go to
    Select Case Command
        Case CSC_NAVIGATEBACK
            cmdBack.Enabled = Enable
        Case CSC_NAVIGATEFORWARD
            cmdForward.Enabled = Enable
        Case CSC_UPDATECOMMANDS
    End Select
End Sub

Private Sub cmdBack_Click()
    ieView.GoBack
End Sub
```

(continued)

```
Private Sub cmdForward_Click()
    ieView.GoForward
End Sub
```

Internet Explorer triggers the NavigateComplete event when the Web page has been displayed and triggers the Quit event when the user closes the application. The following code responds to those events in the Browser add-in:

```
Private Sub ieView_NavigateComplete(ByVal URL As String)
    'Update text box with the final address
    txtAddress.Text = URL
    txtAddress.SelLength = Len(txtAddress)
    'Display the Web page title in the form's caption
    Caption = ieView.LocationName
End Sub

Private Sub ieView_Quit(Cancel As Boolean)
    'Close this application if user closes Internet Explorer
    End
End Sub
```

All the code used to create the Browser add-in can be found on the companion CD-ROM.

 See Also...

- Chapter 25, "Advanced Programming Techniques," and the APIAddin application in Chapter 28, "Development Tools," for more information about creating an add-in

Dear John, How Do I...

Create Applications That Run in Internet Explorer?

Visual Basic includes a new type of container called a user document. User documents form the basis of Visual Basic Document (VBD) files, which can be viewed over the Internet using Microsoft Internet Explorer version 3.0 or later.

User documents are a lot like forms. They can include controls, display message boxes, process data, and call other components. However, they have the following significant differences:

- Data in user documents is not readily available to other parts of your application. You cannot refer to the value of a property in a user document from outside that document.

- Applications based on user documents need Internet Explorer to run. You can't debug them directly from within Visual Basic alone.

- Compiled applications must start from an HTM file that loads the code components of the application before displaying VBD files. You can't start the compiled EXE file or view the VBD files from Internet Explorer without this HTM file.

I'll demonstrate how to deal with these differences using a sample application that runs in Internet Explorer. This isn't meant to be a step-by-step tutorial, but rather an elucidation of the more confusing aspects of programming for the Internet.

Sharing Data Between User Documents

The Future Shock application (FSHOCK.VBP) calculates the cost of sending a child to college. It contains the two user documents shown in Figure 7-3. The CollegeInfo document (COLINFO.DOB) gathers information used to project future college expenses. The DisplayCost document (DISCOST.DOB) presents the results of the calculation.

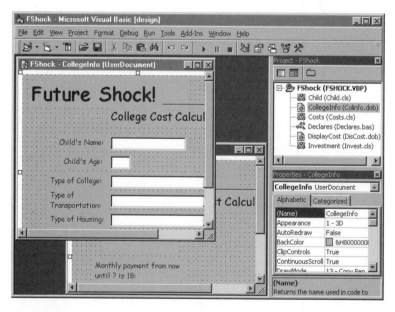

Figure 7-3.
Visual Basic Internet applications use user documents to collect data and display results.

125

In order to share information, the two user documents rely on the global object gchdScholar, which is declared in the code module DECLARES.BAS, as shown here:

```
'Global object that shares data between
'user documents
Public gchdScholar As New Child
```

The gchdScholar object is an instance of the Child class (defined in CHILD.CLS), which includes properties for each of the data fields in the CollegeInfo user document. CollegeInfo sets the values of these properties and then navigates to the DisplayCost user document when the user clicks the Calculate button.

Navigating to an address requires different code during debugging than it does in the released version of an Internet application. During debugging, Visual Basic stores a temporary copy of each compiled document (VBD file) in the Visual Basic home directory. Once the application is final, the VBD files are installed on the Internet server. Future Shock uses the #If...Then...#Else directive to handle this difference.

The following code shows how the CollegeInfo user document initializes its controls, sets the gchdScholar properties, and navigates to the DisplayCost user document:

```
Option Explicit

#Const DEBUG_MODE = True
'Path differs in debug and release versions
#If DEBUG_MODE Then
    'Use local address during debugging
    Const DisplayCost = "C:\Program Files\DevStudio\VB\" & _
        "DisplayCost.VBD"
#Else
    'Use network address at release
    Const DisplayCost = "http:\\msptech\FShock\" & _
        "DisplayCost.VBD"
#End If

Private Sub UserDocument_Initialize()
    'Initialize list boxes
    cmbCollege.AddItem "In-state public college", chdState
    cmbCollege.AddItem "Out-of-state public college", chdOutOfState
    cmbCollege.AddItem "Private college", chdPrivate
    cmbTransport.AddItem "Bike", chdBike
    cmbTransport.AddItem "Bus", chdBus
```

(continued)

```
    cmbTransport.AddItem "Used car", chdUsedCar
    cmbTransport.AddItem "New car", chdNewCar
    cmbHousing.AddItem "Home", chdHome
    cmbHousing.AddItem "Dormitory", chdDorm
    cmbHousing.AddItem "Apartment", chdApartment
End Sub

'Display Costs Web page
Private Sub cmdCalculate_Click()
    'Set Child properties
    gchdScholar.Age = txtAge
    gchdScholar.Name = txtName
    gchdScholar.Transport = cmbTransport.ListIndex
    gchdScholar.Housing = cmbHousing.ListIndex
    gchdScholar.College = cmbCollege.ListIndex
    'Show DisplayCost user document
    Hyperlink.NavigateTo DisplayCost
End Sub
```

Each user document includes a built-in Hyperlink object that you use to navigate to URLs and to go forward or back in Internet Explorer's cache of documents. The NavigateTo method is roughly equivalent to a form's Show method.

When Internet Explorer first navigates to the DisplayCost document, the Initialize event is triggered. The code for this event adds the name of the child to one of the labels on the document. The Initialize event happens only once per Internet Explorer session.

Next the Show event occurs. The code for the user document Show event procedure tells the Child object to calculate his or her college costs (smart kid!) and then displays the results in labels on the document. The Show event is triggered every time the user displays the document.

The Initialize and Show event procedures and the Back command button code for the DisplayCost user document is shown here:

```
Option Explicit

'Use the Initialize event to initialize information that will stay
'the same throughout session
Private Sub UserDocument_Initialize()
    'Fill in name in label
    lblPaymentDesc = Left(lblPaymentDesc, _
        InStr(1, lblPaymentDesc, "?") - 1) & _
        gchdScholar.Name & _
        Right(lblPaymentDesc, _
```

(continued)

127

```
                Len(lblPaymentDesc) - _
                InStr(1, lblPaymentDesc, "?"))
End Sub

'Use the Show event to update information when the
'user revisits this page
Private Sub UserDocument_Show()
    Dim LumpSum, Payment, TotalCost
    'Calculate college costs
    gchdScholar.CollegeCost Payment, LumpSum, TotalCost
    'Display costs
    lblLumpSum = LumpSum
    lblPayment = Payment
    lblTotalCost = TotalCost
End Sub

'Navigate back to the data entry page
Private Sub cmdBack_Click()
    Hyperlink.GoBack
End Sub
```

Actually, I could have put all the Initialize code in the Show event procedure, but I wanted to illustrate the difference. If you click the Back button, enter information for a second child, and then click Calculate, DisplayCost recalculates the costs but doesn't change the name of the child displayed in the second label. This minor bug makes a point: use the Initialize event to set static variables in a document, and use the Show event to set variables you want to refresh every time the user displays the page.

The code used in the Child class (CHILD.CLS), the Costs class (COSTS.CLS), and the Investment class (INVEST.CLS) can be found on the companion CD-ROM.

Debugging Internet Applications

If you load the Future Shock project file in Visual Basic and try to run it, nothing seems to happen. In order to view the application, follow these steps:

1. Place the Future Shock application in run mode by pressing F5 in the Visual Basic programming environment.

2. Start Internet Explorer. If you use dial-up access to the Internet, you can cancel the Connect dialog box and run Internet Explorer without an Internet connection.

3. From Internet Explorer's File menu, choose Open.

4. In the Open dialog box, click Browse.

5. In the second Open dialog box, select the directory in which VB5.EXE is installed (\PROGRAM FILES\DEVSTUDIO\VB by default). Select All Files from the Files Of Type drop-down list, select the COLLEGEINFO.VBD file, and click Open to close the second Open dialog box.

6. Click OK to close the first Open dialog box.

Figure 7-4 below and Figure 7-5 on the following page show the Future Shock application running in Internet Explorer. Enter your child's name, age, and college preferences in the CollegeInfo document, and then click Calculate to view the results.

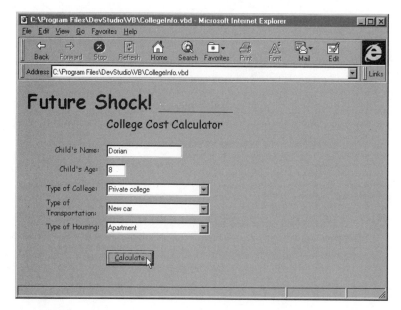

Figure 7-4.
The CollegeInfo document, showing the information used to calculate college expenses.

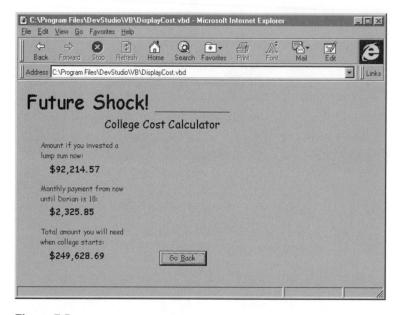

Figure 7-5.
Yow! Well, maybe a new car isn't such a good idea.

While debugging, you can pause the application and step through code in the Visual Basic programming environment. However, if you stop the application you'll need to close and restart Internet Explorer in order to view the document again.

See Also...

- The section "Creating a Browser Add-In" earlier in this chapter for a sample add-in (WEBTOOL.VBP) that makes it easier to view documents while debugging

Testing Compiled Internet Applications

Once you've debugged your Internet application, you can compile it to a dynamic link library (DLL) or an EXE file. Compiling the project also creates a compiled version of each user document in the project. These files can be run locally to test them before distribution over the Internet.

To run a compiled Internet application locally, follow these steps:

1. Register the executable file. For EXE files, simply run the application. To register DLL files, use the REGSVR32.EXE utility found in the \TOOLS\REGUTILS directory of the Visual Basic CD-ROM. The following command line registers FSHOCK.DLL:

   ```
   REGSVR32 FSHOCK.DLL
   ```

2. Open the compiled document (VBD) files in Internet Explorer using the local file address.

The following URL demonstrates the address syntax that Internet Explorer uses when opening local files. (The *file://* portion of the address is optional.)

```
file://C:\VB5dev\Chap07\FShock\CollegeInfo.VBD
```

Based on how the DisplayCost path was configured for compilation, the DisplayCost document may not appear as expected.

 See Also...

- The following section, "Dear John, How Do I...Install Applications over the Internet?" to learn how to view Internet applications over a network

Dear John, How Do I...
Install Applications over the Internet?

You can't run Internet applications by opening VBD files over the Internet. If you do, Internet Explorer simply assumes that you want to copy the VBD file to your disk and displays the Internet Explorer dialog box shown in Figure 7-6 on the following page. If you select Open from this dialog box, the file is copied, and then you are prompted to select an application that will open the file.

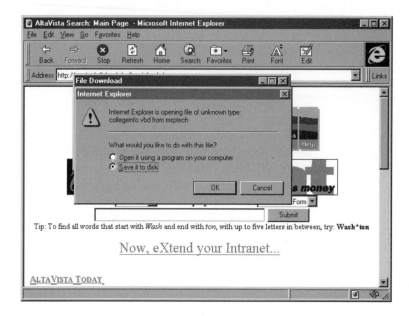

Figure 7-6.
If you open a VBD file over the Internet, Internet Explorer assumes you want to copy the file.

To use a Visual Basic application over the Internet, you need to first create an Internet setup program for the application. Use the Setup Wizard to create this setup program by following these steps:

1. To run the Visual Basic Setup Wizard, choose the Visual Basic program group from the Windows Start button, then choose Application Setup Wizard. This will launch the Setup Wizard, and an Introduction screen will be displayed. Click Next in the Introduction screen to display the Select Project And Options screen, shown on the facing page.

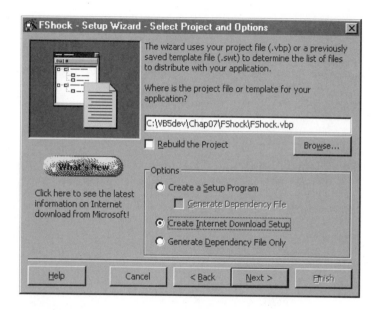

2. Click the Browse button, and select the project file (VBP) for your Internet application. In the Options section, select Create Internet Download Setup, and then click Next to display the Internet Distribution Location screen, shown here:

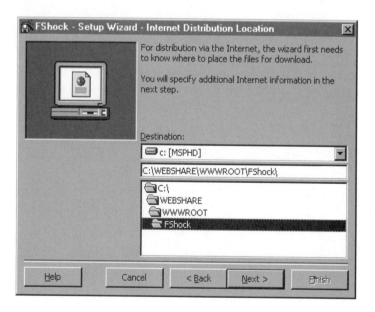

3. Select the target directory for the setup files. You can use the default directory (\TEMP\SWSETUP) and then copy the files to another directory later. If you are working on and have access to your Internet server, you could place the setup files in a subdirectory of your server's Internet root directory so that Internet users can get to the files. Click Next when you have finished. The Setup Wizard displays the Internet Package screen, shown here:

4. The Runtime Components section lets you use the Microsoft servers for the Visual Basic runtime and associated distribution files. If you are using an intranet, you'll probably want to select the Use Alternate Location option so that the Visual Basic runtime and Microsoft OCX files can be copied from the current server or from another location on your network. If the application is being distributed on the Internet, you'll probably want to select the Download From The Microsoft Web Site option so that users always get the latest versions of these files. Click the Safety button to display the Safety dialog box, shown here:

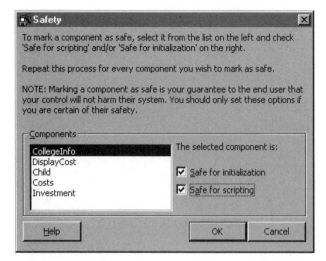

5. The Safety dialog box lets you specify whether components are safe for initialization or scripting. For the Future Shock application, check Safe For Initialization and Safe For Scripting for each of the components. Click OK, and then click Next. The Setup Wizard displays the ActiveX Server Components screen, shown here:

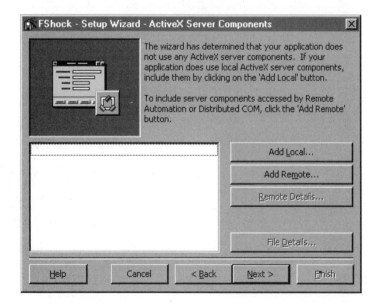

6. The Components screen displays any OCX, DLL, or EXE files referenced in the application's project file. If your application uses other ActiveX components, you need to specify them here. Click Next to display the File Summary screen, shown here:

7. The File Summary screen simply reviews the files to be distributed. Click Next to display the Finished screen. Click Finish to build the Internet setup files.

Based on the options you select, the Setup Wizard generates the types of files listed in the following table. The first three file types are the ones you should copy to your Internet site.

File Type	Description
CAB	Compressed versions of the application's executable and dependent files
HTM	Generated Web page that automatically installs the files from the CAB file on the user's machine and then opens the installed VBD files in the browser
VBD	Compiled user documents

(continued)

continued

File Type	Description
DDF	Project file used by the Setup Wizard to create the CAB file
DEP	Dependency file used by the Setup Wizard
INF	Setup information file used to customize the installation of the application
SWT	Setup Wizard template for the application; used in the Setup Wizard to make changes to the application's installation

Once you copy the setup program files to your Internet site, users can run the application by opening the generated HTM file. This file installs and registers the executable components on the user's machine and then displays the first VBD file in Internet Explorer. The following HTML code shows the HTM file generated for the Future Shock application:

```
<HTML>
<OBJECT ID="Child"
CLASSID="CLSID:80335CD9-8E97-11D0-A269-00A0C908FA50"
CODEBASE="FSHOCK.CAB#version=1,0,0,0">
</OBJECT>

<OBJECT ID="Investment"
CLASSID="CLSID:80335CE2-8E97-11D0-A269-00A0C908FA50"
CODEBASE="FSHOCK.CAB#version=1,0,0,0">
</OBJECT>

<OBJECT ID="Costs"
CLASSID="CLSID:80335CE5-8E97-11D0-A269-00A0C908FA50"
CODEBASE="FSHOCK.CAB#version=1,0,0,0">
</OBJECT>

<SCRIPT LANGUAGE="VBScript">
Sub Window_OnLoad
    Document.Open
    Document.Write "<FRAMESET>"
    Document.Write "<FRAME SRC=""CollegeInfo.VBD"">"
    Document.Write "</FRAMESET>"
    Document.Close
End Sub
</SCRIPT>
</HTML>
```

The CLASSID attributes in the HTM file are the class IDs of the components used in the Future Shock application. It's important to remember that Visual Basic generates new class IDs every time you compile the application. You'll need to run the Setup Wizard again each time you change code and recompile.

Once you've created a setup program and copied the HTM, CAB, and VBD files to your Internet site, you can run the application by following these steps:

1. In Internet Explorer's Address text box, type the URL of your application's HTM file. Internet Explorer checks to see whether the ActiveX components used by the application are registered on your machine. If they aren't registered, Internet Explorer attempts to install the required components from the CAB files.

2. Depending on your Internet Explorer security settings and information gathered by the Setup Wizard, Internet Explorer may display a warning before each component is installed, as shown here:

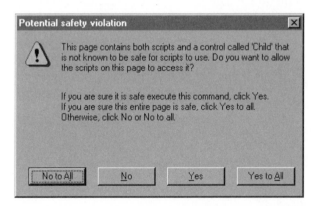

If you respond Yes to each warning, Internet Explorer completes the installation and displays the first document in your application. The Future Shock application is shown here running across an intranet:

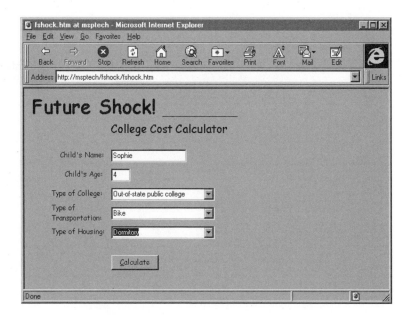

Dear John, How Do I...

Use ActiveX Components in HTML?

The HTML used to create Web pages can include ActiveX controls created in Visual Basic. These controls can be used by VBScript, JavaScript, or Java applets contained in the Web page. For example, Figure 7-7 on the following page shows the Asynchronous Animation control created in Chapter 6, "Reusable Components," being used in a Web page.

The HTML code for this Web page is shown here. Notice that the control is included using the <OBJECT> tag and is automated using VBScript code.

```
<HTML>
<P>
<OBJECT ID="AsyncAni" WIDTH=100 HEIGHT=80
CLASSID="CLSID:3DA62561-785B-11D0-9610-444553540000"
CODEBASE="AsyncAni.CAB#version=1,0,0,0">
</OBJECT>
<P>
<INPUT TYPE="BUTTON" VALUE="Go" NAME="cmdGo">
```

(continued)

```
<SCRIPT LANGUAGE="VBScript">
'Event procedure for the intrinsic button control
Sub cmdGo_OnClick
    'Set a property of the ActiveX control
    AsyncAni.AVIFile = "http://msptech/AsyncAni/Findfile.AVI"
End Sub
</SCRIPT>
</HTML>
```

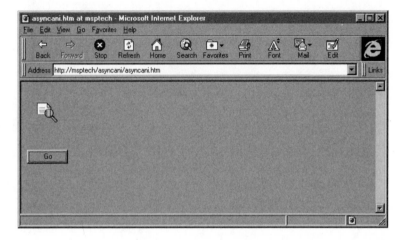

Figure 7-7.
The Asynchronous Animation control embedded in a Web page.

The easiest way to get the class ID and CODEBASE information for the control is by running the Setup Wizard on the control's project file as described in the preceding section, "Dear John, How Do I...Install Applications over the Internet?" The Setup Wizard generates an HTM file with an <OBJECT> tag that includes the control on the page.

You can modify the generated HTM file by adding text, graphics, intrinsic controls, other ActiveX components, and executable scripts. There isn't enough space here to cover all the aspects of programming in HTML using VBScript. There is a pretty good reference on VBScript available at http://www.microsoft.com/vbscript.

Dear John, How Do I...

Access Data on an Internet Server?

The Internet applications described up to now run on the client's machine. When the client accesses the application at its Internet address, the files are copied to his or her machine before they run. Object access, including database access, is local by default. If your application uses a database, that database is copied to the client's machine.

Changes to the client's copy of the database remain local until the client database is synchronized with the server database. Use the Database object's Synchronize method with the dbRepSyncInternet flag to update the server's database with changes from a client. The dbRepSyncInternet flag packages the client's changes with time stamps so that the server can reconcile the client's changes with other modifications that may have been made. The following code updates a server database when a user document terminates:

```
Private Sub UserDocument_Terminate()
    datRS.Synchronize _
        "http://wombat2/samples/chapter7/samples.mdb", _
        dbRepSyncInternet Or dbRepImpExpChanges
End Sub
```

The dpRepImpExpChanges flag tells the server and the client to exchange any differences between the two copies. The package of updates is considerably smaller than the entire database, so these transfers can occur quickly.

Copying a database and synchronizing changes may not be ideal in all situations. For one thing, Synchronize uses *optimistic locking*, meaning that a client can't have exclusive access to a record. One way to get direct access to a database on a server is to use *Microsoft Active Server Pages* (ASP). Active Server Pages are standard text files with an ASP extension that contain HTML and scripting code. Active Server Pages run on the server with access to the server's file system and installed objects. The major benefits of Active Server Pages are that they are fairly easy to create and maintain, and they are not compiled.

Active Server Pages can be installed on Microsoft Windows NT Server version 4.0 with Microsoft Internet Information Server (IIS) version 3.0, Microsoft Windows NT Workstation version 4.0 with Microsoft Peer Web Services version 3.0, and Microsoft Windows 95 with Microsoft Personal Web Server version 1.0a. Although you can create and use Active Server Pages on

Windows NT Workstation and Windows 95, it is recommended that you post your ASP applications on Window NT Server with IIS. Both IIS and ASP are available for free download at http://www.microsoft.com/iis.

All the code for an Active Server Page runs on the server. The client sees only the results in the form of HTML. ASP includes some super documentation and samples. Figures 7-8 and 7-9 show the Future Shock application modified for use as an Active Server Page.

Active Server Pages use the <% and %> characters to identify script code, which is not returned to the browser. Outside of code, the HTML tags are used to identify content just as would happen on an HTM page. The following code for FSHOCK.ASP uses the CreateObject function to create an instance of the Child object from the ActiveX component FSHOCK.DLL created earlier in this chapter.

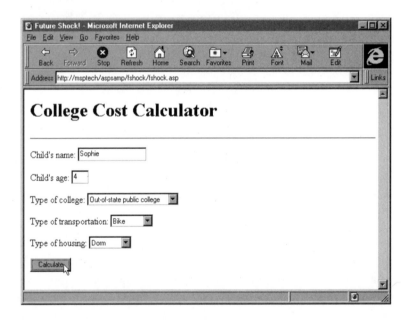

Figure 7-8.
FSHOCK.ASP uses ActiveX objects on the server to perform cost calculations.

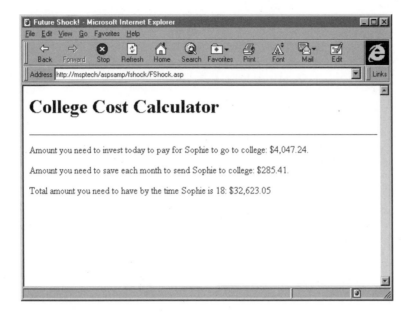

Figure 7-9.
The results of the calculations displayed on FSHOCK.ASP.

```
<HTML>
<HEAD><TITLE>Future Shock!</TITLE></HEAD>
<BODY BGCOLOR=#FFFFFF>
<H1>College Cost Calculator</H1>
<HR>
<%
On Error Resume Next

Dim chdScholar

If Request.Form("sAge") = "" Then
%>
      <FORM METHOD=POST ACTION="FShock.asp">
      <P>
      Child's name: <INPUT TYPE=TEXT SIZE=20 MAXLENGTH=20
      NAME="sName">
      <P>
      Child's age: <INPUT TYPE=TEXT SIZE=2 MAXLENGTH=2 NAME="sAge">
      <P>
```

(continued)

143

```
            Type of college:
            <SELECT NAME="iCollege">
                <OPTION VALUE=0>In-state public college
                <OPTION VALUE=1>Out-of-state public college
                <OPTION VALUE=2>Private college
            </SELECT>
            <P>
            Type of transportation:
            <SELECT NAME="iTransport">
                <OPTION VALUE=0>Bike
                <OPTION VALUE=1>Bus
                <OPTION VALUE=2>Used car
                <OPTION VALUE=3>New car
            </SELECT>
            <P>
            Type of housing:
            <SELECT NAME="iHousing">
                <OPTION VALUE=0>Home
                <OPTION VALUE=1>Dorm
                <OPTION VALUE=2>Apartment
            </SELECT>
            <P>
            <INPUT TYPE="SUBMIT" VALUE="Calculate">
    </FORM>
    <%
    Else
            Dim Payment, LumpSum, TotalCost
            'Create an object variable
            Set chdScholar = CreateObject("FShock.Child")
            'Set object properties
            chdScholar.Name = Request.Form("sName")
            chdScholar.Age = Request.Form("sAge")
            chdScholar.College = Request.Form("College")
            chdScholar.Transport = Request.Form("Transport")
            chdScholar.Housing = Request.Form("Housing")
            'Calculate cost
            chdScholar.CollegeCost Payment, LumpSum, TotalCost
    %>
    <P>
    Amount you need to invest today to pay for <%=chdScholar.Name%> to
    go to college: <%=LumpSum%>.
    <P>
    Amount you need to save each month to send <%=chdScholar.Name%> to
    college: <%=Payment%>.
    <P>
```

(continued)

Total amount you need to have by the time <%=chdScholar.Name%> is 18:
<%=TotalCost%>.

```
<%
End If
%>
```

```
</BODY>
</HTML>
```

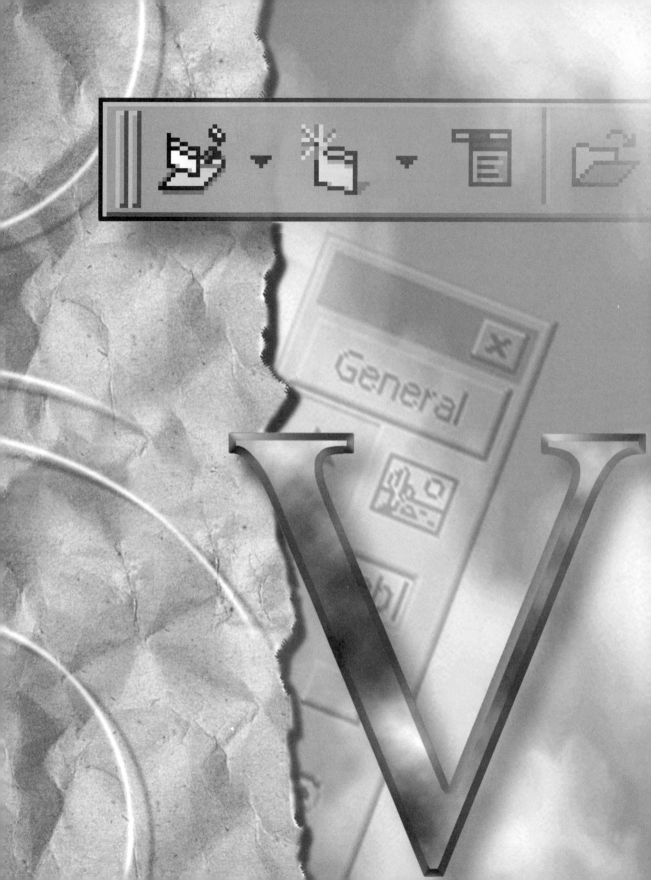

CHAPTER EIGHT

API Functions

A powerful feature of Visual Basic is its ability to call procedures that reside in dynamic link library (DLL) files, including the application programming interface (API) functions that are provided—and used—by Microsoft Windows. The Windows API functions and their syntax are described in the Win32 SDK Help file. Access to the thousands of Windows API functions, as well as other functions contained in DLLs, extends the capabilities of Visual Basic far beyond those of many other programming languages.

In this chapter, I show you a way to declare these functions in an easy-to-read format using Visual Basic's line continuation character, and I demonstrate a few useful functions to give you a head start in using these API calls. I also describe a few simple details and potential gotchas that seem to trip up most of us once or twice as we begin to experiment with API function calling.

Dear John, How Do I...

Call API Functions?

To use API functions, you simply declare them in your source code and then call them just as you would any other function in Visual Basic. We'll take a look at these two steps in more detail in the sections that follow.

Declarations

Because API functions are not internal to Visual Basic, you must explicitly declare them before you can use them. The online help covers the exact syntax for the Declare statement, but I've discovered a few tricks that you will probably find useful.

Some API function declarations are quite long. In the past, either you lived with a long declaration or you somehow condensed the declaration so that it would all fit comfortably on one line. For example, the following code shows the standard declaration for the API function GetTempFileName. In versions of Visual Basic prior to Visual Basic 4, this entire declaration was entered on one line in the source code file:

```
Private Declare Function GetTempFileName Lib "kernel32" Alias
"GetTempFileNameA" (ByVal lpszPath As String, ByVal lpPrefixString
As String, ByVal wUnique As Long, ByVal lpTempFileName As String)
As Long
```

Here's a shortened version of this declaration also entered on one line, which makes the declaration more manageable but somewhat less readable:

```
Private Declare Function GetTempFileName& Lib "kernel32" Alias
"GetTempFileNameA" (ByVal Pth$, ByVal Prf$, ByVal Unq&, ByVal Fnm$)
```

Visual Basic lets you format these declarations in another way, keeping the longer, more readable parameter names but using much shorter lines that are visible in a normal-size edit window. The line continuation character is the key to this improved format. The following code shows the same declaration in a style that I find easy to read. (Feel free to modify the layout to suit your own style.)

```
Private Declare Function GetTempFileName _
Lib "kernel32" Alias "GetTempFileNameA" ( _
    ByVal lpszPath As String, _
    ByVal lpPrefixString As String, _
    ByVal wUnique As Long, _
    ByVal lpTempFileName As String _
) As Long
```

You'll find this style used throughout this book wherever I declare API functions.

32-Bit Function Declarations

Notice in the previous example that the GetTempFileName function name is actually aliased to a function named GetTempFileNameA. In Microsoft Windows 95, 32-bit function declarations involving string parameters have been renamed from their 16-bit predecessors because they've been rebuilt using 32-bit coding specifications, although they still use ANSI strings internally (hence the *A*). Be aware that in 32-bit versions of Visual Basic, Windows API function names are case sensitive.

> NOTE: A third set of functions has been defined for 32-bit Microsoft Windows NT development in which strings are internally manipulated in the system DLLs as Unicode strings. In this case, the original function names now have the suffix *W* (for *Wide* characters). The Unicode function versions are not supported in Windows 95.

To be sure you get the properly formatted function declaration, you can access the Windows API function declarations in the WIN32API.TXT file, which you'll find in the WINAPI directory in your Visual Basic directory. There are several ways to get the function declarations from this file into your application. You can load the file into WordPad and copy the desired declarations into your Visual Basic applications by hand, making the editing changes mentioned above. Or you might prefer to use the API Viewer application, which comes with Visual Basic, to automate this process.

The API Viewer lets you load a text API file or a database API file and easily browse its contents. Items such as function declarations can be selected, copied to the clipboard, and pasted into Visual Basic. You can start the API Viewer by choosing API Text Viewer from the Visual Basic directory on the Windows Start menu or by running the APILOAD.EXE program from the WINAPI directory.

In Chapter 28, "Development Tools," I'll show you how to create an add-in to the Visual Basic environment that helps you insert API function declarations.

Strings

There are a couple of gotchas to watch out for when you are passing strings as arguments to API functions. One is that API functions will not create any string space for you. You must create a string space long enough to handle the longest possible string that could be returned before you pass the string to the function. For example, the following code declares the API function GetWindowsDirectory, which returns the path to the Windows directory. The string buffer for the path must be large enough to hold the data returned by GetWindowsDirectory. Before the function is called, the string variable *WinPath* is built to be 144 bytes in length using the Space$ function, as shown. Failure to build a string parameter to a sufficient length will cause an API function to return no data in the string.

```
Option Explicit

Private Declare Function GetWindowsDirectory _
Lib "kernel32" Alias "GetWindowsDirectoryA" ( _
    ByVal lpBuffer As String, _
    ByVal nSize As Long _
) As Long

Private Sub Form_Click()
    Dim WinPath As String
    Dim Rtn As Integer
```

(continued)

```
        Const MAXWINPATH = 144
        WinPath = Space$(MAXWINPATH)
        Rtn = GetWindowsDirectory(WinPath, MAXWINPATH)
        WinPath = Left$(WinPath, Rtn) 'Truncate at the 0 byte
        Print WinPath
End Sub
```

If you incorporate this code fragment into a program, the Windows directory path, as returned by the GetWindowsDirectory API function, is displayed when the form is clicked. The result is shown in Figure 8-1.

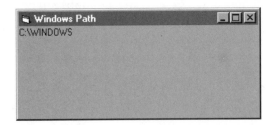

Figure 8-1.
The Windows directory path as returned by GetWindowsDirectory.

Also note that returned strings are terminated by a byte of value 0. In the sample code above, the function returns the length of the string, but in many cases when you use API functions you won't know the actual length of the string data unless you look for the 0 byte. If the API function doesn't return the length of the returned string, here's a way to lop off those extra spaces on the string:

```
WinPath = Left$(WinPath, InStr(WinPath, Chr$(0)) - 1)
```

See Also...

- The APIAddin application in Chapter 28, "Development Tools," for a demonstration of how to select, copy, and paste API functions that are in an easy-to-read format into your source code

Dear John, How Do I...

Pass the Address of a Procedure to an API Function?

Passing the address of a Visual Basic procedure to an API function is a trick that's been reserved for real code gurus up to now. Visual Basic 5 adds the

AddressOf operator, which is used for this C programming technique. In C, this process is known as a *callback*. A callback refers to a Visual Basic procedure that is called while the API function is being executed.

The parameters for the called Visual Basic procedure are determined by the API function. For example, in the following code the EnumChildWindows API function calls the Visual Basic ChildWindowProc function. The code should be placed in a code module (BAS) and not in a form. When the Startup Object is set to Sub Main and this code is executed, the window handles for the Visual Basic programming environment are displayed in the Immediate window.

```
Option Explicit

Private Declare Function GetActiveWindow _
Lib "User32" () As Long

Private Declare Function EnumChildWindows _
Lib "User32" ( _
    ByVal hWnd As Long, _
    ByVal lpWndProc As Long, _
    ByVal lp As Long _
) As Long

Sub Main()
    Dim hWnd As Long
    Dim x As Long
    'Get a handle to the active window
    hWnd = GetActiveWindow()
    If (hWnd) Then
        'Call EnumChildWindows API, which calls
        'ChildWindowProc for each child window and then ends
        x = EnumChildWindows(hWnd, AddressOf ChildWindowProc, 0)
    End If
End Sub

'Called by EnumChildWindows API function
Function ChildWindowProc( _
    ByVal hWnd As Long, _
    ByVal lp As Long _
) As Long
    'hWnd and lp parameters are passed in by EnumChildWindows
    Debug.Print "Window: "; hWnd
    'Return success (in C, 1 is True and 0 is False)
    ChildWindowProc = 1
End Function
```

The EnumChildWindows function passes the *hWnd* and *lp* parameters to ChildWindowProc. The format of the called procedure is described in the Win32 SDK Help topic for EnumChildWindows. By convention, called procedures end with the suffix *Proc*. This suffix tells you that the procedure is not called directly—instead, it is the target of a callback procedure.

Callbacks can generate some confusing results while you are debugging. For instance, the preceding example enumerates all the window handles in the Visual Basic programming environment while the procedure is being executed in Visual Basic. It enumerates a different set of window handles when it is compiled and executed as a stand-alone.

Keep these key points in mind as you work with the AddressOf operator:

■ The AddressOf operator can be used only in a code module (BAS), and then only as part of an argument to a procedure. This prevents you from passing the addresses of procedures that are part of an object or a form.

■ The procedure referenced with the AddressOf operator must be in the same project.

Dear John, How Do I...

Understand ByVal, ByRef, and As Any in an API Function Declaration?

This question is not so important in 32-bit Visual Basic programming because most of the As Any declarations have been replaced with explicit parameter data types. Nonetheless, I'll go ahead and describe a specific case—the 16-bit version of the WinHelp API function—for which this is a concern. Note, however, that the 32-bit version of this function has no As Any parameter declarations. Also bear in mind that Visual Basic 5 doesn't support 16-bit Windows; you'll need Visual Basic 4 or earlier to try this out.

Many 16-bit API function declarations (and a few 32-bit ones) have one or more parameters declared as As Any instead of as a specific data type such as Integer or String. This is so that these parameters can be used to pass a variety of data types, depending on the intended use of the function. For example, in the following code, which uses the 16-bit version of the WinHelp API function to display the Visual Basic help file, consider the WinHelp function's fourth parameter, which is declared as As Any. (This function, in its 32-bit version, will be demonstrated in more detail in Chapter 15, "Help Files.") Depending on the value of wCommand, the last parameter can be used to pass a long integer or a pointer to a string.

```
Option Explicit

Private Declare Function WinHelp _
Lib "User" ( _
    ByVal hWnd As Integer, _
    ByVal lpHelpFile As String, _
    ByVal wCommand As Integer, _
    ByRef dwData As Any _
) As Integer

Private Sub Form_Click()
    Dim x%, y&
    x% = WinHelp(Form1.hWnd, "VB.HLP", vbHelpContents, _
        ByVal y&)
End Sub
```

By convention, all As Any parameters in API functions are declared by reference. (I've added the ByRef keyword to my declarations to explicitly declare them as such, but ByRef is the default when you don't see either ByVal or ByRef in a parameter declaration.) You'll also usually find the ByVal keyword stuck in front of the variable that is passed for the As Any parameter *at the place where the function is called.* This means that you must pay special attention to how you treat these parameters at the place in your application where the function is actually called. In fact, incorrect use of the ByRef and ByVal keywords can cause your application to crash. Take a close look at the sample call to WinHelp in the code. In this case, the long integer *y&* is passed as the fourth parameter using the ByVal modifier, which ensures that a long integer value of *0* is passed.

Dear John, How Do I...
Easily Add API Declarations?

Visual Basic includes the handy API Viewer utility (Apiload) in the WINAPI directory for browsing and inserting the long list of API constants, associated Type structures, and procedure declarations. As an alternative, I've created an add-in utility application named APIAddin that I like even better. I've reformatted the declarations using the line continuation character, and I've made the list accessible directly from Visual Basic's editing environment. I've also prefixed the declarations with the Private keyword, which makes it easier to add them to any form, class, or code module in which you want to use the functions.

 See Also...

- The APIAddin application in Chapter 28, "Development Tools," for a better alternative to the Apiload utility included with Visual Basic

Dear John, How Do I...

Use API Calls to Get System Information?

You can use the Windows API functions to readily access a lot of information that Windows normally keeps hidden from Visual Basic applications. In the previous sections, I gave a general introduction to setting up API function calls in your applications. Let's explore some techniques and API functions that can be used to access system information. The following functions and techniques show how to use standard API calls to access just a few of the many types of data available from the system.

Determining the Version of the Operating System Using the SysInfo Control

A lot of system information that was formerly available only through the Windows API is now available through the SysInfo control. This control provides system version, platform, and system event information. SysInfo is useful for writing code to handle differences between Windows 95 and Windows NT. SysInfo is also particularly useful for the plug-and-play events that occur when a PCMCIA card is inserted in a laptop computer.

To use the SysInfo control, check the Microsoft SysInfo Control check box in the Components dialog box, which is accessible from the Project menu. Once a reference to the SysInfo control has been set, the control is displayed in your Toolbox and can be placed on a form. The following code shows how to use the SysInfo control to display the operating system and version number:

```
Option Explicit

Private Sub Form_Click()
Dim sMsg As String
    'Get platform and version
```

(continued)

```
    Select Case sysInfo1.OSPlatform
        Case 0
            sMsg = "Unidentified"
        Case 1
            sMsg = "Windows 95, version " & CStr(sysInfo1.OSVersion)
        Case 2
            sMsg = "Windows NT, version " & CStr(sysInfo1.OSVersion)
    End Select
    'Display OS information
    Print sMsg
End Sub
```

Figure 8-2 shows an example of the output after the form has been clicked.

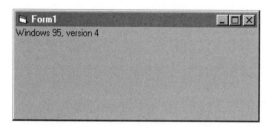

Figure 8-2.
Using the SysInfo control to display the operating system and the
version number.

Unfortunately, the SysInfo control doesn't include a bunch of handy system information, such as system colors, CPU type, and elapsed time. The rest of this section describes how to obtain this information using Windows API functions. The last section of this chapter brings it all together to create an enhanced version of the SysInfo control.

Determining System Colors

The GetSysColor API function returns an RGB color for window items such as captions, menus, and borders. You can get color information about any of 31 window components by passing the appropriate constant to the GetSys-Color function. The code on the following page lists these constants and demonstrates the GetSysColor function by setting the main form's background color to match the current desktop color when you click anywhere on the form. Some of these components are available only in specific versions of Windows—for example, the constants from COLOR_3DDKSHADOW to the end of the list are for Windows 95.

```
Option Explicit

Private Enum SysColor
    COLOR_SCROLLBAR = 0
    COLOR_BACKGROUND = 1
    COLOR_ACTIVECAPTION = 2
    COLOR_INACTIVECAPTION = 3
    COLOR_MENU = 4
    COLOR_WINDOW = 5
    COLOR_WINDOWFRAME = 6
    COLOR_MENUTEXT = 7
    COLOR_WINDOWTEXT = 8
    COLOR_CAPTIONTEXT = 9
    COLOR_ACTIVEBORDER = 10
    COLOR_INACTIVEBORDER = 11
    COLOR_APPWORKSPACE = 12
    COLOR_HIGHLIGHT = 13
    COLOR_HIGHLIGHTTEXT = 14
    COLOR_BTNFACE = 15
    COLOR_BTNSHADOW = 16
    COLOR_GRAYTEXT = 17
    COLOR_BTNTEXT = 18
    COLOR_INACTIVECAPTIONTEXT = 19
    COLOR_BTNHIGHLIGHT = 20
    COLOR_3DDKSHADOW = 21
    COLOR_3DLIGHT = 22
    COLOR_INFOTEXT = 23
    COLOR_INFOBK = 24
    COLOR_DESKTOP = COLOR_BACKGROUND
    COLOR_3DFACE = COLOR_BTNFACE
    COLOR_3DSHADOW = COLOR_BTNSHADOW
    COLOR_3DHIGHLIGHT = COLOR_BTNHIGHLIGHT
    COLOR_3DHILIGHT = COLOR_3DHIGHLIGHT
    COLOR_BTNHILIGHT = COLOR_BTNHIGHLIGHT
End Enum

Private Declare Function GetSysColor _
Lib "user32" ( _
    ByVal nIndex As Long _
) As Long

Private Sub Form_Click()
    Dim SystemColor As Long
    Dim Red As Integer, Green As Integer, Blue As Integer
    'Get color of desktop
    SystemColor = GetSysColor(COLOR_DESKTOP)
```

(continued)

```
                'Set form's background color to same as desktop
                BackColor = SystemColor
                'Split this color into its components
                ColorSplit SystemColor, Red, Green, Blue
                Print "R,G,B = "; Red, Green, Blue
            End Sub

            Function ColorSplit(RGBMix As Long, R%, G%, B%)
            'Extract R, G, and B values from an RGB color
                R% = RGBMix And &HFF
                G% = (RGBMix \ &H100) And &HFF
                B% = (RGBMix \ &H10000) And &HFF
            End Function
```

Notice that I've also provided a handy function, ColorSplit, to extract the red, green, and blue values from the RGB color value returned by these functions. You might find this function useful for other graphics calculations—it's the inverse function of Visual Basic's RGB function, which returns a long integer formed by combining red, green, and blue color values, each in the range 0 through 255.

Figure 8-3 shows an example of the output when the form is clicked.

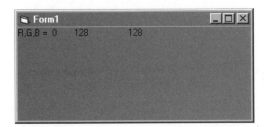

Figure 8-3.
Using the GetSysColor API function to change the form's background color to the desktop color.

 See Also...

- Chapter 12, "Graphics Techniques," if you're interested in another approach to coordinated color schemes

Determining CPU Type

The code on the following page uses the GetSystemInfo API function to determine the type of CPU in the system. By inspecting the SYSTEM_INFO Type structure, you'll find that this function returns several other useful bits of information about the system. In anticipation of more advanced systems that will be available in the near future, this data structure even returns the number of processors on the current system.

```
Option Explicit

Private Type SYSTEM_INFO
    dwOemID As Long
    dwPageSize As Long
    lpMinimumApplicationAddress As Long
    lpMaximumApplicationAddress As Long
    dwActiveProcessorMask As Long
    dwNumberOfProcessors As Long
    dwProcessorType As Long
    dwAllocationGranularity As Long
    dwReserved As Long
End Type

Private Declare Sub GetSystemInfo _
Lib "kernel32" ( _
    lpSystemInfo As SYSTEM_INFO _
)

Private Sub Form_Click()
    Dim Sys As SYSTEM_INFO
    GetSystemInfo Sys
    Print "Processor type: "; Sys.dwProcessorType
    Print "No. Processors: "; Sys.dwNumberOfProcessors
End Sub
```

Figure 8-4 shows an example of the output when the form is clicked.

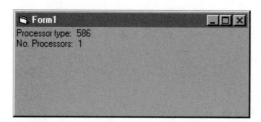

Figure 8-4.
Using GetSystemInfo to determine the type and number of processors.

Determining Elapsed Time

The GetTickCount Windows API function returns the number of milliseconds that have elapsed since Windows was started. Depending on your system, this function returns a value with greater precision than that of Visual Basic's Timer function. The Timer function returns the number of seconds since midnight and includes fractions of seconds that provide the illusion of millisecond accuracy, but Visual Basic actually updates the value returned by Timer only 18.2 times per second. On my Pentium system, the value returned by Get-TickCount is updated almost 100 times each second.

Another advantage of GetTickCount over the Timer function is that crossing the midnight boundary causes no problems. The Timer value returns to *0* at midnight, whereas the GetTickCount value returns to 0 only after about 49.7 days of continuous computer operation. In the following code, when the form is clicked the GetTickCount API function is called and the time elapsed since Windows was started, in milliseconds, is printed on the form. This process is repeated nine more times to show how often the value returned from GetTickCount is updated.

```
Option Explicit

Private Declare Function GetTickCount _
Lib "kernel32" ( _
) As Long

Private Sub Form_Click()
    Dim i, j
    Print "Time elapsed since Windows was started:"
    For i = 1 To 10
        j = GetTickCount
        Do While j = GetTickCount
        Loop
        Print j; " milliseconds"
    Next i
End Sub
```

Figure 8-5 shows an example of the output when the form is clicked.

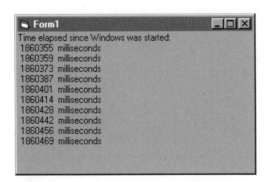

Figure 8-5.
Time elapsed since Windows was started, as reported by GetTickCount and the updated values.

Determining Drive Types

It's easy to determine whether the user's computer has one or two floppy drives or one or more hard drives or is connected to any remote drives; this is accomplished by calling the GetDriveType Windows API function. You might want to use this function in a program that searches all available drives for a specific data file, for instance. In the following code, the GetDriveType function is used to detect all drives that are present on the system:

```
Option Explicit

'GetDriveType return values
Const DRIVE_REMOVABLE = 2
Const DRIVE_FIXED = 3
Const DRIVE_REMOTE = 4
Const DRIVE_CDROM = 5
Const DRIVE_RAMDISK = 6

Private Declare Function GetDriveType _
Lib "kernel32" Alias "GetDriveTypeA" ( _
    ByVal nDrive As String _
) As Long

Private Sub Form_Click()
    Dim i, Drv, D$
    For i = 0 To 25   'All possible drives A to Z
        D$ = Chr$(i + 65) & ":\"
        Drv = GetDriveType(D$)
        Select Case Drv
        Case DRIVE_REMOVABLE
            Print "Drive " & D$ & " is removable."
        Case DRIVE_FIXED
            Print "Drive " & D$ & " is fixed."
        Case DRIVE_REMOTE
            Print "Drive " & D$ & " is remote."
        Case DRIVE_CDROM
            Print "Drive " & D$ & " is CD-ROM."
        Case DRIVE_RAMDISK
            Print "Drive " & D$ & " is RAM disk."
        Case Else
        End Select
    Next i
End Sub
```

The list of available drives is displayed when the form is clicked, as shown in Figure 8-6.

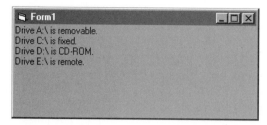

Figure 8-6.
Using GetDriveType to return the types of drives on a system.

Dear John, How Do I...

Add API Calls in an ActiveX Control?

Microsoft left out a lot of useful information when they built the SysInfo control. For example, you can use SysInfo to detect when the user changes the system colors, but you then have to use the Windows API to determine which colors were changed.

Fortunately, you can now create your own controls with Visual Basic 5—and controls make a great home for common API declarations. You can repackage the APIs you use all the time as methods or properties and then call them to get the information you need, without having long, messy API declarations in your code.

Adding API Functions to an ActiveX Control

API declarations can be included in a user control module, just as they can be included in any other module. At the simplest level, all you have to do is create a new ActiveX control project, declare the API function at the control's module level, and then call the API function from a Public procedure. The following code shows a GetTicks method in a control named *TickControl*:

```
Option Explicit

'TickControl control module
'API declaration
Private Declare Function GetTickCount _
Lib "kernel32" ( _
) As Long

Public Function GetTicks() As Long
    'Return number of milliseconds since Windows started
    GetTicks = GetTickCount
End Function
```

161

Notice that the API declaration must be Private. The GetTicks function simply repackages the GetTickCount API function so that it can be called from outside the module.

Testing the New Control

You can't test an ActiveX control by clicking Visual Basic's Start button as you can when you're developing an application in Visual Basic. Because the control is a component, it must have a context in which to exist. To test the new control, follow these steps:

1. Choose Add Project from the File menu, and add a Standard EXE project.

2. Add the TickControl control from the Toolbox to Form1. TickControl will contain the default user control icon. If the TickControl icon is grayed in the Toolbox, close the UserControl window. Size the TickControl control if necessary.

3. Use the methods and properties of the control in code, just as you would any other control.

The following form code shows how to call the GetTicks method of the *TickControl1* control:

```
Option Explicit

Private Sub Form_Click()
    Print TickControl1.GetTicks
End Sub
```

Using the New Control

To use the new control in other projects, follow these steps:

1. Select the user control project, and choose Project Properties from the Project menu to display the Project Properties dialog box. From the Project Type drop-down list, select ActiveX Control, enter a name in the Project Name text box, enter a one-line description in the Project Description text box, and click OK.

2. Choose Make OCX from the File menu, where the OCX name is the name you entered in the Project Name text box.

3. In the Make Project dialog box, select a location in which to save the OCX, enter a name in the File Name text box, and click OK.

4. Start a new Standard EXE project.

5. From the Project menu, choose Components. On the Controls tab of the Components dialog box, add a check box next to the Project Description of the control you just created. Click OK to add this control to the Toolbox.

6. Add the control to a form in the new project.

7. Use the methods and properties of the control in code, just as you would any other control.

See Also...

- Chapter 6, "ActiveX Controls," for more information about creating controls

Enhancing an Existing Control

Controls can contain other controls, which is handy when you want to add features to an existing control but don't have its source code. Remember that you'll have to install both controls on your user's system if you do this.

You can add all sorts of new properties and methods to enhance the SysInfo control by superclassing the control—*superclassing* means that an existing object is included in a new object, keeping all the old object's features and adding your own properties and methods.

Figure 8-7 shows the SysInfo control placed in the UserControl window. Code can be added to enhance, or superclass, the control.

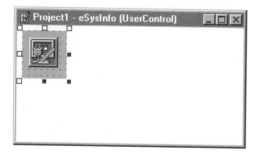

Figure 8-7.
The SysInfo control can be enhanced by superclassing.

To superclass a control, you've got to reproduce all of the properties, methods, and events provided by the base control. The code to accomplish this is trivial but tiresome to type, as shown in the following example:

```
'Delegate to SysInfo Properties
Public Property Get ACStatus() As Integer
    ACStatus = OldSysInfo.ACStatus
End Property
Public Property Get BatteryFullTime() As Long
    BatteryFullTime = OldSysInfo.BatteryFullTime
End Property
Public Property Get BatteryLifePercent() As Integer
    BatteryLifePercent = OldSysInfo.BatteryLifePercent
End Property
Public Property Get BatteryLifeTime() As Long
    BatteryLifeTime = OldSysInfo.BatteryLifeTime
End Property
Public Property Get BatteryStatus() As Integer
    BatteryStatus = OldSysInfo.BatteryStatus
End Property
Public Property Get OSBuild() As Integer
    OSBuild = OldSysInfo.OSBuild
End Property
Public Property Get OSPlatform() As Integer
    OSPlatform = OldSysInfo.OSPlatform
End Property
Public Property Get OSVersion() As Single
    OSVersion = OldSysInfo.OSVersion
End Property
Public Property Get ScrollBarSize() As Single
    ScrollBarSize = OldSysInfo.ScrollBarSize
End Property
Public Property Get WorkAreaHeight() As Single
    WorkAreaHeight = OldSysInfo.WorkAreaHeight
End Property
Public Property Get WorkAreaLeft() As Single
    WorkAreaLeft = OldSysInfo.WorkAreaLeft
End Property
Public Property Get WorkAreaTop() As Single
    WorkAreaTop = OldSysInfo.WorkAreaTop
End Property
Public Property Get WorkAreaWidth() As Single
    WorkAreaWidth = OldSysInfo.WorkAreaWidth
End Property
```

Reproducing properties and methods in this way is called *delegating*. You don't need to delegate common properties such as Name and Parent because these properties are provided by the container.

To reproduce all of the SysInfo events in the Enhanced SysInfo control, declare each event with an Event statement, and then trigger the new event using a RaiseEvent statement in each of the SysInfo control's event procedures. Again, the code is trivial but tedious. An abbreviated version is shown here; see the companion CD-ROM for the complete Event declarations:

```
'Event declarations
Event ConfigChangeCancelled()
Event ConfigChanged( _
    OldConfigNum As Long, _
    NewConfigNum As Long)
Event DeviceArrival( _
    DeviceType As Long, _
    DeviceID As Long, _
    DeviceName As String, _
    DeviceData As Long)
Event DeviceOtherEvent( _
    DeviceType As Long, _
    EventName As String, _
    DataPointer As Long)
Event DeviceQueryRemove( _
    DeviceType As Long, _
    DeviceID As Long, _
    DeviceName As String, _
    DeviceData As Long, _
    Cancel As Boolean)
'And so on...

'Raise all the SysInfo events on the user control
Private Sub OldSysInfo_ConfigChangeCancelled()
    RaiseEvent ConfigChangeCancelled
End Sub
Private Sub OldSysInfo_ConfigChanged( _
    ByVal OldConfigNum As Long, _
    ByVal NewConfigNum As Long)
    RaiseEvent ConfigChanged(OldConfigNum, NewConfigNum)
End Sub
Private Sub OldSysInfo_DeviceArrival( _
    ByVal DeviceType As Long, _
    ByVal DeviceID As Long, _
    ByVal DeviceName As String, _
    ByVal DeviceData As Long)
    RaiseEvent DeviceArrival(DeviceType, DeviceID, DeviceName, DeviceData)
End Sub
```

(continued)

165

```
Private Sub OldSysInfo_DeviceOtherEvent( _
    ByVal DeviceType As Long, _
    ByVal EventName As String, _
    ByVal DataPointer As Long)
    RaiseEvent DeviceOtherEvent(DeviceType, EventName, DataPointer)
End Sub
Private Sub OldSysInfo_DeviceQueryRemove( _
    ByVal DeviceType As Long, _
    ByVal DeviceID As Long, _
    ByVal DeviceName As String, _
    ByVal DeviceData As Long, _
    Cancel As Boolean)
    RaiseEvent DeviceQueryRemove(DeviceType, DeviceID, DeviceName, _
        DeviceData, Cancel)
End Sub
'And so on...
```

Each SysInfo event raises an event of the same name in the enhanced control. After reproducing (or *wrapping*) all the SysInfo events, properties, and methods, you finally get to add some of your own, as shown here:

```
'Declarations for system colors
Public Enum SystemColor
    COLOR_SCROLLBAR = 0
    COLOR_BACKGROUND = 1
    COLOR_ACTIVECAPTION = 2
    COLOR_INACTIVECAPTION = 3
    COLOR_MENU = 4
    COLOR_WINDOW = 5
    COLOR_WINDOWFRAME = 6
    COLOR_MENUTEXT = 7
    COLOR_WINDOWTEXT = 8
    COLOR_CAPTIONTEXT = 9
    COLOR_ACTIVEBORDER = 10
    'Constants omitted for brevity
End Enum

Private Declare Function GetSysColor _
Lib "user32" ( _
    ByVal nIndex As Long _
) As Long

Public Function GetSystemColor(Index As SystemColor)
    GetSystemColor = GetSysColor(Index)
End Function
```

The GetSystemColor method returns the color setting for a specific Windows object. The values in the Enum are displayed in the Object Browser when you use the control in a new application.

See Also...

- Visual Basic's ActiveX Control Interface Wizard for an easy way to create interfaces. This wizard can be added to Visual Basic by checking it in the Add-In Manager, which is accessed from the Add-Ins menu.

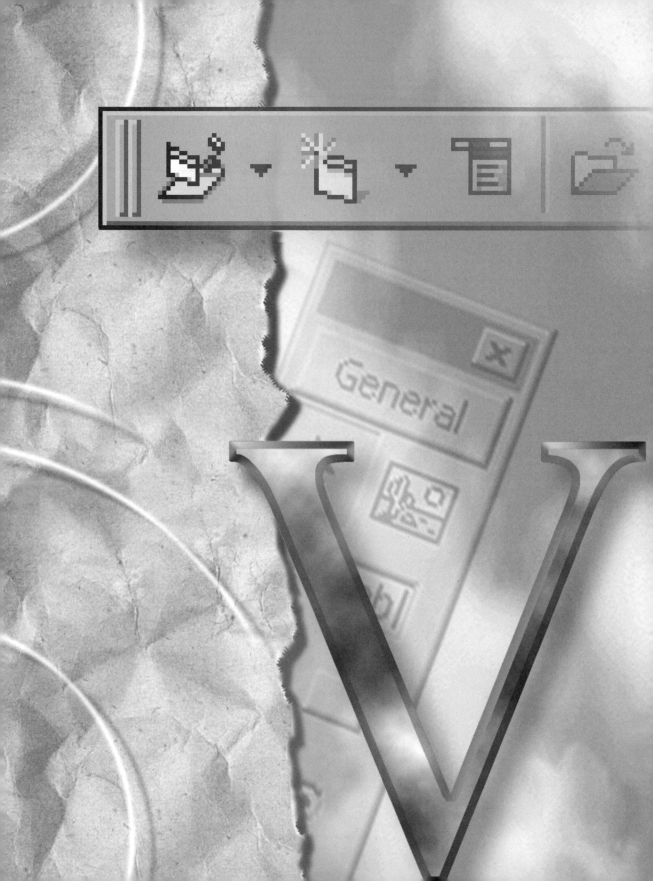

CHAPTER NINE

Multimedia

In this chapter, I show you two ways to add sound files and video clips to your applications. To try the code examples, you need to have a sound board and the appropriate multimedia drivers installed. You also need a sample WAV file to play sound and a sample AVI file to play a video clip.

NOTE: You can find many sample sound and video files on your Microsoft Windows 95 CD-ROM. Right-click on the Start button, and choose Find to search for *.WAV and *.AVI files on your CD-ROM drive.

Dear John, How Do I...

Play a Sound (WAV) File?

There are several ways to play a sound file. Here we take a look at two very straightforward methods: one using the mciExecute API function supplied by Microsoft Windows, and the other using the Multimedia MCI (Media Control Interface) control included with Visual Basic 5.

The mciExecute Function

The following code shows how to declare the mciExecute API function and then use it to play a WAV file. To try this example, add the code to a blank form in a new project, run the application, and click anywhere on the form.

```
Option Explicit

Private Declare Function mciExecute _
Lib "winmm.dll" ( _
    ByVal lpstrCommand As String _
) As Long

Private Sub Form_Click()
    Dim x
    x = mciExecute("Play C:\Windows\Media\Tada.wav")
    'Change filename to name of your sample WAV file
End Sub
```

This same function can be used to send other multimedia commands. For example, we'll soon see how to play a video clip with it.

The Multimedia MCI Control

The Multimedia MCI control included with Visual Basic 5 is an excellent tool for playing sound files. With minor modifications to the code, you can also use this control to play video for Windows (AVI) files and multimedia movie (MMM) files and to control multimedia hardware. Here we concentrate on playing a sound file.

For the example that follows, draw a Multimedia MCI control on a blank form in a new project. If the Multimedia MCI control (whose class name, and thus its ToolTip name, is MMControl) is not in your Toolbox, add it by choosing Components from the Project menu and selecting Microsoft Multimedia Control from the list on the Controls tab of the Components dialog box. Name this control *mciTest,* and set its Visible property to *False.* This example demonstrates how to use an invisible control behind the scenes at runtime, which provides complete programmatic control. For a description of all the buttons on the control and an explanation of how the user can interact with them in the visible mode, refer to the Visual Basic online help.

I've set up the following example to play the sample sound file TADA.WAV when you click anywhere on the form. You can add this code to any event-driven procedure you want, such as an error-trapping procedure or any other event for which you want to give audible notification to the user.

```
Option Explicit

Private Sub Form_Click()
    With mciTest
        .FileName = "C:\Windows\Media\Tada.wav"
        'Change filename to name of your sample WAV file
        .Command = "Sound"
    End With
End Sub
```

Dear John, How Do I...

Play a Video (AVI) File?

It's surprisingly easy to play an AVI file on a system that is configured to play these files. You can use the mciExecute API function supplied by Windows or the Multimedia MCI control.

The mciExecute Function

The code below shows how to declare the mciExecute API function and then use it to play a sample video file. To try this example, add the code to a blank form in a new project, run the application, and click anywhere on the form. I've assumed that you have a Windows 95 CD-ROM in your D drive and will use one of its AVI files as your sample video file. Notice that this code is almost identical to the code for playing a WAV file.

```
Option Explicit

Private Declare Function mciExecute _
Lib "winmm.dll" ( _
    ByVal lpstrCommand As String _
) As Long

Private Sub Form_Click()
    Dim x
    x = mciExecute("Play D:\Funstuff\Videos\Welcome1.avi")
    'Change filename to name of your sample AVI file
End Sub
```

Figure 9-1 shows this form and the video window in action.

Figure 9-1.
A video demonstration initiated by a click on the form.

The Multimedia MCI Control

The Multimedia MCI control included with Visual Basic 5 works well for playing video files. The Visual Basic online help covers the user's interaction with the visible buttons, but I'll show you a simple way to use the control in an "invisible" mode to programmatically play a video.

To try this example, draw a Multimedia MCI control on a blank form in a new project, name it *mciTest,* and set its Visible property to *False.* Add the following code, run the application, and click anywhere on the form. You'll need to change the FileName property setting to the name and location of your AVI file.

```
Option Explicit

Private Sub Form_Click()
    With mciTest
        .FileName = "D:\Funstuff\Videos\Welcome1.avi"
        .Command = "Open"
        .Command = "Play"
    End With
End Sub

Private Sub mciTest_Done(NotifyCode As Integer)
    mciTest.Command = "Close"
End Sub
```

Originally, I tried to put the Close command immediately after the Play command. This didn't work—the video would quit as soon as it started. I solved this problem by putting Close in the Done event code, as shown above. The system tells us automatically when the video has finished playing, at which time it's safe to perform the Close.

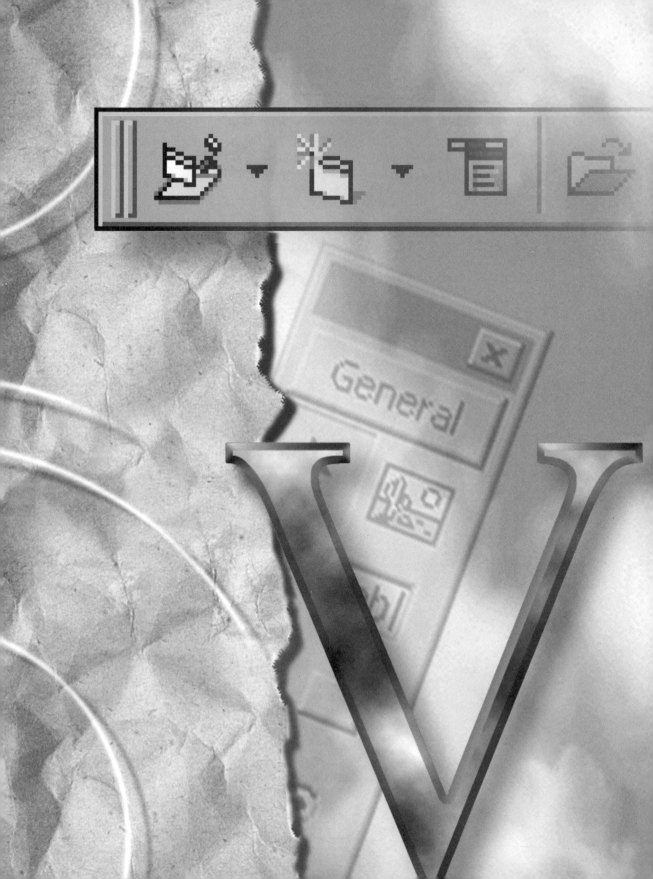

CHAPTER TEN

Dialog Boxes,
Windows,
and Other Forms

In this chapter, I provide several helpful hints and tips for working with forms. Some of these techniques are old standards, such as positioning a form on the screen, and some are newer, such as creating a tabbed form. I've found each of these tips to be a useful addition to my bag of tricks.

Dear John, How Do I...

Add a Standard About Dialog Box?

One of the standard elements of many Microsoft Windows applications is the About dialog box. Usually, the user activates an About dialog box by choosing About from the Help menu. Check out the Help menu of almost any Windows application, and you'll find About there.

You can easily add your own About dialog box to your applications. It doesn't have to be very fancy; in fact, you can use the MsgBox function to create a simple About dialog box. For a display with a more professional appearance, you can create an About dialog box using a form.

I've created a form with the Name property *frmAbout* and saved it as ABOUT.FRM. The *frmAbout* form can easily be loaded into a project. It has three Label controls, named *lblHeading*, *lblApplication*, and *lblCopyright*, and one command button, named *cmdOK*. When the form is called, it will look something like Figure 10-1 on the following page, depending on what strings are passed to it.

Figure 10-1.
A standard About dialog box.

Here is the code for the About form:

```
Option Explicit

Private Sub cmdOK_Click()
    'Cancel About form
    Unload frmAbout
End Sub

Private Sub Form_Load()
    'Center this form
    Left = (Screen.Width - Width) \ 2
    Top = (Screen.Height - Height) \ 2
    'Set defaults
    lblApplication.Caption = "- Application -"
    lblHeading.Caption = "- Heading -"
    lblCopyright.Caption = "- Copyright -"
End Sub

Public Sub Display()
    'Display self as modal
    Me.Show vbModal
End Sub

Property Let Heading(Heading As String)
    'Define string property for Heading
    lblHeading.Caption = Heading
End Property
```

(continued)

```
Property Let Application(Application As String)
    'Define string property for Application
    lblApplication.Caption = Application
End Property

Property Let Copyright(Copyright As String)
    'Build complete Copyright string property
    lblCopyright.Caption = "Copyright © " & Copyright
End Property
```

Notice that in the code I've used Property Let procedures to assign strings to the Heading, Application, and Copyright labels of the About form. By using these property procedures, your calling application can set these properties to whatever strings you want without worrying about public variables or directly referencing the Caption properties of the Label controls on the About form. For example, to have the calling application assign the string *ABOUTDEM* to the application caption on the About form, the code would be this:

```
frmAbout.lblApplication.Caption = "ABOUTDEM"
```

By treating the form as an object and using Property Let procedures, the call would be much easier, as shown here:

```
frmAbout.Application = "ABOUTDEM"
```

Another advantage of using property procedures is that other actions can be initiated by the object when a property is assigned. For example, the string assigned to the Copyright property is concatenated to a standard copyright notice before it's displayed.

The About form code also uses one public method, Display, which I've substituted for the standard Show method. I've added the Display method so that you don't have to include the *vbModal* constant as an argument in the Show method. If the *vbModal* constant is included as an argument, it specifies the form as modal and requires the user to respond to the form before interaction with other forms in an application is allowed. Having the form set as modal is the standard state in which to display the About dialog box. If you use the Display method, which is part of the About form module, you don't need to address the issue of modal or nonmodal state when you display the form. You could also add code to the Display method to enhance the display. For example, you could use a Timer control to display the About dialog box for a specific period and then hide it from view. As a general rule, object-oriented programming (OOP) transfers the responsibility of taking actions to the objects themselves, and this Display method follows that rule.

If you want a different style of generic About dialog box, feel free to modify the About form to your heart's content. Be sure to change the default string property settings to something appropriate for your purposes. These default strings are set in the Form_Load event procedure.

I've used this About dialog box in many of the demonstration applications in Part III of this book. It was easy to add this form to each project: I added an About menu item to the standard Help menu and added a few lines of code to activate the About form when this menu item is selected.

To use this code, you need to create a new project and add the ABOUT.FRM file to the project. For a simple example, which creates an About dialog box similar to the one shown in Figure 10-1 on page 176, create a startup form with a menu to call the About form, and add the following code:

```
Option Explicit

Private Sub mnuAbout_Click()
    'Set properties
    frmAbout.Heading = "Microsoft Visual Basic 5.0 Developer's " & _
        "Workshop"
    frmAbout.Application = "ABOUTDEM"
    frmAbout.Copyright = "1997 John Clark Craig and Jeff Webb"
    'Call a method
    frmAbout.Display
End Sub
```

The About Dialog Form Template

Visual Basic 5 includes many template forms that you can add to your project and customize however you want. One of the template forms is an About Dialog form. One helpful feature of the About Dialog form template is an already created System Info button, which is a familiar feature in many About dialog boxes for Microsoft applications. The System Info button already contains all the necessary code for it to work properly, so it isn't necessary for you to supply additional code. These template forms are located in your Visual Basic directory, in the TEMPLATE directory.

To add the About Dialog form to your project, choose Add Form from the Project menu to display the Add Form dialog box, as shown in Figure 10-2.

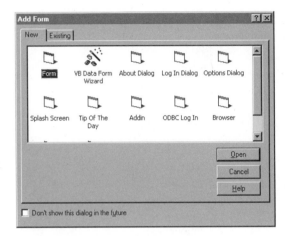

Figure 10-2.
The Add Form dialog box, containing form templates.

On the New tab of the Add Form dialog box, choose the About Dialog icon, and click Open. The About Dialog form is added to your project. The following code shows an example of how you might customize your About Dialog form template:

```
Option Explicit

Private Sub mnuAbout_Click()
    frmAbout.Caption = App.Title
    frmAbout.lblTitle = "ABOUTDEM"
    frmAbout.lblVersion = "Version " & App.Major & "." & App.Minor _
        & "." & App.Revision
    frmAbout.lblDescription = "Microsoft Visual Basic 5.0 " & _
        "Developer's Workshop"
    frmAbout.lblDisclaimer = "Copyright © 1997 John Clark Craig " & _
        "and Jeff Webb"
    frmAbout.Show
End Sub
```

Figure 10-3 on the following page shows the resulting About Dialog form.

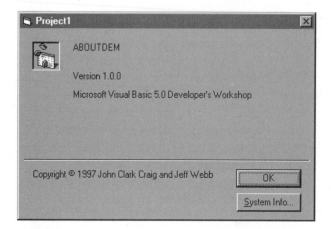

Figure 10-3.
An About dialog box created with Visual Basic's About Dialog form template.

 See Also...

- The Dialogs application in Chapter 32, "Advanced Applications," for a demonstration of the use of an About dialog box

Dear John, How Do I...

Automatically Position a Form on the Screen?

The best place to put code to position a form is in the form's Load procedure. This positions the form before it actually appears on the screen. To center a form, simply add two lines to the form's Load procedure that calculate and specify the location of the upper-left corner of your form, as shown in the following code:

```
Private Sub Form_Load()
    'Center this form
    Left = (Screen.Width - Width) \ 2
    Top = (Screen.Height - Height) \ 2
End Sub
```

NOTE: Notice that the backslash character (\) is used to execute integer division by 2. Integer division is faster than floating-point division, and in many situations (such as when you're centering a form) the result is to be rounded to the nearest integer value anyway. Use \ instead of / whenever it will work just as well.

Figure 10-4 shows a centered form.

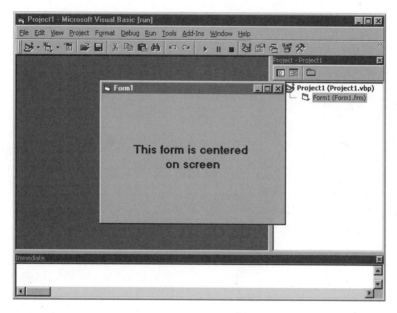

Figure 10-4.
Sample form centered on the screen.

If you want to position a form somewhere else on the screen, it's best to create a general procedure to handle the positioning. For example, the Locate procedure shown here positions the center of your form anywhere on the screen, using absolute coordinates:

```
Private Sub Form_Load()
    'Position this form in left quarter, top third of screen
    Locate 1/4, 1/3
End Sub

Private Sub Locate( _
    Optional Xadjust As Single = 0.5, _
    Optional Yadjust As Single = 0.5 _
)
    Left = Xadjust * Screen.Width - Width \ 2
    Top = Yadjust * Screen.Height - Height \ 2
End Sub
```

The parameters *Xadjust* and *Yadjust* can be any percentage of the screen's dimensions. If you call Locate without any arguments, the default settings will be used. In this case, the default settings will center the form on the screen.

Still another technique for positioning a form on the screen is to use a new feature available in Visual Basic 5, the Form Layout window, shown in Figure 10-5. If the Form Layout window is not currently displayed, you can open it by choosing Form Layout Window from the View menu.

Figure 10-5.
The Form Layout window.

In the Form Layout window, you can visually position the form anywhere on the screen. If you right-click on the screen and choose Resolution Guides from the pop-up menu, dotted lines are drawn indicating the different screen resolutions (640x480, 800x600, and 1024x768). Although this is a very easy way to position a form on the screen, you can't position the form independent of the resolution. If you want a form to always be centered no matter what resolution the user specifies, you should position the form using the preceding code.

See Also...

- The Dialogs application in Chapter 32, "Advanced Applications," for a demonstration of a form-positioning technique

Dear John, How Do I...
Create a Floating Window?

This is a rather loaded question because you can create a form that is modal, floating, or topmost, and the form will stay visible in front of other forms and windows. Let's look at techniques for controlling a form in each of these ways.

Modal Mode

Forms are displayed programmatically using the Show method. If you include the constant *vbModal* as the value for the optional argument in the Show method of a form, the user must attend to the form before any other parts of the application will recognize keypresses or mouse activity. In a sense, you might call this behavior *application modal.* Here's a code line that demonstrates this use of the Show method:

```
frmTest.Show vbModal
```

Note that your modal form must have some way of hiding or unloading itself, directly or indirectly, so that the application can go on from there.

Floating Mode

I consider the floating mode a little different from the topmost mode, which we'll get to next, although the two terms are often used interchangeably. You might think of a floating window as continually bobbing back to the surface.

To create this type of form, add a Timer control to your form, and set its Interval property to the speed at which you want the form to come floating back up. An interval of 500 milliseconds (0.5 second), for instance, is a reasonable value to try. Add the following lines to your Timer1_Timer event procedure to force the form to the top using the ZOrder method:

```
Private Sub Timer1_Timer()
    ZOrder
End Sub
```

Topmost Mode

You can use the Windows API function SetWindowPos to make a form stay on top even while you switch between applications. This creates a better effect than the bobbing motion just described and lets Windows do all the dirty work. Your form will stay on top of all other forms and windows until you close it. I've packaged calls to the SetWindowPos function in an OnTop property for the form. The following code then calls OnTop from the Form_Load and Form_Unload event procedures:

```
Option Explicit

'SetWindowPos flags
Private Const SWP_NOSIZE = &H1
Private Const SWP_NOMOVE = &H2
Private Const SWP_NOZORDER = &H4
Private Const SWP_NOREDRAW = &H8
Private Const SWP_NOACTIVATE = &H10
Private Const SWP_FRAMECHANGED = &H20
Private Const SWP_SHOWWINDOW = &H40
```

(continued)

```
Private Const SWP_HIDEWINDOW = &H80
Private Const SWP_NOCOPYBITS = &H100
Private Const SWP_NOOWNERZORDER = &H200
Private Const SWP_DRAWFRAME = SWP_FRAMECHANGED
Private Const SWP_NOREPOSITION = SWP_NOOWNERZORDER

'SetWindowPos() hwndInsertAfter values
Private Const HWND_TOP = 0
Private Const HWND_BOTTOM = 1
Private Const HWND_TOPMOST = -1
Private Const HWND_NOTOPMOST = -2

Private Declare Function SetWindowPos _
Lib "user32" ( _
    ByVal hwnd As Long, _
    ByVal hWndInsertAfter As Long, _
    ByVal x As Long, _
    ByVal y As Long, _
    ByVal cx As Long, _
    ByVal cy As Long, _
    ByVal wFlags As Long _
) As Long

Private mbOnTop As Boolean

'~~~.OnTop
Private Property Let OnTop(Setting As Boolean)
'Set the form's OnTop property
    If Setting Then
        'Make this form topmost
        SetWindowPos hwnd, HWND_TOPMOST, _
            0, 0, 0, 0, SWP_NOMOVE Or SWP_NOSIZE
    Else
        'Make this form non-topmost
        SetWindowPos hwnd, HWND_NOTOPMOST, _
            0, 0, 0, 0, SWP_NOMOVE Or SWP_NOSIZE
    End If
    mbOnTop = Setting
End Property

Private Property Get OnTop() As Boolean
    'Return the private variable set in Property Let
    OnTop = mbOnTop
End Property

Private Sub Form_Load()
    'Place form on top of all others
```

(continued)

```
    OnTop = True
End Sub

Private Sub Form_Unload(Cancel As Integer)
    'Put form back in normal ZOrder
    OnTop = False
End Sub
```

I've put the code to return the form to normal ZOrder in the Form_Unload event procedure, but you can put this code anywhere in your application. For instance, you could set up the code so that you can toggle the form into and out of the topmost state at will. Using property procedures to contain the SetWindowPos calls makes it easy to toggle the setting. For instance, the following line of code switches the OnTop property on or off, depending on its initial setting:

```
OnTop = Not OnTop
```

You don't actually need to add all of the window position constants to your code. I included all relevant constants for handy reference. You might want to create other form properties that use these constants by combining them with the *wFlags* parameter of SetWindowPos using the Or operator.

Dear John, How Do I...

Create a Splash (Logo) Screen?

Often a large application will take several seconds to get up and running, its loading time varying according to both the amount of initialization needed and the speed of the user's system. One of the best ways to use the screen during this delay is to display a logo, a trademark, or what some have come to call a *splash screen*. Here's a straightforward way to display a splash screen named *frmSplash*:

```
Option Explicit
Private Sub Form_Load()
    'Show this form
    Show
    'Show splash screen
    frmSplash.Show
    DoEvents
    'Perform time-consuming initializations...
    Initialize
    'Erase splash screen
    Unload Splash
End Sub
```

The code in this procedure should be inserted into the application's startup form. Usually, the startup form is the main form that will remain active as long as the application is running. Everything to control the splash screen can be done right here in the Form_Load event procedure because Visual Basic gives us some control over the order of events. The first Show method forces Windows to draw the main form on the screen. (Normally, this doesn't take place until after the Form_Load event procedure has finished.) The next Show method displays the splash screen, which is a form of your own design named *frmSplash*. I've followed this Show method with a DoEvents function to ensure that all elements of the splash screen form are completely drawn right away. The DoEvents function forces Visual Basic to yield control to the operating system until all pending operations are completed. The Initialize function represents the time-consuming tasks that your application performs at startup, such as loading data from files, loading resources from a resource file, loading forms into memory, and so on. After the initialization is complete, the splash screen form is unloaded, and everything's ready to go.

Figure 10-6 shows an example of a splash screen display centered on the application's main form.

Figure 10-6.
Imaginary application's splash screen in action.

The Splash Screen Form Template

As mentioned, Visual Basic 5 includes many template forms. One of the template forms is a splash screen. To add the Splash Screen form to your project, choose Add Form from the Project menu. On the New tab of the Add Form dialog box, select the Splash Screen icon, and click Open. The Splash Screen form is added to your project.

The following code shows an example of how you might customize the Splash Screen form template:

```
Option Explicit

Private Sub Form_Load()
    'Specify splash screen labels
    frmSplash.lblLicenseTo = App.LegalTrademarks
    frmSplash.lblCompanyProduct = App.ProductName
    frmSplash.lblPlatform = "Windows 95"
    frmSplash.lblCopyright = App.LegalCopyright
    frmSplash.lblCompany = App.CompanyName
    frmSplash.lblWarning = "Warning: This program is protected " & _
        "by copyright law, so don't copy"
    'Show splash screen
    frmSplash.Show
    DoEvents
    'Perform time-consuming initializations...
    Initialize
    'Erase splash screen
    Unload frmSplash
End Sub
```

Notice that the App object is used here. The App object can access information about your application. Much of this information is set at design time on the Make tab of the Project Properties dialog box, which can be accessed by choosing Project Properties from the Project menu.

The code in the Splash Screen form template code module is shown here:

```
Private Sub Form_KeyPress(KeyAscii As Integer)
    Unload Me
End Sub

Private Sub Form_Load()
    lblVersion.Caption = "Version " & App.Major & "." & _
        App.Minor & "." & App.Revision
    lblProductName.Caption = App.Title
End Sub

Private Sub Frame1_Click()
    Unload Me
End Sub
```

Notice that the Splash Screen form template code module already has code that sets the version and product name for you, based on the settings on the Make tab of the Project Properties dialog box.

Figure 10-7 on the following page shows an example splash screen.

Figure 10-7.
A splash screen created using the Splash Screen form template.

See Also...

- The Jot application in Chapter 30, "Databases," for a demonstration of the incorporation of a splash screen

Dear John, How Do I...

Use a Tabbed Control?

Visual Basic 5 provides two tabbed controls: the TabStrip control, provided in the file COMCTL32.OCX, and the SSTab control, provided in the file TABCTL32.OCX. The SSTab control is an improved version of the Sheridan SSTab control included in Visual Basic 4.

You can add these tabbed controls to your Toolbox from the Components dialog box. The control description for the TabStrip control is Microsoft Windows Common Controls and for the SSTab control is Microsoft Tabbed Dialog Control.

The SSTab Control

The SSTab control is easier to use than the TabStrip control. The main difference between the TabStrip control and the SSTab control is that the TabStrip control does not provide a container for controls for each tab. For example, when you use the TabStrip control, you typically add a container control, such

188

as a Frame or a PictureBox control, to each tab as a control array. You then draw desired controls in each container and add code to display the appropriate container when the user clicks a tab.

With the SSTab control, shown in Figure 10-8, you can simply draw your controls on each tab at design time; the contents of each tab are then displayed automatically when the user selects a tab. You must draw your controls within the area for each tab instead of drawing the control elsewhere on the form and moving it to the tab area. If you simply move a control to the tab area, that control appears on top of the SSTab control but is not associated with a particular tab.

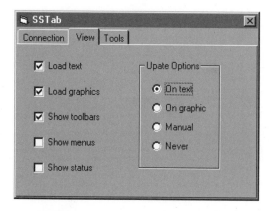

Figure 10-8.
The SSTab control in action.

The SSTab control even includes a property for ToolTips. This is an improvement over the SSTab control included with Visual Basic 4, which did not support ToolTips. The SSTab control has two Style property settings that determine appearance: *ssStyleTabbedDialog* and *ssStylePropertyPage*. If the style is set to *ssStyleTabbedDialog*, the tabs look like those used in some Microsoft Windows version 3.1 applications, and if it is set to *ssStylePropertyPage*, the tabs look like those used in Microsoft Windows 95.

The only time you can't use the SSTab control is when you're programming for 16-bit Windows. In this case, you should use the 16-bit version of the SSTab control provided with Visual Basic 4.

Dear John, How Do I...

Flash a Form to Get the User's Attention?

You can use the FlashWindow API function to toggle, or flash, the title bar of a window. This might be useful for critical conditions that demand user attention. To try this technique, create two forms, *frmControl* and *frmFlash*. Add a Timer control to the *frmFlash* form, and name it *tmrFlash*. Add the following code to the *frmFlash* form:

```
Option Explicit

Private Declare Function FlashWindow _
Lib "user32" ( _
    ByVal hwnd As Long, _
    ByVal bInvert As Long _
) As Long

Private Sub Form_Load()
    tmrFlash.Enabled = False
End Sub

Private Sub tmrFlash_Timer()
    Dim lRtn As Long
    lRtn = FlashWindow(hwnd, CLng(True))
End Sub

Property Let Rate(nPerSecond As Integer)
    tmrFlash.Interval = 1000 / nPerSecond
End Property

Property Let Flash(bState As Boolean)
    tmrFlash.Enabled = bState
End Property
```

Add three command buttons (*cmdFast, cmdSlow,* and *cmdStop*) to the *frmControl* form to control the flashing, and change the Caption properties of these command buttons appropriately. Add the following code to the *frmControl* form:

```
Option Explicit

Private Sub cmdFast_Click()
    frmFlash.Rate = 5
    frmFlash.Flash = True
End Sub
```

(continued)

```
Private Sub cmdStop_Click()
    frmFlash.Flash = False
End Sub

Private Sub cmdSlow_Click()
    frmFlash.Rate = 1
    frmFlash.Flash = True
End Sub

Private Sub Form_Load()
    frmFlash.Show
End Sub
```

Figure 10-9 shows this pair of forms in action.

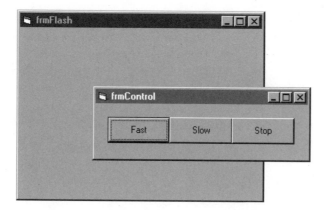

Figure 10-9.
The frmControl *form, which controls the flashing of the* frmFlash *title bar.*

In Figure 10-9, *frmControl* has the focus, but the title bar of *frmFlash* is flashing. Note that if the Windows task bar is visible, the task bar icon for *frmFlash* flashes right along with the title bar of the form itself. This task bar icon will flash even if the flashing form is covered by other windows.

I've set up Rate and Flash as properties of the flashing form, in keeping with the spirit of standard object-oriented programming (OOP) techniques. From anywhere in your application, you set the flash rate (in flashes per second) simply by assigning an integer to the form's Rate property, and you set the Flash property to *True* or *False* to activate or deactivate the flashing effect. Take a look at the code for the *frmControl* command buttons to see how these properties are set.

See Also...

- The Blinker ActiveX control sample in Chapter 6, "ActiveX Controls," to see how this functionality can be incorporated into an ActiveX control

- The Messages application in Chapter 32, "Advanced Applications," to see how a flashing form can be used in an application to get the user's attention

Dear John, How Do I...

Move a Control to a New Container?

This is a slick capability of Visual Basic that could open the door to some creative programming techniques. Controls can be drawn within container controls, which currently include picture boxes and frames. The Container property of most controls is readable and writable, which means that you can make a control jump to a different container!

To see how this works, draw two Frame controls, named *fraLeft* and *fraRight*, on a blank form. Draw a command button named *cmdJump* in the middle of *fraLeft*. Figure 10-10 shows the general layout of this form.

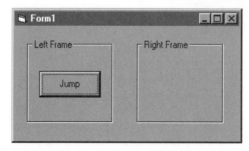

Figure 10-10.
A demonstration of the Container property, which lets controls move into new objects at runtime.

Add the following lines of code to the form:

```
Option Explicit

Private Sub cmdJump_Click()
    Set cmdJump.Container = fraRight
End Sub
```

When you run this program and click the command button, the button will jump to the center of the right frame. This simple demonstration hints at the flexibility in Visual Basic. Objects are much more dynamic and under the control of your program than they used to be.

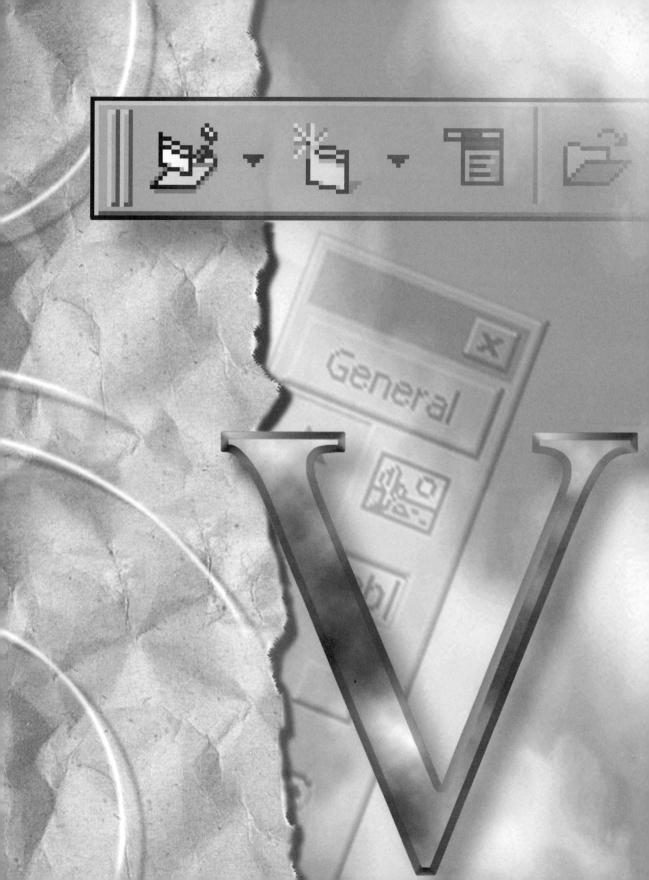

CHAPTER ELEVEN

The Visual Interface

A fundamental change in the Basic programming language was denoted when Microsoft added the word *Visual* to the name. At the very heart of Visual Basic's success has been the enhanced and easy-to-use visual interface that your programs present to the user. With version 5, Visual Basic adds two significant improvements to the visual interface. First, it makes ToolTips a lot easier to create by adding the ToolTipText property to many controls in the Toolbox. Second, it provides many Microsoft Windows 95 controls, including the UpDown control.

This chapter explains and demonstrates techniques for enhancing your program's interface by using features of Visual Basic and Windows and illustrates some creative programming techniques as well.

Dear John, How Do I...

Add a Status Bar to My Application?

Use the StatusBar control, available in the Microsoft Windows Common Controls (COMCTL32.DCX), to add a status bar to your program. A StatusBar control creates a window, usually across the bottom of your form, containing up to 16 Panel objects. Panel objects have a number of properties that let you display text or predefined data, such as an automatically updated time and date. You can combine pictures with your text in each panel too. You can set the number of panels and their properties on the various tabs in the Property Pages dialog box. To access this dialog box, right-click on a positioned StatusBar control and choose Properties from the pop-up menu, or select the positioned StatusBar control, select Custom from the Properties window, and click the displayed ellipsis button.

Figure 11-1 shows a sample form with three StatusBar controls added, one with its alignment set to the bottom of the form and two set to align at the top of the form. The online help provides a good reference for the many properties of the StatusBar control and its associated Panel objects.

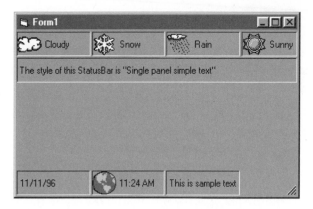

Figure 11-1.
Three sample StatusBar controls in action.

It's also fairly easy to create your own status bars. This can be handy if you are programming with an earlier version of Visual Basic for a 16-bit environment or if you want to customize your status bar to do something a little out of the ordinary. Here's one way I've discovered to create my own status bar: Add a PictureBox control to a form. Set its Align property to *2 - Align Bottom*. Setting the Align property to *Align Bottom* causes the picture box to stretch itself across the bottom edge of the containing form, which is the preferred position for a status bar. Draw any desired controls, such as Label controls, in this picture box. Add code to change the label captions to display status line messages when the program is executed.

From this starting point, you can make several simple improvements to create a more professional looking status bar. You'll probably want to change the BackColor properties of both the PictureBox and the Label controls to light gray. You can also try changing the BorderStyle properties to improve the appearance.

See Also...

- "Dear John, How Do I...Create a Toolbar?" later in this chapter
- The Dialogs application in Chapter 32, "Advanced Applications," for an example of the use of a status bar

Dear John, How Do I...

Add a Horizontal Scrollbar to a List Box?

Sometimes it's hard to predict the width of text that will appear in a list box. The SendMessage Windows API function provides an easy way to tell a list box to add a horizontal scrollbar to itself if the text lines are too long. The following code shows a working example of this technique.

Start a new project, and add a ListBox control and a command button to a form. I've named these controls *lstTest* and *cmdShrinkList*, respectively. Draw the list box so that it is fairly wide on the form—the command button will shrink it during the demonstration.

Add the declarations to your module for the SendMessage API function, as follows:

```
Private Const LB_SETHORIZONTALEXTENT = &H194

Private Declare Function SendMessage _
Lib "user32" Alias "SendMessageA" ( _
    ByVal hwnd As Long, _
    ByVal wMsg As Long, _
    ByVal wParam As Integer, _
    ByVal lParam As Long _
) As Long
```

The SendMessage function takes four arguments. The *hwnd* parameter specifies a window handle. The *wMsg* parameter specifies the message to be sent to the window. In this example, the message will be a constant that indicates that a horizontal scrollbar capability should be added to the list box. The *wParam* and *lParam* parameters specify information related to the message. In this example, *wParam* specifies the width in pixels of the list box at which the horizontal scrollbar should be added and *lParam* is not used.

The code for the command button is shown below. This button's purpose is to shrink the list box width by 10 percent each time the button is clicked. When the list box is so narrow that the text doesn't fit, a horizontal scrollbar will automatically appear at the bottom edge of the list box.

```
Private Sub cmdShrinkList_Click()
    lstTest.Width = lstTest.Width * 9 \ 10
End Sub
```

The horizontal scrollbar capability is added to the list box when the form loads. The following code loads a fairly long string into the list box and then adds the scrollbar by calling the SendMessage function. Because the Send-Message function is expecting a *wParam* value in pixels, you should work in pixel units. The unit of measurement can easily be set to pixels by setting the form's ScaleMode property to *vbPixels*. The threshold width of the list box at which the scrollbar appears can be computed by using the TextWidth function with the longest string. The TextWidth function returns a value in units based on the ScaleMode property—in this case, pixels.

```
Private Sub Form_Load()
Dim Longest$, Rtn As Long
    'Set ScaleMode to Pixels
    ScaleMode = vbPixels
    'Place text in list
    Longest$ = "This is a list of months of the year"
    lstTest.AddItem Longest$
    lstTest.AddItem "January"
    lstTest.AddItem "February"
    lstTest.AddItem "March"
    lstTest.AddItem "April"
    lstTest.AddItem "May"
    lstTest.AddItem "June"
    lstTest.AddItem "July"
    lstTest.AddItem "August"
    lstTest.AddItem "September"
    lstTest.AddItem "October"
    lstTest.AddItem "November"
    lstTest.AddItem "December"
    'Set form's font properties to match list box
    Form1.Font.Size = lstTest.Font.Size
    'Set list box scrollbar threshold width
    Rtn = SendMessage(lstTest.hwnd, LB_SETHORIZONTALEXTENT, _
        Form1.TextWidth(Longest$), ByVal 0&)
End Sub
```

When you run the program, if the list box in its first appearance is wide enough to display the entire string, you'll need to click the Shrink List command button one or more times before the horizontal scrollbar will appear. With each click, the list box width is reduced to 90 percent of its previous width. Figures 11-2 and 11-3 show the list box with and without the horizontal scrollbar.

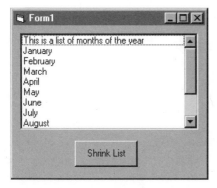

Figure 11-2.
A list box that is wide enough to display the longest string; horizontal scrollbar doesn't appear.

Figure 11-3.
A list box that is too narrow to display the longest string; horizontal scrollbar appears.

The TextWidth method returns the width of a string in the current font of a form, a PictureBox control, or a Printer object, but this method doesn't apply to list boxes. To work around this limitation, and to automatically allow for variations in the list box's font size, I copied the value of the Size property of the list box Font object to the Size property of the form's Font object just before using the form's TextWidth method to determine and set the threshold width at which the list box horizontal scrollbar will appear. If other properties of the list box's Font object are altered, you should also copy these properties to the form's Font object properties.

Dear John, How Do I...

Add ToolTips to My Buttons?

If you're programming for Windows 95 or Microsoft Windows NT, you can use the ToolTipText property to add ToolTips to toolbar buttons and other objects. In Visual Basic 5, the ToolTipText property is available for all the controls that receive input.

If you're programming for 16-bit Windows, you must create your own ToolTip form and display it using the MouseMove event. I describe this technique here for those of you who still need to support 16-bit systems. The behavior of the ToolTips created using this technique is very similar to that of the ToolTips in the Visual Basic development environment—if you pause the pointer over a ToolTip-enabled object, the ToolTip appears in less than a second and remains visible until the pointer is moved off the object.

Creating the ToolTip capability is a one-time chore, and it actually isn't very complicated, considering the complex actions that are required. Modifying a control to be ToolTip-enabled in your applications turns out to be extremely easy. Let's build the ToolTip capability first, and then I'll show an example of the ToolTips in action.

Create a form, and set its Name property to *frmToolTip*. To this form, add a PictureBox control named *picToolTip*, and add a Timer control named *tmrToolTip*. The size and the placement of these controls are not important because these settings will be adjusted automatically at runtime. Change the PictureBox control's BackColor property to white or light yellow, the Appearance property to *0 - Flat*, and the BorderStyle property to *0 - None* to match the standard ToolTip appearance. Set the timer's Interval property to 700 milliseconds (the time that will elapse from the moment the pointer is paused over a control to the moment the ToolTip pops up). The ToolTip form is displayed to allow us to create the ToolTip label, but we don't want the title bar, the border, or the control buttons to appear. You can eliminate all these components by setting the form's BorderStyle property to *0 - None*.

Add the following code to the ToolTip form:

```
'ToolTips
Option Explicit
Private Type POINTAPI
    x As Long
    y As Long
End Type
```

(continued)

```
Private Declare Function GetCursorPos _
Lib "user32" ( _
    lpPoint As POINTAPI _
) As Long

Private Cap$

Public Property Let Label(C$)
    tmrToolTip.Enabled = False
    If C$ = "" Then
        Hide
    Else
        Cap$ = C$
        tmrToolTip.Enabled = True
    End If
End Property

Private Sub tmrToolTip_Timer()
    Dim Papi As POINTAPI
    Dim Wrk$
    Wrk$ = Space$(1) & Trim$(Cap$) & Space$(2)
    picToolTip.Move 0, 0, picToolTip.TextWidth(Wrk$), _
        picToolTip.TextHeight(Wrk$) * 1.1
    GetCursorPos Papi
    Move Papi.x * Screen.TwipsPerPixelX _
        - picToolTip.Width * 0.4, _
        Papi.y * Screen.TwipsPerPixelY _
        + picToolTip.Height * 1.3, _
        picToolTip.Width, picToolTip.Height
    Show
    DoEvents
    picToolTip.Cls
    picToolTip.Print Wrk$
    'Draw box around ToolTip
    picToolTip.Line (0, 0)-( _
        picToolTip.ScaleWidth - Screen.TwipsPerPixelX, _
        picToolTip.ScaleHeight - Screen.TwipsPerPixelY), , B
End Sub
```

The GetCursorPos Windows API function is used to determine the exact location of the pointer so that we can display the ToolTip label at the correct location. POINTAPI is a user-defined Type structure that is filled in by the GetCursorPos function. The string variable *Cap$* stores the text that is to appear in the ToolTip. Your application doesn't touch this variable. (In fact, the variable is declared Private so that you won't be able to call it from outside this form.) I've created a Public property named Label that you interface with. As you'll see, this is the only property that the outside world needs to work with—more about that property in a minute.

Figure 11-4 shows the ToolTip form before we added code to it.

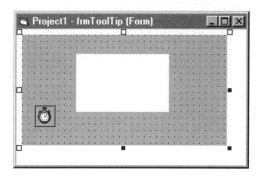

Figure 11-4.
The ToolTip form during development.

Most of the work takes place when the Timer event occurs. The form and its PictureBox control are sized, placed, and displayed to the user with the indicated label.

Now for the surprisingly easy part—adding ToolTip labels to buttons, images, pictures, or other controls. To complete the example shown here, create a startup form that contains a command button, an Image control, and a PictureBox control. Load any desired icons or pictures (I've loaded an icon and a Windows metafile supplied with Visual Basic), and add the following code to the startup form:

```
Option Explicit

Private Sub Command1_MouseMove( _
    Button As Integer, _
    Shift As Integer, _
    x As Single, _
    y As Single _
)
    frmToolTip.Label = "Command1"
End Sub

Private Sub Image1_MouseMove( _
    Button As Integer, _
    Shift As Integer, _
```

(continued)

```
    x As Single, _
    y As Single _
)
    frmToolTip.Label = "An airplane"
End Sub

Private Sub Picture1_MouseMove( _
    Button As Integer, _
    Shift As Integer, _
    x As Single, _
    y As Single _
)
    frmToolTip.Label = "Calendar"
End Sub

Private Sub Form_MouseMove( _
    Button As Integer, _
    Shift As Integer, _
    x As Single, _
    y As Single _
)
    frmToolTip.Label = ""
End Sub
```

Figure 11-5 shows the appearance of a ToolTip label assigned to an image.

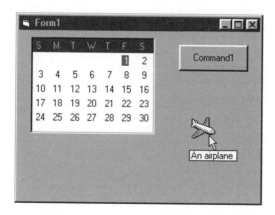

Figure 11-5.
Testing the ToolTips assigned to three controls.

To add ToolTip capability to any control, follow two simple rules: First, in the control's MouseMove event procedure, assign the desired label to the frmToolTip.Label property. Second, assign an empty string to this property from the MouseMove event procedure for the form or containing control. This way, as soon as the pointer moves off the control, the ToolTip will disappear as the label is erased.

See Also...

- The Jot application in Chapter 30, "Databases," for a demonstration of ToolTips

Dear John, How Do I...

Create a Toolbar?

To create a toolbar for 32-bit programming, I suggest using the Toolbar control included with Visual Basic as part of the Microsoft Windows Common Controls (COMCTL32.OCX). To place a series of picture buttons on one of these toolbars, you'll also need to add an ImageList control to your form. The ImageList control lets you store images that can be referenced by their index or key. You can set properties, such as adding images to the ImageList control, in the Property Pages dialog box for each control. To open the Property Pages dialog box, select the positioned Toolbar or ImageList control and double-click on the Custom property in the Properties window. The Property Pages dialog box for the Toolbar control lets you insert buttons, add images from the ImageList control, specify key names, add ToolTips, and set other properties. The Property Pages dialog box for the ImageList control lets you add images, specify the size, and specify color properties.

The Visual Basic online help is a good source for information about using the Toolbar and ImageList controls. The following code shows an example of how to add code for each button on the toolbar:

```
Option Explicit
Private Sub toolbar1_ButtonClick(ByVal Button As ComctlLib.Button)
    Select Case Button.Key
    Case Is = "monitor"
        MsgBox "You clicked the Monitor button."
    Case Is = "plug"
        MsgBox "You clicked the Plug button."
    Case Is = "window"
        MsgBox "You clicked the Window button."
    Case Is = "airplane"
        MsgBox "You clicked the Airplane button."
```

(continued)

```
    Case Is = "wrench"
        MsgBox "You clicked the Wrench button."
    End Select
End Sub
```

Figure 11-6 shows a Toolbar control with images from an associated ImageList control after the Airplane button has been clicked.

Figure 11-6.
The Toolbar control after the Airplane button has been clicked.

For maximum flexibility, or to create a toolbar for the earlier, 16-bit version of Visual Basic, you can simulate a toolbar by using a combination of PictureBox, Image, and perhaps SSPanel controls. This approach is very similar to creating a status bar. Add a PictureBox control to a form, set its Align property to *1 - Align Top*, and add command buttons inside this picture box. The *Align Top* setting causes the picture box to stretch itself across the top edge of the containing form, even if the form is resized by the user.

You'll probably want to set the BackColor property of the picture box to light gray if it is not already that color. You can also try changing the BorderStyle properties to enhance the control's appearance. To improve the effect, also consider adding ToolTip capability to these buttons, as described in the previous section.

See Also...

- "Dear John, How Do I…Add a Status Bar to My Application?" earlier in this chapter

- "Dear John, How Do I…Add ToolTips to My Buttons?" earlier in this chapter

- The Dialogs application in Chapter 32, "Advanced Applications," for an example of the use of a toolbar

Dear John, How Do I...

Dynamically Change the Appearance of a Form?

Here is one useful technique for dynamically changing a form's appearance: At runtime, you can set a control's Top or Left property to move the control off the visible surface of the containing form or control. A safe way to do this is to move the control to a position at twice the width or height of the containing control or form. If you save the original position in the control's Tag property, you have an easy way to later move the control back to its starting position. For example, the following code hides the command button *cmdButton* when you click the button and redisplays the button when you click on the form:

```
Option Explicit
Private Sub cmdButton_Click()
    cmdButton.Tag = cmdButton.Left
    cmdButton.Left = Screen.Width * 2
End Sub

Private Sub Form_Click()
    cmdButton.Left = cmdButton.Tag
End Sub
```

You can position and size controls using the Move method. You typically use the ScaleWidth and ScaleHeight properties of the containing form or control with the Move method. This technique can accommodate a sizeable form and keep controls proportionally spaced as the user changes the form's size or shape. Add code in the form's Resize event to accomplish this.

See Also...

- "Dear John, How Do I...Automatically Position a Form on the Screen?" in Chapter 10 for information about positioning forms

- "Dear John, How Do I...Use a Tabbed Control?" in Chapter 10 for information about using tabbed controls to make your forms more dynamic

Dear John, How Do I...

Dynamically Customize the Menus?

With Visual Basic, you can edit menu objects in the Properties window just as you can edit the properties of the other controls in your application. This feature is easily overlooked, yet it makes the editing of menus a much more manageable task. (Note that you still need to create menu objects by using the Menu Editor.) To get to the menu properties, select the menu from the drop-down list at the top of the Properties window.

NOTE: Another useful method for working with menus is to use menu control arrays, which offer a powerful technique for expanding and shrinking your menus. This subject is covered in the Visual Basic documentation.

Here is a simple trick that isn't too well known, one that provides an easy-to-understand and easy-to-use technique for creating multiple sets of menus. If you set a menu's Visible property to *False*, the menu and all of its submenus will be hidden, both at runtime and in the development environment. So to create two unique File menus, for instance, name the topmost menu item *mnuFile1* for the first File menu and *mnuFile2* for the second File menu. The menus can both have the same Caption property (*File*, in this case), but they must have unique Name properties. The menu items for each File menu can also be entirely unique, or they can share some of the same captions. Just remember to keep each menu item's Name property unique.

Either in the development environment or at runtime, toggle the Visible properties of these two top-level menu items to make one visible and the other hidden. You can set up multiple File menus this way, again by toggling the Visible properties so that only one menu is visible at a time. Note that you don't need to toggle the Visible property for the items on each File menu because they all effectively become invisible when the top-level menu item is made invisible.

You can extend this concept to all the menus to make full use of this technique. You can set up multiple Edit menus or have menu items that come and go depending on the state of the application. You can easily swap out entire sets of menus with replacement sets by using this technique. Figures 11-7 and 11-8 on the following page show two unique sets of menus on the same form, one displayed before and one after the Toggle Menus command button has been clicked.

Figure 11-7.
A form showing the first of two unique sets of menus.

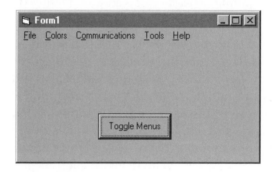

Figure 11-8.
The same form showing the second set of menus.

Dear John, How Do I...

Remove the Title Bar from a Form?

Before you can remove a title bar from a form at design time, you need to eliminate any menu items. Then you can use one of the following two techniques: Using the first technique, if you set the ControlBox property to *False*, delete any text from the Caption property, and set the BorderStyle property to *1 - Fixed Single*, the form will have a single border and no title bar. For the second technique, you set the BorderStyle property to *0 - None*. The form will have no border and no title bar, even if any of the ControlBox, MaxButton, and MinButton properties are set to *True* or you have text in the Caption property. If you want a border around the form, you can draw it yourself.

See Also...

- "Dear John, How Do I...Add ToolTips to My Buttons?" earlier in this chapter for an example of the second technique

Dear John, How Do I...

Create a Progress Indicator?

The easiest way to learn how to use the ProgressBar control included with the Microsoft Windows Common Controls (COMCTL32.OCX) is to create a simple application and put it through its paces. The following short application creates a 3-minute timer, suitable for timing the boiling of eggs as well as demonstrating the ProgressBar control.

On a new form, add a Label control named *lblDone*, a command button named *cmdStart*, a Timer control named *tmrTest*, and a ProgressBar control named *prbEgg*. Set the label's caption to *Ready to start*, and set its font size as desired. Set the Timer's Enabled property to *False* and its Interval property to 1000 milliseconds. I've left the ProgressBar control's properties set to their defaults.

Add the following code to the form to control the action:

```
Option Explicit

Private mfStartTime As Single

Private Sub cmdStart_Click()
    prbEgg.Value = 0
    mfStartTime = 0
    tmrTest.Enabled = True
End Sub

Private Sub tmrTest_Timer()
    Dim Percent
    If mfStartTime = 0! Then
        mfStartTime = Timer
    End If
    Percent = 100 * (Timer - mfStartTime) / 180
    If Percent < 100 Then
        prbEgg.Value = Percent
        lblDone.Caption = "Cooking..."
    Else
        prbEgg.Value = 100
        lblDone.Caption = "Done!"
```

(continued)

```
        Beep
        tmrTest.Enabled = False
    End If
End Sub
```

Figure 11-9 shows the form at runtime, with my egg about two-thirds done.

Figure 11-9.
Using a progress bar as a 3-minute egg timer.

You might want to temporarily change the value of the divisor 180 (the number of seconds in 3 minutes) to something much smaller while you test this program. A value of 10, for instance, will cause the ProgressBar control to fill in 10 seconds instead of 3 minutes. (I wouldn't advise you to eat an egg cooked for this length of time, however.)

You can learn a lot about the ProgressBar control by experimenting with this program. For instance, the number of "chunks" inside the bar is adjusted by changing the height of the bar, an effect that's easier to understand if you try it for yourself instead of just reading about it.

Rolling Your Own Progress Indicator

The ProgressBar control is yet another of those great 32-bit controls that can be used in programs for Windows 95 and Windows NT. But don't despair if you're still stuck in the 16-bit programming world. It's easy to create your own progress bar by using a pair of nested PictureBox controls.

To see how similar this is to the previous example using the ProgressBar control, make these changes: Replace the ProgressBar control with a Picture-Box control named *picProgress*. Draw a second PictureBox control inside the first, and name it *picFill*. Set the BackColor properties of these two controls as desired. I used dark blue for *picFill* and white for *picProgress*, but you can use any color. If you change the *picProgress* control's ScaleWidth property to *100* and its ScaleHeight property to *1*, very little of the program code will require change. Here's the new code, which has only a few modifications:

```
Option Explicit

Private mfStartTime As Single
Private Sub cmdStart_Click()
    mfStartTime = 0
    tmrTest.Enabled = True
End Sub

Private Sub Form_Load()
    picFill.Move 0, 0, 0, 0
End Sub

Private Sub tmrTest_Timer()
    Dim Percent
    If mfStartTime = 0! Then
        mfStartTime = Timer
    End If
    Percent = 100 * (Timer - mfStartTime) / 180
    If Percent < 100 Then
        picFill.Move 0, 0, Percent, 1
        lblDone.Caption = "Cooking..."
    Else
        picFill.Move 0, 0, 100, 1
        lblDone.Caption = "Done!"
        Beep
        tmrTest.Enabled = False
    End If
End Sub
```

This type of progress indicator fills with a solid color instead of using the "chunky" fill style, but the action and appearance are otherwise very similar.

Figure 11-10 shows the egg-timer program in action, again at about the soft-boiled stage.

Figure 11-10.
A homegrown progress indicator in action.

Dear John, How Do I...

Use the Slider Control?

The Slider control included in COMCTL32.OCX is similar to a Scrollbar control except that it has some enhancements that make it a better choice for allowing the user to input numeric values selected from a range. You might think of the scrollbar as a qualitative approach to selecting from a range (it provides visual feedback of an approximate nature) and of the slider as more of a quantitative control (it provides an exact value or a range of values from the range of choices).

An interesting and unique feature of the Slider control is its ability to select either a single value or a range of values. You select a range by setting the SelectRange property to *True* and manipulating the SelStart and SelLength properties to define the range. Microsoft suggests that you programmatically set the range properties when the user holds down the Shift key and moves the slider. The Visual Basic Books Online provides a good working example of this technique using the SelectRange property.

Figure 11-11 shows an imaginary database-filtering application in which the user can select, from a large list of all major cities, cities located in a range of latitudes. The Slider control simplifies this type of range selection, but it can also be used to select a single value from a range, as in setting the volume control of a multimedia device. The online help is the best source of information for the properties and methods of the Slider control.

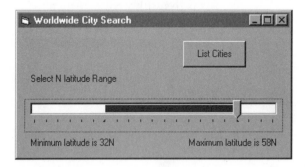

Figure 11-11.
A Slider control being used to select a range of values.

Dear John, How Do I...

Use the UpDown Control?

The UpDown control is a standard Windows 95 and Windows NT control that makes it easier to increment the value of an associated control. The UpDown control is included in the Microsoft Windows Common Controls-2 (COMCT232.OCX) file. Figure 11-12 shows a text box linked to an UpDown control.

Figure 11-12.
An UpDown control being used to increment or decrement the value of a text box.

The UpDown control replaces the scrollbar as a means of incrementing or decrementing a value. In the past, you had to write code to link changes in a scrollbar to the value of a text box. The UpDown control handles this linking automatically through settings on the Buddy tab of its Property Pages dialog box, as shown in Figure 11-13 on the following page.

To link an UpDown control to the value of another control, follow these steps:

1. After adding the UpDown control to your Toolbox, draw the UpDown control and the control you want to link to your form.

2. Select the UpDown control, and double-click on Custom in the Properties window.

3. Select the Buddy tab of the Property Pages dialog box.

4. In the Buddy Control text box, type the name of the control you want to affect. Alternatively, you could check the AutoBuddy check box, which causes the UpDown control to automatically select the control in the previous tab order as its buddy control.

5. In the Buddy Property drop-down list, select the target control property that you want to affect. You will usually want to affect the Default or Value property of the target control. Notice that after you select a Buddy Property value, the SyncBuddy check box automatically appears checked, which indicates that the Value property of the UpDown control is synchronized with a property of the buddy control.

6. Click OK.

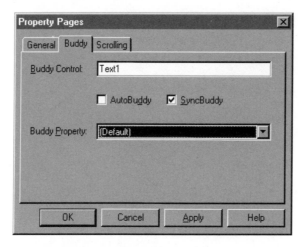

Figure 11-13.
Setting the Buddy properties of an UpDown control to change the value of another control.

When you run this program, the value of the buddy control is incremented or decremented as you click on the UpDown control. Note that you might have to initialize the value of the control—for instance, the default value of *Text1* in a text box control remains *Text1* until you click on the UpDown control.

You set the scroll range and rate of the UpDown control on the Scrolling tab of the Property Pages dialog box, shown in Figure 11-14. The Wrap check box causes the buddy control value to roll over from the minimum to the maximum and vice versa, rather than stopping at the range limits.

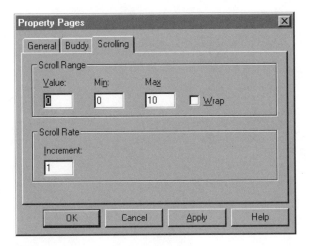

Figure 11-14.
Setting the scroll range and rate of the UpDown control.

 See Also...

- The Blinker ActiveX control sample in Chapter 6, "ActiveX Controls," to see how the UpDown control can be used

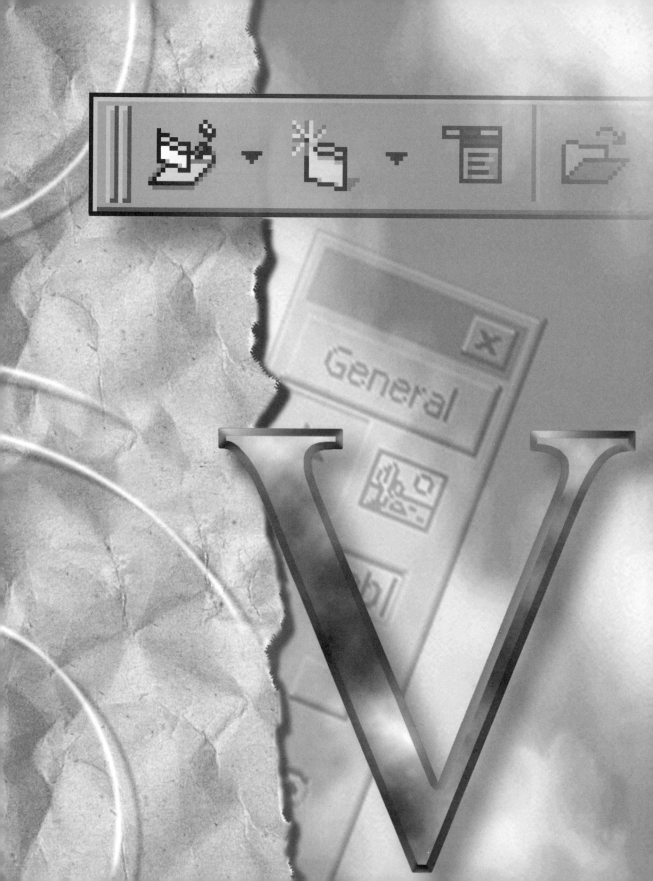

CHAPTER TWELVE

Graphics Techniques

Visual Basic provides a rich set of graphics tools, including, for instance, the PaintPicture method, which is a user-friendly wrapper around the popular BitBlt Windows API function. You'll find PaintPicture used in several places in this chapter—it's a real workhorse for efficient manipulation of graphics images. You'll also find that I've used BitBlt directly, which is the fastest way to create animation. Several other useful API functions are also demonstrated in this chapter, such as those that allow you to create a rubber band selection rectangle, draw polygons efficiently, and perform other graphics magic. Often the best way to implement API functions is to encapsulate them within an object—a technique I've used throughout this chapter.

Dear John, How Do I...

Calculate a Color Constant from RGB or HSV Values?

In Visual Basic, a color is indicated by a single number, the RGB color value. The bit pattern in this number is composed of three values corresponding to color intensity levels: one for red, one for green, and one for blue, each ranging from 0 through 255. The RGB function lets you combine the three intensity levels into the desired color number, but there are no built-in functions for extracting the three intensity levels from a given RGB color value. The code on the following page defines a class that allows you to extract values for red, green, and blue from the combined value of *color*. Add this code to a class module, and name the class *RGB*.

```
'RGB.CLS
Option Explicit

Private mlColor As Long

'~~~Color
Property Let Color(lColor As Long)
    mlColor = lColor
End Property

'~~~Red
Property Get Red() As Byte
    Red = mlColor And &HFF
End Property

'~~~Green
Property Get Green() As Byte
    Green = (mlColor \ &H100) And &HFF
End Property

'~~~Blue
Property Get Blue() As Byte
    Blue = (mlColor \ &H10000) And &HFF
End Property
```

To keep this class simple I've defined the Color property as write-only and the three component color properties as read-only. As an exercise, you might want to make all properties readable and writable.

The following code demonstrates how to use the RGB object to extract the red, green, and blue color components from a color value:

```
Option Explicit

Private Sub Form_Click()
    Dim rgbTest As New RGB
    Dim lColor As Long
    'Combine R,G,and B to create a known color value
    lColor = RGB(17, 53, 220)
    Print "Color:", lColor
    'Use RGB object to extract component colors
    rgbTest.Color = lColor
    Print "Red:", rgbTest.Red
    Print "Green:", rgbTest.Green
    Print "Blue:", rgbTest.Blue
End Sub
```

In addition to the RGB color model, another common way to classify colors is by hue, saturation, and value, or HSV. For some people, the HSV model is more intuitive, and for certain types of graphics these values are definitely easier to work with. For instance, the colors required for a sunset scene might be easier to describe as a group of red colors that vary in value but remain constant in hue and saturation. Hue represents the relative position of a color in the spectrum and, in the HSV system, corresponds to the angle of the color on a color wheel. The range for the hue values is 0 through 360 (360 degrees forming a complete circle). Saturation specifies the purity of the color. The saturation value is a percentage, ranging from 0 (no color) through 100 (the pure color, as specified by the hue value). Value specifies the brightness of the color and is also a percentage, ranging from 0 (black) through 100 (white). Here is a useful class for converting between RGB values and HSV values:

```
'HSV.CLS
Option Explicit

'~~~RGB color properties
Public Red As Integer
Public Green As Integer
Public Blue As Integer

'~~~HSV color properties
Public Hue As Single
Public Saturation As Single
Public Value As Single

'~~~Converts RGB to HSV
Public Sub ToHSV()
    Dim fRed As Single
    Dim fGreen As Single
    Dim fBlue As Single
    Dim fMx As Single
    Dim fMn As Single
    Dim fVa As Single
    Dim fSa As Single
    Dim fRc As Single
    Dim fGc As Single
    Dim fBc As Single
    fRed = Red / 255
    fGreen = Green / 255
    fBlue = Blue / 255
    fMx = fRed
```

(continued)

```
            If fGreen > fMx Then fMx = fGreen
            If fBlue > fMx Then fMx = fBlue
            fMn = fRed
            If fGreen < fMn Then fMn = fGreen
            If fBlue < fMn Then fMn = fBlue
            fVa = fMx
            If fMx Then
                fSa = (fMx - fMn) / fMx
            Else
                fSa = 0
            End If
            If fSa = 0 Then
                Hue = 0
            Else
                fRc = (fMx - fRed) / (fMx - fMn)
                fGc = (fMx - fGreen) / (fMx - fMn)
                fBc = (fMx - fBlue) / (fMx - fMn)
                Select Case fMx
                Case fRed
                    Hue = fBc - fGc
                Case fGreen
                    Hue = 2 + fRc - fBc
                Case fBlue
                    Hue = 4 + fGc - fRc
                End Select
                Hue = Hue * 60
                If Hue < 0 Then Hue = Hue + 360
            End If
            Saturation = fSa * 100
            Value = fVa * 100
        End Sub

        '~~~Converts HSV to RGB
        Public Sub ToRGB()
            Dim fSaturation As Single
            Dim fValue As Single
            Dim fHue As Single
            Dim nI As Integer
            Dim fF As Single
            Dim fP As Single
            Dim fQ As Single
            Dim fT As Single
            Dim fRed As Single
            Dim fGreen As Single
            Dim fBlue As Single
            fSaturation = Saturation / 100
            fValue = Value / 100
```

(continued)

```
        If Saturation = 0 Then
            fRed = fValue
            fGreen = fValue
            fBlue = fValue
        Else
            fHue = Hue / 60
            If fHue = 6 Then fHue = 0
            nI = Int(fHue)
            fF = fHue - nI
            fP = fValue * (1 - fSaturation)
            fQ = fValue * (1 - (fSaturation * fF))
            fT = fValue * (1 - (fSaturation * (1 - fF)))
            Select Case nI
            Case 0
                fRed = fValue
                fGreen = fT
                fBlue = fP
            Case 1
                fRed = fQ
                fGreen = fValue
                fBlue = fP
            Case 2
                fRed = fP
                fGreen = fValue
                fBlue = fT
            Case 3
                fRed = fP
                fGreen = fQ
                fBlue = fValue
            Case 4
                fRed = fT
                fGreen = fP
                fBlue = fValue
            Case 5
                fRed = fValue
                fGreen = fP
                fBlue = fQ
            End Select
        End If
        Red = Int(255.9999 * fRed)
        Green = Int(255.9999 * fGreen)
        Blue = Int(255.9999 * fBlue)
End Sub
```

To use the HSV class in your own application, create an instance of it, set the Red, Green, and Blue or the Hue, Saturation, and Value properties to known values, and use the appropriate method, ToHSV or ToRGB, to convert to the other color model. The RGBHSV application in Chapter 27, "Graphics" provides a complete working example of the use of the HSV object.

To see a similar color scheme in action, take a look at the colors available in Microsoft Windows 95 and Microsoft Windows NT 4.0. In the Control Panel, double-click on the Display icon, and select the Appearance tab of the Display Properties dialog box. Click the Color button, which is to the right of the Item drop-down list. In the list of colors that is displayed, click the Other button. The resulting Color dialog box lets you choose from a range of colors and shows integer values for RGB and HSL (hue, saturation, and luminosity). The HSL color model is similar to the HSV model, although the HSL model uses integer values ranging from 0 through 240, and the conversion algorithm is slightly different. Conceptually and functionally, the two systems are quite similar.

See Also...

- The RGBHSV application in Chapter 27, "Graphics," to see the HSV object in action

Dear John, How Do I...

Convert Between Twips, Points, Pixels, Characters, Inches, Millimeters, and Centimeters?

A form, picture box, or printer object can be scaled using the ScaleMode property. You can scale these objects by custom units or by a close representation of twips, points, pixels, characters, inches, millimeters, or centimeters. I say "close representation" because for many systems Windows can only approximate these units for your display. When used with the printer object and printed on a high-quality printer, these dimensional units are usually represented much more accurately. The following list shows the relationships between some of these units of measure:

1440 twips per inch

567 twips per centimeter

72 points per inch

2.54 centimeters per inch

10 millimeters per centimeter

The character unit is special in that it has one measurement in the horizontal direction and a different measurement in the vertical direction:

120 twips per character in the horizontal direction

240 twips per character in the vertical direction

Two very useful Visual Basic properties, shown in the following table, help you determine the number of twips per pixel for an object. This value can vary widely based on the actual pixel resolution of your display. Again, the number of pixels in the horizontal direction might not be the same as in the vertical, so there are two similar properties for the two directions.

Property	Return Value
TwipsPerPixelX	Twips per pixel in the horizontal direction
TwipsPerPixelY	Twips per pixel in the vertical direction

By combining these properties and the relationships defined above, you can easily convert between any of the various units of measurement.

Dear John, How Do I...

Create One of Those Backgrounds That Fade from Blue to Black?

The following code paints a form's background with boxes of varying shades of blue, from bright blue to black. The trickiest part is getting a continuous and smooth fade effect that works in 256-color mode as well as in the high-color (16-bit) and true-color (24-bit) modes. In 256-color mode, dithering is required for the smooth transition from bright blue to black. Visual Basic's Line method does not allow dithered colors for a straight line, but it does allow a box to be filled with a dithered "solid" color. To accomplish this, use the following procedure to change the form's DrawStyle property to *vbInvisible* and the form's ScaleMode property to *vbPixels*. The DrawStyle property determines the line style, and setting it to *vbInvisible* prevents a black border from being drawn around each blue box. Setting the ScaleMode property to *vbPixels* lets us calculate the dimensions for each box in pixels with no round-off errors; this prevents overlap or blank spaces between the boxes.

```
Option Explicit

Private Sub Form_Paint()
    Dim lY As Long
    Dim lScaleHeight As Long
    Dim lScaleWidth As Long
    ScaleMode = vbPixels
    lScaleHeight = ScaleHeight
    lScaleWidth = ScaleWidth
    DrawStyle = vbInvisible
    FillStyle = vbFSSolid
    For lY = 0 To lScaleHeight
        FillColor = RGB(0, 0, 255 - (lY * 255) \ lScaleHeight)
        Line (-1, lY - 1)-(lScaleWidth, lY + 1), , B
    Next lY
End Sub
```

This procedure fills the form with shades of blue, no matter what size the form is. To create a dramatic full-screen backdrop, set the form's BorderStyle property to *0 - None* and its WindowState property to *2 - Maximized*.

There's a lot of room for you to experiment with this procedure. The FillColor calculation can be modified to produce shades of red instead of blue, for instance. Or you might consider reversing the colors so that bright blue is at the bottom and black is at the top. Figure 12-1 demonstrates the fading effect.

Figure 12-1.
A form that fades from blue to black.

 See Also...

- The Dialogs application in Chapter 32, "Advanced Applications," for a demonstration of a fading screen

Dear John, How Do I...
Create a Rubber Band Selection Rectangle?

The DrawFocusRect Windows API function is great for drawing a rubber band selection rectangle. The following code demonstrates its use. Create a new form, set its AutoRedraw property to *True*, and add these lines of code to try it out. When you run the program, a selection rectangle is created as you hold down the left mouse button and drag the mouse. When you release the button, the selection rectangle is replaced by a permanent red rectangle to indicate the final selection area.

```
Option Explicit

Private Type RECT
    Left As Long
    Top As Long
    Right As Long
    Bottom As Long
End Type

Private Declare Function DrawFocusRect _
Lib "user32" ( _
    ByVal hdc As Long, _
    lpRect As RECT _
) As Long

Private FocusRec As RECT
Private X1, Y1
Private X2, Y2

Private Sub Form_Load()
    'Use units expected by the API function
    Me.ScaleMode = vbPixels
End Sub

Private Sub Form_MouseDown( _
    Button As Integer, _
    Shift As Integer, _
    X As Single, _
    Y As Single _
)
    'Be sure left mouse button is used
    If (Button And vbLeftButton) = 0 Then Exit Sub
```

(continued)

```
                'Set starting corner of box
                X1 = X
                Y1 = Y
            End Sub

            Private Sub Form_MouseMove( _
                Button As Integer, _
                Shift As Integer, _
                X As Single, _
                Y As Single _
            )
                'Be sure left mouse button is pressed
                If (Button And vbLeftButton) = 0 Then Exit Sub
                'Erase focus rectangle if it exists
                If (X2 <> 0) Or (Y2 <> 0) Then
                    DrawFocusRect Me.hdc, FocusRec
                End If
                'Update coordinates
                X2 = X
                Y2 = Y
                'Update rectangle
                FocusRec.Left = X1
                FocusRec.Top = Y1
                FocusRec.Right = X2
                FocusRec.Bottom = Y2
                'Adjust rectangle if reversed
                If Y2 < Y1 Then Swap FocusRec.Top, FocusRec.Bottom
                If X2 < X1 Then Swap FocusRec.Left, FocusRec.Right
                'Draw focus rectangle
                DrawFocusRect Me.hdc, FocusRec
                Refresh
            End Sub

            Private Sub Form_MouseUp( _
                Button As Integer, _
                Shift As Integer, _
                X As Single, _
                Y As Single _
            )
                Dim Ret%
                'Be sure left mouse button is pressed
                If (Button And vbLeftButton) = 0 Then Exit Sub
                'Erase focus rectangle if it exists
                If FocusRec.Right Or FocusRec.Bottom Then
                    DrawFocusRect Me.hdc, FocusRec
                End If
```

(continued)

```
       'Draw indicated rectangle in red
       Line (X1, Y1)-(X2, Y2), QBColor(12), B
       'Zero the rectangle coordinates
       X1 = 0
       Y1 = 0
       X2 = 0
       Y2 = 0
End Sub

Private Sub Swap(A, B)
       Dim T
       T = A
       A = B
       B = T
End Sub
```

Figure 12-2 shows the program in action.

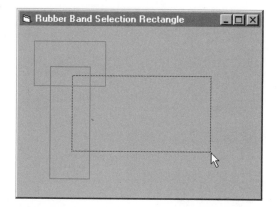

Figure 12-2.
An interactive rubber band selection rectangle in action.

The DrawFocusRect Windows API function draws a dotted selection rectangle. As the mouse is dragged, your code must erase each selection rectangle before the next is drawn. Fortunately, the built-in Xor action of the DrawFocusRect API function makes this easy to do. For example, if you call the DrawFocusRect function a second time using the same coordinates, the selection rectangle will be erased. In the Form_MouseMove event procedure above, you can see that the DrawFocusRect function is called twice, once to erase the previous rectangle and once to draw the next.

Mouse actions in Visual Basic are separated into up, down, and move events. The rubber band selection program uses all three event-driven procedures. MouseDown indicates the start of a rectangle selection, MouseMove indicates the sizing of the rectangle while the mouse button is held down, and MouseUp indicates the completion of the selection.

In this example, only mouse actions on the form itself, and not on any controls it contains, can create a selection rectangle. However, you can draw selection rectangles on any picture box or form by adding the same code to its mouse event procedures. The preceding code will give you a good start on integrating rubber band selection rectangle capabilities into your own applications.

Dear John, How Do I...

Create Graphics Hot Spots?

The Image control is an efficient tool with which to add rectangular hot spot regions to your graphics. Let's walk through an example to see how it's done.

I first loaded a graphic named WORLD.BMP into an Image control named *imgWorld*, and then I carefully drew four more Image controls on top of the image of the world. I named these *imgNAmerica*, *imgSAmerica*, *imgEurope*, and *imgAfrica*. Each rectangle covers the appropriate part of the world. I then added a Label control named *lblHotSpots* to the form.

Figure 12-3 shows a sample of WORLD.BMP with four Image controls.

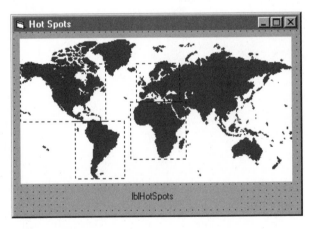

Figure 12-3.
Hot spots shown during application development.

The following code completes the demonstration by displaying a label for each hot spot when the hot spot is clicked:

```
Option Explicit

Private Sub imgAfrica_Click()
    lblHotSpots.Caption = "Africa"
End Sub

Private Sub imgEurope_Click()
    lblHotSpots.Caption = "Europe"
End Sub

Private Sub imgNAmerica_Click()
    lblHotSpots.Caption = "North America"
End Sub

Private Sub imgSAmerica_Click()
    lblHotSpots.Caption = "South America"
End Sub

Private Sub imgWorld_Click()
    lblHotSpots.Caption = "The World"
End Sub
```

Figure 12-4 shows the result when the Africa hot spot rectangle is clicked.

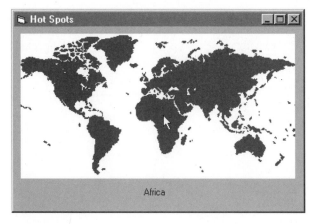

Figure 12-4.
The Africa hot spot activated with a click.

The Image control outlines are visible during development but invisible at runtime. Because these hot spot Image controls are drawn on top of a larger image, click events are acted on by the hot spots rather than by the underlying image.

See Also...

- The VBClock application in Chapter 29, "Date and Time," for a demonstration of graphics hot spots

Dear John, How Do I...
Draw a Polygon Quickly?

You can use the Line method to connect a sequence of points with straight lines and return to the starting point to draw a closed polygon. But the Polygon Windows API function is faster, and it has the advantage of being able to efficiently fill the interior of the polygon with a color. The following Polygon class greatly simplifies the task of drawing polygons by encapsulating the API function and its required data type:

```
'POLYGON.CLS
Option Explicit

Private Type POINTAPI
    x As Long
    y As Long
End Type

Private Declare Function Polygon _
Lib "gdi32" ( _
    ByVal hdc As Long, _
    lpPoint As POINTAPI, _
    ByVal nCount As Long _
) As Long

'Module-level private variables
Private mobjDevice As Object
Private mfSX1 As Single
Private mfSY1 As Single
Private mfXRatio As Single
Private mfYRatio As Single
Private mPointArray() As POINTAPI
```

(continued)

```
'~~~Device
Property Set Device(objDevice As Object)
    Dim fSX2 As Single
    Dim fSY2 As Single
    Dim fPX2 As Single
    Dim fPY2 As Single
    Dim nScaleMode As Integer
    Set mobjDevice = objDevice
    With mobjDevice
        'Grab current scaling parameters
        nScaleMode = .ScaleMode
        mfSX1 = .ScaleLeft
        mfSY1 = .ScaleTop
        fSX2 = mfSX1 + .ScaleWidth
        fSY2 = mfSY1 + .ScaleHeight
        'Temporarily set pixels mode
        .ScaleMode = vbPixels
        'Grab pixel scaling parameters
        fPX2 = .ScaleWidth
        fPY2 = .ScaleHeight
        'Reset user's original scale
        If nScaleMode = 0 Then
            mobjDevice.Scale (mfSX1, mfSY1)-(fSX2, fSY2)
        Else
            mobjDevice.ScaleMode = nScaleMode
        End If
        'Calculate scaling ratios just once
        mfXRatio = fPX2 / (fSX2 - mfSX1)
        mfYRatio = fPY2 / (fSY2 - mfSY1)
    End With
End Property

'~~~Point X,Y
Public Sub Point(fX As Single, fY As Single)
    Dim lN As Long
    lN = UBound(mPointArray) + 1
    ReDim Preserve mPointArray(lN)
    mPointArray(lN).x = XtoP(fX)
    mPointArray(lN).y = YtoP(fY)
End Sub

'~~~Draw
Public Sub Draw()
    Polygon mobjDevice.hdc, mPointArray(1), UBound(mPointArray)
    ReDim mPointArray(0)
End Sub
```

(continued)

```
'Scales X value to pixel location
Private Function XtoP(fX As Single) As Long
    XtoP = (fX - mfSX1) * mfXRatio
End Function

'Scales Y value to pixel location
Private Function YtoP(fY As Single) As Long
    YtoP = (fY - mfSY1) * mfYRatio
End Function

'Initialization
Private Sub Class_Initialize()
    ReDim mPointArray(0)
End Sub
```

I've taken advantage of the behind-the-scenes way Visual Basic handles graphics in order to make the Polygon object easy to use. The Polygon API function always expects pixel parameters, whereas Visual Basic lets you scale your graphics output device in several different ways. Fortunately, Visual Basic doesn't use the API functions for mapping and scaling graphics at a low level; instead it scales user units to pixels just before calling the API functions for drawing lines, circles, and so on. The Polygon object performs the same type of scaling, which turns out to be an efficient way to allow the user to use Visual Basic's different scaling units. Notice that the scaling factors are calculated just once, in the Set Device property procedure. Then, with each coordinate of the polygon set in the Point method, the X and Y values are scaled to pixels using these factors. The only catch here is that the Device property should always be set immediately after any change to the device's scaling mode or scaling units.

Visual Basic uses standard graphical device contexts and brushes in such a way that it's easy to accommodate Visual Basic's FillStyle, FillColor, and similar graphics settings. In fact, nothing special needs to be done within the Polygon object because the Polygon API function automatically uses the output device's current settings. This means, for example, that you can easily draw a polygon of any odd shape, filling its interior with diagonal lines of any desired color.

The following code demonstrates how the Polygon object is implemented in your applications. In this example, a random 17-point polygon is created and filled with a randomly selected solid color. To try it out, add this code to a new form that contains a PictureBox control named *picTest*. Be sure that the Polygon class is named *Polygon*. Run the program, and click on the picture box to draw the polygons.

```
'POLYTEST.FRM
Option Explicit

Dim polyTest As New Polygon

Private Sub Form_Load()
    'Create unique polygon each time
    Randomize
    'Use any desired units and graphics settings
    With picTest
        .Move 0, 0, ScaleWidth, ScaleHeight
        .ScaleMode = vbInches
        .FillStyle = vbSolid
    End With
End Sub

Private Sub picTest_Click()
    Dim nI As Integer
    'Connect picture box as polygon output device
    Set polyTest.Device = picTest
    With picTest
        'Clear output with each click
        .Cls
        'Build 17-point random polygon
        For nI = 1 To 17
            polyTest.Point Rnd * .ScaleWidth, Rnd * .ScaleHeight
        Next nI
        'Create unique fill color each time
        .FillColor = RGB(Rnd * 256, Rnd * 256, Rnd * 256)
        'Draw polygon, filling the interior
        polyTest.Draw
    End With
End Sub
```

Figure 12-5 on the following page shows a 17-point polygon created using the Polygon object.

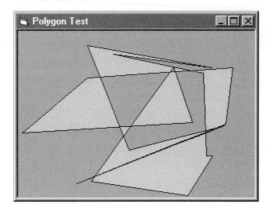

Figure 12-5.
A multipointed polygon drawn using the Polygon object.

See Also...

- "Dear John, How Do I...Draw an Ellipse?" below

- "Dear John, How Do I...Fill an Irregularly Shaped Area with a Color?" later in this chapter

Dear John, How Do I...
Draw an Ellipse?

Visual Basic's Circle method draws an ellipse using its center coordinate, radius, and its aspect ratio. However, in many cases it's more convenient to draw an ellipse using its bounding rectangle. For example, to draw a cylinder you might want the ends of the ellipse (the ellipse forms one end of the cylinder) to just touch the endpoints of the sides. Calculating the center coordinates, radius, and aspect ratio to precisely position an ellipse at the top of such a cylinder can be done, but the math is tricky and prone to errors.

There's a better way to draw ellipses within bounding rectangles: the Ellipse Windows API function is all set up to do exactly this. In fact, Visual Basic itself uses this API function to draw circles and ellipses, converting user information such as the center coordinates, radius, and the aspect ratio to a bounding rectangle. The following Ellipse class encapsulates the Ellipse API function and calls it directly, making it easy for your applications to draw ellipses using their bounding rectangle dimensions:

```
'ELLIPSE.CLS
Option Explicit

Private Declare Function Ellipse _
Lib "gdi32" ( _
    ByVal hdc As Long, _
    ByVal X1 As Long, _
    ByVal Y1 As Long, _
    ByVal X2 As Long, _
    ByVal Y2 As Long _
) As Long

'Module-level private variables
Private mobjDevice As Object
Private mfSX1 As Single
Private mfSY1 As Single
Private mfXRatio As Single
Private mfYRatio As Single

'~~~Device
Property Set Device(objDevice As Object)
    Dim fSX2 As Single
    Dim fSY2 As Single
    Dim fPX2 As Single
    Dim fPY2 As Single
    Dim intScaleMode As Integer
    Set mobjDevice = objDevice
    With mobjDevice
        'Grab current scaling parameters
        intScaleMode = .ScaleMode
        mfSX1 = .ScaleLeft
        mfSY1 = .ScaleTop
        fSX2 = mfSX1 + .ScaleWidth
        fSY2 = mfSY1 + .ScaleHeight
        'Temporarily set pixels mode
        .ScaleMode = vbPixels
        'Grab pixel scaling parameters
        fPX2 = .ScaleWidth
        fPY2 = .ScaleHeight
        'Reset user's original scale
        If intScaleMode = 0 Then
            mobjDevice.Scale (mfSX1, mfSY1)-(fSX2, fSY2)
        Else
            mobjDevice.ScaleMode = intScaleMode
        End If
```

(continued)

```
                    'Calculate scaling ratios just once
                    mfXRatio = fPX2 / (fSX2 - mfSX1)
                    mfYRatio = fPY2 / (fSY2 - mfSY1)
            End With
    End Property

    '~~~Draw X1,Y1,X2,Y2
    Public Sub Draw( _
            fX1 As Single, _
            fY1 As Single, _
            fX2 As Single, _
            fY2 As Single _
    )
            Ellipse mobjDevice.hdc, XtoP(fX1), YtoP(fY1), _
                XtoP(fX2), YtoP(fY2)
    End Sub

    'Scales X value to pixel location
    Private Function XtoP(fX As Single) As Long
            XtoP = (fX - mfSX1) * mfXRatio
    End Function

    'Scales Y value to pixel location
    Private Function YtoP(fY As Single) As Long
            YtoP = (fY - mfSY1) * mfYRatio
    End Function
```

Notice that much of the code in the Ellipse class module is the same as that in the Polygon class described earlier. In particular, the Device property performs the same scaling preparations. You can use the Ellipse (or the Polygon) class module as a template to create other graphics drawing objects based on the many additional graphics API functions. Also, you might want to include these various API functions as methods in a single, all-encompassing Graphics class. The Graphics object would then have one Device property and multiple drawing methods, such as Polygon and Ellipse. I've chosen to place these API functions in separate class modules in order to focus clearly on the implementation of each. If you plan to use only one or two of these new objects in a given application, these smaller, individualized graphics objects provide an efficient option.

The following code demonstrates the Ellipse object by drawing three nested ellipses, each just touching the edge of another ellipse. This is surprisingly difficult to accomplish using Visual Basic's Circle method, due to the way the aspect ratio scales ellipses. To try out the Ellipse object, add the following code to a form that contains a PictureBox control named *picX*. Be sure that the Ellipse class is named *Ellipse*. Run the program, and click on the picture box to draw the ellipses.

```
Option Explicit

Dim ellipseTest As New Ellipse

Private Sub picX_Click()
    picX.ScaleMode = vbCentimeters
    Set ellipseTest.Device = picX
    ellipseTest.Draw 1, 1, 7, 4
    ellipseTest.Draw 2, 1, 6, 4
    ellipseTest.Draw 2, 2, 6, 3
End Sub
```

Figure 12-6 shows the three nested ellipses.

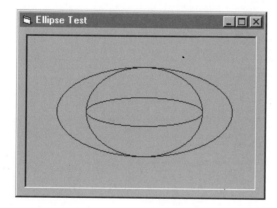

Figure 12-6.
Nested ellipses defined by bounding rectangle coordinates.

See Also...

- "Dear John, How Do I...Draw a Polygon Quickly?" earlier in this chapter

Dear John, How Do I...

Fill an Irregularly Shaped Area with a Color?

The Polygon Windows API function described earlier in this chapter is great for filling an area with a color if you know the boundary coordinates of the area. Sometimes, however, you don't know the boundary coordinates but you do know the boundary color, and you can use this information to fill the area. The FloodFill Windows API function simulates the old Paint command found in earlier versions of Microsoft Basic, which floods an area bounded by a color.

The following class and sample code demonstrates the use of the FloodFill API function to fill the area formed by an overlapping circle and box with color:

```
'PAINT.CLS
Option Explicit

Private Declare Function FloodFill _
Lib "gdi32" ( _
    ByVal hdc As Long, _
    ByVal x As Long, _
    ByVal y As Long, _
    ByVal crColor As Long _
) As Long

'Module-level private variables
Private mobjDevice As Object
Private mfSX1 As Single
Private mfSY1 As Single
Private mfXRatio As Single
Private mfYRatio As Single

Property Set Device(objDevice As Object)
    Dim fSX2 As Single
    Dim fSY2 As Single
    Dim fPX2 As Single
    Dim fPY2 As Single
    Dim nScaleMode As Integer
    Set mobjDevice = objDevice
    With mobjDevice
        'Grab current scaling parameters
        nScaleMode = .ScaleMode
        mfSX1 = .ScaleLeft
        mfSY1 = .ScaleTop
        fSX2 = mfSX1 + .ScaleWidth
        fSY2 = mfSY1 + .ScaleHeight
        'Temporarily set pixels mode
        .ScaleMode = vbPixels
        'Grab pixel scaling parameters
        fPX2 = .ScaleWidth
        fPY2 = .ScaleHeight
        'Reset user's original scale
```

(continued)

```
        If nScaleMode = 0 Then
            mobjDevice.Scale (mfSX1, mfSY1)-(fSX2, fSY2)
        Else
            mobjDevice.ScaleMode = nScaleMode
        End If
        'Calculate scaling ratios just once
        mfXRatio = fPX2 / (fSX2 - mfSX1)
        mfYRatio = fPY2 / (fSY2 - mfSY1)
    End With
End Property

'~~~Flood x,y
Public Sub Flood(fX As Single, fY As Single)
    FloodFill mobjDevice.hdc, XtoP(fX), YtoP(fY), _
        mobjDevice.ForeColor
End Sub

'Scales X value to pixel location
Private Function XtoP(fX As Single) As Long
    XtoP = (fX - mfSX1) * mfXRatio
End Function

'Scales Y value to pixel location
Private Function YtoP(fY As Single) As Long
    YtoP = (fY - mfSY1) * mfYRatio
End Function
```

The code that outlines the circle and the box in red and fills the overlapping area with solid green is as follows:

```
Option Explicit

Dim paintTest As New Paint

Private Sub picX_Click()
    picX.ScaleMode = vbInches
    'Draw overlapping box and circle in red
    picX.Line (0.5, 0.5)-(2, 2), vbRed, B
    picX.Circle (2, 1), 0.7, vbRed
    'Prepare to paint the overlapping area
    picX.FillStyle = vbFSSolid      'Paint style
    picX.FillColor = vbGreen        'Paint color
    picX.ForeColor = vbRed          'Paint boundary color
    Set paintTest.Device = picX
    paintTest.Flood 1.7, 0.9
    'Reset fill style to default
    picX.FillStyle = vbFSTransparent
End Sub
```

Notice that the color boundary is defined by the current ForeColor property and that the fill color itself is defined by the current FillStyle and FillColor properties. The paint fill starts at the specified *xy*-coordinates, filling all pixels with the given fill color and using the given fill style, until pixels with the ForeColor boundary color are reached. This can be very handy for coloring irregularly shaped areas, such as the overlapping circle and box in this example.

To test this example, you will need to name the Paint class *Paint* and add the previous code to a form that contains a PictureBox control named *picX*. Figure 12-7 shows the results of this painting process when the picture box is clicked.

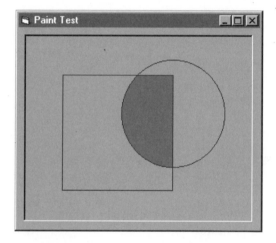

Figure 12-7.
An irregularly shaped area painted using the Paint object.

 See Also...

- "Dear John, How Do I...Draw a Polygon Quickly?" earlier in this chapter

Dear John, How Do I...

Rotate a Bitmap?

The 32-bit function PlgBlt is designed to help you create a generalized polygon transformation of a picture. But although it's been documented in Windows 95, the function has not yet been implemented. I get an error 120 message when I try to call the PlgBlt function, which means that it's still just a stub function, to be implemented later. Stay tuned—this function should be much more efficient than the technique I'll show you here.

The code below will rotate a picture any number of degrees while copying it, pixel by pixel, from one picture box to another. The code is slow, so you'll probably want to use it to rotate individual images while you are building a set of images for an application instead of using it to rotate the images in an application while the application is running.

The Point and PSet methods are used to read and write the pixels, and this short demonstration provides a good example of their use. Be sure to set the ScaleMode to *vbPixels*, as shown here, before using these functions on graphics images.

To try this technique, start a new project and add two picture boxes named *picOne* and *picTwo* and a command button named *cmdRotate* to the form. Assign a bitmap picture to the Picture property of *picOne*, and size *picOne* to display the bitmap. Only the part of the bitmap that is displayed in the picture box will be copied. Size *picTwo* appropriately, and add the code below to the form. The code sets the rotation angle to 45 degrees, but you can set it to any angle. When you run the program, click on the command button to start the rotating and copying process.

```
Option Explicit

Const pi = 3.14159265358979

Private Sub cmdRotate_Click()
    Dim nX As Integer, nY As Integer
    Dim nX1 As Integer, nY1 As Integer
    Dim dX2 As Double, dY2 As Double
    Dim dX3 As Double, dY3 As Double
    Dim dThetaDeg As Double
    Dim dThetaRad As Double
    'Initialize rotation angle
    dThetaDeg = 45
    'Compute angle in radians
    dThetaRad = dThetaDeg * pi / 180
    'Set scale modes to pixels
    picOne.ScaleMode = vbPixels
    picTwo.ScaleMode = vbPixels
    For nX = 0 To picTwo.ScaleWidth
        nX1 = nX - picTwo.ScaleWidth \ 2
        For nY = 0 To picTwo.ScaleHeight
            nY1 = nY - picTwo.ScaleHeight \ 2
```

(continued)

```
                    'Rotate picture by dThetaRad
                    dX2 = nX1 * Cos(-dThetaRad) + nY1 * Sin(-dThetaRad)
                    dY2 = nY1 * Cos(-dThetaRad) - nX1 * Sin(-dThetaRad)
                    'Translate to center of picture box
                    dX3 = dX2 + picOne.ScaleWidth \ 2
                    dY3 = dY2 + picOne.ScaleHeight \ 2
                    'If data point is in picOne, set its color in picTwo
                    If dX3 > 0 And dX3 < picOne.ScaleWidth - 1 _
                        And dY3 > 0 And dY3 < picOne.ScaleHeight - 1 Then
                        picTwo.PSet (nX, nY), picOne.Point(dX3, dY3)
                    End If
            Next nY
        Next nX
End Sub
```

You might want to use the SavePicture statement to save the rotated image as a bitmap file. If you do so, be sure to set the AutoRedraw property of *picTwo* to *True*. The following statement shows an example of how to use the SavePicture statement:

```
SavePicture picTwo.Image, "C:\FINISHROT.BMP"
```

Figure 12-8 shows the demonstration program during development, and Figure 12-9 shows the picture after rotating 45 degrees. The sample image used here is FINISH.BMP, which is located in the Visual Basic directory, in the WIZARDS\TEMPLATE directory.

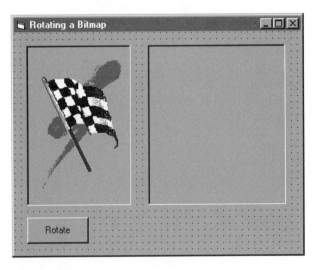

Figure 12-8.
A picture of the finish flag before rotation.

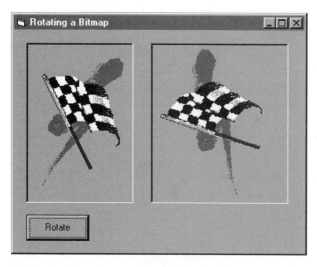

Figure 12-9.
A picture of the finish flag plus a copy rotated 45 degrees.

Dear John, How Do I...

Scroll a Graphics Image?

Visual Basic's PaintPicture method simplifies many graphics manipulation techniques. In the following example, for instance, I use PaintPicture to display a small window of a larger bitmap, with scrollbars to let the user smoothly scroll the image. As shown in Figure 12-10 on the following page, an entire butterfly image appears in the full-size picture box, and a copy of the image appears in the smaller picture box.

> NOTE: The full-size image need not be visible for this program to work. During the development process, you can load the source picture box with a large bitmap and then set its Visible property to *False*. The small picture box will still display the picture.

To try this program, add two picture boxes of different sizes to a new form. Name the larger picture box *picOne* and the smaller one *picTwo*. Add a vertical scrollbar named *vsbScroll* and a horizontal scrollbar named *hsbScroll* to the form, as shown in Figure 12-10. Position these two scrollbar controls adjacent to *picTwo* because they will control the contents of this picture box. Load a bitmap file into the Picture property of *picOne*, and size the picture box—

only the part of the bitmap displayed in the *picOne* picture box can be displayed in the *picTwo* picture box. The program scrolls this image in *picTwo* by copying a rectangular region from *picOne* using the PaintPicture method.

Figure 12-10.
Scrolling a large image in a smaller picture box.

Add the following code to the form. Notice that the program triggers scrollbar Change events from within each scrollbar's Scroll event. This lets you drag the scrollbar box and smoothly scroll the image in real time.

```
Option Explicit

Private Sub Form_Load()
    hsbScroll.Max = picOne.ScaleWidth - picTwo.ScaleWidth
    hsbScroll.LargeChange = hsbScroll.Max \ 10
    hsbScroll.SmallChange = hsbScroll.Max \ 25
    vsbScroll.Max = picOne.ScaleHeight - picTwo.ScaleHeight
    vsbScroll.LargeChange = vsbScroll.Max \ 10
    vsbScroll.SmallChange = vsbScroll.Max \ 25
End Sub

Private Sub hsbScroll_Change()
    UpdatePicTwo
End Sub
```

(continued)

```
Private Sub hsbScroll_Scroll()
    hsbScroll_Change
End Sub

Private Sub vsbScroll_Change()
    UpdatePicTwo
End Sub

Private Sub vsbScroll_Scroll()
    vsbScroll_Change
End Sub

Private Sub UpdatePicTwo()
    picTwo.PaintPicture picOne.Picture, 0, 0, _
        picTwo.ScaleWidth, picTwo.ScaleHeight, _
        hsbScroll.Value, vsbScroll.Value, _
        picTwo.ScaleWidth, picTwo.ScaleHeight, _
        vbSrcCopy
End Sub
```

Dear John, How Do I...

Use BitBlt to Create Animation?

Visual Basic's PaintPicture method is a convenient and fairly fast method for moving irregularly shaped graphics objects around on the screen without disturbing the background. PaintPicture is Visual Basic's equivalent of the BitBlt Windows API function. (Actually, after PaintPicture performs error checking and scaling from the current graphics units, it calls BitBlt.) The only drawback to PaintPicture is its slowness. By calling BitBlt directly, you avoid the overhead of the calculations that PaintPicture must perform before it in turn calls BitBlt. The result is an animated sequence created with BitBlt that is considerably faster, with smoother action—that's why this demonstration program calls BitBlt directly.

The BitBlt API function quickly moves a rectangular block of pixels from a picture box or form to another picture box or form, or to the printer object. BitBlt requires an hDC (handle to a device context) for both the source and the destination of the image transfer. The PictureBox, Form, and Printer objects all provide an hDC property. Note, however, that with the AutoRedraw property set to *True*, the hDC property of a picture box points to the control's Image property, not to its Picture property. The image is a behind-the-scenes copy stored in memory of what you see on the screen; it's where the actual work is performed as you draw or use the BitBlt API function to manipulate the contents of a PictureBox control when AutoRedraw is *True*. The results are transferred from the image to the picture only when the system refreshes a picture box. This works well for our purposes, avoiding flicker and other problems.

The code below animates an image of a UFO, moving it across the standard Windows 95 cloud bitmap without disturbing this background image. This action requires three picture boxes: one containing the UFO's image, a second containing a mask to prepare the background for the UFO's image, and a third to temporarily hold the background that will be restored when the UFO moves on. Much more complicated objects can be animated using the same technique, but for now I chose a simple, small UFO shape.

```
Option Explicit

Private Declare Function BitBlt _
Lib "gdi32" ( _
    ByVal hDestDC As Long, _
    ByVal x As Long, ByVal y As Long, _
    ByVal nWidth As Long, ByVal nHeight As Long, _
    ByVal hSrcDC As Long, _
    ByVal xSrc As Long, ByVal ySrc As Long, _
    ByVal dwRop As Long _
) As Long

  Private Sub cmdAnimate_Click()
    Static lx As Long, ly As Long
    Static lw As Long, lh As Long
    Static BackSavedFlag As Boolean
    Dim lRtn As Long
    'Display hourglass pointer while busy
    Screen.MousePointer = vbHourglass
    'Provide starting location
    lx = -picUfo.ScaleWidth
    ly = picClouds.ScaleHeight
    'Save sizes in local variables once for speed
    lw = picUfo.ScaleWidth
    lh = picUfo.ScaleHeight
    'Loop to animate the UFO
    Do
        'Restore background unless this is first time object is drawn
        If BackSavedFlag = True Then
            lRtn = BitBlt(picClouds.hDC, lx, ly, lw, lh, _
                picBack.hDC, 0, 0, vbSrcCopy)
            'Stop UFO's motion when it gets to the edges
```

(continued)

```
                If lx > picClouds.ScaleWidth Then
                    BackSavedFlag = False
                    picClouds.Refresh
                    Exit Do
                End If
            End If
            'Move UFO to a new location
            lx = lx + 1
                If lx < 0.5 * picClouds.ScaleWidth _
                    Or lx > 0.8 * picClouds.ScaleWidth Then
                    ly = ly - 1
            Else
                ly = ly + 1
            End If
            'Save background at new location
            lRtn = BitBlt(picBack.hDC, 0, 0, lw, lh, _
                picClouds.hDC, lx, ly, vbSrcCopy)
            BackSavedFlag = True
            'Apply mask
            lRtn = BitBlt(picClouds.hDC, lx, ly, lw, lh, _
                picUfoMask.hDC, 0, 0, vbSrcAnd)
            'Draw UFO
            lRtn = BitBlt(picClouds.hDC, lx, ly, lw, lh, _
                picUfo.hDC, 0, 0, vbSrcPaint)
            picClouds.Refresh
        Loop
        'Restore pointer
        Screen.MousePointer = vbDefault
    End Sub
```

To try out this code, start a new project and add to the form a command button named *cmdAnimate* and four PictureBox controls named *picClouds*, *picUfo*, *picUfoMask*, and *picBack*. Now you need three bitmaps: one large bitmap for the background (I used CLOUDS.BMP, which I found on my Windows 95 installation CD-ROM), one of the UFO, and one of the UFO mask. (I created the UFO and UFO mask bitmaps using Windows Paint.) Set the *picClouds* Picture property to CLOUDS.BMP or another background image, and set the AutoRedraw property to *True*. For the other three PictureBox controls, set the *picUfo* Picture property to the UFO bitmap, set the *picUfoMask* Picture property to the UFO mask bitmap, and set the *picBack* Picture property to the UFO bitmap. Size these three controls so that these three picture boxes are the same size, and position them on the form near the top so that you can follow the action when the program is run. For all four of the PictureBox controls, set the AutoSize property to *True* and the ScaleMode property to *3 - Pixel*. Figure 12-11 on the following page shows the form during the development phase.

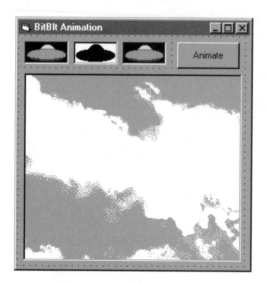

Figure 12-11.
The BitBlt animation example during development.

The UFO and UFO mask bitmaps must be created in a special way. The UFO image here consists of a UFO drawn on a black background. You can use any color except black for an object that is to appear in front of the background. In this case, all the colored pixels that make up the UFO will show. Wherever there are black pixels in an image, however, the background will appear in the animated version. For example, if you want to change the UFO into a doughnut, draw a solid black circle in the center of a nonblack circle.

The UFO mask image is created using the following rule: wherever there are black pixels in the UFO bitmap, make them white in the mask, and wherever there are pixels of any color other than black in the UFO bitmap, make those pixels black in the mask. The mask is a negative image of the primary bitmap and should contain only black and white pixels.

Here's how these bitmaps work to create the animation. First the saved background is restored to erase the UFO at its current location. (Note that this step is skipped the first time the UFO is drawn.) The background at the UFO's next location is saved in the *picBack* picture box. This will be used to restore the background when the UFO moves again. At the new location, the mask image is placed over the background image using a Boolean And operation on a pixel-by-pixel basis. The last parameter in the BitBlt method determines this logical bit-mixing operation. An And operation displays black pixels wherever the applied mask is black and undisturbed background pixels wherever the mask is white. A solid black UFO shape will be displayed on the form at this point, but it will disappear with the next step, before you can see it.

The final step in updating the UFO image to a new location is to apply the primary UFO bitmap (the first picture box) using an Or bitwise operation. The nonblack pixels in the UFO appear where the background is blacked out, and the black pixels leave the background undisturbed. The result is a solid-looking UFO that appears to hover in front of the background scene.

The action is repeated using a loop, causing the UFO to glide across the form from left to right. The UFO is shown in midflight in Figure 12-12.

Figure 12-12.
The animation program in progress, showing the UFO as it moves across the background.

If you are having difficulty getting the UFO to mask properly, the problem could be related to your video driver. Try changing to a different video driver to see whether you experience the same problem.

 See Also...

- The Lottery application in Chapter 27, "Graphics," for a demonstration of animation

Dear John, How Do I...

Use Picture Objects for Animation?

Picture properties have been included in all previous versions of Visual Basic, and starting with version 4, Visual Basic now provides a companion Picture object, which greatly enhances the options you have for manipulating images. A Picture object is an independent entity that you can use to load and store images—you no longer have to use a PictureBox control or an Image control. When you want to access the images, it's easy to copy them from Picture objects to visible controls.

> NOTE: In addition to the Picture object, Visual Basic also provides an ImageList control that lets you load multiple images from a resource file. You might want to try the Picture object or the ImageList control to improve the speed and efficiency of your graphics displays.

Here's some example code for you to experiment with. This program creates an array of Picture objects and loads a sequence of images into each when the form loads. A Timer control named *tmrAnimate* is set to the minimum interval of 1 millisecond, the approximate rate at which it will assign the Picture objects sequentially to a PictureBox control named *picTest*. The result is a smooth, flicker-free animation of the images you've created in the sequence of bitmap files.

```
Option Explicit

Const NUMFRAMES = 15
Dim picArray(1 To NUMFRAMES) As Picture

Private Sub Form_Load()
    Dim sFile As String
    Dim nI As Integer
    For nI = 1 To NUMFRAMES
        sFile = App.Path & "\GLOBE" & _
            Format(nI) & ".BMP"
        Set picArray(nI) = LoadPicture(sFile)
    Next nI
End Sub

Private Sub tmrAnimate_Timer()
    Static nN As Integer
    nN = (nN Mod NUMFRAMES) + 1
    picTest.Picture = picArray(nN)
End Sub
```

I modified the AniGlobe application (see Chapter 27, "Graphics") to create 15 globe images, and named them GLOBE1.BMP, GLOBE2.BMP, and so on, through GLOBE15.BMP. These 15 images are loaded into an array of 15 Picture objects, to be copied and displayed sequentially in a single PictureBox control. The *picTest* PictureBox control's AutoSize property should be set to *True* so that the frames of the animation will automatically fit. Figure 12-13 shows the animation frozen at about the middle of the sequence of frames.

Figure 12-13.
Simple animation sequence created using an array of picture objects.

Dear John, How Do I...

Use the Animation Control?

Windows 95 introduced those tiny, animated Recycle Bins, searching flashlights, file copying, and similar system animations. The Animation control in Visual Basic 5 makes it easy to add any of these animations to your own applications. The following code loads and runs two animations; one that sweeps the flashlight back and forth across a folder, and one that zaps the contents of the Recycle Bin:

```
Option Explicit

Private Sub Form_Load()
    anmOne.Open App.Path & "\SEARCH.AVI"
    anmOne.Play
```

(continued)

```
        anmTwo.Open App.Path & "\FILENUKE.AVI"
        anmTwo.Play
End Sub
```

To try out this code, add two Animation controls to a new form and name them *anmOne* and *anmTwo*. The Animation control, which is part of the Microsoft Windows Common Controls-2 (COMCT232.OCX), enables you to control animation programmatically. Here I've used the Open method to load the animation clips, and I've used the Play method with none of its optional parameters, which results in the animations playing continuously until the form closes. Figure 12-14 shows these two animations in action.

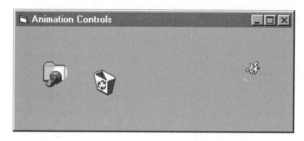

Figure 12-14.
Simple system animations played using the Animation control.

Note that these animations run in their own threads, which means that your program can proceed with other processing.

Not all AVI files can be played using the Animation control. The animations must be silent clips; you'll get an error if you try to play an AVI file containing sound. Check the online help for more information about the fine details and options for the Animation control.

Dear John, How Do I...

Position Text at an Exact Location in a Picture Box?

One advantage a picture box has over a text box or a label is that a picture box lets you print text at any location, with various fonts, in a variety of colors, and intermixed with graphics. You can change the font characteristics using the standard properties of the picture box, and you can position the text for printing at any location in the picture box by using a combination of the

ScaleWidth and ScaleHeight properties and the TextWidth and TextHeight methods of the picture box.

The following code demonstrates how to center a string at a point and how to position a string so that it prints flush with the lower-right corner of the picture box. To try this code, add a PictureBox control named *picTest* to a new form, add the following code, run the application, and resize the form while it's running.

```
Option Explicit

Private Sub Form_Resize()
    Dim nX As Integer
    Dim nY As Integer
    Dim sA As String
    'Reposition the picture box
    picTest.Move 0, 0, ScaleWidth, ScaleHeight
    'Erase previous contents of picture box
    picTest.Cls
    'Determine center of picture box
    nX = picTest.ScaleWidth \ 2
    nY = picTest.ScaleHeight \ 2
    'Draw circle at center for reference
    picTest.Circle (nX, nY), 700
    'Print string centered in picture box
    sA = "CENTER"
    picTest.CurrentX = nX - picTest.TextWidth(sA) \ 2
    picTest.CurrentY = nY - picTest.TextHeight(sA) \ 2
    picTest.Print sA
    'Determine lower-right corner of picture box
    nX = picTest.ScaleWidth
    nY = picTest.ScaleHeight
    'Print string at lower-right corner
    sA = "Lower-right corner..."
    picTest.CurrentX = nX - picTest.TextWidth(sA)
    picTest.CurrentY = nY - picTest.TextHeight(sA)
    picTest.Print sA
End Sub
```

Notice that the TextWidth method returns the effective length of the entire string, taking into account the current font settings, the number of characters in the string, and the proportional spacing for those characters. For this reason, always pass the exact string to be printed to this method just before printing and after any font properties have been set.

Figure 12-15 on the following page shows the result of this code.

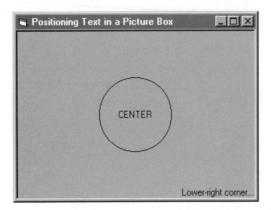

Figure 12-15.
Printing text at exact locations in a picture box.

The above example shows the general technique for exact text placement. By extrapolating from this example, you can print superscript characters, label graph axes, and perform similar tasks.

Dear John, How Do I...

Scale a Font Infinitely?

In earlier versions of Visual Basic, we were limited to a certain fixed set of font sizes, even for the "infinitely scalable" TrueType fonts. Now, it's easy to set the Size property of the Font object of graphical output devices to any font size for TrueType and PostScript fonts. To do so, add the following code on a blank form and set the form's Font property to any TrueType font:

```
Option Explicit

Private Sub Form_Click()
    Dim fSize As Single
    fSize = 1
    Do
        fSize = fSize * 1.2
        Me.Font = "Garamond"
        Me.Font.Size = fSize
        Me.Print "Garamond - "; fSize
    Loop Until fSize > 100
End Sub
```

Figure 12-16 shows the result of running this code.

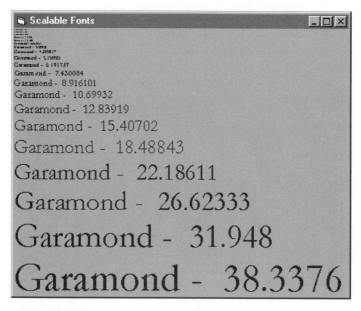

Figure 12-16.
A range of font sizes displayed for the Garamond TrueType font when the form is clicked.

Dear John, How Do I...

Rotate Text to Any Angle?

Visual Basic doesn't let you directly rotate a font to any angle, but with the help of a few Windows API function calls we can still get the job done. The following Rotator class defines an object that encapsulates five API functions, a LOGFONT data type, and a couple of required constants that, working together, let you easily rotate fonts on your screen or in your printed output:

```
'ROTATOR.CLS
Option Explicit

'API constants
Private Const LF_FACESIZE = 32
Private Const LOGPIXELSY = 90
```

(continued)

```
Private Type LOGFONT
    lfHeight As Long
    lfWidth As Long
    lfEscapement As Long
    lfOrientation As Long
    lfWeight As Long
    lfItalic As Byte
    lfUnderline As Byte
    lfStrikeOut As Byte
    lfCharSet As Byte
    lfOutPrecision As Byte
    lfClipPrecision As Byte
    lfQuality As Byte
    lfPitchAndFamily As Byte
    lfFaceName(LF_FACESIZE - 1) As Byte
End Type

Private Declare Function SelectObject _
Lib "gdi32" ( _
    ByVal hdc As Long, _
    ByVal hObject As Long _
) As Long

Private Declare Function DeleteObject _
Lib "gdi32" ( _
    ByVal hObject As Long _
) As Long

Private Declare Function CreateFontIndirect _
Lib "gdi32" Alias "CreateFontIndirectA" ( _
    lpLogFont As LOGFONT _
) As Long

Private Declare Function TextOut _
Lib "gdi32" Alias "TextOutA" ( _
    ByVal hdc As Long, _
    ByVal x As Long, _
    ByVal y As Long, _
    ByVal lpString As String, _
    ByVal nCount As Long _
) As Long

Private Declare Function GetDeviceCaps _
Lib "gdi32" ( _
    ByVal hdc As Long, _
    ByVal nIndex As Long _
) As Long
```

(continued)

```
'Module-level private variables
Private mobjDevice As Object
Private mfSX1 As Single
Private mfSY1 As Single
Private mfXRatio As Single
Private mfYRatio As Single
Private lfFont As LOGFONT
Private mnAngle As Integer

'~~~Angle
Property Let Angle(nAngle As Integer)
    mnAngle = nAngle
End Property
Property Get Angle() As Integer
    Angle = mnAngle
End Property

'~~~Label
Public Sub Label(sText As String)
    Dim lFont As Long
    Dim lOldFont As Long
    Dim lRes As Long
    Dim byBuf() As Byte
    Dim nI As Integer
    Dim sFontName As String
    'Prepare font name, decoding from Unicode
    sFontName = mobjDevice.Font.Name
    byBuf = StrConv(sFontName & Chr$(0), vbFromUnicode)
    For nI = 0 To UBound(byBuf)
        lfFont.lfFaceName(nI) = byBuf(nI)
    Next nI
    'Convert known font size to required units
    lfFont.lfHeight = mobjDevice.Font.Size * _
        GetDeviceCaps(mobjDevice.hdc, LOGPIXELSY) \ 72
    'Set Italic or not
    If mobjDevice.Font.Italic = True Then
        lfFont.lfItalic = 1
    Else
        lfFont.lfItalic = 0
    End If
    'Set Underline or not
    If mobjDevice.Font.Underline = True Then
        lfFont.lfUnderline = 1
    Else
        lfFont.lfUnderline = 0
    End If
    'Set Strikethrough or not
```

(continued)

```
        If mobjDevice.Font.Strikethrough = True Then
            lfFont.lfStrikeOut = 1
        Else
            lfFont.lfStrikeOut = 0
        End If
        'Set Bold or not (use font's weight)
        lfFont.lfWeight = mobjDevice.Font.Weight
        'Set font rotation angle
        lfFont.lfEscapement = CLng(mnAngle * 10#)
        lfFont.lfOrientation = lfFont.lfEscapement
        'Build temporary new font and output the string
        lFont = CreateFontIndirect(lfFont)
        lOldFont = SelectObject(mobjDevice.hdc, lFont)
        lRes = TextOut(mobjDevice.hdc, XtoP(mobjDevice.CurrentX), _
            YtoP(mobjDevice.CurrentY), sText, Len(sText))
        lFont = SelectObject(mobjDevice.hdc, lOldFont)
        DeleteObject lFont
End Sub

'~~~Device
Property Set Device(objDevice As Object)
    Dim fSX2 As Single
    Dim fSY2 As Single
    Dim fPX2 As Single
    Dim fPY2 As Single
    Dim nScaleMode As Integer
    Set mobjDevice = objDevice
    With mobjDevice
        'Grab current scaling parameters
        nScaleMode = .ScaleMode
        mfSX1 = .ScaleLeft
        mfSY1 = .ScaleTop
        fSX2 = mfSX1 + .ScaleWidth
        fSY2 = mfSY1 + .ScaleHeight
        'Temporarily set pixels mode
        .ScaleMode = vbPixels
        'Grab pixel scaling parameters
        fPX2 = .ScaleWidth
        fPY2 = .ScaleHeight
        'Reset user's original scale
        If nScaleMode = 0 Then
            mobjDevice.Scale (mfSX1, mfSY1)-(fSX2, fSY2)
        Else
            mobjDevice.ScaleMode = nScaleMode
        End If
```

(continued)

258

```
        'Calculate scaling ratios just once
        mfXRatio = fPX2 / (fSX2 - mfSX1)
        mfYRatio = fPY2 / (fSY2 - mfSY1)
    End With
End Property

'Scales X value to pixel location
Private Function XtoP(fX As Single) As Long
    XtoP = (fX - mfSX1) * mfXRatio
End Function

'Scales Y value to pixel location
Private Function YtoP(fY As Single) As Long
    YtoP = (fY - mfSY1) * mfYRatio
End Function
```

Even though a lot of code and complicated details are encapsulated in the Rotator object, it's very easy to use this object in your own applications. The following code shows the steps required. An instance of the Rotator object is created, a PictureBox control named *picX* is set as the output device for the object, the angle for the output is set in the Angle property, and a string is passed to the Label method. Notice that the font name and size and the printing location (CurrentX and CurrentY) are set in the picture box's various font properties; the Rotator object uses these current settings to complete the output. For illustration purposes, I've commented out the Bold, Italic, Underline, Strikethrough, and Weight property settings, but you should experiment with these properties to see how they affect the rotated text output.

```
Option Explicit

Dim rotTest As New Rotator

Private Sub picX_Click()
    Dim nA As Integer
    'Prepare the font in the picture box
    picX.Scale (-1, -1)-(1, 1)
    With picX
        .CurrentX = 0
        .CurrentY = 0
        With .Font
            .Name = "Courier New"
            .Size = 11
            '.Bold = True
            '.Italic = True
            '.Strikethrough = True
```

(continued)

```
                '.Underline = True
                '.Weight = 1000
            End With
        End With
        'Connect Rotator object to the picture box
        Set rotTest.Device = picX
        'Label strings at a variety of angles
        For nA = 0 To 359 Step 15
            rotTest.Angle = nA
            rotTest.Label Space(4) & picX.Font.Name & Str(nA)
        Next nA
End Sub
```

Figure 12-17 shows the output of this code.

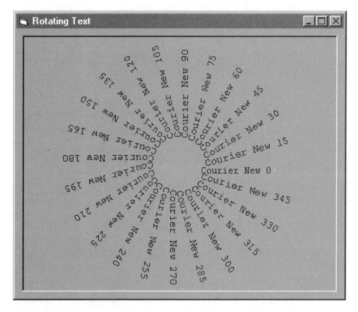

Figure 12-17.
Text printed at a variety of angles using the Rotator object.

Dear John, How Do I...

Use Multiple Fonts in a Picture Box?

The PictureBox control has a full set of properties for font characteristics. Unlike the TextBox and Label controls, the PictureBox control lets you change these properties on the fly, without affecting any text already drawn in the picture box. Simply reset the font properties, print the text, and then move on to print other text using any other combination of these properties. Figure 12-18 shows a few different fonts, all drawn in one picture box.

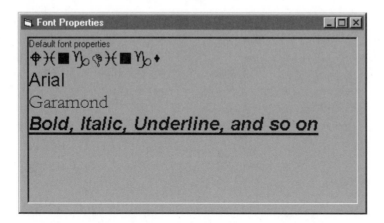

Figure 12-18.
A creative combination of text styles in one picture box.

For backward compatibility, picture boxes support the font properties from earlier versions of Visual Basic, such as FontName and FontSize. The Font property, however, is an object in itself, and it now provides a set of its own properties. Look at the following sample code, which I used to create Figure 12-18, and notice how I set these properties by using the Font object. Keep in mind that you can create a Font object as an independent entity and assign the entire set of its properties to any object having a Font property in one command. For more details, see the online help for Font objects.

```
Option Explicit

Private Sub picTest_Click()
    picTest.Print "Default font properties"
    picTest.Font.Name = "WingDings"
    picTest.Font.Size = 18
    picTest.Print "WingDings"
    picTest.Font.Name = "Arial"
    picTest.Print "Arial"
    picTest.Font.Name = "Garamond"
    picTest.Print "Garamond"
    picTest.Font.Bold = True
    picTest.Font.Italic = True
    picTest.Font.Underline = True
    picTest.Font.Name = "Arial"
    picTest.Print "Bold, Italic, Underline, and so on"
End Sub
```

To try this code, start a new project and add a PictureBox control named *picTest* to the form. Add the code to the form, and at runtime click on the picture box to display the different formats of text in the picture box.

NOTE: For some purposes, Visual Basic's RichTextBox control also provides excellent multifont capabilities. Although the ability to position text at an exact location is not part of the RichTextBox control's properties and methods, you can left align, right align, and center text. You can also use multiple fonts within the same control. Select Microsoft Rich Textbox Control (RICHTX32.OCX) in the Components dialog box to add this control to your Toolbox. Check it out.

See Also...

- Chapter 19, "Text Box and Rich Text Box Tricks," for information about the RichTextBox control

CHAPTER THIRTEEN

File I/O

Visual Basic provides several efficient techniques that you can use to read and write files. This chapter describes some of the most useful techniques for file I/O (input/output), along with several functions that people tend to overlook.

Dear John, How Do I...

Rename, Copy, or Delete a File Efficiently?

Visual Basic has three statements that were specifically designed for renaming, copying, and deleting files. Use the Name statement to rename a file, the FileCopy statement to copy a file, and the Kill statement to delete a file. The following block of code demonstrates all three of these important file manipulation statements in action. When you click on the form, this program creates a simple text file named FILEA, renames it FILEB, copies FILEB to create FILEC.TXT in the directory in which the program resides, displays the contents of FILEC.TXT, and then deletes both FILEB and FILEC.TXT.

```
Option Explicit

Private Sub Form_Click()
    Dim sA As String
    Dim nFileNum As Integer
    'Create a small file
    nFileNum = FreeFile
    Open "FILEA" For Output As #nFileNum
    Print #nFileNum, "This is a test..."
    Close #nFileNum
    'Rename file
    Name "FILEA" As "FILEB"
    'Copy file
    FileCopy "FILEB", App.Path & "\FILEC.TXT"
    'Read and display resulting file
```

(continued)

```
        Open App.Path & "\FILEC.TXT" For Input As #nFileNum
        Line Input #nFileNum, sA
        Close #nFileNum
        MsgBox sA, vbOKOnly, "Contents of the Renamed and Copied File"
        'Delete files
        Kill "FILEB"
        Kill App.Path & "\FILEC.TXT"
End Sub
```

As shown in Figure 13-1, the contents of the copied file are displayed in a message box, verifying the correct operation of the demonstrated statements. When you click OK, FILEB and FILEC.TXT will be deleted.

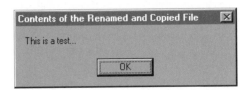

Figure 13-1.
Contents of a renamed and copied file.

Dear John, How Do I...

Work with Directories and Paths?

Visual Basic has several statements that mimic their equivalent MS-DOS commands but don't require your program to shell out to MS-DOS or do any other fancy gymnastics. These statements are discussed in the sections that follow.

MkDir, ChDir, and RmDir

The MkDir statement creates a new directory, ChDir lets you change the current working directory, and RmDir deletes a directory. If you know how to use the commands of the same name at the MS-DOS prompt, you're all set to use them in your Visual Basic applications. Check the online help for more details about these statements.

CurDir and App.Path

Your application can determine the current working directory for any drive by using the CurDir function. Often, however, it's more useful to know the directory that the application itself resides in, rather than the current directory. The Path property of the App object provides this information. For example, with the following lines of code, your application can determine both the current working directory and the directory that the application resides in. The application directory is usually a good location at which to read and write application-specific data files.

```
sCurDirectory = CurDir
sAppDirectory = App.Path
```

Dir

The Dir function is a powerful means of locating files or directories on any drive. The online help describes this function in detail, but I do want to point out that if you call the Dir function with parameters to specify the path or filename pattern and then call the Dir function again without parameters, the function will return the next file that matches the previously specified parameters from the directory currently specified to be searched. This makes possible the sequential collection of all the files in a directory. The following code demonstrates this important feature. This code lists all normal files (hidden files, system files, and directory files are not included) in all directories on the C drive and saves them in a text file named FILETREE.TXT. Add these two procedures to a new form, and run the program to create FILETREE.TXT in the current working directory. The program will automatically unload when it has finished.

```
Option Explicit

Sub RecurseTree(CurrentPath As String)
    Dim nI As Integer, nDirectory As Integer
    Dim sFileName As String, sDirectory List() As String
    'First list all normal files in this directory
    sFileName = Dir(CurrentPath)
    Do While sFileName <> ""
        Print #1, CurrentPath & sFileName
        sFileName = Dir
    Loop
    'Next build temporary list of subdirectories
    sFileName = Dir(CurrentPath, vbDirectory)
    Do While sFileName <> ""
        'Ignore current and parent directories
        If sFileName <> "." And sFileName <> ".." Then
            'Ignore nondirectories
            If GetAttr(CurrentPath & sFileName) _
                    And vbDirectory Then
```

(continued)

265

```
                nDirectory = nDirectory + 1
                ReDim Preserve sDirectoryList(nDirectory)
                sDirectoryList(nDirectory) = CurrentPath & sFileName
            End If
        End If
        sFileName = Dir
        'Process other events
        DoEvents
    Loop
    'Recursively process each directory
    For nI = 1 To nDirectory
        RecurseTree sDirectoryList(nI) & "\"
    Next nI
End Sub

Private Sub Form_Load()
    Dim sStartPath As String
    Me.Show
    Print "Working..."
        Me.MousePointer = vbHourglass
    sStartPath = "C:\"
    Open "FILETREE.TXT" For Output As #1
    RecurseTree sStartPath
    Close #1
        Me.MousePointer = vbDefault
    Unload Me
End Sub
```

This program also illustrates the use of recursive procedures in Visual Basic. In this example, the nesting depth of the recursive calls to RecurseTree is determined by the nested depth of your subdirectories.

You might wonder why RecurseTree builds a dynamically allocated array of subdirectory names instead of simply calling itself each time a subdirectory is encountered. It turns out that the Dir function call, when passed with no parameters, keeps track of the file and path it has most recently found in preparation for the next time Dir is called, regardless of where the function call originated. When it returns from a nested, recursive call, the Dir function will have lost track of its position in the current directory. The string array list of subdirectories, however, is updated accurately with each nested call because at each level a new, local copy of the string array variable is built. This is one of those annoying software details that will drive you up the wall until you realize what's happening!

After you have run this short program, look for a new file on your computer named FILETREE.TXT that contains a list of all files in all directories on your C drive. (Be patient—the program might take a while to finish.)

Figure 13-2 shows an example of FILETREE.TXT in WordPad.

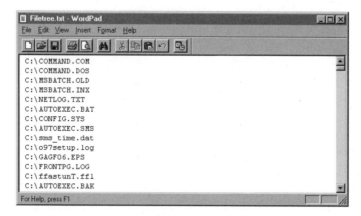

Figure 13-2.
The FILETREE.TXT file in WordPad.

Dear John, How Do I...

Perform Fast File I/O?

The best way to increase the speed of your file I/O operations is to use binary file access whenever possible. You can open any file for binary access, even if it's a text file.

Also, to increase file processing speed, remember to use the FileCopy command whenever it's appropriate, instead of reading and writing from one file to another.

See Also...

- "Dear John, How Do I...Rename, Copy, or Delete a File Efficiently?" earlier in this chapter for information about working with files

- "Dear John, How Do I...Work with Binary Files?" on the following page for information about binary file access

Dear John, How Do I...
Work with Binary Files?

Binary file operations in Visual Basic are fast. Whenever possible, I read and write files using the binary file Get and Put statements. Even if this requires extra processing of the data once the data is loaded into variables, the whole process usually is still faster than using the older Input, Output, and other such functions that have been around since the earliest versions of Microsoft Basic. Today, with Type data structures and very large strings (such as those in 32-bit operating systems), binary file access makes more sense than ever. Let's take a look at a few examples.

Type Data Structures

Type data structures are read from and written to binary files in one fell swoop. For example, the following code writes the same personnel data record to a text file named EMPLOYEE.TXT 10 times when the command button *cmdPut* is clicked. When the command button *cmdGet* is clicked, the personnel data is read from the EMPLOYEE.TXT file.

```
Option Explicit

Private Type Employee
    FirstName As String * 20
    MiddleInitial As String * 1
    LastName As String * 20
    Age As Byte
    Retired As Boolean
    Street As String * 30
    City As String * 20
    State As String * 2
    Comments As String * 200
End Type

Private Sub cmdPut_Click()
    Dim Emp As Employee
    Dim nI
    Open App.Path & "\EMPLOYEE.TXT" For Binary As #1
    For nI = 1 To 10
        Emp.Age = 14
        Emp.City = "Redmond"
        Emp.Comments = "He is a smart guy."
        Emp.FirstName = "Willy"
```

(continued)

```
            Emp.LastName = "Doors"
            Emp.MiddleInitial = "G"
            Emp.Retired = False
            Emp.State = "WA"
            Emp.Street = "One Macrohard Way"
            Put #1, , Emp
        Next nI
        Close #1
    End Sub

    Private Sub cmdGet_Click()
        Dim Emp(1 To 10) As Employee
        Dim nI As Integer
        Open App.Path & "\EMPLOYEE.TXT" For Binary As #1
        For nI = 1 To 10
            Get #1, , Emp(nI)
            Print Emp(nI).FirstName
        Next nI
        Close #1
    End Sub
```

Figure 13-3 shows an example of the output after the Put Data and Get Data buttons are clicked.

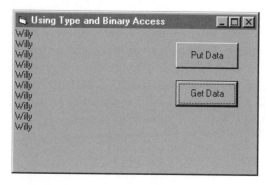

Figure 13-3.
Writing to and reading from a Type data structure using the binary access mode.

Notice that the EMPLOYEE.TXT file is accessed 10 times in this sample program, to read in 10 data records, but that this procedure actually reads 2960 bytes from the file. Each record in the Employee Type data structure contains 296 bytes of data, so the entire structure is read from the file each time the Get statement is executed.

WARNING: As a general rule, you should always read binary file data by using the same Type data structure that was used to write the data. Starting with Visual Basic 4, data layout in memory and in binary files became very tricky and unpredictable because of internal changes necessary for the global programming goals of Unicode and because of the need to make 32-bit applications run faster.

The 32-bit version of Visual Basic internally manipulates all string data, even within Type data structures, as 2-bytes-per-character Unicode data. When performing file I/O, Visual Basic converts all Unicode strings to 1-byte-per-character ANSI strings, which completely changes the overall size of Type data structures that contain strings.

Type data structure items are double word–aligned to achieve the most efficient I/O throughput possible in 32-bit operating systems. This extra padding also changes the exact layout of the data within a Type data structure.

Be careful!

Strings

A fast and flexible method of retrieving a chunk of data from a file is to open the data file in binary mode and then use the Get statement to place the entire chunk of data in a string variable. To retrieve a given number of bytes from a file, first set the size of the string. The Get statement will read bytes until the string is filled, so if the string is one character long, 1 byte will be read from the file. Similarly, if the string is 10,000 bytes long, 10,000 bytes from the file will be loaded. The following code demonstrates this technique using any generic text file named TEST.TXT:

```
Option Explicit

Private Sub Form_Click()
    Dim sA As String * 1
    Open App.Path & "\TEST.TXT" For Binary As #1
    Get #1, , sA
    Print sA
    Close #1
End Sub

Private Sub Text1_Click()
    Dim sB As String
    Open App.Path & "\TEST.TXT" For Binary As #1
```

(continued)

```
        sB = Space(LOF(1))
        Get #1, , sB
        Text1.Text = sB
        Close #1
End Sub
```

In the Form_Click event procedure, a fixed-length string of 1 byte is used to get 1 byte from the TEST.TXT file. In the Text1_Click event procedure, the string *sB* is filled with spaces to set the size of the variable to the size of the file. The Get statement is then used with the *sB* variable to input a chunk of data from the TEST.TXT data file that is equal in length to the string variable *sB*. This results in the variable *sB* being assigned the entire contents of the file.

> **NOTE:** This isn't supposed to work! Microsoft warns us that Unicode character conversions "might" cause binary file data loaded into strings to become corrupted. However, testing the above technique with files containing all 256 possible byte values revealed nothing unexpected. Each byte of the file is assumed to be an ANSI character, and when it is loaded into a string, each byte is padded with a binary byte value of 0 to make it a Unicode character. Everything works as it has in earlier versions of Visual Basic, but in future versions everything might not work that way. The solution is to start using binary arrays now for this type of work instead of strings. Read on!

Note that strings were limited to approximately 65,535 bytes in size in earlier, 16-bit, versions of Microsoft Windows and are now limited to approximately 2 billion bytes in Microsoft Windows NT and Microsoft Windows 95. This means, in most cases, that you can load the entire file into a single string using one Get statement. Just be sure to size the string to the file's size before calling Get by using the LOF function, as shown in the code above.

See Also...

- The Secret application in Chapter 32, "Advanced Applications," for a demonstration of binary file I/O

Byte Arrays

One way to process each byte of a file is to load the file into a string (see above) and then use the ASC function to convert each character of the string to its ASCII numeric value. However, with the introduction of Visual Basic's Byte variable type, byte processing can now be accomplished much more efficiently.

In the following code, I've created a dynamic Byte array that can be dimensioned to match a file's size. You can load the entire file into the array by passing the Byte array variable to the Get statement, as shown here:

```
Option Explicit

Private Sub Form_Click()
    Dim nI As Integer
    Open App.Path & "\TEST.TXT" For Binary As #1
    ReDim byBuf(1 To LOF(1)) As Byte
    Get #1, , byBuf()
    For nI = LBound(byBuf) To UBound(byBuf)
        Print Chr(byBuf(nI));
    Next nI
    Close #1
End Sub
```

The Connection Between Strings and Byte Arrays

The preceding example hints at the connection between strings and Byte arrays. But there's much more to this duality, so I'll describe some of the details you'll need to know to work effectively with the Byte array type.

Byte arrays will be used more and more for the kinds of byte manipulations we used to accomplish with strings. To ease this transition, you can plop a Byte array into the middle of many commands and functions that, in the past, would work only with string parameters. For example, as shown in the following code, you can assign a string to a Byte array and a Byte array to a string:

```
Option Explicit

Private Sub Form_Click()
    Dim nI As Integer
    Dim sA As String, sC As String
    Dim byB() As Byte
    sA = "ABC"
    byB() = sA
    'Displays 65 0 66 0 67 0
    For nI = LBound(byB) To UBound(byB)
        Print byB(nI);
    Next nI
    Print
    sC = byB()
    'Displays ABC
    Print sC
    'Notice actual size of string
    Print sA, Len(sA), LenB(sA)
End Sub
```

Figure 13-4 shows an example of the output when the form is clicked.

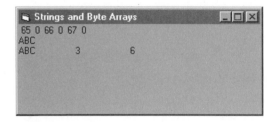

Figure 13-4.
Working with strings and Byte arrays.

Notice that I've declared the Byte array *byB()* as a dynamic array. In general, you should always declare your Byte arrays as dynamic when assigning strings to them. Visual Basic will then be able to automatically expand or collapse the size of the array to match the length of the string, just as it does for dynamic strings.

I suggest you take the time to run the preceding code and study its output carefully. It will help you understand how string variables are maintained in memory as Unicode characters. The 3-byte string *ABC* is shuffled from the string *sA* into the Byte array *byB()*, and then all the bytes in *byB()* are printed out. Instead of the three expected byte values of 65, 66, and 67 (ASCII representations of *A, B,* and *C*), we find that the Byte array actually contains six byte values. This is because the three-character string is maintained in memory in a 6-byte Unicode format and the contents of this string are shuffled straight across, with no conversion back to its 3-byte ANSI string representation upon assignment to the Byte array. Understanding this can help you clearly visualize how Unicode strings are manipulated in memory by Visual Basic.

The 6-byte array is then assigned to a second string, *sC*. Toward the end of the code listing, I added a Print command to display *sA*, its length in number of characters, and its length in actual byte count. Len and LenB, respectively, provide this information.

The StrConv Function

StrConv is a handy conversion function that lets you control the conversion of string data to and from Unicode representation. The code on the following page demonstrates the StrConv function as it forces a 3-byte string to transfer its ANSI characters to a 3-byte array and then shows how you can use StrConv to transfer a 3-byte array into a string.

```
Option Explicit

Private Sub Form_Click()
    Dim nI As Integer
    Dim sA As String
    Dim byB() As Byte
    sA = "ABC"
    byB() = StrConv(sA, vbFromUnicode)
    'Displays 65 66 67
    For nI = LBound(byB) To UBound(byB)
        Print byB(nI);
    Next nI
    Print
    sA = byB()
    'This displays a question mark
    Print sA
    sA = StrConv(byB(), vbUnicode)
    'Displays ABC 3 6
    Print sA, Len(sA), LenB(sA)
End Sub
```

Figure 13-5 shows an example of the output when the form is clicked.

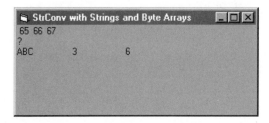

Figure 13-5.
Using the StrConv function with strings and Byte arrays.

> NOTE: What happens if you assign a Byte array to a string when the array bytes are not padded with extra 0 bytes, so as to be in proper internal Unicode format? The bytes transfer into the string, but Visual Basic doesn't know what the heck to do with those strange characters when you try to print the string. You'll get a question mark instead of whatever you might be expecting.

The constants *vbFromUnicode* and *vbUnicode* are just two of several constants defined for the StrConv function. Check the online help for more information about other handy uses for this versatile function.

By understanding the ways in which Byte arrays work hand in hand with strings and how you can control the ANSI/Unicode conversions by using the StrConv function, you will master the fast and efficient capabilities of binary file I/O.

Dear John, How Do I...

Build a General-Purpose File Object?

One of the great advantages of object-oriented programming is the ability to model real-world items in the form of code. These models, or *objects,* simplify programming because they hide from view the intricacies of working with the items. A well-designed object will have a set of intuitive methods and properties. For example, the File class module shown here handles binary file access through FileOpen and FileClose methods and through the Path, Filename, and Text properties:

```
'FILE.CLS
Option Explicit

'API functions for creating temporary files
Private Declare Function GetTempPath _
Lib "kernel32" Alias "GetTempPathA" ( _
    ByVal nBufferLength As Long, _
    ByVal lpBuffer As String _
) As Long

Private Declare Function GetTempFileName _
Lib "kernel32" Alias "GetTempFileNameA" ( _
    ByVal lpszPath As String, _
    ByVal lpPrefixString As String, _
    ByVal wUnique As Long, _
    ByVal lpTempFileName As String _
) As Long

'Internal variables maintained by object
Private msPath As String
Private msFileName As String
Private mlLength As Long
Private mnFileNum As Integer

'Establish default settings for the class
Private Sub Class_Initialize()
```

(continued)

```
        Dim lPathLen As Long
        'Set Path and Filename to temporary values
        'when class is created to provide defaults
        'if no name/path specified in FileOpen
        msPath = Space(144)
        lPathLen = GetTempPath(144, msPath)
        'Trim off null character
        msPath = Left(msPath, lPathLen)
        msFileName = Space(144)
        GetTempFileName msPath, 0, 0, msFileName
        'Trim off null character
        msFileName = Mid(msFileName, 1, InStr(msFileName, Chr(0)) - 1)
        'Trim off path portion
        msFileName = Mid(msFileName, lPathLen + 1)
    End Sub

Public Sub FileOpen( _
    Optional Path As String, _
    Optional Filename As String _
)
        'Check whether file is already open; if it is, display a message
        If mnFileNum Then
            MsgBox "A file is already open. " & _
                "Close before opening another.", , "Error"
            Exit Sub
        End If
        'Use provided path and filename if arguments are included;
        'otherwise, use the defaults (temp path and filename)
        If Path = "" Then
            Path = msPath
        Else
            msPath = Path
        End If
        If Filename = "" Then
            Filename = msFileName
        Else
            msFileName = Filename
        End If
        mnFileNum = FreeFile()
        Open msPath & msFileName For Binary As mnFileNum
    End Sub

'Path read-only property
Public Property Get Path() As String
        Path = msPath
End Property
```

(continued)

```vb
'FileName read-only property
Public Property Get Filename() As String
    Filename = msFileName
End Property

Public Sub FileClose()
    'Close the open file
    Close mnFileNum
    'Reset the file number variable so that the class
    'knows there is no open file
    mnFileNum = 0
End Sub

'Text read/write property
Public Property Get Text() As String
    'Display message if a file is not open
    If mnFileNum = 0 Then
        MsgBox "File is not open."
        Exit Property
    End If
    'Retrieve contents of file
    Dim sText As String
    sText = Space(LOF(msFilenum))
    Get msFilenum, , sText
End Property

Public Property Let Text(Text As String)
    'Display message if a file is not open
    If mnFileNum = 0 Then
        MsgBox "File is not open."
        Exit Property
    End If
    'Close file
    Me.FileClose
    'Delete file
    Kill msPath & msFileName
    'Open file again
    Me.FileOpen msPath, msFileName
    'Write contents of file
    Put mnFileNum, 1, Text
End Property

'Be sure file is closed before destroying object
Private Sub Class_Terminate()
    If mnFileNum Then FileClose
End Sub
```

One of the neat features of the File class is that you don't have to provide a filename to create a file—the name and path simply default to temporary settings provided by Windows. The File class also hides the file number used by the Open and Close statements. This protects the file from being closed outside of the class module.

The Text property of the File class reads or writes the entire contents of the file. The write operation is performed by deleting the file and then creating an entirely new file of the same name. This is the easiest and quickest way to correctly size the file. The following code demonstrates the File object in action:

```
Option Explicit

Private Sub Form_Click()
    'Create a new file object
    Dim filTemp As New File
    'Open a file using temporary file defaults
    filTemp.FileOpen
    'Write some text to file
    filTemp.Text = "Read this"
    'Change text in file
    filTemp.Text = "Now this"
    'Close file
    filTemp.FileClose
    'Display file in Notepad
    Shell "Notepad " & filTemp.Path & filTemp.Filename
End Sub
```

Figure 13-6 shows an example of the file that is displayed in Notepad when the form is clicked.

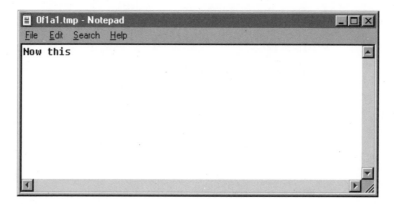

Figure 13-6.
Text file created with the File object.

The File class shown here is a substantial building block. With a few modifications, you can create a file converter or provide easy access to structured data.

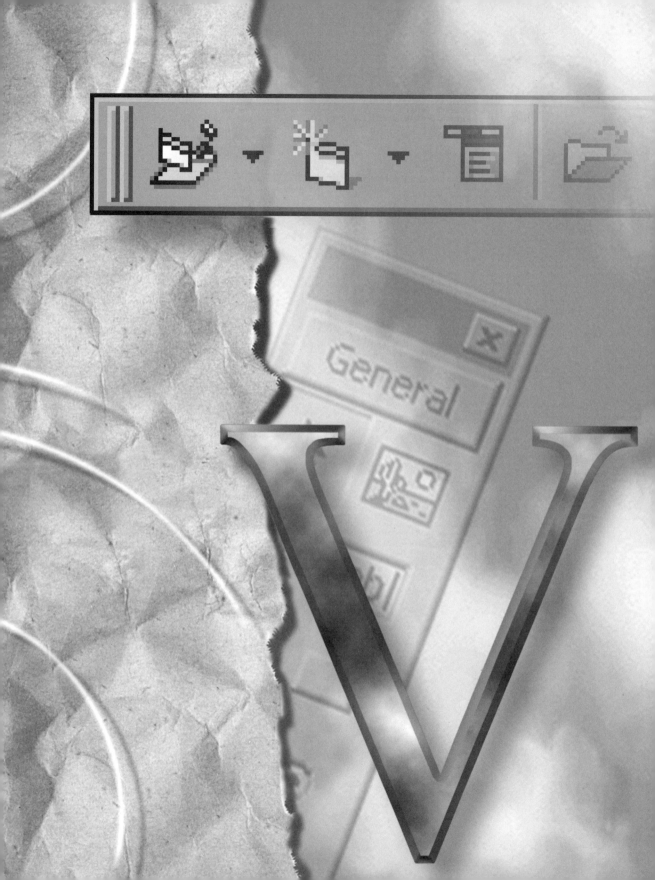

CHAPTER FOURTEEN

The Registry

In 32-bit Microsoft Windows 95 and Microsoft Windows NT, the *Registry* replaces the initialization (INI) files used by most 16-bit Windows-based applications to keep track of information between sessions. The Registry is a systemwide database designed to let all 32-bit applications keep track of application-specific data between runs of the application. The transition from using INI files to using the Registry is easy because Visual Basic provides a handful of functions that simplify the reading and writing of the Registry. Typical information stored in the Registry includes user preferences for colors, fonts, window positions, and the like. This chapter explains and demonstrates these Registry functions.

Dear John, How Do I...

Read and Write to the Registry?

Visual Basic provides four functions that are used for reading and writing to the Registry: GetSetting, SaveSetting, DeleteSetting, and GetAllSettings. The first three functions are, in my opinion, the most important.

As indicated by their names, these functions get or save (read or write) string data (settings) from or to the Registry and delete any settings no longer used. GetAllSettings is a special function that lets you get all settings from a section in one call. This is an extension of the GetSetting function, so I'll leave it up to you to read the online help for more information about this particular function.

To demonstrate the first three functions, I've created a Registry class and a small test application that lets you get and save settings in the Registry. The object defined by the Registry class has properties corresponding to the parameters for the Registry functions as well as methods to get, save, and delete Registry entries based on the property values. The four string properties are Appname, Section, Key, and Setting. The code on the following page defines all of the Registry object's properties and methods.

```
'REGISTRY.CLS
Option Explicit

Private msAppname As String
Private msSection As String
Private msKey As String
Private msSetting As String

'~~~AppName
Public Property Get Appname() As String
    Appname = msAppname
End Property
Public Property Let Appname(ByVal sAppName As String)
    msAppname = sAppName
End Property

'~~~Section
Public Property Get Section() As String
    Section = msSection
End Property
Public Property Let Section(ByVal sSection As String)
    msSection = sSection
End Property

'~~~Key
Public Property Get Key() As String
    Key = msKey
End Property
Public Property Let Key(ByVal sKey As String)
    msKey = sKey
End Property

'~~~Setting
Public Property Get Setting() As String
    Setting = msSetting
End Property
Public Property Let Setting(ByVal sSetting As String)
    msSetting = sSetting
End Property

'~~~RegGet
Public Sub RegGet()
    msSetting = GetSetting(msAppname, msSection, msKey)
End Sub
```

(continued)

```
'~~~RegSave
Public Sub RegSave()
    SaveSetting msAppname, msSection, msKey, msSetting
End Sub

'~~~RegDel
Public Sub RegDel()
    DeleteSetting msAppname, msSection, msKey
End Sub
```

To try out an instance of this new Registry object, start a Standard EXE application and add a class module to it. Change the class Name property to *Registry*, add the previous code to it, and save the file as REGISTRY.CLS. Modify the application's startup form as follows: Change the form's Name property to *Registry_Form1*, and save this form using the same name. (I saved the project itself using the name REGISTRY_TEST.VBP.) Add two text boxes, named *txtKey* and *txtSetting*, and three command buttons, named *cmdSave*, *cmdGet*, and *cmdDel*. If you want, add labels above the TextBox controls and edit the various Text and Caption properties, as shown in Figure 14-1 on the following page. Add the following code to the form:

```
Option Explicit

Dim regTest As New Registry

Private Sub cmdSave_Click()
    regTest.Key = txtKey.Text
    regTest.Setting = txtSetting.Text
    regTest.RegSave
End Sub

Private Sub cmdGet_Click()
    regTest.Key = txtKey.Text
    regTest.RegGet
    txtSetting.Text = regTest.Setting
End Sub

Private Sub cmdDel_Click()
    regTest.Key = txtKey.Text
    regTest.RegDel
End Sub

Private Sub Form_Load()
    regTest.Appname = App.Title
    regTest.Section = "Testing"
End Sub
```

Figure 14-1 shows the form during development.

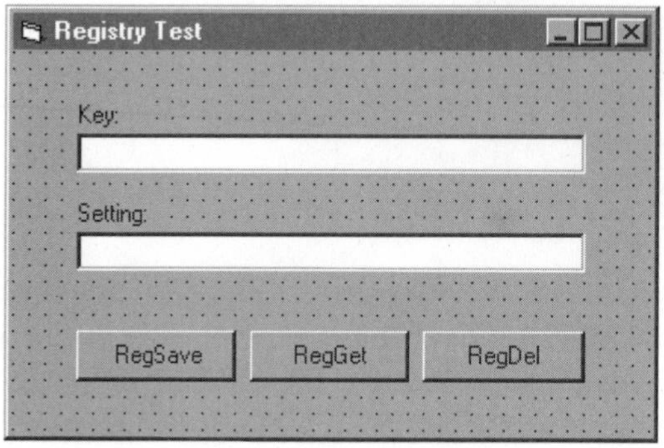

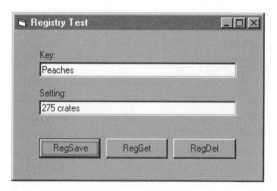

Figure 14-1.
The Registry_Test form at design time.

Notice in the Form_Load event procedure that I've assigned the Title property of the test program's App object to the Appname property of the *regTest* object, and I've hardwired a Section string, *Testing.* You can, of course, change these properties as desired.

At runtime, type a string in the Key text box. To save a setting for your Key, type a string in the Setting text box and click the RegSave button. To access a previously stored setting, enter the identifying Key string and click the RegGet button. Click RegDel to delete the entry for the given Key from the Registry.

Figure 14-2 shows the test application at runtime.

Figure 14-2.
The Registry_Test form at runtime.

A couple of notes about the Registry object's internal code are in order. The RegGet method calls the GetSetting function, which has an optional *default* parameter that I chose not to use here. If you provide a string for this parameter, the default string is returned by the function if the indicated key is not found in the Registry. If you don't provide a *default* parameter, an empty string is returned if nothing is found, and this scenario works just fine for my object.

The best way to see exactly how the Registry is modified as you save and get settings is to run the Registry Editor application included in Windows 95 and Windows NT version 4.0. Click the Start button on the Windows task bar, choose Run, type *Regedit,* and click OK. As shown in Figure 14-3, these Visual Basic functions always save and get settings from the HKEY_CURRENT_USER-\Software\VB and VBA Program Settings section of the Registry, and this is where you should always look for them. Notice that the Appname and Section properties further define the location of saved settings. In this example, the Appname property is *Registry_Test,* and the Section property is *Testing.* These show up as part of the tree structure on the left of the Registry Editor's display. On the right side of the display, you'll find the specific Key and Setting properties. In this example, I entered settings for the three keys: Apples, Oranges, and Peaches. While you are experimenting with the Registry_Test sample application, be sure to refresh the Registry Editor's display after you save or delete settings, either by pressing F5 or by choosing Refresh from the View menu.

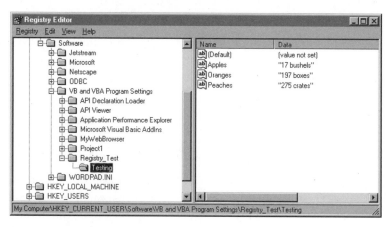

Figure 14-3.
The contents of the Registry as displayed by the Registry Editor.

285

See Also...

- The Ssaver application in Chapter 27, "Graphics," and the VBClock application in Chapter 29, "Date and Time," for a demonstration of the use of the Registry

Dear John, How Do I...

Remember the State of an Application?

The answer to this question is just an extension of the previous section. Use a Registry object's RegSave method to save the current state of your application, and use RegGet to recall the state. An excellent place to put this code is in the Form_Unload and Form_Load event procedures. With this arrangement, when the form is loaded but before it is actually drawn onto the screen, the previous size, shape, location, color, and any other detail of the state of the application can be restored. Similarly, immediately before the form is unloaded, the current state can be written for the next time the application is run.

See Also...

- "Dear John, How Do I...Read and Write to the Registry?" earlier in this chapter for information about manipulating the Registry

- The Ssaver application in Chapter 27, "Graphics," and the VBClock application in Chapter 29, "Date and Time," for a demonstration of the use of the Registry to save and restore an application's state

Dear John, How Do I...

Associate a File Type with an Application?

The Registry stores information about how Windows responds to events on the desktop and in the Windows Explorer. For instance, if you double-click on a desktop file named MYFILE.TXT, Windows opens the file in the Notepad application. This association between files with the extension TXT and NOTEPAD.EXE is set in the Registry.

To examine the Registry entry for a file type, first locate the file type in the Registry Editor. You can find file types under the HKEY_CLASSES_ROOT key. Select the file type branch on the left side of the Registry Editor, and choose Export Registry File from the Registry menu. The Export Registry File dialog box is displayed, as shown in Figure 14-4. Enter a name for the file, verify that the Selected Branch option in the Export Range section is selected, and then click Save.

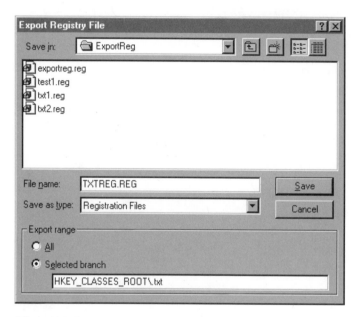

Figure 14-4.
Exporting a branch in the Registry.

The Export Registry File command creates a text file with an REG extension. The following text shows the results of exporting the .txt and txtfile branches of the HKEY_CLASSES_ROOT key and merging them into one REG file. (Note that depending on how your system is configured, you might obtain different results.)

```
REGEDIT4

[HKEY_CLASSES_ROOT\.txt]
"Content Type"="text/plain"
@="txtfile"
```

(continued)

```
[HKEY_CLASSES_ROOT\.txt\ShellNew]
"NullFile"=""

[HKEY_CLASSES_ROOT\txtfile]
@="Text Document"

[HKEY_CLASSES_ROOT\txtfile\DefaultIcon]
@="c:\\windows\\SYSTEM\\shell32.dll,-152"

[HKEY_CLASSES_ROOT\txtfile\shell]

[HKEY_CLASSES_ROOT\txtfile\shell\open]

[HKEY_CLASSES_ROOT\txtfile\shell\open\command]
@="c:\\windows\\NOTEPAD.EXE %1"
```

You can modify the exported Registry file to create your own file type associations. For example, the following REG file creates an association between the file type MYA and MYAPP.EXE:

```
REGEDIT4

[HKEY_CLASSES_ROOT\.mya]
"Content Type"="VBRegSample"
@="MyApp"

[HKEY_CLASSES_ROOT\.mya\ShellNew]
"NullFile"=""

[HKEY_CLASSES_ROOT\MyApp]
@="My File"

[HKEY_CLASSES_ROOT\MyApp\DefaultIcon]
@="c:\\VB Workshop\\Samples\\Chapter 14\\MyApp.EXE,0"

[HKEY_CLASSES_ROOT\MyApp\shell]

[HKEY_CLASSES_ROOT\MyApp\shell\open]

[HKEY_CLASSES_ROOT\MyApp\shell\open\command]
@="c:\\VB Workshop\\Samples\\Chapter 14\\MyApp.EXE %1"
```

The items enclosed in square brackets are the Registry keys. The Registry keys establish the structure of the Registry data. The items to the right of the equal signs are the Registry data. An @ character in front of the equal sign indicates that the data is a default value. The first entry for the file type MYA tells Windows that the information for the application is found under the key [HKEY_CLASSES_ROOT\MyApp].

The following table describes some of the more important Registry keys.

Key	Description
\DefaultIcon	Indicates the file that contains the icon to dis-play for this file type in the Windows shell. The second argument is the index of the icon in the file's resource list. Visual Basic applications seem to support displaying only the first icon (index 0).
\Shell\Open\Command	The command line executed when the user opens a file of this type from the Windows s hell. The %1 argument is the filename passed to the application's command line interface.
\Shell\Print\Command	The command line executed when the user prints a file of this type from the Windows shell. The %1 argument is the filename passed to the application's command line interface.

To add these entries to the Registry, run Regedit with the registration filename as an argument. Add a /s switch to run Regedit silently so that the user doesn't see the process. This command line imports the MYAPP.REG file into the Registry:

```
RegEdit /s MyApp.Reg
```

NOTE: It is always a good idea to make a backup of the Registry before making modifications to it.

Figure 14-5 shows the .mya and MyApp branches in the Registry after MYAPP.REG has been imported.

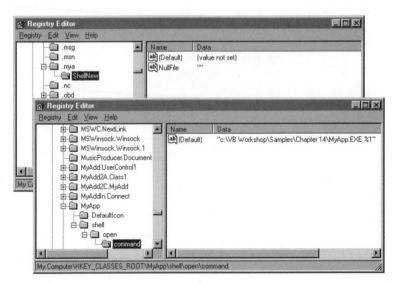

Figure 14-5.
Portions of the Registry after MYAPP.REG has been imported.

Retrieving Command Line Arguments

Now that you've seen how your application's Open, Print, and other command data can be entered in the Registry, let's take a look at how your application can grab and use command line arguments. Applications that respond to Open, Print, and other commands from the Windows shell can accept command line arguments. Using the Visual Basic Command function, the following code shows how to retrieve the command line arguments:

```
Dim mstrFile As String

Private Sub Form_Load()
    'Get command line argument
    mstrFile = Command()
    'If there was an argument, do something
    If Len(mstrFile) Then
        OpenFile 'Or take other action
    End If
End Sub
```

See the online help for the Command function for an example of how to parse multiple arguments from the command line.

 See Also...

- *Inside the Registry for Microsoft Windows 95* by Günter Born (Microsoft Press, 1997) to learn more about the Registry

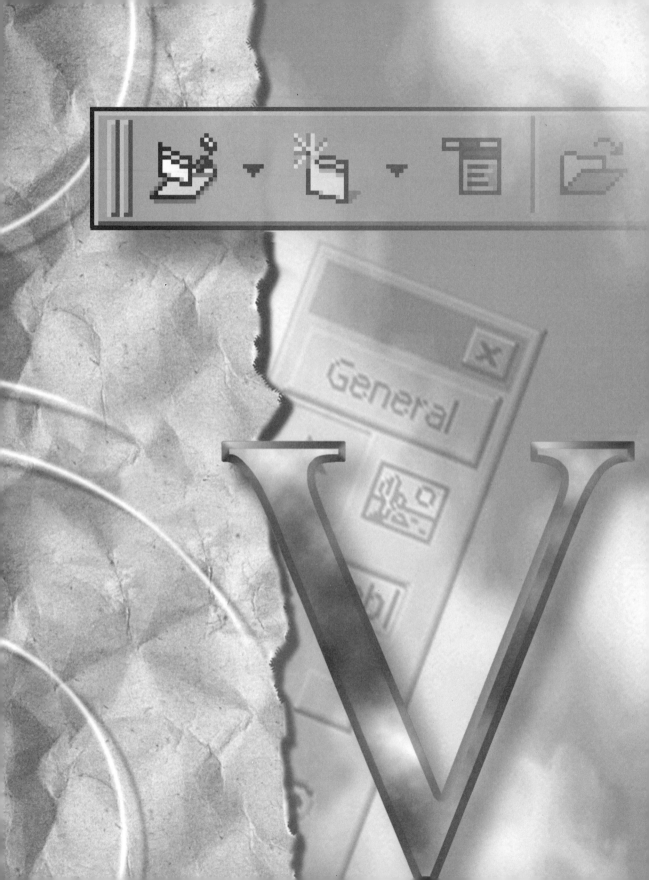

CHAPTER FIFTEEN

Help Files

If your application has users, you'll probably have to tell them how to use it, and the best way to do that is with online help. There are some good help authoring tools on the market, such as RoboHelp, HelpBreeze, and the shareware VBHelp. These tools were essential with previous versions of Visual Basic, when the only help tool available from Microsoft was the Help Compiler. But things have changed a bit.

Visual Basic includes a greatly improved help tool called the Microsoft Help Workshop. This tool is squirreled away in the \TOOLS\HCW directory on the Visual Basic CD-ROM. You can install the Help Workshop by running the setup program in this directory. The Help Workshop finally provides a graphical user interface for organizing help projects and for compiling and debugging help files. The Help Workshop is not a complete authoring environment, but it's definitely worth a look.

Also worth a look are the help features provided by the 32-bit version of WinHelp. You can include a real table of contents, full-text search capabilities, AVI clips, and a bunch of new help macros in your help files. If you choose an add-on help tool, be sure that it's a current version so that you can take advantage of these new features.

In this chapter, I touch on some of the capabilities of the Help Workshop and provide an introduction to the HTML Help Workshop. I haven't included full instructions for creating help files—that's beyond the scope of a single chapter. Besides, the Help Workshop and the HTML Help Workshop include some pretty good help of their own. I also cover how to integrate help into your Visual Basic application. These techniques have never been gathered in one place—until now that is!

Dear John, How Do I...

Create a Help File?

The Help Workshop is a huge improvement over the old command line compiler. For one thing, the Help Workshop handles larger source files without a problem—the old Help Compiler ran out of memory when working with graphics files over a certain size. The Help Workshop also handles long filenames and has a graphical user interface, shown in Figure 15-1.

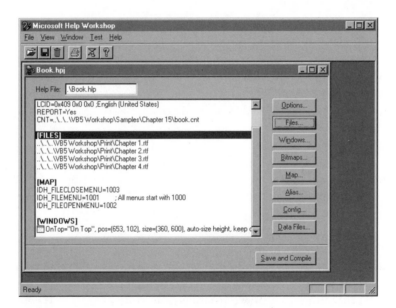

Figure 15-1.
The Microsoft Help Workshop (HCW.EXE).

The Help Workshop creates a help project file (*.HPJ), which lists the source document files used to create the help file. The source documents must be saved in rich-text format (RTF) and can be created using Microsoft Word or another Windows word processor that supports the necessary formatting requirements. The Help Workshop launches the compiler (HCRTF.EXE) and displays compiler errors and warnings once compilation is complete, as shown in Figure 15-2.

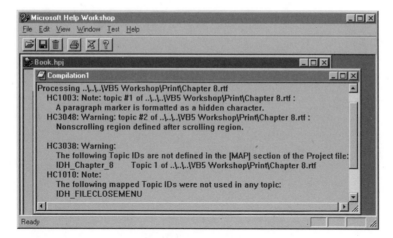

Figure 15-2.

Errors, warnings, and messages are displayed after compilation.

Help Topic Basics

Within a help source file, topics are separated by manual page breaks. You use footnotes to set a topic's title, search keywords, and the unique topic ID used by the Help system to link that topic to other topics. You create links to other topics using underlining and hidden text. Figure 15-3 shows a help topic with its various parts.

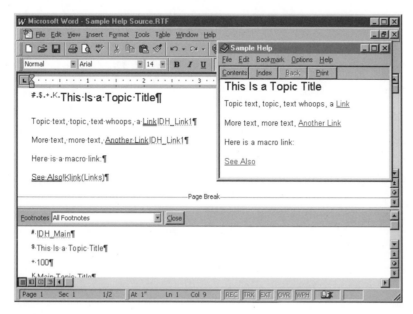

Figure 15-3.

The anatomy of a Help topic.

The footnotes and formatting that you can add to a help topic file are listed below.

Footnotes/Formatting	Meaning
$	Topic title.
#	Topic ID; used to link to this topic from other topics.
K	Search keywords. These keywords will be listed in the help file's Index for this topic; multiple words are separated by semicolons. Can be used with KLink macro to create keyword links.
+	Browse sequence. The number entered for this footnote determines the order of the topics in the help file.
A	Associated keyword. Similar to a K footnote, but the footnote text doesn't appear in the Index. These footnotes are used with the ALink macro to create keyword links.
!	Macro. Help macros entered in the footnote text are run when the topic is displayed.
Double underline	Link to another topic. Links must be followed by hidden text listing the topic ID of the topic to jump to.
Single underline	Pop-up link; used for definitions and other short topics.
Hidden text	Topic ID of link. This ID must match the # footnote of a topic in the help project or an error will occur during compilation.

Creating a Project File

A project file is a text file created using the Help Workshop that contains information about the files to be included in the help file and other settings. A project file has an HPJ extension. To create a new project file, choose New from the File menu to display the New dialog box. Select Help Project, and click OK. In the Project File Name dialog box, select a location, enter a name for the new project file with an HPJ extension, and then click the Save button. Figure 15-4 shows the project window that is displayed.

The Help Workshop project window contains various buttons that will display dialog boxes and allow you to configure your help file. If you click the Files button, you can add any topic files you created to the project file.

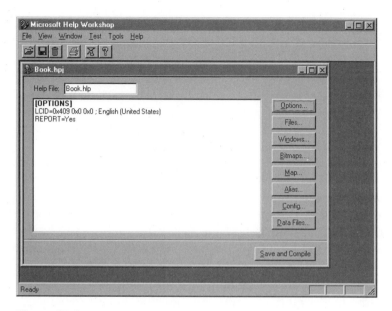

Figure 15-4.
The Help Workshop project window.

Compiling and Testing a Help File

Compiling a help file is a process in which the topic files, graphics, and project file are used to create a help file. You compile a help file by clicking the Save And Compile button in the project window, which launches the compiler (HCRTF.EXE). After compilation, any errors or warnings will be displayed. To test the new help file, click the Run WinHelp button in the Help Workshop and then click the View Help button in the View Help File dialog box.

Mapping Topic IDs

You enter topic IDs in your help file as strings. For example, you might type *IDH_FileMenu* in the # footnote for the help topic explaining the File menu. In your application, you enter the topic ID as a number. For example, you might type 1001 in the HelpContextID property for the File menu. The Help Workshop matches the name to the number in the [MAP] section of the help project file, as shown here:

```
[MAP]
IDH_FILEMENU=1001          ; All menus start with 1000
IDH_FILEOPENMENU=1002
IDH_FILECLOSEMENU=1003
```

Keeping this [MAP] section in sync with your application is essential. Some tools, such as HelpBreeze, generate a BAS module with these values as constants. It is also fairly easy to do this with Enums:

```
Enum HelpContext
    IDH_FILEMENU=1001              ' All menus start with 1000
    IDH_FILEOPENMENU=1002
    IDH_FILECLOSEMENU=1003
End Enum
```

Using Full-Text Search and Table of Contents

Two new help features appeared with Microsoft Windows 95 and Microsoft Windows NT: full-text search and table of contents. The full-text search capability is included with the 32-bit Help Viewer (WINHLP32.EXE). Even help files compiled for Microsoft Windows version 3.1 support this feature when viewed using WINHLP32.EXE.

Windows automatically builds a database of words in the help file for use with Find using the Find Setup Wizard, shown in Figure 15-5.

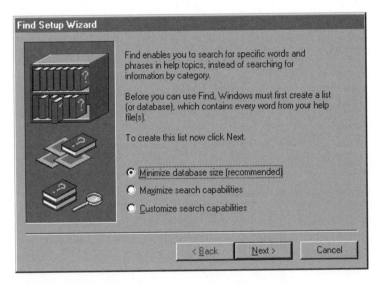

Figure 15-5.
The Find Setup Wizard.

The Help Contents list is built from a text file listed in the Options section of the Help project file. The contents text file has a simple format for each line, as shown in the following text.

```
; From HCW.CNT
1 Getting Started      ; Top-level topic, not a link
2 What is Help Workshop?=BAS_THE_HELP_COMPILER  ; Second-level topic.
2 Help Workshop components=SDK_FILES_DOCS
2 Notational Conventions=SDK_NOTE_CONVENTION
1 What's New in Version 4.0
2 WinHelp 4.0
3 Redesigned User Interface  ; Third-level topic
4 New Help Topics dialog box=NEW_WINHELP_INTERFACE
4 New context menu=NEW_WINHELP_CONTEXT_MENUS
4 New Options menu=NEW_WINHELP_OPTIONS_MENU
4 New annotation capabilities=NEW_ANNOTATION
4 Improved copying=NEW_WINHELP_COPY
4 New printing options=NEW_WINHELP_PRINTING
4 New ESC key function=NEW_KEY
4 Background color override=NEW_COLOR
```

You can maintain the contents file by opening the source file (CNT) in the Help Workshop. This lets you edit the file as it would appear in Help as shown in Figure 15-6.

You use the File New command to create a new contents file from the Help Workshop.

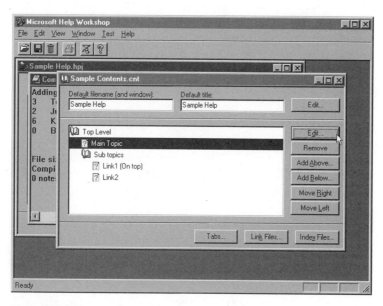

Figure 15-6.
A sample contents text file.

Creating Help Windows

Your help file can display topics in specific Help windows defined in the Help Workshop. To define a Help window in the Help Workshop, click the Windows button in the help project window and complete the dialog box shown in Figure 15-7.

Figure 15-7.
The Window Properties dialog box defining Help window that is always on top.

To display a topic in this window, type *>OnTop* after the topic ID in a link's hidden text. Clicking on that link will then display the topic in the OnTop window. You add window names to the entries in the contents file (CNT) the same way; just type *>OnTop* after the topic ID of the topic. Adding a > footnote to a topic displays the topic in the custom window when the user selects the topic from the Index.

Using Macros

Macros perform special tasks in the Help system. You can run a macro when a topic displays, when the user clicks a button, or when the user clicks on a link. To add a macro to a link, precede the macro name with a ! footnote in the hidden text of the link. For example, *Related Information!KLink(API, WinHelp)* runs the KLink macro to display a list of topics containing the keywords *API* or *WinHelp* when the user clicks Related Information, as shown in Figure 15-8.

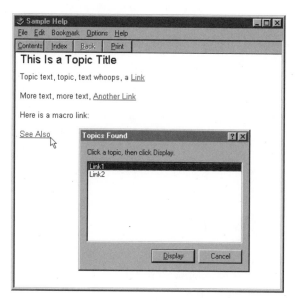

Figure 15-8.
The Topics Found dialog box displaying a list of topics that contain specific keywords.

A list of the help macros you can use can be found in the Help Workshop Help file HCW.HLP.

See Also...

- *Microsoft Windows 95 Help Authoring Kit* (Microsoft Press, 1995) for more information about Windows Help and using the Help Workshop

Dear John, How Do I...

Use the WinHelp API Function to Add Help Files to My Projects?

You can activate a help file using a direct Windows API call, which is the tried-and-true, old-fashioned way to access help. The function is named WinHelp, and you have to add a declaration for it in your application, as shown in the following example. In this sample code, the Contents topic of Visual Basic's main help file pops up when the form is clicked.

```
Option Explicit

Private Declare Function WinHelp _
Lib "user32" Alias "WinHelpA" ( _
    ByVal hWnd As Long, _
    ByVal lpHelpFile As String, _
    ByVal wCommand As Long, _
    ByVal dwData As Long _
) As Long

Const HELP_TAB = &HF

Private Sub Form_Click()
    Dim x
    x = WinHelp(hWnd, "HELP\VB5.HLP", HELP_TAB, 0)
End Sub
```

The *hWnd* parameter is set to the hWnd property of your application's form. The *lpHelpFile* parameter is a string that contains the name of the help file to be activated. The *wCommand* parameter is one of the predefined constants for controlling this function. (Most of these constants are listed under the MSComDlg entry of the Object Browser, after the CommonDialog control is added to the Toolbox; in the online help, under Help Constants; and in the table at the end of this section.) The *dwData* parameter can take on several types of values, depending on the value of *wCommand*. In particular, if *wCommand* is set to *cdlHelpContext*, *dwData*'s value determines which help file topic is displayed.

To demonstrate how this works, the following WinHelp function activates the Visual Basic help file and then displays a specific topic. (You will need to add the Microsoft Common Dialog control to your toolbox, and you may need to edit the path to the location of VB5.HLP on your computer.)

```
Private Sub Form_Click()
    Dim x
    x = WinHelp(hWnd, "HELP\VB5.HLP", cdlHelpContext, 700)
End Sub
```

The Keyword Not Found topic will be displayed when the help file starts because I've set the *wCommand* parameter to the *cdlHelpContext* constant and the *dwData* parameter to the Keyword Not Found topic number. (Some help authoring tools, such as RoboHelp, automate the creation of a BAS file that contains constants for all topics—this is a great time-saver.)

There are several other variations on the function call that you might find useful. Each of the constants listed in the table on the following page, when passed in the *wCommand* parameter, causes a specific action to be carried out by the WinHelp function. (Most of these constants are defined by Visual Basic for the CommonDialog control, hence the *cdl* prefixes.) For example, to display help information about how to use the Help system itself, use the constant *cdlHelpHelpOnHelp*.

Constant	Value	Description
cdlHelpContext	1	Displays help for a particular topic.
cdlHelpQuit	2	Closes the specified help file.
cdlHelpIndex	3	Displays the index of the specified help file.
HELP_FINDER	11	Displays the Help Topics dialog box with the last selected tab displayed. You must define this constant in your application because it is not included in the intrinsic constants.
HELP_TAB	15	Displays the Help Topics dialog box with the tab index specified by *dwData* selected. (The Contents tab is 0, the Index tab is −2, and the Find tab is −1.) You must define this constant in your application because it is not included in the intrinsic constants.
cdlHelpContents	3	Displays the Contents topic in the current help file. This constant is provided for compatibility with earlier versions of help; new applications should display the Help Topics dialog box by using *HELP_FINDER* or *HELP_TAB*.
cdlHelpHelpOnHelp	4	Displays help for using the help application itself.
cdlHelpSetIndex	5	Sets the current index for multi-index help.
cdlHelpSetContents	5	Designates a specific topic as the Contents topic.
cdlHelpContextPopup	8	Displays a topic identified by a context number.

(continued)

continued

Constant	Value	Description
cdlHelpForceFile	9	Creates a help file that displays text in only one font.
cdlHelpKey	257	Displays help for a particular keyword.
cdlHelpCommandHelp	258	Displays help for a particular command.
cdlHelpPartialKey	261	Calls the search engine in Windows Help.

These constants are predefined for the CommonDialog control. You can copy them into your code by using the Object Browser, or you can enable the CommonDialog control in your application, in which case all *cdl* constants will be automatically available. To do so, choose Components from the Project menu and check the Microsoft Common Dialog Control check box.) The constants are also discussed in the description of the HelpCommand property in Visual Basic's online help.

See Also...

- The Lottery application in Chapter 27, "Graphics," for a demonstration of the WinHelp function

Dear John, How Do I...

Add Context-Sensitive F1 Help to My Projects?

Forms, menu items, and most controls have a HelpContextID property that provides a context-sensitive jump to a specific help topic when the F1 key is pressed. The HelpFile property of the App object sets the path and name of the help file for the entire application, and the control with the focus determines which help topic is activated when F1 is pressed. If a control's Help-ContextID property is set to *0* (the default), the containing control or form is checked for a nonzero HelpContextID value. Finally, if the form's Help-ContextID is *0*, the help file's Contents topic is activated as the default.

This scheme works well for accessing context-sensitive help, which is activated when the F1 key is pressed, but how can we activate the help file programmatically without actually pressing the F1 key? Well, here's a slick trick that makes the HelpContextID property much more valuable: simply code your program to send an F1 keypress to your application using the SendKeys command. The SendKeys statement tells Windows to send keypresses to the window that currently has the focus, so the program responds as though the F1 key had been pressed.

The following code fragments demonstrate this technique:

```
Private Sub Form_Load()
    App.HelpFile = "HELP\VB5.HLP"
End Sub

Private Sub cmdHelp_Click()
    cmdHelp.HelpContextID = 700
    SendKeys "{F1}"
End Sub
```

The help file to be accessed is set in the Form_Load event procedure, but you can change the path and filename at any point in your program if you want to access multiple help files. In the cmdHelp_Click event procedure, you activate a specific topic in the help file by setting the HelpContextID property to the context number of the desired topic and then sending the F1 keypress using the SendKeys command. These HelpFile and HelpContextID properties can be set at runtime, as shown above, or you can set them at design time.

Menu items also have a HelpContextID property, but the designated topic in the help file will be activated only if the menu item is highlighted and the F1 key is manually pressed. If you click on the menu item and set up a SendKeys command in the menu event procedure, as shown in the following code, the topic that will be activated will not be determined by the menu item's HelpContextID value but by the HelpContextID value for whatever control currently has the focus:

```
Private Sub mnuHelp_Click()
    SendKeys "{F1}"
End Sub
```

This happens because the menu vanishes as soon as it is clicked on and the focus is returned to the control before the SendKeys command has time to send the F1 keypress. Using a menu command to get context-sensitive help for a control works well, but the behavior seems a little strange until you figure out the sequence of events.

Dear John, How Do I...

Use the CommonDialog Control to Add Help Files to My Projects?

The CommonDialog control provides a powerful and flexible way to access help files. Add a CommonDialog control to your form, set its relevant help file properties, and use the ShowHelp method to activate the Help system. It's that easy—you don't even need to use the control to display a dialog box. For example, the following code activates help for Windows help itself when the *cmdHelpContents* command button is clicked:

```
Private Sub cmdHelpContents_Click()
    dlgCommon.HelpCommand = cdlHelpHelpOnHelp
    dlgCommon.ShowHelp
End Sub
```

> **NOTE:** Setting the HelpCommand property to *cdlHelpContents* displays the first topic in a help file if Windows can't locate the help contents file.

Here's an example that shows the activation of a specific help file topic when a menu item is clicked:

```
Private Sub mnuHelp_Click()
    dlgCommon.HelpFile = "HELP\VB5.HLP"
    dlgCommon.HelpCommand = cdlHelpContext
    dlgCommon.HelpContext = 700
    dlgCommon.ShowHelp
End Sub
```

Dear John, How Do I...

Add WhatsThisHelp to a Form?

Windows 95 provides a few twists to the way help files work. One of the nice features is called WhatsThisHelp. A form that has this feature displays a question-mark button on the title bar that, when clicked, changes the mouse pointer to a special question-mark symbol. Clicking on a control on the form with this special pointer then activates a pop-up topic specific to the object clicked.

It's easy to add WhatsThisHelp to your Visual Basic form and its controls.

Start by setting the form's WhatsThisButton and WhatsThisHelp properties to *True*. The form's BorderStyle property must also be changed from its default setting before you'll see the question-mark box on the title bar. Set BorderStyle to either *1 - Fixed Single* or *3 - Fixed Dialog*. Figure 15-9 shows a form with the question-mark title bar button.

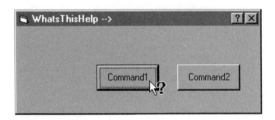

Figure 15-9.
A form showing the question-mark button that activates WhatsThisHelp.

To determine exactly which help file will be activated, you must set the HelpFile property of the App object to the path and name of the help file. You can do this either at design time or at runtime. To set the help file at design time, from the Project menu choose your project's Properties, select the General tab of the Project Properties dialog box, and in the Help File Name text box enter the name of the appropriate help file, including the full path to the file. To set the help file at runtime, assign the pathname and filename to the App.HelpFile property.

Finally, to define the topic in the help file that will pop up when a given control is clicked on, set that control's WhatsThisHelpID property to the topic's ID number.

WhatsThisMode

There's one other way you can use WhatsThisHelp popups. You can programmatically activate the special question-mark mouse pointer by using the WhatsThisMode method of the form. This is a useful technique when you want to add the WhatsThisHelp feature to a form that has its BorderStyle set to *2 - Sizable*. Figure 15-10 on the following page shows a form set up to activate WhatsThisHelp when the Get Help command button is clicked.

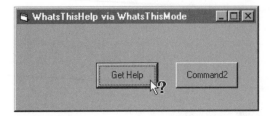

Figure 15-10.
A form showing how WhatsThisHelp can be activated using the WhatsThisMode method.

When the Get Help button is clicked, the mouse pointer changes to the special question mark, and the WhatsThisHelp state operates in exactly the same way as when the title bar question-mark button was clicked in the previous example. To use this WhatsThisHelp technique, all I had to do was set the form's WhatsThisHelp property to *True* and add one line to the command button's Click event. Here's the code:

```
Private Sub cmdGetHelp_Click()
    WhatsThisMode
End Sub
```

Dear John, How Do I...
Link Help to the World Wide Web?

Linking to the Web is probably the newest feature on most Help menus today. In fact, it's a great way to link your company's products to current product information whether you're using it for sales, technical support, or updating software.

Currently, the standards for interaction between standard Windows Help and HTML are being developed, so it is probably best to simply launch a Web browser in a separate window rather than to host a Web page within a help window. This is also the simplest way to implement Web access from within your application.

You can launch a browser application from a link in a help file using the ExecFile macro. For example, the following sample link starts the Internet Explorer and displays the Microsoft home page:

```
Microsoft web site!ExecFile(IExplore.Exe, http://www.microsoft.com)
```

Alternatively, you can add a browser to your application using the Visual Basic Application Wizard. The Application Wizard suggests Microsoft's home page as a default URL, but you can easily change it to your own setting, as shown in Figure 15-11.

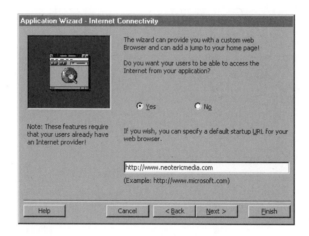

Figure 15-11.
Using the Application Wizard to generate a Web Browser form to add to your application.

Once you've created a Web Browser form, you can add it to any of your applications simply by including it in your existing projects. Display the form from a menu click event. To display a Web page based on the current context of your application, use the WebBrowser control's Navigate property, as shown here:

```
Const AltaVista = "http://www.altavista.digital.com/cgi-bin/" & _
    "query?pg=q&what=web&fmt=.&q="

Private Sub mnuWWW_Click()
    frmBrowser.Show
    frmBrowser.brwWebBrowser.Navigate AltaVista & _
        "Visual+Basic+Workshop"
End Sub
```

Figure 15-12 on the following page shows a Web page displayed in the Web Browser.

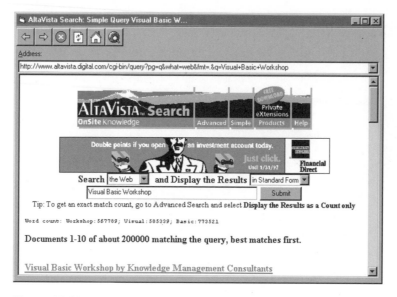

Figure 15-12.
The Web Browser form generated by the Application Wizard.

The preceding code uses AltaVista to demonstrate how you can pass a topic to the Web page you've selected. You can pass any URL string as an argument to Navigate.

See Also...

- Chapter 7, "The Internet Connection," for information about retrieving a file through FTP and using the Internet Transfer control's OpenURL and Execute methods

Dear John, How Do I...

Learn About HTML Help?

Microsoft has proposed a new standard for help based on HTML called Microsoft HTML Help. Eventually, all Microsoft products will use HTML Help. This new standard has similar appearance to WinHelp. Figure 15-13 shows a sample of HTML Help as viewed in the HTML Help browser.

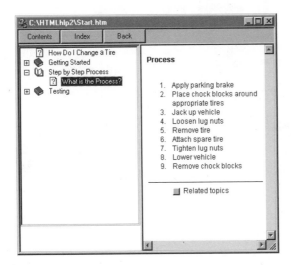

Figure 15-13.
A sample HTML Help file viewed in the HTML Help browser.

You can create HTML help using the Microsoft HTML Help Workshop, which is currently available for download on Microsoft's Web site at the following address: www.microsoft.com/workshop/author/htmhelp/.

The HTML Help Workshop includes the following components:

- The HTML Help Workshop: Lets you create and edit contents, index, and HTML files

- HTML Help ActiveX Control: Adds functionality such as a table of contents, an index, and related topics

- HTML Help Authoring DLL: Provides additional information about table of contents entries

Because the migration to this new help format will be an evolving process, consult Microsoft's Web site frequently for more information about HTML Help and the HTML Help Workshop.

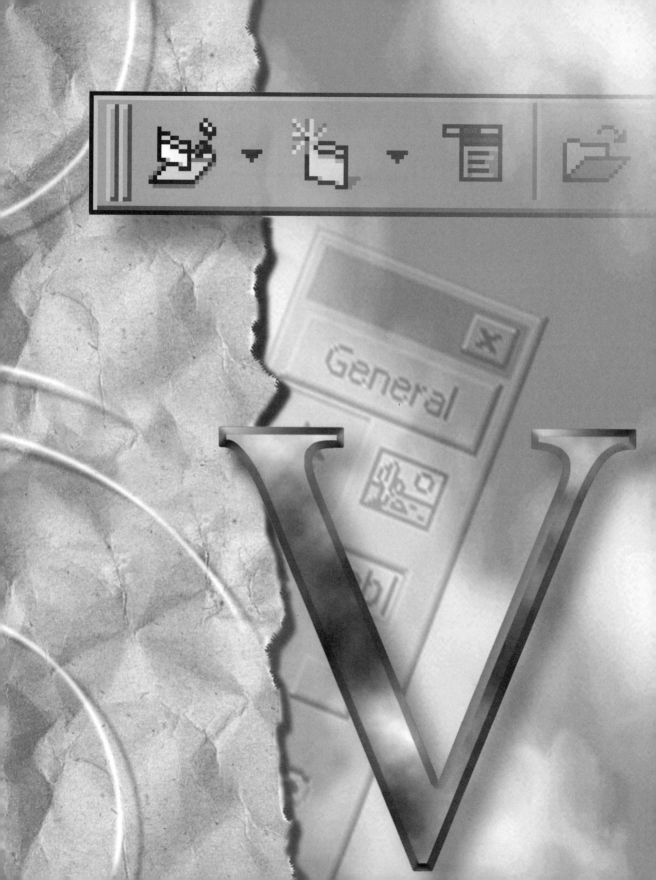

CHAPTER SIXTEEN

Security

Legal issues surrounding software development and software ownership rights can get thorny. One simple device used to prove authorship of an application is a hidden credits dialog box, sometimes referred to as an *Easter egg*. Another handy technique is to embed encrypted messages that declare authorship. Both of these methods are described in this chapter.

Passwords are an integral part of many applications for which security is an issue. It's easy to create a password entry dialog box in Visual Basic; I'll show you how here.

Dear John, How Do I...

Add a Hidden Credits Screen?

Sometimes they're called Easter eggs; sometimes they're not called anything at all. Many applications have a hidden, undocumented feature whereby the authors can put on an impressive little show. Creatively designed Easter eggs, such as the example in Figure 16-1, can be a lot of fun.

Figure 16-1.

A sample Easter egg (semisecret hidden credits screen).

Another purpose of these Easter eggs is to provide some legal protection for the author. If there's ever a disagreement as to who is the original creator of a piece of software, the real author can duly impress everyone by clicking here or there to open a dialog box that will prove authorship. Wouldn't that be fun to do in a court of law someday?

A straightforward approach is to create a special-purpose form to display whatever information you want on your hidden credits screen. The real trick is in deciding how such a form will be activated. I can offer general concepts and a specific example, but there's a lot of room for creativity in determining exactly how to activate your Easter egg.

It's easy to detect where the mouse is clicked on a form or control. The MouseDown and MouseUp events provide *x* and *y* parameters that tell you exactly where the mouse pointer is located when the mouse is clicked. Likewise, it's easy to determine the state of the shift keys (Shift, Ctrl, and Alt) and which mouse button or buttons are pressed. All of this information is passed as parameters to your MouseUp or MouseDown event–driven subprogram. So, for example, your application can check the status of the shift keys and the mouse buttons and then activate the Easter egg only if the right mouse button is pressed while the Shift key is held down and while the mouse pointer is located within 1 centimeter of the upper-right corner of a specific picture box.

Alternatively, by using static variables in your MouseUp or MouseDown event procedure, you can detect a specific sequence of left and right button clicks or watch for something like five clicks in less than 2 seconds.

In a similar way, you can secretly monitor a sequence of specific keypresses by setting the form's KeyPreview property to *True* and using the KeyDown event to keep track of recent keypresses. Let's look at some sample code to see how you might secretly detect the keypress sequence *EGG*. I've created a simple class module named Egg to handle the key code checking. The defined Egg object has just one write-only property, named Char. The object will display a message box if the key codes for *E*, *G*, and *G* are set in this property in exactly that sequence.

```
Option Explicit

Private msKeyPhrase As String * 3

'~~~.Char
Property Let Char(nKey As Integer)
```

(continued)

```
    Select Case nKey
        Case vbKeyE: msKeyPhrase = Mid$(msKeyPhrase, 2) & "E"
        Case vbKeyG: msKeyPhrase = Mid$(msKeyPhrase, 2) & "G"
        Case Else: msKeyPhrase = ""
    End Select
    If msKeyPhrase = "EGG" Then EasterEgg
End Property

Private Sub EasterEgg()
    MsgBox "JC and JW were here!!!"
End Sub
```

To try out the Egg object, add the following code to the main form:

```
Option Explicit

Dim eggTest As New Egg

Sub Form_Load()
    KeyPreview = True
End Sub

Sub Form_KeyDown(nKeyCode As Integer, nShift As Integer)
    eggTest.Char = nKeyCode
End Sub
```

The Form_Load event procedure sets the form's KeyPreview property to *True* so that all keypresses can be checked, no matter which control on the form has the focus. The private EasterEgg procedure in the Egg object displays a simple message box when *EGG* is typed. You'll want to enhance this program for your own use.

The Form_KeyDown event procedure is activated whenever the form, or any control on the form, has the focus and a key is pressed. The *eggTest* instance of the Egg object accumulates the three most recent keypresses by monitoring its Char property, and only if the pattern *EGG* is detected is the private EasterEgg procedure called.

See Also...

- The Dialogs application in Chapter 32, "Advanced Applications," for a hidden message screen that shows more detail and provides a working example of the activation of an Easter egg by a pattern of mouse clicks

Dear John, How Do I...
Create a Password Dialog Box?

In the earliest versions of Visual Basic, you had to jump through hoops and get out the smoke and mirrors to create a password dialog box, but ever since version 3 of Visual Basic this is an easy task.

The goal is to create a dialog box that displays asterisks, or some other chosen character, when the user types a secret password. The asterisks provide visual feedback about the number of characters typed, without giving away the actual password to anyone lurking within eyesight of the screen. The program must keep track of the actual characters typed by the user, of course, so that the password can be verified. A password dialog box is shown in Figure 16-2.

Figure 16-2.
A typical password dialog box.

A TextBox control is usually set up so that the user can enter text from the keyboard. Beginning with Visual Basic 3, the TextBox control has a property named PasswordChar. Set this property to the character that you want to use to hide the password as it is entered. Notice that the Text property will contain the actual characters entered, even though they won't be displayed.

The following code illustrates the basic technique. Add a text box named *txtPassword* and a command button named *cmdOK* to a form. The cmdOK_Click event procedure checks for a password match on *sesame*, but you can modify the code to check for matches with any string you want.

```
Option Explicit

Private Sub cmdOK_Click()
    If txtPassword.Text <> "sesame" Then
        MsgBox "Incorrect password", vbCritical
```

(continued)

```
      Else
           MsgBox "Okay!...Correct password"
      End If
End Sub

Private Sub Form_Load()
      txtPassword.PasswordChar = "*"
      txtPassword.Text=""
End Sub
```

See Also...

- The Secret application in Chapter 32, "Advanced Applications," for a more complete demonstration of this topic

Dear John, How Do I...

Encrypt a Password or Other Text?

Cipher techniques range from simplistic to extremely complex and secure. In most cases, you don't need or really want the level of security required by the National Security Agency; you just don't want the user to scan through your EXE file or a data file to discover copyright strings or other sensitive information. In fact, you've got to be careful about powerful ciphers, especially if there's any chance that your software will be shipped to other countries. The same laws that cover the shipping of munitions overseas apply to the exportation of strong ciphers! The following technique provides an ASCII-to-ASCII cipher suitable for hiding sensitive information from virtually all of the curious people out there. It's not secure enough to keep out the most determined hacker, though.

About the Cipher Class

The Cipher class module defines an object to encrypt and decrypt one string at a time. The two properties and three methods of this object are described here:

- ■ KeyString: This write-only property (there's a Property Let procedure but no corresponding Property Get) sets the string used to define a key for unique encryption or decryption. When this property is set, Visual Basic's internal random number generator is set to a unique starting seed value based on each and every character of the key and the order in which the characters appear in the key.

317

NOTE: To initialize Visual Basic's random number generator to repeat a given sequence, you must use the Rnd function with an optional, negative value parameter and then call the Randomize statement with a value. For example, *Randomize (Rnd(−1.23))* will initialize the generator so that the same sequence of random numbers will be generated each time Rnd is called.

- Text: This property holds the text to be encrypted or decrypted. For example, you might set this property to a readable string, call the following methods to encrypt and stretch the string, and then save the resulting value of this property to a protected file, where it would be unreadable. Later you'd load the Text property with the encrypted string from the file, set the KeyString property to what was used to encrypt the string, call the methods to shrink and decrypt the string, and then display the Text property contents.

- DoXor: This method processes the string contents of the Text property by applying the exclusive-or operator to each byte of the string with the next pseudorandom byte in the sequence defined by the KeyString property. This is a reversible process—a second processing of the string using the same key string–defined sequence of pseudorandom bytes returns the string to its original state. This technique is at the heart of many encryption algorithms.

- Stretch: This method was added to the Cipher object, along with the corresponding Shrink method, to convert any string to a printable, displayable string. In other words, a string that can contain nonprintable or nondisplayable binary byte values is converted to a slightly longer string in which all characters of the string are guaranteed to be displayable and printable. Consider, for instance, a string containing 10 tab characters. (Tab characters have a binary byte value of 9.) If you try to print or display such a string, you'll end up not seeing anything, except perhaps a big gap in your output. When you perform an exclusive-or operation on the bytes of a string using all possible pseudorandom byte values, some of the resulting bytes will be tabs, some will be carriage returns, and some will be stranger yet, such as one of the "graphics" characters. The Stretch method borrows bits from every group of three characters to form a fourth character, and all four characters are then mapped to a range of character byte values that are all printable and displayable. The resulting string can be stored in the Registry or in an INI file, printed on paper, or included in e-mail sent over the Internet.

■ Shrink: This method undoes what the Stretch method does to a string, converting a string containing printable, displayable characters to one that might contain any of the possible set of 256 character byte values.

NOTE: For those interested in such things, I've implemented the Stretch and Shrink methods using an algorithm almost identical to the algorithm in Uuencode. I say "almost" because I've used a different offset value to map the stretched string characters in order to avoid using the space character.

Putting the Cipher Object to Work

The Cipher class uses a simple exclusive-or algorithm based on Visual Basic's random number generator to encrypt your text and uses the same algorithm to decrypt the text. Any string is used as the key, and each unique key will produce a unique encryption.

The Cipher class code listing shows how these properties and methods are implemented. To demonstrate its use, add the following code to a form containing two text boxes, two labels, and two command buttons:

```
Option Explicit

Private Sub cmdEncrypt_Click()
    Dim cipherTest As New Cipher
    cipherTest.KeyString = txtKeyString.Text
    cipherTest.Text = txtClearText.Text
    cipherTest.DoXor
    cipherTest.Stretch
    lblEncryptedText.Caption = cipherTest.Text
End Sub

Private Sub cmdDecrypt_Click()
    Dim cipherTest As New Cipher
    cipherTest.KeyString = txtKeyString.Text
    cipherTest.Text = lblEncryptedText.Caption
    cipherTest.Shrink
    cipherTest.DoXor
    lblDecryptedText.Caption = cipherTest.Text
End Sub
```

This code assumes that *txtClearText* contains the original unencrypted text (sometimes called clear text), *txtKeyString* contains the key string, *lblEncryptedText* contains the encrypted version of the clear text, and *lblDecryptedText* contains the resulting text after it has been decrypted. Clicking *cmdEncrypt* performs the encryption, and clicking *cmdDecrypt* performs the decryption. Notice that the encrypted result is approximately ⁴/₃ the length of the clear text—the effect of the Stretch method.

Figure 16-3 shows an example of the Cipher object in action.

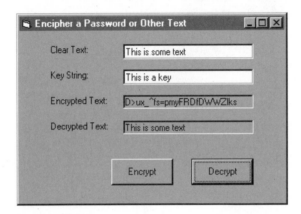

Figure 16-3.
A Cipher object being used to encrypt and decrypt text.

The following should provide you with enough code to implement a simple string ciphering object in your own applications:

```
'CIPHER.CLS
Option Explicit

Private msKeyString As String
Private msText As String

'~~~.KeyString
'A string (key) used in encryption and decryption
Public Property Let KeyString(sKeyString As String)
    msKeyString = sKeyString
    Initialize
End Property
```

(continued)

320

```
'~~~.Text
'Write text to be encrypted or decrypted
Public Property Let Text(sText As String)
    msText = sText
End Property

'Read text that was encrypted or decrypted
Public Property Get Text() As String
    Text = msText
End Property

'~~~.DoXor
'Exclusive-or method to encrypt or decrypt
Public Sub DoXor()
    Dim nC As Integer
    Dim nB As Integer
    Dim lI As Long
    For lI = 1 To Len(msText)
        nC = Asc(Mid(msText, lI, 1))
        nB = Int(Rnd * 256)
        Mid(msText, lI, 1) = Chr(nC Xor nB)
    Next lI
End Sub

'~~~.Stretch
'Convert any string to a printable, displayable string
Public Sub Stretch()
    Dim nC As Integer
    Dim lI As Long
    Dim lJ As Long
    Dim nK As Integer
    Dim lA As Long
    Dim sB As String
    lA = Len(msText)
    sB = Space(lA + (lA + 2) \ 3)
    For lI = 1 To lA
        nC = Asc(Mid(msText, lI, 1))
        lJ = lJ + 1
        Mid(sB, lJ, 1) = Chr((nC And 63) + 59)
        Select Case lI Mod 3
        Case 1
            nK = nK Or ((nC \ 64) * 16)
        Case 2
            nK = nK Or ((nC \ 64) * 4)
```

(continued)

```
            Case 0
                nK = nK Or (nC \ 64)
                lJ = lJ + 1
                Mid(sB, lJ, 1) = Chr(nK + 59)
                nK = 0
            End Select
        Next lI
        If lA Mod 3 Then
            lJ = lJ + 1
            Mid(sB, lJ, 1) = Chr(nK + 59)
        End If
        msText = sB
    End Sub


    '~~~.Shrink
    'Inverse of the Stretch method;
    'result can contain any of the 256-byte values
    Public Sub Shrink()
        Dim nC As Integer
        Dim nD As Integer
        Dim nE As Integer
        Dim lA As Long
        Dim lB As Long
        Dim lI As Long
        Dim lJ As Long
        Dim lK As Long
        Dim sB As String
        lA = Len(msText)
        lB = lA - 1 - (lA - 1) \ 4
        sB = Space(lB)
        For lI = 1 To lB
            lJ = lJ + 1
            nC = Asc(Mid(msText, lJ, 1)) - 59
            Select Case lI Mod 3
            Case 1
                lK = lK + 4
                If lK > lA Then lK = lA
                nE = Asc(Mid(msText, lK, 1)) - 59
                nD = ((nE \ 16) And 3) * 64
            Case 2
                nD = ((nE \ 4) And 3) * 64
            Case 0
                nD = (nE And 3) * 64
                lJ = lJ + 1
```

(continued)

```
        End Select
        Mid(sB, lI, 1) = Chr(nC Or nD)
    Next lI
    msText = sB
End Sub

'Initializes random numbers using the key string
Private Sub Initialize()
    Dim nI As Integer
    Randomize Rnd(-1)
    For nI = 1 To Len(msKeyString)
        Randomize Rnd(-Rnd * Asc(Mid(msKeyString, nI, 1)))
    Next nI
End Sub
```

When using the Cipher object in your own applications, be sure to set the KeyString property immediately before each call to the DoXor method. Setting KeyString causes the pseudorandom numbers to be initialized to a repeatable starting point.

NOTE: These ciphered strings also work well for sending data over a modem because no hidden escape code sequences or control codes will mess up the communication. You won't have to use any complicated binary transfer method. Be aware that you don't have to use the Shrink and Stretch methods if you don't mind working with binary data. Note also that the Shrink and Stretch methods might be useful without the accompanying exclusive-or encryption. Sending binary files (graphics images, for example) through standard e-mail over the Internet is one instance in which you might want to implement Shrink and Stretch without encryption.

Securing Registry Data

Finally, here's an idea for making demonstration software secure. You can keep track of the installation date, number of runs, user name, or other information for an application by encrypting a string and storing it in the Registry entry for the application. Your user's name and organization can be used for the key string to encrypt the data stored in the Registry string. This makes it easy for the program to take appropriate action if the demonstration is out of date, if the maximum number of runs has been reached, or if the user name or organization has been tampered with.

Here's a simple example based on the Cipher class. The following code fragment allows the user to enter a key string and a user name. When the *cmdEncryptUser* button is clicked, an encrypted version of the user name is stored in the Registry. A click of the *cmdDecryptUser* button then displays the decrypted user name. After running this code and entering a sample user name such as *Santa Claus,* you can run Windows 95's Regedit program and search on *User Name* to find the encrypted entry. Don't search on *Santa Claus,* because that string is stored in encrypted format.

```
Option Explicit

Private sAppName As String
Private sSection As String
Private sKey As String
Private sSetting As String

Private Sub cmdEncryptUser_Click()
    Dim cipherTest As New Cipher
    cipherTest.KeyString = txtKeyString.Text
    cipherTest.Text = txtUser.Text
    cipherTest.DoXor
    cipherTest.Stretch
    sSetting = cipherTest.Text
    sAppName = App.Title
    sSection = "Testing"
    sKey = "User Name"
    SaveSetting sAppName, sSection, sKey, sSetting
    lblEncryptUser.Caption = cipherTest.Text
End Sub

Private Sub cmdDecryptUser_Click()
    Dim cipherTest As New Cipher
    sAppName = App.Title
    sSection = "Testing"
    sKey = "User Name"
    cipherTest.Text = GetSetting(sAppName, sSection, sKey)
    cipherTest.KeyString = txtKeyString.Text
    cipherTest.Shrink
    cipherTest.DoXor
    lblDecryptUser.Caption = cipherTest.Text
End Sub
```

Figure 16-4 shows an example of the output.

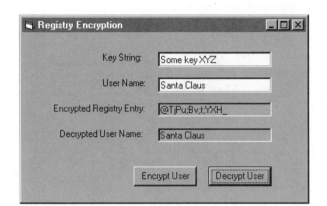

Figure 16-4.
Example of an encrypted user name stored in the Registry.

There's room for creative variations on this theme, but the important concept to note is that strings ciphered with the object presented here are compatible with standard printable and displayable text strings. You can read and write them with no problem, even though they appear to be a random sequence of characters.

See Also...

- The Secret application in Chapter 32, "Advanced Applications," for a thorough demonstration of the cipher algorithm

- Chapter 14, "The Registry," for more information about accessing the Registry

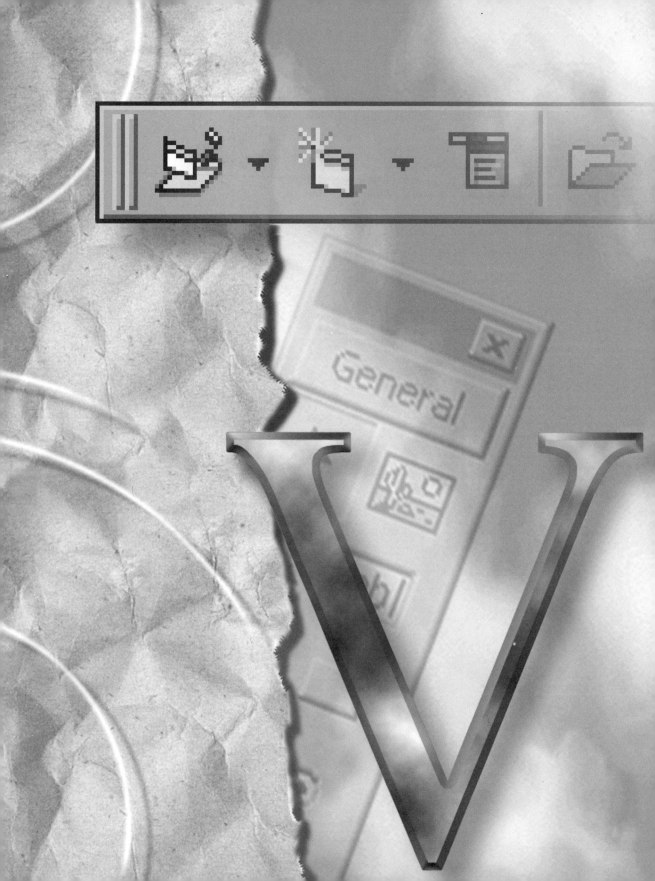

CHAPTER SEVENTEEN

The Mouse

Visual Basic provides 16 standard mouse pointers and also lets you define your own mouse pointer. This chapter explains the manipulation of these pointers and shows you how to easily create custom mouse pointers to use in your applications.

Dear John, How Do I...

Change the Mouse Pointer?

Forms and many visible controls have a property named MousePointer that allows you to control the appearance of the mouse pointer when it is displayed in front of the form or control. This property is usually set programmatically at runtime because the appropriate mouse pointer might vary according to what the program is executing. (For example, while a time-consuming task is being performed it is usually best to set the mouse pointer to an hourglass shape.) The MousePointer property remains set as *vbDefault* in the development environment.

Visual Basic provides a handy collection of constant declarations for setting the MousePointer property. You don't have to load a special file into your project—the following constants are readily available in Visual Basic whenever you need to use them in your program. To view a full list of constants and paste the appropriate constant directly into your code, open the Object Browser, select MousePointerConstants from the Classes list for the VBRUN library, select the constant, press Ctrl-C to copy the constant, and switch to the code window and then press Ctrl-V to paste the constant. The table on the following page lists these constants and describes the appearance of the mouse pointer when the constant is applied to the MousePointer property.

Constant	Value	Mouse Pointer Description
vbDefault	*0*	Default: shape determined by the object
vbArrow	*1*	Arrow
vbCrosshair	*2*	Cross (crosshair pointer)
vbIbeam	*3*	I-beam
vbIconPointer	*4*	Icon
vbSizePointer	*5*	Size: four-headed arrow
vbSizeNESW	*6*	Size: NE-SW double-headed arrow
vbSizeNS	*7*	Size: N-S double-headed arrow
vbSizeNWSE	*8*	Size: NW-SE double-headed arrow
vbSizeWE	*9*	Size: W-E double-headed arrow
vbUpArrow	*10*	Up arrow
vbHourglass	*11*	Hourglass
vbNoDrop	*12*	No drop
vbArrowHourglass	*13*	Arrow and hourglass
vbArrowQuestion	*14*	Arrow and question mark
vbSizeAll	*15*	Size all
vbCustom	*99*	Custom icon specified by the MouseIcon property

Notice that there are four double-headed arrows for sizing. Each one of these arrows points in two directions. The pointing directions are referenced as if your screen were a map, with up as north, down as south, left as west, and right as east. For example, the mouse pointer set with the *vbSizeNS* constant is a double-headed arrow pointing up and down, and the *vbSizeWE* constant specifies a double-headed arrow that points left and right. The other two double-headed arrows point diagonally toward the corners of the screen.

Notice also that the fairly common "hand" pointer is missing from the list of standard mouse pointers. Visual Basic lets you create your own mouse pointer shapes. The MousePtr application presented in Chapter 31, "Utilities," demonstrates how to load and view any icon file as a mouse pointer.

One common use of the MousePointer property is for changing the mouse pointer shape to an hourglass while your program is busy. This pointer lets the user know that something is going on and encourages the user to wait patiently. Figure 17-1 shows the hourglass mouse pointer in action. Be sure to change the pointer back to its previous state when the program has finished its time-consuming task.

Figure 17-1.
The hourglass mouse pointer that appears while the application is busy.

The following lines of code illustrate this technique; the MousePtr application in Chapter 31 provides a more detailed example:

```
frmMain.MousePointer = vbHourglass
ReturnValue = TimeConsumingFunction()
frmMain.MousePointer = vbDefault
```

See Also...

- "Dear John, How Do I...Create a Custom Mouse Pointer?" below for more information about creating and using custom mouse pointers

- The MousePtr application in Chapter 31, "Utilities," for an opportunity to experiment with the mouse pointers and see what they look like

Dear John, How Do I...

Create a Custom Mouse Pointer?

You can use any icon or cursor file as a custom mouse pointer. To do this, set the MousePointer property to *vbCustom*, and set the MouseIcon property to the name of the icon (ICO) or cursor (CUR) file. That's all there is to it! You can quickly switch between any of the standard mouse pointers and the custom pointer by resetting the MousePointer property. If you want to change to a second custom pointer, you'll have to assign a different icon to the MouseIcon property. Figure 17-2 on the following page shows a left-pointing hand icon loaded from the icons included with Visual Basic.

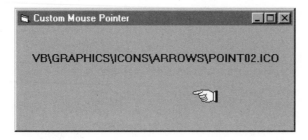

Figure 17-2.
Displaying a custom mouse pointer using an icon file.

NOTE: Animated cursors are not yet supported by Visual Basic's MouseIcon property.

You can load multiple icon files into an ImageList control at design time and access them from the ListImages Picture property to quickly flip through a set of custom mouse pointers. The ImageList control is one of the Microsoft Windows Common Controls (COMCTL32.OCX). The following code uses an ImageList control to display a different custom pointer each time the form is clicked on:

```
Option Explicit

Private Sub Form_Click()
    Static nList As Integer
    nList = nList + 1
    If nList > 3 Then nList = 1
    MousePointer = vbCustom
    MouseIcon = ImageList1.ListImages(nList).Picture
End Sub
```

Dear John, How Do I...

Display an Animated Mouse Pointer?

It puzzles me that Microsoft doesn't include support for 32-bit animated mouse pointers in the MouseIcon property. In order to display an animated pointer for a window, you have to go to the Windows API. This is not terribly difficult, however.

You can load any type of pointer supported by Microsoft Windows using the LoadCursorFromFile Windows API function. To change the pointer for a window, use the SetClassLong Windows API function. The following code shows how this is done:

```
Option Explicit

'Loads cursors and creates pointer handle
Private Declare Function LoadCursorFromFile _
Lib "user32" Alias "LoadCursorFromFileA" ( _
    ByVal lpFileName As String _
) As Long

'Changes class information for a window
Private Declare Function SetClassLong _
Lib "user32" Alias "SetClassLongA" ( _
    ByVal hwnd As Long, _
    ByVal nIndex As Long, _
    ByVal dwNewLong As Long _
) As Long

'Index of pointer in window class structure
Private Const GCL_HCURSOR = (-12)
Private hOldCursor As Long

Private Sub Form_Load()
    Dim hNewCursor As Long
    'Get handle to new animated pointer
    hNewCursor = LoadCursorFromFile _
        ("C:\WINDOWS\CURSORS\HORSE.ANI")
    'Replace window's mouse pointer with new pointer
    hOldCursor = SetClassLong(Form1.hwnd, GCL_HCURSOR, _
        hNewCursor)
End Sub

Private Sub Form_Unload(Cancel As Integer)
    'Restore original pointer to prevent horse pointer
    'from being retained in the design environment
    hOldCursor = SetClassLong(Form1.hwnd, GCL_HCURSOR, _
        hOldCursor)
End Sub
```

Notice that the Form_Unload event procedure resets the mouse pointer to its original state. If you don't do this, the horse pointer is still displayed for the window in the design environment—even after you stop the program. You wouldn't want to hard-code the path to HORSE.ANI in code that you plan to distribute. Instead, use the GetWindowsDirectory Windows API function to get the real Windows directory.

Dear John, How Do I...

Determine Where the Mouse Pointer Is?

The MouseMove, MouseUp, and MouseDown events can provide you with several useful parameters when they are activated. Search Visual Basic's online help for these events to get a full explanation of their parameters. Note that these events all provide *x* and *y* values that tell your application exactly where the mouse pointer is located at the time the event occurs. In most cases, you'll need to copy these *x* and *y* values to more permanent variables to keep track of them, depending on what you're trying to accomplish.

A simple example demonstrates this technique clearly. The following code allows you to draw lines on your form: one endpoint appears where the mouse button is pressed, and the other endpoint appears where the mouse button is released. Notice that the location of the mouse pointer at the MouseDown event is stored in the module-level variables *X1* and *Y1* so that these values are available to the Form_MouseUp event procedure. When the MouseUp event occurs, the *X1* and *Y1* module-level variables are used with the *X* and *Y* local variables as the starting and ending coordinates for the line.

```
Option Explicit

Private X1, Y1

Private Sub Form_MouseDown( _
    Button As Integer, _
    Shift As Integer, _
    X As Single, _
    Y As Single _
)
    X1 = X
    Y1 = Y
End Sub

Private Sub Form_MouseUp( _
    Button As Integer, _
    Shift As Integer, _
    X As Single, _
    Y As Single _
)
    Line (X1, Y1)-(X, Y)
End Sub
```

Figure 17-3 shows this simple line-drawing code in action.

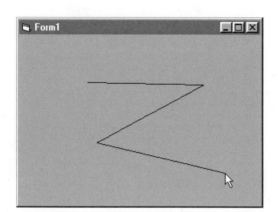

Figure 17-3.
Using the MouseUp and MouseDown events to draw straight line segments.

 See Also...

- The MousePtr application in Chapter 31, "Utilities," for a demonstration of mouse pointer location

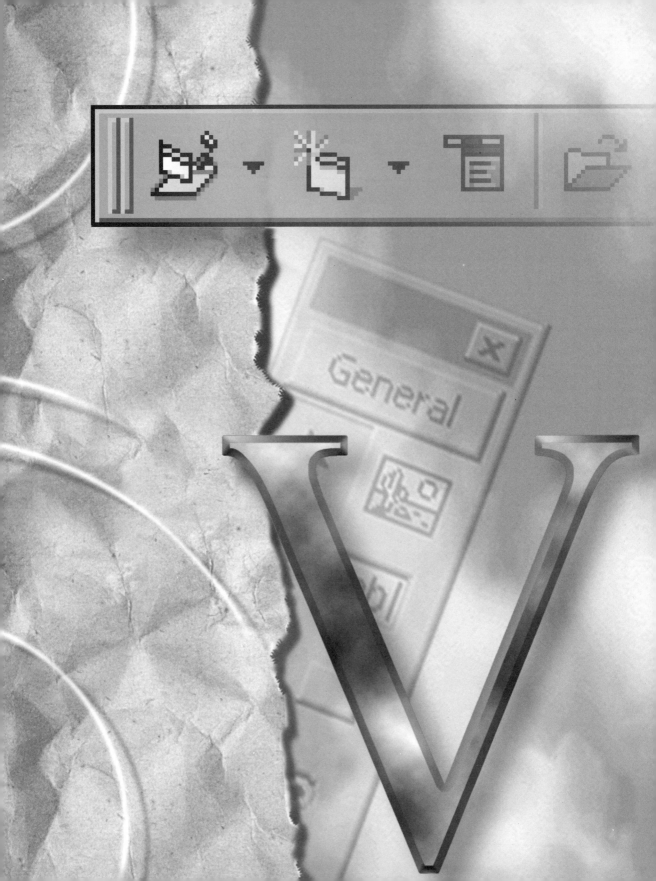

CHAPTER EIGHTEEN

The Keyboard

Here are a few useful ideas for handling user keypresses from within a running Visual Basic application. This chapter covers several techniques that you might otherwise overlook and that you might want to add to your bag of tricks.

Dear John, How Do I...

Change the Behavior of the Enter Key?

Although it's not standard Microsoft Windows programming practice, you might occasionally want to have the Enter key act like a Tab key when the focus is on a particular control—that is, you might want a press of the Enter key to move the focus to the next control instead of having it cause any other action. The following code does the trick for a text box and can be modified to work on any other control that provides a KeyPress event:

```
Private Sub txtText1_KeyPress(KeyAscii As Integer)
    If KeyAscii = vbKeyReturn Then
        SendKeys "{tab}"
        KeyAscii = 0
    End If
End Sub
```

The ASCII code for the pressed key is handed to the KeyPress event in the *KeyAscii* parameter. The ASCII value of the Enter key is *13*, which is the value of the built-in constant *vbKeyReturn*. SendKeys lets your Visual Basic application send any keypress to the window that currently has the focus. (This is a very handy statement because it lets your application send keypresses to other Windows-based applications just as easily as to itself.) The string *{tab}* shows how SendKeys sends a Tab keypress, which will be processed exactly as if the Tab key had really been pressed. To override the default action of the Enter key, set the KeyAscii value to *0*. If you don't do this, you'll get a beep from the control.

If you want to ignore all Enter keypresses when the focus is on a particular control, you can easily set this up: simply assign the value *0* to *KeyAscii* to ignore the Enter key, as above, and don't use SendKeys to substitute any other keypress.

Dear John, How Do I...
Determine the State of the Shift Keys?

The KeyPress event does not directly detect the state of the Shift, Ctrl, and Alt keys (collectively known as the shift keys) at the time of a keypress, but the Shift key state does modify the character that is detected (by making it an uppercase or a lowercase letter, for example). To directly detect the state of these shift keys, you can use the closely related KeyDown and KeyUp events. You can act on the state of these keys directly in the KeyDown and KeyUp event procedures, or you can keep track of their states in module-level variables. I prefer the second technique in many cases because it lets me act on the shift keys' states from within the KeyPress event procedure or from any other code in the module.

The following code immediately updates the state of one of three Boolean variables whenever any of the shift keys is pressed or released. I've used the Visual Basic constants *vbShiftMask*, *vbCtrlMask*, and *vbAltMask* to test for each of the shift states and return a Boolean value. To enable this code for the entire form, be sure to set the form's KeyPreview property to *True*. Then, regardless of which control is active, your code can instantaneously check the state of the three shift keys simply by referring to the current value of these variables.

```
Option Explicit

Private ShiftState As Boolean
Private CtrlState As Boolean
Private AltState As Boolean

Private Sub Form_KeyDown(KeyCode As Integer, Shift As Integer)
    ShiftState = (Shift And vbShiftMask)
    CtrlState = (Shift And vbCtrlMask)
    AltState = (Shift And vbAltMask)
End Sub

Private Sub Form_KeyUp(KeyCode As Integer, Shift As Integer)
    ShiftState = (Shift And vbShiftMask)
```

(continued)

```
    CtrlState = (Shift And vbCtrlMask)
    AltState = (Shift And vbAltMask)
End Sub

Private Sub tmrTest_Timer()
    Cls
    Print "Shift = "; ShiftState
    Print "Ctrl  = "; CtrlState
    Print "Alt   = "; AltState
End Sub
```

To see how this code works, create a new form, add the code to the form, and add a timer named *tmrTest*. Set the timer's Interval property to *100* to sample the state of the keys every 0.1 second. The preceding code will then display the state of the shift keys as you press them. Try holding down combinations of the Shift, Ctrl, and Alt keys to see how all three state variables are updated independently. Figure 18-1 shows the form as it appears when the Ctrl and Alt keys are simultaneously held down.

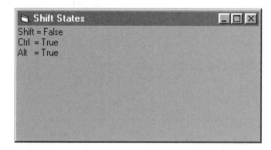

Figure 18-1.
Real-time display of the status of the shift keys.

Dear John, How Do I...

Create Hot Keys?

The KeyPreview property for Visual Basic forms provides an excellent way to set up hot keys. This property lets your application act on any combination of keypresses, such as function keys, shifted function keys, or numeric keypad keys. Here's the general technique: first set your form's KeyPreview property to *True*, and then add code to the form's KeyDown event procedure to check for and act on any desired keypresses. In the code on the following page, I check for F1, F2, and any of the shift keys in combination with the F3 key. I use the Visual Basic constants *vbKeyF1*, *vbKeyF2*, and *vbKeyF3* to identify the key that is pressed. Note that this type of procedure works well to test only one or just a few keys, but the technique in the previous section would help simplify the key tests if we needed to check several function keys for the current shift keys' states.

```
Private Sub Form_KeyDown(KeyCode As Integer, Shift As Integer)
    Select Case KeyCode
    Case vbKeyF1
        Print "F1"
    Case vbKeyF2
        Print "F2"
    Case vbKeyF3
        If (Shift And vbShiftMask) Then
            Print "Shift-F3"
        ElseIf (Shift And vbCtrlMask) Then
            Print "Ctrl-F3"
        ElseIf (Shift And vbAltMask) Then
            Print "Alt-F3"
        Else
            Print "F3"
        End If
    End Select
End Sub
```

Figure 18-2 shows the result of running this code and pressing a few of the function keys. Note that the form intercepts the keypresses before the Command1 button receives them, even though Command1 has the focus.

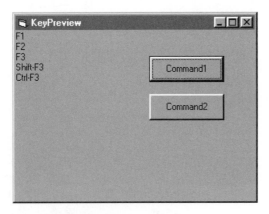

Figure 18-2.
A demonstration of the hot key code.

See Also...

- "Dear John, How Do I...Determine the State of the Shift Keys?" earlier in this chapter

- The Jot application in Chapter 30, "Databases," for a demonstration of this hot key setup

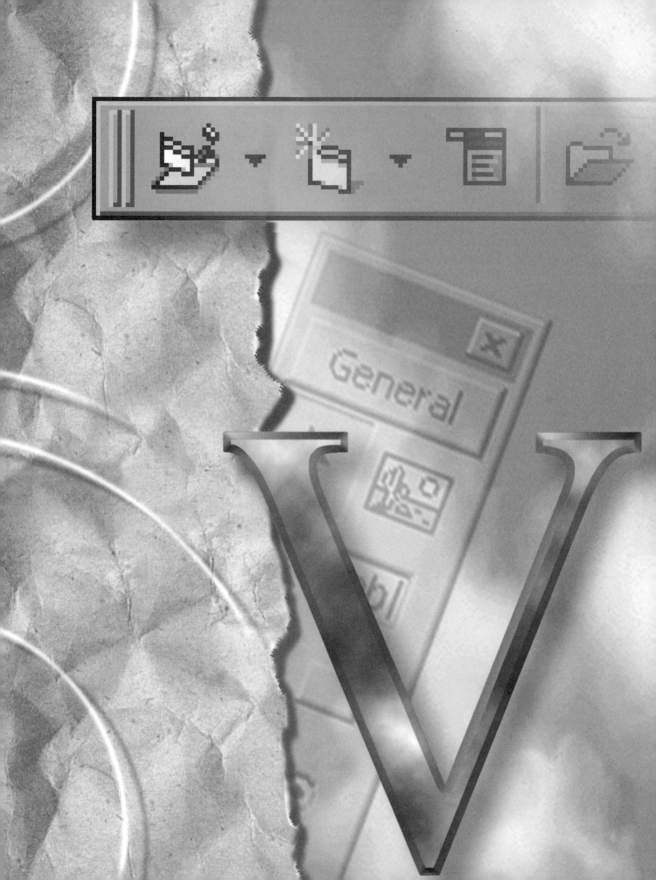

CHAPTER NINETEEN

Text Box and Rich Text Box Tricks

One of the most powerful and useful controls in Visual Basic is the RichText-Box control. With just a few simple changes to the control's property settings, a rich text box can become a decent editor, with capabilities similar to those of Microsoft Windows' WordPad utility. This chapter shows you how to accomplish this and also explains a few other techniques that take your TextBox and RichTextBox control capabilities to new heights.

Dear John, How Do I...

Display a File?

You can set up either a text box or a rich text box as a convenient way to display the contents of a file. The following code loads the AUTOEXEC.BAT file and displays its contents in a scrollable window. To try this example, draw one of these controls on a new form and name it either *txtTest* (if you're using a text box) or *rtfTest* (if you're using a rich text box). If you're using a TextBox control, you'll need to set a couple of the control's properties: set MultiLine to *True* and ScrollBars to *3 - Both*. If you want to view a file other than AUTO-EXEC.BAT, change the filename in the Open statement. In this example, I've used a RichTextBox control to display my AUTOEXEC.BAT file, but you can easily substitute a TextBox control if you want.

```
Option Explicit

Private Sub Form_Load()
    Dim F$
    'Load a file into a string
    Open "C:\AUTOEXEC.BAT" For Binary As #1
```

(continued)

```
    F$ = Space$(LOF(1))
    Get #1, , F$
    Close #1
    'Display file in rich text box
    rtfTest.Text = F$
End Sub
```

Figure 19-1 shows the displayed file.

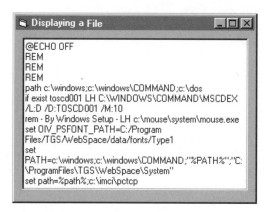

Figure 19-1.
The contents of AUTOEXEC.BAT displayed in a rich text box.

In the above example, the entire AUTOEXEC.BAT file is read into a single string using binary file input. Binary file input is a useful technique because it reads every byte from the file regardless of the content of the byte. This means that when a file with multiple lines is read into a single string, the linefeeds and carriage returns are included in the string. (Chapter 13, "File I/O," goes into greater detail about binary file input/output techniques.)

If you are reading an RTF format file, use the rich text box's TextRTF property instead of the plain Text property. When the RTF file is read, the formatting codes in the file will be interpreted and the text correctly displayed.

Here's another technique that you should know about for building a multiline string: you can concatenate strings (tack them together end to end), but you must insert a carriage return and a linefeed at the end of each string, as demonstrated in the following code. This example performs the same action as the previous example, except that in this case AUTOEXEC.BAT is loaded from the file one line at a time to build up the string for the text box. Compare this code with the previous listing.

```
Option Explicit

Private Sub Form_Load()
    Dim A$, F$
    'Load a file into a string
    Open "C:\AUTOEXEC.BAT" For Input As #1
    Do Until EOF(1)
        Line Input #1, A$
        F$ = F$ & A$ & vbCrLf
    Loop
    Close #1
    'Display file in rich text box
    rtfTest.Text = F$
End Sub
```

NOTE: Prior to Visual Basic 4, you had to create a string of carriage return and linefeed characters yourself. Visual Basic now provides the built-in constant *vbCrLf*, as shown in the example above.

In the past, I have used a TextBox control in both of these examples, but the TextBox control has a maximum limit of roughly 64,000 characters. For smaller files, such as the AUTOEXEC.BAT file shown above, a TextBox control will work just fine, but I suggest using the RichTextBox control because of its greater flexibility.

See Also...

- "Dear John, How Do I...Fit More than 64 KB of Text into a Text Box?" later in this chapter for a workaround for the text box size limitation

Dear John, How Do I...

Create a Simple Text Editor?

If you need a full-featured word processor window in your application, consider using OLE capabilities to embed a Microsoft Word document object. But if you want just a simple text editor along the lines of the Windows NotePad or WordPad utility, a TextBox or RichTextBox control is probably all you need. Let's see how you can do this by building a simple editor on a form. The code on the following page shows how to build the text editor.

```vb
Option Explicit

Private Sub cmdCut_Click()
    'Cut selected text to clipboard
    Dim Work$
    Dim Wstart, Wlength
    'Keep focus on rich text box
    rtfEdit.SetFocus
    'Get working parameters
    Work$ = rtfEdit.Text
    Wstart = rtfEdit.SelStart
    Wlength = rtfEdit.SelLength
    'Copy cut text to clipboard
    Clipboard.SetText Mid$(Work$, Wstart + 1, Wlength)
    'Cut out text
    Work$ = Left$(Work$, Wstart) + _
        Mid$(Work$, Wstart + Wlength + 1)
    rtfEdit.Text = Work$
    'Position edit cursor
    rtfEdit.SelStart = Wstart
End Sub

Private Sub cmdCopy_Click()
    'Copy selected text to clipboard
    'Keep focus on edit box
    rtfEdit.SetFocus
    Clipboard.SetText rtfEdit.SelText
End Sub

Private Sub cmdPaste_Click()
    'Paste text from clipboard
    Dim Work$, Clip$
    Dim Wstart, Wlength
    'Keep focus on rich text box
    rtfEdit.SetFocus
    'Get working parameters
    Work$ = rtfEdit.Text
    Wstart = rtfEdit.SelStart
    Wlength = rtfEdit.SelLength
    'Cut out text, if any, and insert clipboard text
    Clip$ = Clipboard.GetText()
    Work$ = Left$(Work$, Wstart) + Clip$ + _
        Mid$(Work$, Wstart + Wlength + 1)
    rtfEdit.Text = Work$
    'Position edit cursor
    rtfEdit.SelStart = Wstart + Len(Clip$)
End Sub
```

Figure 19-2 shows the completed text editor in action.

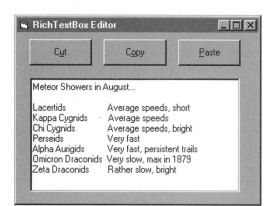

Figure 19-2.
A rich text box editor in action.

In this case, the RichTextBox control is named *rtfEdit*. Set the Right-Margin property to make the text wrap automatically. For instance, the following code makes the text wrap when the user types to the edge of the rich text box:

```
rtfEdit.RightMargin = rtfEdit.Width
```

Set the ScrollBar property to *2 - rtfVertical* to enable text scrolling in long documents.

The form contains three command buttons: *cmdCut, cmdCopy,* and *cmd-Paste.* You don't really need these buttons if you want to rely on the Ctrl-X, Ctrl-C, and Ctrl-V shortcut keys because these keys are automatically processed by the control to cut, copy, and paste without any additional coding on your part. The code I've added for these command buttons allows them to mimic the action of the control keys and provides more flexibility in your programming. You might, for example, want to add a standard Edit menu to the form, and this code is the only convenient way to process menu events. Simply copy the code to the corresponding menu item Click event procedure to set up your own menu-driven cut, copy, and paste procedures.

So when would you want to use a TextBox control instead of a RichText-Box control? In the 32-bit world, the TextBox control is used primarily for simple data entry fields, but in the 16-bit world the TextBox control is your only option, so you must use it for displaying files and collecting text input. The 32-bit RichTextBox control allows much larger pieces of text, supports

OLE drag-and-drop, and displays formatting; virtually anything a text box can do, a rich text box can do better. I haven't even touched on the multiple fonts and the rich set of embedded RTF (rich text format) commands, or the many methods and properties of the RichTextBox control that make it much more powerful and adaptable than the TextBox control. See the online help and printed documentation for more information about all these details.

See Also...

- The Jot application in Chapter 30, "Databases," for a demonstration of the use of a rich text box as a text editor

Dear John, How Do I...

Detect Changed Text?

The Change event is a text box/rich text box event, and you would think that this would make it easy to detect whether a control's contents are edited by the user while a form is displayed. But detecting changed text in a text box or a rich text box can get a little tricky. Usually the initial or default text is loaded into the Text property when the control's form loads. This causes the control's Change event to occur, even though the text has not yet been changed by the user, which is what we're really trying to detect.

The following code solves this problem for a RichTextBox control by manipulating two Boolean flags, but the same method can be used with a TextBox control. The *NotFirstFlag* variable is set to *True* after the first Change event takes place. The *TextChangeFlag* variable is set to *True* only if *NotFirstFlag* is *True*. This happens the second time the control's Change event occurs, which is when the user makes the first change to the text in the *rtfEdit* text box. *TextChangeFlag*'s scope is the entire form, so it's easy to check the value of the flag in the form's Unload event procedure. In the following sample code, the unloading of the form is disabled if the contents have been changed by the user:

```
Option Explicit

Private TextChangeFlag As Boolean

Private Sub Form_Load()
    rtfEdit.Text = "Edit this string..."
    TextChangeFlag = False
End Sub
```

(continued)

```
Private Sub Form_Unload(Cancel As Integer)
    If TextChangeFlag = True Then
        Cancel = True
        MsgBox "Save changes first", 0, _
            "(Testing the Change event...)"
    End If
End Sub

Private Sub rtfEdit_Change()
    Static NotFirstFlag As Boolean
    TextChangeFlag = NotFirstFlag
    NotFirstFlag = True
End Sub
```

When you use this technique in your applications, you might want to perform some other action beyond this simple example. To try this example, place a rich text box named *rtfEdit* on a form. When you run the program, change the text in the rich text box, and then try to unload the form by pressing Alt-F4 or by clicking the Close button to close the form.

Dear John, How Do I...

Fit More than 64 KB of Text into a Text Box?

In 16-bit Visual Basic 4 applications, the Text property for a text box is limited to less than 64 kilobytes (KB) of text. (Actually, depending on how you are using string space, the limit might be around 32 KB.) In Microsoft Windows 95 and Microsoft Windows NT, you can use a RichTextBox control instead of a TextBox control to bypass this limitation. This book focuses on programming for Windows 95, so I considered not addressing this topic. However, the techniques shown here, such as using the Preserve keyword with the ReDim statement, are quite useful for other programming tasks, so I decided to include this topic after all. If you are doing 16-bit programming, you'll find it immediately useful. If you are doing 32-bit programming, read on anyway, because the techniques presented here are useful additions to your bag of tricks.

You can work around the text box string size limitation by placing the text in an array and then assigning an element of the array to the Text property of a TextBox control. With this method, the individual array elements are limited to less than 64 KB, but because arrays can be huge even in 16-bit Visual Basic, a very large amount of text can be contained in the array and subsequently displayed in the text box. In the example shown here, the text box will contain only a handful of lines, but these lines will be quickly updated from a huge dynamic string array that contains more than 64 KB of text. Figure 19-3 shows the result of using this technique to display a text file containing approximately 703,000 bytes in a text box.

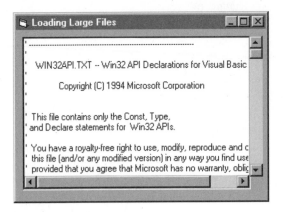

Figure 19-3.
Displaying a large text file in a text box.

To re-create this example, add a text box named *txtTest* and a vertical scrollbar named *vsbTest* to a new form. Set the text box's MultiLine property to *True* and its ScrollBars property to *1 - Horizontal*. The vertical scrollbar takes the place of the text box's built-in scrollbar; move the scrollbar to the right edge of the text box so that it appears to be attached. Add the following code to the form, and change the name of the file in the Open statement to the name of a file on your disk:

```
Option Explicit

Private Const LINES = 15
Private A$()

Private Sub Form_Load()
    Dim n
    'Load dynamic string array from large text file
    Open "C:\WIN32API.TXT" For Input As #1 Len = 1024
    Do Until EOF(1)
        n = n + 1
        ReDim Preserve A$(n + LINES)
        Line Input #1, A$(n)
    Loop
    Close #1
```

(continued)

```
        'Set scrollbar properties
        With vsbTest
            .Min = 1
            .Max = n
            .SmallChange = 1
            .LargeChange = n \ 10
        End With
    End Sub

    Private Sub vsbTest_Change()
    Dim i As Integer
    Dim Tmp$
        'Create display string from array elements
        For i = vsbTest.Value To vsbTest.Value + LINES
            Tmp$ = Tmp$ + A$(i) + vbCrLf
        Next i
        txtTest.Text = Tmp$
    End Sub
```

At form load time, the entire large text file is read into a dynamically allocated string array. This can take a few seconds, so in a real application you might want to load the file while other things are going on so that the user doesn't become anxious. For this demonstration, you can use any text file greater than 64 KB in size, but be prepared to wait if the file is very large.

Once the file is loaded into memory, the string array dimensions are used to set the vertical scrollbar's properties. The text box contents are updated whenever the vertical scrollbar's value changes. A block of strings from the string array are concatenated, with carriage return and linefeed characters inserted at the end of each line, and the resulting temporary string is copied into the text box's Text property.

This demonstration displays only the file's contents and doesn't attempt to keep track of changes made by the user. If you want to turn this text box into a text editor, you'll have to add code to update the string array when there are changes to the text box's contents.

Dear John, How Do I...

Allow the User to Select a Font for a Text Box or a Rich Text Box?

The CommonDialog control provides the most convenient and foolproof way to let the user select a font at runtime. (It's also the best tool for allowing the user to select files, choose colors, set up a printer, and so on.) To experiment with this technique, add a text box named *txtTest*, a command button named *cmdFont*, and a CommonDialog control named *dlgFonts* to a new form. Add the following code to complete the demonstration:

```
Option Explicit

Private Sub cmdFont_Click()
    dlgFonts.Flags = cdlCFScreenFonts
    dlgFonts.ShowFont
    With txtTest.Font
        .Name = dlgFonts.FontName
        .Bold = dlgFonts.FontBold
        .Italic = dlgFonts.FontItalic
        .Size = dlgFonts.FontSize
    End With
End Sub

Private Sub Form_Load()
    txtTest.Text = "ABCDEF abcdef 0123456789"
End Sub
```

The Form_Load event procedure simply loads the text box with some sample text so that the font changes can be seen. The cmdFont_Click event procedure does the interesting stuff. It first sets the CommonDialog control's Flag property to display the system's screen fonts (see the online help for other Flag options), then it activates the ShowFont method to activate the dialog box, and then it sets the text box font properties according to the user's selections. Figures 19-4 and 19-5 show the text box before and after font selection, and Figure 19-6 shows the font selection dialog box itself.

Figure 19-4.
Text box showing font properties at their default settings.

Figure 19-5.
Text box font set to user's font choice.

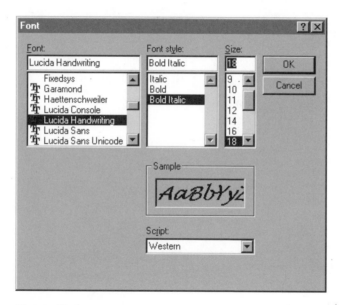

Figure 19-6.
The Font dialog box in action.

NOTE: The TextBox control allows just one font at a time to be in use for the entire control, but the RichTextBox control allows fonts to vary throughout its text contents. Refer to the rich text box properties that start with *Sel* (there are a lot of them) in the Visual Basic online help for a detailed explanation of how to manipulate character fonts within the RichTextBox control.

See Also...

- "Dear John, How Do I...Scale a Font Infinitely?" in Chapter 12, "Graphics Techniques," for information about scaling fonts

Multiple Document Interface

For a lot of applications, the Multiple Document Interface (MDI) metaphor provides an ideal framework for structuring the user interface, but some of the tricky nuances of this interface have prevented many of us from taking full advantage of it. This chapter highlights some of the main concepts behind creating an MDI application and provides a solid background on which to expand your expertise.

Dear John, How Do I...

Create an MDI Application?

This section provides concise coverage of the basic concepts of creating an MDI application. For more details, refer to the Visual Basic online help or Visual Basic Books Online.

When I first started working with MDI forms, I had trouble integrating all the relevant information in such a way that it made sense to me. The following discussion should give you a better foothold than I had.

The MDI Form

A Visual Basic project can have only one MDI form. The MDI form is the container for all the individual child forms. To add an MDI form to your project, choose Add MDI Form from the Project menu and double-click the MDI Form icon. You'll notice that this form has a shorter list of properties than a standard form. The MDI form doesn't have to be the startup form for your application, but you can make it the startup form by choosing Project Properties from the Project menu and, on the General tab of the Project Properties dialog box, selecting the MDI form from the Startup Object drop-down list.

MDI Child Forms

Your project can have any number of child forms contained in an MDI form. (And it can have any number of independent, non-child forms too.) To create a child form, set a standard form's MDIChild property to *True*. The form becomes a child of the MDI form in your project. At runtime, the program code is responsible for loading these child forms and for showing, hiding, or unloading them as desired. Notice that, at design time, child forms look and act just like standard forms. The big difference in their behavior shows up at runtime.

Figure 20-1 shows a running MDI application with an assortment of child forms. I've minimized some of the child forms and displayed others.

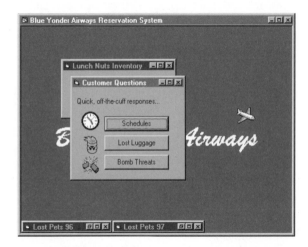

Figure 20-1.
A sample MDI form with an assortment of child forms.

The ActiveForm and ActiveControl Properties

When used together, the ActiveForm and ActiveControl properties let your MDI form refer to controls on the child form that currently has the focus. For example, your MDI application might have identical text controls on several child forms. When text is highlighted in a text box on one of these child forms, and when a Copy menu item is chosen, the ActiveForm.ActiveControl.SelText property refers to the text selected in the currently active text box on the currently active child form.

The Me Keyword

The Me keyword functions like a variable, referring to the identity of the active child window. When multiple instances of a child form are created, Me provides a way for the code that was designed for the original form to operate on the specific instance of that form that currently has the focus.

The Tag Property

The Tag property provides a handy way to uniquely identify exact copies of child forms. As each new copy is created, have a number or string placed into its Tag property. This creates an index, somewhat like an array index, that keeps track of forms that are otherwise identical copies of one another.

Fundamental MDI Features

The MDI form is unique when compared to other forms. The following features of the MDI form should be kept in mind when you are designing and coding MDI applications:

- Child forms always appear in the MDI form and never appear elsewhere. Even when minimized, the child form icons appear only in the MDI form. They ride along with the MDI form—for instance, when the MDI form is minimized you'll see nothing of the child forms it contains.

- If a child form has a menu, that menu shows up on the MDI form when that child form has the focus. At runtime, you'll never see menus on any child forms; they instantly migrate to the parent MDI form.

- You can add a menu to the MDI form at design time, but the only controls that can be added are those with an Align property. (There is a way to work around this, though—simply draw a picture box on the MDI form and draw your controls inside this box.) When a control is placed on the MDI form, child windows cannot overlap any part of the control.

- You can create multiple instances of a single child form at runtime using the Dim As New statement. In many MDI applications, this is an extremely important feature. As mentioned above, the ActiveForm, ActiveControl, and Tag properties and the Me keyword are very useful for working with multiple copies of child forms. Take a look at the online help for more information.

■ A useful MDIForm property, Picture, lets you install a bitmap or other graphics image onto the backdrop of the MDI form. This is handy for displaying graphics such as company logos.

See Also...

- The Jot application in Chapter 30, "Databases," to see how a single child edit form is mass-produced to let the user edit in multiple windows

Dear John, How Do I...

Add a Logo (Splash Screen) to an MDI Form?

It's tricky to place an image in the center of an MDI form. The Picture property always plops an image in the upper-left corner, and only aligned controls can be placed on an MDI form. But an MDI form makes a good backdrop for an entire application, and it's nice to be able to position your company logo right in the middle of things. Here's a workaround that displays a logo (or any image) in the middle of your MDI form. With this technique, the logo stays centered even if the form is resized. Figure 20-2 shows an imaginary application at startup. In this application, the MDI form is set as the startup form and the company logo appears centered on the MDI form.

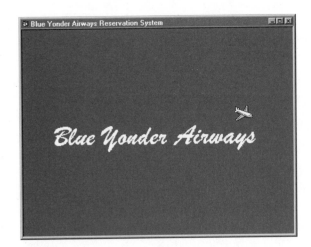

Figure 20-2.
An MDI form displaying a centered logo.

To try this example, create a new project containing an MDI form and one child form named *frmLogo*. Add an Image control named *imgLogo* to the child form. You can't add the Image control directly to the MDI form, and if you use a picture box to contain the Image control (or to directly display the logo), you won't be able to center the logo if the MDI form is resized. By placing the Image control on the child form, you can always center the child form and thus center the logo. So the trick here is to size *frmLogo* to the size of the image, remove *frmLogo*'s borders and title bar, and then keep *frmLogo* centered on the MDI form. Set *frmLogo*'s MDIChild property to *True*, and set the Border-Style property to *0 - None*. Load a bitmap logo file into *imgLogo*. Don't worry about the placement of this image on *frmLogo*—the runtime code shown below will take care of these details. Add this code to the MDI form, and give it a try:

```
Option Explicit

Private Sub MDIForm_Resize()
    'Move logo to upper-left corner of Image control
    frmLogo.imgLogo.Move 0, 0
    'Size form to size of image it contains
    frmLogo.Width = frmLogo.imgLogo.Width
    frmLogo.Height = frmLogo.imgLogo.Height
    'Center logo form on MDI form
    frmLogo.Left = (ScaleWidth - frmLogo.Width) \ 2
    frmLogo.Top = (ScaleHeight - frmLogo.Height) \ 2
    'Show logo
    frmLogo.Show
End Sub
```

The image is moved to the upper-left corner of its containing form. The form is then resized to match the image size and is relocated to the center of the MDI form. I've put this code in the MDIForm_Resize event procedure so that the logo will always shift to the center of the MDI form if the form is resized.

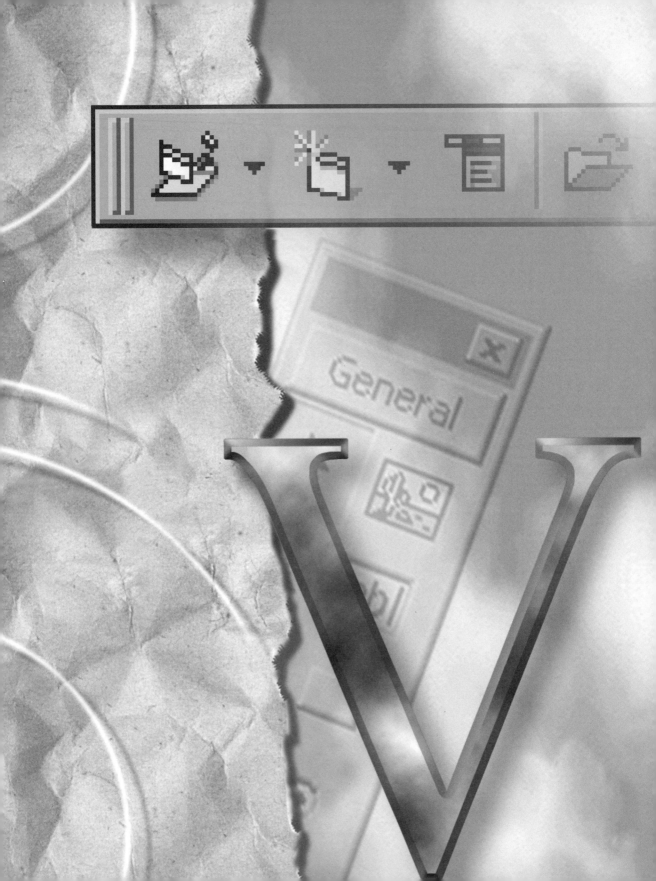

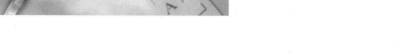

CHAPTER TWENTY-ONE

Database Access

Microsoft's evolving approach to data access has been increasingly evident in recent versions of Visual Basic. Visual Basic has many important and powerful features that make it an ideal language for all of your database programming requirements. Although a full discussion of database programming is beyond the scope of this book, this chapter provides a short introduction to give you a feel for this important subject. For more in-depth information, see Visual Basic's Books Online and online help. Excellent coverage is also provided in the Microsoft Office Developer's Kit (ODK), and your local bookstore probably carries several books devoted entirely to the subject of database programming.

This chapter covers the new wizards available in Visual Basic 5 that help you get up and running with databases in record time and presents two different ways to connect a Visual Basic application to a database. The first technique uses the Data control and is a simple and straightforward approach that requires very little programming, and the second uses data access objects (DAOs), which provide flexible, complete control of a database.

Dear John, How Do I...

Use Wizards in My Database Development Cycle?

You can save a lot of time and energy by leveraging the tools Microsoft packages with Visual Basic and Microsoft Access. For example, Visual Basic includes two new wizards that can greatly simplify the task of adding a data-enabled form to your applications. These wizards create a simplified version of a typical database form, but if you think about it, most of the time this is all you really need. For those occasions when further customization is required, the forms created by these wizards still provide an excellent starting point.

If you know you will be adding a data-enabled form to a new Visual Basic project, you can save development time and effort by stepping through the

Application Wizard. To start this wizard, choose New Project from the File menu and double-click the VB Application Wizard icon in the New Project dialog box. In addition to several other useful forms, menus, and similar parts that make up a standard application, the Application Wizard will optionally add a database form to the new project. You should definitely become familiar with the Application Wizard—it can save a lot of time in the typical application development cycle.

For even more options and control over the creation of a database form, you can run the Data Form Wizard whenever you add a new form to your project. To start this wizard, choose Add Form from the Project menu and double-click the VB Data Form Wizard icon. The Data Form Wizard steps you through several design decisions and then uses your input to create a complete, working form connected to a database of your choice.

One of the nice features of the Data Form Wizard is the choice of fundamental database form types. Often, a form that shows one record at a time from a table or query is all that's required; at other times, you might want a full grid of records. Both of these form types are automatically generated by the Data Form Wizard. A third form type, Master/Detail, is also very useful. This form type displays a single record from a table or query and a grid of data from the same database. The single record and the grid are connected through one of the common fields. For example, using the BIBLIO.MDB sample database found in the VB directory, the Data Form Wizard can easily create a form that displays data for one publisher at a time along with an associated grid of all books published by that publisher, as shown in Figure 21-1. As you proceed from record to record through the publisher information, the grid automatically fills with the relevant book titles.

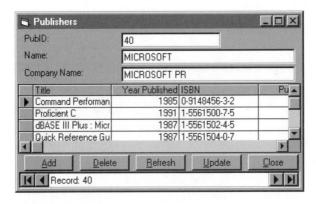

Figure 21-1.
Master/Detail-type form created with the Data Form Wizard.

Rather than describe the Data Form Wizard's steps in detail here, I recommend that you experiment with the wizard directly. It's easy to use and self-explanatory, and with a few minutes of exploration up front you'll probably save many hours of labor down the road when you need to get data-enabled forms up and running as quickly as possible. The BIBLIO.MDB database provides an excellent database to experiment with.

If you want to get database forms up and running quickly, an excellent approach is to combine tools, using Access for the creation and maintenance of each database and using the Data Form Wizard whenever possible. As you'll see in the next few sections, you can use Visual Basic itself to create and maintain your databases and to create custom data-enabled forms, but for maximum leverage you can't beat using Access and the Data Form Wizard.

Dear John, How Do I...
Use the Data Control to Connect an Application to a Database?

Let's put together a very simple database using a Data control. You must take two basic steps to accomplish this: first create a database, and then create the user interface.

Creating a Database Using the Visual Data Manager

You can programmatically create a database, which we'll do in the next section, or you can create a database using the add-in Visual Data Manager tool. When I am working with a Data control, I prefer to use the Visual Data Manager for this one-time task. This utility lets you create a database by defining its tables and fields.

To create a database using the Visual Data Manager utility, follow these steps:

1. From the Add-Ins menu, choose Visual Data Manager.

2. Click No if a dialog box appears that asks, "Add SYSTEM.MD? (Microsoft Access Security File) to INI File?" For this example, you do not need file security. The Visual Data Manager utility starts, and the Visual Data Manager window is displayed.

3. From the Visual Data Manager's File menu, choose New, choose Microsoft Access as the database type from the first submenu, and choose Version 7.0 MDB from the second submenu. The Select Microsoft Access Database To Create dialog box appears.

4. Select a location in which to save the database, type *BDAY* in the File Name text box to name the database, and click Save. The file-name extension MDB is automatically added to the filename. The Database and SQL Statement windows appear. At this point, the database exists, but it contains no table or field definitions.

5. Right-click in the Database window, and choose New Table from the pop-up menu to add a new table. The Table Structure dialog box appears.

6. Type *Birthdays* in the Table Name text box. This is the name of our one and only table.

7. Click the Add Field button to display the Add Field dialog box. Type *Name* in the Name text box to define the first field of the table.

8. The Type drop-down list already displays *Text*, so you don't need to change the setting in this case.

9. Type *30* in the Size text box to define the maximum number of characters that can be contained in the Name field.

10. Click the OK button to add the field definition to the list of fields in the current table. You can now enter the definitions for the second field.

11. Type *Birthday* in the Name text box, select Date/Time from the Type drop-down list, and click the OK button to define the second field and add the field definition to the list of fields.

12. Click the Close button to close the Add Field dialog box. Figure 21-2 shows the resulting Table Structure dialog box.

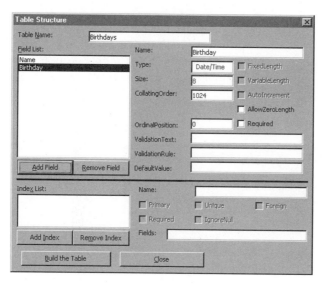

Figure 21-2.
Adding fields to the Birthdays table.

13. Click the Build The Table button to complete the process and close the Birthdays table. Figure 21-3 shows the BDAY database.

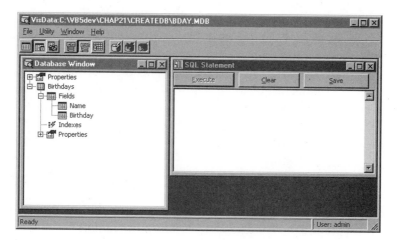

Figure 21-3.
The BDAY database created with the Visual Data Manager.

14. Exit from the Visual Data Manager to return to Visual Basic.

We have now properly defined the database, although it contains no valid records yet.

Creating the User Interface

Our database now needs a user interface. Start with a new Standard EXE project, and draw three controls on Form1: a text box named *txtName*, a second text box named *txtBirthday*, and a Data control named *datBDay*. You can add optional labels if you want, as I've done in this example, but they aren't required. The completed form, containing sample data, is shown in Figure 21-4.

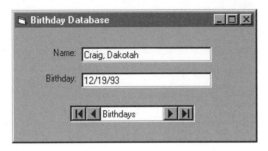

Figure 21-4.
A simple birthday database application using a Data control.

The key to using the Data control and associated data-bound controls is to set the properties correctly. Always start with the Data control by setting its DatabaseName property to the name of the database file to be connected. In this case, set DatabaseName to *BDAY.MDB*, the file we just created with the Visual Data Manager. Set the Data control's RecordSource property to *Birthdays*, the name of the table in the database that this Data control is to reference. Generally speaking, one Data control is associated with one table in a database.

In this example, we have one other property to set on the Data control. We need to be able to add new records when the application runs. Set the EOFAction property to *2 - Add New*. Now when the user scrolls to the blank record at the end of the database and fills in a new name and birth date, the database is automatically updated to contain the new record.

The Data control doesn't do much by itself. What we need to do is to associate other controls with the Data control. When they are associated, or data-bound, the controls become tools for working with the database. In our example, we use the DataSource and DataField properties of the text boxes to make these controls data-bound to the *datBDay* Data control. Set the DataSource property of each text box to *datBDay*, and set the DataField property of each text box to the name of the field it's to be associated with. Set *txtName*'s DataField to *Name* and *txtBirthday*'s DataField to *Birthday*. These database-related properties provide a drop-down list of available tables and fields after the Data control connection has been made, making it easier to set these properties.

Running the Application

That's it! You don't need to write any code to work with the database. Run the application, enter a new name and birth date, and click on the Data control's next record scrollbar arrow. You'll probably want to add some code and modify some of the properties to customize the application.

This simple example doesn't let you delete records or search for specific names or dates in the database. To turn this into a real application, you'd need to add code to provide capabilities along these lines.

Dear John, How Do I...

Use Data Access Objects to Connect an Application to a Database?

Objects are everywhere in Visual Basic, and one of the areas in which they've enhanced the language most is data access. Let's use these objects, without touching a Data control at all, to build another simple database application. But first let's chart out the data access objects in Visual Basic.

Data Access Objects

One of the best ways to understand the organization of objects in Visual Basic is to study a chart that shows the hierarchy of these objects, called an object model. The hierarchy of data access objects is shown in Figure 21-5 on the following page. As I learned about data objects, this chart helped me see where collections and objects fit into the scheme of things, and with its help I was able to get the syntax down pat for accessing these nested objects.

I've added (s) to object names that can also be names of collections of objects. For example, there's a Workspace object, and then there's the Workspaces collection, of which Workspaces(0) is the first Workspace object. All object names follow this scheme: the pluralizing s is added to the name of a type of object to name the collection. Notice in Figure 21-5 that the only data access object that is not part of a collection is DBEngine. There's only one DBEngine.

The sample code presented in this section provides examples that declare and use these objects. Compare the notation I've used to access these objects with the structure shown in Figure 21-5. If any of this notation seems confusing, be sure to search the online help for these object names and study the examples and explanations you'll find there.

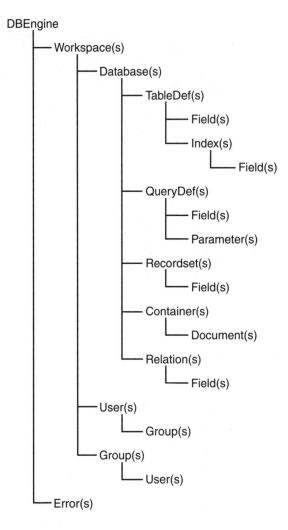

Figure 21-5.
The structure of data access objects in Visual Basic.

Creating a Database Using Data Access Objects

The following short program creates a telephone number database from scratch, using only data access objects (no Data control). I've made this database similar to the birthday database we created earlier so that you can easily compare the two. In this case, two text fields are created: one for a name, and one for its associated telephone number (or any other text you want to enter, such as an e-mail address).

To create this example, start a new Standard EXE project and add one command button named *cmdCreate* to Form1. Set the button's Caption property to *Create*. Be sure that you have included the data access object (DAO) library as a reference, or you will get an error. If the DAO library is not referenced, choose References from the Project menu and check the Microsoft DAO 3.5 Object Library check box. Add the following code to the form. Be sure to change the database path and filename as desired if you don't want the new database to be saved in the root directory of your C drive.

```
Option Explicit

Private Sub cmdCreate_Click()
    'Create data access object variables
    Dim dbWorkspace As Workspace
    Dim dbDatabase As Database
    Dim dbTableDef As TableDef
    Dim dbName As Field
    Dim dbNumber As Field
    'Create data access objects
    Set dbWorkspace = DBEngine.Workspaces(0)
    Set dbDatabase = dbWorkspace.CreateDatabase( _
        "C:\PHONES.MDB", dbLangGeneral)
    Set dbTableDef = dbDatabase.CreateTableDef("Phones")
    Set dbName = dbTableDef.CreateField("Name", dbText)
    Set dbNumber = dbTableDef.CreateField("Number", dbText)
    'Set field properties
    dbName.Size = 30
    dbNumber.Size = 30
    'Append each field object to its table object
    dbTableDef.Fields.Append dbName
    dbTableDef.Fields.Append dbNumber
    'Append each table to its database
    dbDatabase.TableDefs.Append dbTableDef
    'Close completed database
    dbDatabase.Close
    MsgBox "Database Created", , "Create Phones"
End Sub
```

Figure 21-6 on the following page shows this short program in action. All you have to do is click the Create button once to create the new database. I've put a lot of comments in the code to describe the action, but the overall design of the routine is as follows: In the first half of the preceding code, all object variables are declared, and then objects are created and set to be referenced by these variable names. The rest of the code deals with these new objects and their properties and methods. The Size property of the two text fields is set, and then the various objects are linked to each other using the Append method of each. This completes the creation of the structure of the new database.

Figure 21-6.
Creating a database with the click of a button.

Note that although the new Phones database contains no valid data, the internal structure is complete and ready to go. We've created one table, Phones, and two text fields in this table, Name and Number. These two text fields are fixed to a maximum length of 30 characters.

NOTE: If, in the course of your experimentation, you want to start all over with the Phones database, simply delete the PHONES.MDB file and rerun this program.

Accessing the Database

Now let's create a simple program to access the Phones database, again without using a Data control. I've kept this demonstration simple: the following application lets you move forward and backward through the table's records, append new records, and type any text (up to 30 characters) to change the records as desired. To enhance this application, you'd probably want to add code to delete records, search and sort, and so on.

Start with a new Standard EXE project, and add two command buttons to Form1. Name the buttons *cmdprevious* and *cmdNext*, and set their caption properties to *Previous* and *Next*. Then add two text boxes, and name them *txtName* and *txtNumber*. Figure 21-7 shows how I placed and sized these controls.

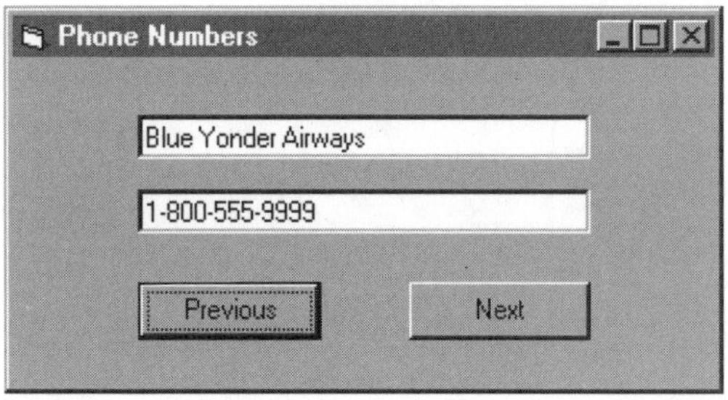

Figure 21-7.
The simple phone number database program in action.

The following code completes the demonstration. Add it to your form, and when you run it you'll have a working, albeit simple, database editor. Check that the database's path name and filename match the location of the Phones database we created in the previous short program and that your project references the Microsoft DAO 3.5 Object Library. If the DAO library is not referenced, choose References from the Project menu and check the Microsoft DAO 3.5 Object Library check box.

```
Option Explicit

'Create new data access object variables
Private dbWorkspace As Workspace
Private dbDatabase As Database
Private dbTable As Recordset
Private dbName As Field
Private dbNumber As Field

Private Sub cmdNext_Click()
    'Move only if current record isn't a blank one
    If txtName.Text <> " " And txtNumber.Text <> " " Then
        'Save any changes to current record
        UpdateRecord
        'Move to next record
        dbTable.MoveNext
        'Prepare new record if at end of table
        If dbTable.EOF Then NewRecord
        'Display data from record
        DisplayFields
    End If
```

(continued)

```
        'Keep focus on text boxes
        txtName.SetFocus
    End Sub

    Private Sub cmdPrevious_Click()
        'Save any changes to current record
        UpdateRecord
        'Step back one record
        dbTable.MovePrevious
        'Don't go past first record
        If dbTable.BOF Then dbTable.MoveNext
        'Display data from record
        DisplayFields
        'Keep focus on text boxes
        txtName.SetFocus
    End Sub

    Private Sub Form_Load()
        'Create data access objects
        Set dbWorkspace = DBEngine.Workspaces(0)
        'Change database path if neccessary
        Set dbDatabase = dbWorkspace.OpenDatabase("C:\PHONES.MDB")
        Set dbTable = dbDatabase.OpenRecordset("Phones", dbOpenTable)
        'Use special handling if new database
        If dbTable.BOF And dbTable.EOF Then NewRecord
        'Start on first record
        dbTable.MoveFirst
        'Display data from record
        DisplayFields
    End Sub

    Private Sub NewRecord()
        'Add new record
        dbTable.AddNew
        'Install a space in each field
        dbTable!Name = " "
        dbTable!Number = " "
        'Update database
        dbTable.Update
        'Move to new record
        dbTable.MoveLast
    End Sub

    Private Sub UpdateRecord()
        'Prepare table for editing
        dbTable.Edit
        'Copy text box contents into record fields
```

370

```
        dbTable!Name = txtName.Text
        dbTable!Number = txtNumber.Text
        'Update database
        dbTable.Update
    End Sub

    Private Sub DisplayFields()
        'Display fields in text boxes
        txtName.Text = dbTable!Name
        txtNumber.Text = dbTable!Number
    End Sub
```

To make things simple, I have set up this code so that it automatically updates the current record whenever you click the Previous or Next button. Notice that because we're not using data-bound text controls, it is entirely up to the program's code to coordinate what appears in the text boxes with what's in the fields of the current record. This takes a little more coding than a program that uses a Data control would require, but it is a lot more flexible.

For example, I've chosen to update the current record as the user moves to the next or the previous record. But it would be easy to update the record whenever any change occurs in either text box or to add an Update button and change the record if and only if this button is clicked. Data access object programming is much more flexible than using Data controls, although it requires a little more effort up front.

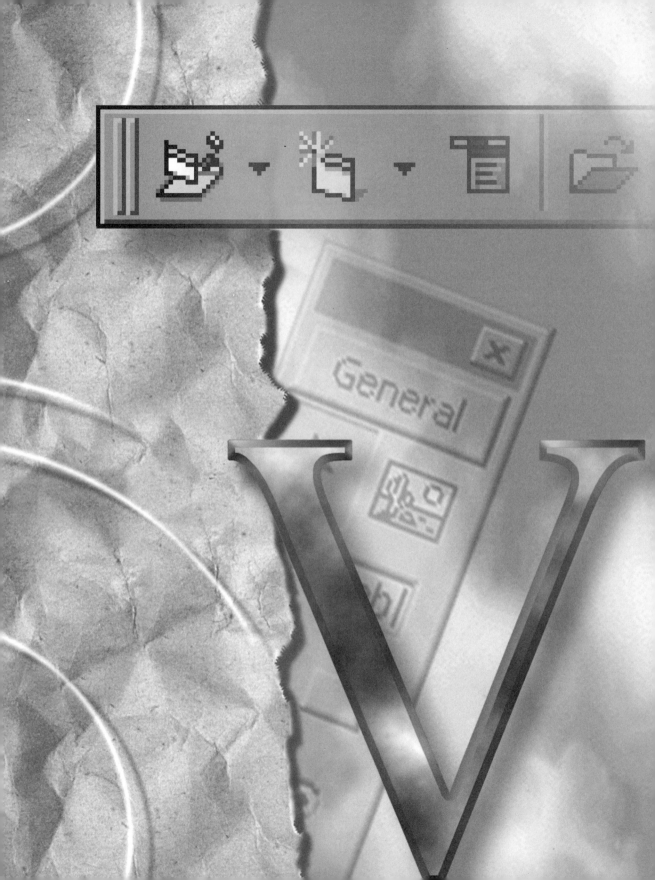

CHAPTER TWENTY TWO

ActiveX Objects in Other Applications

ActiveX is an important part of Microsoft's vision for Microsoft Windows and the Internet. Central to the overall ActiveX picture is Automation, the technology that enables objects to be easily shared between applications. More and more applications will begin to provide Automation objects to the external world, and Visual Basic will be able to immediately take advantage of those objects. As shown in Chapter 5, "Object-Oriented Programming," Visual Basic itself lets you create class modules that define ActiveX objects for use by external applications. The inclusion of Automation capabilities makes Visual Basic a logical choice for software development in Windows.

This chapter presents a sampling of common and useful tasks that are simplified by the Automation technology provided in Microsoft Word and Microsoft Excel.

Dear John, How Do I...

Use ActiveX to Perform Spell Checking?

All of the Microsoft Office 97 applications provide ActiveX objects you can use in Visual Basic. As the two premier applications in Microsoft Office, Microsoft Word and Microsoft Excel are of particular interest. Each exposes an extensive library of objects that programmers can easily tap into. Let's see how we can use Automation from Visual Basic to access the spell checker available in each of these applications and return the corrected spelling to our Visual Basic application.

Microsoft Word Spell Checking

The following code creates a Word Document object and manipulates a few of the object's properties and methods to perform spell checking on a string from within a Visual Basic application. The Document object lets you create and control a document in Word. I've added many comments to the code to help you follow the action, but here's the basic scenario: The Document object is created, the text is inserted into it, and the spell checker engine is activated for this document. The results are then copied back to the text box, where they replace the original text. (This code is designed to work with Microsoft Word 97.)

```
Option Explicit

Dim mdocSpell As New Document
Dim mbVisible As Boolean

Private Sub Form_Load()
    'Check whether application is visible
    '(used in Unload to determine whether this
    'application started Word application)
    mbVisible = mdocSpell.Application.Visible
End Sub

'Check spelling of text box contents
Private Sub cmdSpell_Click()
    'Add text to a Word Range object
    mdocSpell.Range.Text = txtSpell
    'IMPORTANT: You must perform the following two steps
    'before using the CheckSpelling method!!
    'Be sure that Word is visible
    mdocSpell.Application.Visible = True
    'Activate Word application
    AppActivate mdocSpell.Application.Caption
    'Check spelling
    mdocSpell.Range.CheckSpelling
    'Update text box with changes from Word
    txtSpell = mdocSpell.Range.Text
    'Trim off null character that Word adds
    txtSpell = Left(txtSpell, Len(txtSpell) - 1)
    'Activate this application
    AppActivate Caption
End Sub
```

(continued)

```
'Clean up
Private Sub Form_Unload(Cancel As Integer)
    'Check whether this application started Word application
    If mbVisible Then
        'Close document
        mdocSpell.Close savechanges:=False
    Else
        'Shut down Word
        mdocSpell.Application.Quit savechanges:=False
    End If
End Sub
```

This code switches activation back and forth between Word and the sample application. The CheckSpelling method is modal, so the Visual Basic code does not continue until the user has closed the spell checker. Be sure to make Word visible before calling any modal method; otherwise, the user won't be able to switch to Word and your application will appear to hang.

To try this example, create a new Visual Basic application. Establish a reference to the Microsoft Word 8.0 Object Library. Add a command button named *cmdSpell* and a text box named *txtSpell,* and name the form *frmSpell.* Add the preceding code to the form module, and run the application. Figure 22-1 shows some incorrectly spelled text just before the Check Spelling button is clicked, and Figure 22-2 on the following page shows Word's spell checker dialog box in action. Figure 22-3 on the following page shows the results of running Word's spell checker on the text.

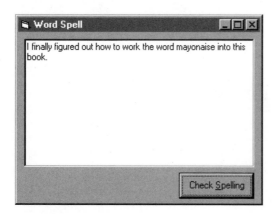

Figure 22-1.
Text as it appears before Word's spell checker is invoked.

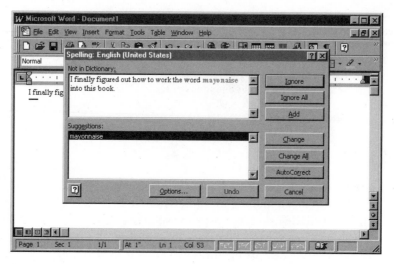

Figure 22-2.
Changing the spelling of the text using Word's spell checker.

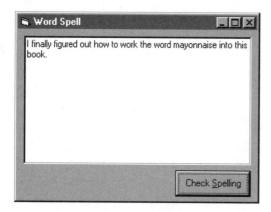

Figure 22-3.
Results of invoking Word's spell checker.

The Word spell checker is also available through the global method GetSpellingSuggestions. Use the GetSpellingSuggestions method to check the spelling of a single word. The following code displays a list of suggestions when the user selects a word and presses the F7 key:

```
Const KEY_F7 = 118

'Check spelling of a single word
Private Sub txtSpell_KeyDown(KeyCode As Integer, Shift As Integer)
    Dim Corrections
    If KeyCode = KEY_F7 Then
        If txtSpell.SelLength = 0 Then
            'Select the word
            SendKeys "+^{Right}"
        End If
        'Check spelling of selection
        Set Corrections = GetSpellingSuggestions(txtSpell.SelText)
        'If misspelled, display suggestions
        If Corrections.Count Then
            frmCorrections.Display Corrections
        End If
    End If
End Sub

'Called by frmCorrections to replace text
Friend Sub Replace(Word As String)
    txtSpell.SelText = Word
End Sub
```

The preceding code displays the collection of spelling suggestions using a second form named *frmCorrections*. This form contains a list box, named *lstCorrections*, and two command buttons, named *cmdReplace* and *cmdCancel*, that allow the user to select the correction or cancel the operation. Here is the code for *frmCorrection*:

```
'Called by frmSpell to display suggestions from Word
Friend Sub Display(Corrections)
    Dim Word
    For Each Word In Corrections
        lstCorrections.AddItem Word
    Next Word
    'Select first suggestion
    lstCorrections.Selected(0) = True
    'Display the form
    Show vbModal
End Sub
```

(continued)

377

```
'Replace word with selection
Private Sub cmdReplace_Click()
    frmSpell.Replace lstCorrections.List(lstCorrections.ListIndex)
    Unload Me
End Sub

'Cancel correction
Private Sub cmdCancel_Click()
    Unload Me
End Sub
```

Figure 22-4 shows the GetSpellingSuggestions method in action, after the misspelled word *vehements* is selected and the F7 key is pressed. You may notice that the GetSpellingSuggestions method executes faster than the CheckSpelling method and that both methods execute much faster if Word is already running. Speed of execution can be an important factor when you are designing applications that make use of ActiveX objects—most objects require the entire application to be running; others may run independently, loading only a few modules of an application.

Figure 22-4.
Microsoft Word's GetSpellingSuggestions method in action.

Microsoft Excel Spell Checking

Programming through Automation to access the spell checker engine in Excel is similar to the Word example. The code for this example accomplishes the same results, as shown in Figures 22-5 and 22-6. (This code is designed to work with Microsoft Excel 97.)

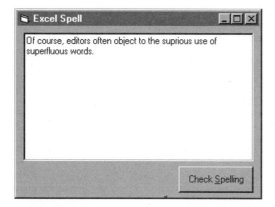

Figure 22-5.
Text as it appears before Excel's spell checker is invoked.

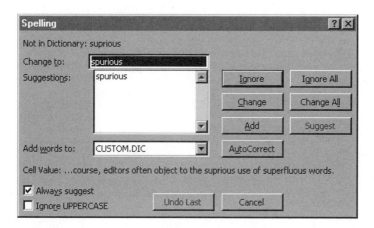

Figure 22-6.
Results of invoking Excel's spell checker.

In this code, an Excel Sheet object is created, the Visual Basic text string is loaded into a single cell of the sheet object, Excel's spell checker is invoked, and the cell's contents are copied back to the Visual Basic text box:

```
Option Explicit

Dim xl As Object

Private Sub cmdSpell_Click()
    'Use Automation to create an Excel object
    Set xl = CreateObject("Excel.Sheet")
```

(continued)

```
            'Get programmable reference (apparently a bug in Excel)
            Set xl = xl.Application.ActiveWorkbook.ActiveSheet
            'Copy from text box to sheet
            xl.Range("A1").Value = txtSpell.Text
            'Check spelling
            xl.CheckSpelling
            'Copy back to text box
            txtSpell.Text = xl.Range("A1").Value
            'Remove object from memory
            Set xl = Nothing
            'Be sure that this application is active
            AppActivate Caption
End Sub
```

To run this code, create a new form containing a command button named *cmdSpell* and a text box named *txtSpell*. Add the code to the form, and give it a try.

Notice that the AppActivate function is being used. If AppActivate was not used and this program was run with Excel already loaded, Excel would stay active after the spell checking was completed. To prevent this problem, the Visual Basic AppActivate function was used to reactivate your application when you have finished using Excel's spell checker.

Also notice the following line of code:

```
Set xl = xl.Application.ActiveWorkbook.ActiveSheet
```

Normally, you would not need to include this line, but due to an apparent bug in Excel 97, this line of code is necessary.

Early vs. Late Binding

You can use either early or late binding when working with ActiveX objects. *Early binding* lets you use specific types for your ActiveX objects. This enables Visual Basic's command-completion feature and enables the Object Browser for the referenced ActiveX object library. Early binding also writes the ActiveX object's class ID into your application's executable file. This results in faster object access. Early binding is demonstrated in the Word spelling example, which uses the Visual Basic References dialog box to establish a reference to the Word object library.

Late binding uses a generic Object data type for ActiveX object variables and then creates a reference to the specific ActiveX object at runtime. The ActiveX application's class ID is not written into your application's executable file, and object access takes a little longer. Late binding is demonstrated in the Excel spell checking example, which uses the CreateObject method to establish a reference to the Excel object library.

Whether or not the class ID is written into your application's executable file is very important because class IDs are likely to change with each new version of a product. If a new version of Word or Excel is released, applications that use their objects through early binding must be revised and redistributed. Applications that use late binding may not need to be redistributed, although you should test them to be sure that changes to Word or Excel don't have adverse affects on your application.

Dear John, How Do I...

Use ActiveX to Count Words?

Let's take a look at one more example of Automation with Word, this time to count the words in a string. In the following code, access to Word is achieved through the Document object, as was shown in the spell checking example. A second object variable, *dlg*, is created to access and hold the settings of Word's Document Properties dialog box.

```
Private Sub cmdWords_Click()
    Dim dlg As Word.Dialog
    'Copy text into Word document
    mdocSpell.Range = txtSpell.Text
    'Create an object to hold dialog box settings
    Set dlg = mdocSpell.Application.Dialogs _
        (wdDialogDocumentStatistics)
    'Count words and characters
    dlg.Execute
    'Display results in a Label control
    Caption = Str(dlg.Words) & " words, " _
        & Str(dlg.Characters) & " characters"
End Sub
```

In this example, I've grabbed the number of words and the number of characters from the object holding the dialog box settings, but there are other properties you can access if you want. Search Word's Visual Basic online help for the Dialogs collection to learn more about the contents of this and other dialog boxes.

Figure 22-7 shows the word and character count for a small sample of text.

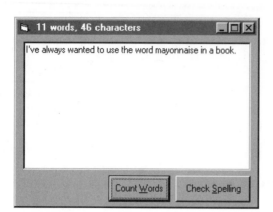

Figure 22-7.
Counting words and characters using Word's Word Count feature.

To run this example, start with the form created in the section "Microsoft Word Spell Checking," and add a command button named *cmdWords*. At runtime, type several words of text into the text box, and then click the command button.

Dear John, How Do I...

Use Microsoft Excel's Advanced Math Functions?

Microsoft Excel contains a number of math functions that are not available in Visual Basic. The following procedure uses Automation to create an Excel Sheet object and then access one of Excel's functions to perform a calculation on a value passed to the object from the Visual Basic program. More important, this example shows how you can use Excel to create bigger and better Visual Basic programs.

In this example, I use two cells in the Excel Sheet object for input and two other cells for reading back the results of the calculation performed on the values placed in the first two cells. Excel's ATAN2 function is used to calculate the angle between the positive *x*-axis and a line drawn from the origin to the point represented by these two data values. The angle is returned in radians, which can easily be converted to degrees. Unlike Visual Basic's Atn function, which uses the ratio of two sides of a triangle to return a value of $-\pi/2$ to $\pi/2$ radians, Excel's ATAN2 function uses the coordinates of the point to return a value between $-\pi$ and π radians. In this way, the return value of ATAN2 is correctly calculated for the quadrant that the given point is in.

The following code creates an Excel Sheet object, places the coordinates for the point into two cells of the Excel Sheet object, has Excel calculate the arctangent using the ATAN2 function, and returns the value to the Visual Basic application:

```
Option Explicit

Private Sub cmdAngle_Click()
    Dim xl As Object
    'Use Automation to create an Excel object
    Set xl = CreateObject("Excel.Sheet")
    'This solves the Excel bug mentioned earlier
    Set xl = xl.Application.ActiveWorkbook.ActiveSheet
    'Set known values in cells
    xl.Range("A1").Value = txtX.Text
    xl.Range("A2").Value = txtY.Text
    'Calculate third cell
    xl.Range("A3").Formula = "=ATAN2(A1,A2)"
    xl.Range("A4").Formula = "=A3*180/PI()"
    'Display result in a Label control
    lblRadians.Caption = xl.Range("A3").Value
    lblDegrees.Caption = xl.Range("A4").Value
    'Remove object from memory
    Set xl = Nothing
End Sub
```

To try this example, create a new form and add to it two text boxes, named *txtX* and *txtY*; two labels, named *lblRadians* and *lblDegrees*; and a command button, named *cmdAngle*. As shown in Figure 22-8 on the following page, an *xy*-coordinate pair entered into the text boxes is processed when the button is clicked to calculate the angle from the *x*-axis to the given point. I've set up two calculations, the first to find the angle in radians and the second to convert this measurement to degrees. The results of these two Excel calculations are copied back to the labels for display. I've also added labels to the form to clarify the identity of the input text boxes and output labels.

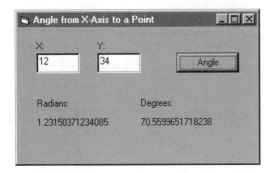

Figure 22-8.
An advanced Excel math function called from Visual Basic.

This technique of using an Excel Sheet object can be adapted to work with varying amounts of data, types of calculations, and levels of complexity, and the final result of all the number crunching can be copied back to your Visual Basic application. You'll find that using an Excel object for some types of data manipulations and calculations is easier and more efficient than trying to code the entire process in Visual Basic.

CHAPTER TWENTY-THREE

Screen Savers

It's actually fairly easy to create a screen saver using Visual Basic. In this chapter, I cover how to create a basic screen saver. But I also go further into the subject, showing you how to enhance the screen saver and make it work with the Microsoft Windows 95 screen saver controls. The enhancements include ensuring that only one instance of the program is run, turning off the mouse cursor, speeding up the graphics, detecting different user actions to terminate the screen saver, and using the current screen contents as part of a screen saver. I also look at how to use Windows controls to preview the screen saver and let the user set options.

Dear John, How Do I...

Create a Screen Saver?

Screen savers were originally created to protect screens from the "burn-in" that can be caused by pixels that don't change very often. Perhaps screen savers are now used more for entertainment than for screen protection, but the underlying principle of toggling all pixel locations through a variety of colors over time is still the foundation of their design. For this reason, a screen saver should display some sort of graphics that always move and change.

Any Visual Basic application can run as a screen saver. Of course, some programs will work better than others for this purpose. A basic screen saver is quite simple: a form that takes up the entire screen, code to create moving and changing graphics, and code to terminate the program when the user executes some action. This is all that is required to create a simple screen saver, but you will probably want to use the enhancements discussed in the following sections to improve the operation of your application.

To make your application function as a screen saver in the Windows environment, you need to compile the program as a screen saver. To do this, choose Make Project from the File menu, and make the following change in the Make Project dialog box: instead of creating an executable file with the extension EXE, change the extension to SCR by typing over EXE in the File Name text box. Click the OK button to finish building the executable screen saver. Copy the resulting SCR file into your Windows directory so that it can be located and its options set from the Display applet in the Control Panel.

> NOTE: Be aware that if you give your screen saver a name starting with two uppercase S's, Windows will remove them and SSaver1.scr will be listed as "aver1" in the Display Properties dialog box. This occurs because of the way earlier versions of Windows handled screen savers.

The following listing presents a simple screen saver application. The application does not handle some of the more complex features that are normally integrated into a screen saver. To act as a proper screen saver, your application should end when the mouse is moved or clicked or when a key is pressed. It should also not allow multiple instances of itself to run, and in Windows 95, it should gracefully handle the Settings, Preview, and Password options that are accessed from the Screen Saver tab of the Display Properties dialog box.

In this application, the screen saver does not respond to all of the control options in the Display Properties dialog box (except the Wait setting, which is handled by the system). The screen saver ends when you press a key, but it does not respond to any mouse movement. Adding all these features to the application is discussed in the sections following this one.

To create this screen saver, start a new Standard EXE project, and add a Timer control named *tmrExitNotify* to Form1. Set the timer's Interval property to *1* and its Enabled property to *False*. Set the form's BorderStyle property to *0 - None* and its WindowState property to *2 - Maximized,* and add the following code:

```
'Ssaver1
Option Explicit

'Declare module-level variables
Dim QuitFlag As Boolean

Private Sub Form_Click()
    'Quit if mouse is clicked
    QuitFlag = True
End Sub
```

(continued)

```
Private Sub Form_KeyDown(KeyCode As Integer, Shift As Integer)
    'Quit if any key is pressed
    QuitFlag = True
End Sub

Private Sub Form_Load()
    'Proceed based on command line
    Select Case UCase$(Left$(Command$, 2))
    'Put the show on the road
    Case "/S"
        'Display full size
        Show
        'Display different graphics every time
        Randomize
        'Initialize graphics parameters
        Scale (0, 0)-(1, 1)
        BackColor = vbBlack
        'Loop to create graphics
        Do
            'Occasionally change line color and width
            If Rnd < 0.03 Then
                ForeColor = QBColor(Int(Rnd * 16))
                DrawWidth = Int(Rnd * 9 + 1)
            End If
            'Draw circle
            Circle (Rnd, Rnd), Rnd
            'Yield execution
            DoEvents
        Loop Until QuitFlag = True

        'Can't quit in this context; let timer do it
        tmrExitNotify.Enabled = True
    Case Else
        Unload Me
        Exit Sub
    End Select
End Sub

Private Sub tmrExitNotify_Timer()
    'Time to quit
    Unload Me
End Sub
```

Create an SCR file, as described earlier, and place it in your Windows directory. Right-click on the desktop, select Properties, and click on the Screen Saver tab of the Display Properties dialog box. Here you should be able to select Ssaver1 from the drop-down list and test the screen saver by clicking the Preview button.

When activated, this screen saver draws random circles of varying thickness and color over a black background, as shown in Figure 23-1.

Figure 23-1.
The Ssaver1 screen saver program in action.

See Also...

- The other sections in this chapter for details about enhancements to this screen saver

- The Ssaver application in Chapter 27, "Graphics," for an example of a more complete screen saver application

Dear John, How Do I...

Prevent Two Instances of a Screen Saver from Running at the Same Time?

Visual Basic provides an App object that has a PrevInstance property set to *True* if a previous instance of the current Visual Basic application is already running. This handy property makes it easy to bail out of an application quickly, during the Form_Load event procedure, to avoid running multiple instances of a screen saver simultaneously. The following code shows how App.PrevInstance is typically implemented in a screen saver application:

```
'Don't allow multiple instances of program
If App.PrevInstance = True Then
    Unload Me
    Exit Sub
End If
```

Dear John, How Do I...
Hide the Mouse Pointer in a Screen Saver?

The ShowCursor Windows API function allows you to hide or show the mouse pointer in a Visual Basic application. To hide the mouse pointer, pass *False* to ShowCursor, and to show it again, pass *True*.

In a screen saver application, I declare the ShowCursor function and call it where appropriate to temporarily hide or reshow the mouse pointer.

NOTE: In Visual Basic, we refer to the mouse *pointer,* but in Visual C++ it's called the mouse *cursor.* This is why the function name is ShowCursor instead of ShowPointer, which would be more logical to us Visual Basic types.

Here is the declaration for the API function ShowCursor:

```
Private Declare Function ShowCursor _
Lib "user32" ( _
    ByVal bShow As Long _
) As Long
```

Here are two examples of the use of the ShowCursor function, one that hides and one that shows the mouse pointer:

```
'Hide mouse pointer
x = ShowCursor(False)

'Show mouse pointer
x = ShowCursor(True)
```

Be sure to pair these functions so that the mouse pointer is properly restored at the termination of the program.

Dear John, How Do I...
Speed Up the Graphics in a Screen Saver?

The first time I created a screen saver using Visual Basic, I put each iteration of the graphics into a timer event, with the timer's Interval property set to the fastest possible value, 1 millisecond. This worked well, but there's an even faster technique. Here's the basic outline to follow:

```
Private Sub Form_Load()
    Show
    Do
        '(Display graphics here)
        DoEvents    'Yield execution to the system
    Loop
End Sub
```

The execution of the program actually stays in the Form_Load event procedure until the program is terminated. The DoEvents command lets the system perform housekeeping tasks, such as checking for keypresses and mouse activity, but control is returned to the graphics generating loop as soon as possible.

You'll need to add code to allow the execution to exit from this loop when mouse or keyboard activity is detected, and you'll need to add code to prepare the graphics display. Take a look at the screen saver listing in the section "Dear John, How Do I...Create a Screen Saver?" earlier in this chapter to see how a keypress causes the execution to exit the loop. The concept to grasp here is that the tight looping lets the graphics updating proceed as quickly as the system will allow while still letting the system monitor for keyboard and mouse activity.

Dear John, How Do I...
Detect Mouse Movement or a
Mouse Click to Terminate a Screen Saver?

The most obvious place to detect mouse movement is in the MouseMove event, but this presents a problem. The MouseMove event is triggered once when the application starts, even if the mouse doesn't physically move. The workaround for this problem is to detect the first MouseMove event and to stop the screen saver only if the mouse actually moves from its starting position. Here's the code that accomplishes this technique:

```
Private Sub Form_MouseMove( _
    Button As Integer, _
    Shift As Integer, _
    X As Single, _
    Y As Single _
)
    Static Xlast, Ylast
    Dim Xnow As Single
    Dim Ynow As Single
    'Get current position
    Xnow = X
    Ynow = Y
    'On first move, simply record position
    If Xlast = 0 And Ylast = 0 Then
        Xlast = Xnow
        Ylast = Ynow
        Exit Sub
    End If
    'Quit only if mouse actually changes position
    If Xnow <> Xlast Or Ynow <> Ylast Then
        QuitFlag = True
    End If
End Sub
```

The static variables *Xlast* and *Ylast* keep track of the starting position of the mouse pointer. The program terminates if and only if the MouseMove event occurs and the mouse is no longer at the starting location. It's assumed that the mouse is always at a nonzero location to begin with, but even if the mouse is at the location (0, 0) when the screen saver starts, the program will still terminate correctly when the mouse starts to move.

Mouse clicks are easier to detect. A form's Click event can cause the screen saver to terminate, as shown in the following code:

```
Private Sub Form_Click()
    'Quit if mouse is clicked
    QuitFlag = True
End Sub
```

> **NOTE:** If your screen saver contains other controls on its main form, you'll probably want to handle mouse clicks on those objects too. Simply add the above code to the Click event for each of the objects.

Dear John, How Do I...

Detect a Keypress to Terminate a Screen Saver?

The form's KeyPress event can be used to detect keyboard activity, but this doesn't actually catch all keyboard activity. For example, pressing and releasing a shift key does not cause the form's KeyPress event to fire. Instead, I chose to watch for keyboard activity by using the form's KeyDown event. This stops the screen saver the moment any key, including one of the shift keys, is pressed:

```
Private Sub Form_KeyDown(KeyCode As Integer, Shift As Integer)
    'Quit if any key is pressed
    QuitFlag = True
End Sub
```

Dear John, How Do I...

Use an Image of the Screen as a Screen Saver?

A lot of nifty screen savers act on the current display without permanently affecting any running applications. Perhaps you've seen those screen savers that cause the display to melt and drip away or to swirl down a drain. By using a few Windows API functions, you can easily copy the current display into a full screen form on which you can do whatever you want to the pixels without actually affecting the "real" display.

Below is the listing for a screen saver that demonstrates this effect. This program is similar to Ssaver1, which was introduced in the first section of this chapter. The main difference is the addition of the API functions used to grab the screen contents and some enhancements based on some of the other sections in this chapter. Notice the declarations at the start of the listing for the API functions BitBlt, GetDesktopWindow, GetDC, and ReleaseDC, which are all required to copy the screen onto the form. These functions are called in the Form_Load event procedure to display a copy of the screen on the main form. I've named this screen saver example Ssaver2.

Follow the same procedure as in the first section to compile this application to an executable file in the Windows directory with the extension SCR. Also, for proper operation, be sure to set the following properties of the form: set AutoRedraw to *True*, BorderStyle to *0 - None*, KeyPreview to *True*, and WindowState to *2 - Maximized*. Finally, add a Timer control named *tmrExitNotify* to the form and set its Enabled property to *False* and its Interval property to *1*.

Here's the code:

```
'Ssaver2
Option Explicit

'Declare API to hide or show mouse pointer
Private Declare Function ShowCursor _
Lib "user32" ( _
    ByVal bShow As Long _
) As Long

'Declare API to get a copy of entire screen
Private Declare Function BitBlt _
Lib "gdi32" ( _
    ByVal hDestDC As Long, _
    ByVal x As Long, ByVal y As Long, _
    ByVal nWidth As Long, _
    ByVal nHeight As Long, _
    ByVal hSrcDC As Long, _
    ByVal XSrc As Long, ByVal YSrc As Long, _
    ByVal dwRop As Long _
) As Long

'Declare API to get handle to screen
Private Declare Function GetDesktopWindow _
Lib "user32" () As Long

'Declare API to convert handle to device context
Private Declare Function GetDC _
Lib "user32" ( _
    ByVal hwnd As Long _
) As Long

'Declare API to release device context
Private Declare Function ReleaseDC _
Lib "user32" ( _
    ByVal hwnd As Long, _
    ByVal hdc As Long _
) As Long

'Define module-level variables
Dim QuitFlag As Boolean

Private Sub Form_Click()
    'Quit if mouse is clicked
    QuitFlag = True
End Sub
```

(continued)

```
Private Sub Form_KeyDown(KeyCode As Integer, Shift As Integer)
    'Quit if any key is pressed
    QuitFlag = True
End Sub

Private Sub Form_Load()
    Dim x As Long, y As Long
    Dim XSrc As Long, YSrc As Long
    Dim dwRop As Long, hwndSrc As Long, hSrcDC As Long
    Dim Res As Long
    Dim PowerOfTwo
    Dim m1, m2
    Dim n1, n2
    Dim PixelColor, PixelCount
    'Don't allow multiple instances of screen saver
    If App.PrevInstance = True Then
        Unload Me
        Exit Sub
    End If

    'Hide mouse pointer
    x = ShowCursor(False)
    'Proceed based on command line
    Select Case UCase$(Left$(Command$, 2))
    'Put the show on the road
    Case "/S"
        'Display different graphics every time
        Randomize
        'Copy entire desktop screen into picture box
        ScaleMode = vbPixels
        Move 0, 0, Screen.Width + 1, Screen.Height + 1
        dwRop = &HCC0020
        hwndSrc = GetDesktopWindow()
        hSrcDC = GetDC(hwndSrc)
        Res = BitBlt(hdc, 0, 0, ScaleWidth, _
            ScaleHeight, hSrcDC, 0, 0, dwRop)
        Res = ReleaseDC(hwndSrc, hSrcDC)
        'Display full size
        Show
        'First time use high power of 2
        PowerOfTwo = 128
        'Graphics loop
        Do
            'Map screen into rectangular blocks
            Scale (0, 0)-(PowerOfTwo, PowerOfTwo)
            'Set a random solid color
            PixelColor = (PixelColor * 9 + 7) Mod 16
```

(continued)

```
            PixelCount = 0
            'Algorithm to hit each location on screen
            m1 = Int(Rnd * (PowerOfTwo \ 4)) * 4 + 1
            m2 = Int(Rnd * (PowerOfTwo \ 4)) * 4 + 1
            n1 = Int(Rnd * (PowerOfTwo \ 2)) * 2 + 1
            n2 = Int(Rnd * (PowerOfTwo \ 2)) * 2 + 1
            Do
                'Jump to next coordinate
                x = (x * m1 + n1) Mod PowerOfTwo
                If x <> 0 Then
                    y = (y * m2 + n2) Mod PowerOfTwo
                Else
                    'Let system do its thing
                    DoEvents
                End If
                'Fill rectangular block with solid color
                Line (x, y)-(x + 1, y + 1), QBColor(PixelColor), BF
                PixelCount = PixelCount + 1
                'Exit this loop only to quit screen saver
                If QuitFlag = True Then Exit Do
            Loop Until PixelCount = PowerOfTwo * PowerOfTwo
            PowerOfTwo = 2 ^ (Int(Rnd * 5) + 2)
        Loop Until QuitFlag = True
        'Can't quit in this context; let timer do it
        tmrExitNotify.Enabled = True
    Case Else
        Unload Me
        Exit Sub
    End Select
End Sub

Private Sub Form_MouseMove( _
    Button As Integer, _
    Shift As Integer, _
    X As Single, _
    Y As Single _
)
    Static Xlast, Ylast
    Dim Xnow As Single
    Dim Ynow As Single
    'Get current position
    Xnow = X
    Ynow = Y
    'On first move, simply record position
    If Xlast = 0 And Ylast = 0 Then
        Xlast = Xnow
        Ylast = Ynow
```

(continued)

```
        Exit Sub
    End If
    'Quit only if mouse actually changes position
    If Xnow <> Xlast Or Ynow <> Ylast Then
        QuitFlag = True
    End If
End Sub

Private Sub tmrExitNotify_Timer()
    'Time to quit
    Unload Me
End Sub

Private Sub Form_Unload(Cancel As Integer)
    Dim x
    'Show mouse pointer
    x = ShowCursor(True)
End Sub
```

The graphics update loop in the Form_Load event procedure draws solid rectangular blocks of color, causing the display to gradually dissolve to the given color. Figure 23-2 shows the effect, with the original display dissolving to a solid gray.

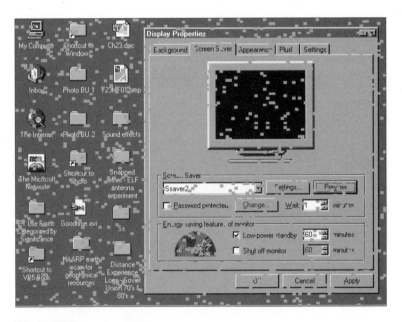

Figure 23-2.
The dissolving-display screen saver in action.

See Also...

- The Ssaver application in Chapter 27, "Graphics," for additional creative screen saver effects

Dear John, How Do I...

Add Password and Setup Capabilities to a Screen Saver?

Windows automatically passes a command line parameter to the screen saver when it starts it up, based on how, and in what mode, the program is started. These command parameters and their descriptions are as follows:

/a   The Change password button has been clicked in the Display Properties dialog box.

/p   A preview is shown in the Display Properties dialog box whenever the Screen Saver tab is activated.

/c   The Settings button has been clicked in the Display Properties dialog box.

/s   The Preview button has been clicked in the Display Properties dialog box, or the application was started normally by the system.

I check for these parameters in the Form_Load event procedure and take appropriate action based on the way the screen saver was started. In the two sample screen savers already presented in this chapter, I check only for the /s command parameter and terminate the program whenever any other parameter is used. This could be approached in a more user-friendly way by looking for some of the other command parameters and showing a message about the options, as shown here:

```
'Configuration command
Case "/C"
    'Temporarily show mouse pointer
    x = ShowCursor(True)
    'Perform any user interaction
    MsgBox "No setup options for this screen saver"
    'Hide mouse pointer
    x = ShowCursor(False)
    'Configuration is completed
    Unload Me
    Exit Sub
'Password setting command
Case "/A"
```

(continued)

```
'Temporarily show mouse pointer
x = ShowCursor(True)
'Get and record new password here
MsgBox "No password for this screen saver"
'Hide mouse pointer
x = ShowCursor(False)
'Setting of new password is completed
Unload Me
Exit Sub
```

I've created a third screen saver, Ssaver3, which demonstrates the addition of a configuration setup form. Adding password capabilities can be done in a similar way. To implement password capabilities, you would use a form to create and verify a password when the application is started with the /a command parameter and another form to enter the password when the user tries to terminate the program after it has been started with the /s command parameter.

This program displays stars randomly on the screen and lets the user specify the number of points for the stars. Very different effects are created when you set different numbers of star points, as you'll discover if you try settings such as 3, 7, 17, and 97 points.

To create this screen saver, start with a new Standard EXE project, and add a Timer control named *tmrExitNotify* to Form1. Set the timer's Interval property to *1* and its Enabled property to *False*. Also, set the form's BorderStyle property to *0 - None* and its WindowState property to *2 - Maximized*.

The number of points the user specifies is saved and retrieved from the Registry using the SaveSetting and GetSetting functions. These functions are described in Chapter 14, "The Registry." Here is the complete listing for Ssaver3:

```
'Ssaver3
Option Explicit

'Declare API to hide or show mouse pointer
Private Declare Function ShowCursor _
Lib "user32" ( _
    ByVal bShow As Long _
) As Long

'Define data structure for Polygon API function
Private Type POINTAPI
    x As Long
    y As Long
End Type
```

(continued)

```
'Declare API to draw polygonal "stars"
Private Declare Function Polygon _
Lib "gdi32" ( _
    ByVal hdc As Long, _
    lpPoint As POINTAPI, _
    ByVal nCount As Long _
) As Long

'Declare module-level variables
Dim QuitFlag As Boolean

Private Sub Form_Click()
    'Quit if mouse is clicked
    QuitFlag = True
End Sub

Private Sub Form_KeyDown(KeyCode As Integer, Shift As Integer)
    'Quit if any key is pressed
    QuitFlag = True
End Sub

Private Sub Form_Load()
    Dim i As Integer, j As Integer
    Dim x As Long
    Dim nPoints As Long
    Dim xCenter As Long, yCenter As Long
    Dim Radius As Single, Angle As Single
    'Don't allow multiple instances of screen saver
    If App.PrevInstance = True Then
        Unload Me
        Exit Sub
    End If
    'Hide mouse pointer
    x = ShowCursor(False)
    'Proceed based on command line
    Select Case UCase$(Left$(Command$, 2))
    'Display Properties dialog box quick preview mode
    Case "/P"
        Unload Me
        Exit Sub
    'Configuration command
    Case "/C"
        'Temporarily show mouse pointer
        x = ShowCursor(True)
        'Perform any user interaction
        SS3Setup.Show vbModal
```

(continued)

```
            'Hide mouse pointer
            x = ShowCursor(False)
            'Configuration is completed
            Unload Me
            Exit Sub
        'Password setting command
        Case "/A"
            'Temporarily show mouse pointer
            x = ShowCursor(True)
            'Get and record new password here
            MsgBox "Password is not available for this screen saver"
            'Hide mouse pointer
            x = ShowCursor(False)
            'Setting of new password is completed
            Unload Me
            Exit Sub
        'Put the show on the road
        Case "/S"
            'Display full size
            Show
            'Display different graphics every time
            Randomize
            'Get current setting from the Registry
            nPoints = Val(GetSetting("Ssaver3", _
                "Startup", "Points", "5"))
            'Size array for number of star points
            ReDim P(nPoints) As POINTAPI
            'Initialize graphics parameters
            Scale (0, 0)-(1, 1)
            BackColor = vbBlack
            ScaleMode = vbPixels
            FillStyle = vbSolid
            'Loop to create graphics
            Do
                'Generate a somewhat random radius
                Radius = (1 + Rnd) * ScaleWidth / 20
                'Generate random center of star
                xCenter = Rnd * ScaleWidth
                yCenter = Rnd * ScaleHeight
                'Build array of polygon coordinates
                For i = 0 To nPoints - 1
                    j = (j + nPoints \ 2) Mod nPoints
                    Angle = j * 6.2831853 / nPoints
                    P(i).x = xCenter + Radius * Cos(Angle)
```

(continued)

```
                P(i).y = yCenter + Radius * Sin(Angle)
        Next i
        'Create unique fill color each time
        FillColor = RGB(Rnd * 256, Rnd * 256, Rnd * 256)
        'Draw polygon, filling the interior
        x = Polygon(hdc, P(0), UBound(P))
        'Yield execution
        DoEvents
    Loop Until QuitFlag = True
    'Can't quit in this context; let timer do it
    tmrExitNotify.Enabled = True
    Case Else
        Unload Me
        Exit Sub
    End Select
End Sub

Private Sub Form_MouseMove( _
    Button As Integer, _
    Shift As Integer, _
    X As Single, _
    Y As Single _
)
    Static Xlast, Ylast
    Dim Xnow As Single
    Dim Ynow As Single
    'Get current position
    Xnow = X
    Ynow = Y
    'On first move, simply record position
    If Xlast = 0 And Ylast = 0 Then
        Xlast = Xnow
        Ylast = Ynow
        Exit Sub
    End If
    'Quit only if mouse actually changes position
    If Xnow <> Xlast Or Ynow <> Ylast Then
        QuitFlag = True
    End If
End Sub

Private Sub tmrExitNotify_Timer()
    'Time to quit
    Unload Me
End Sub
```

(continued)

```
Private Sub Form_Unload(Cancel As Integer)
    Dim x
    'Show mouse pointer
    x = ShowCursor(True)
End Sub
```

The dialog box used to make the configuration settings is a form named *SS3Setup*, which is activated from the main form when the command line contains the */c* command parameter. To create this dialog box, add a new form, and add a label, a text box named *txtPoints*, and a command button named *cmdOK*, as shown in Figure 23-3.

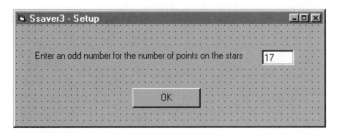

Figure 23-3.
The SS3Setup *form at design time.*

Add the following code to *SS3Setup* to handle the maintenance of the number-of-points setting:

```
'SS3Setup
Option Explicit

Private Sub Form_Load()
    'Center this form
    Left = (Screen.Width - Width) \ 2
    Top = (Screen.Height - Height) \ 2
    'Get current setting from the Registry
    txtPoints.Text = GetSetting("Ssaver3", _
        "Startup", "Points", "5")
End Sub

Private Sub cmdOK_Click()
    Dim nPoints As Integer
    'Get user input value
    nPoints = Val(txtPoints.Text)
```

(continued)

```
'Make sure nPoints is odd and greater than 1
If ((nPoints And 1) = 0) Or (nPoints < 3) Then
    Beep
    MsgBox "You must enter an odd number greater than 1", _
        vbExclamation, "Ssaver3"
    Exit Sub
End If
'Save the setting
SaveSetting "Ssaver3", _
    "Startup", "Points", txtPoints.Text
Unload Me
End Sub
```

Figure 23-4 shows the *SS3Setup* form displayed when the settings button is clicked in the Display Properties dialog box for the Ssaver3 screen saver. Figure 23-5 on the following page shows the screen saver as it appears when it has been given a setting of *17*, which creates 17-point stars on the display in random colors and at random locations.

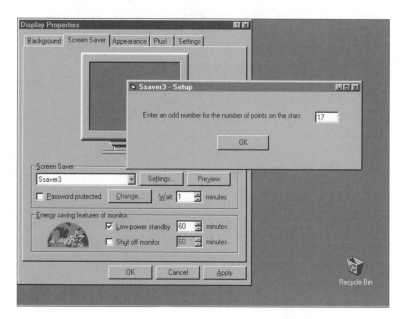

Figure 23-4.
The Ssaver3 Settings dialog box.

Figure 23-5.
The Ssaver3 screen saver in action, showing 17-point stars.

 See Also...

- The Ssaver application in Chapter 27, "Graphics," for an example of a more complete screen saver application

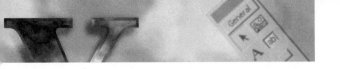

CHAPTER TWENTY-FOUR

Project Development

This chapter presents a few tricks I've picked up along the way that are useful for overall project development. The first section shows you a very simple but often overlooked technique for grabbing images of your running application so that they can be added to your help file. (Help files, which are an important part of any complete application, are covered more fully in Chapter 15, "Help Files.")

The second and third sections in this chapter explain how to use resource files and string databases to internationalize applications. These techniques will give you a great start on building applications for users around the world.

Dear John, How Do I...

Grab a Running Form and Save It as a Bitmap?

Here's a simple technique for grabbing all or part of the display to convert it to a bitmap (BMP) file, a technique that you might already know: simply press the Print Screen key to copy the entire screen to the clipboard. You can do this at any time while Microsoft Windows is running. (If you want to copy only the form that currently has the focus, press Alt-Print Screen.) You won't hear a beep or notice anything other than perhaps a slight delay in the current program's operation, but the screen's contents (or the form's contents) will quickly be copied to the system's clipboard. Most of the forms shown in this book were grabbed using the Alt-Print Screen technique.

Pasting the Graphic into Paint

To process the clipboard's graphics contents, run the Windows Paint application, and paste the clipboard's contents into it. You should see the upper-left corner of the captured display in Paint's workspace, as shown in Figure 24-1. With Paint, you can scroll to any part of the image, and you can use its tools to make editing changes.

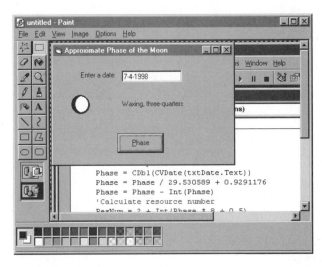

Figure 24-1.
A portion of a captured display, as shown in Paint.

Save As vs. Copy To

Choose Save As from the File menu to save the image as a BMP file. To save a smaller region of the image, select part of the image using the rectangle selection tool, and then choose Copy To from Paint's Edit menu. This menu option prompts for a filename. Unlike the Save As option, the Copy To option saves only the area of the image within the selection rectangle. Figure 24-2 shows the selection rectangle delineating a small part of the entire original screen image, and Figure 24-3 shows this small image after it has been reloaded into Paint from the BMP file it was written to.

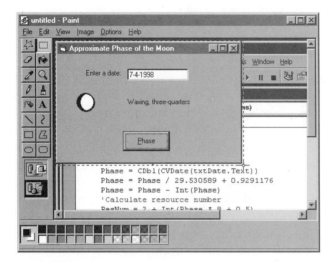

Figure 24-2.
A selection rectangle delineating a portion of a larger image.

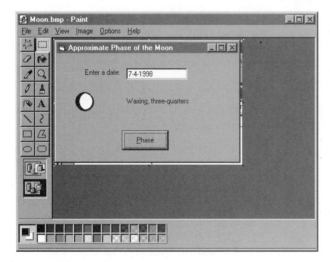

Figure 24-3.
The selected image loaded into Paint.

Dear John, How Do I...

Use Resource Files?

Resource file capability was added to Visual Basic primarily to make it easier to internationalize applications. Before resource files were available, you had to edit all the captions, labels, and other strings for an application within the Visual Basic project itself if you wanted your application to appear in another language. (I'm referring to spoken languages here, of course, not computer programming languages.) But now you can isolate all of your application's strings in a resource file, making it much easier to edit the strings for a second language. I've also found another useful feature of resource files: they allow you to easily include numerous graphics bitmap and icon files directly in your project. These images can then be loaded and manipulated from resource files much faster than from individual external files.

You can load one, and only one, resource file into your Visual Basic project. But you can stuff a lot of strings, icons, bitmaps, sound files, and even video clips into a single resource file. On the following pages, I demonstrate the process of building a small resource file and then provide an example application that uses its contents.

Creating a Resource File

Start by creating an RC file using any text editor, such as Notepad. For this example, enter the following short file, which defines a collection of eight icons and eight strings for our resource file:

```
// MOON.RC - Resource file for moon phases example
//
// D:\TOOLS\RESOURCE\RC /R /FO MOON.RES MOON.RC

// Icons
2   ICON   "C:\VB\Graphics\icons\elements\Moon01.ico"
3   ICON   "C:\VB\Graphics\icons\elements\Moon02.ico"
4   ICON   "C:\VB\Graphics\icons\elements\Moon03.ico"
5   ICON   "C:\VB\Graphics\icons\elements\Moon04.ico"
6   ICON   "C:\VB\Graphics\icons\elements\Moon05.ico"
7   ICON   "C:\VB\Graphics\icons\elements\Moon06.ico"
8   ICON   "C:\VB\Graphics\icons\elements\Moon07.ico"
9   ICON   "C:\VB\Graphics\icons\elements\Moon08.ico"

// Strings
STRINGTABLE
```

(continued)

```
BEGIN
    2   "New"
    3   "Waxing, one-quarter"
    4   "Waxing, one-half"
    5   "Waxing, three-quarters"
    6   "Full"
    7   "Waning, three-quarters"
    8   "Waning, one-half"
    9   "Waning, one-quarter"
END
```

There are several details to note about this resource file listing:

■ Comment lines begin with two slashes and are ignored during compilation.

■ I've stayed away from using the resource number *1* because Visual Basic reserves this resource number for your application's internally stored icon.

■ Strings are defined in one or more string tables in your resource file. In my listing, you'll see one such table. It starts with a STRINGTABLE declaration, and all strings are defined in a block between BEGIN and END lines.

■ You include binary resources indirectly, by listing the full paths to the files in which the data resides. At compile time, the contents of each file will be pulled into the final RES file. My listing includes the eight phase-of-the-moon icons from the Visual Basic CD-ROM. (You will need to change these paths.) Binary file types you might find useful in resource files include bitmaps (BMP files), sound clips (WAV files), video clips (AVI files), and others. Refer to the Visual Basic online help, under the LoadResData function, for more information.

If your application has a large resource file that is likely to be used frequently, you should be aware of some further details of resource files. There are options that control when each resource is actually loaded into memory behind the scenes and when a resource can be discarded. Also, resources with resource numbers in the same block of 16 numbers (that is, those for which the most significant 12 bits of their 16-bit integer resource numbers are identical) will be loaded by the system simultaneously whenever any one of the resources is loaded by Visual Basic. You will probably want to work with this feature instead of against it, especially if your resources are large chunks of binary data and speed is your goal.

Notice that I've typed the compiler command line into a comment line at the beginning of my listing. This helps me remember exactly how to run the resource compiler. (For more information about using the resource compiler, check the Microsoft Developer Network CD-ROM, or look for a file named RESOURCE.TXT in the TOOLS\RESOURCE directory on your Visual Basic CD-ROM.) This command line runs the RC.EXE program directly from the Visual Basic CD-ROM. (Be sure you have your Visual Basic CD-ROM in the drive before running this command.) If your RC.EXE program is in a different location, be sure you modify this command line appropriately.

When the file has been successfully compiled, a sample resource file named MOON.RES will be created. Use this file in the next step of our example.

Using a Resource File in Your Application

I designed this simple resource file to demonstrate the loading of strings and one type of binary data file (the Moon icons). The sample program I describe here loads these resources as required, to show a very approximate phase-of-the-moon report for any given date. Start a new Standard EXE project, and add a TextBox control named *txtDate*, a Label control named *lblString*, an Image control named *imgMoon*, and a command button named *cmdPhase*. Refer to Figure 24-4 for the placement and appearance of these controls. If you want, you can add a prompting label next to the text box and change the form's caption to spruce up the form a little. Add the compiled resource file to the project: from the Project menu, choose Add File, and then select MOON.RES.

Add the following code to the form:

```
Option Explicit

Private Sub cmdPhase_Click()
    Dim Phase, ResNum
    'Calculate phase
    Phase = CDbl(CVDate(txtDate.Text))
    Phase = Phase / 29.530589 + 0.9291176
    Phase = Phase - Int(Phase)
    'Calculate resource number
    ResNum = 2 + Int(Phase * 8 + 0.5)
    If ResNum = 10 Then ResNum = 2
    'Load bitmap and string
```

(continued)

```
        imgMoon.Picture = LoadResPicture(ResNum, vbResIcon)
        lblString.Caption = LoadResString(ResNum)
End Sub

Private Sub Form_Load()
        txtDate.Text = Date$
        cmdPhase_Click
End Sub
```

Most of this code is used for the calculation of the approximate phase of the moon for any given date. Once the phase is determined, a corresponding image and a string description are loaded from the project's resource file. The LoadResPicture and LoadResString functions do the loading. Figure 24-4 shows the Approximate Phase of the Moon form during development.

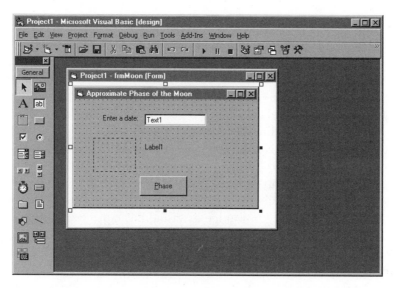

Figure 24-4.
The Approximate Phase of the Moon form under construction.

Figure 24-5 on the following page shows the program in action, displaying and describing the approximate phase of the moon for July 4, 1998.

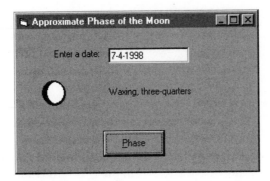

Figure 24-5.
The Approximate Phase of the Moon program in action.

When to Use a Resource File

As mentioned, the original motivation behind Microsoft's decision to add resource file capabilities to Visual Basic was to make it easier for applications to be internationalized. In a form's Load event procedure, for example, you can easily load string resources into the Caption properties of command buttons, forms, and Label controls. Menus, sounds, pictures, text boxes—you name it—can all be modified at runtime to reflect the language of the user. The big advantage of this approach is that the task of reconstructing an application for one or more foreign languages is reduced to the single task of duplicating and editing an external ASCII resource file. You can then turn the resource file over to a skilled translator, who can create a new ASCII resource file without any working knowledge of Visual Basic programming.

In addition to making it easier to internationalize, resource files provide a few other advantages worth mentioning: For one thing, application speed is improved—graphics images load faster as resources than from external files. A second advantage is that multiple images are easier to manipulate. With earlier versions of Visual Basic, a common technique for manipulating multiple images was to load them into multiple controls. The Moon icons, for example, can be loaded into separate Image or PictureBox controls, and these controls can then be manipulated to display one moon image at a time. Since Visual Basic 4, however, you can store the bitmaps in a resource file and then load each bitmap into a single control as needed, thus avoiding the complexity and processing time of manipulating multiple controls.

Dear John, How Do I...

Use a String Database for Internationalization?

You can use a database to store strings that need to be translated and load those strings as needed. This lets you use Microsoft Access or Visual Basic to build tools that simplify the translation process. In general, resource files are simpler and easier to program than databases, but when localization is a primary concern it's hard to beat a string database.

The structure of a string database can be very simple. In the example shown in Figure 24-6, a single record set contains all the translated versions of each control on a form. Three option buttons on the start form determine which language to use.

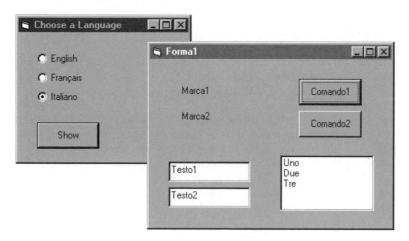

Figure 24-6.
Choose a language, and then click Show to display the translated version of a form.

Entries in the database are indexed by the control's name, so a For Each loop can get the translated version of each control's caption or text based on the name of the control. A Select Case statement decides which property to change, based on the control type, which can be determined using the TypeName function. The code is shown on the following page.

```
Option Explicit

Private Sub cmdShow_Click()
    'Translate the test form into the
    'selected language
    If optLanguage(0) Then
        ShowLocal frm1, "English"
    ElseIf optLanguage(1) Then
        ShowLocal frm1, "French"
    Else
        ShowLocal frm1, "Italian"
    End If
End Sub


'Translate the strings on the form
Sub ShowLocal(frmLocal As Object, Language As String)
    Dim wrkDatabase As Workspace
    Dim dbStrings As Database
    Dim recStrings As Recordset
    Dim arString As Variant
    Dim iCount As Integer
    Dim cntIndex As Control
    'Create workspace, open database, and get set of records
    Set wrkDatabase = CreateWorkspace("", "admin", "", dbUseJet)
    Set dbStrings = wrkDatabase.OpenDatabase("strings.mdb")
    Set recStrings = dbStrings.OpenRecordset("Strings")
    'Use names of controls as index in record set
    recStrings.Index = "ControlName"
    'Internationalize each control name
    For Each cntIndex In frmLocal.Controls
        recStrings.Seek "=", cntIndex.Name
        Select Case TypeName(cntIndex)
            'Change Text property for text boxes
            Case "TextBox"
                cntIndex.Text = recStrings.Fields(Language)
            'Change captions on others
            Case "Label", "OptionButton", "CheckBox", "Frame", _
                "CommandButton"
                cntIndex.Caption = recStrings.Fields(Language)
            'Change List property for list boxes (record contains
            'an array)
```

(continued)

414

```
            Case "ListBox", "ComboBox"
                arString = MakeArray(recStrings.Fields(Language))
                For iCount = 0 To UBound(arString)
                    cntIndex.AddItem arString(iCount)
                Next iCount
            'Ignore pictures, timers, scrollbars, and so on
            Case Else
        End Select
    Next cntIndex
    'Internationalize form name
    recStrings.Seek "=", frmLocal.Name
    frmLocal.Caption = recStrings.Fields(Language)
    'Close record set and database
    recStrings.Close
    dbStrings.Close
    'Show the form
    frmLocal.Show
End Sub


'Utility function to convert a semicolon-delineated list
'to an array
Function MakeArray(strSource As String) As Variant
    Dim arTemp()
    Dim iCount As Integer, iPos As Integer
    Do
        ReDim Preserve arTemp(iCount)
        iPos = InStr(strSource, ";")
        If iPos Then
            arTemp(iCount) = Left(strSource, iPos - 1)
            strSource = Right(strSource, Len(strSource) - (iPos + 1))
            iCount = iCount + 1
        Else
            arTemp(iCount) = strSource
            Exit Do
        End If
    Loop
    MakeArray = arTemp
End Function
```

I've included an Edit button on the start form so that you can easily modify the database that contains all the string information. I created the form shown in Figure 24-7 on the following page using the Data Form Wizard on the STRINGS.MDB database. STRINGS.MDB was created using Microsoft Access.

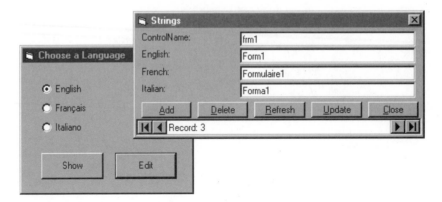

Figure 24-7.
Click Edit to modify the string database.

You can use the DebugBuild flag to control the display of the Edit button, preventing users from changing the string database. Just set the Edit button's Visible property to *False,* and use the following code to change it for debug builds:

```
#Const DebugBuild = 1

#If DebugBuild Then
    Private Sub Form_Load()
        'Display Edit button only on debug builds
        cmdEdit.Visible = True
    End Sub

    Private Sub cmdEdit_Click()
        'Display data entry form for the database
        frmStrings.Show
    End Sub
#End If
```

In this way, you can create applications that contain built-in tools for maintaining translated versions.

See Also...

- The Designing International Software and General Considerations When Writing International Code topics in Visual Basic Books Online for more information about internationalization issues

CHAPTER TWENTY-FIVE

Advanced Programming Techniques

With Visual Basic, it's easy to streamline and extend the capabilities of your applications. This chapter presents a few advanced programming techniques that will help you make your Visual Basic applications more efficient and robust.

First I show you how to create a dynamic link library (DLL), which is a great way to speed up the execution of critical sections of your Visual Basic applications. Prior to Visual Basic 4, the only way you could create a DLL was by using another programming language, such as C. C is still a good choice, but you can also now use Visual Basic itself to create high-speed, compiled DLL modules using the in-process ActiveX technology. I'll show you examples of both DLL creation techniques.

Although not new to Visual Basic, *remote automation* makes its debut in this chapter. Remote automation lets you access objects running on servers from your local machine. The Visual Basic Enterprise Edition can create remote applications that run on Microsoft Windows NT and Microsoft Windows 95 servers. I'll walk you through creating, debugging, installing, and using a simple remote application. Plus I'll give you some troubleshooting tips for working with remote automation.

The final section introduces another feature of Visual Basic: the ability to create add-ins for Visual Basic's Integrated Development Environment (IDE). In this section, you will learn how to create a simple add-in using Visual Basic itself.

Dear John, How Do I...
Use Visual Basic to Create an ActiveX DLL?

You can use Visual Basic to create DLLs for 32-bit Windows-based applications. Visual Basic uses in-process ActiveX technology to accomplish this. A DLL created in this manner is a real DLL, complete with the filename extension DLL. The main difference between an in-process ActiveX DLL and a conventional DLL for earlier versions of Windows is the way that calling programs interface with the provided routines. For example, you create and access an ActiveX DLL by declaring a variable of the object's type, and then you use that object's properties and methods to achieve the desired results. With the old DLL calling convention, you use the Declare statement to define functions within the DLL, which is not possible with the new type of DLL. ActiveX DLLs provide objects, not just functions and procedures.

The Fraction Object

In this example, you will create a simple in-process ActiveX DLL, step by step, to see how this works. For complete information about all the technical details and guidelines for creating DLLs of this type, see the Visual Basic documentation. However, if you follow all the steps listed here, you should be able to create this example DLL with no complications. You'll create an in-process ActiveX DLL component named Math that provides a Fraction class, which will let a calling program perform simple math operations with fractions. The Fraction object will provide two public properties, Num and Den, and four methods for performing addition, subtraction, multiplication, and division of fractions. One private method within the Fraction class will assist in reducing fractions to lowest terms.

Start a new project, and double-click the ActiveX DLL icon in the New Project window. Visual Basic will add a class module to your project and set the project type to ActiveX DLL. In the Properties window, change the class module's Name property to *Fraction*. This is the name other applications will use to create instances of this object. From the File menu, choose Save Fraction As, and save the class module as MATHFRAC.CLS. This is the name of the file itself—I like to combine the name of the project and the name of the class to identify the file.

This project will contain only the Fraction class module, but let's suppose that we want to add more object definitions of a related, mathematical nature at a later time. For this reason, set the project's Name property to *Math* (instead of *Fraction*). To do this, choose Project Properties from the Project menu to display the Project Properties dialog box. In the Project Name text box, type *Math*, and then click OK. Then choose the Save Project As option from the File menu, and save the project as MATHPROJ.VBP.

It's useful to keep in mind the distinction between the names of files that make up the development of a component and the Name properties of the various parts within that component. For example, the project's filename—in this case, MATHPROJ.VBP—is important only during the development cycle of the project. However, the project's Name property—in this case, *Math*—can be important for programmatically identifying the component containing the Fraction object. For example, if several ActiveX DLLs are used by an application, there might be two Fraction objects defined in different components. If so, you can explicitly identify a particular Fraction object by prefixing references to it with the name of its component. The following line, for example, would create an instance of the Fraction object that's defined within the Math project, even if some other Fraction object is defined in a different component:

```
Public Frac As New Math.Fraction
```

If only one Fraction class is defined within all components that make up an application, the following line suffices to create an instance of the object:

```
Public Frac As New Fraction
```

The next step is to fill out the Fraction class module with code to define its two public properties, four public methods, and one private method. Add the following code to MATHFRAC.CLS:

```
Option Explicit

Public Num
Public Den

Public Sub Add(Num2, Den2)
    Num = Num * Den2 + Den * Num2
    Den = Den * Den2
    Reduce
End Sub

Public Sub Sbt(Num2, Den2)
    Num = Num * Den2 - Den * Num2
    Den = Den * Den2
    Reduce
End Sub
```

(continued)

```
Public Sub Mul(Num2, Den2)
    Num = Num * Num2
    Den = Den * Den2
    Reduce
End Sub

Public Sub Div(Num2, Den2)
    Mul Den2, Num2
End Sub

Private Sub Reduce()
Dim s, t, u
    s = Abs(Num)
    t = Abs(Den)
    If t = 0 Then Exit Sub
    Do
        u = (s \ t) * t
        u = s - u
        s = t
        t = u
    Loop While u > 0
    Num = Num \ s
    Den = Den \ s
    If Den < 0 Then
        Num = -Num
        Den = -Den
    End If
End Sub
```

The Public properties Num and Den let a calling application set and read values that define a fraction. The four public methods Add, Sbt, Mul, and Div perform fraction math on the Num and Den properties using a second fraction that is passed as two parameters. (Notice that I couldn't use the more logical Sub abbreviation to name the subtract procedure, because this is reserved by Visual Basic for naming subroutines.) The Reduce method is private and is used internally by the DLL to reduce all fraction results to lowest terms.

We're almost ready to compile and test the Math ActiveX DLL, but first open the Project menu and choose Math Properties to display the Project Properties dialog box. Notice that the Startup Object field is already set to *(None)* because we didn't add a Sub Main procedure to our project as a startup point. If your object needs to perform any initialization steps, add a Sub Main procedure and change the Startup Object setting in this dialog to *Sub Main.* In this case, our Fraction object gets along just fine without any initialization code, so leave the setting as *(None).*

The Project Description field is blank, but you should always enter a short description of your project here. This is the text users will see later when they are adding a reference to your component to their projects, and it helps identify the purpose of your component. In this case, type in *Demonstration of Fraction Object* or something similar and click OK.

The final step is to compile the Math project to create a completed ActiveX DLL. Choose Make MATHPROJ.DLL from the File menu to take this final step. In the Make Project dialog box, select a location in which to save the DLL and click OK. This compiles the DLL and registers it in your computer, and you're good to go! Since Visual Basic 5 now lets us load and work with multiple projects simultaneously, let's proceed by testing the Math component right in the Visual Basic development environment.

Testing in the Development Environment

One of Visual Basic 5's new features is the capability to load multiple projects into the development environment simultaneously. This provides a great way for you to test and debug components without having to jump through a bunch of hoops.

To test an ActiveX DLL in the development environment, choose Add Project from the File menu and double-click the Standard EXE icon in the Add Project dialog box. Notice that both ActiveX DLL and Standard EXE projects are listed in the Project Explorer window. Our new project won't be anything fancy—it's designed simply to test our new Fraction object in the Math component—so leave the form name as Form1 and the project name as Project1. We do need to make Project1 the startup project, however, because nothing will happen if you try to run with the Math DLL as the startup project. Right-click on Project1 within the Project Explorer window to display a pop-up menu. Choose Set As Start Up from this menu, and notice that the highlight moves from the Math project to Project1.

Now that a specific project in our project group has been selected as the startup project, we need to make the project aware of the Math component and the objects it defines. From the Project menu, choose References, and in the References dialog box, check the Math check box. Recall that this is the setting we specified for the Math project's Name property. Click OK to close the References dialog box.

Before proceeding with the construction of the test project, save the entire current development environment configuration as a project group. The project group is a new feature starting with Visual Basic 5—it's simply an extension of the concept of saving modules and forms in a project. Only the project group saves information about the currently loaded group of projects.

A project filename extension is VBP, and a project group filename extension is VBG. From the File menu, choose Save Project Group As. Save Form1 as FORM1.FRM, the standard EXE project as PROJECT1.VBP, and the project group as MATHDEMO.VBG.

To Form1, add six text boxes and four buttons in a layout similar to that shown in Figure 25-1. Notice that I added a few Line controls and some labels to improve the appearance a little—you can add these extras if you want to.

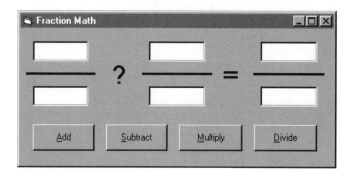

Figure 25-1.
A form for testing the new Fraction object.

Name the text controls *txtN1, txtD1, txtN2, txtD2, txtN3,* and *txtD3* to represent the numerators and denominators for three fractions as viewed from left to right. Name the command buttons *cmdAdd, cmdSubtract, cmdMultiply,* and *cmdDivide,* and change their captions to match their functions. Finally, add the following code to the form to complete the application:

```
Option Explicit

Public Frac As New Math.Fraction

Private Sub cmdAdd_Click()
    Frac.Num = txtN1.Text
    Frac.Den = txtD1.Text
    Frac.Add txtN2.Text, txtD2.Text
    txtN3.Text = Frac.Num
    txtD3.Text = Frac.Den
End Sub

Private Sub cmdDivide_Click()
    Frac.Num = txtN1.Text
    Frac.Den = txtD1.Text
```

(continued)

```
    Frac.Div txtN2.Text, txtD2.Text
    txtN3.Text = Frac.Num
    txtD3.Text = Frac.Den
End Sub

Private Sub cmdMultiply_Click()
    Frac.Num = txtN1.Text
    Frac.Den = txtD1.Text
    Frac.Mul txtN2.Text, txtD2.Text
    txtN3.Text = Frac.Num
    txtD3.Text = Frac.Den
End Sub

Private Sub cmdSubtract_Click()
    Frac.Num = txtN1.Text
    Frac.Den = txtD1.Text
    Frac.Sbt txtN2.Text, txtD2.Text
    txtN3.Text = Frac.Num
    txtD3.Text = Frac.Den
End Sub
```

At the form level, I've declared the variable *Frac* as an object reference of type Fraction, as defined in the Math DLL. The Frac object is defined at the module level, but it's not actually created until the first time you click any of the four command buttons. The Frac object is destroyed automatically when its reference goes out of scope—that is, when the form unloads.

At this point, you're ready to run the test application and let it create and use a Fraction object as defined in the Math DLL. Enter numbers for the numerators and denominators of the two fractions on the left side of the dialog box, and click the four buttons, one at a time, to perform the fraction math. The result, displayed on the right, should always be a fraction reduced to its lowest terms. Figure 25-2 shows the result of multiplying $\frac{3}{4}$ by $\frac{5}{6}$.

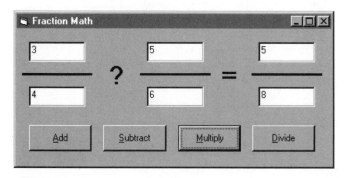

Figure 25-2.
The Fraction Math test in action.

Creating and Using the Final DLL Module

Once your DLL has been debugged and is ready to roll, you'll want to compile your in-process ActiveX project to create a shippable DLL module. All you have to do to achieve this is choose Make MATHPROJ.DLL from the File menu. It's that simple. The DLL will automatically be registered on your computer and is immediately available to any application capable of using ActiveX components.

When your DLL is in the hands of an end user, it must be registered with the user's system before it will show up in the list of references or before any external application will be able to load the DLL into its running space so that it can use the objects the DLL defines. The simplest way to register a DLL with your user's system is to use Visual Basic's Setup Wizard to create an installation disk. The registration of a DLL is set up automatically by the Setup Wizard.

Dear John, How Do I...

Use C to Create a DLL?

Visual Basic's great strength is in the speed with which it allows you to produce applications for Windows; it's hard to beat the Visual Basic programming environment on the productivity score. On the other hand, C is the language of choice for speed-critical sections of code, which you can often write as a standard block of functions in an old-fashioned (as opposed to an ActiveX) DLL file.

With the latest Visual C++ compilers, creating a DLL is easier than ever. Because this book focuses on using Microsoft tools to create applications for the 32-bit Windows 95 environment, I've streamlined the following example DLL code. This should make it easier for you to focus on the essential points of the DLL creation task. (If you need to program for the 16-bit Windows environment, or if you're using a version of C other than Microsoft Visual C++ version 2.2 or later, you'll need to make adjustments to the listings.) For the best in-depth explanation of every aspect of DLL creation, refer to the documentation that comes with your compiler.

The Two C Files

The following two listings are the only two files you'll need in your Visual C++ project. Start a new project in the 32-bit version of Visual C++, and select Dynamic Link Library as the type of project to be built. Create a DEF file as part of your project, enter the following few lines, and name this file MYDLL.DEF:

```
; Mydll.def
LIBRARY Mydll

CODE PRELOAD MOVEABLE DISCARDABLE
DATA PRELOAD MOVEABLE

EXPORTS
    TestByte          @1
    TestInteger       @2
    TestLong          @3
    TestSingle        @4
    TestDouble        @5
    ReverseString     @6
```

The DEF file tells the outside world the names of exported functions. In other words, this file provides the list of functions you can call from your Visual Basic applications.

This DLL project has just one C source code file. Enter the following lines of code in a file, save the file as MYDLL.C, and be sure the file is included in your Visual C++ project:

```c
#include <windows.h>
#include <ole2.h>

BYTE _stdcall TestByte( BYTE a, LPBYTE b )
{
    *b = a + a;
    return( *b + a );
}

short _stdcall TestInteger( short a, short far * b )
{
    *b = a + a;
    return( *b + a );
}

LONG _stdcall TestLong( LONG a, LPLONG b )
{
    *b = a + a;
    return( *b + a );
}

float _stdcall TestSingle( float a, float far * b )
{
    *b = a + a;
    return( *b + a );
}
```

(continued)

```
double _stdcall TestDouble( double a, double far * b )
{
    *b = a + a;
    return( *b + a );
}

void _stdcall ReverseString( BSTR a )
{
    int i, iLen;
    BSTR b;
    LPSTR pA, pB;

    iLen = strlen( (LPCSTR)a );
    b = SysAllocStringLen( NULL, iLen );

    pA = (LPSTR)a;
    pB = (LPSTR)b + iLen -1;

    for ( i = 0; i < iLen; i++ )
        *pB-- = *pA++;

    pA = (LPSTR)a;
    pB = (LPSTR)b;

    for ( i = 0; i < iLen; i++ )
        *pA++ = *pB++;

    SysFreeString( b );
}
```

Click the Build All button in the Visual C++ environment to compile and link the two files in your project and create a small DLL module named MYDLL.DLL. Move or copy MYDLL.DLL to your Windows SYSTEM directory so that your Visual Basic Declare statements will be able to locate the DLL file automatically.

Testing the DLL

It's easy to try out the functions in your new DLL file from Visual Basic. To test the six functions in MYDLL.DLL, I started a new Visual Basic project and added the following code to a form containing a single command button named *cmdGo*:

```
Option Explicit

Private Declare Function TestByte _
Lib "mydll.dll" ( _
    ByVal a As Byte, _
    ByRef b As Byte _
) As Byte

Private Declare Function TestInteger _
Lib "mydll.dll" ( _
    ByVal a As Integer, _
    ByRef b As Integer _
) As Integer

Private Declare Function TestLong _
Lib "mydll.dll" ( _
    ByVal a As Long, _
    ByRef b As Long _
) As Long

Private Declare Function TestSingle _
Lib "mydll.dll" ( _
    ByVal a As Single, _
    ByRef b As Single _
) As Single

Private Declare Function TestDouble _
Lib "mydll.dll" ( _
    ByVal a As Double, _
    ByRef b As Double _
) As Double

Private Declare Sub ReverseString _
Lib "mydll.dll" ( _
    ByVal a As String _
)

Private Sub cmdGo_Click()
    Dim bytA As Byte
    Dim bytB As Byte
    Dim bytC As Byte
    Dim intA As Integer
    Dim intB As Integer
    Dim intC As Integer
```

(continued)

427

```
        Dim lngA As Long
        Dim lngB As Long
        Dim lngC As Long
        Dim sngA As Single
        Dim sngB As Single
        Dim sngC As Single
        Dim dblA As Double
        Dim dblB As Double
        Dim dblC As Double
        Dim strA As String

        bytA = 17
        bytC = TestByte(bytA, bytB)
        Print bytA, bytB, bytC

        intA = 17
        intC = TestInteger(intA, intB)
        Print intA, intB, intC

        lngA = 17
        lngC = TestLong(lngA, lngB)
        Print lngA, lngB, lngC

        sngA = 17
        sngC = TestSingle(sngA, sngB)
        Print sngA, sngB, sngC

        dblA = 17
        dblC = TestDouble(dblA, dblB)
        Print dblA, dblB, dblC

        strA = "This string will be reversed"
        Print strA
        ReverseString (strA)
        Print strA
End Sub
```

When you run this program and click the Go button, each of the new DLL functions will be called and the results will be printed on the form, as shown in Figure 25-3.

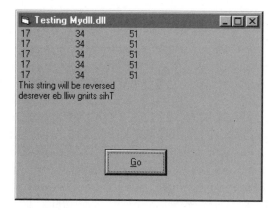

Figure 25-3.
The results of testing the functions in MYDLL.DLL.

A few words of explanation about this simple DLL are in order. Each of the five numeric functions demonstrates the passing of one data type in two ways. The first parameter is passed using the ByVal keyword, and the second is passed using ByRef. Parameters passed with ByVal can't be changed by the DLL function, but parameters passed with ByRef can be. In this test program, each function is passed a numeric value of *17* in the first parameter, which the DLL function doubles and stores in the second. Each of the numeric functions also returns a value of the same data type, and the value returned by the DLL to the Visual Basic test program is simply the sum of the two parameters. The results displayed in Figure 25-3 show how these values are modified by the DLL functions. In the Visual Basic declarations of the test program, I explicitly declared the ByRef parameters using that keyword, but because this is the default for all parameter passing in Visual Basic, you can drop the ByRef if you want to. The ByVal keyword is not optional, however, and I find it less confusing if I go ahead and explicitly declare both types of parameters. This is a matter of style, and you might prefer to drop all the ByRef keywords in your declarations.

You might have noticed in the source code that I didn't use C's int data type in the function that expects Visual Basic's Integer parameters; instead I used the keyword short. This is because in 32-bit Microsoft C an int is actually a 32-bit integer, rather than the 16-bit size that Visual Basic's Integer declaration refers to. Fortunately, if you use short you're guaranteed a 16-bit integer in all versions of Microsoft C.

Strings are now handled internally as BSTR types, both in C code, if they are declared as such, and automatically in Visual Basic. In this example, I used a Visual Basic ByVal declaration to pass a string to the ReverseString function in MYDLL.DLL. You can pass a string using ByRef, but because BSTR strings are passed around by address anyway, a string passed with ByVal can be altered, as shown in this example, and little is gained by passing a string ByRef.

In the ReverseString function, you'll notice the use of the functions SysAllocStringLen and SysFreeString. These are just two of several API functions that can be used to manipulate BSTR strings, all of which make it easier than ever to manipulate Visual Basic strings within a C-language DLL. The long list of things you can do with strings in your DLLs is beyond the scope of this book; refer to the Visual C++ documentation for all the details. The simple example functions I've provided here can help you get your feet wet.

See Also...

- The BitPack application in Chapter 32, "Advanced Applications," for a demonstration of the creation and use of another DLL

Dear John, How Do I...

Create an Application That Runs Remotely?

The Visual Basic Enterprise Edition can create applications that run on remote computers but provide properties and methods to applications on your local machine. This is part of a concept known as *distributed computing*, in which processing tasks are shared across CPUs through part of the ActiveX technology called remote automation.

Just about any application that provides public properties and methods can be configured to run remotely. The concepts involved in creating remote applications are the same as those in local ActiveX applications, with just a few more compiler options and the added complexity of managing the system registration for both the remote and the local machines.

In this section, I walk you through creating and running a simple remote application that finds prime numbers. It's best to start with a simple application because most of the gotchas that arise in remote automation involve system configuration.

Creating a Remote Application

To create a remote application, start with any ActiveX EXE application and check the Remote Server Files check box on the Component tab of the Project Properties dialog box, as shown in Figure 25-4. The Remote Server Files option tells Visual Basic to generate files that enable client machines to use the remote application. When you compile your application, Visual Basic will generate a registration file (VBR) and a type library (TLB) for use on the client machines.

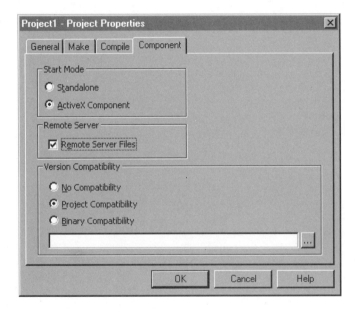

Figure 25-4.
The Component tab of the Project Properties dialog box.

The Prime number sample application (PRIME.VBP) demonstrates how you can offload a processor-intensive task to a remote machine. The application provides one object, Number, with a Value property. You set Value to any positive integer, and Prime finds the nearest prime number that's less than or equal to the initial value.

One of the interesting features built in to the Prime number application is its asynchronous processing. Finding large prime numbers around, say, 1 billion takes a lot of time. The Prime number application lets you poll the Value property—if the returned value is nonzero, it is the requested prime number. This lets you find large prime numbers without tying up your local machine.

The following listing shows the Number class module in the Prime number application:

```
'NUMBER.CLS
Dim mlMaxNumber As Long
Dim mlFound As Long

Property Get Value() As Long
    'Return prime number
    'Note that Value is 0 until number is
    'found
    Value = mlFound
End Property

Property Let Value(Setting As Long)
    'Initialize module-level variables
    mlMaxNumber = Setting
    mlFound = 0
    'Launch asynchronous calculation
    frmLaunch.Launch Me
End Property

Friend Sub ProcFindPrime()
    Dim Count As Long
    For Count = 2 To mlMaxNumber \ 2
        DoEvents
        If mlMaxNumber Mod Count = 0 Then
            mlMaxNumber = mlMaxNumber - 1
            ProcFindPrime
            Exit Sub
        End If
    Next Count
    mlFound = mlMaxNumber
End Sub
```

The Prime number application uses a Timer control to launch the ProcFindPrime procedure after control has returned to the calling application. This may look like a hack, but it is a useful technique nonetheless. Here is the code for the Launch form named *frmLaunch*, which contains a Timer control named *tmrLaunch*:

```
'LAUNCH.FRM
Dim mnumObject As Number

Public Sub Launch(numObject As Number)
    Set mnumObject = numObject
```

(continued)

```
        tmrLaunch.Enabled = True
        trmLaunch.Interval = 1
End Sub

Private Sub tmrLaunch_Timer()
    'Turn off timer
    tmrLaunch.Enabled = False
    'Launch calculation within object
    mnumObject.ProcFindPrime
End Sub
```

Registering the Remote Application

The remote application is installed on the server machine and registered on both the server and the client machines. To register the application on the server, simply run the EXE application once on the server. Visual Basic applications are self-registering.

To register the application on the client machine, copy the application's VBR and TLB files to the client, and run the CLIREG32.EXE utility included on the Visual Basic CD-ROM in the \VB\CLISVR directory. The following command line registers the Prime number application on a client machine and specifies the server named WOMBAT2:

```
CLIREG32 PRIME.VBR -t PRIME.TLB -s WOMBAT2
```

The CLIREG32 utility displays a dialog box that lets you modify the registration entries for the application, as shown in Figure 25-5.

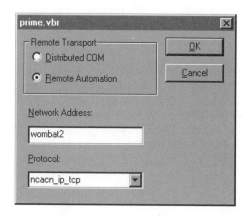

Figure 25-5.
Using the CLIREG32 dialog box to set the network protocol for remote access.

Remote automation supports a number of network protocols: TCP/IP, IPX, and NetBEUI. In general, if one protocol fails, remote automation will attempt to use the other supported protocols that are installed on the client machine. The protocol options registered for the application determine the search order of the protocols.

CLIREG32 doesn't do anything magical; it simply provides a front end to the registration file created by Visual Basic. Most registration files in Windows have REG suffixes; you could simply change the suffix of the VBR file to REG, replace the first two lines with REGEDIT4 and a blank line, and use RegEdit to register the application. However, you would also need to add server and protocol information to the Registry file. The following listing shows a sample of the Prime number application's VBR file:

```
VB5SERVERINFO
VERSION=1.0.0
HKEY_CLASSES_ROOT\Typelib\{942D0A51-A0E1-11D0-99AE-00805F502907}\
2.0\0\win32 = Prime.exe
HKEY_CLASSES_ROOT\Typelib\{942D0A51-A0E1-11D0-99AE-00805F502907}\
2.0\FLAGS = 0
HKEY_CLASSES_ROOT\Prime.Number\CLSID =
{942D0A53-A0E1-11D0-99AE-00805F502907}
HKEY_CLASSES_ROOT\CLSID\{942D0A53-A0E1-11D0-99AE-00805F502907}\
ProgID = Prime.Number
HKEY_CLASSES_ROOT\CLSID\{942D0A53-A0E1-11D0-99AE-00805F502907}\
Version = 2.0
HKEY_CLASSES_ROOT\CLSID\{942D0A53-A0E1-11D0-99AE-00805F502907}\
Typelib = {942D0A51-A0E1-11D0-99AE-00805F502907}
HKEY_CLASSES_ROOT\CLSID\{942D0A53-A0E1-11D0-99AE-00805F502907}\
LocalServer32 = Prime.exe
HKEY_CLASSES_ROOT\INTERFACE\{942D0A52-A0E1-11D0-99AE-00805F502907} =
Number
HKEY_CLASSES_ROOT\INTERFACE\{942D0A52-A0E1-11D0-99AE-00805F502907}\
ProxyStubClsid = {00020420-0000-0000-C000-000000000046}
HKEY_CLASSES_ROOT\INTERFACE\{942D0A52-A0E1-11D0-99AE-00805F502907}\
ProxyStubClsid32 = {00020420-0000-0000-C000-000000000046}
HKEY_CLASSES_ROOT\INTERFACE\{942D0A52-A0E1-11D0-99AE-00805F502907}\
Typelib = {942D0A51-A0E1-11D0-99AE-00805F502907}
HKEY_CLASSES_ROOT\INTERFACE\{942D0A52-A0E1-11D0-99AE-00805F502907}\
Typelib\"version" = 2.0
```

Running the Remote Application

To use an application through remote automation, the server must be running the Automation Manager application (AUTMGR32.EXE) and the server machine's security settings must allow the user to perform the required actions.

To start the Automation Manager, choose Automation Manager from the Windows Visual Basic Start menu. The Automation Manager displays a small dialog box that indicates the server's status, as shown in Figure 25-6.

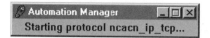

Figure 25-6.
The Automation Manager dialog box.

Windows NT provides full security profiles for each user. To use objects from a remote automation server, a user must have access privileges to the server. To start an application that is not already running, the application must allow remote creation. The Remote Automation Connection Manager (RACMGR32.EXE) provides a front end to the System Registry remote automation settings, as shown in Figure 25-7.

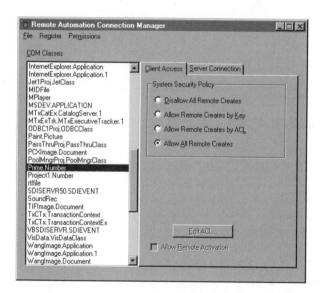

Figure 25-7.
Using the Remote Automation Connection Manager on the server machine to set user access to the remote application.

For debugging purposes, set Client Access to Allow All Remote Creates. Later you can restrict access to the server application as needed.

NOTE: Because of differences in the security models, Access Control List (ACL) features available in the Remote Automation Connection Manager are available only on computers running Windows NT and not those running Windows 95.

Accessing the Remote Application

Once you've set up your remote application and registered the application on both the remote and the client machines, you can use objects from the remote server just as you would any local objects. For programming purposes, establish a reference to the application's TLB file. This file can reside locally because it simply provides information about the remote application and does not contain executable code.

The following code shows a simple test of the Prime number application:

```
Option Explicit

Private Sub Form_Load()
    Dim x As New Prime.Number
    x.Value = 42
    Debug.Print x.Value
End Sub
```

Figure 25-8 shows a sample of the output.

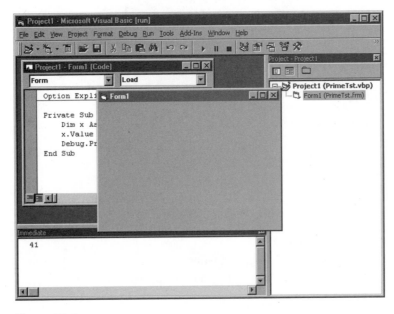

Figure 25-8.
Results returned from the remote Prime number application.

Returning Errors from Remote Applications

Errors that occur in a remote application are passed back to the client application, just as they are with local ActiveX applications. You can display user-defined error messages to notify the client applications when something goes wrong. The modifications to the Value property below show how to return an error to the client application:

```
Property Let Value(Setting As Long)
    'Raise error for negative values
    If Setting <= 0 Then
        Err.Raise 8001, "Prime.Number", _
            "Value must be a positive integer."
        Exit Property
    End If
    'Initialize module-level variables
    mlMaxNumber = Setting
    mlFound = 0
    'Launch asynchronous calculation
    frmLaunch.Launch Me
End Property
```

Figure 25-9 shows the displayed error message.

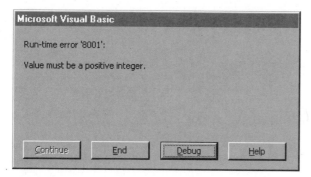

Figure 25-9.
Error message displayed if a negative value is entered.

Debugging Remote Applications

You should thoroughly debug remote applications locally before installing them on the server and testing them for remote access. Once you've installed and registered a remote application on the server and client machines, any change to the application requires you to completely reregister the application on both the server and the client machines.

Remote applications may remain loaded in the server machine's memory after remote access, so be sure to check the Windows Task Manager for phantom instances of the application by pressing Ctrl-Alt-Del, as shown in Figure 25-10. End these applications before you reregister new versions of the remote application.

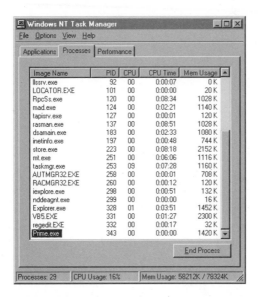

Figure 25-10.
Checking the Windows Task Manager for phantom instances of your remote application before you install new versions.

Troubleshooting Remote Automation

Unfortunately, the error messages from remote automation are very general. Most can apply to many different problems, and tracking down all the possible causes can be frustrating. The table on the following page shows a selection of automation errors and lists some of the most likely causes drawn from my experience.

As a rule, remote automation either works well or not at all, and most problems are simple ones—for instance, mistakenly including \\ with the server name or mistakenly including the share name with the server name in the System Registry.

Error Number (&H)	Message Text	Likely Causes
&H800706ba	The RPC server is unavailable.	The server name is wrong in the client machine's System Registry entry for the remote application.
		The remote application has shut down on the server.
		The remote application's EXE file was not found on the server.
&H800706be	The remote procedure call failed.	Network connection to the server was dropped or timed-out waiting for a response.
&H800706d9	There are no more endpoints from the endpoint mapper.	The Automation Manager (AUTMGR32.EXE) is not running on the server machine.

Dear John, How Do I...

Create an Add-In for the Visual Basic Development Environment?

A Visual Basic *add-in* is a special program that can be attached to the Visual Basic development environment to add extra or customized functionality to the environment. For example, you could use an add-in to add some capabilities to the environment in the form of new menu items on Visual Basic's menus or to perform housekeeping chores whenever you load or save forms or code modules. One obviously useful type of add-in is a source code librarian, such as the Microsoft Visual SourceSafe product that ships with the Enterprise Edition of Visual Basic.

Two sample add-in applications, TabOrder and VisData, are included in Visual Basic's SAMPLES directory, but I found these samples to be somewhat confusing at first because of their complex use of the Visual Basic Extensibility object model. Visual Basic also includes an Add-In project template that you can use when creating add-ins. Again, the template's code can be a bit overwhelming without a good explanation of the basic parts.

In this section, I present a streamlined example to help you better understand the mechanics of creating and running an add-in program. Once you have a clear understanding of this example, you'll find the examples provided with Visual Basic much easier to master.

Basic Concepts

As mentioned, a Visual Basic add-in is simply a specially constructed Visual Basic program. The example program presented here will start in the procedure Main, which is located in a code module (BAS file). This portion of the routine will do nothing more than ensure that the appropriate entry is made in VBADDIN.INI. This entry enables Windows to find and load the add-in when you want it. Registering an add-in is a one-time-only process that is best accomplished by simply running the add-in program once during the installation of the add-in. Because you're creating your own add-in instead of installing a commercial product, you'll run the program once manually, after you have built it.

When you choose Add-In Manager from the Visual Basic Add-Ins menu, all registered add-ins will be available for either loading into or unloading out of the currently running instance of the Visual Basic development environment. For this example, you'll create a special class within the add-in program that implements Visual Basic's extensibility interface, IDTExtensibility. To implement this interface, use the Implements keyword, as shown here:

```
Implements IDTExtensibility
```

Interfaces are a contract with another program—in this case, Visual Basic—that says your program will implement specific procedures that the other program can call. In the case of IDTExtensibility, you must implement four procedures that are called at various times, as described in the following table.

Procedure Name	Occurs When
IDTExtensibility_OnAddInsUpdate	The Visual Basic environment starts with this add-in loaded. This occurs early in Visual Basic's startup.
IDTExtensibility_OnStartupComplete	The add-in has finished loading in the Visual Basic environment. This occurs after Visual Basic has completed its startup.

(continued)

440

continued

Procedure Name	Occurs When
IDTExtensibility_OnConnection	The user selects the add-in from the Add-In Manager.
IDTExtensibility_OnDisconnection	The user deselects the add-in from the Add-In Manager.

The IDTExtensibility_OnConnection procedure provides a *VBInst* parameter that gives access to the Visual Basic extensibility root object (VBIDE.VBE). From *VBInst,* you can make changes to the Visual Basic menus and toolbars, connect procedures to events in the environment, and perform other actions.

NOTE: Visual Basic 4 used the ConnectEvents method to associate event procedures in a class module with events in the Visual Basic environment. The new Visual Basic extensibility object model provides access to many more aspects of the development environment.

The really cool work is accomplished in the MenuHandler_Click event procedure or in other event-driven procedures provided in the add-in. In this example, you'll use a small subset of the Visual Basic object hierarchy to locate and resize all command buttons on the currently active form within the Visual Basic environment. This is a small example of what can be accomplished with an add-in, yet I find it quite useful. I'm always tweaking my command buttons to make them all the same size in a project, and this little add-in lets me instantly resize all my command buttons to a fixed, standard size.

Building an Add-In

The following paragraphs provide a recipe-style series of steps to show you how to build your relatively simple add-in. When I was building my first add-in, I stumbled over several not-so-obvious details, mostly because I had to wade around in the Microsoft documentation to determine what I had done wrong. The steps presented here should help you breeze through these details.

Start with a new ActiveX EXE project, and insert a second class module and one code module. Name the code module Myaddin, and name the class modules Connect and Sizer. You'll need to make some important property settings in the project before you try to run the add-in, but you should enter all the source code first and take care of the property settings when you have finished.

Add the following code to Myaddin. Note that the only task performed by the Main procedure is to register this add-in with Windows. The Main code runs quickly, and the program terminates almost immediately, with no activity visible to the outside world.

```
Option Explicit

'Declare API to write to INI file
Declare Function WritePrivateProfileString _
Lib "Kernel32" Alias "WritePrivateProfileStringA" ( _
    ByVal AppName$, _
    ByVal KeyName$, _
    ByVal keydefault$, _
    ByVal FileName$ _
) As Long

'Declare API to read from INI file
Declare Function GetPrivateProfileString _
Lib "Kernel32" Alias "GetPrivateProfileStringA" ( _
    ByVal AppName$, _
    ByVal KeyName$, _
    ByVal keydefault$, _
    ByVal ReturnString$, _
    ByVal NumBytes As Long, _
    ByVal FileName$ _
) As Long

Sub Main()
    Dim ReturnString As String
    Dim Section As String
    'Be sure you are in the VBADDIN.INI file
    Section = "Add-Ins32"
    ReturnString = String$(255, Chr$(0))
    GetPrivateProfileString Section, _
        "cmdSizer.Connect", "NotFound", _
        ReturnString, Len(ReturnString) + 1, "Vbaddin.Ini"
    If InStr(ReturnString, "NotFound") Then
        WritePrivateProfileString Section, "cmdSizer.Connect", _
            "0", "vbaddin.ini"
    End If
End Sub
```

The Connect class module provides the IDTExtensibility_OnConnection and IDTExtensibility_OnDisconnection event procedures that Visual Basic will automatically call when the user loads or unloads this add-in into or out of the Visual Basic environment. It's enlightening to realize that the previously mentioned Main procedure will run *once per installation* of this add-in, whereas the procedures in the Connect class module will run *once per load or unload*. Continuing this pattern, the routines in the other class module will run *once per menu click*. Mentally partitioning this activity will help you understand better what's going on here. Add this code to the Connect class module:

```
Option Explicit

'Indicate that this class implements the extensibility
'interface for Visual Basic
Implements IDTExtensibility

Dim VBInstance As VBIDE.VBE
Dim mnuSize As Office.CommandBarControl
Dim SizerHandler As Sizer

'Set these constants as desired
Const CMDBTNWIDTH = 1200
Const CMDBTNHEIGHT = 400

Private Sub IDTExtensibility_OnConnection _
    (ByVal VBInst As Object, _
    ByVal ConnectMode As vbext_ConnectMode, _
    ByVal AddInInst As VBIDE.AddIn, _
    custom() As Variant)
    'Save this instance of Visual Basic so you can refer to it later
    Set VBInstance = VBInst
    'Add menu item to Visual Basic's Add-Ins menu
    Set mnuSize = VBInstance.CommandBars("Add-Ins").Controls.Add(1)
    mnuSize.Caption = "&Size Command Buttons"
    'Create Sizer object
    Set SizerHandler = New Sizer
    'Establish a connection between menu events
    'and Sizer object
    Set SizerHandler.MenuHandler = _
        VBInst.Events.CommandBarEvents(mnuSize)
    'Pass VBInstance to Sizer object
    Set SizerHandler.VBInstance = VBInstance
    'Set command button sizing properties
    SizerHandler.ButtonWidth = CMDBTNWIDTH
    SizerHandler.ButtonHeight = CMDBTNHEIGHT
End Sub
```

(continued)

```
'Removes menu item when user deselects this add-in in
'the Add-In Manager
Private Sub IDTExtensibility_OnDisconnection _
    (ByVal RemoveMode As VBIDE.vbext_DisconnectMode, _
    custom() As Variant)
    'Remove menu item
    VBInstance.CommandBars("Add-Ins").Controls _
        ("&Size Command Buttons").Delete
End Sub

'The following empty procedures are required because this
'class implements the IDTExtensibility interface
Private Sub IDTExtensibility_OnAddInsUpdate(custom() As Variant)

End Sub

Private Sub IDTExtensibility_OnStartupComplete(custom() As Variant)

End Sub
```

Notice that I've defined two constants in this module, *CMDBTNWIDTH* and *CMDBTNHEIGHT*, which define the size to which all command buttons processed by this add-in will be set. Feel free to change these constants if you want. Better yet, if you feel energetic, you might consider adding a dialog box to this add-in to let the user enter the desired sizing constants on the fly. I decided to keep this example simple by just using constants, which works well for almost all of my command buttons anyway.

The VBInstance object helps you stay in control if the user runs multiple copies of Visual Basic simultaneously. There will be only one instance of your add-in in memory at a time, even if multiple copies of Visual Basic are running. By storing the VBIDE.VBE object passed by Visual Basic to the IDTExtensibility_OnConnection event procedure, you can refer to the forms and controls in that particular instance of Visual Basic when a user clicks on the new menu item.

The other class module, Sizer, contains the code to be activated when the user clicks on the new menu item. This module contains one event procedure, MenuHandler_Click, which is automatically called by the system when its containing object is connected to that menu. Add the following source code to the Sizer class module:

```
Option Explicit

'Sizer object properties
Public ButtonWidth As Long
Public ButtonHeight As Long
Public VBInstance As VBIDE.VBE

'Declare menu event handler
Public WithEvents MenuHandler As CommandBarEvents

'This event fires when menu is clicked in IDE
Private Sub MenuHandler_Click _
    (ByVal CommandBarControl As Object, _
    Handled As Boolean, CancelDefault As Boolean)
    Dim AllControls
    Dim Control As Object
    'Get collection containing all controls on form
    Set AllControls = _
        VBInstance.SelectedVBComponent.Designer.VBControls
    'For each control on the active form...
    For Each Control In AllControls
        '...if the control is a command button...
        If Control.ClassName = "CommandButton" Then
            '...resize it
            With Control.Properties
                .Item("Width") = ButtonWidth
                .Item("Height") = ButtonHeight
            End With
        End If
    Next Control
End Sub
```

When the user clicks on the new menu item, this subprogram wades through all the controls on the currently selected form within the user's Visual Basic project. If a control is a command button, its Width and Height properties are set to the predetermined constant values. Later, when you try out this add-in, you'll see all the command buttons on your current form snap to a fixed size.

Before you run this program as an add-in, you need to set some important project properties, as shown in Figure 25-11 on the following page. Choose Project Properties from the Project menu, and click on the General tab of the Project Properties dialog box that appears. Set the Startup Object to *Sub Main* so that the correct procedure will run when this program is executed for the first time. Type *cmdSizer* in the Project Name field. This name must be the same as the first part of the string *cmdSizer.Connect* used in the system registration process executed in the Main procedure. If the two don't match, you won't be able to load this add-in using Visual Basic's Add-In Manager tool. This is one of those fine points that tripped me up the first time. Type *Command Button Sizer Add-In* in the Project Description field. This text appears in the Object Browser and helps identify the exposed objects.

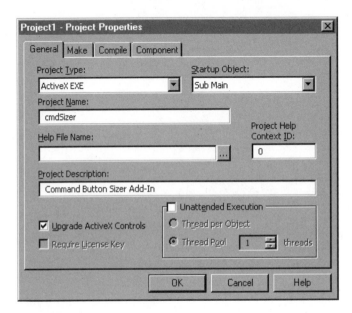

Figure 25-11.
Project property settings for the cmdSizer *add-in.*

Next click on the Component tab of the Project Properties dialog box, and select ActiveX Component from the StartMode options. An add-in executable contains ActiveX code to be activated from an external application; in this case, the Visual Basic environment uses ActiveX technology to connect to the various objects within our add-in program. Finally, click OK in the dialog box to set your options.

Another trip-up detail is remembering to enable the Microsoft Office objects and the VBIDE.VBE object on which this whole add-in application depends so heavily. Choose References from the Project menu, check the Microsoft Office 8.0 Object Library and Microsoft Visual Basic 5.0 Extensibility items in the Available References list, and then click OK. If you forget to enable these references, an error message will be displayed when you try to run the program.

The Connect class module must have its Instancing property set to *5 - MultiUse*. The Instancing setting allows this add-in to be loaded into multiple concurrent instances of Visual Basic. The Instancing property can be set to *1 - Private* in the Sizer class module.

Running the Add-In for the First Time

Your new add-in must be run once to be registered with Windows. While you are debugging, you can run an add-in from within the Visual Basic environment. Once the add-in has been compiled to an EXE file it can be run using the Run command on the Windows Start menu. The system will load the EXE file and make its ActiveX objects available normally, but these objects can still be accessed during debugging if the program is left in the run state.

To try this, click the Run button, and then click the Break button. In the Immediate window, type *Main* and press the Enter key to register the add-in in VBADDIN.INI. Next click the Continue button, and minimize the entire Visual Basic environment while your add-in is still running.

Start a second instance of Visual Basic, and try loading your new add-in using the Add-In Manager item on the Add-Ins menu. If all has gone smoothly, you'll see the *cmdSizer* add-in listed in the Add-In Manager dialog box.

> **NOTE:** Since the add-in's project Start Mode is set to ActiveX Component, the Main procedure won't run when you start the program in the Visual Basic environment. You need to run the program manually the first time to register the add-in.

Another approach is to create an EXE file for the add-in. When compilation is successful, exit Visual Basic, run the new CMDSIZER.EXE file once (noticing that nothing much appears to happen while it quickly registers itself with the system), and then start Visual Basic again to see whether you can then load the new add-in. Remember that you need to run the add-in's EXE file only once, to let it register and effectively install itself in the Windows system.

Using the Add-In

To test this add-in, start Visual Basic and choose Add-In Manager from the Add-Ins menu. Select the cmdSizer.Connect option, and then click OK. As shown in Figure 25-12 on the following page, a new menu item, Size Command Buttons, should become available at the bottom of the Add-Ins menu.

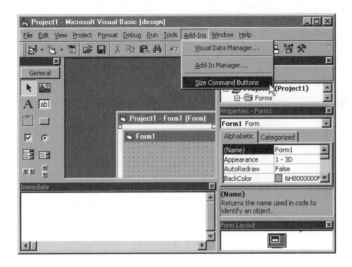

Figure 25-12.
The new menu item installed by the add-in.

Throw a handful of odd-sized command buttons onto a form, and give this new menu option a try. You should see all the command buttons quickly snap to the same size. Figure 25-13 shows a form before command button resizing, and Figure 25-14 shows the same form after I have clicked on the new menu item.

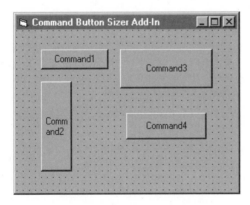

Figure 25-13.
Command buttons ready to be resized.

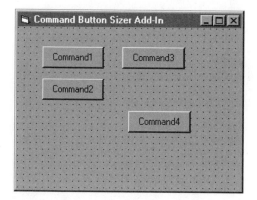

Figure 25-14.
Command buttons resized by the add-in.

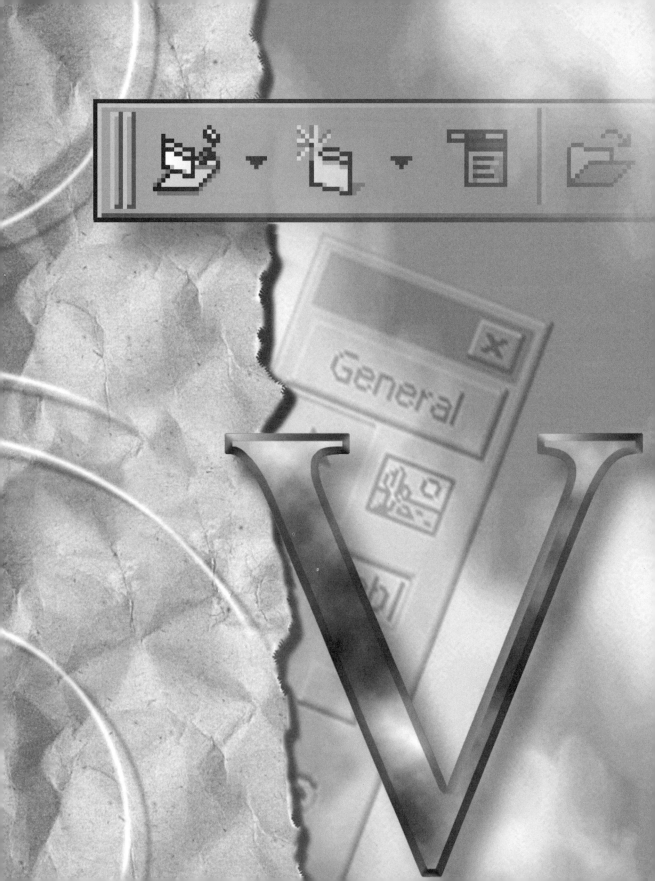

CHAPTER TWENTY-SIX

Miscellaneous Techniques

In this chapter, I cover a few odds and ends that don't quite fit anywhere else but that are still valuable tricks for the Visual Basic programmer to know.

One of the complaints I've heard in the past about the Basic language in general is its lack of pointers and data structures, features that a competent C programmer wouldn't know what to do without. Earlier in this book, I show how Variants allow great flexibility in the creation of structured data, and in the first section in this chapter I show you how the Collection object lets you create dynamic data structures that support very sophisticated data manipulation techniques. As a simple example, I create the equivalent of a linked list.

Two other techniques that are useful to know are how to detect the operating system version and how to programmatically reboot the computer. You might want to do this, for example, as part of a setup or an initialization application.

The fourth section shows you how your application can dial a phone by sending commands to the modem through the serial port. This is a common programming task, and it turns out to be quite simple to accomplish.

Finally, the last topic shows a generalized technique for inline error trapping that has advantages over the On Error GoTo Label technique of the past.

Dear John, How Do I...

Create a Linked List?

Using a linked list to create, manage, and reorder a sequential series of data has long been a powerful C programming tool. When you create a linked list of data structures in C, you must rely on pointer variables to hold the addresses of linked members in the list. Visual Basic doesn't have explicit pointer variables, but it does provide several of its own techniques to handle references to objects and variables. Behind the scenes, Visual Basic does keep track of pointers, but you don't have to worry about those details. You can focus instead on the higher level data handling concepts.

In this example, you will create the equivalent of a linked list of strings, in which you can insert strings as new members of the list while maintaining alphabetic order. The Collection object is a powerful tool for accomplishing this task efficiently. Start a new project, add a command button named *cmdBuildList* to a blank form, and add the following lines of code:

```
Option Explicit

Private colWords As New Collection

Sub Insert(V As Variant)
    Dim i, j, k
    'Determine whether this is first item to add
    If colWords.Count = 0 Then
        colWords.Add V
        Exit Sub
    End If
    'Get the range of the collection
    i = 1
    j = colWords.Count
    'Determine whether this should be inserted before first item
    If V <= colWords.Item(i) Then
        colWords.Add V, before:=i
        Exit Sub
    End If
    'Determine whether this should be inserted after last item
    If V >= colWords.Item(j) Then
        colWords.Add V, after:=j
        Exit Sub
    End If
    'Conduct binary search for insertion point
    Do Until j - i <= 1
        k = (i + j) \ 2
        If colWords.Item(k) < V Then
            i = k
        Else
            j = k
        End If
    Loop
    'Insert item where it belongs
    colWords.Add V, before:=j
End Sub
```

(continued)

```
Private Sub cmdBuildList_Click()
    Dim i
    Insert "One"
    Insert "Two"
    Insert "Three"
    Insert "Four"
    Insert "Five"
    Insert "Six"
    Insert "Seven"
    Insert "Eight"
    Insert "Nine"
    Insert "Ten"
    For i = 1 To colWords.Count
        Print colWords.Item(i)
    Next i
End Sub
```

I've declared the *colWords* Collection object at the module level to ensure that it exists for the duration of this program. As with other local variables, if you declare a Collection object within a procedure, it is automatically removed from memory when that procedure ends. When you declare a Collection object at the module level, it exists as long as the form is loaded. Also, it's common to create several procedures that process the same collection, and this technique allows all the procedures to share the same module-level Collection object.

Collection objects can contain two types of members: Objects and Variants. Of course, a Variant-type variable can contain a wide variety of data types, so a Collection object can actually contain just about anything you want it to contain. In this example, strings are passed and handled as Variants for insertion into the list. Visual Basic Books Online explains in detail how to wrap a Collection object within a class module to better control the type of data that can be added to a collection. This would be important, for instance, if you were to use a Collection object within an ActiveX component that you plan to distribute commercially, in which you might want the Collection object to contain only one type of data. In the example code above, there's nothing to prevent me from passing something other than a string to the Insert procedure, even though that would not make sense in the context of what my program is trying to accomplish.

Collection members can be directly accessed via a key string or an index number representing the member's position within the list. In this example, I use the index number to control the order in which the members are accessed. A Collection object's index allows you to insert, delete, and generally perform the same kinds of manipulations that a true linked list requires. A Collection

object is like a linked list (and unlike an array) in that the insertion and deletion of members from anywhere within the Collection object are handled by
Visual Basic efficiently, automatically, and without wasting memory.

The Collection object's Add method is used to insert each string. Two
named arguments of the Add method, *before* and *after*, allow you to add a new
string just before or just after an indexed location in the object. I use both of
these named arguments to insert each string into the object based on alphabetic order. This way the list of strings, when accessed sequentially through
the Collection object's index, returns the strings in alphabetic order without
requiring any further processing. Figure 26-1 shows the results of printing the
Collection object's sorted contents on the form.

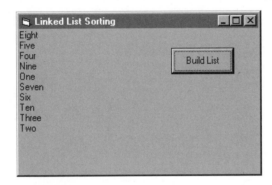

Figure 26-1.
Results of using an insertion sort in a linked list collection.

Be sure to study Visual Basic Books Online for more information about
the Collection object. This powerful and flexible construct, when combined
with the flexibility of Variant data types and class module objects, frees you
from many of the constraints that were imposed by the Basic language in the
past, allowing you to program in ways never before possible.

Dear John, How Do I...

Respond to O/S Version Differences?

In an ideal world, elves would upgrade everyone's hardware and software silently and simultaneously in the night, all software would be 100 percent
upwardly compatible, and everyone would buy *two* copies of this book. Unfortunately, there are still a lot of machines running 16-bit versions of Microsoft
Windows, and even my Mom will only chip in for one copy of this book.

There are several strategies for managing applications that have to run on 16-bit and 32-bit systems, but I believe the best is really the simplest: freeze development of your 16-bit application, migrate the code to 32-bit, and incorporate only the new features in the 32-bit version. Trying to maintain equivalent versions of an application for both 16-bit and 32-bit platforms will either seriously hobble the 32-bit version or more than double your workload.

Now, with philosophy and humor out of the way, let's deal with how you detect operating system versions. To tell the difference between a 16-bit and a 32-bit system, you have to write a 16-bit application using Visual Basic 4 or earlier. (Version 5 does not provide a 16-bit environment.) The following code shows how to create a stub application that launches the 16-bit or 32-bit version of a setup application based on the current operating system:

```
'LAUNCH.BAS
Option Explicit

#If Win16 Then
Declare Function GetVersion Lib "Kernel" () _
    As Long
#Else
Declare Function GetVersion Lib "Kernel32" () _
    As Long
#End If

'Demonstrates how to get Windows version information
'for 16-bit and 32-bit systems
Sub Main()
    Dim lWinInfo As Long
    Dim strWinVer As String
    Dim strDosVersion As String
    'Retrieve Windows version information
    lWinInfo = GetVersion()
    'Parse Windows version number from returned
    'Long integer value
    strWinVer = LoByte(LoWord(lWinInfo)) & "." & _
        HiByte(LoWord(lWinInfo))
    'If version number is earlier than 3.5 (Win NT 3.5)...
    If Val(strWinVer) < 3.5 Then
        Shell "Setup1.EXE"        'Run 16-bit setup;
    Else                          'otherwise,
        Shell "Setup132.EXE"      'run 32-bit setup
    End If
End Sub
```

(continued)

455

```
Function LoWord(lArg)
    LoWord = lArg And (lArg Xor &HFFFF0000)
End Function

Function HiWord(lArg)
    If lArg > &H7FFFFFFF Then
        HiWord = (lArg And &HFFFF0000) \ &H10000
    Else
        HiWord = ((lArg And &HFFFF0000) \ &H10000) Xor &HFFFF0000
    End If
End Function

Function HiByte(iArg)
    HiByte = (iArg And &HFF00) \ &H100
End Function

Function LoByte(iArg)
    LoByte = iArg Xor (iArg And &HFF00)
End Function
```

Notice that I've included conditional code for the 16-bit and 32-bit GetVersion API functions. This lets me develop and debug the application on either platform. The final version must be compiled using 16-bit Visual Basic to create a 16-bit application, however.

> NOTE: To run a compiled 16-bit Visual Basic application on a 32-bit system, the 16-bit Visual Basic runtime dynamic link library (DLL) VB40016.DLL must be installed.

Dear John, How Do I...

Exit and Restart Windows?

Rebooting Microsoft Windows 95 from your application is not something you're likely to do frequently, but there are times when the ability to reboot can be useful. A detected security violation, for instance, can be counteracted with a programmatic reboot of the system. Some specialized application installation and setup procedures require a reboot to update current paths and Registry settings. It's easy to reboot from your code; just be sure you save any open files, including this project, before you try the following code!

To try this example, add a command button named *cmdReboot* to a form, add this code, save the form, and then run it and click the command button:

```
Option Explicit

Private Declare Function ExitWindowsEx _
Lib "user32" ( _
    ByVal uFlags As Long, _
    ByVal dwReserved As Long _
) As Long

Private Sub cmdReboot_Click()
    ExitWindowsEx &H43, 0
End Sub
```

Once you have clicked the command button, there's no turning back—the system will shut down and begin the reboot process.

Dear John, How Do I...

Dial a Phone from My Application?

The Microsoft Comm control is a complete, powerful, and easy-to-use control for handling all your serial communications requirements. One of the most common communications programming tasks is simply dialing a telephone. The NISTTime application in Chapter 29, "Date and Time," provides an example of a more sophisticated use of the MSComm control, but here I provide the few lines of code required for a quick dial of the phone.

To make this example more useful, I've assumed that the phone number has been copied to the clipboard. This way, you can mark and copy a telephone number from just about anywhere and use it to dial the phone. To try this out, start a new project. If the MSComm control is not available, choose Components from the Project menu, and check the Microsoft Comm Control check box on the Controls tab of the Components dialog box. To a blank form, add an MSComm control named *comOne* and a command button named *cmdDial.* Then add the following code:

```
Option Explicit

Private Sub cmdDial_Click()
    Dim A$
    A$ = Clipboard.GetText(vbCFText)
    If A$ = "" Then
        MsgBox "Mark and copy a number first."
        Exit Sub
```

(continued)

```
      End If
      comOne.CommPort = 1
      comOne.Settings = "9600,N,8,1"
      comOne.PortOpen = True
      comOne.Output = "ATDT" & A$ & vbCr
      MsgBox "Dialing " & A$ & vbCrLf & "Pick up the phone...", _
          vbOKOnly, "Dial-A-Phone"
      comOne.PortOpen = False
End Sub
```

Figure 26-2 shows the program in action.

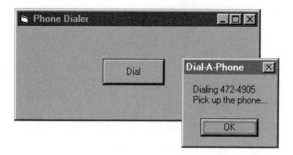

Figure 26-2.
The phone-dialing program waiting for the user to pick up the phone.

You will need to change the CommPort property setting to *2* if your modem is installed on COM2 instead of COM1, and in rare cases you might need to change some of the other properties for your hardware. In the vast majority of situations, however, the above property settings will work fine.

The MsgBox command delays the program just before the PortOpen property is set to *False*. As soon as the user clicks the OK button in the message box, the phone is hung up by the MSComm control. This gives the user time to pick up the phone before the program proceeds and disconnects the line at the modem.

See Also...

- The NISTTime application in Chapter 29, "Date and Time," for a demonstration of a more sophisticated use of the MSComm control

Dear John, How Do I...
Use Inline Error Trapping?

The most commonly suggested way to set up error-trapping code in a Visual Basic program is to add a labeled section of code with an automatic On Error GoTo Label branch set up at the beginning of the procedure. Here's a simple example of this type of error trapping:

```
Private Sub cmdTest_Click()

    On Error GoTo ErrorTrap
    Print 17 / 0   '(math error)
    Exit Sub

ErrorTrap:
    Print "Illegal to divide by zero."
    Resume Next

End Sub
```

There are several reasons why you might prefer a more inline approach to error trapping, though. First, the error-trap label above is reminiscent of the GOTO labels of ancient spaghetti coding days. Modern structured programming techniques, like those used for much of Visual Basic, have gotten us away from code containing discontinuous jumps and branches, a style that can be identified by the presence of a GOTO command. True, a simple error-trapping GoTo is not as confusing as a lot of Basic code I've seen in the past, but the action is still not as clear as it is when you use other techniques. Even more discouraging, especially when you are dealing with objects in your code, is the confusion you might experience when you are using this method and would like to know exactly where the error occurred and what in your procedure triggered the error. Although the old Err variable is now an enhanced object with properties of its own, the Err object provides limited information, especially in larger procedures.

Inline Error Trapping

The error-trapping approach taken in C programming is to check for returned error information immediately after each function call. The best example of this technique is the way you check for errors in Visual Basic after calling an

API function. For example, immediately after you call the mciExecute API function to play a sound file, you can check the returned value to see whether the call was successful:

```
x = mciExecute("Play c:\windows\tada.wav")
If x = 0 Then MsgBox "There was a problem."
```

There is a way to set up generalized error trapping in your Visual Basic code to check for errors immediately after they occur. I like this technique much better than the standard error-trapping method, and Microsoft's documentation does suggest using this technique when you are working with objects. The trick is to use an On Error Resume Next statement at the start of your procedure and to check for possible errors immediately after the lines of code in which errors might occur. The following subprogram demonstrates this technique:

```
Option Explicit

Private Sub cmdTest_Click()
    Dim X, Y
    For X = -3 To 3
        Y = Reciprocal(X)
        Print "Reciprocal of "; X; " is "; Y; ""
        If IsError(Y) Then Print Err.Description
    Next X
End Sub

Function Reciprocal(X)
    Dim Y
    On Error Resume Next
    Y = 1 / X
    If Err.Number = 0 Then
        Reciprocal = Y
    Else
        Reciprocal = CVErr(Err.Number)
    End If
End Function
```

Here I've taken advantage of the fact that a Variant can actually be set to a value of type Error using the CVErr conversion function, which is an excellent way to signal back to a calling procedure that an error has occurred. You can, of course, return a value from your functions to indicate an error, but the advantage of signaling an error implicitly through the returned data type is that the error can be indicated even if your function can theoretically return any numeric value.

Figure 26-3 shows the results of running this sample code on a form. Notice that I print the contents of the returned Variant *Y* even in the case of an error. Because the returned value is a Variant, an error message instead of a number is returned.

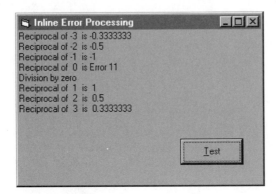

Figure 26-3.
Inline error trapping detecting and reporting a divide-by-zero condition.

The Err object provides several properties and methods that greatly enhance what you can do with error handling. For example, the Err object's Raise method lets you create your own errors, a handy technique for passing errors back from objects you create. Be sure to review Visual Basic's documentation to learn about all the error-handling features.

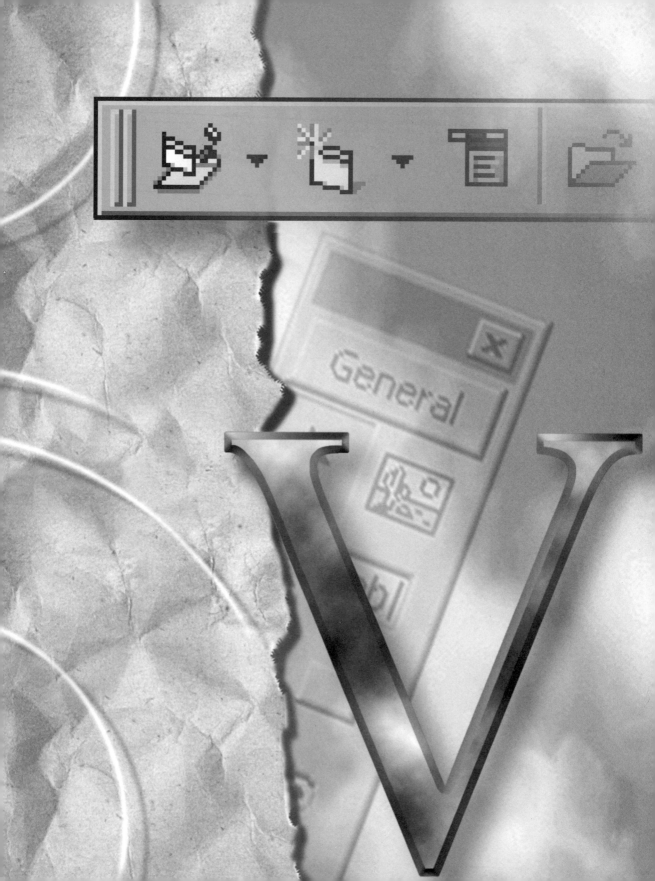

PART III

SAMPLE
APPLICATIONS

The samples in this part of the book are complete, stand-alone applications that demonstrate many of the solutions described in the previous chapters; they also demonstrate other tricks and techniques I've picked up during my programming experiences. Some of these applications are useful utilities, some are informative, and some are just for fun. As you follow along and learn how each of these programs works, I hope you'll find new and creative approaches that you can use in your own applications in Visual Basic. I've tried to include a variety of types of applications, but no matter what your field of interest might be, I think you'll find several interesting applications here. All the forms and source code for each application in this part of the book are included on the companion CD-ROM.

CHAPTER TWENTY-SEVEN

Graphics

This chapter contains a handful of fun applications that demonstrate some of the graphics techniques and features discussed in Part II of this book. The RGBHSV application is a handy utility for selecting colors. The Animate application demonstrates a few ways to create simple animated graphics on your Visual Basic forms. The Lottery application might not guarantee that you'll win a million dollars, but it will at least provide some fun graphics experimentation, and the Ssaver application provides a full-blown screen saver that includes multiple options.

The RGBHSV Application

The RGBHSV application is a simple utility to help you select any shade of color using either the RGB (red, green, blue) system or the HSV (hue, saturation, value) system of color definition. This application creates an instance of the HSV object presented in Chapter 12, "Graphics Techniques," in order to make the necessary conversions between the two color systems. This conversion is accomplished by adding the HSV.CLS class module to this project and creating an instance of the HSV object.

Like many of the programs in Part III, this application includes menu items. Some of the items are not enabled and appear grayed out, waiting for you to add code to give them purpose. All the items on the Help menu, however, are enabled, giving you access to my standard About dialog box and a help file created for this collection of programs. Use of the About dialog box is described in Chapter 10, "Dialog Boxes, Windows, and Other Forms." Notice in the source code that the path to the help file is a relative path. By starting with the application's path and then working up a couple of directories and then down to the HELP directory, you can locate the help file regardless of the drive you use for your CD-ROM or even if you copied the contents of the CD-ROM into a directory on your hard drive without changing the basic directory structure.

One line of code might cause you to do a double take. In the Update procedure, the hexadecimal value of the currently selected color value is displayed in a Label control named *lblColor*, just above the picture box that displays the color itself. To create the standard Visual Basic notation for a hexadecimal number, I added an ampersand (&) and an uppercase *H* prefix to the displayed hexadecimal value. Notice, however, that the string in my program line contains two ampersands in a row:

```
lblColor = "Color = " & "&&H" & Hex$(RGBColor)
```

A single ampersand just before the *H* causes the label to display an underlined *H*, a handy feature when you want it, but a nuisance when you want to actually display an ampersand. When you use two ampersands in a row, Visual Basic knows to display a single ampersand instead of an underlined character.

Figures 27-1 through 27-3 show runtime and development-time details of the RGBHSV application. Figure 27-1 shows the RGBHSV application in action. As each slider is moved, RGBHSV displays the color within the picture box to match the slider position and all other Slider controls are adjusted programmatically. Figure 27-2 shows the contents of the Project window, which provides a list of all the forms and modules that make up this application. Figure 27-3 shows the RGBHSV form during the development process. The numbers on the form identify the form's objects, as listed in the "RGBHSV.FRM Objects and Property Settings" table on page 468.

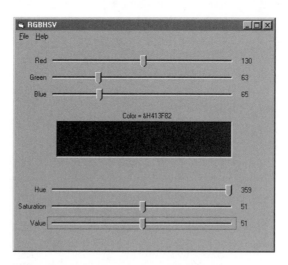

Figure 27-1.
The RGBHSV application in action.

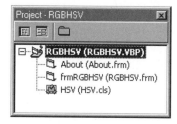

Figure 27-2.
The RGBHSV project list.

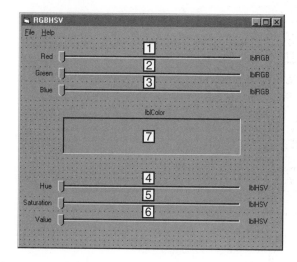

Figure 27-3.
RGBHSV.FRM during development.

To create this application, use the tables and source code on the following pages to add the appropriate controls, set any nondefault properties as indicated, and enter the source code as shown. I've included the source code for the About form and the HSV class modules for easy reference, but refer to Chapter 10, "Dialog Boxes, Windows, and Other Forms," for a complete description of the About form and Chapter 12, "Graphics Techniques," for a complete description of the HSV class.

RGBHSV.FRM Menu Design Window Entries

Caption	Name	Indentation	Enabled
&File	mnuFile	0	True
&New	mnuNew	1	False
&Open...	mnuOpen	1	False
&Save	mnuSave	1	False
Save &As...	mnuSaveAs	1	False
-	mnuFileDash1	1	True
E&xit	mnuExit	1	True
&Help	mnuHelp	0	True
&Contents	mnuContents	1	True
&Search for Help on...	mnuSearch	1	True
-	mnuHelpDash1	1	True
&About...	mnuAbout	1	True

RGBHSV.FRM Objects and Property Settings

ID No.*	Property	Value
Slider		
1	Name	sliRGB
	Index	0
	Max	255
	LargeChange	10
Slider		
2	Name	sliRGB
	Index	1
	Max	255
	LargeChange	10
Slider		
3	Name	sliRGB
	Index	2
	Max	255
	LargeChange	10

*   The number in the ID No. column corresponds to the number in Figure 27-3 that identifies
the location of the object on the form.

(continued)

RGBHSV.FRM Objects and Property Settings *continued*

ID No.	Property	Value
Slider		
4	Name	*sliHSV*
	Index	*0*
	Max	*359*
Slider		
5	Name	*sliHSV*
	Index	*1*
	Max	*100*
Slider		
6	Name	*sliHSV*
	Index	*2*
	Max	*100*
Label		
	Name	*Label1*
	Index	*0*
	Caption	*Red*
Label		
	Name	*Label1*
	Index	*1*
	Caption	*Green*
Label		
	Name	*Label1*
	Index	*2*
	Caption	*Blue*
Label		
	Name	*Label2*
	Index	*0*
	Caption	*Hue*
Label		
	Name	*Label2*
	Index	*1*
	Caption	*Saturation*

(continued)

RGBHSV.FRM Objects and Property Settings *continued*

ID No.	Property	Value
Label		
	Name	*Label2*
	Index	*2*
	Caption	*Value*
Label		
	Name	*lblRGB*
	Index	*0*
Label		
	Name	*lblRGB*
	Index	*1*
Label		
	Name	*lblRGB*
	Index	*2*
Label		
	Name	*lblHSV*
	Index	*0*
Label		
	Name	*lblHSV*
	Index	*1*
Label		
	Name	*lblHSV*
	Index	*2*
Label		
	Name	*lblColor*
PictureBox		
7	Name	*picColor*

Source Code for RGBHSV.FRM

```
Option Explicit

Private Declare Function WinHelp _
Lib "user32" Alias "WinHelpA" ( _
    ByVal hwnd As Long, _
    ByVal lpHelpFile As String, _
    ByVal wCommand As Long, _
    ByVal dwData As Long _
) As Long

Const RgbToHsv = 1
Const HsvToRgb = 2

Dim RGBColor
Dim hsvTest As New HSV

Private Sub Form_Load()
    Dim i
    'Set a random starting color
    Randomize
    hsvTest.Red = Int(Rnd * 256)
    hsvTest.Green = Int(Rnd * 256)
    hsvTest.Blue = Int(Rnd * 256)
    Update RgbToHsv
    Update HsvToRgb
End Sub

Private Sub mnuAbout_Click()
    'Set properties
    About.Application = "RGBHSV"
    About.Heading = _
        "Microsoft Visual Basic 5.0 Developer's Workshop"
    About.Copyright = "1997 John Clark Craig and Jeff Webb"
    'Call a method
    About.Display
End Sub

Private Sub mnuContents_Click()
    WinHelp hwnd, App.Path & "\..\..\Help\Mvbdw.hlp", _
        cdlHelpContents, 0
End Sub
```

(continued)

Source Code for RGBHSV.FRM *continued*

```
Private Sub mnuExit_Click()
    Unload Me
End Sub

Private Sub mnuSearch_Click()
    WinHelp hwnd, App.Path & "\..\..\Help\Mvbdw.hlp", _
        cdlHelpPartialKey, 0
End Sub

Private Sub HSV_Changed(Index As Integer)
    hsvTest.Hue = sliHSV(0).Value
    hsvTest.Saturation = sliHSV(1).Value
    hsvTest.Value = sliHSV(2).Value
    Update HsvToRgb
End Sub

Private Sub RGB_Changed(Index As Integer)
    hsvTest.Red = sliRGB(0).Value
    hsvTest.Green = sliRGB(1).Value
    hsvTest.Blue = sliRGB(2).Value
    Update RgbToHsv
End Sub

Sub Update(Direction)
    Dim i
    Select Case Direction
    Case RgbToHsv
        hsvTest.ToHsv
        sliHSV(0).Value = hsvTest.Hue
        sliHSV(1).Value = hsvTest.Saturation
        sliHSV(2).Value = hsvTest.Value
    Case HsvToRgb
        hsvTest.ToRgb
        sliRGB(0).Value = hsvTest.Red
        sliRGB(1).Value = hsvTest.Green
        sliRGB(2).Value = hsvTest.Blue
    End Select
    'Update RGB color labels
    lblRGB(0).Caption = Format$(hsvTest.Red, "##0")
    lblRGB(1).Caption = Format$(hsvTest.Green, "##0")
    lblRGB(2).Caption = Format$(hsvTest.Blue, "##0")
    'Update HSV color labels
    lblHSV(0).Caption = Format$(hsvTest.Hue, "##0")
    lblHSV(1).Caption = Format$(hsvTest.Saturation, "##0")
```

(continued)

Source Code for RGBHSV.FRM *continued*

```
    lblHSV(2).Caption = Format$(hsvTest.Value, "##0")
    'Update the displayed color
    RGBColor = RGB(hsvTest.Red, hsvTest.Green, hsvTest.Blue)
    picColor.BackColor = RGBColor
    'Update the color's number
    lblColor = "Color = " & "&&H" & Hex$(RGBColor)
End Sub

Private Sub sliRGB_Scroll(Index As Integer)
    RGB_Changed (Index)
End Sub

Private Sub sliHSV_Scroll(Index As Integer)
    HSV_Changed (Index)
End Sub
```

Source Code for HSV.CLS

```
Option Explicit

'RGB color properties
Public Red As Integer
Public Green As Integer
Public Blue As Integer

'HSV color properties
Public Hue As Single
Public Saturation As Single
Public Value As Single
'Converts RGB to HSV
Public Sub ToHsv()
    Dim sngRed As Single
    Dim sngGreen As Single
    Dim sngBlue As Single
    Dim sngMx As Single
    Dim sngMn As Single
    Dim sngVa As Single
    Dim sngSa As Single
    Dim sngRc As Single
    Dim sngGc As Single
    Dim sngBc As Single
    sngRed = Red / 255
    sngGreen = Green / 255
```

(continued)

Source Code for HSV.CLS *continued*

```
        sngBlue = Blue / 255
        sngMx = sngRed
        If sngGreen > sngMx Then sngMx = sngGreen
        If sngBlue > sngMx Then sngMx = sngBlue
        sngMn = sngRed
        If sngGreen < sngMn Then sngMn = sngGreen
        If sngBlue < sngMn Then sngMn = sngBlue
        sngVa = sngMx
        If sngMx Then
            sngSa = (sngMx - sngMn) / sngMx
        Else
            sngSa = 0
        End If
        If sngSa = 0 Then
            Hue = 0
        Else
            sngRc = (sngMx - sngRed) / (sngMx - sngMn)
            sngGc = (sngMx - sngGreen) / (sngMx - sngMn)
            sngBc = (sngMx - sngBlue) / (sngMx - sngMn)
            Select Case sngMx
            Case sngRed
                Hue = sngBc - sngGc
            Case sngGreen
                Hue = 2 + sngRc - sngBc
            Case sngBlue
                Hue = 4 + sngGc - sngRc
            End Select
            Hue = Hue * 60
            If Hue < 0 Then Hue = Hue + 360
        End If
        Saturation = sngSa * 100
        Value = sngVa * 100
End Sub

'Converts HSV to RGB
Public Sub ToRgb()
    Dim sngSaturation As Single
    Dim sngValue As Single
    Dim sngHue As Single
    Dim intI As Integer
    Dim sngF As Single
    Dim sngP As Single
    Dim sngQ As Single
    Dim sngT As Single
    Dim sngRed As Single
```

(continued)

Source Code for HSV.CLS *continued*

```
    Dim sngGreen As Single
    Dim sngBlue As Single
    sngSaturation = Saturation / 100
    sngValue = Value / 100
    If Saturation = 0 Then
        sngRed = sngValue
        sngGreen = sngValue
        sngBlue = sngValue
    Else
        sngHue = Hue / 60
        If sngHue = 6 Then sngHue = 0
        intI = Int(sngHue)
        sngF = sngHue - intI
        sngP = sngValue * (1 - sngSaturation)
        sngQ = sngValue * (1 - (sngSaturation * sngF))
        sngT = sngValue * (1 - (sngSaturation * (1 - sngF)))
        Select Case intI
        Case 0
            sngRed = sngValue
            sngGreen = sngT
            sngBlue = sngP
        Case 1
            sngRed = sngQ
            sngGreen = sngValue
            sngBlue = sngP
        Case 2
            sngRed = sngP
            sngGreen = sngValue
            sngBlue = sngT
        Case 3
            sngRed = sngP
            sngGreen = sngQ
            sngBlue = sngValue
        Case 4
            sngRed = sngT
            sngGreen = sngP
            sngBlue = sngValue
        Case 5
            sngRed = sngValue
            sngGreen = sngP
            sngBlue = sngQ
        End Select
    End If
    Red = Int(255.9999 * sngRed)
    Green = Int(255.9999 * sngGreen)
    Blue = Int(255.9999 * sngBlue)
End Sub
```

Source Code for ABOUT.FRM

```
Option Explicit

Private Sub cmdOK_Click()
    'Cancel About form
    Unload About
End Sub

Private Sub Form_Load()
    'Center this form
    Left = (Screen.Width - Width) \ 2
    Top = (Screen.Height - Height) \ 2
    'Set defaults
    lblApplication.Caption = "- Application -"
    lblHeading.Caption = "- Heading -"
    lblCopyright.Caption = "- Copyright -"
End Sub

Public Sub Display()
    'Display self as modal
    Me.Show vbModal
End Sub

Property Let Application(Application As String)
    'Define string property for Application
    lblApplication.Caption = Application
End Property

Property Let Heading(Heading As String)
    'Define string property for Heading
    lblHeading.Caption = Heading
End Property

Property Let Copyright(Copyright As String)
    'Build complete Copyright string property
    lblCopyright.Caption = "Copyright © " & Copyright
End Property
```

The Animate Application

The Animate application demonstrates a couple of graphics techniques you might find useful in designing your own applications. In the code module ANIMATE.BAS, Sub Main displays two forms, each demonstrating a unique graphics technique. First let's take a look at the source code for the entire code module, and then we'll dive right into the two forms in this project.

Source Code for ANIMATE.BAS

```
Option Explicit
DefDbl A-Z

Public Const PI = 3.14159265358979
Public Const RADPERDEG = PI / 180

Sub Main()
    App.HelpFile = App.Path & "\..\..\Help\Mvbdw.hlp"
    frmClock.Show vbModeless
    frmGlobe.Show vbModeless
End Sub

Sub RotateX(X, Y, Z, Angle)
    Dim Radians, Ca, Sa, Ty
    Radians = Angle * RADPERDEG
    Ca = Cos(Radians)
    Sa = Sin(Radians)
    Ty = Y * Ca - Z * Sa
    Z = Z * Ca + Y * Sa
    Y = Ty
End Sub

Sub RotateY(X, Y, Z, Angle)
    Dim Radians, Ca, Sa, Tx
    Radians = Angle * RADPERDEG
    Ca = Cos(Radians)
    Sa = Sin(Radians)
    Tx = X * Ca + Z * Sa
    Z = Z * Ca - X * Sa
    X = Tx
End Sub

Sub RotateZ(X, Y, Z, Angle)
    Dim Radians, Ca, Sa, Tx
    Radians = Angle * RADPERDEG
    Ca = Cos(Radians)
    Sa = Sin(Radians)
    Tx = X * Ca - Y * Sa
    Y = Y * Ca + X * Sa
    X = Tx
End Sub

Sub PolToRec(Radius, Angle, X, Y)
    Dim Radians
```

(continued)

Source Code for ANIMATE.BAS *continued*

```
    Radians = Angle * RADPERDEG
    X = Radius * Cos(Radians)
    Y = Radius * Sin(Radians)
End Sub

Sub RecToPol(X, Y, Radius, Angle)
    Dim Radians
    Radius = Sqr(X * X + Y * Y)
    If X = 0 Then
        Select Case Y
        Case Is > 0
            Angle = 90
        Case Is < 0
            Angle = -90
        Case Else
            Angle = 0
        End Select
    ElseIf Y = 0 Then
        Select Case X
        Case Is < 0
            Angle = 180
        Case Else
            Angle = 0
        End Select
    Else
        If X < 0 Then
            If Y > 0 Then
                Radians = Atn(Y / X) + PI
            Else
                Radians = Atn(Y / X) - PI
            End If
        Else
            Radians = Atn(Y / X)
        End If
        Angle = Radians / RADPERDEG
    End If
End Sub
```

Notice that I've used the DefDbl A-Z statement in all of the forms and modules of this project to cause all variables to default to double-precision floating-point values. This program will run just fine if you delete these statements and let all variables default to Variants, but operation is slightly quicker if all variables are defined as Double as shown.

Unlike most of the applications in Part III, these graphics demonstration forms don't have menus; hence, they have no menu selections to access the help file. However, this is a convenient place to demonstrate how to connect the F1 key to this application's help file so that the user can activate the Help system at any time by pressing the F1 key. To do this, I simply set the application's HelpFile property in Sub Main to the path and filename of my help file.

An alternative to defining the HelpFile property in your code is to set the filename and optionally the full path of the help file in your project file. To do this, choose Project Properties from the Project menu to display the Project Properties dialog box. In the Help File Name text box, enter the name of the help file, and leave the Project Help Context ID text box set to *0*, which displays the Contents topic in the help file.

I set the program to start with Sub Main instead of one of the forms. To do this, I chose Project Properties from the Project menu to open the Project Properties dialog box. From the Startup Object drop-down list in this dialog box, I selected Sub Main. The Sub Main code block is very short; its purpose is to show both of the animation demonstration forms and set the application's HelpFile property. The rest of the code in this module is a collection of handy procedures for rotating Cartesian coordinates around each of the three axes and for converting coordinates between rectangular and polar. These procedures are useful for three-dimensional graphics computations, such as the ones I use to display a spinning globe. We get into that in more detail later, but first let's look at the animated clock form.

ANICLOCK.FRM

This form creates a real-time clock using only a single Line control and a Timer control. Figure 27-4 shows these two controls on the form at design time, and Figure 27-5 on the following page shows the clock at runtime.

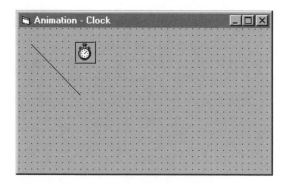

Figure 27-4.
The clock form at design time, with only two controls.

479

Figure 27-5.
The clock form at runtime.

You might be wondering how in the world all the straight-line elements of the clock face are drawn. The trick is to make 14 copies of the original Line control using the Load statement, with the endpoint-coordinate properties of each instance of this control array set to properly place each line on the clock face. Twelve of these copies are placed once, to mark the hour positions on the clock face, and three of the Line controls, the hands of the clock, are updated each second to give the illusion of movement.

Notice that no Line methods were used to create this clock and that no lines are ever erased directly by our application code. All the technical work of erasing and redrawing each hand as it moves is taken care of by Visual Basic when we update the endpoints of each Line control. Sometimes you don't need fancy graphics statements and commands—even a simple Line control can do amazing things.

You can change the appearance of the clock by adjusting property settings in the code. For example, you can create thinner or fatter lines by changing the setting of each Line control's BorderWidth property. To create this application, use the following table to add the appropriate controls, and set any nondefault properties as indicated.

ANICLOCK.FRM Objects and Property Settings

Property	Value
Form	
Name	*frmClock*
Caption	*Animation - Clock*
MinButton	*False*
Timer	
Name	*tmrClock*
Interval	*100*
Line	
Name	*linClock*
Index	*0*

Notice that I set the timer's Interval property to *100*, which is $\frac{1}{10}$ of a second. It might seem that logic would dictate a setting of 1000 milliseconds, or once per second, as ideal for updating the hands of the clock. However, this timing interval is not precise because Visual Basic's timers are designed to provide a delay that is at least as long as the specified interval, but there is no guarantee that every delay will be of exactly the same duration. Because of the slight variability in delay intervals, occasionally the second hand will "miss a beat," causing a noticeably jerky cycle in the movement of the second hand. To solve this timing unpredictability, I chose to check at the rate of 10 times per second to see whether a new second has arrived. This results in a maximum error of approximately $\frac{1}{10}$ of a second in the precision of each movement of the second hand, which is well within the tolerance of smooth operation for visual perception. About 9 out of 10 times the timer event procedure runs, it bails out immediately because the current second hasn't changed, wasting very little of the system's time.

Much of the work of *tmrClock*'s timer event procedure is in recalculating and resetting the endpoint-coordinate properties X1, Y1, X2, and Y2. The source code for the AniClock form is shown on the following pages.

Source Code for ANICLOCK.FRM

```
Option Explicit
DefDbl A-Z

Private Sub Form_Load()
    Width = 4000
    Height = 4000
    Left = Screen.Width \ 2 - 4100
    Top = (Screen.Height - Height) \ 2
End Sub

Private Sub Form_Resize()
    Dim i, Angle
    Static Flag As Boolean
    If Flag = False Then
        Flag = True
        For i = 0 To 14
            If i > 0 Then Load linClock(i)
            linClock(i).Visible = True
            linClock(i).BorderWidth = 5
            linClock(i).BorderColor = RGB(0, 128, 0)
        Next i
    End If
    For i = 0 To 14
        Scale (-1, 1)-(1, -1)
        Angle = i * 2 * Atn(1) / 3
        linClock(i).x1 = 0.9 * Cos(Angle)
        linClock(i).y1 = 0.9 * Sin(Angle)
        linClock(i).x2 = Cos(Angle)
        linClock(i).y2 = Sin(Angle)
    Next i
End Sub

Private Sub tmrClock_Timer()
    Const HourHand = 0
    Const MinuteHand = 13
    Const SecondHand = 14
    Dim Angle
    Static LastSecond
    'Position hands only on the second
    If Second(Now) = LastSecond Then Exit Sub
    LastSecond = Second(Now)
    'Position hour hand
    Angle = 0.5236 * (15 - (Hour(Now) + Minute(Now) / 60))
    linClock(HourHand).x1 = 0
```

(continued)

Source Code for ANICLOCK.FRM *continued*

```
    linClock(HourHand).y1 = 0
    linClock(HourHand).x2 = 0.3 * Cos(Angle)
    linClock(HourHand).y2 = 0.3 * Sin(Angle)
    'Position minute hand
    Angle = 0.1047 * (75 - (Minute(Now) + Second(Now) / 60))
    linClock(MinuteHand).x1 = 0
    linClock(MinuteHand).y1 = 0
    linClock(MinuteHand).x2 = 0.7 * Cos(Angle)
    linClock(MinuteHand).y2 = 0.7 * Sin(Angle)
    'Position second hand
    Angle = 0.1047 * (75 - Second(Now))
    linClock(SecondHand).x1 = 0
    linClock(SecondHand).y1 = 0
    linClock(SecondHand).x2 = 0.8 * Cos(Angle)
    linClock(SecondHand).y2 = 0.8 * Sin(Angle)
End Sub
```

ANIGLOBE.FRM

This form displays sequential images of a sphere's lines of latitude and longitude, creating the illusion of a spinning globe. The technique used here is an ImageList control that stores the sequential images and provides them for quick, animated copying to a PictureBox control. Figure 27-6 shows the AniGlobe form during development, with PictureBox, ImageList, and Timer controls for creating the animation effect.

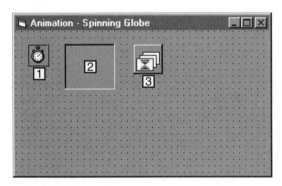

Figure 27-6.
The AniGlobe form at development time.

This form updates itself each time its *tmrGlobe* timer event fires. For the first 15 iterations, a new image is drawn, using the various 3D graphics procedures you'll find in the ANIMATE.BAS module. As each image is drawn, it is quickly saved in an ImageList control declared at the module level. After all 15 images have been tucked away for safekeeping, the program begins to display them sequentially by updating the PictureBox's Picture property to refer to each image, as shown in Figure 27-7. This image transfer operation is fast and smooth, providing a great general technique for creating animated sequences.

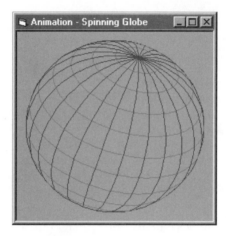

Figure 27-7.
The AniGlobe form in action.

The following table specifies the AniGlobe form's settings.

ANIGLOBE.FRM Objects and Property Settings

ID No.*	Property	Value
Form		
	Name	*frmGlobe*
	Caption	*Animation - Spinning Globe*
Timer		
1	Name	*tmrGlobe*
	Interval	*1*

* The number in the ID No. column corresponds to the number in Figure 27-6 that identifies the location of the object on the form.

(continued)

ANIGLOBE.FRM Objects and Property Settings *continued*

ID No.	Property	Value
PictureBox		
2	Name	*picGlobe*
	AutoRedraw	*True*
ImageList		
3	Name	*imlGlobe*

In the source code below, I've isolated constants that define the forward and sideways tilt angles of the globe. Try changing the *TILTSOUTH* and *TILTEAST* constants to see the dramatic changes in the appearance of the spinning globe.

The ImageList control is especially useful when associated with other controls, such as the ListView, ToolBar, TabStrip, and TreeView controls. For more information about this powerful image manipulation tool, see the Visual Basic documentation.

The source code for the AniGlobe form is shown below.

Source Code for ANIGLOBE.FRM

```
Option Explicit
DefDbl A-Z

Const TILTSOUTH = 37
Const TILTEAST = 27

Private Sub Form_Load()
    Width = 4000
    Height = 4000
    Left = Screen.Width \ 2 + 100
    Top = (Screen.Height - Height) \ 2
End Sub

Private Sub tmrGlobe_Timer()
    Dim Lat, Lon, Radians
    Dim R, A, i
    Dim x1, y1, x2, y2
    Dim Xc(72), Yc(72), Zc(72)
    Dim imgX As ListImage
```

(continued)

Source Code for ANIGLOBE.FRM *continued*

```
Static ImageIndex, ImageNum
Select Case ImageNum
'Pump next image to  display
Case -1
    ImageIndex = (ImageIndex Mod 15) + 1
    Set picGlobe.Picture = imlGlobe.ListImages _
        (ImageIndex).Picture
    Exit Sub
'Initialize  PictureBox
Case 0
    picGlobe.Move 0, 0, ScaleWidth, ScaleHeight
    picGlobe.Scale (-1.1, 1.1)-(1.1, -1.1)
    Caption = "Animation ... PREPARATION"
    ImageNum = ImageNum + 1
    Exit Sub
'Flag that last image has been drawn and saved in image list
Case 16
    Caption = "Animation - Spinning Globe"
    ImageNum = -1
    Exit Sub
End Select
'Erase any previous picture in PictureBox control
Set picGlobe.Picture = Nothing
'Draw edge of globe
picGlobe.ForeColor = vbBlue
For i = 0 To 72
    PolToRec 1, i * 5, Xc(i), Yc(i)
Next i
For i = 1 To 72
    picGlobe.Line (Xc(i - 1), Yc(i - 1))-(Xc(i), Yc(i))
Next i
'Calculate and draw latitude lines
picGlobe.ForeColor = vbRed
For Lat = -75 To 75 Step 15
    'Convert latitude to radians
    Radians = Lat * RADPERDEG
    'Draw circle size based on latitude
    For i = 0 To 72
        PolToRec Cos(Radians), i * 5, Xc(i), Zc(i)
        Yc(i) = Sin(Radians)
        'Tilt globe's north pole toward us
        RotateX Xc(i), Yc(i), Zc(i), TILTSOUTH
        'Tilt globe's north pole to the right
        RotateY Xc(i), Yc(i), Zc(i), TILTEAST
```

(continued)

Source Code for ANIGLOBE.FRM *continued*

```
            Next i
            'Draw front half of rotated circle
            For i = 1 To 72
                If Zc(i) >= 0 Then
                    picGlobe.Line (Xc(i - 1), Yc(i - 1))-(Xc(i), Yc(i))
                End If
            Next i
        Next Lat
        'Calculate and draw longitude lines
        picGlobe.ForeColor = vbBlue
        For Lon = 0 To 165 Step 15
            'Start with xy-plane circle
            For A = 0 To 72
                PolToRec 1, A * 5, Xc(A), Yc(A)
                Zc(A) = 0
            Next A
            'Rotate points for current line of longitude
            For i = 0 To 72
                RotateY Xc(i), Yc(i), Zc(i), Lon + ImageNum
                'Tilt globe's north pole toward us
                RotateX Xc(i), Yc(i), Zc(i), TILTSOUTH
                'Tilt globe's north pole to the right
                RotateY Xc(i), Yc(i), Zc(i), TILTEAST
            Next i
            'Draw front half of rotated circle
            For i = 1 To 72
                If Zc(i) >= 0 Then
                    picGlobe.Line (Xc(i - 1), Yc(i - 1))-(Xc(i), Yc(i))
                End If
            Next i
        Next Lon
        'Update PictureBox state
        picGlobe.Refresh
        picGlobe.Picture = picGlobe.Image
        'Add this image to our image list
        Set imgX = imlGlobe.ListImages.Add(, , picGlobe.Picture)
        'Prepare to draw next image
        ImageNum = ImageNum + 1
End Sub
```

The Lottery Application

The Lottery application is modeled after the Colorado lottery, in which a cylindrical basket tumbles numbered Ping-Pong balls. With minor modifications, this application can model other similar games of chance. The concept is fairly simple: 42 Ping-Pong balls, numbered 1 through 42, are tossed into a basket and jumbled. Six balls are then selected, one at a time, in a random manner. The six numbers drawn from the set of numbers 1 through 42 represent the winning ticket. The prize money can be a huge amount, but the chance of hitting all six numbers is extremely small, so the state wins big on the average. In the Lottery application, each time you click the Next Ball command button, one of the balls is selected and placed at the bottom of the screen. Figure 27-8 shows the application in action, after three of the numbers have been selected. After you've finished selecting six balls, you can see how lucky you are—I've added an option to simulate the purchase of 1000 lottery tickets so that you can see how hard it is to hit the jackpot even if you buy a lot of tickets. As you'll discover, it's very rare that you'll match even five out of the six numbers.

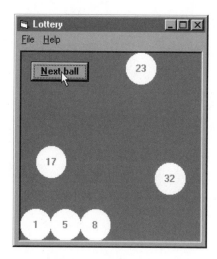

Figure 27-8.
The Lottery program in action.

This application demonstrates a Random object I've created that generates random numbers with a much greater sequence length than the generator built into Visual Basic. The application also demonstrates one of the simplest methods of animation, which is simply to redraw a picture repeatedly with enough speed to make it appear that the action is continuous.

In addition to the main Lottery form, which displays the tumbling Ping-Pong balls, this project contains a class module named RANDOM.CLS and the standard About form I described in Chapter 10, "Dialog Boxes, Windows, and Other Forms." Figure 27-9 shows the Lottery project list.

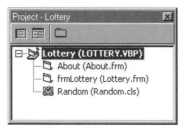

Figure 27-9.
The Lottery project list.

LOTTERY.FRM

LOTTERY.FRM is the main startup form for this application. The *picTumble* PictureBox control displays the tumbling balls and the selected balls, the two command buttons control the action, and the *tmrPingPong* Timer control triggers each update of the action. Figure 27-10 shows this form during development, and the tables and source code on the following pages define the form's design.

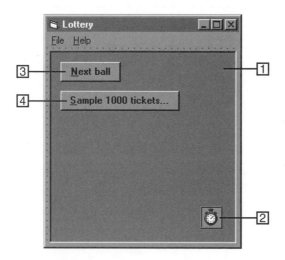

Figure 27-10.
The Lottery form during development.

LOTTERY.FRM Menu Design Window Entries

Caption	Name	Indentation	Enabled
&File	mnuFile	0	True
&New	mnuNew	1	False
&Open...	mnuOpen	1	False
&Save	mnuSave	1	False
Save &As...	mnuSaveAs	1	False
-	mnuFileDash1	1	True
E&xit	mnuExit	1	True
&Help	mnuHelp	0	True
&Contents	mnuContents	1	True
&Search for Help on...	mnuSearch	1	True
-	mnuHelpDash1	1	True
&About...	mnuAbout	1	True

LOTTERY.FRM Objects and Property Settings

ID No.*	Property	Value
Form		
	Name	frmLottery
	Caption	Lottery
PictureBox		
1	Name	picTumble
	AutoRedraw	True
	BackColor	&H00FF0000&
	Height	3600
	Width	3600
Timer		
2	Name	tmrPingPong
	Interval	50
CommandButton		
3	Name	cmdNextBall
	Caption	&Next Ball

* The number in the ID No. column corresponds to the number in Figure 27-10 that identifies the location of the object on the form.

(continued)

LOTTERY.FRM Objects and Property Settings *continued*

ID No.*	Property	Value
CommandButton		
4	Name	*cmdSample*
	Caption	*&Sample 1000 tickets...*

Source Code for LOTTERY.FRM

```
Option Explicit
DefLng A-Z

Private Declare Function WinHelp _
Lib "user32" Alias "WinHelpA" ( _
    ByVal hwnd As Long, _
    ByVal lpHelpFile As String, _
    ByVal wCommand As Long, _
    ByVal dwData As Long _
) As Long


Const MAXNUM = 42

Dim PPBall(6)
Dim R As New Random

Private Sub cmdNextBall_Click()
    Dim i, j
    'Set command button caption
    cmdNextBall.Caption = "&Next ball"
    cmdSample.Visible = False
    'Get current count of selected balls
    i = PPBall(0)
    'If all balls were grabbed, start over
    If i = 6 Then
        For i = 0 To 6
            PPBall(i) = 0
        Next i
        Exit Sub
    End If
    'Select next unique Ping-Pong ball
    GrabNext PPBall()
```

(continued)

Source Code for LOTTERY.FRM *continued*

```
        'Change command button caption,
        'and show sample command button
        If PPBall(0) = 6 Then
            cmdNextBall.Caption = "Start &over"
            cmdSample.Visible = True
        End If
    End Sub

    Private Sub cmdSample_Click()
        Dim i, j, k, n
        Dim Ticket(6)
        Dim Hits(6)
        Dim Msg$
        'Display hourglass mouse pointer
        MousePointer = vbHourglass
        'Now simulate 1000 "quick pick" tickets
        For i = 1 To 1000
            'Generate a ticket
            Ticket(0) = 0
            For j = 1 To 6
                GrabNext Ticket()
            Next j
            'Tally the hits
            n = 0
            For j = 1 To 6
                For k = 1 To 6
                    If Ticket(j) = PPBall(k) Then
                        n = n + 1
                    End If
                Next k
            Next j
            'Update statistics
            Hits(n) = Hits(n) + 1
        Next i
        'Display default mouse pointer
        MousePointer = vbDefault
        'Display summarized statistics
        Msg$ = "Sample of 1000 tickets..." & vbCrLf & vbCrLf
        Msg$ = Msg$ & Space$(10) & "Hits   Tally" & vbCrLf
        For i = 0 To 6
            Msg$ = Msg$ & Space$(12) & Format$(i) & Space$(6)
            Msg$ = Msg$ & Format$(Hits(i)) & vbCrLf
        Next i
        MsgBox Msg$, , "Lottery"
    End Sub
```

(continued)

Source Code for LOTTERY.FRM *continued*

```
Private Sub Form_Load()
    'Seed new random numbers
    Randomize
    R.Shuffle Rnd
    'Set range of random integers
    R.MinInt = 1
    R.MaxInt = MAXNUM
    'Center form
    Left = (Screen.Width - Width) \ 2
    Top = (Screen.Height - Height) \ 2
    'Hide sample command button for now
    cmdSample.Visible = False
    'Prepare tumble animation
    picTumble.Scale (0, 12)-(12, 0)
    picTumble.FillStyle = vbSolid
    picTumble.FillColor = vbWhite
    picTumble.ForeColor = vbRed
End Sub

Private Sub picTumble_Paint()
    Dim i, x, y, n$
    'Erase previous tumble animation
    picTumble.Cls
    For i = 1 To 6
        'Determine whether ball has been selected
        If PPBall(i) > 0 Then
            x = i * 2 - 1
            y = 1
            n$ = Format$(PPBall(i))
        Else
            x = Rnd * 10 + 1
            y = Rnd * 8 + 3
            n$ = Format$(R.RandomInt)
        End If
        'Draw each Ping-Pong ball
        picTumble.Circle (x, y), 1, vbWhite
        picTumble.CurrentX = x - picTumble.TextWidth(n$) / 2
        picTumble.CurrentY = y - picTumble.TextHeight(n$) / 2
        'Label each Ping-Pong ball
        picTumble.Print n$
    Next i
End Sub
```

(continued)

Source Code for LOTTERY.FRM *continued*

```vb
Private Sub tmrPingPong_Timer()
    picTumble_Paint
End Sub

Private Sub mnuAbout_Click()
    'Set properties
    About.Application = "Lottery"
    About.Heading = _
        "Microsoft Visual Basic 5.0 Developer's Workshop"
    About.Copyright = "1997 John Clark Craig and Jeff Webb"
    About.Display
End Sub

Private Sub mnuExit_Click()
    Unload Me
End Sub

Private Sub mnuContents_Click()
    WinHelp hwnd, App.Path & "\..\..\Help\Mvbdw.hlp", _
        cdlHelpContents, 0
End Sub

Private Sub mnuSearch_Click()
    WinHelp hwnd, App.Path & "\..\..\Help\Mvbdw.hlp", _
        cdlHelpPartialKey, 0
End Sub

Private Sub GrabNext(Ary())
    Dim i, j
    'Store index in first array element
    Ary(0) = Ary(0) + 1
    i = Ary(0)
    'Get next unique Ping-Pong ball number
    Do
        Ary(i) = R.RandomInt
        If i > 1 Then
            For j = 1 To i - 1
                If Ary(i) = Ary(j) Then
                    Ary(i) = 0
                End If
            Next j
        End If
    Loop Until Ary(i)
End Sub
```

Long integers are the most common type of variable in this application, so I simplified the declarations of my variables by adding the DefLng A–Z statement at the module level.

NOTE: The WinHelp API function is used to activate the help file when the appropriate menu items are clicked. In some of the applications in Part III, I'll add a CommonDialog control to the project to provide the connection to the help file, even in cases in which the menu is identical to the menu shown here. Both techniques produce identical results, and it's largely a matter of personal preference as to the method you choose.

Notice in the Form_Load event procedure that I use an object of type Random. This type of object is defined by the Random class module, which I'll describe next.

RANDOM.CLS

The Random class module provides the template for creating objects of type Random. At the core of the Random objects is a technique that greatly expands the sequence length of the random-number generator built into Visual Basic. I've used an array of type Double to add a shuffling and mixing action to the generation of the random numbers.

The following public properties are defined in RANDOM.CLS:

- MinInt: Minimum value for the range of generated random integers

- MaxInt: Maximum value for the range of generated random integers

- Random: Random double number in the range 0 through 1

- RandomInt: Random integer in the range defined by MinInt and MaxInt

The one public method defined in RANDOM.CLS is Shuffle, which initializes the random-number sequence.

The random-number generator in Visual Basic is very good, but I've heard of some concerns. First, it's not at all clear how to initialize Visual Basic's random-number generator to a repeatable sequence. OK, I'll let you in on a little secret—there is a simple, albeit tricky, way to reinitialize Visual Basic's random-number generator to a repeatable sequence. You need to call Randomize immediately after passing a negative value to the Rnd function, as in the following example:

```
Randomize Rnd(-7)
```

Every time you pass -7 to these two functions, as shown, you'll initialize Visual Basic's random numbers to the same sequence. I've used this technique, modified slightly, in the Shuffle method of my Random object to initialize the object's sequence. For flexibility, if you pass a negative value to Shuffle, a repeatable sequence is initialized. A positive or 0 value results in a completely unpredictable sequence.

Another concern I've heard, especially from cryptographers, is that the random numbers generated by Visual Basic don't take into account such phenomena as subtle patterns and entropy, reducing the value of the generated sequences for high-quality cryptography work. My Random object maintains an array of double-precision numbers that effectively shuffle and randomize Visual Basic's sequence by many orders of magnitude, while maintaining a good distribution of numbers in the range 0 through 1. Study the Random public property procedure to see how this is accomplished.

The RandomInt property procedure modifies a value returned by the Random procedure to provide an integer in the range defined by the user-set properties MinInt and MaxInt. The distribution of these pseudorandom integers is as good as the distribution of the values returned by Random.

There are two private procedures in the Random class module. The Zap procedure initializes the array and its indexes to a known state during the initialization performed by the Shuffle method. The Stir private method helps warm up the generator.

Source Code for RANDOM.CLS

```
Option Explicit

Const SIZE = 17

Public MinInt As Long
Public MaxInt As Long

Private dSeed(SIZE - 1) As Double
Private iP1 As Integer
Private iP2 As Integer

Public Sub Shuffle(dX As Double)
```

(continued)

Source Code for RANDOM.CLS *continued*

```
    Dim sN
    Dim i As Integer
    Zap
    sN = Str$(dX)
    For i = 1 To Len(sN)
        Stir 1 / Asc(Mid$(sN, i, 1))
    Next i
    Randomize Rnd(dSeed(iP1) * Sgn(dX))
    For i = 1 To SIZE * 2.7
        Stir Rnd
    Next i
End Sub

Property Get Random() As Double
    iP1 = (iP1 + 1) Mod SIZE
    iP2 = (iP2 + 1) Mod SIZE
    dSeed(iP1) = dSeed(iP1) + dSeed(iP2) + Rnd
    dSeed(iP1) = dSeed(iP1) - Int(dSeed(iP1))
    Random = dSeed(iP1)
End Property

Property Get RandomInt() As Long
    RandomInt = Int(Random() * (MaxInt - MinInt + 1)) + MinInt
End Property

Private Sub Zap()
    Dim i As Integer
    For i = 1 To SIZE - 1
        dSeed(i) = 1 / i
    Next i
    iP1 = SIZE \ 2
    iP2 = SIZE \ 3
    If iP1 = iP2 Then
        iP1 = iP1 + 1
    End If
End Sub

Private Sub Stir(dX As Double)
    iP1 = (iP1 + 1) Mod SIZE
    iP2 = (iP2 + 1) Mod SIZE
    dSeed(iP1) = dSeed(iP1) + dSeed(iP2) + dX
    dSeed(iP1) = dSeed(iP1) - Int(dSeed(iP1))
End Sub
```

The Ssaver Application

The Ssaver application expands on the examples presented in Chapter 23, "Screen Savers." I've added a larger set of graphics options that let the user set a wide variety of effects without a lot of additional code. Figure 27-11 shows this screen saver in action, although you should try the many combinations of settings to get the full effect of its many graphics variations.

Figure 27-11.
The Ssaver application in action.

As shown in Figure 27-12, this project contains only two form modules. SSAVER.FRM is the main startup form, and SSETUP.FRM is activated when the user clicks the Settings button in the Screen Saver dialog box on the Microsoft Windows 95 desktop.

Figure 27-12.
The Ssaver project list.

SSAVER.FRM

The SSAVER.FRM form is where all the graphical screen saver action takes place. Notice that I set the form's WindowState property to *2 - Maximized* and turned off all visible parts of the form—for example, setting the MinButton and MaxButton properties to *False*. This lets the form provide a drawing surface covering the entire screen.

The only control on this form, as shown in Figure 27-13, is a Timer control. The graphics update happens in a continuous loop during the form's Load event. Visual Basic generates an error if your program tries to unload itself from within the Load event, so the timer is a tricky way to allow the form to unload quickly after exiting from the graphics loop within the Load event. I wouldn't normally suggest structuring a program to continuously loop within the Load event in this way, but I did it this way because it's slightly faster than letting a timer trigger each update of the graphics and because the system doesn't interact with the user while a screen saver is running.

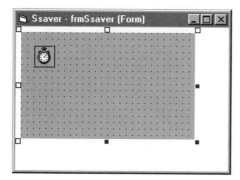

Figure 27-13.
SSAVER.FRM during development.

The following table and source code define the form's design.

SSAVER.FRM Objects and Property Settings

Property	Value
Form	
Name	*frmSsaver*
BorderStyle	*0 - None*

(continued)

SSAVER.FRM Objects and Property Settings *continued*

Property	Value
Form	
ControlBox	*False*
MaxButton	*False*
MinButton	*False*
WindowState	*2 - Maximized*
Timer	
Name	*tmrExitNotify*
Interval	*1*
Enabled	*False*

Source Code for SSAVER.FRM

```
Option Explicit
DefLng A-Z

'Declare API to hide and reshow the mouse pointer
Private Declare Function ShowCursor _
Lib "user32" ( _
    ByVal bShow As Long _
) As Long

'Declare module-level variables
Dim mlXai, mlYai
Dim mlXbi, mlYbi
Dim mlLineCount
Dim mlLineWidth
Dim mlActionType
Dim mlXmax, mlYmax
Dim mlInc
Dim mlColorNum()
Dim mlDx1() As Double, mlDx2() As Double
Dim mlDy1() As Double, mlDy2() As Double
Dim mlXa(), mlXb()
Dim mlYa(), mlYb()
Dim bQuitFlag As Boolean
```

(continued)

Source Code for SSAVER.FRM *continued*

```vb
Private Sub Form_Click()
    'Quit if mouse is clicked
    bQuitFlag = True
End Sub

Private Sub Form_KeyDown(KeyCode As Integer, Shift As Integer)
    'Quit if any key is pressed
    bQuitFlag = True
End Sub

Private Sub Form_Load()
    Dim lX
    'Don't allow multiple instances of screen saver
    If App.PrevInstance = True Then
        Unload Me
        Exit Sub
    End If
    'Proceed based on command line
    Select Case UCase$(Left$(Command$, 2))
    'Show quick preview
    Case "/P"
        Unload Me
        Exit Sub
    'Configure screen saver
    Case "/C"
        'Perform any user interaction
        frmSsetup.Show vbModal
        'Continue after configuring screen saver
        Unload Me
        Exit Sub
    'Set password
    Case "/A"
        'Get and record new password here
        MsgBox "No password for this screen saver"
        'Continue after setting new password
        Unload Me
        Exit Sub
    'Get this show on the road
    Case "/S"
        'Create different display each time
        Randomize
        'Display full size
```

(continued)

Source Code for SSAVER.FRM *continued*

```
Show
'Set control values
mlInc = 5
mlXmax = 300
mlYmax = 300
'Get current user settings from Registry
mlActionType = Val(GetSetting("Ssaver", "Options", _
    "Action", "1"))
mlLineCount = Val(GetSetting("Ssaver", "Options", _
    "LineCount", "1"))
mlLineWidth = Val(GetSetting("Ssaver", "Options", _
    "LineWidth", "1"))
'Initialize graphics
BackColor = vbBlack
DrawWidth = mlLineWidth
Scale (-mlXmax, -mlYmax)-(mlXmax, mlYmax)
'Size arrays
ReDim mlColorNum(0 To mlLineCount)
ReDim mlXa(1 To mlLineCount), mlXb(1 To mlLineCount)
ReDim mlYa(1 To mlLineCount), mlYb(1 To mlLineCount)
'Action types above 4 are a little different
If mlActionType < 5 Then
    ReDim mlDx1(1 To mlLineCount), mlDx2(1 To mlLineCount)
    ReDim mlDy1(1 To mlLineCount), mlDy2(1 To mlLineCount)
Else
    ReDim mlDx1(0), mlDx2(0)
    ReDim mlDy1(0), mlDy2(0)
    mlDx1(0) = Rnd * mlInc
    mlDx2(0) = Rnd * mlInc
    mlDy1(0) = Rnd * mlInc
    mlDy2(0) = Rnd * mlInc
End If
'Hide mouse pointer
lX = ShowCursor(False)
'Do main processing as a loop
Do
    'Update display
    DoGraphics
    'Yield execution
    DoEvents
Loop Until bQuitFlag = True
'Show mouse pointer
lX = ShowCursor(True)
'Can't quit in this context; let timer do it
tmrExitNotify.Enabled = True
```

(continued)

Source Code for SSAVER.FRM *continued*

```
    Case Else
        Unload Me
        Exit Sub
    End Select
End Sub

Private Sub Form_MouseMove(Button As Integer, Shift As Integer, _
    x As Single, y As Single)
    Static lXlast, lYlast
    Dim lXnow
    Dim lYnow
    'Get current position
    lXnow = x
    lYnow = y
    'On first move, simply record position
    If lXlast = 0 And lYlast = 0 Then
        lXlast = lXnow
        lYlast = lYnow
        Exit Sub
    End If
    'Quit only if mouse actually changes position
    If lXnow <> lXlast Or lYnow <> lYlast Then
        bQuitFlag = True
    End If
End Sub

Private Sub tmrExitNotify_Timer()
    'Time to quit
    Unload Me
End Sub

Sub ColorReset()
    Dim i
    'Randomize set of colors
    If mlActionType <= 4 Then
        For i = 1 To mlLineCount
            mlColorNum(i) = RGB(Rnd * 256, Rnd * 256, Rnd * 256)
        Next i
    'Use bright colors for action types 5 or 6
    Else
        mlColorNum(0) = QBColor(Int(8 * Rnd) + 8)
    End If
End Sub
```

(continued)

Source Code for SSAVER.FRM *continued*

```
Sub DoGraphics()
    Dim i
    Static dColorTime As Double
    'Shuffle line colors every so often
    If Timer > dColorTime Then
        ColorReset
        If mlLineCount < 5 Then
            dColorTime = Timer + mlLineCount * Rnd + 0.3
        Else
            dColorTime = Timer + 5 * Rnd + 0.3
        End If
    End If
    'Process based on count of lines
    For i = 1 To mlLineCount
        'Handle action types above 4 with special procedures
        If mlActionType < 5 Then
            'Keep ends of lines in bounds
            If mlXa(i) <= 0 Then
                mlDx1(i) = mlInc * Rnd
            End If
            If mlXb(i) <= 0 Then
                mlDx2(i) = mlInc * Rnd
            End If
            If mlYa(i) <= 0 Then
                mlDy1(i) = mlInc * Rnd
            End If
            If mlYb(i) <= 0 Then
                mlDy2(i) = mlInc * Rnd
            End If
            If mlXa(i) >= mlXmax Then
                mlDx1(i) = -mlInc * Rnd
            End If
            If mlXb(i) >= mlXmax Then
                mlDx2(i) = -mlInc * Rnd
            End If
            If mlYa(i) >= mlYmax Then
                mlDy1(i) = -mlInc * Rnd
            End If
            If mlYb(i) >= mlYmax Then
                mlDy2(i) = -mlInc * Rnd
            End If
            'Increment position of line ends
            mlXa(i) = mlXa(i) + mlDx1(i)
            mlXb(i) = mlXb(i) + mlDx2(i)
```

(continued)

Source Code for SSAVER.FRM *continued*

```
            mlYa(i) = mlYa(i) + mlDy1(i)
            mlYb(i) = mlYb(i) + mlDy2(i)
            'Set each line with a unique color
            ForeColor = mlColorNum(i)
        Else
            'Set action types 5 and 6 with the same color
            ForeColor = mlColorNum(0)
        End If
        'Draw lines based on action type
        Select Case mlActionType
        Case 1
            Line (mlXa(i), mlYa(i))-(mlXb(i), mlYb(i))
            Line (-mlXa(i), -mlYa(i))-(-mlXb(i), -mlYb(i))
            Line (-mlXa(i), mlYa(i))-(-mlXb(i), mlYb(i))
            Line (mlXa(i), -mlYa(i))-(mlXb(i), -mlYb(i))
        Case 2
            Line (mlXa(i), mlYa(i))-(mlXb(i), mlYb(i)), , B
            Line (-mlXa(i), -mlYa(i))-(-mlXb(i), -mlYb(i)), , B
            Line (-mlXa(i), mlYa(i))-(-mlXb(i), mlYb(i)), , B
            Line (mlXa(i), -mlYa(i))-(mlXb(i), -mlYb(i)), , B
        Case 3
            Circle (mlXa(i), mlYa(i)), mlXb(i)
            Circle (-mlXa(i), -mlYa(i)), mlXb(i)
            Circle (-mlXa(i), mlYa(i)), mlXb(i)
            Circle (mlXa(i), -mlYa(i)), mlXb(i)
        Case 4
            Line (mlXa(i), mlYa(i))-(mlXb(i), -mlYb(i))
            Line -(-mlXa(i), -mlYa(i))
            Line -(-mlXb(i), mlYb(i))
            Line -(mlXa(i), mlYa(i))
        'Handle action types above 4 a little differently
        Case 5, 6
            If mlActionType = 5 Then
                Line (mlXa(i), mlYa(i))-(mlXb(i), mlYb(i)), _
                    BackColor
            Else
                Line (mlXa(i), mlYa(i))-(mlXb(i), mlYb(i)), _
                    BackColor, B
            End If
            If mlXai <= -mlXmax Then
                mlDx1(0) = mlInc * Rnd + 1
            End If
            If mlXbi <= -mlXmax Then
                mlDx2(0) = mlInc * Rnd + 1
```

(continued)

Source Code for SSAVER.FRM *continued*

```
                    End If
                    If mlYai <= -mlYmax Then
                        mlDy1(0) = mlInc * Rnd + 1
                    End If
                    If mlYbi <= -mlYmax Then
                        mlDy2(0) = mlInc * Rnd + 1
                    End If
                    If mlXai >= mlXmax Then
                        mlDx1(0) = -mlInc * Rnd + 1
                    End If
                    If mlXbi >= mlXmax Then
                        mlDx2(0) = -mlInc * Rnd + 1
                    End If
                    If mlYai >= mlYmax Then
                        mlDy1(0) = -mlInc * Rnd + 1
                    End If
                    If mlYbi >= mlYmax Then
                        mlDy2(0) = -mlInc * Rnd + 1
                    End If
                    mlXai = mlXai + mlDx1(0)
                    mlXbi = mlXbi + mlDx2(0)
                    mlYai = mlYai + mlDy1(0)
                    mlYbi = mlYbi + mlDy2(0)
                    mlXa(i) = mlXai
                    mlXb(i) = mlXbi
                    mlYa(i) = mlYai
                    mlYb(i) = mlYbi
                    If mlActionType = 5 Then
                        Line (mlXa(i), mlYa(i))-(mlXb(i), mlYb(i))
                    Else
                        Line (mlXa(i), mlYa(i))-(mlXb(i), mlYb(i)), , B
                    End If
            End Select
        Next i
End Sub
```

This code acts on the standard command line parameters that the system passes to any screen saver. In particular, the /C parameter causes the display of the Ssetup form, and the /S parameter activates the main graphics display loop. For a more in-depth explanation of the way screen savers interact with the system, refer to Chapter 23, "Screen Savers."

I've set up six unique types of graphics animations, with variations on the number of lines and the thickness of each line in pixels. Much of the code is only slightly different for these various modes, although the effects can be dramatically different. For example, the B parameter that is added to the Line method causes the same command to draw a series of boxes instead of diagonal lines.

SSETUP.FRM

As mentioned, the Ssetup form is activated when the user clicks the Settings button after selecting this screen saver. You can select a screen saver by right-clicking on the Windows 95 desktop, choosing Properties, and then clicking on the Screen Saver tab in the Display Properties dialog box that appears.

SSETUP.FRM is a dialog box that lets you select one of six types of graphics displays and lets you modify each of these by selecting the number of lines and the thickness in pixels of each line. These settings are read from and written to the System Registry using the GetSetting and SaveSetting statements. The dialog box always displays the current settings when it opens. Figure 27-14 shows the Ssetup form during the development process.

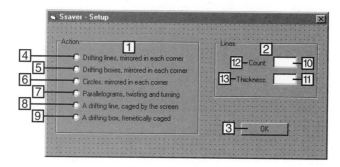

Figure 27-14.
The Ssetup form during development.

The following table and source code define the form:

SSETUP.FRM Objects and Property Settings

ID No.*	Property	Value
Form		
	Name	*frmSsetup*
	BorderStyle	*3 - Fixed Dialog*
	Caption	*Ssaver - Setup*
	ScaleMode	*3 - Pixel*

* The number in the ID No. column corresponds to the number in Figure 27-14 that identifies the location of the object on the form.

(continued)

SSETUP.FRM Objects and Property Settings *continued*

ID No.	Property	Value
Frame		
1	Name	*Frame1*
	Caption	*Action*
Frame		
2	Name	*Frame2*
	Caption	*Lines*
CommandButton		
3	Name	*cmdOK*
	Caption	*OK*
OptionButton		
4	Name	*optAction*
	Index	*0*
	Caption	*Drifting lines, mirrored in each corner*
OptionButton		
5	Name	*optAction*
	Index	*1*
	Caption	*Drifting boxes, mirrored in each corner*
OptionButton		
6	Name	*optAction*
	Index	*2*
	Caption	*Circles, mirrored in each corner*
OptionButton		
7	Name	*optAction*
	Index	*3*
	Caption	*Parallelograms, twisting and turning*
OptionButton		
8	Name	*optAction*
	Index	*4*
	Caption	*A drifting line, caged by the screen*

(continued)

SSETUP.FRM Objects and Property Settings *continued*

ID No.	Property	Value
OptionButton		
9	Name	*optAction*
	Index	*5*
	Caption	*A drifting box, frenetically caged*
TextBox		
10	Name	*txtLineCount*
TextBox		
11	Name	*txtLineWidth*
Label		
12	Name	*Label1*
	Caption	*Count:*
Label		
13	Name	*label2*
	Caption	*Thickness:*

Source Code for SSETUP.FRM

```
Option Explicit

Dim msAction As String

Private Sub Form_Load()
    'Center this form
    Left = (Screen.Width - Width) \ 2
    Top = (Screen.Height - Height) \ 2
    'Get current settings from the Registry
    msAction = GetSetting("Ssaver", "Options", "Action", "1")
    optAction(Val(msAction) - 1).Value = True
    txtLineCount.Text = GetSetting("Ssaver", "Options", _
        "LineCount", "5")
    txtLineWidth.Text = GetSetting("Ssaver", "Options", _
        "LineWidth", "1")
End Sub

Private Sub cmdOK_Click()
    Dim lN As Long
```

(continued)

Source Code for SSETUP.FRM *continued*

```
    'Check line count option
    lN = Val(txtLineCount.Text)
    If lN < 1 Or lN > 1000 Then
        MsgBox "Line count should be a small positive integer", _
            vbExclamation, "Ssaver"
        Exit Sub
    End If
    'Check line thickness option
    lN = Val(txtLineWidth.Text)
    If lN < 1 Or lN > 100 Then
        MsgBox _
            "Line thickness should be a small positive integer", _
            vbExclamation, "Ssaver"
        Exit Sub
    End If
    'Save the settings
    SaveSetting "Ssaver", "Options", "Action", msAction
    SaveSetting "Ssaver", "Options", "LineCount", _
        txtLineCount.Text
    SaveSetting "Ssaver", "Options", "LineWidth", _
        txtLineWidth.Text
    'Close the Setup dialog box
    Unload Me
End Sub

Private Sub optAction_Click(Index As Integer)
    msAction = Format$(Index + 1)
End Sub
```

Most of the code in this form is used to read and write settings to and from the Registry. I used defaults in the GetSetting statements to guarantee a valid setting even if the setting doesn't yet exist in the Registry.

To complete the screen saver, you must compile it as an executable file with an SCR extension—for example, MYSSAVER.SCR. Copy the resulting SCR file into your Windows directory. Your screen saver should then be listed in the drop-down list on the Screen Saver tab of the Display Properties dialog box. For more information about screen savers and how to compile a screen saver, see Chapter 23, "Screen Savers."

CHAPTER TWENTY-EIGHT

Development Tools

This chapter contains three applications that help you control your Visual Basic programming environment. The ColorBar application helps you adjust your monitor so that you can see all the color characteristics your users will see. The APIAddin application is an add-in to the Visual Basic development environment that lets you locate, copy, and paste constants, types, and declarations for Microsoft Windows 32-bit API functions. The Metric application demonstrates one way to extend your set of application development tools—in this case, by putting much of the functionality of the application in a help file and using Visual Basic to do the tasks it does best.

The ColorBar Application

The ColorBar application is quite simple, but I've found it very useful for adjusting my monitor to balance the colors and brightness. It also demonstrates a couple of programming techniques you'll probably find useful elsewhere. Figure 28-1 on the following page shows the ColorBar application in action, and Figure 28-2 shows the project list.

When you run ColorBar, you see a form filled with 16 rectangles, each containing one of the 16 primary colors defined by the QBColor function. Make sure the yellow block doesn't look brown. (I had a monitor like that a few years ago, and it drove me nuts!) Also make sure each color is distinct from all the others—for example, you should see two distinct shades of gray. Click with the left mouse button on the form to rotate the color blocks one way, and click with the right button to rotate them the other way. After 16 clicks in either direction, the blocks return to their original locations.

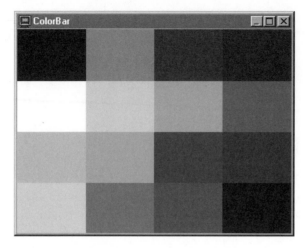

Figure 28-1.
The ColorBar application in action.

Figure 28-2.
The ColorBar project list.

COLORBAR.FRM

Take note of a couple of details about this form. The MinButton property is set to *False* to prevent an error condition. Each time the user resizes the form, the surface of the form is rescaled to simplify the drawing of the blocks. The Scale statement generates an error if the form is minimized to an icon. Because this utility serves little purpose in the minimized state, I decided to simply eliminate the MinButton option. As shown in Figure 28-1, the button is still visible even when the form's MinButton property is set to *False*. Notice, however, that the button is grayed and inactive.

The only control on the form is a timer, as shown in Figure 28-3. Originally I put the block drawing code in the form's Paint event procedure, a technique that worked great as long as I stretched the form to a larger size at runtime, triggering a Paint event. But when I shrank the form a little, the Paint event was not called. To get around this result, I activated the timer at the various places in my program where I wanted to redraw the blocks of color. The timer is set up as a one-shot event, which means its code is activated once and then the timer shuts itself off. This one-shot action is triggered by setting the timer's Enabled property to *True* whenever the blocks are to be updated. By setting this property within the Resize event, I effectively enabled the program to redraw the blocks whenever the form is resized either larger or smaller. This also makes it easy to redraw the blocks when the mouse is clicked to rotate the order of the blocks.

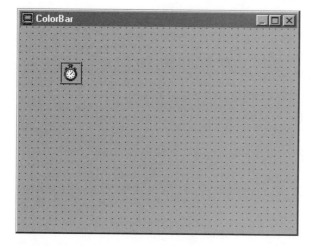

Figure 28-3.
The ColorBar form during development.

To create this application, use the table and source code on the following page to add the Timer control, set any nondefault properties as indicated, and enter the source code lines as shown.

COLORBAR.FRM Objects and Property Settings

Property	Value
Form	
Name	*frmColorBar*
Caption	*ColorBar*
MinButton	*False*
Icon	*Monitr01.ico*
Timer	
Name	*tmrDrawBars*
Interval	*1*

Source Code for COLORBAR.FRM

```
Option Explicit

Dim nColorShift As Integer

Private Sub Form_Load()
    'Center form on screen
    Left = (Screen.Width - Width) \ 2
    Top = (Screen.Height - Height) \ 2
End Sub

Private Sub Form_MouseDown(Button As Integer, _
Shift As Integer, X As Single, Y As Single)
    'Shift color bars based on mouse button
    nColorShift = (nColorShift - Button * 2 + 19) Mod 16
    'Activate timer to draw color bars
    tmrDrawBars.Enabled = True
End Sub

Private Sub Form_Resize()
    'Activate timer to draw color bars
    tmrDrawBars.Enabled = True
End Sub
```

(continued)

Source Code for COLORBAR.FRM *continued*

```
Private Sub tmrDrawBars_Timer()
    Dim nX As Integer
    Dim nY As Integer
    'Deactivate timer so that color bars are drawn only once
    tmrDrawBars.Enabled = False
    'Scale form for convenience
    Scale (4, 4)-(0, 0)
    'Fill in colors
    For nX = 0 To 3
        For nY = 0 To 3
            nColorShift = (nColorShift + 1) Mod 16
            Line (nX, nY)-(nX + 1, nY + 1), _
                QBColor(nColorShift), BF
        Next nY
    Next nX
End Sub
```

The APIAddin Application

The APIAddin application is an add-in to the Visual Basic development environment. I include it to provide a working example of an add-in and because I like the way I've structured the API declarations better than the way this information is presented in WIN32API.TXT, a file you'll find in the WINAPI subdirectory of the Visual Basic installation.

The line continuation character makes it easy to format declarations in an easier-to-read, multiline layout. Throughout this book, I've taken advantage of this capability, and this application lets you easily add API functions to your applications in the same format. Figure 28-4 on the following page shows the APIAddin application in action, displaying a few of the multiline API function declarations. Notice that once the application is installed as an add-in, the dialog box that this application creates is accessed directly from the Visual Basic menu, letting you quickly and easily locate API functions and copy and paste them into your applications.

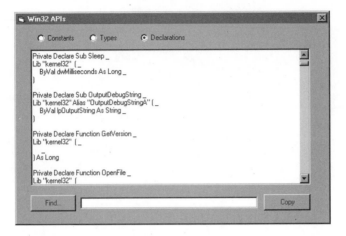

Figure 28-4.
The APIAddin application in action.

Converting the WIN32API.TXT File

Before I describe the APIAddin application itself, I want to make you aware that the original WIN32API.TXT file must be modified to provide three new working files that the APIAddin application loads at runtime. This conversion process is performed only once, and because I've provided the resulting files on the companion CD-ROM, you won't even need to run it once. However, I'll include the source code for the conversion process here in case you are interested in modifying the format even further or you have a newer version of the WIN32API.TXT file and you want to perform an update conversion.

The following code can be plopped into a fresh, blank form. I've provided no controls or other modifications. Simply click once on the running form, and wait until a "Done" message is displayed on the form. (This demonstrates, by the way, a handy way to create a small utility program for your own use, when there's no need for a fancy user interface.) You'll need to either move the WIN32API.TXT file, normally located in your Visual Basic subdirectory, to the directory containing your application or modify the path in the code so that the program can find the file. This code can be found in the CVTAPITX.VBP project on the companion CD-ROM.

Source Code for WIN32API.TXT Conversion

```
Option Explicit

Private Sub Form_Click()
    Dim sA As String
    Dim sT As String
    Dim nState As Integer
    Dim I As Integer
    Dim j As Integer
    Dim k As Integer
    Dim n As Integer
    Print "Working..."
    Open App.Path & "\Win32api.txt" For Input As #1
    Open App.Path & "\W32cons.txt" For Output As #2
    Open App.Path & "\W32type.txt" For Output As #3
    Open App.Path & "\W32decl.txt" For Output As #4
    Do Until EOF(1)
        Line Input #1, sA
        If InStr(sA, "Const ") Then nState = 2
        If InStr(LTrim(sA), "Type ") = 1 Then
            sA = "Private " & sA
            nState = 3
        End If
        If InStr(LTrim(sA), "Declare ") = 1 Then
            nState = 4
        End If
        If nState = 2 Then
            I = InStr(sA, "=")
            j = InStr(I, sA, "'")
            If j > I Then
                sA = Trim(Left(sA, j - 1))
            End If
            Print #2, "Private" & Mid(sA, 7)
        End If
        If nState = 3 Then
            If Left(sA, 1) = " " Then
                sA = Space(4) & Trim(sA)
            End If
            j = InStr(sA, "'")
            If j > 0 Then
                sA = RTrim(Left(sA, j - 1))
            End If
            Print #3, sA
        End If
```

(continued)

Source Code for WIN32API.TXT Conversion *continued*

```
If nState = 4 Then
    n = 2
    If Trim(sA) = "" Then
        Print #4, ""
    Else
        'Lop off comments
        I = InStr(sA, ")")
        j = InStr(I, sA, "'")
        If j > I Then sA = Trim(Left(sA, j - 1))
        'Drop Alias if not different from original function
        I = InStr(sA, "Alias")
        If I Then
            j = InStr(I, sA, Chr(34))
            k = InStr(j + 1, sA, Chr(34))
            sT = Mid(sA, j + 1, k - j - 1)
            sT = Space(1) & sT & Space(1)
            If InStr(sA, sT) Then
                sA = Left(sA, I - 1) & Mid(sA, k + 1)
            End If
        End If
        'Locate "Lib"
        I = InStr(sA, " Lib")
        'Insert "Private"
        Print #4, "Private Declare " & _
            Mid(sA, 9, I - 8) & "_"
        sA = Mid(sA, I + 1)
        'Locate left parenthesis
        I = InStr(sA, "(")
        Print #4, Left(sA, I) & " _"
        sA = Mid(sA, I + 1)
        'Locate each parameter
        Do
            I = InStr(sA, ", ")
            If I = 0 Then Exit Do
            Print #4, Space(4) & Left(sA, I) & " _"
            n = n + 1
            sA = Mid(sA, I + 2)
        Loop
        'Locate right parenthesis
        I = InStr(sA, ")")
        Print #4, Space(4) & Left(sA, I - 1) & " _"
        Print #4, Mid(sA, I)
    End If
```

(continued)

Source Code for WIN32API.TXT Conversion *continued*

```
         End If
         If nState = 2 Then nState = 0
         If nState = 3 And InStr(sA, "End Type") > 0 Then
             nState = 0
             Print #3, ""
         End If
         If nState = 4 Then
             nState = 0
             Print #4, ""
         End If
     Loop
     Close #1
     Close #2
     Close #3
     Close #4
     Print "Done"
 End Sub
```

When you run this code, WIN32API.TXT is split into three files: W32CONS.TXT contains a list of all constants, W32TYPE.TXT contains all type structure definitions, and W32DECL.TXT contains all the declarations for all API functions. The program removes all extraneous comments and extra blank lines in order to keep the files small and quick to load. The Private declaration is added to minimize the scope of all declarations. For explanations and descriptions of these functions, you'll need to consult the Win32 SDK Reference Help or another source. These trimmed-down files are designed to provide the declarations as efficiently as possible and not to explain their use.

I discovered an interesting fact about Visual Basic while creating these files. On one of the first iterations using these files, I left all the Alias modifiers within the Declare statements. However, when you enter a Declare statement in which the aliased function name is identical to the original name, Visual Basic automatically deletes the Alias part. This is cool, except that the extra Alias text, which is going to get zapped automatically by your Visual Basic application anyway, takes up some space in the W32DECL.TXT file, and my goal is to condense this file as much as possible. So my preparation program strips out the Alias modifiers when the original name is identical to the aliased name. Compare the contents of W32DECL.TXT and WIN32API.TXT to see the difference in the functions when this modification is performed.

One final note: keep these three text files in the same directory as the APIAddin application's executable file. I've used the App.Path property to locate these files as they are needed, simplifying the housekeeping.

Building the APIAddin Application

The easiest way to begin building an add-in application is to start a new project and double-click the Addin icon in the New Project dialog box. An almost complete application is created, containing one form, one class module, and one code module—the framework for your new add-in application. That's how I first created the APIAddin application. From this point on, I'll describe the changes that were required to modify this application to display the API data files.

First rename and save the form that was automatically created and named for you. Name the form *frmAPIAddin,* and save it as APIADDIN.FRM. Save the Addin code module as ADDIN.BAS, and save the Connect class module as CONNECT.CLS. Finally, name the project APIAddin, and save it as APIADDIN.VBP. Figure 28-5 shows the project list after these changes have been made.

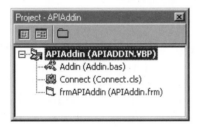

Figure 28-5.
The project list for the APIAddin application.

CONNECT.CLS

There's not a lot of code in these three files, and both the code module and the class module require just a few changes from the code that was created automatically. The biggest change to the Connect class module code is a global replacement of all occurrences of *frmAddIn* with *frmAPIAddin.* I did make a few other changes though, so do check each line of your code carefully to be sure it matches the following listing. Here's the code as it should appear in the edited CONNECT.CLS class module.

Source Code for CONNECT.CLS

```
Option Explicit

Implements IDTExtensibility

Public FormDisplayed        As Boolean
Public VBInstance           As VBIDE.VBE
Dim mcbMenuCommandBar        As Office.CommandBarControl
Dim mfrmAPIAddin             As New frmAPIAddin
Public WithEvents MenuHandler As CommandBarEvents

Sub Hide()
    On Error Resume Next
    FormDisplayed = False
    mfrmAPIAddin.Hide
End Sub

Sub Show()
    On Error Resume Next
    If mfrmAPIAddin Is Nothing Then
        Set mfrmAPIAddin = New frmAPIAddin
    End If
    Set mfrmAPIAddin.VBInstance = VBInstance
    Set mfrmAPIAddin.Connect = Me
    FormDisplayed = True
    mfrmAPIAddin.Show
End Sub

'This method adds the Add-In to VB
Private Sub IDTExtensibility_OnConnection( _
ByVal VBInst As Object, ByVal ConnectMode As vbext_ConnectMode, _
ByVal AddInInst As VBIDE.AddIn, custom() As Variant)
    On Error GoTo error_handler
    'save the vb instance
    Set VBInstance = VBInst
    If ConnectMode = vbext_cm_External Then
        'Used by the wizard toolbar to start this wizard
        Me.Show
    Else
        Set mcbMenuCommandBar = AddToAddInCommandBar("API Addin")
        'sink the event
        Set Me.MenuHandler = VBInst.Events.CommandBarEvents _
            (mcbMenuCommandBar)
    End If
    Exit Sub
```

(continued)

Source Code for CONNECT.CLS *continued*

```
error_handler:
    MsgBox Err.Description
End Sub


'This method removes the Add-In from VB
Private Sub IDTExtensibility_OnDisconnection( _
ByVal RemoveMode As vbext_DisconnectMode, custom() As Variant)
    On Error Resume Next
    'delete the command bar entry
    mcbMenuCommandBar.Delete
    'shut down the Add-In
    If FormDisplayed Then
        SaveSetting App.Title, "Settings", "DisplayOnConnect", "1"
        FormDisplayed = False
    Else
        SaveSetting App.Title, "Settings", "DisplayOnConnect", "0"
    End If
    Unload mfrmAPIAddin
    Set mfrmAPIAddin = Nothing
End Sub


Private Sub IDTExtensibility_OnStartupComplete(custom() As Variant)
'No action at this time
End Sub


Private Sub IDTExtensibility_OnAddInsUpdate(custom() As Variant)
'No action at this time
End Sub


'This event fires when the menu is clicked in the IDE
Private Sub MenuHandler_Click(ByVal CommandBarControl As Object, _
handled As Boolean, CancelDefault As Boolean)
    Me.Show
End Sub


Function AddToAddInCommandBar(sCaption As String) As _
Office.CommandBarControl
    Dim cbMenuCommandBar As Office.CommandBarControl
    Dim cbMenu As Object
    On Error GoTo AddToAddInCommandBarErr
    'see if we can find the Add-Ins menu
    Set cbMenu = VBInstance.CommandBars("Add-Ins")
    If cbMenu Is Nothing Then
        'not available so we fail
        Exit Function
```

(continued)

Source Code for CONNECT.CLS *continued*

```
    End If
    'add it to the command bar
    Set cbMenuCommandBar = cbMenu.Controls.Add(1)
    'set the caption
    cbMenuCommandBar.Caption = sCaption
    Set AddToAddInCommandBar = cbMenuCommandBar
    Exit Function
AddToAddInCommandBarErr:
End Function
```

The Connect object's purpose is to provide the connections to the Visual Basic Integrated Development Environment (IDE). This object provides the code that connects actions to menus, toolbar buttons, or to other events in your Visual Basic environment. Be sure to study the explanations and examples in Visual Basic Books Online to gain a thorough understanding of all the ways the Connect object can be modified to suit your purposes.

ADDIN.BAS

The ADDIN.BAS code module is even easier to edit, as it contains just a few lines of code, as shown.

Source Code for ADDIN.BAS

```
Option Explicit

Private Declare Function WritePrivateProfileString _
Lib "kernel32" Alias "WritePrivateProfileStringA" ( _
    ByVal lpApplicationName As String, _
    ByVal lpKeyName As Any, _
    ByVal lpString As Any, _
    ByVal lpFileName As String _
) As Long


    '=========================================================
    'This sub should be executed from the Immediate window
    'in order to get this app added to the VBADDIN.INI file.
    'You must change the name in the 2nd argument to reflect
    'the correct name of your project.
    '=========================================================
Sub AddToINI()
    Dim ErrCode As Long
    ErrCode = WritePrivateProfileString( _
        "Add-Ins32", "APIAddin.Connect", _
        "0", "vbaddin.ini")
End Sub
```

The single procedure in this code module is designed to help you easily edit the VBADDIN.INI file, which must contain entries for all add-ins in the Visual Basic environment. This procedure is run just once from the Immediate window. For a shippable, commercial-quality add-in, you would probably want to automate this process during the setup procedure instead of relying on this manual method.

APIADDIN.FRM

The APIAddin form displays one of three files in a RichTextBox control, depending on which option button is selected along the top of the form. For efficiency, each of the three files is loaded into a string variable only if it's requested by the user, and it's loaded only once per run of the application. When selected, the contents of the appropriate string are copied into the rich text box's Text property. Figure 28-6 shows the APIAddin form during the development process, and Figure 28-7 shows the form in action, with the list of constants displayed.

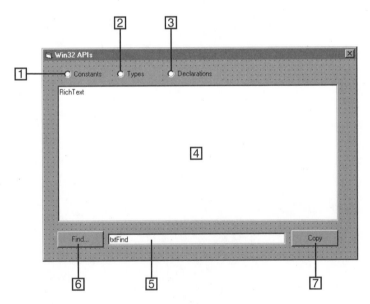

Figure 28-6.
The APIAddin form during development.

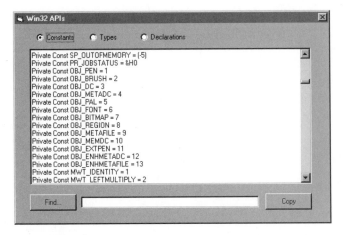

Figure 28-7.
The APIAddin form, displaying the list of constants.

The APIAddin form creates an instance of the Connect object to make the connection to Visual Basic's Add-Ins menu, and it displays the API constants, types, and declarations when the new menu item is selected. To create this form, use the following table and source code to add the appropriate controls, set any nondefault properties for APIADDIN.FRM as indicated, and enter the source code lines as shown.

APIADDIN.FRM Objects and Property Settings

ID No.*	Property	Value
Form		
	Name	*frmAPIAddin*
	Caption	*Win32 APIs*
	BorderStyle	*3 - Fixed Dialog*
OptionButton		
1	Name	*optAPI*
	Caption	*Constants*
	Index	*0*

*   The number in the ID No. column corresponds to the number in Figure 28-6 that identifies the location of the object on the form.

(continued)

APIADDIN.FRM Objects and Property Settings *continued*

ID No.	Property	Value
OptionButton		
2	Name	*optAPI*
	Caption	*Types*
	Index	*1*
OptionButton		
3	Name	*optAPI*
	Caption	*Declarations*
	Index	*2*
RichTextBox		
4	Name	*rtfAPI*
	HideSelection	*False*
	Scrollbars	*3 - rtfBoth*
TextBox		
5	Name	*txtFind*
CommandButton		
6	Name	*cmdFind*
	Caption	*Find…*
CommandButton		
7	Name	*cmdCopy*
	Caption	*Copy*

Source Code for APIADDIN.FRM

```
Option Explicit

Public VBInstance As VBIDE.VBE
Public Connect As Connect

Private sCon As String
Private sTyp As String
Private sDec As String
```

(continued)

Source Code for APIADDIN.FRM *continued*

```
Private Sub cmdCopy_Click()
    'Copy selected text to clipboard
    Clipboard.SetText rtfAPI.SelText
    'Return to user's project
    Unload Me
End Sub

Private Sub cmdFind_Click()
    Dim lPtr As Long
    Dim sFind As String
    'Put focus on rich text box
    rtfAPI.SetFocus
    'Grab search string
    sFind = txtFind.Text
    'Determine where to begin search
    If rtfAPI.SelLength Then
        lPtr = rtfAPI.SelStart + rtfAPI.SelLength
    Else
        lPtr = 0
    End If
    'Use rich text box's Find method
    lPtr = rtfAPI.Find(sFind, lPtr)
    If lPtr = -1 Then
        MsgBox "Search text not found"
    End If
End Sub

Private Sub Form_Load()
    'Startup showing declarations
    optAPI(2).Value = True
    txtFind.Text = ""
    Me.Show
    Me.ZOrder
End Sub

Private Sub optAPI_Click(Index As Integer)
    Select Case Index
    'Constants
    Case 0
        If sCon = "" Then
            LoadUp sCon, "W32cons.txt"
        End If
        rtfAPI.Text = sCon
    'Type structures
```

(continued)

Source Code for APIADDIN.FRM *continued*

```
      Case 1
          If sTyp = "" Then
              LoadUp sTyp, "W32type.txt"
          End If
          rtfAPI.Text = sTyp
      'Declarations
      Case 2
          If sDec = "" Then
              LoadUp sDec, "W32decl.txt"
          End If
          rtfAPI.Text = sDec
      End Select
End Sub

Private Sub LoadUp(sA As String, sFile As String)
    Open App.Path & "\" & sFile For Binary As #1
    sA = Space(LOF(1))
    Get #1, , sA
    Close #1
End Sub

Private Sub rtfAPI_SelChange()
    If rtfAPI.SelLength Then
        cmdCopy.Enabled = True
    Else
        cmdCopy.Enabled = False
    End If
End Sub

Private Sub txtFind_Change()
    If Len(txtFind.Text) Then
        cmdFind.Enabled = True
    Else
        cmdFind.Enabled = False
    End If
End Sub
```

The rich text box turns out to be very easy to use for this application. Scrollbars allow manual scanning of the large amount of text, and the RichTextBox control provides its own Find method. This Find method solves a lot of implementation details that would be complicated otherwise. For example, once a fragment of text is searched for and found, the rich text box automatically scrolls to the appropriate spot and highlights the text, just as the user would expect. Likewise, the special properties related to text selection simplify the task of identifying a block of text to be copied to the clipboard. See the descriptions of the SelStart, SelLength, and SelText properties in Visual Basic's online help for more information about text selection within a RichTextBox control.

Compiling the Add-In

Before compiling this or any other add-in project, be sure to enable the references to Microsoft Visual Basic 5.0 Extensibility and to the Microsoft Office 8.0 Object Library. To do so, choose References from the Project menu, and verify that these items are checked in the References dialog box.

An add-in is an ActiveX component and can be built in either a dynamic link library (DLL) or an EXE file. In most cases, you'll want to create an ActiveX DLL, as is done with this APIAddin project. From the Project menu, choose APIAddIn Properties, and verify that Project Type is set to *ActiveX DLL* in the Project Properties dialog box.

To compile the add-in, choose Make APIADDIN.DLL from the File menu. Save the resulting APIADDIN.DLL file in the same directory in which you saved the three API text files. I've used the App.Path property to locate these files, and the application assumes that they're located in the same directory as the DLL. During the compiling process, an entry in the Registry is automatically created for you, and the Registry remembers where the DLL is stored.

Visual Basic itself needs to be made aware of this new add-in at each project startup, so you should now go to the Immediate window, type *AddToINI*, and press Enter. When you run this small subprogram, it creates an entry in the VBADDIN.INI file indicating the existence of the new add-in.

To try out the APIAddin add-in, start a new Standard EXE project. From the Add-Ins menu, choose Add-In Manager. You should see the new My Add-In item in the Add-In Manager dialog box. (The items are in alphabetic order.) Check the My Add-In check box to activate the new add-in, and click OK. Open the Add-Ins menu again, and notice that there's now an API Addin menu option. Choose the new menu option, and you should see the new Win32 APIs dialog box.

The purpose of the Win32 APIs dialog box is to provide quick and easy access to the 32-bit API declarations, constants, and type structures. Click the three option buttons at the top of the dialog box to see how each of these types of API data lists are displayed. To find a specific entry, type part or all of the text in the text box at the bottom of the dialog box and click the Find button. Once you've found what you're looking for, highlight the lines and click the Copy button. The dialog box will disappear, and you'll be returned to your project, ready to paste the selected text from the clipboard.

The Metric Application

The Metric application is rather simple, but it demonstrates the powerful technique of combining a Visual Basic application with a help file to achieve a symbiotic relationship that incorporates the best features of each. I've created a very short example tutorial on the metric system of weights and measures using this technique. The METRIC.HLP file displays easy-to-read text and has pop-up windows and hypertext hot spots; METRIC.EXE, the Visual Basic half of the team, plays sound files and video clips, performs metric conversions for the user, and displays a quiz to test the user's understanding. Help files in Microsoft Windows 95 can do much more than help files in earlier versions of Windows, but when you connect to Visual Basic the possibilities are virtually limitless.

When you run METRIC.EXE, it first checks to see whether you used any command line parameters. Assuming that you start the program by double-clicking on its name or icon, there won't be any parameters, and the program immediately runs the METRIC.HLP file. I've provided several buttons in the main topic window of the help file that jump back into the METRIC.EXE program, each passing a different set of command line parameters. The METRIC.EXE program takes action based on these parameters and then terminates, allowing the user to interact once again with the help file.

METRIC.EXE effectively lets a help file play a sound file or a video clip, display a full-blown dialog box, perform mathematical computations, or do just about anything else you can imagine. The Metric application demonstrates each of these techniques. For example, when you click the Video Clip button in the main topic window of the help file, a short sample video clip plays. Likewise, when you click the Quiz button, a dialog box full of quiz questions is displayed, as shown in Figure 28-8. Study the source code listings to see how easily this was accomplished. Note that both METRIC.EXE and METRIC.HLP should be in the same directory at runtime. Also, to view the video clip T_PG01.AVI, copy the file from the VB\VBONLINE\MEDIA directory on the Visual Basic CD-ROM to the directory containing the Metric application.

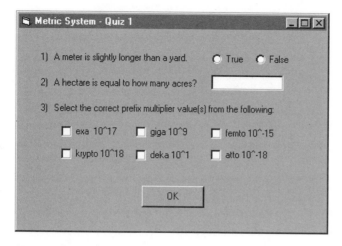

Figure 28-8.
The quiz activated from within the METRIC.HLP file.

Building the Metric Application

The Visual Basic part of the Metric application consists of three files, as shown in the project list in Figure 28-9.

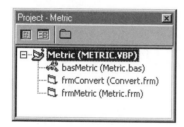

Figure 28-9.
The Metric project list.

The METRIC.BAS code module contains most of the code for this application, including the startup routine Sub Main, in which action decisions based on the command line parameters are made. The METRIC.FRM form displays the sample quiz, and the CONVERT.FRM form lets the user perform conversions from meters to feet and from centimeters to inches.

METRIC.BAS

The METRIC.BAS code module contains the Sub Main startup point for the Visual Basic half of this application. Sub Main calls a useful procedure named GetParms, which analyzes and parses an application's command line parameters, returning an array of parameters that's often much easier to process than Visual Basic's Command function. The public dynamic array vParm returns each parameter, and even in the case in which no command line parameters were given, vParm(0) returns the full pathname and filename of the executable file.

Based on the evaluated command line parameters, Sub Main plays a multimedia file, displays a quiz, or performs metric conversions. You can easily add other capabilities by modifying the Select Case statements to intercept and process command line parameters of your own design.

Source Code for METRIC.BAS

```
Option Explicit

Private Declare Function WinExec _
Lib "kernel32" ( _
    ByVal lpCmdLine As String, _
    ByVal nCmdShow As Long _
) As Long

Private Declare Function mciExecute _
Lib "winmm.dll" ( _
    ByVal lpstrCommand As String _
) As Long

Public vParm()

Sub Main()
    GetParms
    Select Case UBound(vParm)
    Case 0
        TakeAction
    Case 1
        TakeAction vParm(1)
    Case 2
        TakeAction vParm(1), vParm(2)
    End Select
End Sub
```

(continued)

Source Code for METRIC.BAS *continued*

```
Private Sub TakeAction(Optional vCmd, Optional vFil)
    'If no parameters, open help file
    If IsMissing(vCmd) Then
        WinExec "Winhelp.exe " & App.Path & "\Metric.hlp", 1
        Exit Sub
    End If
    'First parameter determines action to take
    Select Case UCase(vCmd)
    'Display units conversion form
    Case "M2F", "C2I"
        frmConvert.Show
    'Play a sound file


    Case "WAV"
        Select Case vFil
        Case 1
            mciExecute "Play Sound1.wav"
        End Select
    'Play a video clip
    Case "AVI"
        Select Case vFil
        Case 1
            mciExecute "Play T_pg01.avi"
        End Select
    'Display a quiz form
    Case "QUIZ"
        frmMetric.Show
    End Select
End Sub

Private Sub GetParms()
    Dim nP As Integer
    Dim nN As Integer
    Dim sCmd As String
    ReDim vParm(0)
    sCmd = Command
    'Always return full path of this application
    If Right(App.Path, 1) <> "\" Then
        vParm(0) = App.Path & "\" & App.EXEName
    Else
```

(continued)

Source Code for METRIC.BAS *continued*

```
        vParm(0) = App.Path & App.EXEName
    End If
    'Trim and add one space to command line
    sCmd = Trim(sCmd) + Space(1)
    'Extract each parameter from command line
    Do
        nP = InStr(sCmd, Space(1))
        If nP <= 1 Then Exit Do
        nN = nN + 1
        ReDim Preserve vParm(nN)
        vParm(nN) = Left(sCmd, nP - 1)
        sCmd = LTrim$(Mid$(sCmd, nP + 1))
    Loop
End Sub
```

METRIC.BAS uses two API functions: one to play the multimedia files, and one to start the METRIC.HLP file. Notice that I've used yet another technique to start up a help file. (See Chapter 15, "Help Files," for other ways to do this.) The WinExec API function lets your Visual Basic application start any Windows application—WinHelp, in this case. You could use this function to start the Calculator application, for instance, which might be a handy addition to a tutorial.

The TakeAction procedure demonstrates the use of optional parameters by accepting none, one, or two parameters.

METRIC.FRM

This form displays a sample quiz when the Quiz button in the help file is clicked. (Read on to see how the help file handles this button click.) To keep this sample application simple, I've created a nongraded quiz that displays one true/false question, one fill-in-the-blank question, and one multiple-choice question. It's a start, but I'm sure you'd want to enhance a real quiz dialog box beyond this simple example. Figure 28-10 shows the Metric form during development; Figure 28-8 on page 531 shows the form in action after it has been activated from within the help file.

To create this application, use the following table and source code to add the appropriate controls, set any nondefault properties as indicated, and enter the source code lines as shown.

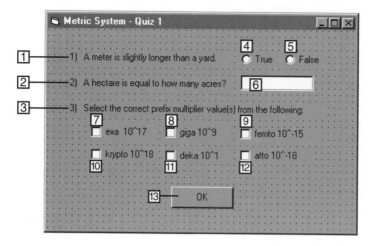

Figure 28-10.
The Metric form during development.

METRIC.FRM Objects and Property Settings

ID No.*	Property	Value
Form		
	Name	*frmMetric*
	Caption	*Metric System - Quiz 1*
Label		
1	Name	*Label1*
	Caption	*1) A meter is slightly longer than a yard.*
Label		
2	Name	*Label2*
	Caption	*2) A hectare is equal to how many acres?*
Label		
3	Name	*Label3*
	Caption	*3) Select the correct prefix multiplier value(s) from the following:*

*   The number in the ID No. column corresponds to the number in Figure 28-10 that identifies the location of the object on the form.

(continued)

METRIC.FRM Objects and Property Settings *continued*

ID No.	Property	Value
Option1		
4	Caption	*True*
Option2		
5	Caption	*False*
Text1		
6	Text	(blank)
Check1		
7	Caption	*exa 10^17*
Check2		
8	Caption	*giga 10^9*
Check3		
9	Caption	*femto 10^−15*
Check4		
10	Caption	*krypto 10^18*
Check5		
11	Caption	*deka 10^1*
Check6		
12	Caption	*atto 10^−18*
CommandButton		
13	Name	*cmdOK*
	Caption	*OK*

Source Code for METRIC.FRM

```
Option Explicit

Private Sub cmdOK_Click()
    MsgBox "This example quiz is not graded."
    Unload Me
End Sub
```

CONVERT.FRM

The Convert form displays a dialog box that lets the user perform mathematical calculations—in this case, conversions of meters to feet and centimeters to inches. Once again, this example is greatly simplified, and a full suite of conversions would probably be in order for a real application along these lines. I've included enough in this dialog box to get you started and to demonstrate the core technique of using Visual Basic to add computational abilities to a help file. Figure 28-11 shows the CONVERT.FRM form during development, and Figure 28-12 shows the form at runtime, after the user has clicked one of the buttons in the Conversions section of the help file.

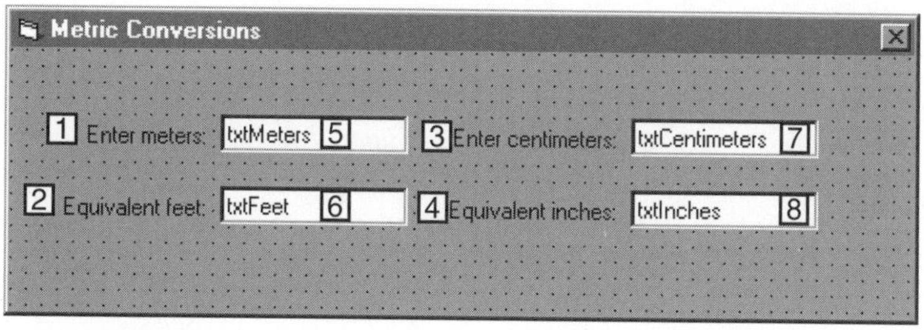

Figure 28-11.
The Convert form during development.

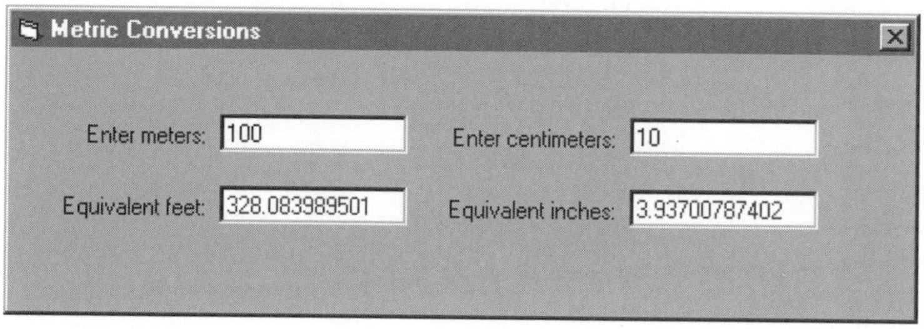

Figure 28-12.
The Metric Conversions dialog box when activated by a button in the Metric help file.

To create this application, use the following table and source code to add the appropriate controls, set any nondefault properties as indicated, and enter the source code lines as shown.

CONVERT.FRM Objects and Property Settings

ID No.*	Property	Value
Form		
	Name	*frmConvert*
	Caption	*Metric Conversions*
	BorderStyle	*3 - Fixed Dialog*
Label		
1	Name	*lblMeters*
	Caption	*Enter meters:*
Label		
2	Name	*lblFeet*
	Caption	*Equivalent feet:*
Label		
3	Name	*lblCentimeters*
	Caption	*Enter centimeters:*
Label		
4	Name	*lblInches*
	Caption	*Equivalent inches:*
TextBox		
5	Name	*txtMeters*
TextBox		
6	Name	*txtFeet*
	Enabled	*False*
TextBox		
7	Name	*txtCentimeters*
TextBox		
8	Name	*txtInches*
	Enabled	*False*

* The number in the ID No. column corresponds to the number in Figure 28-11 that identifies the location of the object on the form.

Source Code for CONVERT.FRM

```
Option Explicit

Private Sub Form_Load()
    txtMeters.Tex = "0"
    txtCentimeters = "0"
End Sub

Private Sub txtCentimeters_Change()
    txtInches.Text = Val(txtCentimeters.Text) * 0.393700787402
End Sub

Private Sub txtMeters_Change()
    txtFeet.Text = Val(txtMeters.Text) * 3.28083989501
End Sub
```

METRIC.HLP

Perhaps you've been wondering how the METRIC.EXE application is activated, complete with a variety of command line parameters, from within the METRIC.HLP file. It's beyond the scope of this book to go into all the details of building a help file, but I will describe this critical part of the process. I used RoboHelp 95, from Blue Sky Software, to create the METRIC.HLP file. (RoboHelp 95 is a great product for enhancing your 32-bit Visual Basic applications with full-blown 32-bit help files using all the latest techniques.) RoboHelp makes it easy to add macros to buttons or hot spots, and these macros are the key to activating an external application such as METRIC.EXE. You can also insert the buttons and macros using other help-building tools, such as the Microsoft Help Workshop that comes with Visual Basic (HCW.EXE), or you can even code everything directly using footnotes in a Rich Text File (RTF) document. See the online help for the Microsoft Help Workshop for the button and macro syntax. For reference, here are the macros embedded in the METRIC.RTF source code for the buttons that appear in the main topic window of the help file:

Conversions:

{button Meters to feet, ExecProgram("Metric.exe M2F")}

{button Centimeters to inches, ExecProgram("Metric.exe C2I")}

To hear a {button Sound, ExecProgram("Metric.exe wav 1")} click on this button, and to see a sample {button Video clip, ExecProgram("Metric.exe avi 1")} click here. When you're ready, click on this {button Quiz, Exec-Program("Metric.exe QUIZ 1")} button.

For each button, everything between the braces is processed by the help file compiler to create a button that activates an external application named METRIC.EXE, passing the necessary command line parameters. Macros such as these are a standard feature of help files. RoboHelp explains the use of macros in detail, but no matter what tool you use to edit and compile help files, the documentation should provide an explanation of the inclusion of macros. Figure 28-13 shows this primary help topic in action. All the buttons providing macros leading back to the METRIC.EXE application are shown in this first help topic.

Figure 28-13.
The METRIC.HLP file displaying the first help topic.

CHAPTER TWENTY-NINE

Date and Time

This chapter provides several applications to handle date and time tasks: a calendar form (VBCal) that enhances the way users of your applications can select a date, a visually appealing analog clock (VBClock) that displays the current system time, and a utility that dials in to the National Institute of Standards and Technology (NIST) to set your computer's clock precisely.

The VBCal Application

A common task in many business applications is to let the user select a date. The easiest way to do this is to simply have the user type a date into a text box. This method, however, requires careful attention to validation of the entered date and to internationalization issues—for example, does the string *3/5/97* indicate March 5 or May 3? A better approach is to display a visual calendar sheet and let the user click on the date. The VBCal form lets the user select any date from January 1, 1000, to December 31, 9899.

> NOTE: The date functions in Visual Basic are valid for dates from January 1, 100, to December 31, 9999. I've limited the range of VBCal's dates to a subset of this range to prevent complications and errors in my program at the limiting values.

It's a Wizard

I've designed this application as a simple wizard, which is a useful concept in itself. The wizard metaphor, first used by Microsoft in several products, is a convenient and standard way to perform interactions with the user in a linear, sequential manner. The VBCal form is the core calendar sheet form, and the rest of the forms in this project are used to step through the wizard action. The code module VBCALWIZ.BAS contains only two lines of code, which make the dates the user selected available to all the forms. These forms have one or more command buttons, a visual element in the left half of each form, and step-by-step instructions in the upper right. In general, most wizards are laid out the same way. Figures 29-1 through 29-5 show these wizard forms in action.

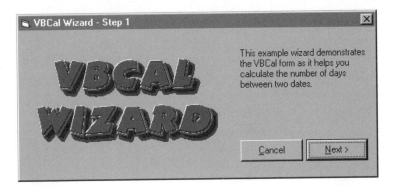

Figure 29-1.
Step 1 of the VBCal Wizard.

Figure 29-2.
Step 2 of the VBCal Wizard, prompting for the first date.

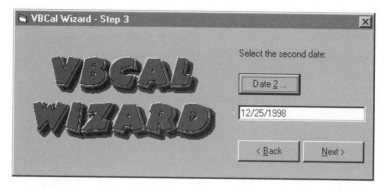

Figure 29-3.

Step 3 of the VBCal Wizard, prompting for the second date.

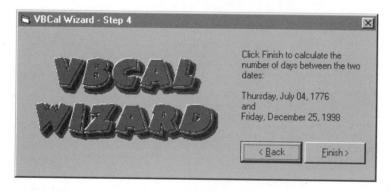

Figure 29-4.

Step 4 of the VBCal Wizard, preparing for the final step.

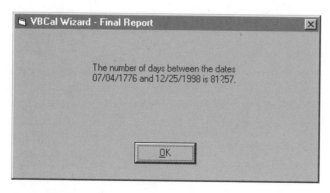

Figure 29-5.

The report display for the VBCal Wizard, displaying the final results.

VBCAL.FRM

> NOTE: Microsoft Access provides a Calendar control that you can use in your applications if you have Access installed. VBCal provides a good alternative if you don't have Access.

When you click the Date button in the VBCal Wizard, the VBCal form is called. The VBCal form displays a one-month calendar sheet with scrollbars to efficiently flip through the months, years, and centuries. I've added a Today button to quickly jump back to the current day and month and OK and Cancel buttons to accept the selection or to cancel it. To select a date, the user selects the day number on the calendar sheet and then clicks the OK button. Figure 29-6 shows the VBCal form in action with the date July 4, 1776, selected.

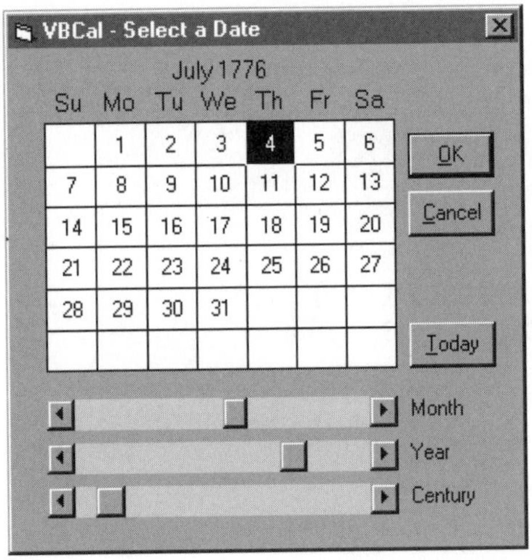

Figure 29-6.
The VBCal form in action.

The VBCal form interacts with a calling procedure through two public variables. The Boolean variable *gbDateSelectedFlag* has the value *True* if a date was selected by the user or *False* if the Cancel button was used to cancel the selection. The Date variable *gdtDateNum* holds the selected date. The code for the Date1 button in the second step of the wizard shows how these two variables are accessed:

```
Private Sub cmdDate1_Click()
    frmVBCal.Show vbModal
    If frmVBCal.gbDateSelectedFlag Then
        txtDate1.Text = Format(frmVBCal.gdtDateNum, "mm/dd/yyyy")
    End If
End Sub
```

Figure 29-7 shows the project list for the VBCal application. The form *frmVBCalWiz1* is set as the startup form. Most of the files in this project define the steps of the wizard action. The source code, tables, and illustrations on the following pages describe the construction of each of these forms.

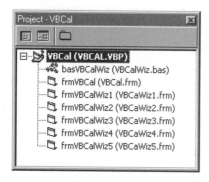

Figure 29-7.
The VBCal project list.

The VBCal form comprises two PictureBox controls, three scrollbars, three command buttons, and three descriptive labels. To enhance performance and reduce the use of resources, I used a single PictureBox control instead of an array of Text or Label controls to display the days of the month. Figure 29-8 shows the VBCal form during development.

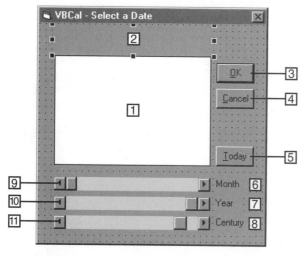

Figure 29-8.
The VBCal form during development.

To create this form, use the following table and source code to add the appropriate controls, set any nondefault properties as indicated, and enter the source code lines as shown.

VBCAL.FRM Objects and Property Settings

ID No.*	Property	Value
Form		
	Name	*frmVBCal*
	Caption	*VBCal - Select a Date*
	BorderStyle	*3 - Fixed Dialog*
PictureBox		
1	Name	*picMonth*
	Appearance	*0 - Flat*
PictureBox		
2	Name	*picTitle*
	Appearance	*0 - Flat*
	BackColor	*&H00C0C0C0&*
	BorderStyle	*0 - None*
CommandButton		
3	Name	*cmdOK*
	Caption	*&OK*
	Default	*True*
CommandButton		
4	Name	*cmdCancel*
	Caption	*&Cancel*
	Cancel	*True*

---

* The number in the ID No. column corresponds to the number in Figure 29-8 that identifies the location of the object on the form.

(continued)

VBCAL.FRM Objects and Property Settings *continued*

ID No.	Property	Value
CommandButton		
5	Name	*cmdToday*
	Caption	*&Today*
Label		
6	Name	*lblMonth*
	Caption	*Month*
	Appearance	*0 - Flat*
Label		
7	Name	*lblYear*
	Caption	*Year*
	Appearance	*0 - Flat*
Label		
8	Name	*lblCentury*
	Caption	*Century*
	Appearance	*0 - Flat*
HScrollBar		
9	Name	*hsbMonth*
	Min	*1*
	Max	*12*
HScrollBar		
10	Name	*hsbYear*
	Max	*99*
	LargeChange	*10*
HScrollBar		
11	Name	*hsbCentury*
	Min	*10*
	Max	*98*
	LargeChange	*10*

Source Code for VBCAL.FRM

```
Option Explicit

Public gdtDateNum As Date
Public gbDateSelectedFlag As Boolean

Private mlCenturyNum As Long
Private mlYearNum As Long
Private mlMonthNum As Long
Private mlDayNum As Long
Private mlMarkedDay As Long
Private mbFirstTime As Boolean
Private mfMouseX As Single, mfMouseY As Single
Private mdStartDate As Double

Private Sub cmdCancel_Click()
    'Signal that no date was selected
    gbDateSelectedFlag = False
    'All done
    Unload Me
End Sub

Private Sub cmdOK_Click()
    'Build serial date number for selected date
    gdtDateNum = DateSerial(mlCenturyNum * 100 + mlYearNum, _
        mlMonthNum, mlDayNum)
    'Signal that date was selected
    gbDateSelectedFlag = True
    'All done
    Unload frmVBCal
End Sub

Private Sub cmdToday_Click()
    'Reset selected date to today
    gdtDateNum = Now
    'Redraw calendar
    picTitle.Cls
    picMonth.Cls
    Form_Load
    Form_Paint
End Sub

Private Sub DrawLines()
    Dim nX As Integer
    Dim nY As Integer
```

(continued)

Source Code for VBCAL.FRM *continued*

```
    'Draw lines that separate days
    picMonth.Scale (0, 0)-(7, 6)
    picMonth.DrawMode = 13
    'Draw vertical lines
    For nX = 1 To 6
        picMonth.Line (nX, 0)-(nX, 6)
    Next nX
    'Draw horizontal lines
    For nY = 1 To 5
        picMonth.Line (0, nY)-(7, nY)
    Next nY
End Sub

Private Sub FillCal()
    Dim dSerial1 As Double
    Dim dSerial2 As Double
    Dim lNumDays As Long
    Dim nDayOffset As Integer
    Dim i As Integer
    'Get serial date number for 1st of current month
    dSerial1 = DateSerial(mlCenturyNum * 100 + mlYearNum, _
        mlMonthNum, 1)
    'Get serial date number for 1st of next month
    dSerial2 = DateSerial(mlCenturyNum * 100 + mlYearNum, _
        mlMonthNum + 1, 1)
    'Calculate number of days in month
    lNumDays = dSerial2 - dSerial1
    'Skip over blank days at start of month
    nDayOffset = WeekDay(dSerial1) - 1
    For i = 1 To lNumDays
        PutNum i + nDayOffset, i
    Next i
End Sub

Private Sub Form_Activate()
    Sketch
End Sub

Private Sub Form_Load()
    'Center form
    Move (Screen.Width - Width) \ 2, _
        (Screen.Height - Height) \ 2
    'Default to no date selected
    gbDateSelectedFlag = False
```

(continued)

Source Code for VBCAL.FRM *continued*

```
    'Record starting date
    mdStartDate = gdtDateNum
    'If no starting date, use current date
    If gdtDateNum = 0 Then gdtDateNum = Now
    'Keep track of marked day
    mlMarkedDay = 0
    'Extract date parts
    mlCenturyNum = Year(gdtDateNum) \ 100
    mlYearNum = Year(gdtDateNum) Mod 100
    mlMonthNum = Month(gdtDateNum)
    mlDayNum = Day(gdtDateNum)
    'Flag that this is first time through
    mbFirstTime = True
    'Initialize scrollbars
    hsbCentury.Value = mlCenturyNum
    hsbYear.Value = mlYearNum
    hsbMonth.Value = mlMonthNum
    'Flag first time setting scrollbars is done
    mbFirstTime = False
End Sub

Private Sub Form_Paint()
    'Display names of days at top
    WeekDayNames
    'Draw lines that form calendar
    DrawLines
    'Fill calendar with day numbers
    FillCal
    'Update month name
    UpdateTitle
    'Mark currently selected day
    MarkDay
End Sub

Private Sub hsbMonth_Change()
    'Get new month number
    mlMonthNum = hsbMonth.Value
    'Redraw calendar, and mark first day
    If mbFirstTime = False Then
        mlDayNum = 1
        Sketch
    End If
End Sub
```

(continued)

Source Code for VBCAL.FRM *continued*

```
Private Sub hsbYear_Change()
    'Get new year number
    mlYearNum = hsbYear.Value
    'Redraw calendar, and mark first day
    If mbFirstTime = False Then
        mlDayNum = 1
        Sketch
    End If
End Sub


Private Sub hsbCentury_Change()
    'Get new century number
    mlCenturyNum = hsbCentury.Value
    'Redraw calendar, and mark first day
    If mbFirstTime = False Then
        mlDayNum = 1
        Sketch
    End If
End Sub


Private Sub MarkDay()
    Dim nTheDay As Integer
    Dim i As Integer
    Dim dSerial As Double
    Dim nDayBox As Integer
    Dim nX As Integer
    Dim nY As Integer
    Dim nX1 As Single
    Dim nY1 As Single
    Dim nX2 As Single
    Dim nY2 As Single
    'Record day number
    nTheDay = mlDayNum
    'Erase previous mark, and then mark current day
    For i = 1 To 2
        'Calculate box number for day
        dSerial = DateSerial(mlCenturyNum * 100 + mlYearNum, _
            mlMonthNum, 1)
        nDayBox = WeekDay(dSerial) + mlDayNum - 1
        'Calculate location of box number
        nX = ((nDayBox - 1) Mod 7) + 1
        nY = ((nDayBox - 1) \ 7) + 1
        'Get first corner location of box
        nX1 = (nX - 1) * picMonth.ScaleWidth / 7
```

(continued)

Source Code for VBCAL.FRM *continued*

```
            nY1 = (nY - 1) * picMonth.ScaleHeight / 6
            'Get second corner location of box
            nX2 = nX1 + picMonth.ScaleWidth / 7
            nY2 = nY1 + picMonth.ScaleHeight / 6
            'XOR box pixels
            picMonth.DrawMode = 7
            picMonth.Line (nX1, nY1)-(nX2, nY2), QBColor(15), BF
            'Quit if no previously marked day
            If mlMarkedDay = 0 Then
                Exit For
            'Prepare to mark currently selected day
            Else
                mlDayNum = mlMarkedDay
            End If
        Next i
        'Reset day number
        mlDayNum = nTheDay
        'Record marked day for next trip through here
        mlMarkedDay = mlDayNum
End Sub

Private Sub picMonth_Click()
    Dim nX As Integer
    Dim nY As Integer
    Dim nDayBox As Integer
    Dim nLastDay As Integer
    Dim nFirstDay As Integer
    Dim dSerial As Double
    Dim nNewDay As Integer
    'Get current location of mouse
    nX = Int(mfMouseX) + 1
    nY = Int(mfMouseY) + 1
    'Calculate which day-number box mouse pointer is on
    nDayBox = nX + (nY - 1) * 7
    'Get serial date number for first of month
    dSerial = DateSerial(mlCenturyNum * 100 + mlYearNum, _
        mlMonthNum, 1)
    'Get last serial date number for month
    nLastDay = DateSerial(mlCenturyNum * 100 + mlYearNum, _
        mlMonthNum + 1, 1) - dSerial
    'Find day of week for first day
    nFirstDay = WeekDay(dSerial)
    'Determine day number selected
    nNewDay = nDayBox - nFirstDay + 1
    'Handle selection of blank box before first day
```

(continued)

Source Code for VBCAL.FRM *continued*

```
        If nDayBox < nFirstDay Then
            Beep
            Exit Sub
        End If
        'Handle selection of blank box after end of month
        If nDayBox - nFirstDay + 1 > nLastDay Then
            Beep
            Exit Sub
        End If
        'Continued if selection passed tests; new day selected
        mlDayNum = nNewDay
        'Re-mark selected day
        MarkDay
    End Sub


    Private Sub picMonth_DblClick()
        'Get currently selected date
        gdtDateNum = DateSerial(mlCenturyNum * 100 + mlYearNum, _
            mlMonthNum, mlDayNum)
        'Signal that a date was selected
        gbDateSelectedFlag = True
        'All done
        Unload frmVBCal
    End Sub


    Private Sub picMonth_MouseMove(Button As Integer, _
        Shift As Integer, x As Single, y As Single)
        'Keep track of mouse location when on calendar
        mfMouseX = x
        mfMouseY = y
    End Sub


    Private Sub PutNum(nSquare As Integer, nNum As Integer)
        Dim sN As String
        Dim nX As Integer
        Dim nY As Integer
        'Build string of day-number digits
        sN = LTrim$(Str$(nNum))
        'Calculate location of box
        nX = ((nSquare - 1) Mod 7) + 1
        nY = (nSquare - 1) \ 7 + 1
        'Set print position
        picMonth.CurrentX = nX - 0.5 - picMonth.TextWidth(sN) / 2
        picMonth.CurrentY = nY - 0.5 - picMonth.TextHeight(sN) / 2
```

(continued)

Source Code for VBCAL.FRM *continued*

```
    'Display day number
    picMonth.Print sN
End Sub

Private Sub Sketch()
    'Clear out previous stuff
    picMonth.Cls
    picTitle.Cls
    frmVBCal.Cls
    'Redraw calendar
    mlMarkedDay = 0
    Form_Paint
End Sub

Private Sub UpdateTitle()
    Dim dWorkDate As Double
    Dim sTmp As String
    Dim sT As String
    'Build long date string for selected month
    dWorkDate = DateSerial(mlCenturyNum * 100 + mlYearNum, _
        mlMonthNum, 1)
    sTmp = Format$(dWorkDate, "long date")
    'Remove day of week
    sTmp = Mid$(sTmp, InStr(sTmp, ",") + 2)
    'Remove day number from string
    sT = Left$(sTmp, InStr(sTmp, " ") - 1)
    sTmp = sT + Right$(sTmp, 5)
    'Display month and year at top
    picTitle.CurrentX = 3.5 - picTitle.TextWidth(sTmp) / 2
    picTitle.CurrentY = 0
    picTitle.Print sTmp
End Sub

Private Sub WeekDayNames()
    Dim i As Integer
    Dim sD As String
    'Scale for displaying seven day names
    picTitle.Scale (0, 0)-(7, 1)
    'Display each weekday name
    For i = 0 To 6
        'Get three-letter abbreviation
        sD = Format$(CDbl(i + 1), "ddd")
        'Use two characters if user's font is too wide
```

(continued)

Source Code for VBCAL.FRM *continued*

```
        If picTitle.TextWidth("Wed") > 1 Then
            sD = Left$(sD, 2)
        End If
        'Display each weekday name
        picTitle.CurrentX = i + 0.5 - _
            picTitle.TextWidth(sD) / 2
        picTitle.CurrentY = 1 - picTitle.TextHeight(sD)
        picTitle.Print sD
    Next i
End Sub
```

To create the wizards for this application, use the following tables and source code to add the appropriate controls, set any nondefault properties as indicated, and enter the source code lines as shown.

VBCAWIZ1.FRM Objects and Property Settings

Property	Value
Form	
Name	*frmVBCalWiz1*
Caption	*VBCal Wizard - Step 1*
BorderStyle	*3 - Fixed Dialog*
Image	
Name	*imgCal*
Picture	*VBCAL.BMP*
Stretch	*True*
Label	
Name	*lblPrompt*
CommandButton	
Name	*cmdNext*
Caption	*&Next>*
Default	*True*
CommandButton	
Name	*cmdCancel*
Caption	*&Cancel*
Cancel	*True*

Source Code for VBCAWIZ1.FRM

```
Option Explicit

Private Sub cmdCancel_Click()
    Unload Me
End Sub

Private Sub cmdNext_Click()
    frmVBCalWiz2.Show
    Unload Me
End Sub

Private Sub Form_Load()
    Dim sT As String
    'Preset today's date
    If gdtDate1 = 0 Then
        gdtDate1 = Date
        gdtDate2 = Date
    End If
    'Display the prompting text
    sT = "This example wizard demonstrates "
    sT = sT & "the VBCal form as it helps you "
    sT = sT & "calculate the number of days "
    sT = sT & "between two dates."
    lblPrompt.Caption = sT
    'Center form
    Move (Screen.Width - Width) \ 2, _
        (Screen.Height - Height) \ 2
    Show
    cmdNext.SetFocus
End Sub
```

VBCAWIZ2.FRM Objects and Property Settings

Property	Value
Form	
Name	*frmVBCalWiz2*
Caption	*VBCal Wizard - Step 2*
BorderStyle	*3 - Fixed Dialog*
Image	
Name	*imgCal*
Picture	*VBCAL.BMP*
Stretch	*True*

(continued)

VBCAWIZ2.FRM Objects and Property Settings *continued*

Property	Value
Label	
Name	*lblPrompt*
Caption	*Select the first date:*
CommandButton	
Name	*cmdNext*
Caption	*&Next>*
Default	*True*
CommandButton	
Name	*cmdBack*
Caption	*<&Back*
CommandButton	
Name	*cmdDate1*
Caption	*Date &1…*
TextBox	
Name	*txtDate1*

Source Code for VBCAWIZ2.FRM

```
Option Explicit

Private Sub cmdBack_Click()
    gdtDate1 = txtDate1.Text
    frmVBCalWiz1.Show
    Unload Me
End Sub

Private Sub cmdDate1_Click()
    frmVBCal.Show vbModal
    If frmVBCal.gbDateSelectedFlag Then
        txtDate1.Text = Format(frmVBCal.gdtDateNum, "mm/dd/yyyy")
    End If
End Sub
```

(continued)

557

Source Code for VBCAWIZ2.FRM *continued*

```
Private Sub cmdNext_Click()
    gdtDate1 = txtDate1.Text
    frmVBCalWiz3.Show
    Unload Me
End Sub

Private Sub Form_Load()
    'Center form
    Move (Screen.Width - Width) \ 2, _
        (Screen.Height - Height) \ 2
    txtDate1.Text = Format(gdtDate1, "mm/dd/yyyy")
    Show
    cmdNext.SetFocus
End Sub
```

VBCAWIZ3.FRM Objects and Property Settings

Property	Value
Form	
Name	*frmVBCalWiz3*
Caption	*VBCal Wizard - Step 3*
BorderStyle	*3 - Fixed Dialog*
Image	
Name	*imgCal*
Picture	*VBCAL.BMP*
Stretch	*True*
Label	
Name	*lblPrompt*
Caption	*Select the second date:*
CommandButton	
Name	*cmdNext*
Caption	*&Next>*
Default	*True*
CommandButton	
Name	*cmdBack*
Caption	*<&Back*

(continued)

VBCAWIZ3.FRM Objects and Property Settings *continued*

Property	Value
CommandButton	
Name	*cmdDate2*
Caption	*Date &2...*
TextBox	
Name	*txtDate2*

Source Code for VBCAWIZ3.FRM

```
Option Explicit

Private Sub cmdBack_Click()
    gdtDate2 = txtDate2.Text
    frmVBCalWiz2.Show
    Unload Me
End Sub

Private Sub cmdDate2_Click()
    frmVBCal.Show vbModal
    If frmVBCal.gbDateSelectedFlag Then
        txtDate2.Text = Format(frmVBCal.gdtDateNum, "mm/dd/yyyy")
    End If
End Sub

Private Sub cmdNext_Click()
    gdtDate2 = txtDate2.Text
    frmVBCalWiz4.Show
    Unload Me
End Sub

Private Sub Form_Load()
    'Center form
    Move (Screen.Width - Width) \ 2, _
        (Screen.Height - Height) \ 2
    txtDate2.Text = Format(gdtDate2, "mm/dd/yyyy")
    Show
    cmdNext.SetFocus
End Sub
```

VBCAWIZ4.FRM Objects and Property Settings

Property	Value
Form	
Name	*frmVBCalWiz4*
Caption	*VBCal Wizard - Step 4*
BorderStyle	*3 - Fixed Dialog*
Image	
Name	*imgCal*
Picture	*VBCAL.BMP*
Stretch	*True*
Label	
Name	*lblPrompt*
CommandButton	
Name	*cmdFinish*
Caption	*&Finish>*
Default	*True*
CommandButton	
Name	*cmdBack*
Caption	*<&Back*

Source Code for VBCAWIZ4.FRM

```
Option Explicit

Private Sub cmdBack_Click()
    frmVBCalWiz3.Show
    Unload Me
End Sub

Private Sub cmdFinish_Click()
    frmVBCalWiz5.Show
    Unload Me
End Sub

Private Sub Form_Load()
    Dim sT As String
    sT = "Click Finish to calculate the number "
    sT = sT & "of days between the two dates:"
```

(continued)

560

Source Code for VBCAWIZ4.FRM *continued*

```
    sT = sT & vbCrLf & vbCrLf
    sT = sT & Format$(gdtDate1, "long date")
    sT = sT & vbCrLf & "and " & vbCrLf
    sT = sT & Format$(gdtDate2, "long date")
    lblPrompt.Caption = sT
    'Center form
    Move (Screen.Width - Width) \ 2, _
        (Screen.Height - Height) \ 2
End Sub
```

VBCAWIZ5.FRM Objects and Property Settings

Property	Value
Form	
Name	*frmVBCalWiz5*
Caption	*VBCal Wizard - Final Report*
BorderStyle	*3 - Fixed Dialog*
Label	
Name	*lblReport*
CommandButton	
Name	*cmdOK*
Caption	*&OK*

Source Code for VBCAWIZ5.FRM

```
Option Explicit

Private Sub cmdOK_Click()
    Unload Me
End Sub

Private Sub Form_Load()
    'Center this form
    Move (Screen.Width - Width) \ 2, _
        (Screen.Height - Height) \ 2
    lblReport.Caption = "The number of days between the dates " _
    & Format$(gdtDate1, "mm/dd/yyyy") & " and " _
    & Format$(gdtDate2, "mm/dd/yyyy") & " is " _
    & Abs(gdtDate1 - gdtDate2) & "."
End Sub
```

Source Code for VBCALWIZ.BAS

```
Option Explicit

Public gdtDate1 As Date
Public gdtDate2 As Date
```

The VBClock Application

This application creates a visually appealing and fun analog clock that displays the system time. The VBClock application also demonstrates several graphics techniques and an alternative approach to adding a generic About box to your applications. As shown in Figure 29-9, the VBClock form's background is a colorful bitmap graphic. I created this bitmap using a public domain program that generates fractals based on the Mandelbrot set, but you can load any bitmap file into the *picBackGround* PictureBox control to customize the clock.

Figure 29-9.
The VBClock application in action.

The Options menu provides selections to manually set the time and to change the colors of the clock's hands. To set the time, I added a simple InputBox function to the program. To change the hand colors, I used a dialog box form that demonstrates a useful hot spot graphics technique. The Help menu provides access to the Contents and Search entry points into the associated help file.

NOTE: A great way to update your system time is to use the NISTTime application, described later in this chapter. You can run NISTTime and VBClock simultaneously to see the clock adjustment in real time.

Figure 29-10 shows the project list for the VBClock application. Each of the three files is explained in more detail below.

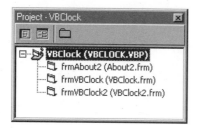

Figure 29-10.
The VBClock project list.

VBCLOCK.FRM

The VBClock form displays the analog clock image and updates the clock's hands once per second. This form has only three controls: a PictureBox control to display the background and the clock hands, a Timer control to update the clock, and a CommonDialog control to provide the interface to the associated help file. You can load any bitmap image into the PictureBox control or change the startup hand colors to suit your taste.

NOTE: AutoRedraw is an important property of the PictureBox control. It should be set to *True* so that the clock hands are drawn smoothly and crisply. If AutoRedraw is set to *False*, you'll probably see some flickering of the image as the hands are erased and redrawn.

Figure 29-11 shows the VBClock form during development.

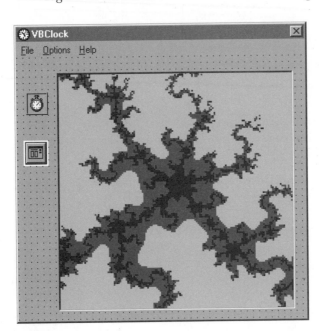

Figure 29-11.
The VBClock form during development.

To create this form, use the following tables and source code to add the appropriate controls, set any nondefault properties as indicated, and enter the source code lines as shown.

VBCLOCK.FRM Menu Design Window Entries

Caption	Name	Indentation	Enabled
&File	mnuFile	0	True
&New	mnuNew	1	False
&Open...	mnuOpen	1	False
&Save	mnuSave	1	False
Save &As...	mnuSaveAs	1	False
-	mnuFileDash1	1	True

(continued)

VBCLOCK.FRM Menu Design Window Entries *continued*

Caption	Name	Indentation	Enabled
E&xit	mnuExit	1	True
&Options	mnuOption	0	True
&Set Time...	mnuSetTime	1	True
&Hand Colors...	mnuHandColors	1	True
&Help	mnuHelp	0	True
&Contents	mnuContents	1	True
&Search For Help On...	mnuSearch	1	True
-	mnuHelpDash1	1	True
&About...	mnuAbout	1	True

VBCLOCK.FRM Objects and Property Settings

Property	Value
Form	
Name	frmVBClock
Caption	VBClock
BorderStyle	3 - Fixed Dialog
Timer	
Name	tmrClock
Interval	100
CommonDialog	
Name	cdlOne
PictureBox	
Name	picBackGround
AutoRedraw	True
AutoSize	True
Picture	Mandel1.bmp

Source Code for VBCLOCK.FRM

```
Option Explicit

Public gnHourHandColor As Integer
Public gnMinuteHandColor As Integer
Public gnSecondHandColor As Integer

Private mnHnum As Integer
Private mnMnum As Integer
Private mnSnum As Integer
Private mlHcolor As Long
Private mlMcolor As Long
Private mlScolor As Long
Private mfHlen As Single
Private mfMlen As Single
Private mfSlen As Single
Private msAppname As String
Private msSection As String
Private msKey As String
Private msSetting As String

Private Const Pi = 3.14159265358979
Private Const TwoPi = Pi + Pi
Private Const HalfPi = Pi / 2

Private Sub Form_Load()
    'Fill form exactly with background image
    picBackGround.Move 0, 0
    Width = picBackGround.Width + (Width - ScaleWidth)
    Height = picBackGround.Height + (Height - ScaleHeight)
    'Change the scaling of the clock face
    picBackGround.Scale (-2, -2)-(2, 2)
    'Center form
    Left = (Screen.Width - Width) \ 2
    Top = (Screen.Height - Height) \ 2
    'Set width of hands in pixels
    picBackGround.DrawWidth = 5
    'Set length of hands
    mfHlen = 0.8
    mfMlen = 1.5
    mfSlen = 1
    'Set colors of hands from Registry settings
    msAppname = "VBClock"
    msSection = "Hands"
    msKey = "mlHcolor"
```

(continued)

Source Code for VBCLOCK.FRM *continued*

```
        msSetting = GetSetting(msAppname, msSection, msKey)
        gnHourHandColor = Val(msSetting)
        msKey = "mlMcolor"
        msSetting = GetSetting(msAppname, msSection, msKey)
        gnMinuteHandColor = Val(msSetting)
        msKey = "mlScolor"
        msSetting = GetSetting(msAppname, msSection, msKey)
        gnSecondHandColor = Val(msSetting)
End Sub

Private Sub Form_Unload(Cancel As Integer)
        'Save current hand colors
        msKey = "mlHcolor"
        msSetting = Str$(gnHourHandColor)
        SaveSetting msAppname, msSection, msKey, msSetting
        msKey = "mlMcolor"
        msSetting = Str$(gnMinuteHandColor)
        SaveSetting msAppname, msSection, msKey, msSetting
        msKey = "mlScolor"
        msSetting = Str$(gnSecondHandColor)
        SaveSetting msAppname, msSection, msKey, msSetting
End Sub

Private Sub mnuAbout_Click()
        frmAbout2.Display
End Sub

Private Sub mnuExit_Click()
        Unload Me
End Sub

Private Sub mnuContents_Click()
        cdlOne.HelpFile = App.Path & "\..\..\Help\Mvbdw.hlp"
        cdlOne.HelpCommand = cdlHelpContents
        cdlOne.ShowHelp
End Sub

Private Sub mnuHandColors_Click()
        'Show form for selecting hand colors
        frmVBClock2.Show vbModal
End Sub

Private Sub mnuSearch_Click()
        cdlOne.HelpFile = App.Path & "\..\..\Help\Mvbdw.hlp"
```

(continued)

Source Code for VBCLOCK.FRM *continued*

```
        cdlOne.HelpCommand = cdlHelpPartialKey
        cdlOne.ShowHelp
    End Sub

    Private Sub tmrClock_Timer()
        Dim dHang As Double
        Dim dMang As Double
        Dim dSang As Double
        Dim dHx As Double
        Dim dHy As Double
        Dim dMx As Double
        Dim dMy As Double
        Dim dSx As Double
        Dim dSy As Double
        'Keep track of current second
        Static LastSecond
        'Check to see if new second
        If Second(Now) = LastSecond Then
            Exit Sub
        Else
            LastSecond = Second(Now)
        End If
        'Update time variables
        mnHnum = Hour(Now)
        mnMnum = Minute(Now)
        mnSnum = Second(Now)
        'Calculate hand angles
        dHang = TwoPi * (mnHnum + mnMnum / 60) / 12 - HalfPi
        dMang = TwoPi * (mnMnum + mnSnum / 60) / 60 - HalfPi
        dSang = TwoPi * mnSnum / 60 - HalfPi
        'Calculate endpoints for each hand
        dHx = mfHlen * Cos(dHang)
        dHy = mfHlen * Sin(dHang)
        dMx = mfMlen * Cos(dMang)
        dMy = mfMlen * Sin(dMang)
        dSx = mfSlen * Cos(dSang)
        dSy = mfSlen * Sin(dSang)
        'Restore background image
        picBackGround.Cls
        'Draw new hands
        picBackGround.Line (0, 0)-(dMx, dMy), QBColor(gnMinuteHandColor)
        picBackGround.Line (0, 0)-(dHx, dHy), QBColor(gnHourHandColor)
        picBackGround.Line (0, 0)-(dSx, dSy), QBColor(gnSecondHandColor)
    End Sub
```

(continued)

Source Code for VBCLOCK.FRM *continued*

```
Private Sub mnuSetTime_Click()
    Dim sPrompt As String
    Dim sTitle As String
    Dim sDefault As String
    Dim sStartTime As String
    Dim sTim As String
    Dim sMsg As String
    'Ask user for new time
    sPrompt = "Enter the time, using the format 00:00:00"
    sTitle = "VBClock"
    sDefault = Time$
    sStartTime = sDefault
    sTim = InputBox$(sPrompt, sTitle, sDefault)
    'Check if user clicked Cancel
    'or clicked OK with no change to time
    If sTim = "" Or sTim = sStartTime Then
        Exit Sub
    End If
    'Set new time
    On Error GoTo ErrorTrap
    Time$ = sTim
    Exit Sub
ErrorTrap:
    sMsg = "The time you entered is invalid. " + sTim
    MsgBox sMsg, 48, "VBClock"
    Resume Next
End Sub
```

The Timer control's Interval property is set to *100 milliseconds* ($^{1}/_{10}$ of a second) instead of *1000 milliseconds* (1 second). The hands need to be updated at the rate of once per second, but setting the timer to a rate of once per second causes intermittent jerkiness in the movement of the hands. The jerkiness occurs because a Visual Basic timer isn't based on an exact timing between activations. Instead, the timer activates after the indicated interval, as soon as the system can get back to the timer after that interval has transpired. This causes a slight, unpredictable variation in the actual activations of timer events. (Activations are probably more accurate in faster computers and less accurate in slower ones.) Every so often, this unpredictable delay can cause the VBClock application's clock hands to jump to the next second erratically.

To fix this problem, set the timer's Interval property to something less than half a second. I chose *100 milliseconds*. The result is that the hands are updated much more accurately and are never off by more than about a tenth of a second. This updating action is smooth enough that the user won't notice any variation in the beat. The Timer event procedure checks the system time against the previously updated second shown by the hands of the clock. If a new second has not yet arrived, the procedure exits, causing very little delay to the overall system's speed.

Using the Registry

The user has the option of changing the color of the clock's hands. To maintain this color information between sessions, the application uses the Registry to retrieve the last known color settings during the form's Load event and saves the current color settings during the form's Unload event. This simple example demonstrates the use of the Registry to save the state of an application. Using these same techniques, you can use the Registry to store any details about the state of the application that you may want to add.

VBCLOCK2.FRM

The VBClock2 form provides a graphical way to select the colors for the three hands of the clock. My goal here was to allow the user to select one of the 16 main colors for each of the hands, but I didn't want to complicate the form with a lot of verbal descriptions of the colors. The solution was to draw all 16 colors in each of three picture boxes and let the user select the colors visually. Figure 29-12 shows the VBClock2 form in action. This approach is simple and uncluttered, and the user sees exactly what color he or she is selecting. Besides, like they always say, a picture is worth two thousand bytes!

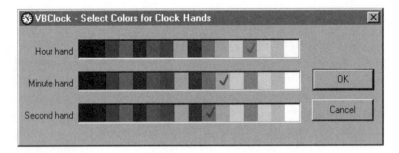

Figure 29-12.
The VBClock2 form, which lets the user select clock hand colors.

During the form's Load event procedure, I scaled the three picture boxes to divide them into 16 regions. The height of each picture box is scaled from 0 to 1, and the width from 0 to 16. Regardless of the actual size of the picture boxes, each one will display the 16 main colors in rectangular regions of equal size. Likewise, when the user clicks anywhere on a picture box, the *x*-coordinate converts to a number from 0 to 15, indicating the selected color.

Image Hot Spots

The Click event doesn't provide the required information to determine exactly where in a picture box the mouse click happened. The best way to determine the location of the click is to maintain the last known position of the mouse pointer using a global variable. The picture box's MouseMove event does provide *x* and *y* pointer location information, so it's easy to update the global variables (in this case, *mnHourMouseX*, *mnMinuteMouseX*, and *mnSecondMouseX*) to keep track of the mouse. The values stored in these variables at the time of a Click event determine what color the user is selecting. This technique can be used to define hot spots on your graphics. In fact, by mathematically scrutinizing the current *xy*-coordinates of the mouse pointer, you can define hot spots in your graphics that are circular, polygonal, or whatever shape and size you want.

Figure 29-13 shows the VBClock2 form during the development process.

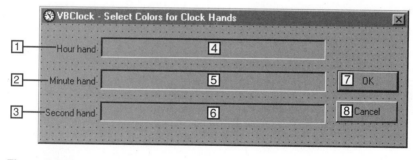

Figure 29-13.
The VBClock2 form during development.

To create this form, use the table and source code on the following pages to add the appropriate controls, set any nondefault properties as indicated, and enter the source code lines as shown.

VBCLOCK2.FRM Objects and Property Settings

ID No.*	Property	Value
Form		
	Name	*frmVBClock2*
	Caption	*VBClock - Select Colors for Clock Hands*
	BorderStyle	*3 - Fixed Dialog*
	Icon	*CLOCK02.ICO*
Label		
1	Name	*lblHourHand*
	Caption	*Hour hand*
	Alignment	*1 - Right Justify*
Label		
2	Name	*lblMinuteHand*
	Caption	*Minute hand*
	Alignment	*1 - Right Justify*
Label		
3	Name	*lblSecondHand*
	Caption	*Second hand*
	Alignment	*1 - Right Justify*
PictureBox		
4	Name	*picHourColor*
PictureBox		
5	Name	*picMinuteColor*
PictureBox		
6	Name	*picSecondColor*
CommandButton		
7	Name	*cmdOK*
	Caption	*OK*
	Default	*True*
CommandButton		
8	Name	*cmdCancel*
	Caption	*Cancel*
	Cancel	*True*

*   The number in the ID No. column corresponds to the number in Figure 29-13 that identifies the location of the object on the form.

Source Code for VBCLOCK2.FRM

```
Option Explicit

Private mnHourMouseX As Integer
Private mnMinuteMouseX As Integer
Private mnSecondMouseX As Integer
Private mnHourHand As Integer
Private mnMinuteHand As Integer
Private mnSecondHand As Integer

Private Sub cmdCancel_Click()
    'Cancel without changing hand colors
    Unload Me
End Sub

Private Sub cmdOK_Click()
    'Reset hand colors
    frmVBClock.gnHourHandColor = mnHourHand
    frmVBClock.gnMinuteHandColor = mnMinuteHand
    frmVBClock.gnSecondHandColor = mnSecondHand
    'Return to clock form
    Unload Me
End Sub

Private Sub Form_Activate()
    Form_Paint
End Sub

Private Sub Form_Load()
    'Get current hand colors
    mnHourHand = frmVBClock.gnHourHandColor
    mnMinuteHand = frmVBClock.gnMinuteHandColor
    mnSecondHand = frmVBClock.gnSecondHandColor
    'Scale picture boxes
    picHourColor.Scale (0, 0)-(16, 1)
    picMinuteColor.Scale (0, 0)-(16, 1)
    picSecondColor.Scale (0, 0)-(16, 1)
End Sub

Private Sub Form_Paint()
    Dim i As Integer
    'Draw the 16 colors in each color "bar"
    For i = 0 To 15
        'Draw colored boxes
        picHourColor.Line (i, 0)-(i + 1, 1), QBColor(i), BF
```

(continued)

Source Code for VBCLOCK2.FRM *continued*

```
        picMinuteColor.Line (i, 0)-(i + 1, 1), QBColor(i), BF
        picSecondColor.Line (i, 0)-(i + 1, 1), QBColor(i), BF
    Next i
    'Draw check marks for current colors
    picHourColor.DrawWidth = 2
    picHourColor.Line (mnHourHand + 0.3, 0.5) _
        -(mnHourHand + 0.5, 0.7), QBColor(mnHourHand Xor 15)
    picHourColor.Line (mnHourHand + 0.5, 0.7) _
        -(mnHourHand + 0.8, 0.2), QBColor(mnHourHand Xor 15)
    picMinuteColor.DrawWidth = 2
    picMinuteColor.Line (mnMinuteHand + 0.3, 0.5) _
        -(mnMinuteHand + 0.5, 0.7), QBColor(mnMinuteHand Xor 15)
    picMinuteColor.Line (mnMinuteHand + 0.5, 0.7) _
        -(mnMinuteHand + 0.8, 0.2), QBColor(mnMinuteHand Xor 15)
    picSecondColor.DrawWidth = 2
    picSecondColor.Line (mnSecondHand + 0.3, 0.5) _
        -(mnSecondHand + 0.5, 0.7), QBColor(mnSecondHand Xor 15)
    picSecondColor.Line (mnSecondHand + 0.5, 0.7) _
        -(mnSecondHand + 0.8, 0.2), QBColor(mnSecondHand Xor 15)
End Sub

Private Sub picHourColor_Click()
    'Determine selected hour hand color
    mnHourHand = mnHourMouseX
    Form_Paint
End Sub

Private Sub picHourColor_MouseMove(Button As Integer, _
    Shift As Integer, X As Single, Y As Single)
    'Keep track of mouse location
    mnHourMouseX = Int(X)
End Sub

Private Sub picMinuteColor_Click()
    'Determine selected minute hand color
    mnMinuteHand = mnMinuteMouseX
    Form_Paint
End Sub

Private Sub picMinuteColor_MouseMove(Button As Integer, _
    Shift As Integer, X As Single, Y As Single)
    'Keep track of mouse location
    mnMinuteMouseX = Int(X)
End Sub
```

(continued)

Source Code for VBCLOCK2.FRM *continued*

```
Private Sub picSecondColor_Click()
    'Determine selected second hand color
    mnSecondHand = mnSecondMouseX
    Form_Paint
End Sub

Private Sub picSecondColor_MouseMove(Button As Integer, _
    Shift As Integer, X As Single, Y As Single)
    'Keep track of mouse location
    mnSecondMouseX = Int(X)
End Sub
```

ABOUT2.FRM

In Chapter 10, "Dialog Boxes, Windows, and Other Forms," I provided a generic, fill-in-the-blanks About dialog box that you can easily plug into your own applications. To further demonstrate the App properties and how they can automate the About dialog box even further, I created ABOUT2.FRM. This form is completely generic in that all displayed data is modified by the calling application, yet the only line of source code required to activate this form is a call to the frmAbout2.Display method.

Figure 29-14 shows the About2 form as it is displayed by the VBClock application.

Figure 29-14.
The About2 form as activated by VBClock.

So when, where, and how does the information displayed by the About2 form get set? The trick is to set properties of the App object during the development process. From the Visual Basic Project menu, choose Project Properties to display the Project Properties dialog box, and then click on the Make tab, as shown in Figure 29-15.

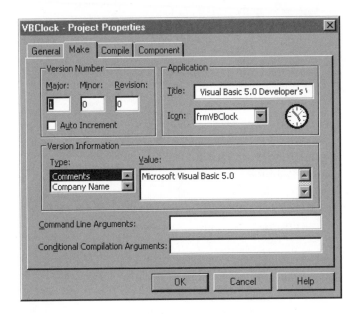

Figure 29-15.
The Project Properties dialog box, in which many of the App properties are set.

Visual Basic's App object now provides a long list of useful properties, many of which you can set using the Project Properties dialog box. The version numbers, title, and all properties listed in the Version Information section of the Make tab can be set here, and they can be accessed programmatically by referring to properties of the application's App object.

The About2 form accesses four App properties to set the Caption properties of four Label controls. Here's the code that loads these labels, which you'll find in the form's Load event procedure:

```
'Set labels using App properties
lblHeading.Caption = App.Title
lblApplication.Caption = App.ProductName
lblVB.Caption = App.Comments
lblCopyright.Caption = App.LegalCopyright
```

Feel free to modify the About2 form to display any other App properties you want. For example, you might want to display the version number information or the trademark text. I chose only four of the properties in order to make this About dialog box similar to the original About dialog box so that you can easily compare the two techniques. Figure 29-16 shows the About2 form during development.

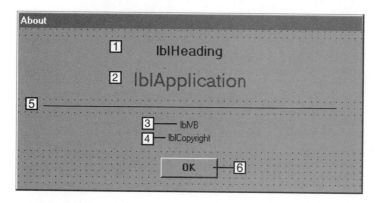

Figure 29-16.
The About2 form during development.

To create this form, use the following table and source code to add the appropriate controls, set any nondefault properties as indicated, and enter the source code lines as shown.

ABOUT2.FRM Objects and Property Settings

ID No.*	Property	Value
Form		
	Name	*frmAbout2*
	Caption	*About*
	BorderStyle	*3 - Fixed Dialog*
Label		
1	Name	*lblHeading*
	Alignment	*2 - Center*
	Font	*MS Sans Serif, Bold, 12*

*   The number in the ID No. column corresponds to the number in Figure 29-16 that identifies the location of the object on the form.

(continued)

ABOUT2.FRM Objects and Property Settings *continued*

ID No.	Property	Value
Label		
2	Name	*lblApplication*
	Alignment	*2 - Center*
	Font	*MS Sans Serif, Regular, 18*
	ForeColor	*&H00008000&*
Label		
3	Name	*lblVB*
	Alignment	*2 - Center*
Label		
4	Name	*lblCopyright*
	Alignment	*2 - Center*
Line		
5	Name	*linSeparator*
CommandButton		
6	Name	*cmdOK*
	Caption	*OK*

Source Code for ABOUT2.FRM

```
Option Explicit

Private Sub cmdOK_Click()
    Unload Me
End Sub

Private Sub Form_Load()
    'Center form
    Left = (Screen.Width - Width) \ 2
    Top = (Screen.Height - Height) \ 2
    'Set labels using App properties
    lblHeading.Caption = App.Title
    lblApplication.Caption = App.ProductName
    lblVB.Caption = App.Comments
    lblCopyright.Caption = App.LegalCopyright
End Sub
```

(continued)

```
Public Sub Display()
    'Display self as modal
    Me.Show vbModal
End Sub
```

The NISTTime Application

This little utility automatically dials up and connects with the National Institute of Standards and Technology (NIST) in Boulder, Colorado. You can use it to adjust your computer's clock to something better than 1-second accuracy. I say "something better" because various factors can limit the efficiency of the processing, such as modem throughput speed, the speed and efficiency of your computer at setting its clock, telephone line delays, and so on. The NIST time service does attempt to adjust for this delay by sending the "on mark" character 45 milliseconds before the actual time. As a result, the NISTTime application can set your clock's time far more accurately than you can set it manually.

How NISTTime Works

The NISTTime application uses the MSComm control to handle the modem connection over the telephone to the NIST facility. This control makes it simple to set up the correct baud rate, telephone number, and other modem parameters, as shown in the relevant lines of code in the form's Load event procedure. Originally, the baud rate for this service was limited to either 300 or 1200 baud, but NIST has installed modems that adjust automatically to the baud rate of the modem making the call. As shown in the source code listing, I've set my modem speed to 14,400 baud, which has worked fine for me. If you experience any line noise or inconsistent connections, try a lower baud rate.

Once connected, the service sends a header message, followed by a line of information repeated once per second. At the end of this line of data, an asterisk is transmitted, marking the exact time. The NISTTime application reads and stores this data as it arrives, watching for two occurrences of the asterisk time marks. When the second asterisk arrives, the NISTTime application extracts minute and second information from the string of data and sets the system clock to these values.

The string of incoming data provides other useful information, such as the modified Julian date; the year, month, day, and hour numbers for Coordinated Universal Time; and even a number indicating a possible leap second adjustment at the end of the current month. All of this extra data is ignored in the NISTTime application because your clock is probably already close to the correct local time and only an adjustment for minutes and seconds will be necessary.

NOTE: To get a full accounting and description of the information broadcast by this service, dial in to the same number using a terminal program such as HyperTerminal. Once you are connected, type a question mark to receive several pages of detailed information.

The NISTTime form uses two timers to control the communications interaction: one timer's interval is set to 1 millisecond to process incoming bytes; the other control is set to trigger after 1 minute. Normally, the NISTTime application makes the connection, sets your clock, and hangs up just a few seconds after dialing. However, if anything is amiss, the 1-minute timer disconnects the phone at the end of a minute. The service itself disconnects after roughly 1 minute of operation—all of which makes the chances of accidentally running up long-distance bills highly unlikely. I added this second watchdog timer as a redundant safety mechanism.

As NISTTime runs, several short messages are displayed to indicate its progress. No interaction with the user is required, and the application unloads shortly after the clock is set. Figures 29-17 through 29-19 show the normal sequence of these messages during the few seconds of operation.

NOTE: To monitor your system's time, either run the VBClock program presented in the previous section, or double-click on the time displayed in your Microsoft Windows 95 desktop task bar to display the Date/Time Properties dialog box.

Figure 29-17.
The NISTTime application as it dials in to NIST.

Figure 29-18.
The application receiving the data used to set the system clock.

Figure 29-19.
The NISTTime message displayed while disconnecting from NIST.

NISTTIME.FRM

The NISTTime form is small—just big enough to display progress messages in the upper-left corner of your display. The form contains two Timer controls, an MSComm control, and a Label control to display progress messages.

Figure 29-20 shows the form during development.

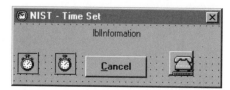

Figure 29-20.
The NISTTime form during development.

To create this form, use the table and source code on the following pages to add the appropriate controls, set any nondefault properties as indicated, and enter the source code lines as shown.

NISTTIME.FRM Objects and Property Settings

Property	Value
Form	
Name	*frmNISTTime*
Caption	*NIST - Time Set*
BorderStyle	*3 - Fixed Dialog*
Icon	*CLOCK01.ICO*
Timer	
Name	*tmrGetBytes*
Interval	*1*
Enabled	*False*
Timer	
Name	*tmrWatchDog*
Interval	*60000*
Enabled	*False*
MSComm	
Name	*comControl*
Handshaking	*2 - comRTS*
CommandButton	
Name	*cmdCancel*
Caption	*&Cancel*
Label	
Name	*lblInformation*
Alignment	*2 - Center*

Source Code for NISTTIME.FRM

```
Option Explicit

Const PORT = 1
Const TELEPHONE = "1-303-494-4774"
Const BUFSIZ = 3000

Dim nNistNdx As Integer
Dim sNistBuf As String * BUFSIZ
```

(continued)

Source Code for NISTTIME.FRM *continued*

```
Private Sub cmdCancel_Click()
    Unload Me
End Sub

Private Sub Form_Load()
    'Locate form near upper-left corner
    Left = (Screen.Width - Width) * 0.1
    Top = (Screen.Height - Height) * 0.1
    'Display first informational message
    lblInformation.Caption = _
        "Dialing National Institute of Standards " & _
        "and Technology Telephone Time Service"
    'Show form and first message
    Show
    'Set up Communications control parameters
    comControl.CommPort = PORT
    comControl.Settings = "14400,N,8,1"
    'Set to read entire buffer
    comControl.InputLen = 0
    comControl.PortOpen = True
    'Send command to dial NIST
    comControl.Output = "ATDT" + TELEPHONE + vbCr
    'Activate timers
    tmrGetBytes.Enabled = True
    tmrWatchDog.Enabled = True
    'Enable Cancel button
    cmdCancel.Enabled = True
End Sub

Private Sub Form_Unload(Cancel As Integer)
    'This usually hangs up phone
    comControl.DTREnable = False
    'The following also hangs up phone
    Pause 1500
    'Update message for user
    lblInformation.Caption = "Hanging up"
    Refresh
    'Send commands to control modem
    comControl.Output = "+++"
    Pause 1500
    comControl.Output = "ATH0" + vbCrLf
    'Close down communications
    comControl.PortOpen = False
End Sub
```

(continued)

Source Code for NISTTIME.FRM *continued*

```
Private Sub Pause(millisec)
    Dim EndOfPause As Double
    'Determine end time of delay
    EndOfPause = Timer + millisec / 1000
    'Loop away time
    Do
    Loop While Timer < EndOfPause
End Sub

Private Sub SetTime(sA As String)
    Dim nHo As Integer
    Dim nMi As Integer
    Dim nSe As Integer
    Dim dTimeNow As Double
    'Extract current hour from system
    nHo = Hour(Now)
    'Extract minute and second from NIST string
    nMi = Val(Mid(sA, 22, 2))
    nSe = Val(Mid(sA, 25, 2))
    'Construct new time
    dTimeNow = TimeSerial(nHo, nMi, nSe)
    'Set system clock
    Time = Format(dTimeNow, "hh:mm:ss")
End Sub

Private Sub tmrGetBytes_Timer()
    Static ConnectFlag As Boolean
    Dim sTmp As String
    Dim nBytes As Integer
    Dim nP1 As Integer
    Dim nP2 As Integer
    'Check for incoming nBytes
    If comControl.InBufferCount = 0 Then
        Exit Sub
    Else
        sTmp = comControl.Input
        nBytes = Len(sTmp)
        If nBytes + nNistNdx >= BUFSIZ Then
            lblInformation.Caption = "Hanging up"
            tmrGetBytes.Enabled = False
            tmrWatchDog.Enabled = False
            Unload Me
        Else
```

(continued)

Source Code for NISTTIME.FRM *continued*

```
                Mid(sNistBuf, nNistNdx + 1, nBytes) = sTmp
                nNistNdx = nNistNdx + nBytes
            End If
        End If
        'Check for sign that we've connected
        If ConnectFlag = False Then
            If InStr(sNistBuf, "*" & vbCrLf) Then
                lblInformation.Caption = "Connected... setting clock"
                ConnectFlag = True
            End If
        Else
            'Check for time marks
            nP1 = InStr(sNistBuf, "*")
            nP2 = InStr(nP1 + 1, sNistBuf, "*")
            'Time received if two time marks found
            If nP2 > nP1 Then
                SetTime Mid(sNistBuf, nP1, nP2 - nP1 + 1)
                Unload Me
            End If
        End If
    End Sub

Private Sub tmrWatchDog_Timer()
    'Activate safety time-out if no connection
    Beep
    Unload Me
End Sub
```

Two constants are declared at the beginning of the code that you may need to change. The *PORT* constant indicates the COM port your modem is connected to. If your modem is at COM1, *PORT* should be set to *1* as shown, but if your modem is at COM2, COM3, or COM4, change *PORT* to *2*, *3*, or *4*.

If you happen to live in the Denver metropolitan area, you can remove the long-distance digits from the *TELEPHONE* constant. I'm lucky enough to live near Denver, so my NISTTime program's *TELEPHONE* constant is set to *494-4774*. Similarly, if you need to dial 9 to get an outside line, you will want to add this to the string constant, along with a comma for a delay. A typical string that dials 9 first would be *9,1-303-494-4774*.

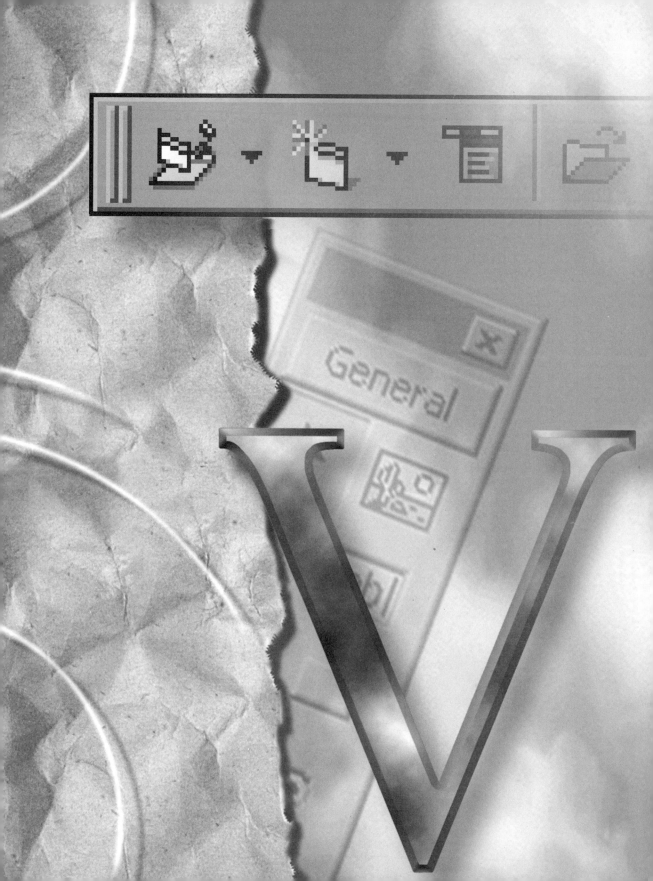

CHAPTER THIRTY

Databases

Visual Basic is playing an increasingly important role in the corporate environment, especially since its database capabilities have been enhanced to make it a powerful development and front-end tool. The three applications in this chapter—AreaCode, DataDump, and Jot—provide examples of just how easy it is to work with Microsoft Access or other databases using Visual Basic.

The AreaCode Application

The AreaCode application consists of two forms, AREACODE.FRM and the generic ABOUT.FRM. AREACODE.FRM uses two Data controls to access the same database of telephone area codes in different ways. The first Data control, in the top half of the form, accesses a table of area codes in the database file AREACODE.MDB, which was created using Microsoft Access 97. The Data control in the bottom half of the form accesses a query in the same database file. The table tapped by the first Data control presents area code data in ascending (201 through 970) area code order. The query provides the same table of area code data in ascending state abbreviation order (AK through WY). This application makes it easy either to look up where a call came from when all you know is the area code or to look up an area code for a known state.

The single form for the AreaCode application uses few database-related lines of code because the Data control and several TextBox controls have properties that simplify the connection to the database. To create the form, I drew the controls and then set a handful of properties to make the connection to the database. I added a few lines of code to handle minor details of the search process—and then I was done!

Connecting controls to a database in this way is a two-step process. First a Data control is connected to the database file by setting the DatabaseName property, and then it is connected to a specific table or query within that database by setting the RecordSource property. In general, each Data control connects to a single table or query. Many other types of controls, such as Label and ListBox controls, now have properties that make the final connection to the database by connecting to a specific Data control. In this case, I've used several TextBox controls. All I had to do was set each TextBox control's DataSource property to the name of one of the Data controls and then set each of their DataField properties to indicate the specific field within the table or query.

Although you can navigate the database table or query by clicking on the Data control, I've added some code to demonstrate another way to manipulate the database records. In the top half of the form, the *txtAreaCode* text box lets the user type in a three-digit area code. After the user enters the three digits, a bookmark is set at the current record (so that the current record can be displayed again if the search fails), and several RecordSet properties of the Data control are set to cause the txtAreaCode_Change event procedure to begin searching for a matching area code in the database immediately.

Similarly, when the user types a two-character state abbreviation in the *txtStateAbbrev1* text box in the bottom half of the form, a search for the state abbreviation is performed and the first record for that state is displayed. The user can then click the Next Record button of the Data control to see the records with the additional area codes for that state.

Figure 30-1 shows the AreaCode form after a successful search for the area code 303 in the top half and after a successful search for the state of Washington in the bottom half. Note how the top and bottom halves of the form work independently of each other, even though they access the same database.

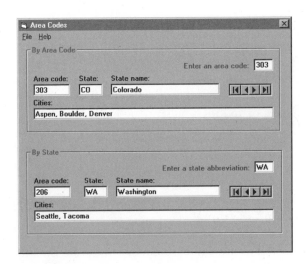

Figure 30-1.
The AreaCode form after locating area code 303 in the top half and an area code for Washington state in the bottom half.

AREACODE.FRM

The AreaCode form contains two nearly identical sets of controls: one set for the top half of the form, and one set for the bottom half. Two Data controls connect to the same database, and several TextBox controls connect to fields through the associated Data control. To organize the TextBox controls, I've grouped them with some descriptive labels within Frame controls. A single CommonDialog control provides access to the associated help file by using the control's *ShowHelp* method. I assigned the name of the database file to the Data controls' DatabaseName property in the Form_Load event procedure, and I use the App.Path property to identify the location of the database. If your database is in a location other than the directory containing the application, assign the full path to the database.

Figure 30-2 shows the AreaCode form during development.

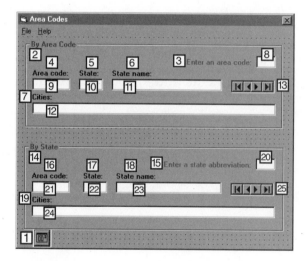

Figure 30-2.
The AreaCode form during development.

To create this form, use the tables and source code on the following pages to add the appropriate controls, set any nondefault properties as indicated, and enter the source code lines as shown.

AREACODE.FRM Menu Design Window Entries

Caption	Name	Indentation	Enabled
&File	mnuFile	0	True
&New	mnuNew	1	False
&Open...	mnuOpen	1	False
&Save	mnuSave	1	False
Save &As...	mnuSaveAs	1	False
-	mnuFileDash1	1	True
E&xit	mnuExit	1	True
&Help	mnuHelp	0	True
&Contents	mnuContents	1	True
&Search for Help on...	mnuSearch	1	True
-	mnuHelpDash1	1	True
&About...	mnuAbout	1	True

AREACODE.FRM Objects and Property Settings

ID No.*	Property	Value
Form		
	Name	frmAreaCode
	Caption	Area Codes
	BorderStyle	3 - Fixed Dialog
CommonDialog		
1	Name	cdlOne
Frame		
2	Name	fraByAreaCode
	Caption	By Area Code
	ForeColor	&H000000FF&
Label		
3	Name	lblPrompt2
	Caption	Enter an area code:
	ForeColor	&H00FF0000&

*   The number in the ID No. column corresponds to the number in Figure 30-2 that identifies the location of the object on the form.

(continued)

AREACODE.FRM Objects and Property Settings *continued*

ID No.	Property	Value
Label		
4	Name	*lblAreaCode2*
	Caption	*Area code:*
Label		
5	Name	*lblState2*
	Caption	*State:*
Label		
6	Name	*lblStateName2*
	Caption	*State name:*
Label		
7	Name	*lblCities2*
	Caption	*Cities:*
TextBox		
8	Name	*txtAreaCode*
	Alignment	*2 - Center*
TextBox		
9	Name	*txtAreaCode2*
	DataSource	*datAreaCode2*
	DataField	*AreaCode*
TextBox		
10	Name	*txtState2*
	DataSource	*datAreaCode2*
	DataField	*State*
TextBox		
11	Name	*txtStateName2*
	DataSource	*datAreaCode2*
	DataField	*StateName*
TextBox		
12	Name	*txtCities2*
	DataSource	*datAreaCode2*
	DataField	*Cities*

(continued)

AREACODE.FRM Objects and Property Settings *continued*

ID No.	Property	Value
Data		
13	Name RecordSource	*datAreaCode2* *AreaCode*
Frame		
14	Name Caption ForeColor	*fraByState* *By State* *&H000000FF&*
Label		
15	Name Caption ForeColor	*lblPrompt1* *Enter a state abbreviation:* *&H00FF0000&*
Label		
16	Name Caption	*lblAreaCode1* *Area code:*
Label		
17	Name Caption	*lblState1* *State:*
Label		
18	Name Caption	*lblStateName1* *State name:*
Label		
19	Name Caption	*lblCities1* *Cities:*
TextBox		
20	Name Alignment	*txtStateAbbrev1* *2 - Center*
TextBox		
21	Name DataSource DataField	*txtAreaCode1* *datAreaCode1* *AreaCode*

(continued)

AREACODE.FRM Objects and Property Settings *continued*

ID No.	Property	Value
TextBox		
22	Name	*txtState1*
	DataSource	*datAreaCode1*
	DataField	*State*
TextBox		
23	Name	*txtStateName1*
	DataSource	*datAreaCode1*
	DataField	*StateName*
TextBox		
24	Name	*txtCities1*
	DataSource	*datAreaCode1*
	DataField	*Cities*
Data		
25	Name	*datAreaCode1*
	RecordSource	*ByState*

Source Code for AREACODE.FRM

```
Option Explicit

Private Sub Form_Load()
    'Center this form
    Left = (Screen.Width - Width) \ 2
    Top = (Screen.Height - Height) \ 2
    datAreaCode1.DatabaseName = App.Path & "\AreaCode.mdb"
    datAreaCode2.DatabaseName = App.Path & "\AreaCode.mdb"
End Sub

Private Sub txtAreaCode_Change()
    Dim sBookmark
    Dim sCriteria
    'Wait for user to enter all three digits
    If Len(txtAreaCode.Text) = 3 Then
        'Record current record
        sBookmark = datAreaCode2.Recordset.Bookmark
```

(continued)

Source Code for AREACODE.FRM *continued*

```
            'Search for first matching area code
            sCriteria = "AreaCode = " + txtAreaCode.Text
            datAreaCode2.Recordset.FindFirst sCriteria
            'Handle unmatched area code
            If datAreaCode2.Recordset.NoMatch Then
                Beep
                datAreaCode2.Recordset.Bookmark = sBookmark
            End If
        End If
    End If
End Sub

Private Sub txtAreaCode_KeyPress(KeyAscii As Integer)
    If Len(txtAreaCode.Text) = 3 Then
        txtAreaCode.Text = ""
    End If
End Sub

Private Sub txtStateAbbrev1_Change()
    Dim sBookmark
    Dim sCriteria
    'Wait for user to enter two-letter abbreviation
    If Len(txtStateAbbrev1.Text) = 2 Then
        'Record current record
        sBookmark = datAreaCode1.Recordset.Bookmark
        'Search for first matching state
        sCriteria = "State = '" + txtStateAbbrev1.Text + "'"
        datAreaCode1.Recordset.FindFirst sCriteria
        'Handle unmatched state abbreviation
        If datAreaCode1.Recordset.NoMatch Then
            Beep
            datAreaCode1.Recordset.Bookmark = sBookmark
        End If
    End If
End Sub

Private Sub txtStateAbbrev1_KeyPress(KeyAscii As Integer)
    KeyAscii = Asc(UCase$(Chr$(KeyAscii)))
    If Len(txtStateAbbrev1.Text) = 2 Then
        txtStateAbbrev1.Text = ""
    End If
End Sub

Private Sub mnuAbout_Click()
    'Set properties
```

(continued)

Source Code for AREACODE.FRM *continued*

```
        About.Application = "AreaCode"
        About.Heading = _
            "Microsoft Visual Basic 5.0 Developer's Workshop"
        About.Copyright = "1997 John Clark Craig and Jeff Webb"
        About.Display
    End Sub

    Private Sub mnuExit_Click()
        Unload Me
    End Sub

    Private Sub mnuContents_Click()
        cdlOne.HelpFile = App.Path & "\..\..\Help\Mvbdw.hlp"
        cdlOne.HelpCommand = cdlHelpContents
        cdlOne.ShowHelp
    End Sub

    Private Sub mnuSearch_Click()
        cdlOne.HelpFile = App.Path & "\..\..\Help\Mvbdw.hlp"
        cdlOne.HelpCommand = cdlHelpPartialKey
        cdlOne.ShowHelp
    End Sub
```

This code relies on a query within the database to sort the AreaCode records by state, but there is a simple alternative to creating the query. We can set the Data control's RecordSource property to a structured query language (SQL) string, which provides a flexible and powerful tool for manipulating data. For example, you can add the following line of code to the form's Load event procedure to produce the same result as setting the RecordSource property to the ByState query:

```
datAreaCode1.RecordSource = "Select * from AREACODE order by State"
```

If you add this line to the program listing, you can delete the ByState query from the database. Both Data controls now access the same database table: one using the default area code order of the records, and the other using the SQL command to reorder the records by state.

The DataDump Application

With Visual Basic, it's easy to manipulate database files programmatically. The data access object (DAO) model provides a structured hierarchy of objects that lets you access and modify any part of a database. (See Chapter 21, "Database

Access," for more about the DAO model.) The DataDump application described here is a streamlined utility that demonstrates how you can loop through the various parts of this hierarchy to determine the layout of any field in any table of any database.

Unlike the AreaCode application, this program contains no Data controls or other data-bound controls. DataDump contains only a TextBox control for displaying the analyzed internal structure of a user-selected database and a CommonDialog control for selecting a database file to analyze. All analysis of the database file contents is performed by looping through various objects within the DAO model.

This application provides a list of all tables within the database and all fields within each table. Each field is described by name, type, and data size in bytes. I've found this utility useful for quickly reviewing the contents of a database's tables without having to run Access. If you want, you can easily extend the current code to include a listing of any queries stored in the database in the analysis. Visual Basic Books Online provides a good explanation of the complete DAO hierarchy for those interested in digging into the subject even deeper.

At load time, the DataDump form prompts for a database filename by using the CommonDialog control, as shown in Figure 30-3. It then proceeds to analyze the selected database, concatenating all the results into a single string variable. The database structure is traversed just once per run of the program, and the results string is displayed in the TextBox control whenever the form is resized.

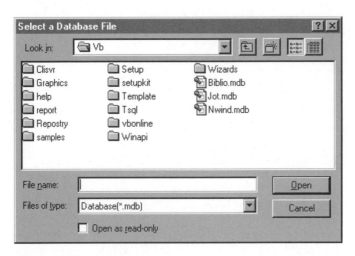

Figure 30-3.
The CommonDialog control that lets the user select a database file for analysis.

To improve the readability of the output, I have formatted the string using *vbCrLf* constants and extra spaces for padding. The font of the text box is set to Courier New, which is a monospace font that provides consistent alignment of the indented text lines. The TextBox control has scrollbars that let you view the data list no matter how long it gets, and the control adjusts automatically to fill the form whenever the form is resized.

Figure 30-4 shows the structure of the BIBLIO.MDB database that ships with Visual Basic.

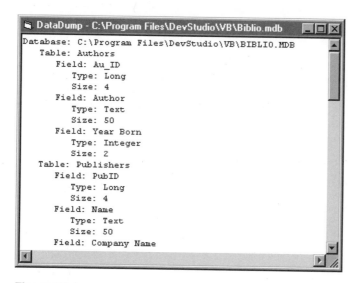

Figure 30-4.
The DataDump application in action, showing the tables and fields in BIBLIO.MDB.

DATADUMP.FRM

Figure 30-5 on the following page shows the DataDump form during development. The TextBox control is smaller than the form but is resized at runtime to the size of the form.

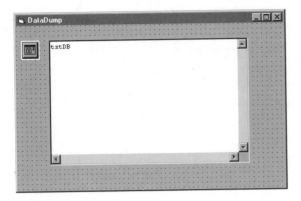

Figure 30-5.
The DataDump form during development.

To create this form, use the following table and source code to add the appropriate controls, set any nondefault properties as indicated, and enter the source code lines as shown.

DATADUMP.FRM Objects and Property Settings

Property	Value
Form	
Name	*frmDataDump*
Caption	*DataDump*
CommonDialog	
Name	*cdlOne*
TextBox	
Name	*txtDB*
Font	*Courier New*
MultiLine	*True*
Scrollbars	*3 - Both*

Source Code for DATADUMP.FRM

```
Option Explicit

Dim sDBFileName
Dim sDB

Private Sub Form_Load()
    'Center this form
    Left = (Screen.Width - Width) \ 2
    Top = (Screen.Height - Height) \ 2
    'Prompt user for database filename
    cdlOne.DialogTitle = "Select a Database File"
    cdlOne.Filter = "Database(*.mdb)|*.mdb"
    cdlOne.CancelError = True
    'Check for Cancel button click
    On Error Resume Next
    cdlOne.ShowOpen
    If Err = cdlCancel Then End
    'Prepare to analyze database
    sDBFileName = cdlOne.filename
    Me.Caption = "DataDump - " & sDBFileName
    GetStructure
End Sub

Private Sub Form_Resize()
    'Size text box to fit form
    txtDB.Move 0, 0, ScaleWidth, ScaleHeight
    'Display analysis string in text box
    txtDB.Text = sDB
End Sub

Private Sub GetStructure()
    'Looping variables
    Dim i As Integer
    Dim j As Integer
    'Database objects
    Dim db As Database
    Dim rs As Recordset
    Dim td As TableDef
    Dim fd As Field
    'Open the database
    Set db = Workspaces(0).OpenDatabase(sDBFileName)
    sDB = "Database: " & db.Name & vbCrLf
    'Process each table
    For i = 0 To db.TableDefs.Count - 1
        Set td = db.TableDefs(i)
        If Left(td.Name, 4) <> "MSys" Then
```

(continued)

Source Code for DATADUMP.FRM *continued*

```
                'Get table's name
                sDB = sDB & Space(3) & "Table: "
                sDB = sDB & td.Name & vbCrLf
                'Process each field in each table
                For j = 0 To td.Fields.Count - 1
                    Set fd = td.Fields(j)
                    'Get field's name
                    sDB = sDB & Space(6) & "Field: "
                    sDB = sDB & fd.Name & vbCrLf
                    'Get field's data type
                    sDB = sDB & Space(9) & "Type: "
                    Select Case fd.Type
                    Case dbBoolean
                        sDB = sDB & "Boolean" & vbCrLf
                    Case dbByte
                        sDB = sDB & "Byte" & vbCrLf
                    Case dbInteger
                        sDB = sDB & "Integer" & vbCrLf
                    Case dbLong
                        sDB = sDB & "Long" & vbCrLf
                    Case dbCurrency
                        sDB = sDB & "Currency" & vbCrLf
                    Case dbSingle
                        sDB = sDB & "Single" & vbCrLf
                    Case dbDouble
                        sDB = sDB & "Double" & vbCrLf
                    Case dbDate
                        sDB = sDB & "Date" & vbCrLf
                    Case dbText
                        sDB = sDB & "Text" & vbCrLf
                    Case dbLongBinary
                        sDB = sDB & "LongBinary" & vbCrLf
                    Case dbMemo
                        sDB = sDB & "Memo" & vbCrLf
                    Case Else
                        sDB = sDB & "(unknown) & vbCrLf"
                    End Select
                    'Get field's size in bytes
                    If fd.Type <> dbLongBinary And _
                        fd.Type <> dbMemo Then
                        sDB = sDB & Space(9) & "Size: "
                        sDB = sDB & fd.Size & vbCrLf
                    End If
                Next j
            End If
        Next i
        'Close database
        db.Close
End Sub
```

Testing the DataDump Application

To test the DataDump application, you'll need to set a reference to the Microsoft DAO 3.5 Object Library in the References dialog box.

The Jot Application

The Jot application uses a Multiple Document Interface (MDI) form to display multiple note windows. To make this a commercial application, you'd probably want to add a lot of features and modify the design, but the application is fully functional as is and it demonstrates a number of useful Visual Basic programming features.

I've included features that demonstrate how to create multiple copies of MDI child forms, how to use hot keys on an MDI form, how to create a database from scratch programmatically, and one way to center an image on an MDI form.

Figure 30-6 shows the Jot application at runtime. Buttons on the toolbar let you create new note windows and delete them when you have finished. Other buttons arrange the note windows and their minimized windows. When you close Jot, all notes are saved in a database; when you run Jot the next time, these notes reappear.

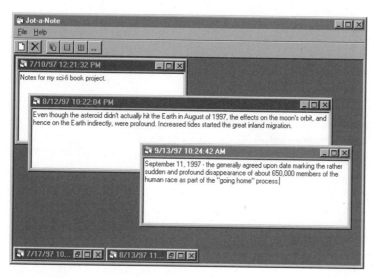

Figure 30-6.
The Jot application in action.

Multiple Child Forms

The first button on the toolbar creates a new, blank note window: I created a single Note child form named *frmNote* at design time and placed a call in the toolbar button's ButtonClick event procedure to a procedure named Make-NewNote, which creates a new copy of the Note form. If you look in the MakeNewNote procedure, you'll see two lines of code that create and display each new copy of the Note form:

```
Dim newNote As New frmNote
newNote.Show
```

Each copy of this child form shares the same event-driven procedures. To refer to the properties of the current copy of the child form (the Note form with the focus) in these procedures, I've used the *Me* prefix. For example, during the child form's Unload event procedure, its Caption property is saved in a field of the database. To record the caption of the child form currently unloading, the Unload event procedure refers to Me.Caption.

MDI Form Hot Key

The Note form's KeyPreview property is set to *True* so that all keypresses are intercepted before they are processed further by the form or its controls. The only keypress the Note form intercepts is Ctrl-T, which updates the date and time displayed in the current Note form's caption to the current date and time. Normally the date and time of each note are fixed at the time the note is created. This hot key combination lets you update the caption when you want. Even if you assign your own hot key combinations, you can still use the standard Windows shortcut key combinations Ctrl-X, Ctrl-C, and Ctrl-V to cut, copy, and paste as you edit these notes. The Ctrl-T command works much like these built-in commands. You can easily add code to process any other keys or combinations of keys in the same KeyDown event procedure. If you do process any key combinations, remember to set KeyAscii to *0* to prevent the form from further acting on the intercepted keys.

Figures 30-7 and 30-8 show a Note form just before and just after Ctrl-T is pressed to update the date and time in the caption.

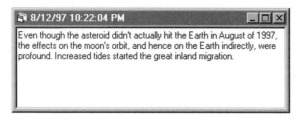

Figure 30-7.

A note originally created on August 12, 1997.

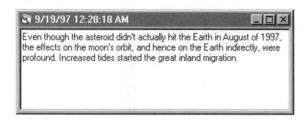

Figure 30-8.
The same note updated to the current date and time.

Creating a Database

When the Jot form loads, it attempts to open the JOT.MDB database file to read any previously saved notes. If this database file doesn't exist, which is true the first time you run the Jot application, the Jot form ignores the request. The database is not created until the first Note child form is unloaded. When a Note child form unloads and there is no database, a special block of code creates the database automatically. Understanding how these lines of code work provides concepts you'll find useful for mastering a lot of other database programming techniques. Here is the code that creates the new database (if the database doesn't already exist) in the Note child form's Unload event procedure:

```
'Create empty database
Set db = Workspaces(0).CreateDatabase("Jot.mdb", dbLangGeneral)
'Create table
Set td = db.CreateTableDef("JotTable")
'Create field
Set fd = td.CreateField("JotDateTime", dbDate)
```

(continued)

603

```
'Add new field to table's Fields collection
td.Fields.Append fd
'Create second field
Set fd = td.CreateField("JotNote", dbMemo)
'Add it to table
td.Fields.Append fd
'Add new table to TableDefs collection
db.TableDefs.Append td
'New database is now open
```

The CreateDatabase, CreateTableDef, and CreateField methods, as their names imply, create a Database object, a TableDef object, and a Field object. However, these methods don't actually hook the created objects into their parent objects—they just allocate memory and create all the behind-the-scenes details of the database objects. It takes an explicit second step to connect each new object to the structure of the parent object that created it. The code above shows several Append methods used to hook the new objects into the structure of the containing collection. For example, the TableDef object contains a collection named Fields, which contains all Field objects in the defined table. The Append method of the Fields collection is called to hook the freshly created Field object into this collection. It's a two-step process: create an object, and then append it to a collection to tie everything together. As shown above, this same two-step process is used to create fields and tables, append fields to tables, and append tables to a database.

Centering an Image on an MDI Form

The types of controls that can be placed on an MDI form are limited. In general, only controls with Align properties can be placed on an MDI form, and these controls will always be aligned at the top, bottom, left, or right of the form. An MDI form does have a Picture property, but any image loaded into this property is also aligned at the top-left corner of the form. So how did the Jot application end up with a bitmap image that always moves to the center of the MDI form as the form is resized? It's a useful trick to know.

You can move a child form to any relative position within the MDI parent form, including dead center, with a little bit of calculation. I've taken advantage of this by centering the Splash form in the Jot form's Resize event procedure.

The Splash form doesn't display anything except a picture because its BorderStyle property has been set to *0 - None* and the form is sized to match the size of the Image control it contains. As a result, when the Splash form is placed in the center of the MDI Jot form, the user sees only a centered bitmap picture. Figures 30-9 and 30-10 show the Jot form with the centered image before and after the form is resized.

Figure 30-9.
The Jot form with a centered image.

Figure 30-10.
The image still centered after the Jot form is resized.

JOT.FRM

As shown in the project list in Figure 30-11, the Jot application contains five files. JOT.FRM is the main MDI startup form, so we'll take a look at it first.

Figure 30-11.
The Jot application's project list.

Figure 30-12 shows the Jot form during development.

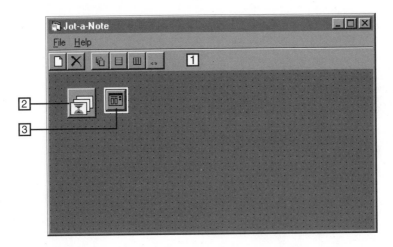

Figure 30-12.
The MDI Jot form during development.

To create this form, add an MDI form to a new Standard EXE project and use the following tables to add the appropriate controls and set any nondefault properties.

JOT.FRM Menu Design Window Entries

Caption	Name	Indentation	Enabled
&File	*mnuFile*	0	*True*
&New	*mnuNew*	1	*False*
&Open...	*mnuOpen*	1	*False*
&Save	*mnuSave*	1	*False*
Save &As...	*mnuSaveAs*	1	*False*
-	*mnuFileDash1*	1	*True*
E&xit	*mnuExit*	1	*True*
&Help	*mnuHelp*	0	*True*
&Contents	*mnuContents*	1	*True*
&Search for Help on...	*mnuSearch*	1	*True*
-	*mnuHelpDash1*	1	*True*
&About...	*mnuAbout*	1	*True*

JOT.FRM (MDI) Objects and Property Settings

ID No.*	Property	Value
Form		
	Name	*frmJot*
	Caption	*Jot-a-Note*
Toolbar		
1	Name	*tlbToolBar*
ImageList		
2	Name	*imlIcons*
CommonDialog		
3	Name	*cdlOne*

*   The number in the ID No. column corresponds to the number in Figure 30-12 that identifies the location of the object on the form.

Toolbars, Buttons, and ToolTips

In earlier versions of Visual Basic, you could create toolbars with buttons and ToolTips by using a variety of tricks and techniques or third-party custom controls, but Visual Basic 5 now makes this easier than ever to accomplish. Here I'll describe how to create the toolbar with buttons that appears on the Jot form, shown in Figure 30-12 on page 606.

First load the button images into the ImageList control. Right-click on the ImageList control, and select Properties to edit this control's properties. Change the image size option to *16 x 16*. Click on the Images tab, and click the Insert Picture button to add each button's image.

The following table lists the images to be inserted into the ImageList control.

Image Index	Image
1	NEW.BMP
2	DELETE.BMP
3	CASCADE.BMP
4	TILEH.BMP
5	TILEV.BMP
6	ARNGICON.BMP

The first two images in this table, NEW.BMP and DELETE.BMP, are found in the GRAPHICS\BITMAPS\TLBR_W95 directory of the Visual Basic CD-ROM. The CASCADE.BMP, TILEH.BMP, TILEV.BMP, and ARNGICON.BMP images were created using the Microsoft Paint utility and can be found on the companion CD-ROM.

Figure 30-13 shows the ImageList control's Property Pages dialog box after all the button images have been inserted.

Once the ImageList control has its button images loaded, you can connect this control to the Toolbar control. Right-click on the toolbar, and select Properties. Set the ImageList entry to *imlIcons* to make the connection. To explicitly create buttons and assign images from the list to them, click on the Buttons tab. Figure 30-14 shows the Toolbar control's Property Pages dialog box.

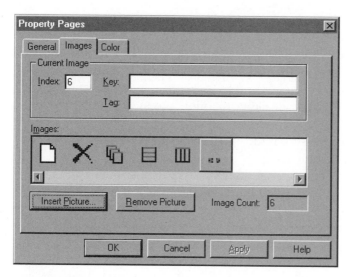

Figure 30-13.
Button images inserted into the ImageList control.

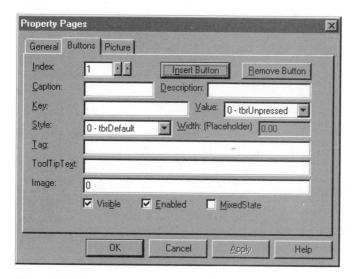

Figure 30-14.
The Toolbar control's Property Pages dialog box.

The toolbar buttons are added one at a time by clicking the Insert Button button. For each button, fill in the fields with the appropriate data. The text you type in the ToolTipText field will appear as the button's ToolTip. Enter a descriptive label in the Key field—this text will be used in the program to determine which button the user clicks, and an appropriate entry here will make your program code easier to follow and more self-documenting. In the Image field, enter the number of the image to be associated from the ImageList control—this is the entry that makes the connection between each button and a specific image.

The Style property determines the type of button; this property is normally left at the default setting of *0 - tbrDefault*. To add a space between buttons on the toolbar, simply add a button and set its Style property to *3 - tbrSeparator*. You won't need to assign an image or a key to these separator buttons. Other useful properties are available to control the appearance and behavior of your buttons, but we won't need them in this example application. (You should take the time to become familiar with the full set of properties later.)

The following table shows the button settings for the *tlbToolBar* control.

Button Index	Key	Style	ToolTipText	Image Index
1	*New*	*0 - tbrDefault*	*New*	*1*
2	*Delete*	*0 - tbrDefault*	*Delete*	*2*
3		*3 - tbrSeparator*		*0*
4	*Cascade*	*0 - tbrDefault*	*Cascade*	*3*
5	*TileHorizontally*	*0 - tbrDefault*	*Tile Horizontally*	*4*
6	*TileVertically*	*0 - tbrDefault*	*Tile Vertically*	*5*
7	*ArrangeIcons*	*0 - tbrDefault*	*Arrange Icons*	*6*

That's all there is to setting up a toolbar with buttons and ToolTips! If you've worked with Visual Basic ToolTip techniques in the past, you'll quickly appreciate the ease with which they can now be implemented.

Enter the following source code for the Jot form, which includes code to make your toolbar buttons active.

Source Code for JOT.FRM

```
Option Explicit

Public bSaveFlag

Private Sub MDIForm_Load()
    'Center this form on screen
    Move (Screen.Width - Width) \ 2, _
        (Screen.Height - Height) \ 2
    'Load all previous notes from database
    LoadNotes
    'Display splash image
    frmSplash.Show
End Sub

Private Sub MDIForm_QueryUnload(Cancel As Integer, _
    UnloadMode As Integer)
    'Prepare to save all current notes
    bSaveFlag = True
End Sub

Private Sub MDIForm_Resize()
    'Move splash image to center of MDI form
    frmSplash.Move (Me.ScaleWidth - frmSplash.Width) \ 2, _
        (Me.ScaleHeight - frmSplash.Height) \ 2
End Sub

Private Sub mnuAbout_Click()
    'Set properties and display About form
    About.Application = "Jot"
    About.Heading = _
        "Microsoft Visual Basic 5.0 Developer's Workshop"
    About.Copyright = "1997 John Clark Craig and Jeff Webb"
    About.Display
End Sub

Private Sub mnuExit_Click()
    Unload Me
End Sub

Private Sub mnuContents_Click()
    cdlOne.HelpFile = App.Path & "\..\..\Help\Mvbdw.hlp"
    cdlOne.HelpCommand = cdlHelpContents
    cdlOne.ShowHelp
End Sub
```

(continued)

611

Source Code for JOT.FRM *continued*

```vb
Private Sub mnuSearch_Click()
    cdlOne.HelpFile = App.Path & "\..\..\Help\Mvbdw.hlp"
    cdlOne.HelpCommand = cdlHelpPartialKey
    cdlOne.ShowHelp
End Sub

Private Sub LoadNotes()
    Dim db As Database
    Dim rs As Recordset
    'Open database of previous notes
    On Error Resume Next
    Set db = Workspaces(0).OpenDatabase("Jot.mdb")
    'If database doesn't exist, nothing to display
    If Err Then Exit Sub
    On Error GoTo 0
    'Open table of notes
    Set rs = db.OpenRecordset("JotTable")
    'RecordCount will be 1 if there are any records
    If rs.RecordCount Then
        'Create note window for each note
        Do Until rs.EOF
            MakeNewNote Format(rs!JotDateTime, _
                "General Date"), rs!JotNote
            rs.MoveNext
        Loop
    End If
    'Empty database table for now
    db.Execute "Delete * from JotTable"
    'Close recordset and database
    rs.Close
    db.Close
End Sub

Private Sub MakeNewNote(sdtDateTime As String, sNote As String)
    'Create new copy of Note form
    Dim newNote As New frmNote
    'Set caption and note contents
    newNote.rtfNote.Text = sNote
    newNote.Caption = sdtDateTime
    'Display new Note form
    newNote.Show
End Sub
```

(continued)

Source Code for JOT.FRM *continued*

```
Private Sub tlbToolBar_ButtonClick(ByVal Button As ComctlLib.Button)
    Select Case Button.Key
    Case "New"
        MakeNewNote Format(Now, "General Date"), ""
    Case "Delete"
        Unload ActiveForm
    Case "Cascade"
        frmJot.Arrange vbCascade
    Case "TileVertically"
        frmJot.Arrange vbTileVertical
    Case "TileHorizontally"
        frmJot.Arrange vbTileHorizontal
    Case "ArrangeIcons"
        frmJot.Arrange vbArrangeIcons
    Case Else
    End Select
End Sub
```

SPLASH.FRM

This borderless form displays the Jot logo in the center of the main Jot form, as explained previously. The form contains one Image control, which you can load at design time using the JOT.BMP bitmap image file (found on the companion CD-ROM). Figure 30-15 shows the Splash form during development. Notice that the form's border is not visible because the BorderStyle property is set to *0 - None.*

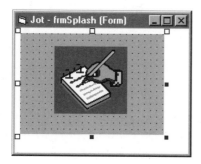

Figure 30-15.
The Splash form during development.

To create this form, position an Image control on a blank form and set the nondefault settings for the form and control as shown on the following page.

613

SPLASH.FRM Objects and Property Settings

Property	Value
Form	
Name	*frmSplash*
Caption	*frmSplash*
BorderStyle	*0 - None*
MDIChild	*True*
ShowInTaskBar	*False*
Image	
Name	*imgSplash*
Picture	*JOT.BMP*

The code for this form is contained in the Form_Load event procedure. When the form loads, the Image control is moved to the upper-left corner of the form and the form is sized to the dimensions of the Image control.

Source Code for SPLASH.FRM

```
Option Explicit

Private Sub Form_Load()
    'Move image to upper-left corner
    imgSplash.Move 0, 0
    'Size this form to size of splash image
    Width = imgSplash.Width
    Height = imgSplash.Height
End Sub
```

NOTE.FRM

The Note form is created once during development and duplicated as needed at runtime. Each copy of this form holds a single user-edited note. I chose to use a RichTextBox control for the actual note-editing control on the Note form, but a TextBox control would work well too. If you want to enhance the Jot application, the RichTextBox control offers more formatting capabilities.

Figure 30-16 shows the Note form during development with a single RichTextBox control.

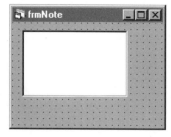

Figure 30-16.
The Note form during development.

To create this form, position a RichTextBox control on a blank form, set the nondefault settings for the form and control, and enter the source code lines as shown.

NOTE.FRM Objects and Property Settings

Property	Value
Form	
Name	*frmNote*
Caption	*frmNote*
KeyPreview	*True*
MDIChild	*True*
RichTextBox	
Name	*rtfNote*
ScrollBars	*3 - rtfBoth*

Source Code for NOTE.FRM

```
Option Explicit

Private Sub Form_KeyDown(KeyCode As Integer, Shift As Integer)
    'Update date and time in caption with hot key Ctrl-T
    If KeyCode = 84 And Shift = 2 Then
        Me.Caption = Format(Now, "General Date")
    End If
End Sub
```

(continued)

Source Code for NOTE.FRM *continued*

```
Private Sub Form_Resize()
    rtfNote.Move 0, 0, ScaleWidth, ScaleHeight
End Sub

Private Sub Form_Unload(Cancel As Integer)
    Dim db As Database
    Dim rs As Recordset
    Dim td As TableDef
    Dim fd As Field
    Dim vErrorNumber As Variant
    Dim dtDateTime As Date
    Dim sNote As String
    'bSaveFlag means save this note
    If frmJot.bSaveFlag = False Then Exit Sub
    'Open database to save this note
    On Error Resume Next
    Set db = Workspaces(0).OpenDatabase("Jot.mdb")
    vErrorNumber = Err
    On Error GoTo 0
    'Create database if it does not already exist
    If vErrorNumber Then
        'Create empty database
        Set db = Workspaces(0).CreateDatabase( _
            "Jot.mdb", dbLangGeneral)
        'Create table
        Set td = db.CreateTableDef("JotTable")
        'Create field
        Set fd = td.CreateField("JotDateTime", dbDate)
        'Add new field to table's Fields collection
        td.Fields.Append fd
        'Create second field
        Set fd = td.CreateField("JotNote", dbMemo)
        'Add it to the table
        td.Fields.Append fd
        'Add new table to TableDefs collection
        db.TableDefs.Append td
        'New database is now open
    End If
    'Get working recordset
    Set rs = db.OpenRecordset("JotTable", dbOpenTable)
    'Add new record
    rs.AddNew
    'Prepare data for placing in record
    dtDateTime = Me.Caption
```

(continued)

Source Code for NOTE.FRM *continued*

```
      sNote = Me.rtfNote.Text
      If sNote = "" Then sNote = " "
      'Load fields in new record
      rs!JotDateTime = dtDateTime
      rs!JotNote = sNote
      'Be sure database is updated
      rs.Update
      'Close recordset and database
      rs.Close
      db.Close
  End Sub
```

Testing the Jot Application

To test the Jot application, you'll need to set a reference to the Microsoft DAO 3.5 Object Library in the References dialog box. Also, in the Project Properties dialog box, set the Startup Object property to *frmJot*. Although Jot is a simple program, it provides a solid foundation for creating your own MDI applications.

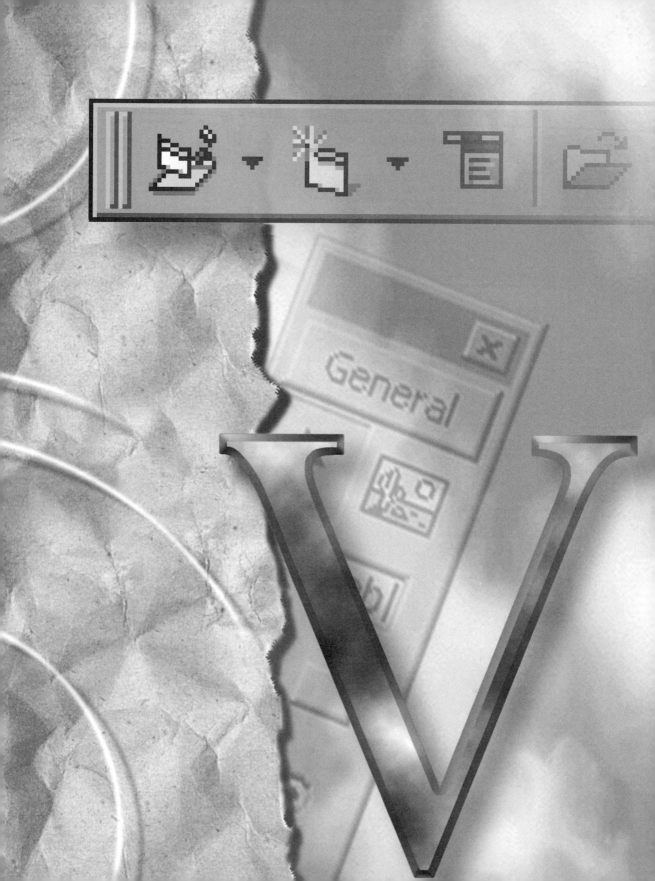

CHAPTER THIRTY-ONE

Utilities

It can be extremely easy to create a very useful little utility in Visual Basic. Sometimes such utilities are useful tools that can help you during the development of other Visual Basic applications, and sometimes they're just good ways to learn more about Visual Basic programming in general. This chapter presents three utilities: one that lets you experiment with the mouse pointer, one that lets you quickly view or listen to multimedia files anywhere on your system, and even one that tells you today's windchill index.

The MousePtr Application

The MousePtr application is a handy utility you can use to quickly review any of the 16 standard mouse pointers and to load and view any icon file as a mouse pointer.

Figure 31-1 on the following page shows the MousePtr form at runtime. When you select a mouse pointer option, the mouse pointer changes to reflect your choice. To use an icon as a mouse pointer, select the last setting, *99 - Custom Icon*. The first time you select this option, the Select An Icon File dialog box appears. This dialog box allows you to choose the icon to be displayed. Subsequent selection of the *99 - CustomIcon* setting displays the same custom icon. To change the icon that is displayed, click the Select Icon button and choose a different icon in the Select An Icon File dialog box.

I've provided a TextBox control as a learning tool and a memory aid. Selecting the *0 - Default* or *1 - Arrow* setting appears to display the same standard arrow. You'll see the difference in the way these mouse pointers behave when you move them across the face of the TextBox control. The default mouse pointer changes to an I-beam when it's located over editable text in a text box, as shown in Figure 31-1, whereas the arrow mouse pointer remains an arrow no matter which controls it passes over.

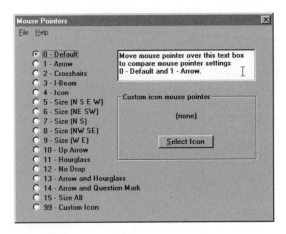

Figure 31-1.
The MousePtr form in action.

Figure 31-2 shows the EARTH.ICO icon as a mouse pointer. You'll find this icon and many others in the ICONS directory on the Visual Basic CD-ROM. If you plan to use several icon files as custom mouse pointers in an application, you might want to store them in a resource file, as described in Chapter 24, "Project Development."

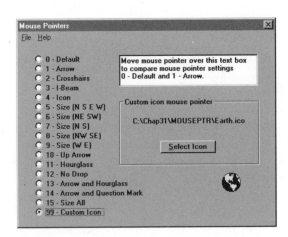

Figure 31-2.
Using the EARTH.ICO icon as an interesting mouse pointer.

As shown in the project list in Figure 31-3, this project contains two files. The About form displays the standard About dialog box for this application.

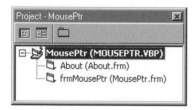

Figure 31-3.
The MousePtr project list.

MOUSEPTR.FRM

The MousePtr form displays an array of option buttons you can click to select a mouse pointer. The Index property of each option button corresponds to the value assigned to the form's MousePointer property, which displays the type of mouse pointer. These numbers range from 0 through 15, with a big jump to 99 for the special case in which an icon file is loaded as a user-defined (custom) mouse pointer. If you build this form manually, be sure to set the last option button's Index property to *99*.

Figure 31-4 shows the MousePtr form during development.

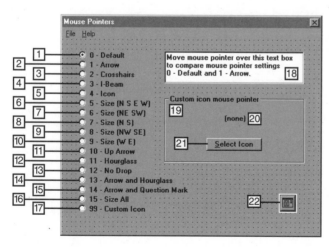

Figure 31-4.
The MousePtr form during development.

To create this form, use the following tables and source code to add the appropriate controls, set any nondefault properties as indicated, and enter the source code lines as shown.

MOUSEPTR.FRM Menu Design Window Entries

Caption	Name	Indentation	Enabled
&File	mnuFile	0	True
&New	mnuNew	1	False
&Open...	mnuOpen	1	False
&Save	mnuSave	1	False
Save &As...	mnuSaveAs	1	False
-	mnuFileDash1	1	True
E&xit	mnuExit	1	True
&Help	mnuHelp	0	True
&Contents	mnuContents	1	True
&Search for Help on...	mnuSearch	1	True
-	mnuHelpDash1	1	True
&About...	mnuAbout	1	True

MOUSEPTR.FRM Objects and Property Settings

ID No.*	Property	Value
Form		
	Name	frmMousePtr
	Caption	Mouse Pointers
	BorderStyle	3 - Fixed Dialog
OptionButton		
1	Name	optMousePtr
	Caption	0 - Default
	Index	0

* The number in the ID No. column corresponds to the number in Figure 31-4 that identifies the location of the object on the form.

(continued)

MOUSEPTR.FRM Objects and Property Settings *continued*

ID No.	Property	Value
OptionButton		
2	Name	*optMousePtr*
	Caption	*1 - Arrow*
	Index	*1*
OptionButton		
3	Name	*optMousePtr*
	Caption	*2 - Crosshairs*
	Index	*2*
OptionButton		
4	Name	*optMousePtr*
	Caption	*3 - I-Beam*
	Index	*3*
OptionButton		
5	Name	*optMousePtr*
	Caption	*4 - Icon*
	Index	*4*
OptionButton		
6	Name	*optMousePtr*
	Caption	*5 - Size (N S E W)*
	Index	*5*
OptionButton		
7	Name	*optMousePtr*
	Caption	*6 - Size (NE SW)*
	Index	*6*
OptionButton		
8	Name	*optMousePtr*
	Caption	*7 - Size (N S)*
	Index	*7*
OptionButton		
9	Name	*optMousePtr*
	Caption	*8 - Size (NW SE)*
	Index	*8*

(continued)

MOUSEPTR.FRM Objects and Property Settings *continued*

ID No.	Property	Value
OptionButton		
10	Name	*optMousePtr*
	Caption	*9 - Size (W E)*
	Index	*9*
OptionButton		
11	Name	*optMousePtr*
	Caption	*10 - Up Arrow*
	Index	*10*
OptionButton		
12	Name	*optMousePtr*
	Caption	*11 - Hourglass*
	Index	*11*
OptionButton		
13	Name	*optMousePtr*
	Caption	*12 - No Drop*
	Index	*12*
OptionButton		
14	Name	*optMousePtr*
	Caption	*13 - Arrow and Hourglass*
	Index	*13*
OptionButton		
15	Name	*optMousePtr*
	Caption	*14 - Arrow and Question Mark*
	Index	*14*
OptionButton		
16	Name	*optMousePtr*
	Caption	*15 - Size All*
	Index	*15*
OptionButton		
17	Name	*optMousePtr*
	Caption	*99 - Custom Icon*
	Index	*99*

(continued)

MOUSEPTR.FRM Objects and Property Settings *continued*

ID No.	Property	Value
TextBox		
18	Name	*txtTestArea*
	Text	*Move mouse pointer over this text box to compare mouse pointer settings 0 - Default and 1 - Arrow.*
	Multiline	*True*
Frame		
19	Name	*fraSelect*
	Caption	*Custom icon mouse pointer*
Label		
20	Name	*lblIcon*
	Caption	*(none)*
CommandButton		
21	Name	*cmdSelect*
	Caption	*&Select Icon*
CommonDialog		
22	Name	*cdlOne*

Source Code for MOUSEPTR.FRM

```
Option Explicit

Private Sub cmdSelect_Click()
    'Prompt user for database filename
    cdlOne.DialogTitle = "Select an Icon File"
    cdlOne.Filter = "Icon(*.ico)|*.ico"
    cdlOne.CancelError = True
    'Check for Cancel button click
    On Error Resume Next
    cdlOne.ShowOpen
    If Err <> cdlCancel Then
        'Load icon as mouse pointer
        frmMousePtr.MouseIcon = LoadPicture(cdlOne.filename)
        'Display current icon path
```

(continued)

Source Code for MOUSEPTR.FRM *continued*

```
            lblIcon.Caption = cdlOne.filename
            'Select mouse pointer type 99
            optMousePtr(99).SetFocus
        End If
    End Sub

    Private Sub Form_Load()
        'Center this form
        Left = (Screen.Width - Width) \ 2
        Top = (Screen.Height - Height) \ 2
        'Move focus off text box and onto option buttons
        Show
        optMousePtr(0).SetFocus
    End Sub

    Private Sub optMousePtr_Click(Index As Integer)
        'Set selected mouse pointer
        frmMousePtr.MousePointer = Index
        'Open dialog box if no icon file previously specified
        If Index = 99 And lblIcon = "(none)" Then
            cmdSelect_Click
        End If
    End Sub

    Private Sub mnuAbout_Click()
        'Set properties
        About.Application = "MousePtr"
        About.Heading = "Microsoft Visual Basic 5.0 Developer's Workshop"
        About.Copyright = "1997 John Clark Craig and Jeff Webb"
        About.Display
    End Sub

    Private Sub mnuExit_Click()
        Unload Me
    End Sub

    Private Sub mnuContents_Click()
        cdlOne.HelpFile = App.Path & "\..\..\Help\Mvbdw.hlp"
        cdlOne.HelpCommand = cdlHelpContents
        cdlOne.ShowHelp
    End Sub

    Private Sub mnuSearch_Click()
        cdlOne.HelpFile = App.Path & "\..\..\Help\Mvbdw.hlp"
        cdlOne.HelpCommand = cdlHelpPartialKey
        cdlOne.ShowHelp
    End Sub
```

The ShowTell Application

The ShowTell application is simple in its design, yet it provides a handy utility for quickly reviewing many types of image files (bitmap, icon, JPG, GIF, and Windows metafile), listening to sound files (WAV), or viewing video clips (AVI and MPG).

The startup form, *frmShowTell*, provides a button for each type of image or multimedia file. The various types of files fall into two broad categories: those that provide a static picture or image that can be loaded into an Image control, and those that are more dynamic and require activation using the mciExecute multimedia API function. I've set up the application to handle the differences in the types of files automatically.

Figure 31-5 shows the startup form at runtime.

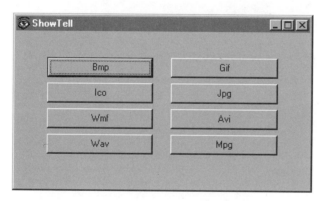

Figure 31-5.
The ShowTell application startup form.

When one of the buttons is clicked, a CommonDialog control is used to display an open dialog box that lets you choose a file of the indicated type located anywhere on your system. Static images are displayed on a second form, *frmImage*, and dynamic multimedia files are played using an API function call. Immediately after the user closes the displayed image, or when a sound or video clip automatically finishes playing, the open dialog box reappears, allowing the user to select another file of the same type. To close the dialog box and return to the main form, click the Cancel button instead of selecting a file.

In Figure 31-6 on the following page, a sample JPG file is displayed, and in Figure 31-7 a sample AVI file is displayed.

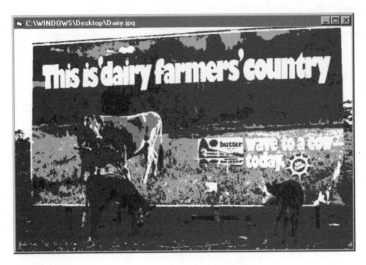

Figure 31-6.
The ShowTell application displaying a JPG file.

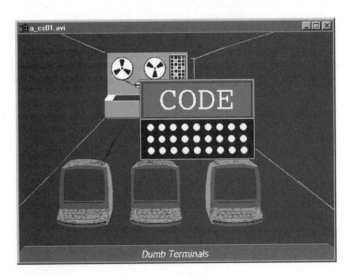

Figure 31-7.
The ShowTell application displaying a video clip (AVI).

As shown in Figure 31-8, the ShowTell project consists of two forms.

Figure 31-8.
The ShowTell project list.

SHOWTELL.FRM

As mentioned, the ShowTell form uses a CommonDialog control to display an open dialog box that allows the user to select a file to be displayed or played. While the open dialog box is visible and the selected image or multimedia file is displayed, the ShowTell form is hidden. When static images are displayed, the ShowTell form stays hidden until the image is closed by the user, but when multimedia files are played, the ShowTell program displays the open dialog box as soon as the multimedia file has started.

Figure 31-9 shows the ShowTell form during development. This form contains eight command buttons and one CommonDialog control.

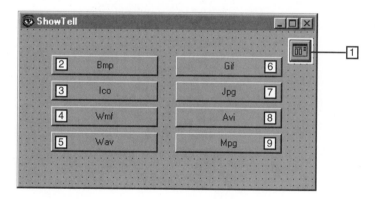

Figure 31-9.
The ShowTell form during development.

To create the ShowTell form, use the table and source code on the following pages to add the appropriate controls, set any nondefault properties as indicated, and enter the source code lines as shown.

SHOWTELL.FRM Objects and Property Settings

ID No.*	Property	Value
Form		
	Name	*frmShowTell*
	Caption	*ShowTell*
	Icon	*Eye.ico*
Common Dialog		
1	Name	*cdlOne*
CommandButton		
2	Name	*cmdShow*
	Caption	*Bmp*
	Index	*0*
CommandButton		
3	Name	*cmdShow*
	Caption	*Ico*
	Index	*1*
CommandButton		
4	Name	*cmdShow*
	Caption	*Wmf*
	Index	*2*
CommandButton		
5	Name	*cmdShow*
	Caption	*Wav*
	Index	*3*
CommandButton		
6	Name	*cmdShow*
	Caption	*Gif*
	Index	*4*

* The number in the ID No. column corresponds to the number in Figure 31-9 that identifies the location of the object on the form.

(continued)

SHOWTELL.FRM Objects and Property Settings *continued*

ID No.	Property	Value
CommandButton		
7	Name	*cmdShow*
	Caption	*Jpg*
	Index	*5*
CommandButton		
8	Name	*cmdShow*
	Caption	*Avi*
	Index	*6*
CommandButton		
9	Name	*cmdShow*
	Caption	*Mpg*
	Index	*7*

Source Code for SHOWTELL.FRM

```
Option Explicit

Private Declare Function mciExecute _
Lib "winmm.dll" ( _
    ByVal lpstrCommand As String _
) As Long

Private Sub Form_Load()
    'Center this form on screen
    Move (Screen.Width - Width) \ 2, _
        (Screen.Height - Height) \ 2
End Sub

Private Sub cmdShow_Click(Index As Integer)
    Me.Hide
    Select Case Index
    Case 0
        ShowMedia "bmp"
    Case 1
        ShowMedia "ico"
```

(continued)

Source Code for SHOWTELL.FRM *continued*

```
    Case 2
        ShowMedia "wmf"
    Case 3
        PlayMedia "wav"
    Case 4
        ShowMedia "gif"
    Case 5
        ShowMedia "jpg"
    Case 6
        PlayMedia "avi"
    Case 7
        PlayMedia "mpg"
    End Select
    Me.Show
End Sub

Private Sub PlayMedia(sFileExt As String)
    'Process multimedia files
    Dim sFilter As String
    Dim sFile As String
    Dim nX As Long
    sFilter = "*." & sFileExt & "|*." & sFileExt
    Do
        sFile = GetFileName(sFilter)
        If sFile = "" Then Exit Do
        nX = mciExecute("Play " & sFile)
    Loop
End Sub

Private Sub ShowMedia(sFileExt As String)
    'Process static images
    Dim sFilter As String
    Dim sFile As String
    Dim nX As Long
    sFilter = "*." & sFileExt & "|*." & sFileExt
    Do
        sFile = GetFileName(sFilter)
        If sFile = "" Then Exit Do
        frmImage.Display sFile
    Loop
End Sub

Private Function GetFileName(sFilter As String) As String
    'Use CommonDialog control to display a dialog box that allows
    'user to select media file
```

(continued)

Source Code for SHOWTELL.FRM *continued*

```
    With cdlOne
        .DialogTitle = "ShowTell"
        .Flags = cdlOFNHideReadOnly
        .Filter = sFilter
        .filename = ""
        .CancelError = True
        On Error Resume Next
        .ShowOpen
        On Error GoTo 0
        GetFileName = .filename
    End With
End Function
```

FRMIMAGE.FRM

The *frmImage* form loads and displays an image from a file. The form's code comprises just one public method, Display, which is responsible for handling all aspects of the display of the graphics image. Display's one parameter is the path and filename of the file to be loaded and displayed. This filename is automatically placed in the form's Caption property for easy reference. The image is then loaded from the file, and the form is sized and moved to display the full image at the center of the screen.

To create this form, add a second form to your ShowTell project and set its Name property to *frmImage*. Add an Image control named *imgOne*, and enter the following code on the form:

Source Code for FRMIMAGE.FRM

```
Option Explicit

Public Sub Display(sFileName As String)
    Dim nWedge As Long
    Dim nHedge As Long
    Me.Caption = sFileName
    With imgOne
        .Picture = LoadPicture(sFileName)
        .Move 0, 0
        nWedge = Width - ScaleWidth
        nHedge = Height - ScaleHeight
        Me.Move (Screen.Width - (.Width + nWedge)) \ 2, _
            (Screen.Height - (.Height + nHedge)) \ 2, _
            .Width + nWedge, .Height + nHedge
    End With
    Me.Show vbModal
End Sub
```

The WindChil Application

The WindChil application uses the same equation the National Weather Service uses to calculate the effective windchill given the actual air temperature and the wind speed. (If the scientific and technical aspects defining the windchill factor interest you, search for the keywords *wind chill* on the World Wide Web. I've found several sites with excellent explanations.)

This application demonstrates the Slider control, which I've set up to let the user select the current air temperature and wind speed. Figure 31-10 shows the WindChil form in action: the two sliders are set to a wind speed of 17 miles per hour and a temperature of 32 degrees Fahrenheit.

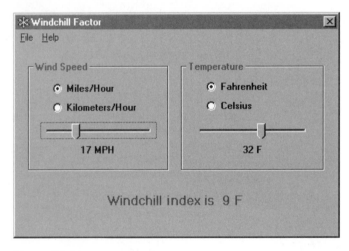

Figure 31-10.
The WindChil form in action.

This application has some advantages over the standard charts you'll find posted on the World Wide Web and elsewhere. In my application, the temperature and wind speed can be set to any values in the ranges provided by the Slider controls, whereas the charts round off values to the nearest 5 or 10 degrees or miles per hour. The biggest advantage, however, is that with the addition of a few option buttons, I've made it easy to use metric values if you want. You have your choice of temperature scales (Fahrenheit or Celsius) and your choice of wind speed units (miles per hour or kilometers per hour). When you click an option button, the current settings of the sliders are retained and the numbers are converted to the alternative units. Figure 31-11 shows the same settings as in Figure 31-10, here converted to metric units.

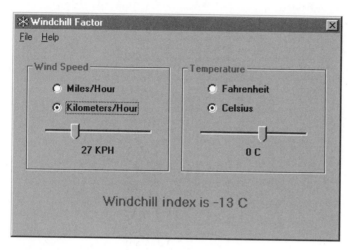

Figure 31-11.
The WindChil form, showing values in metric units.

WINDCHIL.FRM

The Min and Max properties of the two sliders are set to the full range of accuracy for the windchill equation: 5 through 50 miles per hour for wind speed, and –50 through +90 degrees Fahrenheit for temperature. Values outside these ranges are invalid. The use of sliders, instead of text box data entry fields, simplifies the process of validating the numbers a user enters. If you use a Slider control, there's no way a user can enter an invalid wind speed or temperature value and no code is needed to check and enforce the entered values. In the "WINDCHIL.FRM Objects and Property Settings" table beginning on page 637, notice that the LargeChange property of the Slider controls is set to *1*. This allows the user to click the slider at either side of the slider's knob and adjust the setting by 1 degree or 1 unit of wind speed. This technique works well for the range of values selected.

NOTE: I don't use Variant data types routinely, mostly because explicit data typing generally results in slightly faster code and more predictable intermediate calculation results, but in this program I decided to dimension most of the numeric variables as Variants as an experiment. It worked well. The program runs plenty fast enough, and the displayed results exactly match the various wind-chill charts I found on the Internet. Some people argue that Variants are actually easier to program than explicit variable types. I think this depends on the particular program and its design. Automatic conversions between strings and numbers can be very tricky, for instance, and I've seen some mighty strange and hard-to-track-down results from unexpected automatic type conversions. On the other hand, in some applications, such as WindChill, Variants work just great.

Figure 31-12 shows the WindChil form during development. I've set the ForeColor property of some of the text labels to red or blue to brighten the appearance of the form. You might prefer the default black ForeColor setting for your labels. You can experiment with the appearance of this form without affecting its calculations.

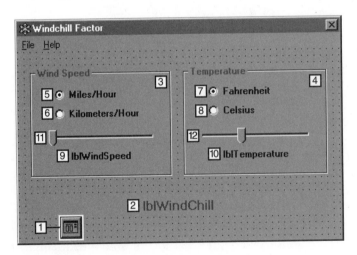

Figure 31-12.
The WindChil form during development.

To create this form, use the following tables and source code to add the appropriate controls, set any nondefault properties as indicated, and enter the source code lines as shown.

WINDCHIL.FRM Menu Design Window Entries

Caption	Name	Indentation	Enabled
&File	mnuFile	0	True
&New	mnuNew	1	False
&Open...	mnuOpen	1	False
&Save	mnuSave	1	False
Save &As...	mnuSaveAs	1	False
-	mnuFileDash1	1	True
E&xit	mnuExit	1	True
&Help	mnuHelp	0	True
&Contents	mnuContents	1	True
&Search for Help on...	mnuSearch	1	True
-	mnuHelpDash1	1	True
&About...	mnuAbout	1	True

WINDCHIL.FRM Objects and Property Settings

ID No.*	Property	Value
Form		
	Name	frmWindChill
	Caption	Windchill Factor
	BorderStyle	3 - Fixed Dialog
	Icon	Snow.ico
CommonDialog		
1	Name	cdlOne
Label		
2	Name	lblWindChill
	Alignment	2 - Center
	Font	MS Sans Serif Bold 12
	ForeColor	&H00FF0000&

*   The number in the ID No. column corresponds to the number in Figure 31-12 that
identifies the location of the object on the form.

(continued)

WINDCHIL.FRM Objects and Property Settings *continued*

ID No.	Property	Value
Frame		
3	Name	*fraWindSpeed*
	Caption	*Wind Speed*
	ForeColor	*&H000000FF&*
Frame		
4	Name	*fraTemperature*
	Caption	*Temperature*
	ForeColor	*&H000000FF&*
OptionButton		
5	Name	*optMPH*
	Caption	*Miles/Hour*
	Value	*True*
OptionButton		
6	Name	*optKPH*
	Caption	*Kilometers/Hour*
OptionButton		
7	Name	*optFahrenheit*
	Caption	*Fahrenheit*
	Value	*True*
OptionButton		
8	Name	*optCelsius*
	Caption	*Celsius*
Label		
9	Name	*lblWindSpeed*
	Alignment	*2 - Center*
Label		
10	Name	*lblTemperature*
	Alignment	*2 - Center*

(continued)

WINDCHIL.FRM Objects and Property Settings *continued*

ID No.	Property	Value
Slider		
11	Name	*hslWindSpeed*
	LargeChange	*1*
	Max	*50*
	Min	*5*
Slider		
12	Name	*hslTemperature*
	LargeChange	*1*
	Max	*90*
	Min	*−50*

Source Code for WINDCHIL.FRM

```
Option Explicit

Private Sub mnuAbout_Click()
    'Set properties
    With About
        .Application = "WindChil"
        .Heading = "Microsoft Visual Basic 5.0 Developer's Workshop"
        .Copyright = "1997 John Clark Craig and Jeff Webb"
        .Display
    End With
End Sub

Private Sub mnuExit_Click()
    Unload Me
End Sub

Private Sub mnuContents_Click()
    With cdlOne
        .HelpFile = App.Path & "\..\..\Help\Mvbdw.hlp"
        .HelpCommand = cdlHelpContents
        .ShowHelp
    End With
End Sub
```

(continued)

Source Code for WINDCHIL.FRM *continued*

```vb
Private Sub mnuSearch_Click()
    With cdlOne
        .HelpFile = App.Path & "\..\..\Help\Mvbdw.hlp"
        .HelpCommand = cdlHelpPartialKey
        .ShowHelp
    End With
End Sub

Private Function Celsius(vF)
    'Convert Fahrenheit to Celsius
    Celsius = (vF + 40) * 5 / 9 - 40
End Function

Private Sub ChillOut()
    Dim vWind
    Dim vTemp
    Dim vChill
    Dim sY As String
    'Get working values from scrollbars
    vWind = hslWindSpeed.Value
    vTemp = hslTemperature.Value
    'Convert to MPH if KPH selected
    If optKPH.Value = True Then
        vWind = Mph(vWind)
    End If
    'Convert to Fahrenheit if Celsius selected
    If optCelsius.Value = True Then
        vTemp = Fahrenheit(vTemp)
    End If
    'Calculate windchill index
    vChill = Int(0.0817 * (Sqr(vWind) * 3.71 + _
        5.81 - 0.25 * vWind) * (vTemp - 91.4) + 91.4)
    'Convert back to Celsius if selected
    If optCelsius.Value = True Then
        vChill = Celsius(vChill)
    End If
    'Display windchill index
    sY = "Windchill index is " & Str$(CInt(vChill))
    If optFahrenheit.Value = True Then
        lblWindChill.Caption = sY & " F"
    Else
        lblWindChill.Caption = sY & " C"
    End If
End Sub
```

(continued)

Source Code for WINDCHIL.FRM *continued*

```
Private Sub cmdCancel_Click()
    'End if Cancel button clicked
    Unload frmWindChill
End Sub

Private Function Fahrenheit(vC)
    'Convert Celsius to Fahrenheit
    Fahrenheit = (vC + 40) * 9 / 5 - 40
End Function

Private Sub Form_Load()
    'Force scrollbars to update
    hslWindSpeed_Change
    hslTemperature_Change
End Sub

Private Sub hslTemperature_Change()
    Dim vTmp
    'Get temperature
    vTmp = hslTemperature.Value
    'Display using selected units
    If optCelsius.Value = True Then
        lblTemperature.Caption = vTmp & " C"
    Else
        lblTemperature.Caption = vTmp & " F"
    End If
    'Calculate windchill index
    ChillOut
End Sub

Private Sub hslTemperature_Scroll()
    'Update when slider knob moves
    hslTemperature_Change
End Sub

Private Sub hslWindSpeed_Change()
    Dim vTmp
    'Get wind speed
    vTmp = hslWindSpeed.Value
    'Display using selected units
    If optKPH.Value = True Then
        lblWindSpeed.Caption = vTmp & " KPH"
    Else
```

(continued)

Source Code for WINDCHIL.FRM *continued*

```vb
        lblWindSpeed.Caption = vTmp & " MPH"
    End If
    'Calculate windchill index
    ChillOut
End Sub

Private Sub hslWindSpeed_Scroll()
    'Update when slider knob moves
    hslWindSpeed_Change
End Sub

Private Function Kph(vMph)
    'Convert MPH to KPH
    Kph = vMph * 1.609344
End Function

Private Function Mph(vKph)
    'Convert KPH to MPH
    Mph = vKph / 1.609344
End Function

Private Sub optCelsius_Click()
    Dim vC
    'Convert current temperature to Celsius
    vC = Celsius(hslTemperature.Value)
    If vC < -45 Then vC = -45
    'Reset scrollbar for Celsius
    hslTemperature.Min = -45
    hslTemperature.Max = 32
    hslTemperature.Value = CInt(vC)
    hslTemperature_Change
End Sub

Private Sub optFahrenheit_Click()
    Dim vF
    'Convert current temperature to Fahrenheit
    vF = Fahrenheit(hslTemperature.Value)
    If vF < -50 Then vF = -50
    'Reset scrollbar for Fahrenheit
    hslTemperature.Min = -50
    hslTemperature.Max = 90
    hslTemperature.Value = CInt(vF)
    hslTemperature_Change
End Sub
```

(continued)

Source Code for WINDCHIL.FRM *continued*

```
Private Sub optKPH_Click()
    Dim vK
    'Convert current wind speed to KPH
    vK = Kph(hslWindSpeed.Value)
    'Reset scrollbar for KPH
    hslWindSpeed.Min = 8
    hslWindSpeed.Max = 80
    hslWindSpeed.Value = vK
    hslWindSpeed_Change
End Sub

Private Sub optMPH_Click()
    Dim vM
    'Convert current wind speed to MPH
    vM = Mph(hslWindSpeed.Value)
    'Reset scrollbar for MPH
    hslWindSpeed.Min = 5
    hslWindSpeed.Max = 50
    hslWindSpeed.Value = vM
    hslWindSpeed_Change
End Sub
```

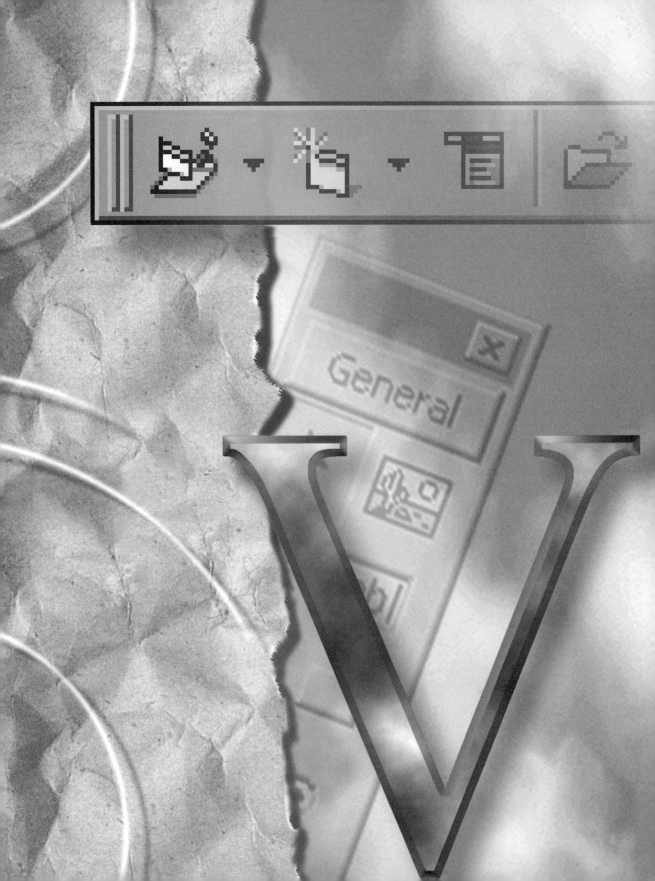

CHAPTER THIRTY TWO

Advanced Applications

This chapter covers a few advanced programming techniques that can enhance your Visual Basic development productivity. The Messages application
demonstrates one way you can use commands embedded in an externally
edited text file to control an application's behavior. The Secret application
pieces together several forms and techniques presented earlier in this book
to create a file encryption program. BitPack provides a working demonstration of a C-language dynamic link library (DLL) that enhances speed and
utility, and the Dialogs application demonstrates several creative techniques
that can enhance your Visual Basic forms.

The Messages Application

You can create your own programming, or scripting, language to perform
specific tasks. I've created the Messages application as a simple example. This
application displays a series of text boxes containing messages on the screen.
It accomplishes this by declaring and using Message objects. The Message objects are defined by the class module MSG.CLS and its associated MSG.FRM file.

A Message object has a FileName property, which is set to the name of
a specially formatted text file with the extension MES (a message file).
(I describe the syntax of these message files below.) The MSG.CLS and
MSG.FRM files work together to display messages from the message file. I've
set up two special commands that can be typed into the message files to control the appearance and behavior of the displayed messages. I've kept these
commands simple, but it would be easy to expand on the concept presented
here if you want more creative control over the messages displayed.

Message File Syntax

Each message file contains blocks of text to be displayed. Three tilde characters (~~~) mark the start of each text block, and a message file can contain as many text blocks as you want. All messages in the selected message file are displayed sequentially. You can control the display of each message somewhat by including commands on the same line as each block separator.

An example message file helps clarify how this works. Here's the sample MESSAGE.MES file I've provided with this sample application on the companion CD-ROM:

```
MESSAGE.MES

This message file provides a sampling of the
features demonstrated in the Messages application.

Note that all of these lines appearing before
the first text block header will be ignored.


~~~
This is the first text block in the MESSAGE.MES file.
Notice that the display window sizes automatically for
the dimensions of the message.

Close this display window to proceed to the next text
block in this file. Click the Close button in the
upper-right corner of this message.
~~~ .P 10
This message should automatically disappear in 10 seconds.
You may close it manually before then if you want.
~~~ F 2
This message should be in a flashing window, with the
flash rate set to 2 times per second.
~~~ F 5
This message should be in a flashing window, with the
flash rate set to 5 times per second.
~~~ P 20 F 1
This is the last message in this file. The flash rate is 1
time per second, and the message will disappear automatically
in 20 seconds if you don't close it manually before then.
```

This file defines five messages to be displayed sequentially by the Message object when it is activated in the Messages application. The first message is displayed in a nonflashing window and stays displayed until the user closes the window. The second text block's header contains the P command, which indicates that the message is to disappear after being displayed for the specified number of seconds. In this case, the second message disappears (and the next message appears) after a pause of 10 seconds. The third message is controlled by the F command, which sets a flash rate for the display window. The number after the F command is the toggle rate for the flashing—in this case, twice per second. Notice that in the final message of the file, both commands are given; this message will be displayed for 20 seconds, with a flash rate of once per second.

I've provided only the P and F commands, but it would be easy to add others. For example, you might want to add a C command to control the color of the message text. By studying the way these two commands work, you can easily add other commands on your own.

Figure 32-1 shows the first message as it's displayed, and Figure 32-2 shows the third message.

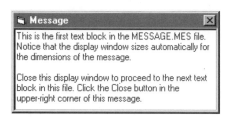

Figure 32-1.
A message displayed by the Messages application.

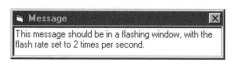

Figure 32-2.
A message window that flashes to catch the user's attention.

Why Use Message Files?

It would be fairly straightforward to embed the messages shown directly in an application's source code. Using external ASCII text files has some advantages, however. For example, to change the displayed messages you simply edit the message file using Notepad, WordPad, or any other text editor. Also, creating multiline text messages in Visual Basic code requires you to concatenate the lines using the *vbCrLf* constant, and making changes to these somewhat messy lines in your application can be tedious. An external message file has the same advantage as a resource file if you're creating applications to distribute internationally. Instead of editing and recompiling the application's source code for each foreign language, you need only change the message file's contents.

Figure 32-3 shows the project list for the Messages application. To add the messaging capabilities to your own applications, add the MSG.CLS file, the MSG.FRM file, and activation code similar to that found in the MESSAGES.FRM demonstration form.

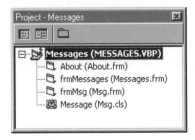

Figure 32-3.
The Messages project list.

MESSAGES.FRM

MESSAGES.FRM is the main startup form for the Messages application. In the source code for this application, you'll notice that a single instance of a Message object, *msgOne*, is declared and manipulated by this form. To sequentially display all messages defined in the MESSAGE.MES file, this form sets the declared Message object's FileName property to the selected file's path and filename and then calls the object's Display method. The rest of the displayed message's appearance is controlled by commands embedded within the message file itself.

I've added a CommonDialog control and a Command button to this form so that you can select any other message file or files you might want to create for experimentation purposes. Figure 32-4 shows the Messages form during development.

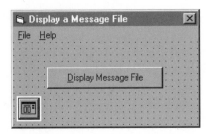

Figure 32-4.
The Messages form during development.

To create this form, use the following tables and source code to add the appropriate controls, set any nondefault properties as indicated, and enter the source code lines as shown.

MESSAGES.FRM Menu Design Window Entries

Caption	Name	Indentation	Enabled
&File	mnuFile	0	True
&New	mnuNew	1	False
&Open...	mnuOpen	1	False
&Save	mnuSave	1	False
Save &As...	mnuSaveAs	1	False
-	mnuFileDash1	1	True
E&xit	mnuExit	1	True
&Help	mnuHelp	0	True
&Contents	mnuContents	1	True
&Search for Help on...	mnuSearch	1	True
-	mnuHelpDash1	1	True
&About...	mnuAbout	1	True

MESSAGES.FRM Objects and Property Settings

Property	Value
Form	
Name	frmMessages
BorderStyle	3 - Fixed Dialog
Caption	Display a Message File
CommandButton	
Name	cmdMessages
Caption	&Display Message File
CommonDialog	
Name	cdlOne

Source Code for MESSAGES.FRM

```
Option Explicit

Private Sub cmdMessages_Click()
    'Declare new Message object
    Dim msgOne As New Message
    'Prompt user for message file (*.MES)
    cdlOne.DialogTitle = "Message Files"
    cdlOne.Flags = cdlOFNHideReadOnly
    cdlOne.Filter = "Messages(*.mes)|*.mes"
    cdlOne.CancelError = True
    On Error Resume Next
    cdlOne.ShowOpen
    'Quit if user canceled or closed dialog box
    If Err Then Exit Sub
    On Error GoTo 0
    'Display message file
    With msgOne
        .FileName = cdlOne.FileName
        .Display
    End With
End Sub

Private Sub Form_Load()
    'Center this form
    Left = (Screen.Width - Width) \ 2
    Top = (Screen.Height - Height) \ 2
End Sub

Private Sub mnuAbout_Click()
    'Set properties
    About.Application = "Messages"
    About.Heading = _
        "Microsoft Visual Basic 5.0 Developer's Workshop"
    About.Copyright = "1997 John Clark Craig and Jeff Webb"
    About.Display
End Sub

Private Sub mnuExit_Click()
    Unload Me
End Sub

Private Sub mnuContents_Click()
    cdlOne.HelpFile = App.Path & "\..\..\Help\Mvbdw.hlp"
```

(continued)

Source Code for MESSAGES.FRM *continued*

```
    cdlOne.HelpCommand = cdlHelpContents
    cdlOne.ShowHelp
End Sub

Private Sub mnuSearch_Click()
    cdlOne.HelpFile = App.Path & "\..\..\Help\Mvbdw.hlp"
    cdlOne.HelpCommand = cdlHelpPartialKey
    cdlOne.ShowHelp
End Sub
```

MSG.CLS

The MSG.CLS class module is the blueprint used to create Message objects. This particular class module requires an associated MSG.FRM file that provides the visual elements of the Message object. If you want to add Message objects to your applications, be sure to add both of these files.

Each Message object provides one property, FileName, which the calling application must set in order to display messages. Set the FileName property to the full path and filename of a selected message file. The only method provided by each Message object is Display, which starts the sequential display of all messages contained in the indicated message file.

There are quite a few lines of code in the Display method. This code interacts with, and controls, the properties and methods of the associated *frmMsg* form. Commands embedded within the given message file are interpreted in the Display method, and the *frmMsg* form is controlled from here to provide the indicated operation.

Source Code for MSG.CLS

```
Option Explicit

'Property that defines message file to be displayed
Public FileName As String

'Method to display message file
Public Sub Display()
    Dim sH As String
    Dim sJ As String
    Dim sA As String
    Dim sB As String
    Dim sC As String
```

(continued)

Source Code for MESSAGES.FRM *continued*

```
        Dim nFilNum As Integer
        Dim lNdx As Long
        Dim lFlashRate As Long
        Dim lPauseTime As Long
        Dim lHeight As Long
        Dim lWidth As Long
        Dim TwTest As Long
        'Get next available file I/O number
        nFilNum = FreeFile
        'Trap error if filename is invalid
        On Error Resume Next
        Open FileName For Input As #nFilNum
        If Err Then
            MsgBox "File not found: " & FileName
            Exit Sub
        End If
        On Error GoTo 0
        'Find start of first text block
        Do Until EOF(nFilNum)
            Line Input #nFilNum, sH
            'Skip lines until three tilde characters found
            If InStr(sH, "~~~") = 1 Then
                sJ = UCase$(sH)
                Exit Do
            End If
        Loop
        'Loop through all text blocks
        Do Until EOF(nFilNum)
            sB = ""
            sH = sJ
            lWidth = 0
            lHeight = 0
            'Load all of current text block
            Do Until EOF(nFilNum)
                Line Input #nFilNum, sA
                'End of block is at start of next one
                If InStr(sA, "~~~") = 1 Then
                    sJ = UCase$(sA)
                    Exit Do
                End If
                'Keep track of widest line of text
                TwTest = frmMsg.TextWidth(sA & "XX")
                If TwTest > lWidth Then lWidth = TwTest
                'Keep track of total height of all lines
```

(continued)

Source Code for MESSAGES.FRM *continued*

```
            lHeight = lHeight + 1
            'Accumulate block of text lines
            If lHeight > 1 Then
                sB = sB & vbCrLf & sA
            Else
                sB = sA
            End If
        Loop
        'Check for flash rate in block header
        lNdx = InStr(sH, "F")
        If lNdx Then
            lFlashRate = Val(Mid$(sH, lNdx + 1))
        Else
            lFlashRate = 0
        End If
        'Check for pause time in block header
        lNdx = InStr(sH, "P")
        If lNdx Then
            lPauseTime = Val(Mid$(sH, lNdx + 1))
        Else
            lPauseTime = 0
        End If
        'Prepare message form's text box
        With frmMsg.txtMsg
            .Text = sB
            .Left = 0
            .Top = 0
            .Width = lWidth
            .Height = (lHeight + 1) * frmMsg.TextHeight("X")
        End With
        'Prepare message form
        With frmMsg
            .Width = .txtMsg.Width + (.Width - .ScaleWidth)
            .Height = .txtMsg.Height + (.Height - .ScaleHeight)
            .Left = (Screen.Width - .Width) \ 2
            .Top = (Screen.Height - .Height) \ 2
            'Set flash and pause properties if given
            If lPauseTime > 0 Then .Pause = lPauseTime
            If lFlashRate > 0 Then .Flash = lFlashRate
        End With
        'Show message and wait until it closes
        frmMsg.Show vbModal
    Loop
End Sub
```

MSG.FRM

The *frmMsg* form is the working partner of the MSG.CLS class module. Together they form the basis for a Message object. Notice that MSG.FRM interacts only with the MSG.CLS module. The main Messages form does not directly set any of the *frmMsg* form's properties, call any of its methods, or in any way directly interact with it. In this way, the *frmMsg* form becomes an integral part of the Message objects defined by the MSG.CLS class module.

MSG.FRM has four controls: two Timer controls, a TextBox control to display the messages, and a dummy command button, which will be explained shortly. Figure 32-5 shows MSG.FRM during the development process.

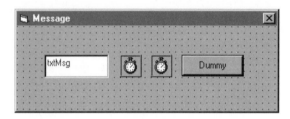

Figure 32-5.
The frmMsg *form during development.*

To create this form, use the following table and source code to add the appropriate controls, set any nondefault properties as indicated, and enter the source code lines as shown.

MSG.FRM Objects and Property Settings

Property	Value
Form	
Name	*frmMsg*
Caption	*Message*
BorderStyle	*3 - Fixed Dialog*
TextBox	
Name	*txtMsg*
ForeColor	*&H00FF0000&*
MultiLine	*True*
Locked	*True*

(continued)

MSG.FRM Objects and Property Settings *continued*

Property	Value
Timer	
Name	*tmrTerminate*
Timer	
Name	*tmrFlash*
CommandButton	
Name	*cmdDummy*
Default	*True*
Caption	*Dummy*

Source Code for MSG.FRM

```
Option Explicit

Private Declare Function FlashWindow _
Lib "user32" ( _
    ByVal hwnd As Long, _
    ByVal bInvert As Long _
) As Long

Private Sub Form_Paint()
    'Remove focus from text box
    cmdDummy.Left = Screen.Width * 2
    cmdDummy.SetFocus
End Sub

Private Sub tmrTerminate_Timer()
    Unload Me
End Sub

Private Sub tmrFlash_Timer()
    'Toggle form flashing
    FlashWindow hwnd, CLng(True)
End Sub

Property Let Flash(PerSecond As Integer)
    'Set and activate form flashing rate
    tmrFlash.Interval = 1000 / PerSecond
    tmrFlash.Enabled = True
End Property
```

(continued)

Source Code for MSG.FRM *continued*

```
Property Let Pause(Seconds As Double)
    'Set and activate auto-unload timing
    tmrTerminate.Interval = 1000 * Seconds
    tmrTerminate.Enabled = True
End Property
```

The FlashWindow API function is called from the tmrFlash_Timer event procedure to toggle the flashing of the MSG.FRM form. The Interval property of this timer determines the flash rate.

The Dummy command button's only purpose is to get the focus, and the flashing cursor, out of the text box while the message is displayed. As this form is painted, the Dummy command button's Left property is set to twice the width of the screen, guaranteeing that the button will be out of sight. By setting the button's Default property to *True*, you ensure that the focus goes with it.

The Flash and Pause properties are not set directly by a calling application. Instead, these properties are set by the MSG.CLS module to control the form's behavior.

The Secret Application

There's a lot of talk about privacy and security nowadays, particularly in reference to the transfer of financial or other proprietary information over the Internet. The Secret application shouldn't be used for critical security situations, but it does provide a modest level of personal privacy for your e-mail or for any file that you'd rather not have others view indiscriminately.

NOTE: The level of security provided by this application is not foolproof, and determined attackers, as the experts call them, could crack messages encrypted with this program. Realistically, though, your messages and files will be secure from the prying eyes of over 99 percent of the population.

To keep this application very simple, and very legal for exporting overseas, I've used a private key technique rather than the sophisticated but slightly messy public key technology. If you use this application to encrypt e-mail, both you and the party at the other end must agree on a password phrase in advance. Any password phrase of reasonable length can be used as the private key, but the password string is hashed by the program to 24 bits of unique key data—well within the 40 bits allowed by the authorities. Visual Basic's random number generator is used as the source of the pseudorandom bytes; it's generally accepted in the cryptography world that this is not a highly secure technique.

Even so, someone would have to be highly motivated to go to the trouble of cracking your Secret messages and files. If you need an extremely secure cipher, go with one of the commercial products on the market. If you just want a tool that will provide reasonable privacy and that's very easy to use, the Secret application will do the trick.

> **NOTE:** A hash of a string is a one-way calculation, kind of like a check sum, that's repeatable but not easily reversible. The same password will always hash to the same result, but given the result of the hash, there's no easy way to determine the original password.

How Does the Secret Application Work?

Here's how: You can select any file to encrypt or decrypt. A small header line is inserted at the beginning of encrypted files to allow Secret to detect whether a selected file is currently encrypted. Before you click either the Encrypt or the Decrypt button, enter a password in the appropriate field or fields. You must enter the same password twice for encryption, but it needs to be entered only once for decryption. This is a commonly used method that requires the user to type the password correctly in each box, thus preventing typographical errors from creeping in. Any mistyping of the password will prevent the file from being encrypted. The encrypted file is saved in a displayable, printable, e-mailable ASCII format, even if the original file contained binary data not suitable for these forms of output.

I've used an interesting technique that causes the message to appear different each time it's encrypted, even if the same password is used. This is accomplished by adding eight pseudorandom "salt" characters to the header line and hashing a combination of these salt characters with the password to form the rest of the header data. These 16 header characters are then used to encrypt the file, resulting in a unique result each time the file is encrypted. The header characters also provide a way to quickly check the accuracy of a password before the file is decrypted. The password and salt characters are hashed and the result is compared with the header line. An incorrect password results in the wrong hash.

Figure 32-6 on the following page shows the Secret application just after a text file named TEST.TXT has been selected and the short password *HAARP* has been entered twice. Because this file is not yet encrypted, the Encrypt button is enabled and the Decrypt button is not. Figure 32-7 shows the interface after the Encrypt button has been clicked; the file is now encrypted. Notice that the Decrypt button is now enabled, the Encrypt button is not enabled, and the second password field is not enabled.

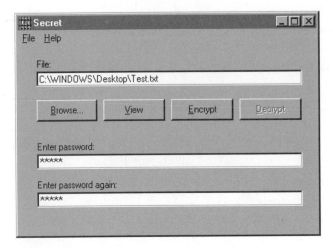

Figure 32-6.
The TEST.TXT file selected to be encrypted by the Secret application.

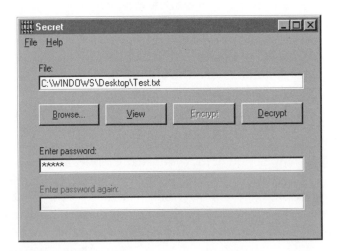

Figure 32-7.
The TEST.TXT file, now in its encrypted state.

Figure 32-8 shows the sample TEST.TXT file before it's encrypted, and Figure 32-9 shows its contents in the encrypted state. Both of these views of the file contents were obtained by clicking the View button. Figure 32-10 on the following page shows the same file after it has been decrypted and then encrypted a second time using the same password. Notice that the results of the two encryptions are entirely different, even though both versions decrypt to the same original file.

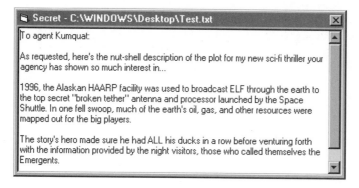

Figure 32-8.
The original TEST.TXT file displayed using the View button.

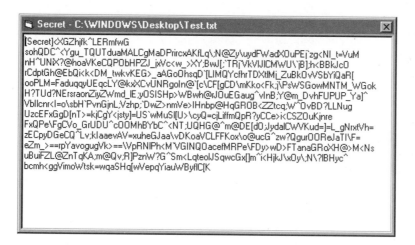

Figure 32-9.
The encrypted TEST.TXT file displayed using the View button.

Figure 32-10.
TEST.TXT encrypted a second time using the same password.

The Secret project comprises four files, as shown in the project list window in Figure 32-11. The CIPHER.CLS class module contains the same cipher class module that was presented in Chapter 16, "Security." The Secret form includes a Hash function that converts any string to a repeatable but unpredictable sequence of eight characters. This hash value is used to verify a user's password before a file is decrypted. The View form is a simple file-contents viewer that displays the contents of a selected file, ciphered or not, to let the user review the file in read-only mode.

Figure 32-11.
The project list for the Secret application.

SECRET.FRM

SECRET.FRM is the main startup form for the Secret application. As shown in Figure 32-12, the form contains a text box for selecting a file to be processed, two text boxes for entering the password, and four command buttons that control all operations on the file. The CommonDialog control is used during the file selection process.

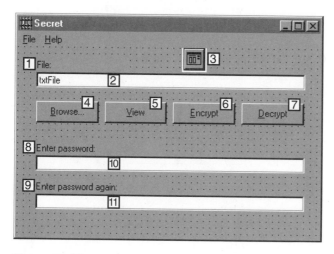

Figure 32-12.
The Secret form during development.

To create this form, use the following tables and source code to add the appropriate controls, set any nondefault properties as indicated, and enter the source code lines as shown.

SECRET.FRM Menu Design Window Entries

Caption	Name	Indentation	Enabled
&File	*mnuFile*	0	*True*
&New	*mnuNew*	1	*False*
&Open...	*mnuOpen*	1	*False*
&Save	*mnuSave*	1	*False*
Save &As...	*mnuSaveAs*	1	*False*

(continued)

SECRET.FRM Menu Design Window Entries *continued*

Caption	Name	Indentation	Enabled
-	*mnuFileDash1*	1	*True*
E&xit	*mnuExit*	1	*True*
&Help	*mnuHelp*	0	*True*
&Contents	*mnuContents*	1	*True*
&Search for Help on…	*mnuSearch*	1	*True*
-	*mnuHelpDash1*	1	*True*
&About…	*mnuAbout*	1	*True*

SECRET.FRM Objects and Property Settings

ID No.*	Property	Value
Form		
	Name	*frmSecret*
	Caption	*Secret*
	Icon	*Secur03.ico*
Label		
1	Name	*lblFile*
	Caption	*File:*
TextBox		
2	Name	*txtFile*
CommonDialog		
3	Name	*cdlOne*
CommandButton		
4	Name	*cmdBrowse*
	Caption	*&Browse…*
CommandButton		
5	Name	*cmdView*
	Caption	*&View*

* The number in the ID No. column corresponds to the number in Figure 32-12 that identifies the location of the object on the form.

(continued)

SECRET.FRM Objects and Property Settings *continued*

ID No.	Property	Value
CommandButton		
6	Name Caption	*cmdEncrypt* *&Encrypt*
CommandButton		
7	Name Caption	*cmdDecrypt* *&Decrypt*
Label		
8	Name Caption	*lblPassword1* *Enter password:*
Label		
9	Name Caption	*lblPassword2* *Enter password again:*
TextBox		
10	Name PasswordChar Text	*txtPassword1* * (blank)
TextBox		
11	Name PasswordChar Text	*txtPassword2* * (blank)

Source Code for SECRET.FRM

```
Option Explicit

Private Sub cmdBrowse_Click()
    'Prompt user for filename
    cdlOne.DialogTitle = "Secret"
    cdlOne.Flags = cdlOFNHideReadOnly
    cdlOne.Filter = "All files (*.*)|*.*"
    cdlOne.CancelError = True
    On Error Resume Next
    cdlOne.ShowOpen
```

(continued)

Source Code for SECRET.FRM *continued*

```
        'Grab filename
        If Err = 0 Then
            txtFile.Text = cdlOne.filename
        End If
        On Error GoTo 0
    End Sub

    Private Sub cmdEncrypt_Click()
        'Make sure both passwords match exactly
        If txtPassword1.Text <> txtPassword2.Text Then
            MsgBox "The two passwords are not the same!", _
                vbExclamation, "Secret"
            Exit Sub
        End If
        'Encrypt file
        MousePointer = vbHourglass
        cmdEncrypt.Enabled = False
        cmdDecrypt.Enabled = False
        cmdView.Enabled = False
        cmdBrowse.Enabled = False
        Refresh
        Encrypt
        txtFile_Change
        MousePointer = vbDefault
    End Sub

    Private Sub cmdDecrypt_Click()
        MousePointer = vbHourglass
        cmdEncrypt.Enabled = False
        cmdDecrypt.Enabled = False
        cmdView.Enabled = False
        cmdBrowse.Enabled = False
        Refresh
        Decrypt
        txtFile_Change
        MousePointer = vbDefault
    End Sub

    Private Sub cmdView_Click()
        Dim sA As String
        Dim lZndx As Long
        MousePointer = vbHourglass
        'Get file contents
```

(continued)

Source Code for SECRET.FRM *continued*

```
    Open txtFile.Text For Binary As #1
    sA = Space$(LOF(1))
    Get #1, , sA
    Close #1
    Do
        lZndx = InStr(sA, Chr$(0))
        If lZndx = 0 Or lZndx > 5000 Then Exit Do
        Mid$(sA, lZndx, 1) = Chr$(1)
    Loop
    'Display file contents
    MousePointer = vbDefault
    frmView.rtfView.Text = sA
    frmView.Caption = "Secret - " & txtFile.Text
    frmView.Show vbModal
End Sub

Private Sub Command1_Click()
    MsgBox Date & Str(Timer)
End Sub

Private Sub Form_Load()
    'Center this form
    Left = (Screen.Width - Width) \ 2
    Top = (Screen.Height - Height) \ 2
    'Disable most command buttons
    cmdEncrypt.Enabled = False
    cmdDecrypt.Enabled = False
    cmdView.Enabled = False
    'Initialize filename field
    txtFile.Text = ""
End Sub

Private Sub mnuAbout_Click()
    'Set properties
    About.Application = "Secret"
    About.Heading = _
        "Microsoft Visual Basic 5.0 Developer's Workshop"
    About.Copyright = "1997 John Clark Craig and Jeff Webb"
    About.Display
End Sub

Private Sub mnuExit_Click()
    Unload Me
End Sub
```

(continued)

Source Code for SECRET.FRM *continued*

```
Private Sub mnuContents_Click()
    cdlOne.HelpFile = App.Path & "\..\..\Help\Mvbdw.hlp"
    cdlOne.HelpCommand = cdlHelpContents
    cdlOne.ShowHelp
End Sub

Private Sub mnuSearch_Click()
    cdlOne.HelpFile = App.Path & "\..\..\Help\Mvbdw.hlp"
    cdlOne.HelpCommand = cdlHelpPartialKey
    cdlOne.ShowHelp
End Sub

Private Sub txtFile_Change()
    Dim lFileLen As Long
    Dim sHead As String
    'Check to see whether file exists
    On Error Resume Next
    lFileLen = Len(Dir(txtFile.Text))
    'Disable buttons if filename isn't valid
    If Err <> 0 Or lFileLen = 0 Or Len(txtFile.Text) = 0 Then
        cmdEncrypt.Enabled = False
        cmdDecrypt.Enabled = False
        cmdView.Enabled = False
        lblPassword1.Enabled = False
        txtPassword1.Enabled = False
        lblPassword2.Enabled = False
        txtPassword2.Enabled = False
        txtPassword2.Text = ""
        Exit Sub
    End If
    'Get first 8 bytes of selected file
    Open txtFile.Text For Binary As #1
    sHead = Space(8)
    Get #1, , sHead
    Close #1
    'Check to see whether file is already encrypted
    If sHead = "[Secret]" Then
        cmdEncrypt.Enabled = False
        cmdDecrypt.Enabled = True
        lblPassword2.Enabled = False
        txtPassword2.Enabled = False
        txtPassword2.Text = ""
    Else
        cmdEncrypt.Enabled = True
        cmdDecrypt.Enabled = False
```

(continued)

Source Code for SECRET.FRM *continued*

```
            lblPassword2.Enabled = True
            txtPassword2.Enabled = True
        End If
        lblPassword1.Enabled = True
        txtPassword1.Enabled = True
        cmdBrowse.Enabled = True
        cmdView.Enabled = True
    End Sub


Sub Encrypt()
    Dim sHead As String
    Dim sT As String
    Dim sA As String
    Dim cphX As New Cipher
    Dim n As Long
    Open txtFile.Text For Binary As #1
    'Load entire file into sA
    sA = Space$(LOF(1))
    Get #1, , sA
    Close #1
    'Prepare header string with salt characters
    sT = Hash(Date & Str(Timer))
    sHead = "[Secret]" & sT & Hash(sT & txtPassword1.Text)
    'Do the encryption
    cphX.KeyString = sHead
    cphX.Text = sA
    cphX.DoXor
    cphX.Stretch
    sA = cphX.Text
    'Write header
    Open txtFile.Text For Output As #1
    Print #1, sHead
    'Write encrypted data
    n = 1
    Do
        Print #1, Mid(sA, n, 70)
        n = n + 70
    Loop Until n > Len(sA)
    Close #1
End Sub

Sub Decrypt()
    Dim sHead As String
    Dim sA As String
    Dim sT As String
    Dim cphX As New Cipher
```

(continued)

Source Code for SECRET.FRM *continued*

```
    Dim n As Long
    'Get header (first 18 bytes of encrypted file)
    Open txtFile.Text For Input As #1
    Line Input #1, sHead
    Close #1
    'Check for correct password
    sT = Mid(sHead, 9, 8)
    If InStr(sHead, Hash(sT & txtPassword1.Text)) <> 17 Then
        MsgBox "Sorry, this is not the correct password!", _
            vbExclamation, "Secret"
        Exit Sub
    End If
    'Get file contents
    Open txtFile.Text For Input As #1
    'Read past the header
    Line Input #1, sHead
    'Read and build the contents string
    Do Until EOF(1)
        Line Input #1, sT
        sA = sA & sT
    Loop
    Close #1
    'Decrypt file contents
    cphX.KeyString = sHead
    cphX.Text = sA
    cphX.Shrink
    cphX.DoXor
    sA = cphX.Text
    'Replace file with decrypted version
    Kill txtFile.Text
    Open txtFile.Text For Binary As #1
    Put #1, , sA
    Close #1
End Sub

Function Hash(sA As String) As String
    Dim cphHash As New Cipher
    cphHash.KeyString = sA & "123456"
    cphHash.Text = sA & "123456"
    cphHash.DoXor
    cphHash.Stretch
    cphHash.KeyString = cphHash.Text
    cphHash.Text = "123456"
    cphHash.DoXor
    cphHash.Stretch
    Hash = cphHash.Text
End Function
```

VIEW.FRM

This relatively simple form provides a read-only file viewer window for the Secret application. Figure 32-13 shows the View form during development. The only control this form contains is a RichTextBox control to display the selected file.

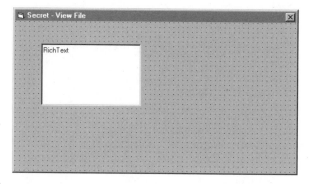

Figure 32-13.
The View form during development.

To create this form, use the following table and source code to add the appropriate control, set any nondefault properties as indicated, and enter the source code lines as shown.

VIEW.FRM Objects and Property Settings

Property	Value
Form	
Name	*frmView*
Caption	*Secret - View File*
MaxButton	*False*
MinButton	*False*
RichTextBox	
Name	*rtfView*
Scrollbars	*3 - Both*
Locked	*True*

Source Code for VIEW.FRM

```
Option Explicit

Private Sub Form_Resize()
    'Center this form
    Left = (Screen.Width - Width) \ 2
    Top = (Screen.Height - Height) \ 2
    'Size RichTextBox to fill form
    rtfView.Move 0, 0, ScaleWidth, ScaleHeight
End Sub
```

CIPHER.CLS

This class module provides the cipher engine at the heart of the Secret application. The Cipher object is described in Chapter 16, "Security," but I'll present it again here for easy reference.

To create the Cipher class, add a new class module to your project, name it Cipher, and enter the source code lines as shown.

Source Code for CIPHER.CLS

```
Option Explicit

Private msKeyString As String
Private msText As String

'~~~.KeyString
Public Property Let KeyString(sKeyString As String)
    msKeyString = sKeyString
    Initialize
End Property

'~~~.Text
Public Property Let Text(sText As String)
    msText = sText
End Property
Public Property Get Text() As String
    Text = msText
End Property

'~~~.DoXor
Public Sub DoXor()
    Dim intC As Integer
    Dim intB As Integer
```

(continued)

Source Code for CIPHER.CLS *continued*

```
    Dim lngI As Long
    For lngI = 1 To Len(msText)
        intC = Asc(Mid(msText, lngI, 1))
        intB = Int(Rnd * 256)
        Mid(msText, lngI, 1) = Chr(intC Xor intB)
    Next lngI
End Sub


'~~~.Stretch
Public Sub Stretch()
    Dim intC As Integer
    Dim lngI As Long
    Dim lngJ As Long
    Dim intK As Integer
    Dim lngA As Long
    Dim sB As String
    lngA = Len(msText)
    sB = Space(lngA + (lngA + 2) \ 3)
    For lngI = 1 To lngA
        intC = Asc(Mid(msText, lngI, 1))
        lngJ = lngJ + 1
        Mid(sB, lngJ, 1) = Chr((intC And 63) + 59)
        Select Case lngI Mod 3
        Case 1
            intK = intK Or ((intC \ 64) * 16)
        Case 2
            intK = intK Or ((intC \ 64) * 4)
        Case 0
            intK = intK Or (intC \ 64)
            lngJ = lngJ + 1
            Mid(sB, lngJ, 1) = Chr(intK + 59)
            intK = 0
        End Select
    Next lngI
    If lngA Mod 3 Then
        lngJ = lngJ + 1
        Mid(sB, lngJ, 1) = Chr(intK + 59)
    End If
    msText = sB
End Sub


'~~~.Shrink
Public Sub Shrink()
    Dim intC As Integer
    Dim intD As Integer
```

(continued)

Source Code for CIPHER.CLS *continued*

```
    Dim intE As Integer
    Dim lngA As Long
    Dim lngB As Long
    Dim lngI As Long
    Dim lngJ As Long
    Dim lngK As Long
    Dim sB As String
    lngA = Len(msText)
    lngB = lngA - 1 - (lngA - 1) \ 4
    sB = Space(lngB)
    For lngI = 1 To lngB
        lngJ = lngJ + 1
        intC = Asc(Mid(msText, lngJ, 1)) - 59
        Select Case lngI Mod 3
        Case 1
            lngK = lngK + 4
            If lngK > lngA Then lngK = lngA
            intE = Asc(Mid(msText, lngK, 1)) - 59
            intD = ((intE \ 16) And 3) * 64
        Case 2
            intD = ((intE \ 4) And 3) * 64
        Case 0
            intD = (intE And 3) * 64
            lngJ = lngJ + 1
        End Select
        Mid(sB, lngI, 1) = Chr(intC Or intD)
    Next lngI
    msText = sB
End Sub

'Initializes random numbers using the Key string
Private Sub Initialize()
    Dim intI As Integer
    Randomize Rnd(-1)
    For intI = 1 To Len(msKeyString)
        Randomize Rnd(-Rnd * Asc(Mid(msKeyString, intI, 1)))
    Next intI
End Sub
```

The BitPack Application

I developed the BitPack application while experimenting with C-language DLLs to see how much extra speed I could squeeze out of Visual Basic. Even with the native code compiler available in Visual Basic 5, for certain types of problems a C DLL can make a real difference in the speed-critical sections of your applications. The BitPack application demonstrates this well.

I designed BITPACK.DLL to manipulate individual bits in a byte array, which is a task that Visual Basic is not particularly well suited for. This DLL provides three functions: BitGet, to return the current state of a bit; BitSet, to set the bit at the given location to *1*; and BitClr, to set the bit to *0*. You pass a byte array to these functions, along with a bit number, and the C code does the rest. For example, to retrieve bit number 542 from a byte array, the C code in the BitGet routine efficiently locates bit number 6 from byte number 67 in the array, extracts the bit, and returns *1* if that bit is set or *0* if it isn't. Byte arrays can be huge in 32-bit Visual Basic, so a practically unlimited store of bits can be accessed by these routines, all stored in a single byte array.

Generating a Table of Prime Numbers (Sieve of Eratosthenes)

A practical use for these functions is in the field of data acquisition and process control. The state of thousands of switches, contact closures, and the like can be maintained in a byte array using only the three functions in the BitPack application (BitGet, BitSet, and BitClr). For this book, however, I created a small program to generate a table of prime numbers using the well-known sieve of Eratosthenes. Each bit in the byte array represents an odd integer. Using a couple of nested loops, it's easy to toggle all bits representing nonprime numbers to 1s, leaving all primes as 0s. Because of the DLL's speed, we can generate a table of primes in the range 1 through 1,000,000, for example, in just a few seconds. When you realize how many times the BitSet and BitGet functions are called to generate this table, you begin to get a sense of how much the C-language DLL functions can speed up some types of code!

Creating the BitPack DLL Project Files

Before creating the Visual Basic application to generate the prime numbers table, you must create the DLL that is at the core of its operation.

NOTE: With the latest Microsoft Visual C++ compilers, creating a DLL is easier than ever. Because this book focuses on using Microsoft tools to create applications for the 32-bit Microsoft Windows 95 environment, I've streamlined the following example DLL code. This should make it easier for you to focus on the essential points of the DLL creation task. If you're using a version of C other than Microsoft Visual C++ version 2.2, you might need to make some adjustments to the following listings and development steps. For the best in-depth explanation of every aspect of DLL creation, refer to the documentation that comes with your compiler.

The following two listings are for the only two files you'll need in your Visual C++ project. Start a new project in the 32-bit version of Visual C++, and select Dynamic Link Library as the type of project to be built. Create a DEF file as part of your project, enter the following few lines, and name this file BITPACK.DEF:

```
;BitPack.def
LIBRARY BitPack

CODE PRELOAD MOVEABLE DISCARDABLE
DATA PRELOAD MOVEABLE

EXPORTS
        BitGet          @1
        BitSet          @2
        BitClr          @3
```

The DEF file tells the outside world the names of exported functions—in other words, this file provides the list of functions you can call from your Visual Basic applications.

The BITPACK.C source code file is another short file. The efficient single-line functions perform all the addressing, masking, and other bit manipulations required to access or process a single bit anywhere in a huge byte array. Enter the following lines in a file, save the file as BITPACK.C, and be sure it's included in your Visual C++ project:

```
#include <windows.h>
#include <ole2.h>

BYTE _stdcall BitGet( LPBYTE bytes, LONG bitpos )
{
    return( bytes[bitpos >> 3] & ( 1 << ( bitpos % 8 )) ? 1 : 0 );
}

BYTE _stdcall BitSet( LPBYTE bytes, LONG bitpos )
{
    return( bytes[bitpos >> 3] |= ( 1 << ( bitpos % 8 )));
}

BYTE _stdcall BitClr( LPBYTE bytes, LONG bitpos )
{
    return( bytes[bitpos >> 3] &= ~( 1 << ( bitpos % 8 )));
}
```

Click the Build All button in the Visual C++ environment to compile and link the two files in your project and create a small DLL module named BITPACK.DLL. Move or copy BITPACK.DLL to your Windows SYSTEM directory so that your Visual Basic Declare statements will be able to locate the DLL file automatically. BitPack's three functions can then be declared and called from a Visual Basic program located anywhere in your system.

BITPACK.FRM

This form prompts the user for the largest desired prime number. It then calls the functions within the BitPack DLL to generate a table of prime numbers represented by bits in a byte array and creates an output file of the results. I've added a progress indicator bar to the form so that you can monitor the speed of the prime number calculations. On my computer, the generation of the prime numbers table is faster than the creation of the output file! Figure 32-14 shows the BitPack form in action, as it calculates all prime numbers up to 1,000,000.

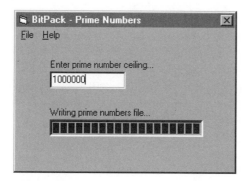

Figure 32-14.
The BitPack form in action.

The output file of prime numbers is written to the file C:\WINDOWS\ DESKTOP\PRIMES.TXT, but you can change the location or the filename. The path and filename string is isolated for easy maintenance in a constant named *FileName,* near the top of the BITPACK.FRM source code. If you elect to generate a large table of prime numbers, this file can become fairly large. To roughly predict the size of the output file, cut the largest prime number value in half. For example, the generation of prime numbers up to 200,000 creates a PRIMES.TXT file of just a little over 100,000 bytes in size.

Figure 32-15 shows the first lines of the contents of PRIMES.TXT after the BitPack application has generated prime numbers up to 1,000,000.

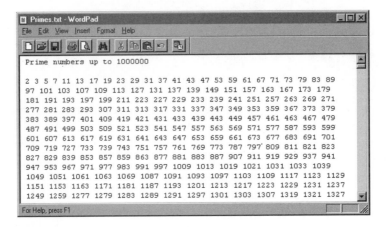

Figure 32-15.
The PRIMES.TXT file listing the generated prime numbers.

The BitPack form provides a working example of the ProgressBar control. It monitors the progress of the application as it creates the prime numbers table, and also while it creates the PRIMES.TXT output file. I've toggled the Visible properties of the ProgressBar and CommandButton controls so that you'll always see one or the other, but not both at the same time.

Figure 32-16 shows the BitPack form during development.

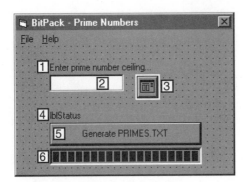

Figure 32-16.
The BitPack form during development.

To create this form, use the following tables and source code to add the appropriate controls, set any nondefault properties as indicated, and enter the source code lines as shown.

BITPACK.FRM Menu Design Window Entries

Caption	Name	Indentation	Enabled
&File	mnuFile	0	True
&New	mnuNew	1	False
&Open...	mnuOpen	1	False
&Save	mnuSave	1	False
Save &As...	mnuSaveAs	1	False
-	mnuFileDash1	1	True
E&xit	mnuExit	1	True
&Help	mnuHelp	0	True
&Contents	mnuContents	1	True
&Search for Help on...	mnuSearch	1	True
-	mnuHelpDash1	1	True
&About...	mnuAbout	1	True

BITPACK.FRM Objects and Property Settings

ID No.*	Property	Value
Form		
	Name	frmBitPack
	BorderStyle	3 - Fixed Dialog
	Caption	BitPack - Prime Numbers
Label		
1	Name	lblPrompt
	Caption	Enter prime number ceiling...
TextBox		
2	Name	txtMaxPrime

* The number in the ID No. column corresponds to the number in Figure 32-16 that identifies the location of the object on the form.

(continued)

BITPACK.FRM Objects and Property Settings *continued*

ID No.	Property	Value
CommonDialog		
3	Name	*cdlOne*
Label		
4	Name	*lblStatus*
CommandButton		
5	Name	*cmdPrimes*
	Caption	*Generate PRIMES.TXT*
ProgressBar		
6	Name	*prgOne*

Source Code for BITPACK.FRM

```
Option Explicit

Private Declare Function BitGet _
Lib "BitPack.dll" ( _
    ByRef b As Byte, _
    ByVal n As Long _
) As Byte

Private Declare Function BitSet _
Lib "BitPack.dll" ( _
    ByRef b As Byte, _
    ByVal n As Long _
) As Byte

Private Declare Function BitClr _
Lib "BitPack.dll" ( _
    ByRef b As Byte, _
    ByVal n As Long _
) As Byte

'Change output path or filename here
Const FileName = "C:\Windows\Desktop\Primes.txt"

Private Sub cmdPrimes_Click()
    Dim n As Long
```

(continued)

Source Code for BITPACK.FRM *continued*

```
    Dim i As Long
    Dim j As Long
    Dim k As Long
    Dim lNextVal As Long
    Dim lLastVal As Long
    Dim byAry() As Byte
    Dim sP As String
    MousePointer = vbHourglass
    cmdPrimes.Visible = False
    prgOne.Top = cmdPrimes.Top
    prgOne.Visible = True
    prgOne.Value = 0
    'Get largest prime number specified
    n = Abs(Val(txtMaxPrime.Text))
    'Match only odd numbers to bits in byte array
    ReDim byAry(n \ 16)
    'Keep user informed of progress
    lblStatus.Caption = "Generating prime numbers table..."
    Refresh
    'Process byte array; 0 bits represent prime numbers
    k = (n - 3) \ 2
    For i = 0 To k
        'If next number is prime...
        If BitGet(byAry(0), i) = 0 Then
            '...set bits that are multiples
            For j = 3 * i + 3 To k Step 2 * i + 3
                BitSet byAry(0), j
            Next j
            'Update progress bar, but not too often
            lNextVal = Int(100 * i / k)
            If lNextVal <> lLastVal Then
                lLastVal = lNextVal
                prgOne.Value = lNextVal
            End If
        End If
    Next i
    'Keep user informed
    lblStatus.Caption = "Writing prime numbers file..."
    lLastVal = 0
    prgOne.Value = 0
    Refresh
    'Write primes to file on desktop
    Open FileName For Output As #1
    'Bit table starts at 3, so output 2 as prime
    Print #1, "Prime numbers up to" & Str$(n) & vbCrLf
```

(continued)

Source Code for BITPACK.FRM *continued*

```
    sP = "2"
    For i = 0 To k
        'If prime number...
        If BitGet(byAry(0), i) = 0 Then
            'Concatenate number to string for output
            sP = sP & Str$(i + i + 3)
            'If string is long enough...
            If Len(sP) > 65 Then
                'Output string to file
                Print #1, LTrim$(sP)
                'Prepare for next line of output
                sP = ""
                'Update progress bar, but not too often
                lNextVal = Int(100 * i / k)
                If lNextVal > lLastVal Then
                    lLastVal = lNextVal
                    prgOne.Value = lNextVal
                End If
            End If
        End If
    Next i
    'Print any last-line primes
    Print #1, LTrim$(sP)
    Close #1
    'Set form to original visible state
    lblStatus.Caption = ""
    cmdPrimes.Visible = True
    prgOne.Visible = False
    MousePointer = vbDefault
End Sub

Private Sub Form_Load()
    txtMaxPrime.Text = ""
    lblStatus.Caption = ""
End Sub

Private Sub mnuAbout_Click()
    'Set properties
    About.Application = "BitPack"
    About.Heading = _
        "Microsoft Visual Basic 5.0 Developer's Workshop"
    About.Copyright = "1997 John Clark Craig and Jeff Webb"
    About.Display
End Sub
```

(continued)

Source Code for BITPACK.FRM *continued*

```
Private Sub mnuExit_Click()
    Unload Me
End Sub

Private Sub mnuContents_Click()
    cdlOne.HelpFile = App.Path & "\..\..\Help\Mvbdw.hlp"
    cdlOne.HelpCommand = cdlHelpContents
    cdlOne.ShowHelp
End Sub

Private Sub mnuSearch_Click()
    cdlOne.HelpFile = App.Path & "\..\..\Help\Mvbdw.hlp"
    cdlOne.HelpCommand = cdlHelpPartialKey
    cdlOne.ShowHelp
End Sub
```

On the BitPack form, all calls to the bit manipulation functions in BITPACK.DLL pass the first member of the byte array *byAry()*. You can also pass a single nonarray byte variable to these functions, in which case the *BitPos* parameter should stay in the range 0 through 7. For maximum speed, I elected not to include range-checking code within the DLL, so it's up to you to develop the code to prevent your application from passing *BitPos* values outside the range of a byte value or of a byte array. Because there are 8 bits per byte-array element, an array dimensioned with the value *100*, for example, has a range of legal *BitPos* values from 0 through 807.

To compute prime numbers using the sieve of Eratosthenes, I mapped the odd integers 3, 5, 7,... to the bits 0, 1, 2,... in the byte array. This allows a range of 16 integers to be covered in each 8-bit byte element. Because Visual Basic supports huge byte arrays, you can theoretically compute primes up to a huge value using this program.

The Dialogs Application

The CommonDialog control provides many powerful options for interacting with users in a standard way. The Dialogs application illustrates the five common dialog boxes provided by this one control. I've set up five buttons in a toolbar to activate the Open, Save As, Color, Font, and Print dialog boxes. The user's options in each dialog box are displayed for verification, but no files or settings are affected. You can select any file on your system while the Save As dialog box is displayed, for instance, but the file is left unaffected.

Figure 32-17 shows the Dialogs application at runtime, and Figures 32-18 through 32-22 show the dialog boxes that appear when you click the associated buttons on the toolbar.

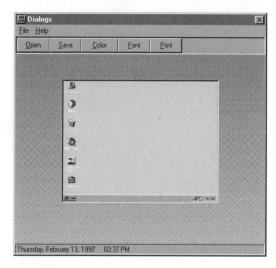

Figure 32-17.
The Dialogs application in action.

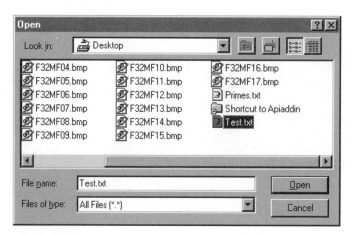

Figure 32-18.
The CommonDialog control's Open dialog box.

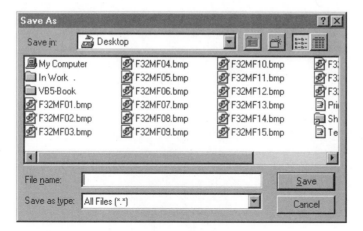

Figure 32-19.
The CommonDialog control's Save As dialog box.

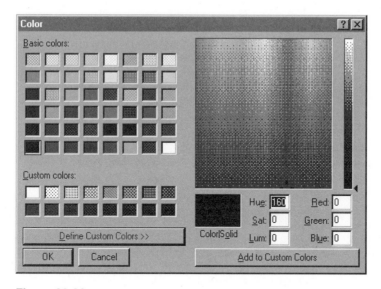

Figure 32-20.
The CommonDialog control's Color dialog box.

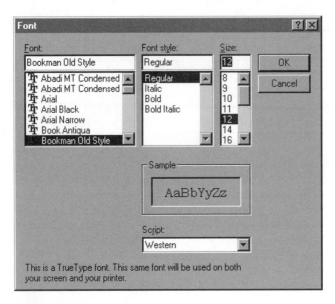

Figure 32-21.
The CommonDialog control's Font dialog box.

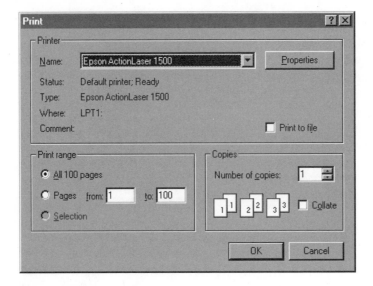

Figure 32-22.
The CommonDialog control's Print dialog box.

I like to keep this application handy while I'm working on new applications. When I need to set up a color selection feature in my new application, for example, I simply copy the relevant code from the Dialogs application, add a CommonDialog control, and modify the code for any unique requirements of the new application. Often this method saves me time compared to searching the online help to recall how to set up the CommonDialog control.

Some Special Features

The Dialogs application contains several unique features that demonstrate some handy techniques.

About and About2

Two types of About dialog boxes are shown by this program. The Help menu has both an About item and an About2 item. The About dialog box is the one I've used in many of the applications in this book, and the About2 dialog box provides the alternative About dialog box I presented in the VBClock application in Chapter 29, "Date and Time." Although both forms create similar About dialog boxes in the application, they are created using different techniques. I've included both of them here so that you can make a direct comparison of the two techniques.

The Sunset Background

There are a few other interesting twists to this application. By a simple modification of the blue-to-black fade algorithm presented in Chapter 12, "Graphics Techniques," this form's background fades from red to yellow, like a colorful sunset. It's easy to tweak this code to fade from any color to another color that you specify. A more subtle color gradation would probably be more appropriate for many forms, but I liked the bright colors for this demonstration application.

The Hidden Message

I've also added a hidden message to this application, along the lines of the Easter egg presented in Chapter 16, "Security." Hidden messages, such as author credits, can be activated in a nearly infinite number of ways. In this application, I keep track of the locations of the last four mouse clicks on the main form. When the correct sequence of clicks occurs near each of the corners of the picture box in the middle of the form, a hidden message window pops up for 5 seconds. Try clicking just outside the picture box, near the upper-left corner, the upper-right corner, the lower-right corner, and finally the lower-left corner. If the order and locations of these four clicks are correct, you'll see a bright yellow message, as shown in Figure 32-23.

Figure 32-23.
The hidden message.

Form Position

Throughout this book, I've centered most forms on the screen during each form's Load event procedure. A slight modification of this technique allows you to position a form at any location on the screen. To see how this works, click anywhere on the screen graphic in the center of the Dialog application's main form. If you click one-quarter of the way across the image of the screen and three-quarters of the way down from its top, the entire form will jump to the same relative position on the real screen. After a 2-second delay, the form relocates to the center of the screen again, so you can experiment further. Take a look at the picScreen_Click event procedure in the source code to see how the form's center is moved temporarily to the relative position indicated by the mouse click in the picture box.

Figure 32-24 shows the mouse at roughly the position described above, and Figure 32-25 shows the form's new, temporary location on the screen.

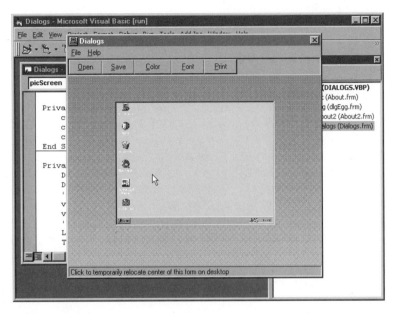

Figure 32-24.
Clicking in the picture box to cause the application to temporarily relocate.

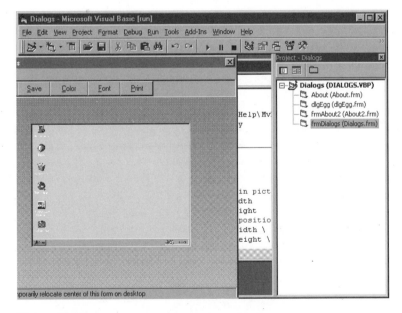

Figure 32-25.
The entire application temporarily located in the indicated position on the screen.

The Application Files

The Dialogs project contains four files. In addition to the main Dialogs form, two types of About dialog forms and a special hidden messages form are part of the project. Figure 32-26 shows the project list.

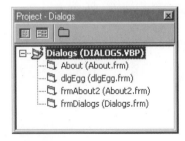

Figure 32-26.
The Dialogs application project list.

DIALOGS.FRM

The Dialogs form displays what looks like the Windows 95 desktop within a form. Actually, a picture box in the center of the form displays a reduced image of the Windows 95 desktop. (As described above, a click anywhere on this image causes the form to temporarily jump to the same relative position on the real desktop.)

Figure 32-27 shows the Dialogs form during development.

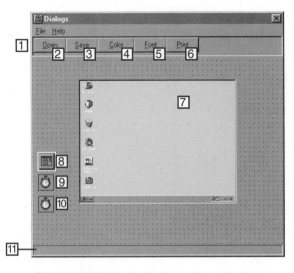

Figure 32-27.
The Dialogs form during development.

To create this form, use the following tables and source code to add the appropriate controls, set any nondefault properties as indicated, and enter the source code lines as shown.

DIALOGS.FRM Menu Design Window Entries

Caption	Name	Indentation	Enabled
&File	mnuFile	0	True
&New	mnuNew	1	False
&Open...	mnuOpen	1	False
&Save	mnuSave	1	False
Save &As...	mnuSaveAs	1	False
-	mnuFileDash1	1	True
E&xit	mnuExit	1	True
&Help	mnuHelp	0	True
&Contents	mnuContents	1	True
&Search for Help on...	mnuSearch	1	True
-	mnuHelpDash1	1	True
&About...	mnuAbout	1	True
About&2...	mnuAbout2	1	True

DIALOGS.FRM Objects and Property Settings

ID No.*	Property	Value
Form		
	Name	frmDialogs
	Caption	Dialogs
	BorderStyle	3 - Fixed Dialog
	Icon	Pc01.ico
PictureBox		
1	Name	picTop
	Align	1 - Align Top

*   The number in the ID No. column corresponds to the number in Figure 32-27 that identifies the location of the object on the form.

(continued)

DIALOGS.FRM Objects and Property Settings *continued*

ID No.	Property	Value
CommandButton		
2	Name	*cmdOpen*
	Caption	*&Open*
CommandButton		
3	Name	*cmdSave*
	Caption	*&Save*
CommandButton		
4	Name	*cmdColor*
	Caption	*&Color*
CommandButton		
5	Name	*cmdFont*
	Caption	*&Font*
CommandButton		
6	Name	*cmdPrint*
	Caption	*&Print*
PictureBox		
7	Name	*picScreen*
	AutoSize	*True*
	Picture	*DESKTOP.BMP*
CommonDialog		
8	Name	*cdlOne*
Timer		
9	Name	*tmrClock*
	Interval	*100*
Timer		
10	Name	*tmrRelocate*
	Enabled	*False*
	Interval	*2000*
StatusBar		
11	Name	*stbBottom*
	Align	*2 - vbAlignBottom*
	Style	*1 - sbrSimple*

Source Code for DIALOGS.FRM

```
Option Explicit

Dim mvX, mvY
Dim mvLastSec
Dim mvEggX(1 To 4)
Dim mvEggY(1 To 4)

Private Sub Form_Click()
    Dim i As Integer
    'Keep track of last four clicks on form
    For i = 1 To 3
        mvEggX(i) = mvEggX(i + 1)
        mvEggY(i) = mvEggY(i + 1)
    Next i
    mvEggX(4) = mvX
    mvEggY(4) = mvY
    'Check for correct sequence and position
    If Abs(mvEggX(1) - 70) < 30 And _
        Abs(mvEggY(1) - 60) < 30 And _
        Abs(mvEggX(2) - 360) < 30 And _
        Abs(mvEggY(2) - 60) < 30 And _
        Abs(mvEggX(3) - 360) < 30 And _
        Abs(mvEggY(3) - 290) < 30 And _
        Abs(mvEggX(4) - 70) < 30 And _
        Abs(mvEggY(4) - 290) < 30 Then
        'Display hidden message
        dlgEgg.Show vbModal
    End If
End Sub

Private Sub Form_Load()
    'Center this form
    Left = (Screen.Width - Width) \ 2
    Top = (Screen.Height - Height) \ 2
    'Adjust button bar height
    picTop.Height = cmdOpen.Height + _
        (picTop.Height - picTop.ScaleHeight)
End Sub

Private Sub Form_MouseMove(Button As Integer, Shift As Integer, _
    X As Single, Y As Single)
    'Signal timer to update status bar
```

(continued)

Source Code for DIALOGS.FRM *continued*

```
    mvLastSec = -1
    'Keep track of mouse location
    mvX = X
    mvY = Y
End Sub

Private Sub Form_Paint()
    Dim n As Long
    ScaleMode = vbPixels
    DrawStyle = 5 'Transparent
    DrawWidth = 1
    'Draw sunset background (fade from red to yellow)
    For n = 0 To ScaleHeight Step ScaleHeight \ 16
        Line (-1, n - 1)-(ScaleWidth, n + ScaleHeight \ 16), _
            RGB(255, n * 255 \ ScaleHeight, 0), BF
    Next n
End Sub

Private Sub mnuAbout_Click()
    'Set properties for the About dialog
    About.Application = "Dialogs"
    About.Heading = _
        "Microsoft Visual Basic 5.0 Developer's Workshop"
    About.Copyright = "1997 John Clark Craig and Jeff Webb"
    About.Display
End Sub

Private Sub mnuAbout2_Click()
    'Display the About2 dialog box
    frmAbout2.Display
End Sub

Private Sub mnuExit_Click()
    Unload Me
End Sub

Private Sub mnuContents_Click()
    cdlOne.HelpFile = App.Path & "\..\..\Help\Mvbdw.hlp"
    cdlOne.HelpCommand = cdlHelpContents
    cdlOne.ShowHelp
End Sub
```

(continued)

Source Code for DIALOGS.FRM *continued*

```
Private Sub mnuSearch_Click()
    cdlOne.HelpFile = App.Path & "\..\..\Help\Mvbdw.hlp"
    cdlOne.HelpCommand = cdlHelpPartialKey
    cdlOne.ShowHelp
End Sub

Private Sub picScreen_Click()
    Dim vXpct
    Dim vYpct
    'Determine mouse's relative position in picture
    vXpct = 100 * mvX \ picScreen.ScaleWidth
    vYpct = 100 * mvY \ picScreen.ScaleHeight
    'Move form's center to same relative position on screen
    Left = Screen.Width * vXpct \ 100 - Width \ 2
    Top = Screen.Height * vYpct \ 100 - Height \ 2
    'Set timer to move form back later
    tmrRelocate.Enabled = True
End Sub

Private Sub picScreen_MouseMove(Button As Integer, _
    Shift As Integer, X As Single, Y As Single)
    'Keep track of mouse location
    mvX = X
    mvY = Y
    'Update status message at bottom of form
    stbBottom.SimpleText = "Click to temporarily relocate " & _
        "center of this form on desktop"
    'Signal timer not to display date and time in status bar
    mvLastSec = -2
End Sub

Private Sub cmdColor_Click()
    'Set flags for Color dialog box
    cdlOne.Flags = cdlCCRGBInit
    'Show Color dialog box
    cdlOne.ShowColor
    'Display selected color value
    MsgBox "&H" & Hex$(cdlOne.Color), , _
        "Selected color..."
End Sub
```

(continued)

Source Code for DIALOGS.FRM *continued*

```
Private Sub cmdFont_Click()
    Dim sTab2 As String
    sTab2 = vbTab & vbTab
    'Set flags for Font dialog box
    cdlOne.Flags = cdlCFWYSIWYG + cdlCFBoth + cdlCFScalableOnly
    'Show Font dialog box
    cdlOne.ShowFont
    'Display selected font values
    MsgBox _
        "Font Name:" & vbTab & cdlOne.FontName & vbCrLf & _
        "Font Size:" & sTab2 & cdlOne.FontSize & vbCrLf & _
        "Bold:" & sTab2 & cdlOne.FontBold & vbCrLf & _
        "Italic:" & sTab2 & cdlOne.FontItalic, , _
        "Selected font..."
End Sub

Private Sub cmdOpen_Click()
    'Set up sample filter for Open dialog box
    Dim sBat As String
    Dim sTxt As String
    Dim sAll As String
    sBat = "Batch Files (*.bat)|*.bat"
    sTxt = "Text Files (*.txt)|*.txt"
    sAll = "All Files (*.*)|*.*"
    cdlOne.Filter = sBat & "|" & sTxt & "|" & sAll
    'Set default filter to third one listed
    cdlOne.FilterIndex = 3
    'Hide "ReadOnly" check box
    cdlOne.Flags = cdlOFNHideReadOnly
    'Deselect previously selected file, if any
    cdlOne.filename = ""
    'Show Open dialog box
    cdlOne.ShowOpen
    'Display selected filename
    If cdlOne.filename = "" Then Exit Sub
    MsgBox cdlOne.filename, , "Selected file..."
End Sub

Private Sub cmdPrint_Click()
    Dim sPrintToFile As String
    'Set flags for Print dialog box
    cdlOne.Flags = cdlPDAllPages + cdlPDNoSelection
    'Set imaginary page range
    cdlOne.Min = 1
```

(continued)

694

Source Code for DIALOGS.FRM *continued*

```
    cdlOne.Max = 100
    cdlOne.FromPage = 1
    cdlOne.ToPage = 100
    'Show Print dialog box
    cdlOne.ShowPrinter
    'Extract some printer data
    If cdlOne.Flags And cdlPDPrintToFile Then
        sPrintToFile = "Yes"
    Else
        sPrintToFile = "No"
    End If
    'Display selected print values
    MsgBox _
        "Begin Page:" & vbTab & cdlOne.FromPage & vbCrLf & _
        "End Page:" & vbTab & cdlOne.ToPage & vbCrLf & _
        "No. Copies:" & vbTab & cdlOne.Copies & vbCrLf & _
        "Print to File:" & vbTab & sPrintToFile _
        , , "Selected print information..."
End Sub

Private Sub cmdSave_Click()
    'Set up filter for Save As dialog box
    Dim sBat As String
    Dim sTxt As String
    Dim sAll As String
    sBat = "Batch Files (*.bat)|*.bat"
    sTxt = "Text Files (*.txt)|*.txt"
    sAll = "All Files (*.*)|*.*"
    cdlOne.Filter = sBat & "|" & sTxt & "|" & sAll
    'Set default filter to third one listed
    cdlOne.FilterIndex = 3
    'Hide ReadOnly check box
    cdlOne.Flags = cdlOFNHideReadOnly
    'Deselect previously selected file, if any
    cdlOne.filename = ""
    'Show the Save As dialog box
    cdlOne.ShowSave
    'Display the selected file
    If cdlOne.filename = "" Then Exit Sub
    MsgBox cdlOne.filename, , "'Save As' file..."
End Sub

Private Sub tmrRelocate_Timer()
    'Relocating form once per move
```

(continued)

Source Code for DIALOGS.FRM *continued*

```
        tmrRelocate.Enabled = False
        'Center this form
        Left = (Screen.Width - Width) \ 2
        Top = (Screen.Height - Height) \ 2
    End Sub

    Private Sub tmrClock_Timer()
        Dim vSec
        vSec = Second(Now)
        If vSec = mvLastSec Then Exit Sub
        If mvLastSec = -2 Then Exit Sub
        mvLastSec = vSec
        'Update date and time in status line
        stbBottom.SimpleText = Format(Date, "Long Date") & _
            Space$(5) & Format(Time, "hh:mm AMPM")
    End Sub
```

DLGEGG.FRM

DLGEGG.FRM is a simple form that displays a secret message when the user clicks on the specified locations in the correct sequence. A timer causes the form to unload itself after a 5-second delay, although you could easily modify this form to unload when the user clicks anywhere on the form. Feel free to change the message or enhance the form as you want.

Figure 32-28 shows the *dlgEgg* form during development.

Figure 32-28.
The dlgEgg *form during development.*

To create this form, use the following table and source code to add the appropriate controls, set any nondefault properties as indicated, and enter the source code lines as shown.

DLGEGG.FRM Objects and Property Settings

Property	Value
Form	
Name	*dlgEgg*
Caption	*dlgEgg*
BackColor	*&H0000FFFF&*
BorderStyle	*1 - Fixed Single*
ControlBox	*False*
MaxButton	*False*
MinButton	*False*
WindowState	*0 - Normal*
Label	
Name	*lblEgg*
Alignment	*2 - Center*
Caption	*This "Easter egg" (hidden message) will disappear in 5 seconds.*
Font	*Arial - Italic - 14*
BackColor	*&H0000FFFF&*
Timer	
Name	*tmrQuit*
Enabled	*True*
Interval	*5000*

Source Code for DLGEGG.FRM

```
Option Explicit

Private Sub tmrQuit_Timer()
    Unload Me
End Sub
```

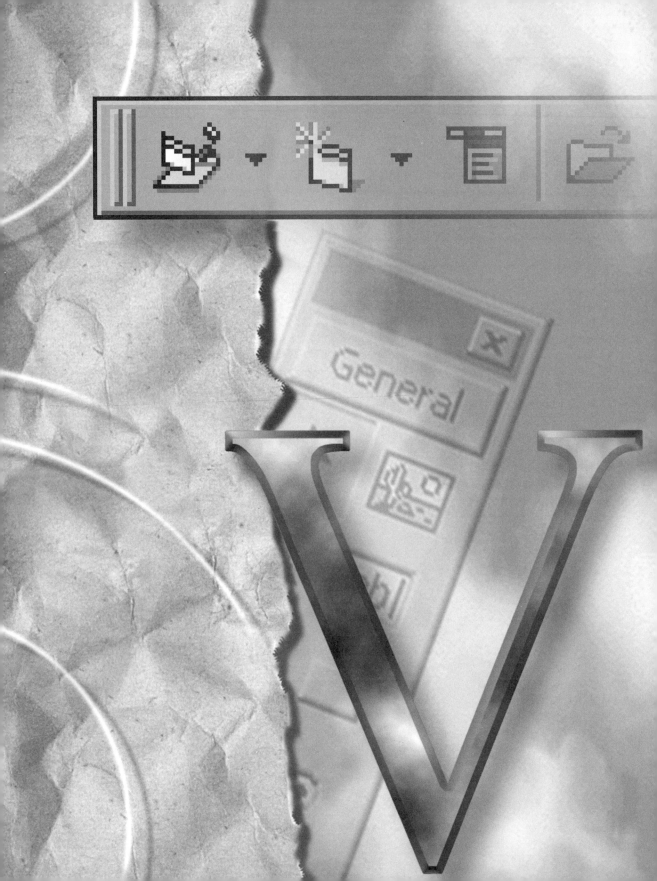

INDEX

Italicized page references indicate figures, tables, or program listings.

John Clark Craig

John Clark Craig is the author of 15 books on personal computing, including titles from Microsoft Press covering all versions of Microsoft Visual Basic for Windows, Microsoft Visual Basic for MS-DOS, Microsoft QuickBasic, and Microsoft QuickC. John was the technical editor for both the first and the second editions of *Microsoft Mouse Programmer's Reference* (Microsoft Press, 1989, 1991), and he authored parts of *Microsoft Word Developer's Kit* (Microsoft Press, 1993) and *Microsoft Windows 3.1 Developer's Workshop* (Microsoft Press, 1994). He lives with his family in Castle Rock, Colorado. His software design company is Craig Software, and he can be reached at JohnCraig@msn.com (http://ourworld.compuserve.com/homepages/johncr/).

Jeff Webb

Jeff Webb is a former senior member of the Microsoft Visual Basic product team. While at Microsoft, he worked on all things Basic, including Basic PDS, QuickBasic, Visual Basic, Visual Basic for Applications, and OLE Automation. He lives in Sanibel, Florida, and when he's not fishing, he can be reached at JeffWebb@msn.com.

The manuscript for this book was prepared and submitted to Microsoft Press in electronic form. Text files were prepared using Microsoft Word 7.0 for Windows 95. Pages were composed by Microsoft Press using Adobe PageMaker 6.0 for Windows 95, with text in New Baskerville and display type in Helvetica bold. Composed pages were delivered to the printer as electronic prepress files.

Cover Graphic Designer
Greg Erickson

Cover Illustrator
Glenn Mitsui

Interior Graphic Designer
Pamela Hidaka

Interior Graphic Artists
Michael Victor, Joel Panchot

Compositors
Elisabeth Thébaud Pong, Paul Vautier

Indexer
Foxon-Maddocks Associates

Register Today!

Return this
*Microsoft® Visual Basic® 5.0
Developer's Workshop, Fourth Edition*
registration card for
a Microsoft Press® catalog

U.S. and Canada addresses only. Fill in information below and mail postage-free. Please mail only the bottom half of this page.

1-57231-436-2   ***MICROSOFT® VISUAL BASIC® 5.0***   *Owner Registration Card*
                       DEVELOPER'S WORKSHOP, FOURTH EDITION

_____
NAME

_____
INSTITUTION OR COMPANY NAME

_____
ADDRESS

_____

_____
CITY   STATE   ZIP

Microsoft® Press
Quality Computer Books

For a free catalog of
Microsoft Press® products, call
1-800-MSPRESS